老子道德 上篇
第一章
道可道，非常道。名可名，非常名。
無名天地之始。有名萬物之母。
故常無，欲以觀其妙；常有，欲以觀其徼。
此兩者同出而異名。同謂之玄。玄之又玄，眾妙之門。

A TREASURY OF
MYSTIC TERMS

A TREASURY OF MYSTIC TERMS

PART II

SPIRITUAL GUIDES & PRACTITIONERS

VOLUME 10

JOHN DAVIDSON

SCIENCE OF THE SOUL RESEARCH CENTRE

Published by:
G. P. S. Bhalla
Science of the Soul Research Centre
c/o Radha Soami Satsang Beas
5 Guru Ravi Dass Marg, Pusa Road
New Delhi 110 005, India

For internet orders, please visit:
www.ScienceoftheSoul.org
For book orders within India, please write to:
Science of the Soul Research Centre
c/o Radha Soami Satsang Beas
BAV Distribution Centre, 5 Guru Ravi Dass Marg
Pusa Road, New Delhi 110 005

First edition 2016

21 20 19 18 17 16 8 7 6 5 4 3 2 1

ISBN 978-93-80077-47-5

Printed in India: Thomson Press (India) Ltd.

EDITED AND LARGELY WRITTEN BY

JOHN DAVIDSON

WITH THE HELP OF AN INTERNATIONAL TEAM

A Treasury of Mystic Terms has been compiled using the collective skills of an international team of researchers, contributors, assistant editors and readers with a wide variety of religious and cultural backgrounds. All members of the team are spiritual seekers, most of whom have found inspiration and encouragement in the teachings of the mystics of Beas in India. All those involved have given freely to this project, both as a source of inspiration for themselves, and as a way of showing to others the essential unity behind all the apparent variety in religion, philosophy, and mysticism.

Everybody has a perspective or a bias – coloured glasses through which they view the world. So although every attempt has been made to handle each entry within its own religious or mystical context, if any particular perspective is detected, it will inevitably be that of the contributors and their perception of mysticism. This does not mean, of course, that the contributors have always been in agreement. The preparation of the *Treasury* has often resulted in healthy debate!

RESEARCHERS AND CONTRIBUTORS

Prem Singh Alam MA, LLB (Sufism)
Janine Archer (Māori tradition)
Brian Bocking PhD (Buddhism)
Miriam Bokser Caravella BA (Judaism)
Jacqueline Carter BFA (Buddhism)
Roma Chadha-Sood MA (Jainism)
Beverly Chapman MA (Sufism)
Kevin Sagohawihdah Connelly PhD (Native North American)
John Davidson MA (Buddhism, Christianity, Western Classical, Gnosticism, Indian traditions, Jainism, Sufism, Zoroastrianism)
Lucie Davidson M ès L (Editorial)
Carole Devillers (Haitian, Native North American)
Shiv Singh Dhatt BA, Adib Fazil, GD Art (Sikhism)
Tom Gillen MA (Native traditions)
Prem Kathpalia MA (Buddhism, Indian traditions, Sufism)
K.K. Khurana BA (Indian traditions)
Shraddha Liertz (Indian traditions)
Farideh Maleki (Sufism)
Donka Markus PhD (Western Classical)
Jeremy Miller (Buddhism, Daoism)
K.S. Narang MA (Sikhism)
Antoine Nohra BSc (Buddhism, Sufism)
Christian O'Brien MA (Gnosticism)
Tony Pitman BA (Western Classical)
Janak Puri MA (Indian traditions)
Carolyn Ralston MA (Paraguayan Guaraní)
Thomas Richman MA (Western Classical)
K. Sankaranarayanan MA, LLB, DBM (Indian traditions)
V.K. Sethi MA (Indian traditions)
T.R. Shangari PhD (Indian traditions)
Judith Sankaranarayan MA (Indian traditions)
Jo Tennent (Siddha tradition)
Sylvia Xiaowen Shi MA (Buddhism, Daoism)
Faith Singh (Editorial)
K.N. Upadhyaya PhD (Buddhism, Indian traditions)
Frank Vogel JD, PhD (Sufism)

CONTENTS

Acknowledgements
ix

Abbreviations
xiii

7.3 Powers, Attributes, Characteristics
1

7.4 Baptism, Initiation, Mysteries
183

7.5 Spiritual Association
309

Acknowledgements

In the course of compiling the *Treasury,* the editorial team have consulted two major sources. Firstly, the scriptures and writings of mystics and others who have written on spiritual and mystical matters. Secondly, the works of scholars concerning these texts and their associated traditions. To all of these, we will be forever grateful. Among the mystics, we owe especial gratitude to the masters of Beas who have been, and who remain, the primary source of spiritual inspiration for most of the editorial team.

Among the many scholars and other writers, all sources and references have been cited in the appropriate places. In particular:

The translations of the Buddhist *Dhammapada* are founded mostly upon the work of S. Radhakrishnan and Narada Thera.

Most of the translations of the *Bhagavad Gītā* have drawn upon the earlier translations of S. Radhakrishnan and Swami Tapasyananda.

Quotations from the *Ādi Granth* are from the English translations of Manmohan Singh, Dr Gopal Singh, Dr Gurbachan Singh Talib, and Dr Sant Singh Khalsa.

The sayings of Heraclitus are found only as fragments, quoted in the works of other writers of antiquity. Various scholarly numbering systems exist for these fragments, the system employed here being that used by Philip Wheelwright in *Heraclitus* (Princeton University Press, 1959).

Most of the translations of Rūmī's *Maśnavī* are based upon the work of R.A. Nicholson.

Many scholarly translations of Zarathushtra's *Gāthās* into European languages have been made from defective Pahlavi translations. The translations here are from the Avestan, and are based largely on the original work of Dr I.R.S. Taraporewala.

The indigenous Guaraní of eastern Paraguay, made up of three large subgroups – the Mbyá, the Paí Cayuá, and the Avá-Chiripá – are described in books and articles by the most notable experts in this field, Miguel Alberto Bartolomé, León Cádogan, Alfred Métraux, and Egon Schaden. Most of the information used for the Guaraní mystical terms derives from these scholars' studies of the Mybá and Avá-Chiripá. If a term is general to all indigenous Guaraní, it is labelled (G); if a term is known only to apply to the Avá-Chiripá subgroup, it is labelled (AC). The transliteration conventions used for all Avá-Chiripá terms are the same as those used in Miguel Alberto Bartolomé's article, *Shamanism and Religion Among the Avá-Chiripá,* which resulted from his field studies in the northeastern region of Paraguay in 1968 and 1969. Bartolomé explains that since Paraguayan Guaraní has an officially recognized written form, he does not use phonetic symbols except the letter 'y' for the sixth guttural vowel.

Special mention must be made of the extensive compilation of material made by Dr Javad Nurbakhsh in his 15-volume *Farhang-i Nūrbakhsh: Iṣṭilāḥāt-i Taṣawwuf,* translated by Terry Graham *et al.* (1984–2001) as *Sufi Symbolism: The Nurbakhsh Encyclopedia of Sufi Terminology.* Dr Nurbakhsh's considerable contribution to Sufi literature has been of great help to us in the compilation of the *Treasury,* and we have made significant use of this material, both the Persian and its English translation.

Existing dictionaries and encyclopaedias are naturally of great assistance when preparing a work such as the *Treasury.* We gladly acknowledge the particular help we have received from *Encyclopedic Dictionary of Yoga,* Georg Feuerstein (Paragon House, New York, 1990); *Encyclopaedia of Islam,* ed. H.A.R. Gibb *et al.* (Brill, Leiden, 1960–2005); *The Illustrated Encyclopedia of Zen Buddhism,* Helen Baroni (Rosen, New York, 2002); *Japanese-English Buddhist Dictionary,* Daito Shuppansha (Tokyo, 1965); *Oxford Dictionary of Buddhism,* Damien Keown (Oxford University Press, 2003); *Buddhist Dictionary: Manual of Buddhist Terms and Doctrines,* Ven. Nyanatiloka (Buddhist Publication Society, Sri Lanka, 1988); *The Princeton Dictionary of Buddhism,* Robert Buswell & Donald Lopez (Princeton University Press, New Jersey, 2014); *A Comprehensive Etymological Dictionary of the Hebrew Language for Readers of English,* ed. Ernest Klein (Carta Jerusalem, University of Haifa, 1987); *Encyclopedia Judaica* (Judaica Multimedia, Jerusalem, 1997); *Jewish Encyclopedia* (Funk & Wagnalls, New York, 1901–6, www.jewishencyclopedia.com); *The Catholic Encyclopedia* (Robert Appleton Co., 1907–14); *Wikipedia* (wikipedia.org, 2001–); *Hawaiian Dictionary,* Mary Kawena Pukui & Samuel Elbert (University of Hawaii Press, Honolulu, 1986); *Te Aka: Māori-English, English-Māori Dictionary and Index,* John Moorfield (www.maoridictionary.co.nz); *A Dictionary of the Maori Language*, Herbert Williams (nzetc.victoria.ac.nz/tm/scholarly/tei-WillDict.html); and *The A to Z of Jainism,* Kristi Wiley (Vision, New Delhi, 2006).

We also greatly appreciate the publishers, copyright holders and administrators for giving their specific permission to include excerpts, as below. In all instances, all rights are reserved by the copyright holders. Full bibliographical details can be found in the bibliography. Excerpts from:

Drops of Nectar – Khenpo Kunpal's Commentary on Shantideva's Entering the Conduct of the Bodhisattvas, etc., tr. Andreas Kretschmar, copyright © 2003 by Andreas Kretschmar; reprinted by permission of Andreas Kretschmar (www.kunpal.com).

The Feats of the Knowers of God (Manāqeb al-ʿārefin), Shams al-Dīn Aḥmad-e Aflākī, tr. John O'Kane (Brill, 2002), copyright © 2002 by Koninklijke Brill NV; reprinted by permission of Brill, Leiden, The Netherlands.

The Jerusalem Bible, published and copyright © 1966, 1967 and 1968 by Darton, Longman and Todd Ltd., and Doubleday, a division of Random House Inc.; reprinted by permission.

The New Jerusalem Bible, published and copyright © 1985 by Darton, Longman and Todd Ltd., and Doubleday, a division of Random House Inc.; reprinted by permission.

The Authorized (King James) Version. Rights in the *Authorized Version* in the United Kingdom are vested in the Crown. Reproduced by permission of the Crown's patentee, Cambridge University Press.

Black Elk: The Sacred Ways of a Lakota, Wallace H. Black Elk and William S. Lyon PhD., copyright © 1990 by Wallace H. Black Elk and William S. Lyon, pp.xi, xi–xii, xviii–xix, 4, 6–8, 43–44, 136–37; reprinted by permission of HarperCollins Publishers.

Tanakh: The Holy Scriptures in *The CD-ROM Judaic Classics Library (The Bible),* copyright © David Mandel 1998; reprinted by permission of David Mandel.

The Jerusalem Bible, English text rev. & ed. Harold Fisch; copyright © 1972, 1994 by Koren Publishers Jerusalem; reprinted by permission of Koren Publishers Jerusalem Ltd.

Translation from the Buddhist Pali *Suttas* by Thanissaro Bhikkhu, published by Access to Insight (www.accesstoinsight.org), copyright © by Thanissaro Bhikkhu; reprinted by permission of Thanissaro Bhikkhu.

Fools Crow: Wisdom and Power, Thomas E. Mails, copyright © Thomas E. Mails 1991; reprinted by permission of Tri S Foundation, available from www.millichapbooks.com.

Zen and the Brain: Towards an Understanding of Meditation and Consciousness, James H. Austin, copyright © by James H. Austin, 1999; reprinted by permission of the publishers, The MIT Press.

Sufi Symbolism: The Nurbakhsh Encyclopedia of Sufi Terminology, 15 vols., Dr Javad Nurbakhsh, tr. Terry Graham *et al.,* copyright © Dr Javad Nurbakhsh 1984–2000; reprinted by permission of Khaniqahi-Nimatullahi Publications.

Tohunga – The Revival: Ancient Knowledge for the Modern Era, Samuel Timoti Robinson (Penguin, Rosedale, New Zealand), copyright © by Samuel Robinson 2005; reprinted by permission of Samuel Robinson.

The Complete Dead Sea Scrolls in English, Geza Vermes (Allen Lane, Penguin Press, 1997), copyright © by Geza Vermes, 1962, 1965, 1968, 1975, 1995, 1997, 2004; *The Conference of the Birds,* Farid ud-Din Attar, tr. Afkham Darbandi and Dick Davis (Penguin Classics, 1984), copyright © 1984 by Afkham Darbandi and Dick Davis; *The Penguin Book of*

Hebrew Verse, ed. T. Carmi (Allen Lane, 1981), copyright © by T. Carmi 1981; *The Ladder of Perfection,* Walter Hilton, translated by Leo Sherley Price, introduction by Clifton Wolters (Penguin Classics, 1957, reissued 1988), translation copyright © Leo Sherley Price, introduction copyright © 1988 Clifton Wolters; reprinted by permission of Penguin Books Ltd.

The Philokalia: The Complete Text, Compiled by St Nikodimos of the Holy Mountain and St Makarios of Corinth, ed. & tr. G.E.H. Palmer, Philip Sherrard, Kallistos Ware (Faber & Faber, London), copyright © by The Eling Trust (1979, 1981, 1984, 1995); reprinted by permission of Metropolitan Kallistos and The Eling Trust.

The Lotus Sutra and Its Opening and Closing Sutras, tr. Burton Watson (Soka Gakkai, 2009), copyright © by Soka Gakkai (Tokyo) 2009; reprinted by permission of Soka Gakkai International. In these excerpts, to allow for standard *Treasury* usage, some terms have been replaced by the Sanskrit, or the Chinese term has been added in brackets. For the original, see: www.nichirenlibrary.org/en/lsoc/toc/.

The Sufi Path of Love: The Spiritual Teachings of Rūmī, William C. Chittick, the State University of New York Press, copyright © 1984, State University of New York; reprinted by permission of the State University of New York Press, all rights reserved.

The Sufi Path of Knowledge: Ibn al-ʿArabi's Metaphysics of Imagination, William Chittick, the State University of New York Press, copyright © 1989, State University of New York; reprinted by permission of the State University of New York Press, all rights reserved.

The Teachings and Practices of the Early Quanzhen Taoist Masters, Stephen Eskildsen; State University of New York Press, copyright © 2006, State University of New York; reprinted by permission of the State University of New York Press, all rights reserved.

Middle Length Discourses of the Buddha: A New Translation of the Majjhima Nikāya, tr. Bhikkhu Ñāṇamoli, ed. & rev. Bhikkhu Bodhi, copyright © Bhikkhu Bodhi 1995; *The Long Discourses of the Buddha: A Translation of the Dīgha Nikāya,* tr. Maurice Walshe, copyright © Maurice Walshe 1995; *The Connected Discourses of the Buddha: A Translation of the Saṃyutta Nikāya,* 2 vols., tr. Bhikkhu Bodhi, copyright © Bhikkhu Bodhi 2000; reprinted by permission of Wisdom Publications.

We have done our best to track down all the relevant copyright holders or administrators for all material for which it seemed that copyright permission would be required. In the event of any errors or omissions, please advise us, so that matters may be rectified.

Thanks are also due to Dr John Smith, now retired from the Faculty of Oriental Studies, Cambridge University, for his Unicode character fonts.

Abbreviations

General

Abbreviations that are a common part of written language are not included in this list.

C4th	fourth century (*e.g.)*
cf.	*confero,* compare (L. I compare)
col.	column
fol.	folio
ff.	and the following (pages, lines, *etc.*)
lit.	literally
n.	foot- or endnote(s)
passim	here and there throughout (L)
p.	page
pp.	pages
pron.	pronounced
ret.	retrieved web page, followed by the month and year of retrieval
▸1 ▸3 ▸4	Indicates a yet-to-be-published entry in Parts I, III, or IV

Dates

b.	born
c.	circa, about
d.	died
fl.	flourished
r.	reigned or ruled
AH	*Anno Hegirae,* Muslim lunar calendar, from 622 CE, the Hegira *(al-Hijrah),* the year of Muḥammad's flight to Madīnah
BCE	Before Common Era, equivalent to BC.
CE	Common Era, equivalent to AD.
SH	Solar Hijri, the official solar calendar of Iran and Afghanistan, starting on the vernal equinox.

Languages

A	Arabic	C	Chinese	Gk	Greek
AC	Avá-Chiripá	Es	Spanish	H	Hindi
Am	Aramaic	Fr	French	He	Hebrew
Av	Avestan	G	Guaraní	Hw	Hawaian

J	Japanese	P	Persian	S	Sanskrit
L	Latin	Pa	Pali	Su	Sumerian
M	Marathi	Pk	Prakrit	T	Tibetan
Md	Mandaean	Pu	Punjabi	U	Urdu
Mo	Māori	Pv	Pahlavi		

Sources Cited

See *Bibliography* for full details of published works. Published collections of the writings of Indian Saints have been referred to in source references as below. Other collections published as the *Bānī, Granthāvalī, Padāvalī* or *Shabdāvalī* of various Indian Saints have been similarly abbreviated.

Bullā Sāhib kā Shabd Sār	*Shabd Sār*
Charaṇdās Jī kī Bānī	*Bānī*
Dariyā Sāhib ke chune hue Shabd	*Chune hue Shabd*
Dhanī Dharamdās Jī kī Shabdāvalī	*Shabdāvalī*
Kabīr Granthāvalī	*Granthāvalī*
Kabīr Sāhib kā Bījak	*Bījak*
Kabīr Sākhī Sangrah	*Sākhī Sangrah*
Keshavdās Jī kī Amīghūnt	*Amīghūnt*
Kullīyāt-i Bulleh Shāh	*Kullīyāt*
Mīrā Bṛihat Padāvalī	*Bṛihat Padāvalī*
Mīrā Sudhā Sindhu	*Sindhu*
Nāmdev kī Hindi Padāvalī	*Padāvalī*
Ravidās Darshan	*Darshan*
Sant Guru Ravidās Vāṇī	*Vāṇī*
Shrī Nāmdev Gāthā	*Gāthā*
Tulsīdās kī Bārahmāsī	*Bārahmāsī*
Tulsī Sāhib Hāthrasvale kī Shabdāvalī	*Shabdāvalī*

Other books and texts cited are abbreviated as follows:

AAA	*The Apocryphal Acts of the Apostles,* ed. & tr. W.R. Wright (English).
AASZ	*Ano Ano: The Seed,* Kristin Zambucka.
ABC	*Apocalypse of Baruch,* tr. R.H. Charles.
ABCD	*Atthasālinī,* ed. Edward Müller.
ADP	*Abandonment to Divine Providence,* J.-P. de Caussade, tr. J. Beevers.
AF1–2	*The Apostolic Fathers,* 2 vols., tr. Kirsopp Lake.
AGG	*Sri Guru Granth Sahib,* 4 vols., tr. Dr Gopal Singh.
AGK	*Sri Guru Granth Sahib: Khalsa Consensus Translation,* tr. Dr Sant Singh Khalsa.

AH1–2	*Against Heresies,* in *The Writings of Irenaeus,* 2 vols., tr. A. Roberts & W.H. Rambaud.
AJT	*Annales,* 15 vols., Abū Jaʿfar Muḥammad ibn Jarīr al-Ṭabarī.
AKN1–2	*The Apadāna of the Khuddaka Nikāya,* 2 vols., ed. Mary Lilley.
AKRT	*Abhinavagupta,* John Dupuche.
AMAS	*Al-Muʿjam al-Ṣūfī,* Khānam Dr Suʿād al-Ḥakīm.
AMBF	*Aḥādīś-i Maśnavī,* B. Furūzānfar.
AMEI	*Te Aka: Māori-English, English-Māori Dictionary and Index,* John Moorfield.
AMM	*Dīvān-i Ḥakīm Abū al-Majd Majdūd ibn-i Ādam Sanāʾī Ghaznavī,* ed. Mudarris Riżavī.
AMMB	*Some Aspects of Maori Myth and Religion,* Elsdon Best.
ANNP	*Anguttara Nikaya,* Nyanaponika Thera.
ANST	*Anguttara Nikaya,* tr. Soma Thera.
ANT	*The Apocryphal New Testament,* tr. M.R. James.
ANTB	*Anguttara Nikaya,* tr. Thanissaro Bhikkhu. See *Acknowledgements.*
ANTH	*The Authentic New Testament,* tr. H.J. Schonfield.
AOT	*The Apocryphal Old Testament,* ed. H.E.D. Sparks.
ARSR	*Adhyatma Ramayana,* tr. Swami Tapasyananda.
ARTM	*Ancestral Recordings of Tainui,* Mitaki Ra.
ATS1–2	*Asrār al-Tawḥīd fī Maqāmāt al-Shaykh Abī Saʿīd,* 2 vols., M. ibn Munavvar, ed. & intro. M. Rażā Shafāʾī Kadkanī.
AYA	*The Holy Qurʾān,* tr. & comm. ʿAbdullah Yūsuf ʿAlī.
AZJW	*The A to Z of Jainism,* Kristi Wiley.
BBAV	*Bahiṇā Bāī,* Justin Abbott.
BBH	*The Book of Balance and Harmony,* tr. Thomas Cleary.
BC	*The Books of Jeu and the Untitled Text in the Bruce Codex,* tr. Violet MacDermot.
BDB	*Beiträge zur Kenntnis der religiösen Dichtung Balai's,* K.V. Zetterstéen.
BDBS	*The Bodhisattva Doctrine in Buddhist Sanskrit Literature,* Har Dayal.
BDC	*The Book of Divine Consolation of the Blessed Angela of Foligno,* tr. M. Steegman.
BDV1–6	*The Book of the Discipline (Vinaya-Piṭaka),* 6 vols., tr. I.B. Horner.
BESW	*Black Elk: The Sacred Ways of a Lakota,* Wallace Black Elk & William Lyon. See *Acknowledgements.*
BFFM	*Bodhisattvas of the Forest and the Formation of the Mahāyāna,* Daniel Boucher.
BGT	*Bhagavad Gītā,* tr. Swāmī Tapasyānanda.
BLD1–3	*Buddhist Legends,* 3 vols., Buddhaghosa, tr. E.W. Burlingame.
BMC1–2	*Buddhist Monastic Code,* 2 parts, tr. & comm. Ṭhānissaro Bhikkhu.
BOS	*Badāyiʾ,* ed. & tr. Lucas White King.

BPT1–5	*The Bhāgavata Purāṇa,* 5 vols., tr. & ann. G.V. Tagare.
BSFD	*Branching Streams Flow in the Darkness,* Shunryu Suzuki, ed. M. Weitsman & M. Wenger.
BSPS	*Bulleh Shah,* J.R. Puri & T.R. Shangari.
BTIC	*The Buddhist Tradition in India, China and Japan,* ed. William De Bary.
BTLD	*Buddhism in Tibet,* Emil Schlagintweit.
BTOT	*The Buddhist Teaching of Totality,* Garma C.C. Chang.
BWIC	*Ibn 'Ata' Illah: The Book of Wisdom,* tr. V. Danner, and *Kwaja Abdullah Ansari: Intimate Conversations,* tr. W. Thackston.
CBD	*The Conference of the Birds,* Farid ud-Din Attar, tr. Afkham Darbandi & Dick Davis. See *Acknowledgements.*
CBET	*The Concept of the Buddha,* Guang Xing.
CCED	*Cosmos and Community,* Livia Kohn.
CDBB	*The Connected Discourses of the Buddha,* 2 vols., tr. Bhikkhu Bodhi. See *Acknowledgements.*
CDP	*The Collected Dialogues of Plato,* ed. E. Hamilton & H. Cairns.
CDSV	*The Complete Dead Sea Scrolls in English,* Geza Vermes (2004). See *Acknowledgements.*
CGAP	*St Augustine: Concerning the City of God against the Pagans,* tr. Henry Bettenson.
CH	*The Clementine Homilies,* tr. Thomas Smith *et al.*
CMMD	*Concentration and Meditation,* Christmas Humphreys.
CPM	*The Canonical Prayerbook of the Mandaeans,* tr. E.S. Drower.
CSM	*Die Chroniken der Stadt Mekka,* ed. Wustenfeld.
CSRK	"Socrates, the Freethinker," R. Janko.
CTIH	*Chuang Tzu,* tr. David Hinton.
CTSU	*Commentary on Tattvārtha Sūtra of Vācaka Umāsvāti,* Pandit Sukhalalji, tr. K.K. Dixit.
CU	*The Cloud of Unknowing,* tr. William Johnston.
CVAB	*The Call of the Vedas,* A.C. Bose.
CW	*Angelus Silesius: The Cherubinic Wanderer,* tr. Maria Shrady.
CWCT	*The Complete Works of Chuang Tzu,* tr. Burton Watson.
CWJC1–3	*The Complete Works of Saint John of the Cross,* 3 vols., ed. & tr. E. Allison Peers.
CWSV1–9	*Complete Works of Swami Vivekananda,* 9 vols.
CWT1–3	*The Collected Works of St. Teresa of Avila,* 3 vols., tr. Kieran Kavanaugh & Otilio Rodriquez.
CWTA1–3	*The Complete Works of Saint Teresa of Jesus,* 3 vols., ed. & tr. E. Allison Peers.
DASN	*Dīvān-i 'Aṭṭār,* incl. *Qaṣā'id, Tarjī'āt, va Ghazaliyāt,* ed. Sa'īd Nafīsī.
DBGT	*A Dictionary of Buddhism,* Trevor Ling.
DBRD	*Dialogues of the Buddha,* Part I, tr. T.W. Rhys Davids.

DCBP	*The Dhammapada and Commentary,* tr. Nārada Thera, ed. Bhikkhu Pesala.
DCMU	*Dadu: The Compassionate Mystic,* K.N. Upadhyaya.
DDB1–2	*Dādū Dayāl kī Bānī,* 2 vols.
DDMW	*Dynamic and Different: Mana Wahine,* Rosemary Madden.
DDRR	*Rubâi'yât,* Mawlânâ Djalâl-od-Dîn Rûmî, tr. Eva de Vitray-Meyerovitch & Djamchid Mortazavi.
DG1–2	*Dariyā Granthāvalī,* 2 vols., D.B. Shāstrī.
DHA	*Dīvān-i Khwājah Ḥāfiẓ Shīrāzī,* ed. Abū al-Qāsim Anjavī Shīrāzī.
DHHM	*Dīvān-i Ḥāfiẓ,* Ḥājjī Malik Dīn Muḥammad & Sons, Lahore.
DHK1–2	*Daoism Handbook,* 2 vols., ed. Livia Kohn.
DHM	*Dīvān-i Ḥāfiẓ,* Malik Ghulām Muḥammad & Sons.
DHWC	*The Dīvān-i-Ḥāfiẓ,* 2 vols., tr. H. Wilberforce Clarke.
DIH	*Dīvān-i Ḥāfiẓ,* ed. Qāzi Sajjād Ḥusayn.
DKK	*Dīvān-i Kamāl al-Dīn Mas'ūd-i Khujandī,* ed. 'Azīz Dawlatābādī.
DL	*Divine Light,* Maharaj Charan Singh.
DMHS	*Dīvān-i Ḥājjī Mullā Hādī-yi Sabzavārī (Asrār),* ed. Sayyid Muḥammad Riżā Dā'i-Javād.
DNK1–5	*Drops of Nectar,* 5 vols., tr. Andreas Kretschmar. See *Acknowledgements.*
DNTB	*Digha Nikaya,* tr. Thanissaro Bhikkhu. See *Acknowledgements.*
DNVS	*Digha Nikaya,* tr. Sister Vajira & Francis Story.
DP1–4	*The Dialogues of Plato,* 4 vols., tr. B. Jowett.
DPN	*The Dhammapada,* Narada Thera.
DPR	*The Dhammapada,* tr. S Radhakrishnan.
DR	*The Divine Romance,* John Davidson.
DRA	*Discourses of Rūmī,* tr. & comm. A.J. Arberry.
DSMR	*Dīvān-i Kāmil-i Shams-i Maghribī,* Muḥammad Shīrīn Maghribī.
DSSE	*The Dead Sea Scrolls in English,* Geza Vermes (1988).
DSSK	*Dariya Sahib: Saint of Bihar,* K.N. Upadhyaya.
DSSM	*The Dead Sea Scrolls,* Millar Burrows.
DTDG	*Dohāvalī,* Tulsīdās.
DTL	*Die to Live,* Maharaj Charan Singh.
EDYF	*Encyclopedic Dictionary of Yoga,* Georg Feuerstein.
EIM	*Early Islamic Mysticism,* Michael Sells.
EPR1–2	*St Ephraim's Prose Refutations of Mani, Marcion and Bardaisan,* 2 vols., C.W. Mitchell, A. A. Bevan & F.C. Burkitt.
ETCA	"The Excerpta ex Theodoto," R.P. Casey.
FFNA	*Fawā'id al-Fu'ād,* Niẓām al-Dīn Awliyā', Kvājah Amīr Ḥasan 'Alā Sijzī, Khvājah Ḥasan Śānī Niẓāmī.
FJFC	*Five Játakas,* tr. V. Fausböll.
FKG	*The Feats of the Knowers of God,* Shams al-Dīn Aḥmad-e Aflākī, tr. John O'Kane. See *Acknowledgements.*

FLML	*The Fire of Love and The Mending of Life,* Richard Rolle, tr. Richard Misyn, ed. Frances Comper.
FLRR	*The Fire of Love,* Richard Rolle, tr. Clifton Wolters.
FMIA1–9	*Futūḥāt al-Makkīyah,* 9 vols., Ibn al-ʿArabī, ed. Aḥmad S. al-Dīn.
FNI1–15	*Farhang-i Nūrbakhsh: Iṣṭilāḥāt-i Taṣawwuf,* 15 vols., Dr Javād Nūrbakhsh.
FOSC	*The Flower Ornament Scripture,* Thomas Cleary.
G12A	*The Gospel of the Twelve Apostles,* ed. & tr. J. Rendel Harris.
GCK	*Ghazālī's Book of Counsel for Kings,* tr. F.R.C. Bagley.
GDDS	*Gyān Dīpak,* Dariyā Sāhib.
GFAJ	*George Fox: An Autobiography,* ed. Rufus Jones.
GGG	*From Glory to Glory,* ed. & tr. H. Musurillo.
GJ	*The Gospel of Jesus,* John Davidson.
GJB	*The Gnostic John the Baptizer,* G.R.S. Mead.
GLMT	*The Great Liberation (Mahānirvāna Tantra),* tr. Arthur Avalon.
GLTS	*The Golden Letters, etc.,* tr. John Reynolds.
GR1–2	*Ghaṭ Rāmāyaṇ,* 2 vols., Tulsī Sāhib.
GRPS	*Guru Ravidas: The Philosopher's Stone,* K.N. Upadhyaya.
GRSS	*Gulshan-i Raz,* ed. & tr. E.H. Whinfield.
GS	*The Gnostic Scriptures,* Bentley Layton.
GSBM	*Ginzā der Schatz oder das Grosse Buch der Mandäer,* M. Lidzbarski.
GSR	*Gnosis on the Silk Road,* tr. H-J. Klimkeit.
GSV	*Gheranda Samhita,* tr. Rai Bahadur Srisa Chandra Vasu.
GT	*The Gospel of Truth,* K. Grobel.
GZAG	*A Guide to the Zohar,* Arthur Green.
HAG	*Hermetica,* ed. & tr. Walter Scott.
HC	*The History of the Church,* Eusebius, tr. G.A. Williamson.
HCPF	*Heraclitus: The Complete Philosophical Fragments,* tr. W. Harris.
HDMG	*History and Doings of the Maoris,* Thomas Gudgeon.
HEDA	*The Hymns and Homilies of Ephraim the Syrian and the Demonstrations of Aphrahat the Persian Sage,* tr. J. Gwynn.
HFJD	*The Heart and the Fountain,* ed. Joseph Dan.
HGCH	*Hermetica,* tr. Brian Copenhaver.
HHG	*The First Book of the Ḥadīqatu'l-Ḥaqīqat,* tr. J. Stephenson (English).
HHGP	*The First Book of the Ḥadīqatu'l-Ḥaqīqat,* J. Stephenson (Persian).
HJBB	*A Handbook of Jainology,* Acharyadeo Shri Bhuvanbhanijsoorishwarji, tr. K. Ramappa.
HJP1–3	*The History of the Jewish People in the Age of Jesus Christ,* 3 vols., E. Schürer, rev., ed. & tr. G. Vermes *et al.*
HMJS	*From the Holy Mountain,* William Dalrymple.

HMV	*W.B. Henning Memorial Volume,* ed. Mary Boyce & Ilya Gershevitch.
HPPS	*The Heart of Prajna Paramita Sutra,* comm. Master Hsuan Hua, tr. Buddhist Text Translation Society.
HSB	*Hadith Sahih al-Bukhari,* tr. Muhsin Khan.
HSDM	*The Hunger of the Soul: A Spiritual Diary,* Nancy Mayorga.
HSL2	*The Heritage of Sufism,* vol. 2, ed. Leonard Lewisohn.
HSM	*Hadith Sahih Muslim,* tr. Abdul Hamid Siddiqui.
HTBS	*Handbook of Tibetan Buddhist Symbols,* Robert Beer.
HYP	*Hatha Yoga Pradipika,* tr. Pancham Sinh.
HYPM	*Hatha Yoga Pradipika,* Swami Muktibodhananda & Swami Satyananda Saraswati.
IBTH	*An Introduction to Buddhism,* Peter Harvey.
IC	*The Imitation of Christ,* Thomas à Kempis, tr. R. Whitford (*c.*1530), ed. Harold Gardiner.
ICTK	*The Imitation of Christ,* Thomas à Kempis, tr. Leo Sherley Price.
IEZB	*The Illustrated Encyclopedia of Zen Buddhism,* Helen Baroni.
IKMH	*An Introduction to the Kabbalah,* Moshe Hallamish, tr. Ruth Bar-Ilan & Ora Wiskind-Elper.
IMRI	*An Introduction to Maori Religion,* James Irwin.
ITCT	*Illustrated Tirthankar Charitra,* ed. Shri Amar Muni.
J1–10	*Josephus,* 10 vols., tr. H. Thackeray *et al.*
JB	*The Jerusalem Bible* (1966). See *Acknowledgements.*
JBLB	*Jainism in Buddhist Literature,* Bhagchandra Jain Bhaskar.
JCL	*Tanakh: The Holy Scriptures* in *Judaic Classics Library.* See *Acknowledgements.*
JE	JewishEncyclopaedia, www.jewishencyclopedia.com.
JEDS	*Japanese-English Buddhist Dictionary,* Daito Shuppansha.
JEMS	*The Jade Emperor's Mind Seal Classic,* tr. Stuart Olson.
JGF1–2	*Journal of George Fox,* 2 vols., ann. Wilson Armistead.
JH1–108	*Dàozàng jīnghuá,* 108 titles.
JM	*Das Johannesbuch der Mandäer,* M. Lidzbarski (German).
JMKS	*Jewish Mysticism and Kabbalah,* ed. Frederick Greenspahn.
JMM	*Das Johannesbuch der Mandäer,* M. Lidzbarski (Mandaean).
JPP1–2	*Jain Philosophy and Practice,* 2 vols., comp. Jaina Education Committee.
JPPR	*Jaina Perspective in Philosophy and Religion,* Ramjee Singh.
JSB1–2	*Jagjīvan Sāhib kī Bānī,* 2 vols.
JSBB1–7	*The Jātaka or Stories of the Buddha's Former Births,* 7 vols., ed. E.B Cowells.
JTPB	*Jain Theory of Perception,* Pushpa Bothra.
JVLK	*Jaina View of Life,* T.G. Kalghati.

JWW	*The Jewish War,* Josephus, tr. G.A. Williamson.
KA1–10	*Kashf al-Asrār va-ʿUddat al-Abrār,* 10 vols., Abū al-Fażl Rashīd al-Dīn Maybudī, ed. ʿAlī Aṣghar Ḥikmat.
KB	*The Jerusalem Bible,* English text rev. & ed. Harold Fisch. See *Acknowledgements.*
KBS	*Kullīyāt-i Bulleh Shāh,* Faqīr Muḥammad.
KDRM	*Al-Kawākib al-Durrīyah fī Tarājim al-Sādah al-Ṣūfīyah,* ʿAbd al-Raʾūf al-Munāwī.
KDT1–2	*Al-Kawākib al-Durriyyah fī Tarājim al-Sādah al-Ṣūfiyyah,* 2 vols., al-Munāwi, ed. Aḥmad Farīd al-Mizyadi.
KFF	*Kitāb Fīhi mā Fīhi,* Jalāl al-Dīn Rūmī, ed. B. Furūzānfar.
KG	*Kabīr Granthāvalī,* ed. Shyām Sundardās.
KGME	*Kabir: The Great Mystic,* I.A. Ezekiel.
KHI	*Kullīyāt-i Shaykh Fakhr al-dīn Ibrāhīm Hamadānī ʿIrāqī,* ed. Saʿīd Nafīsī.
KIFT1–4	*Kashshāf Iṣṭilāḥāt al-Funūn,* 4 vols., al-Tahānawī, ed. A.H. Basaj.
KJV	*The Bible: The Authorized (King James) Version.* See *Acknowledgements.*
KM	*Kashf al-Mahjūb,* al-Hujwīrī, ed. & tr. R.A. Nicholson.
KMA1–4	*Kitāb al-Mawāʿiẓ wa al-Iʿtibār bi Dhikr al-Khiṭaṭ wa al-Āthār,* 4 vols., Aḥmad ibn ʿAlī ibn ʿAbd al-Qādir al-Maqrīzī.
KMM	*Kashf al-Maḥjūb,* Hujwīrī, ed. V.A. Zhukovsky.
KNLG	*Kullīyāt,* Bhāʾī Nand Lāl Goyā, ed. Gandā Singh.
KNTB	*Khuddaka Nikaya,* tr. Thanissaro Bhikkhu. See *Acknowledgements.*
KODW	*Kingitanga,* Mitaki Ra.
KOT	*The Kephalaia of the Teacher,* Iain Gardner.
KPA	*The Koran: With a Parallel Arabic Text,* tr. N.J. Dawood.
KSB	*Kabīr Sāhib kā Bījak.*
KSD1–10	*Kullīyāt-i Shams yā Dīvān-i Kabīr,* 10 vols., ed. B. Furūzānfar.
KSS	*Kabīr Sākhī Sangrah.*
KSS1–4	*Kabīr Sāhib kī Shabdāvalī,* 4 vols.
KSSL	*Kashmir Shaivism: The Secret Supreme,* Swami Lakshman Jee.
KSSS	*Kullīyāt-i Saʿdī,* Shaykh Muṣliḥ Dīn Saʿdī Shīrazī.
KSTK	*Khulāṣah-ʾi Sharḥ-i Taʿarruf,* ed. Aḥmad ʿAlī Rajāʾī.
KTA	*Kitāb al-Taʿrīfāt,* al-Jurjānī, ed. I. al-Ābyārī.
KTAA	*Kulārṇava Tantra,* Arthur Avalon, readings M.P. Pandit.
KTJ	*Kitāb al-Taʿrīfāt,* al-Jurjānī, ed. ʿĀdil Anwar Khiḍr.
KTS	*Kitāb Ṭabaqāt al-Ṣūfīyah,* Sulamī, ed. Johannes Pedersen.
KWGN	*Kabir: The Weaver of God's Name,* V.K. Sethi.
LBBN	*The Life of the Buddha,* tr. Bhikkhu Ñāṇamoli.
LBFD	*Scripture of the Lotus Blossom of the Fine Dharma,* tr. L. Hurvitz.
LGMD	*Laṭīfah-ʾi Ghaybī,* Muḥammad ibn Muḥammad al-Dārābī.

LMTB	"The Legend of Mahu and Taewha," Elsdon Best.
LOSM	*Light on Sant Mat,* Maharaj Charan Singh.
LPH	*The Ladder of Perfection,* Walter Hilton, tr. Leo Sherley Price. See *Acknowledgements.*
LSGR	*The Lotus Sutra,* tr. Gene Reeves.
LSMC	*Light on Saint Matthew,* Maharaj Charan Singh.
LSMH	"Lower (Second?) Section of the Manichaean Hymns," tr. T. Chi.
LSOC	*The Lotus Sutra and Its Opening and Closing Sutras,* tr. Burton Watson. See *Acknowledgements.*
LTJG	*The Living Talmud,* Judah Goldin.
LWKT	*The Lore of the Whare-wānanga,* Te Matorohanga, tr. S.P. Smith.
MAA	"The Mythological Acts of the Apostles," A.S. Lewis.
MAFG	*Majmūʻah-ʼi Āsar-i Fārsī,* Aḥmad Ghazālī, ed. Aḥmad Mujāhid.
MARB	*Mashrab al-Arwāḥ,* Rūzbihān Baqlī, ed. ʻĀsim Ibrāhim al-Kayālī.
MASA1–2	*Manāqib al-ʻĀrifīn,* 2 vols., al-Aflākī al-ʻĀrifī, ed. Taḥsīn Yāzījī.
MBB	*Ein Manichäisches Bet- und Beichtbuch,* W.B. Henning.
MBDF	*Mahāyāna Buddhism: The Doctrinal Foundations,* Paul Williams.
MBST	*Bon-zo-Kan-Wa shi-yaku tai ko (Mahāvyutpatti),* 2 vols, ed. Ryōzaburō Sakaki.
MCLM	*Manu's Code of Law,* Patrick Olivelle.
MDB	*Malūkdās Jī kī Bānī.*
MDBB	*Middle Length Discourses of the Buddha,* tr. Bhikkhu Ñāṇamoli, ed. & rev. Bhikkhu Bodhi. See *Acknowledgements.*
MDI	*Mystical Dimensions of Islam,* Annemarie Schimmel.
MDLS	*Mira: The Divine Lover,* V.K. Sethi.
MDT	"Manichäische Dogmatik aus chinesischen und iranischen Texten," E. Waldschmidt & W. Lentz.
MEM	"Mesopotamian Elements in Manichaeism," G. Widengren.
MGK	*The Meaning of the Glorious Koran,* Marmaduke Pickthall.
MH	"Ein Manichäisches Henochbuch," W.B. Henning.
MHCP	*The Manichaean Hymn-Cycles in Parthian,* tr. M. Boyce.
MHK	*Miṣbāḥ al-Hidāyah wa-Miftāḥ al-Kifāyah,* ʻIzz al-Dīn Maḥmūd Qāshānī, ed. Jalāl al-Dīn Humāʼī.
MHN	*Morals for the Heart,* tr. Bruce Lawrence.
MHVA	*Mahāvastu-Avadāna,* 3 vols., ed. Émile Senart.
MJR1–8	*The Mathnawī of Jalālu'ddīn Rūmī,* 8 vols., ed., tr. & comm. R.A. Nicholson.
ML	*Manichaean Literature,* J.P. Asmussen.
MMS	*Sri Guru Granth Sahib,* 8 vols., tr. Manmohan Singh.
MMSY	*Mahayana Mahaparinirvana Sutra,* tr. Kosho Yamamoto, ed. Tony Page (2007).
MNNB	*Majjhima Nikaya,* tr. Nanamoli Thera & Bhikkhu Bodhi. See *Acknowledgements.*

MNNP	*Majjhima Nikaya,* tr. Nyanaponika Thera.
MP1–2	*Mystical Poems of Rumi,* 2 vols., tr. A.J. Arberry.
MPAS	"Maori Personifications," Elsdon Best.
MPB	*A Manichaean Psalm-Book,* Part II, ed. & tr. C.R.C. Allberry.
MRG	"Maori Religion," Walter Gudgeon.
MRJA	"Maori Religion," Johannes Andersen.
MRM1–2	*Maori Religion and Mythology,* 2 parts, Elsdon Best.
MSAN	*Maśnavīhā-yi Sanā'ī,* ed. ʿAbd al-Rażā Sayf & Ghulām Ḥusayn.
MSLB	*The Maori School of Learning,* Elsdon Best.
MSM	*Muslim Saints and Mystics,* Farid al-Din Attar, tr. A.J. Arberry.
MSS	*Mīrā Sudhā Sindhu.*
MTAN	*Manṭiq al-Ṭayr, Shaykh ʿAṭṭār Nīshābūrī,* ed. Muḥammad Rażā Shafāʿī Kadkanī.
MTIN	*Mystic Treatises by Isaac of Nineveh,* tr. A.J. Wensinck.
MTSB	*Midrash Tanḥuma,* ed. Solomon Buber.
MTTL	*Mahānirvāna Tantra,* tr. & comm. Arthur Avalon.
MVJ1–3	*The Mahāvastu,* 3 vols., tr. J. J. Jones.
MVOS	*Many Voices, One Song,* Judith Sankaranarayan.
NARB	*Native American Religion,* Nancy Bonvillain.
NAWB	"Notes on the Art of War, *etc.*" Elsdon Best.
NBST	*Nārada Bhakti Sūtras,* Swāmī Tyāgīśānanda.
NDBB	*The Numerical Discourses of the Buddha,* tr. Bhikkhu Bodhi. See *Acknowledgements.*
NEB	*The New English Bible.*
NEL	*Nourishing the Essence of Life,* tr. Eva Wong.
NHS15	*Nag Hammadi Studies* XV, ed. Birger Pearson.
NHS20	*Nag Hammadi Studies* XX, vol. 1, ed. Bentley Layton.
NHS21	*Nag Hammadi Studies* XXI, vol. 2, ed. Bentley Layton.
NHS22	*Nag Hammadi Studies* XXII, vol. 1, ed. Harold Attridge.
NHS28	*Nag Hammadi Studies* XXVIII, ed. Charles Hedrick.
NHS30	*Nag Hammadi Studies* XXX, ed. Birger Pearson.
NHS31	*Nag Hammadi Studies* XXXI, ed. John Sieber.
NHS33	*Nag Hammadi Studies* XXXIII, ed. M. Waldstein & F. Wisse.
NHS4	*Nag Hammadi Studies* IV, ed. A. Böhlig & F. Wisse.
NJB	*The New Jerusalem Bible* (1985). See *Acknowledgements.*
NKK1–2	*Nānā I Ke Kumu,* 2 vols., Mary Kawena Pukui *et al.*
NKTF	*Nuṣūṣ al-Khuṣūṣ fi Tarjamah al-Fuṣūṣ,* Rukn al-Dīn ibn ʿAbd Allāh Shīrāzī.
NR1–2	*The Nestorians and Their Rituals,* 2 vols., G.P. Badger.
NUJ	*Nafaḥāt al-Uns,* ʿAbd al-Raḥmān Jāmī, ed. Mahdī Tawhīdīpūr.
OCM	*The Origins of the Christian Mystical Tradition,* A. Louth.
ODB	*Oxford Dictionary of Buddhism,* Damien Keown.
OPJ	*On the Prayer of Jesus,* Ignatius Brianchaninov, tr. Father Lazarus.

OSD	*The Odes of Solomon,* John Davidson.
OSDP	*Œuvres spirituelles,* Diadoque de Photicé, tr. Édouard des Places.
OTP1–2	*The Old Testament Pseudoepigrapha,* 2 vols., ed. J.H. Charlesworth.
OWKG	"The Occupation of Wounded Knee," Tom Gillen.
PAS	*8 Chapters on Perfection & Angels' Song,* Walter Hilton, tr. Rosemary Dorward.
PBD	*Buddhist Dictionary,* Ven. Nyanatiloka.
PCCV	*Play of Consciousness,* Swami Muktananda.
PCT1–5	*The Philokalia,* 4 vols., ed. & tr. G.E.H. Palmer, Philip Sherrard, Kallistos Ware. See *Acknowledgements.*
PCW1–10	*Philo,* 10 vols., tr. F.H. Colson & G.H. Whitaker.
PDB	*The Princeton Dictionary of Buddhism,* R. Buswell & D. Lopez.
PDPM	*The Path of Discrimination,* tr. Bhikkhu Ñānamoli.
PES	*Panarion of Epiphanius of Salamis,* tr. F. Williams.
PG1–161	*Patrologiae cursus completus... Series Graeca,* 161 vols., ed. J.-P. Migne.
PMA	*The Persian Mystics: Ansāri of Herat,* Jogendra Singh.
PMB1–15	*Plutarch's Moralia,* 15 vols., tr. F.C. Babbitt *et al.*
PMS1–5	*Philosophy of the Masters,* 5 vols., Huzur Maharaj Sawan Singh.
PNC	*A Pair of Naṣoraean Commentaries,* tr. E.S. Drower.
PPHS	*The Prajna Paramita Heart Sutra,* comm. Grand Master T'an Hsu, tr. Master Lok To.
PPVM	*The Path of Purification,* Buddhaghosa, tr. Bhikkhu Ñāṇamoli.
PS	*Pistis Sophia,* tr. Violet MacDermot.
PSB1–3	*Paltū Sāhib kī Bānī,* 3 vols.
PSGG	*Pistis Sophia: A Gnostic Gospel,* G.R.S. Mead.
PSHC	*Physician of the Soul, Healer of the Cosmos,* Lawrence Fine.
PSSL	*The Pratyutpanna Samādhi Sūtra,* tr. Paul Harrison.
PSW	*The Prodigal Soul,* John Davidson.
PTSA1–6	*The Aṅguttara-nikāya,* 6 vols., ed. R. Morris & E. Hardy.
PTSD1–3	*The Dīgha-nikāya,* 3 vols., ed. T.W. Rhys Davids & J.E. Carpenter.
PTSDA1–5	*The Commentary on the Dhammapada,* 5 vols., ed. H.C. Norman & H. Smith.
PTSI	*Itivuttaka,* ed. E. Windisch.
PTSJ1–8	*Jātaka with Commentary,* 8 vols., ed. V. Fausbøll.
PTSM1–4	*The Majjhima-nikāya,* 4 vols., ed. V. Trenckner & R. Chalmers.
PTSN	*Suttanipāta,* ed. D. Anderson & Helmer Smith.
PTSP	*Puggala-paññati,* ed. R. Morris, and *Puggala-paññatti-atthakathā,* ed. G. Landsberg & C.A.F. Rhys Davids.
PTSP1–2	*Paṭisambhidāmagga,* 2 vols., ed. A.C. Taylor.
PTSQ	*Milindapañha,* ed. V. Trenckner.
PTSS1–6	*Samyutta-nikāya,* 6 vols., ed. L. Feer.

PTST	*Theragāthā and Therīgāthā,* ed. H. Oldenberg & R. Pischel.
PTSU	*Udāna,* ed. P. Steinthal.
PTSV	*The Visuddhi-Magga of Buddhaghosa,* ed. C.A.F. Rhys Davids.
PTSV1–5	*Vinaya-piṭaka,* 5 vols., ed. H. Oldenberg.
PU	*The Principal Upaniṣads,* tr. S. Radhakrishnan.
RAIH	*The Religions of the American Indians,* Åke Hultkrantz, tr. Monica Setterwall.
RBDS	*Refuge,* Thanissaro Bhikkhu.
RCML	*Śrī Rāmacaritamānasa,* Tulasīdāsa.
RDL	*Revelations of Divine Love,* Julian of Norwich, tr. C. Wolters.
RIS	*Rubaiyat-i-Sarmad,* ed. & tr. Fażl Maḥmūd Asīrī (English).
RISP	*Rubaiyat-i-Sarmad,* ed. & tr. Fażl Maḥmūd Asīrī (Persian).
RLRI	*Risālah-'i Lam'āt va Risālah-'i Iṣṭilaḥāt,* Fakhr al-Dīn Ibrāhīm 'Irāqī, ed. Javād Nūrbakhsh.
RM	*Rabi'a the Mystic and her Fellow-Saints in Islam,* M. Smith.
RMP	*A Reader in Manichaean Middle Persian and Parthian,* Mary Boyce.
RNV1–4	*Rasā'il Shāh Ni'matullāhī Valī,* 4 vols., ed. Javād Nūrbakhsh.
RQQQ	*Al-Risālah al-Qushayrīyah,* Abū al-Qāsim Qushayrī, ed. Muṣṭafā al-Bābī al-Ḥalabī.
RSV	*The Holy Bible: The Revised Standard Version* (1952).
RTHM	*Rangitāne: A Tribal History,* J.M. McEwen.
SA	*The Secret Adam: A Study of Naṣoraean Gnosis,* E.S. Drower.
SAGH	*Sefer Ari ve-Gurav,* ed. Ya'akov Hillel.
SB1–18	*Śrīmad Bhāgavatam of Kṛṣṇa-Dvaipāyana Vyāsa,* 18 vols., A.C. Bhaktivedanta Swami Prabhupada.
SBAT	*Sar Bachan: An Abstract of the Teachings of Soami Ji Maharaj.*
SBB	*Sahajobāī kī Bānī.*
SBE	*Sultan Bahu,* J.R. Puri & K.S. Khak.
SBE11	*Buddhist Suttas,* tr. T.W. Rhys Davids.
SBE25	*The Laws of Manu,* tr. George Bühler.
SBE35–36	*The Questions of King Milinda,* 2 vols., tr. T.W. Rhys Davids.
SBF	"The Symbolism of Birds and Flight in the Writings of Rūzbehān Baqli," C.W. Ernst.
SBP	*Sār Bachan Chhand-Band (Sār Bachan Poetry),* Swāmī Shiv Dayāl Singh.
SBPS	*Sar Bachan Poetry (Selections),* Soami Shiv Dayal Singh.
SBU	*Ḥażrat Sulṭān Bāhū,* Radha Soami Satsang Beas (Urdu).
SBWG	*Srimad Bhagavatam: The Wisdom of God,* tr. Swami Prabhavananda.
SCM1–2	"Spiritual Concepts of the Maori," 2 parts, Elsdon Best.
SDBZ	*The Shambhala Dictionary of Buddhism and Zen,* Ingrid Fischer-Schreiber, Franz-Karl Ehrhard, Michael Diener, tr. Michael Kohn.

SDST	*Selected Poems from the Dīvāni Shamsi Tabrīz,* ed. & tr. R.A. Nicholson.
SDT1–4	*Shōbōgenzō,* 4 vols., tr. Gudo Wafu Nishijima & Chodo Cross.
SG	*Spiritual Gems,* Maharaj Sawan Singh Ji.
SGB	*The Seeker's Glossary of Buddhism,* Sutra Translation Committee of the United States and Canada.
SGHV	*Sha'ar ha-Gilgulim,* Ḥayyim Vital, ed. Yehudah Ashlag.
SGR	*Mafātiḥ al-I'jāz fī Sharḥ-i Gulshan-i Rāz-i Maḥmūd Shabistarī,* Shaykh Muḥammad Lāhījī, ed. Kayvān Samī'ī.
SGRV	*Sant Guru Ravidās Vāṇī,* ed. B.P. Sharmā.
SHHV	*Sefer ha-Ḥezyonot,* Ḥayyim Vital, ed. Aaron Zeev Aescoly.
SIM	*Studies in Islamic Mysticism,* R.A. Nicholson.
SIS	*Sawāniḥ,* Aḥmad Ghazzālī, tr. Nasrollah Pourjavady.
SL	*Spiritual Letters,* Baba Jaimal Singh Ji (1998).
SLO	*Spiritual Letters,* Baba Jaimal Singh Ji (1984).
SMIK1–13	*The Sufi Message of Hazrat Inayat Khan,* 13 vols., Hazrat Inayat Khan.
SNG	*Shrī Nāmdev Gāthā.*
SNPS	*Saint Namdev,* J.R. Puri & V.K. Sethi.
SNVF	*The Sutta-Nipâta,* tr. V. Fausböll.
SOA	*Sufis of Andalusia,* tr. R.W.J. Austin.
SOU	*Signs of The Unseen,* tr. W.M.Thackston Jr.
SP1–3	*Spiritual Perspectives,* 3 vols., Maharaj Charan Singh.
SPBS	*Sahaj Prakash,* Sahajo Bai, ed. & tr. H. Aveling & S. Joshi.
SPK	*The Sufi Path of Knowledge,* William Chittick. See *Acknowledgements.*
SPL	*The Sufi Path of Love,* William Chittick. See *Acknowledgements.*
SPLT	*Saint Paltu: His Life and Teachings,* Isaac Ezekiel.
SPM	*The Sacrament of the Present Moment,* J.-P. de Caussade, tr. Kitty Muggeridge.
SPS1–4	*Śiva Purāṇa,* 4 vols., tr. J.L. Shastri.
SRK1–5	*Sri Sri Ramakrishna Kathamrita,* 5 vols., Mahendra Nath Gupta.
SRVU	*A Study on the Ratnagotravibhāga,* tr. Jikidō Takasaki.
SS1–8	*The Shurangama Sutra,* 8 vols., expl. Ven. Master Hsuan Hua, tr. Buddhist Text Translation Society.
SSE1–15	*Sufi Symbolism: The Nurbakhsh Encyclopedia of Sufi Terminology,* 15 vols., Dr Javad Nurbakhsh, tr. T. Graham *et al.* See *Acknowledgements.*
SSG1–2	*Shrī Sakal Santa Gāthā,* 2 vols., ed. R.R. Gosavi.
SSG1–6	*Shirei Shlomo ben Yehuda ibn Gebirol,* 5 vols., ed. Hayym Bialik & Yehoshu'a Ravnitzky.
SSI1–10	*Sacred Songs of India,* 10 vols., V.K. Subramanian.
SSJV	*Samaṇ Suttaṁ,* comp. Jinēndra Varṇī, tr. T.K. Tukol & K.K. Dixit.

SSL	*The Seven Steps of the Ladder of Spiritual Love,* Jan van Ruysbroeck, tr. F. Sherwood Taylor.
SSRF	*Safed Spirituality,* tr. Lawrence Fine.
SSSK	*Shūrangama-Samādhi Sūtra,* tr. John McRae.
SSV	*The Siva Samhita,* tr. Rai Bahadur Srisa Chandra Vasu.
STG1–3	*Sārtha Tukārām Gāthā,* 3 vols., Tukārām, ed. P.N. Joshi.
STHT	*Shōbōgenzō,* Eihei Dogen, tr. Hubert Nearman.
SVD1–3	*Sumaṅgala-vilāsinī,* Buddhaghosa, 3 vols., ed. T.W. Rhys Davids, J.E. Carpenter & W. Stede.
SVEB	*Sutra of the Past Vows of Earth Store Bodhisattva,* tr. Bhiksu Heng Ching, rev. Bhiksuni Heng Ch'ih.
SVSL	*'Umar ibn al-Fâriḍ: Sufi Verse, Saintly Life,* tr. Th. Emil Homerin.
SWP	*Select Works of Plotinus,* tr. Thomas Taylor.
T1–100	*Taishō Shinshū Daizōkyō,* 100 vols., ed. Takakusu Junjirō & Watanabe Kaigokyu.
TAN1–2	*Tadhkiratu 'l-Awliya,* 2 parts, ed. R.A. Nicholson.
TAT	*Taṣawwuf va-Adabīyāt-i Taṣawwuf,* Y.E. Bertels, tr. Sirus Izadi.
TBLD	*The Long Discourses of the Buddha,* tr. Maurice Walshe. See *Acknowledgements.*
TCC1–4	*The Taoist Classics,* 4 vols., Thomas Cleary.
TCSD	*Tukaram: The Ceaseless Song of Devotion,* Chandravati Rajwade.
TCVC	*Tao Te Ching: Tao Virtue Classic,* ann. & expl. Derek Lin.
TEAK	*The Taoist Experience: An Anthology,* Livia Kohn.
TGH1–3	*Thrice-Greatest Hermes,* 3 vols., G.R.S. Mead.
TGTD	*The Teachings of Goswami Tulsidas,* K.N. Upadhyaya.
TMC1–3	*Türkische Manichaica aus Chotscho,* 3 vols., Albert von Le Coq.
TMED	*Taoist Meditation,* tr. Thomas Cleary.
TMSC	*A Treasury of Mahāyāna Sūtras,* ed. G.C.C. Chang.
TMU	*Thirty Minor Upaniṣads,* tr. K. Narayanasvami Aiyar.
TNB1–4	*Tuḥfat al-Nuẓẓār,* 4 vols., Ibn Baṭṭūtah, ed. C. Defrémery & B.R. Sanguinetti.
TOS	*Tayyibat,* tr. Lucas White King.
TPEF	*Tantra: The Path of Ecstasy,* Georg Feuerstein.
TPEQ	*The Teachings and Practices of the Early Quanzhen Taoist Masters,* Stephen Eskildsen. See *Acknowledgements.*
TRAK	*Tohunga – The Revival,* Samuel Timoti Robinson. See *Acknowledgements.*
TSH1–2	*Tulsī Sāhib Hāthrasvale kī Shabdāvalī,* 2 vols.
TSP1–6	*Triṣaṣṭiśalākāpuruṣacaritra,* 6 vols., Hemacandra, tr. H. Johnson.
TSR	*The Triumphal Sun,* Annemarie Schimmel.
TSSH	*Tulsi Sahib: Saint of Hathras,* J.R. Puri & V.K. Sethi.
TSTD	*Tulsī Satsai,* Tulsīdās. ed. Śyām Sundar Dās.
TT1–2	*The Texts of Taoism,* 2 vols., tr. James Legge.

TTCT	*Tao Te Ching: A New Translation,* tr. Ch'u Ta-Kao.
TTEP	*Taoist Texts,* ed. & tr. Frederic Balfour.
TTQ	*The Thousand and Twelve Questions,* E.S. Drower.
TTTT	*Tikao Talks,* Herries Beattie.
TVW1–5	*The Treatise on the Great Virtue of Wisdom of Nāgārjuna,* 5 vols., tr. Étienne Lamotte & Gelongma Karma Migme Chōdrōn.
TYPY	*The Textbook of Yoga Psychology,* Rammurti Mishra.
TYVL	*A Translation of Yoga-Vâsishta: Laghu,* tr. K.N. Aiyer.
UHMD	Unpublished handwritten manuscripts, *Shabds* of Dariyā Sāhib.
UJM1–2	*Understanding Jewish Mysticism,* 2 vols., David Blumenthal.
UMDC	*The Union of Mahamudra and Dzogchen,* Chökyi Nyima Rinpoche.
VCSM	*Viveka-cūḍāmaṇi of Śrī Śaṅkarācārya,* tr. Swāmī Mādhavānanda.
VE	*The Vedic Experience,* Raimundo Panikkar.
VHAM	*Voodoo in Haiti,* Alfred Métraux.
VTP3	*Vinaya Texts,* Part III, tr. T.W. Rhys Davids & H. Oldenberg.
WBC1–4	*The Works of Bernard of Clairvaux, On the Song of Songs,* 4 vols., tr. K. Walsh & I.M. Edmonds.
WCA1–2	*The Writings of Clement of Alexandria,* 2 vols., tr. W. Wilson.
WLT	*The Wisdom of Laotse,* ed. & tr. Lin Yutang.
WMPT	*Kunzang Lama'i Shelung,* Patrul Rinpoche, tr. Padmakara Translation Group.
WPJ1–4	*The Works of Philo Judaeus,* 4 vols., tr. C.D. Yonge.
YDSP	*The Yoga-Darśana,* tr. Gangânâtha Jhâ.
YSPB	*The Yoga System of Patañjali or the Ancient Hindu Doctrine of Concentration of Mind,* tr. J.H. Woods.
YU	*The Yoga Upaniṣads,* tr. T.R. S'rīnivāsa Ayyaṅgār.
YVV1–4	*Yoga-Vāsiṣṭha of Vālmīki,* 4 vols., tr. V.L. Mitra, ed. R.P. Arya.
ZBMC	*Zen and the Brain,* James Austin. See *Acknowledgements.*
ZSS1–5	*The Zohar,* 5 vols., tr. Harry Sperling & Maurice Simon.
ZW1–991	*Zángwài dàoshū,* 991 titles in 36 vols.

7.3 Powers, Attributes, Characteristics

Spiritual experience is inwardly powerful, and as the mind concentrates and consciousness expands as a result of spiritual practice, practitioners may begin to realize that they are developing various faculties beyond those of ordinary human experience.

According to mystical perception, the physical realm is actually a level of consciousness. Its material substance and everything that happens here come about through higher and hidden operations of the mind. Spiritual practice and meditation involve the exploration of realms of consciousness that give the practitioner not only a direct awareness of these processes, but also the ability to manipulate them at will.

To an observer who knows nothing of such processes, any event that appears to contravene natural laws is perceived as a miracle and often as something to be marvelled at. In fact, there is something miraculous even in the natural 'laws' as understood by science, for the origin of these laws remains a mystery. They may be observed and described in scientific terminology, but there is no real understanding of how they come into being in the first place.

The lives of mystics are remarkable in many ways, and many of those who have had close association with them have been aware of an utterly other-worldly atmosphere surrounding them, where happenings of a seemingly miraculous nature appear as commonplace. These powers and the supernormal characteristics of those who possess them form the basis of the entries in this section.

abhijñā (S), **abhiññā** (Pa), **mngon shes** (T), **shénlì, shéntōng** (C), **jinzu, rokutsu** (J) *Lit.* knowing, clever, skilful; direct knowledge, comprehension, awareness; hence also, spiritual power or powers, super-knowledge, supernatural wisdom, mystical understanding; also, the six supernormal forms of intuitive knowledge (S. *ṣaḍ-abhijñā,* Pa. *chalabhiññā*), awareness or ability developed by means of concentration *(samādhi)* and contemplation *(jhāna),* and said to be among the attributes of a *buddha, tathāgata,* or *arhat.* In common with many other spiritual traditions, Buddhist texts generally maintain that such powers are not to be used for personal benefit.

The two Chinese terms, *shénlì,* meaning occult force, power of a god or spirit, or spiritual power(s), and *shéntōng,* meaning remarkable ability, or supernatural or magical power(s) are often used interchangeably.

The six *abhijñās* are:

1. *Dibba-cakkhu* (Pa), *divya-chakshu* (S). *Lit.* the divine *(dibba)* eye *(cakkhu);* the celestial eye; the ability to see all that is happening in heaven and earth, whether near or far; also, knowledge of the death and rebirth of all sentient beings (*cutūpapāta-ñāṇa,* knowledge of disappearance and reappearance), in accordance with their good and bad deeds *(kamma),* also known as *yathākammūpaga-ñāṇa* (knowledge according to the result of actions). When describing this *abhiññā,* some texts speak of universal vision, others of the ability to see the *karma* of all beings.

2. *Dibba-sota* (Pa), *divya-shrotra* (S). *Lit.* the divine *(dibba)* ear *(sota),* the ability to hear earthly and heavenly sounds, whether near or far.

3. *Parassa ceto-pariya-ñāṇa* (Pa), *cetaḥ-paryāya-jñāna, para-chitta-jñāna* (S). *Lit.* penetrating *(pariya)* knowledge *(ñāṇa, jñāna)* of another's *(para, parassa, paryāya)* thoughts *(ceta, chitta);* penetration of others' minds; awareness of the thinking processes of others; acquired, according to the *Yoga Sūtras* of Patañjali, by focused attention *(saṃyama)* upon the mental processes of others;[1] also called *manaḥ-paryāya-jñāna,* knowledge of another's mind *(manas),* especially in Jainism.

4. *Pubbe-nivāsānussati, pubbe-nivāsa-ñāṇa* (Pa), *pūrva-nivāsa-anusmṛiti* (S). *Lit.* knowledge *(ñāṇa)* of former *(pubba)* abodes or habitations *(nivāsa);* remembrance of one's past lives, remembrance of one's previous existences. A *buddha* has the ability to recall all his past lives; for others, this awareness is limited.

5. *Iddhi-vidha* (Pa), *ṛiddhi* (S). *Lit.* forms of *(vidha)* power *(iddhi);* various miraculous powers, such as the ability to walk on water, levitate, fly in the air, pass through solid objects, project bodily replicas of oneself through

mental power, adopt another form, touch the sun and moon (inwardly), and ascend through the lower heavens to the highest heaven.

6. *Āsravakkhaya* (Pa), *āshravakshaya* (S). *Lit.* cessation *(khaya)* of all mental effluents *(āsava);* the elimination of impurities, specifically, the imperfections of: desire for things of the senses *(kāma),* coming into being *(bhava),* ignorance (Pa. *avijjā,* S. *avidyā*), and opinion (Pa. *diṭṭhi,* S. *dṛishṭi*).

The first five *abhiññās* are sometimes categorized as mundane or worldly *(lokiya),* attainable by meditative concentration *(samādhi)* through the practice of contemplation (Pa. *jhāna,* S. *dhyāna*); the sixth is regarded as supramundane or transcendental *(lokuttara),* acquired through the practice of deep meditation *(vipassanā),* often translated as 'insight'. The former are regarded as attainable by spiritual practitioners of other traditions. They arise as a natural result of meditation and spiritual evolution, but are not indicators of supreme enlightenment. The latter is traditionally regarded as being attainable only by the practice of Buddhist *vipassanā,* and is a companion to the highest enlightenment.

Remembrance of past lives, the divine eye, and the elimination of all impurities also appear as the threefold higher knowledge (S. *trividyā,* Pa. *tevijjā*). Although the sixfold *abhiññās* are listed in the Pali canon, the term *abhiññā* is not used for them (though it does appear in its ordinary sense), leading to the supposition that the use of *abhiññā* for supernormal and miraculous powers is a later introduction.

A deeply concentrated and focused mind, trained by long meditation and contemplation, becomes aware of the subtle connections between mental and material energies that are invisible to normal sensory awareness. Along with this awareness comes the power to manipulate these forces by tapping into the hidden currents of causality that underlie the material and mental events comprising existence in this world. To the mystic, there is nothing unusual or even miraculous about this, although it may appear so to the ordinary person. The stock description of the six *abhiññās* found in the Pali canon attributes the attainment of such powers to concentration of the mind:

> With a concentrated mind,... he (a monk) applies and directs his mind to the various supernormal powers *(iddhi-vidha).* He then enjoys different powers, such as being one, he becomes many; and having become many, he again becomes one. He becomes visible and invisible. Without hindrance, he passes through walls and mountains, as if through air. He sinks into the ground and emerges from it as if it were water. He walks on water without sinking, as if on land. He flies cross-legged through the air, like a winged bird. With his hand he touches and feels the sun and moon (experiences the light within),

mighty and powerful as they are; and he travels in the body as far as the *Brahmā* world....

With the divine ear *(dibba-sota),* purified and surpassing that of human beings, he hears sounds both heavenly and human, far and near....

He knows the minds of other beings *(parassa ceto-pariya-ñāṇa)* or other persons, by penetrating them with his own mind. He knows the mind with passion to be with passion, and the mind without passion to be without passion. He knows the hating mind to be hating, and the non-hating mind to be non-hating. He knows the deluded mind to be deluded, and the undeluded mind to be undeluded. He knows the narrow mind to be narrow, and the broad mind to be broad;... the expanded mind to be expanded, and the unexpanded mind to be unexpanded;... the surpassed mind to be surpassed, and the unsurpassed mind to be unsurpassed;... the concentrated mind to be concentrated, and the distracted mind to be distracted;... the liberated mind to be liberated, and the unliberated mind to be unliberated....

He remembers many former existences *(pubbe-nivāsānussati):* one birth, two, three, four, five births, ten, twenty, thirty, forty, fifty births, a hundred, a thousand, a hundred thousand births; and he remembers many formations and dissolutions of worlds: "There my name was so-and-so; my clan was so-and-so; my caste was so-and-so; my food was such-and-such; I experienced such-and-such pleasant and painful conditions; I lived for so long. Having vanished from there, I reappeared here;... and having vanished from there, I reappeared here." Thus he remembers many former existences, always together with their circumstances and peculiarities....

With the divine eye *(dibba-cakkhu),* purified and surpassing that of humans, he sees beings vanishing and reappearing: base and noble, beautiful and ugly, going to happy and unhappy destinations as their *kamma* (S. *karma*) leads them, and he knows: "These beings, on account of their misconduct in body, word and thought, disparaged the noble ones, held evil views, and reaped the kammic consequences of their evil views. At the dissolution of their body, after death, they have reappeared in lower worlds, a bad destination, in a state of suffering, in hell. But those other beings, on account of their good conduct in body, word and thought, praised the noble ones, held right views, and reaped the kammic consequences of their right views. At the dissolution of their body, after death, they have reappeared in a good destination, a heavenly world." Thus, with the divine eye,... he sees beings vanishing and reappearing....

And he with mind concentrated, purified and cleansed, unblemished, free from impurities, malleable, workable, established and

> having gained imperturbability, applies and directs his mind to the knowledge of the extinction of all defilements *(āsavakkhaya)*. He knows, as it really is: "This is suffering, . . . the origin of suffering, . . . the cessation of suffering, . . . the path leading to the cessation of suffering." And he knows, as it really is: "These are the impurities *(āsava)*, . . . the origin of the impurities, . . . the cessation of the impurities, . . . the path leading to the cessation of the impurities." And through his knowing and seeing his mind is delivered from the impurities of sense desire, . . . of becoming, . . . of ignorance, and the knowledge arises in him: "This is deliverance!", and he knows: "Birth is finished; the holy life has been led; done is what had to be done, and there is nothing more to be done."[2]
>
> *Dīgha Nikāya 2, Sāmaññaphala Sutta, PTSD1 pp.77–84; cf. TBLD pp.105–8*

Although the *abhiññās* are regarded as attributes of all *buddhas*, the open display of such knowledge or power is generally discouraged. Nevertheless, Buddhist texts contain many stories in which the Buddha demonstrates his possession of miraculous powers, and where he praises his disciples for such attainment. The point is made, however, that not only should such powers be used with discrimination, but that their possession is no proof of true spirituality and wisdom. The real miracle, he says, is the miracle of instruction *(anusāsanī-pāṭihāriya)* by which a true spiritual teacher is able to transform a disciple. If these texts accurately represent the Buddha's teaching rather that that of his later followers, the Buddha seems to be giving credence to the miraculous powers so esteemed in the yogic tradition of his times, while simultaneously pointing out the nature of the true miracle performed by a *buddha*.

In the *Kevaḍḍha Sutta*, a young householder, Kevaḍḍha, suggests to the Buddha that he should enable one of the assembled monks to perform "superhuman feats of miraculous power *(uttarimanussadhammā iddhi-pāṭihāriya)*", so that the crowd of lay devotees would be impressed, resulting in a strengthening of their faith and devotion. The Buddha explains, however, that were a monk to display such powers, the people would not benefit, but would simply explain away the miracles as magic tricks.[3]

Despite such strictures against the display of miracles, people have always been fascinated by them, and *bodhisattvas* and *buddhas*, as well as Buddhist tantric *gurus*, and even the Buddha himself, are commonly portrayed as possessing and using supernormal powers. Likewise, Buddhist cults, such as those centred around the Buddha's disciples Mahākāshyapa and Upagupta, generally attribute the possession of such powers to their chosen figureheads.

Abhiññā is sometimes understood under two categories. Firstly, there is *samatha-abhiññā*, which is supernormal knowledge or awareness attained by the practice of meditative calm and inner quietude *(samatha).* This form of knowledge encompasses the *abhiññās* already mentioned. Secondly, there is *dhamma-abhiññā,* which refers to the knowledge or wisdom by which the things relating to the *Dhamma* (Way, teachings) are understood. This is further subdivided into:

1. *Sutamaya-ñāṇa.* Knowledge *(ñāṇa)* acquired by *(maya)* learning *(suta).*

2. *Cintāmaya-ñāṇa.* Knowledge acquired by reasoning and thought *(cintā).*

3. *Bhāvanāmaya-ñāṇa.* Knowledge acquired by meditation *(bhāvanā).* This is further subdivided into *anubodha-ñāṇa* and *paṭivedha-ñāṇa. Anubodha-ñāṇa* (understanding knowledge) is an outer, theoretical understanding of the truths of the *Dhamma. Paṭivedha-ñāṇa* (penetration knowledge) is inner realization of the true meaning of the *Dhamma,* rather than its expression in language.

Some of the *Mahāyāna sūtras* describe the powers of a *buddha* in a fantastical manner. The *Avataṃsaka Sūtra,* for instance, in a spiritual adventure story, describes how the spiritual seeker Sudhana – "by the spiritual power *(shénlì)* of Maitreya (the *buddha*-to-be)"[4] – is granted an inner vision of innumerable magnificent worlds and unimaginable scenes, and meets an amazing assembly of countless *buddhas* and *bodhisattvas.* He witnesses a beauty his outer eyes have never seen, and grasps a kind of wisdom never previously accessible to him; and he hears and understands the higher teachings coming straight from the mouths of the Buddha, Maitreya, and many other highly evolved beings. After some time, Maitreya brings the vision to a close by snapping his fingers:[5]

> At the sound of the finger snap, Sudhana awoke from his state of focused contemplation and absorption *(samādhi).* And Maitreya said to him, "Now you have witnessed the *bodhisattvas'* inconceivable mastery of liberation and have experienced the bliss of their meditation. You have had visions of various magnificently adorned palaces sustained by the *bodhisattvas'* spiritual power *(shénlì),* supported by their practices, and manifested by their will and wisdom. You have witnessed the enlightenment practices of the *bodhisattvas,* heard their teachings, learnt of their virtues, and seen the fulfilment of the Tathāgata's wish."
>
> Sudhana said, "Indeed, O saint. What I have seen is by the exalted spiritual power of the grace and blessings of spiritual friends *(shànzhīshi).*"
>
> *Avataṃsaka Sūtra 39, T10 279:437c21–26*

The wonderstruck Sudhana then asks Maitreya, "Where has that magnificent display gone?" Maitreya replies teasingly, "Where it came from;" and when Sudhana presses his point, asking once more, "Where did it come from?", Maitreya replies:

> "It came from the *bodhisattvas'* spiritual power *(shénlì)* of wisdom, and it is sustained by the spiritual power *(shénlì)* of their wisdom. It has no permanent location or place of residence. It does not come into existence by being built or by accumulation. It does not remain unchangingly the same. There is no particular place where it exists.
>
> "It is like the rainfall of the water spirits – the rain does not fall from their body or mind, yet everyone can see the rain. It is by the power of the mind of the water spirits that the timely and nurturing rains pour down upon the world; it is the wondrous nature of their realm.
>
> "Likewise, these sublime manifestations are neither internal nor external, yet they can be seen. It is by the exalted spiritual power of the *bodhisattvas,* and by the power of your own roots of goodness, that you have had these visions.
>
> "It is like a magician's performance, in which things seem to appear out of nowhere and disappear into nowhere. Although they seem to appear out of and disappear into nowhere, it is actually the magician's skill that is making them seem that way. Likewise, these sublime manifestations appear out of nowhere and disappear into nowhere. And although they seem to appear out of and disappear into nowhere, they are manifest as such by the well-practised, inconceivable magic power of wisdom, by a mastery of wisdom empowered by past vows."
>
> *Avataṃsaka Sūtra 39, T10 279:438a3–14*

See also: **dibba-cakkhu** (▸3), **divya-shrotra** (▸3).

1. Patañjali, *Yoga Sūtras* 3:19.
2. *Cf. Dīgha Nikāya* 34, *Dasuttara Sutta, PTSD3* pp.281–82; *Majjhima Nikāya* 4 *(Bhayabherava Sutta),* 77 *(Mahāsakuludāyi Sutta), PTSM1* pp.22–23, *PTSM2* pp.18–22; *Anguttara Nikāya* 3:60, *Sangārava Sutta, PTSA1* pp.170–73; *Puggala-Paññatti* 271, 239.
3. *Dīgha Nikāya* 11, *Kevaḍḍha Sutta, PTSD1* p.215; see also *Vinaya Piṭaka* 5:8.1–2, *VTP3* pp.78–81.
4. *Avataṃsaka Sūtra* 39, *T10* 279:435b2.
5. *Avataṃsaka Sūtra* 39, *T10* 279:434c29–437c20.

abracadabra A seemingly nonsensical word used to invoke magic or healing powers; a kind of magical formula.

The first known occurrence of the word is in the third-century Latin text *Liber Medicinalis* ('Book of Medicines') of Quintus Serenus Sammonicus, physician to the Roman emperor Caracella (*r.* 198–217). In chapter fifty-one, Sammonicus recommends wearing an amulet containing the word *abracadabra* as a cure for those suffering from malaria. He maintains that such an amulet possesses the power to dispel deadly diseases. He instructs that *abracadabra* is to be written in the form of an inverted triangle, each row of letters containing one less letter than the row above, and it is often in this form that it appears in ancient amulets. The word has had a long history of use. It was current as a charm among the superstitious even in the seventeenth century, where it was written on doorways to ward off disease during the Great Plague of London (1665–1666). Nowadays, it is used by stage magicians, or as a facetious or humorous observation concerning the solution to some seemingly difficult or impossible problem.

It is possible that the word is related to *Abrasax,* a name of the great *archon,* ruler of the 365 spheres or realms, who appears in the teachings of the gnostic Basilidēs, and in the Nag Hammadi text the *Holy Book of the Great Invisible Spirit. Abrasax* also makes an appearance in the *Papyri Graecae Magicae* (Greek Magical Papyri) originating in Graeco-Roman Egypt. The word *Abrasax* was written on gemstones, which were known as *Abraxas* stones and used as amulets and charms. The original Greek word written on such stones was *Abrasax, Abraxas* probably originating from confusion between the Greek letters *sigma* and *xi,* when transliterated from Greek into Latin.

The origin of the word *abracadabra* is uncertain, but since both *abracadabra* and *Abraxas* were used as magic charms, it is thought that it may be a corruption of *Abraxas.* Another theory traces its origin to the Hebrew *evra ca-davra,* meaning 'I create as I speak' or 'I create through speech', or from its Aramaic translation. There are, however, significant problems with this etymology.

The broader concept of creation through speech stems from the scriptural references to the creation resulting from the *Memra* (Word), Speech, or Name of God – the creative power emanating from the divine Source, as in the opening lines of *Genesis,* "And God said, 'Let there be...'" *etc.*[1] Some Jewish mystics, who tried to utilize occult powers, believed that they could imitate God if they had knowledge of the divine Name through which He had brought forth the creation. They were labouring under the mistaken assumption that the true divine Name is a name or word that can be spoken, written, or pronounced.

The use of names in occult, magical or theurgic practices was an attempt by some mystics to use powers gained in their spiritual exercises to control natural forces for a number of purposes, including healing, foretelling the future, and so on.

See also: **hashba'ot** (▸3), **kavanot** (▸3).

1. *Genesis* 1:1–30, *KJV.*

adhishṭhāna (S), **adhiṭṭhāna** (Pa), **byin brlabs** (T), **jiāchí** (C), **kaji** (J) *Lit.* basis, base, support, substratum, foundation, resting place, seat; in Buddhism, supernatural or miraculous power used by *buddhas* and *bodhisattvas* to transform something in the material world in order to help sentient beings understand the *Dharma* (Way, teachings); the spiritual power of a *buddha* that sustains a *bodhisattva* throughout his spiritual evolution; hence, a blessing; a notion peculiar to the *Mahāyāna* tradition. In *Vedānta, adhishṭhāna* is *Brahman,* the absolute Reality, the support of the universe.

Adhishṭhāna is sometimes translated into Japanese as *kaji,* which means blessings, grace, or empowerment. In this sense, *kaji* is a blessing or grace of spiritual empowerment granted to people to expand their horizons, and help them understand the path to liberation. *Adhishṭhāna* assists human beings to rid themselves of illusion and perceive the underlying Reality, rather than the superficial appearance – to understand things beyond the faculties of reason and the conceptualizing intellect. In esoteric Buddhism, *kaji* often takes the form of a prayer or ritual directed towards a particular deity or celestial being for spiritual blessings and empowerment. In this context, *kaji* also includes faith healing and incantation.

In a fantastical, spiritual adventure story, the *Avataṃsaka Sūtra* describes how the spiritual seeker Sudhana, "by the spiritual power *(shénlì)* of Maitreya (the *buddha*-to-be)"[1] is granted an inner vision of innumerable magnificent worlds and unimaginable scenes, and meets an amazing assembly of numerous *buddhas* and *bodhisattvas,* and "by the power *(jiāchí)* of Maitreya . . . senses the passing of billions of ages".[2]

In Pali, *adhiṭṭhāna* means resolution, will, determination. It is one of the ten perfections *(pāramitās)* of character developed by a *bodhisatta* over many lifetimes, that enable him to teach others and progress towards enlightenment. There are also said to be four foundations *(adhiṭṭhāna)* to an *arhat*'s inner being – wisdom *(paññā),* truthfulness *(sacca),* generosity *(cāga),* and peace *(upasama). Adhiṭṭhānā-iddhi* (power of determination) is also one of the many supernatural powers *(iddhis)* that enables a practitioner to control the length of time he remains in one of the *jhānas* (states of meditative absorption). More generally, it refers to supernatural powers brought about by an act of determined will. *Adhiṭṭhānā-iddhi* is also said to manifest the saying regarding one of a *buddha*'s supernatural powers, "Being one, he becomes many; and having become many he again becomes one,"[3] which implies that his consciousness can be both individual and universal, as he chooses.

See also: **abhijñā**, **iddhi**.

1. *Avataṃsaka Sūtra* 39, *T10* 279:435b2.
2. *Avataṃsaka Sūtra* 39, *T10* 279:435c2–3.
3. *Dīgha Nikāya* 2, *Sāmaññaphala Sutta, PTSD1* p.78; *cf. TBLD* p.105.

advandva (S) *Lit.* non *(a-)* duality *(dvandva);* release from duality; rising above duality, going beyond the pairs of opposites. See **siddhi**.

agni-arkāmbu-vishādīnām pratishṭambhaḥ (S) *Lit.* countering the influence *(pratishṭambhaḥ)* of fire *(agni),* sun *(arka),* water *(ambu),* poison *(visha),* and so on *(ādīnām);* the power to neutralize the influence of fire, sun, water, poison, and other material elements. See **siddhi**.

aishvarya (S) *Lit.* lordship, sovereignty, supremacy, power; mastery over the subtle elemental forces of nature from which all other forms are manifested; the power to manipulate the forces of nature from an inner level, resulting in apparent miracles in the manifested universe; also called *pradhāna-jaya* (mastery of nature); an alternative name for the *siddhis.*

See also: **siddhi**.

ājñā apratihatā gati (S) *Lit.* power *(gati)* of unhindered *(apratihatā)* command *(ājñā);* irresistible or unimpeded command; the power to ensure that all one's orders are obeyed.[1] See **siddhi**.

1. *Bhāgavata Purāṇa* 11:15.7.

ākāsha-gamana (S) *Lit.* space *(ākāsha)* moving *(gamana);* moving at will through space, levitation. See **siddhi**.

akualele (Hw) *Lit.* a god who flew across the sky on a mission of evil or destruction; a fireball; a meteorite entering the atmosphere.

When a *kahuna 'anā'anā* performed black magic to hurt another, the energy was sent to the victim via an *akualele.* This *'anā'anā* or black magic was carried by a god, and when he flew across the sky, he was seen as a fireball in the night.

See also: **'anā'anā**.

'anā'anā (Hw) *Lit.* evil sorcery; black magic in Hawaiian culture; the casting of evil spells; practised by a *kahuna 'anā'anā.*

The casting of evil spells required the performance of certain rituals. Spells could cause madness, sickness, loss of bodily functions, death, weakness of the limbs, and so on. Before the ritual was performed, the *kāhuna* needed some personal effects from the victim. Often some hair, nails, clothing or even bodily excretions were used. This is why Hawaiians were very careful to hide all such things by burying them in secret places. These articles *(kameha'i* or *maunu)* were considered to have the person's *mana* or personal power. Once the *kahuna* had obtained these articles, he would have power over the items and thus have power over the person to whom they belonged.

Mary Kawena Pukui, co-author of the book *Nānā I Ke Kumu,* relates how this would unfold:

> When the *kahuna 'anā'anā* had obtained the needed *maunu,* he first called on his gods of sorcery and then recited the particular prayer designed to bring about a specific doom. One example is the *pule 'umi,* literally 'prayer to choke'. For this the sorcerer had to recite, all in one breath:
>
> Faint, be faint, faint, faint.
> Fall down, let him fall down, down, down.
> Consciousness goes, it departs.
> He gasps, gasps.
> Now pinch him, strangle him,
> pinch his eyes to blind him.
> His nose, pinch it, too.
> His mouth, pinch it, close it.
> His windpipe seize, choke, strangle!
>
> In the geographically stable, closely knit communities of early Hawaii, word easily reached the victim of his doom. Before long, *ho'upu'upu* (planting a thought in another's mind) went to work. Under the 'strangulation spell', the victim would attempt to eat the head of a live *manini* or *aholehole* fish. Both fish have sharp bones in the dorsal fin which, lodged in the throat, can cause strangulation. However, the victim, his air passage closing from fear and fish bone, could be saved by a counter-sorcerer called *kahuna pale* (*pale* means 'to ward off'). The *kahuna pale* said the counter-prayer. The first few lines seem

addressed to the fish, but because the human was sometimes called ‘two-legged fish’, this could be symbolic. Certainly the second part of the prayer was said directly *to* the victim. The prayer goes:

> Though he chokes, yet he lives.
> Strangles, yet he lives.
> O fish, be softened, be cooked.
> Be pliable; be very soft.
> O bones, be reduced to ashes.
> Though you have swallowed a *manini* and be choked,
>   yet Life comes to the rescue.
> Though you become crooked, a paralytic,
>   yet Life comes to the rescue.
> Though you eat of the *aholehole* and choke,
>   life shall deliver you.
> Though you be broken, paralysed,
>   life comes to your rescue.
> And health be with you to the end of your days.

This counterspell, said to the frightened victim in a ritual-accompanied ‘doctor-patient’ relationship, must have been vastly reassuring. It may have been hypnotic.

In the following spell, this one to inflict harm, the hypnotic content and cadence come through clearly even in translation:

> Numbness, numbness, numbness, numbness,
> Spreads, spreads, spreads, spreads,
> Stiffens, stiffens, stiffens, stiffens.
> Your head droops, droops, droops,
> Bends over, bends over,
> It droops, droops.

For the victim who knew he was under a spell, rescue lay either in a counterspell or through *‘oki,* severing or cutting off a spell by prayer. In current case histories, *‘oki* sometimes includes both Hawaiian and Christian prayers.

What about the victim who did not know he was under a spell? In his case, the family and the ‘family doctor’, the *kahuna lapa‘au,* took over. The family gathered in *ho‘oponopono,* the family conference which worked, through prayers and frank confession of error and restitution for wrongdoing, to find solutions to family crises. In the case of *‘anā‘anā,* the family joined in trying to help the victim remember what he might have done that would lead to sickness. The *kahuna lapa'au* examined the victim, praying to his *'aumakua* (ancestor gods) for medical insight. There were causes and effects to investigate. Did the victim have a swollen hand, sign that he had stolen? This might mean that the one he had stolen from had employed a sorcerer to cast a spell on him. Prayer, detective work and a medical *kahuna* often discovered the spell in time for countermeasures.

"'Anā'anā," Nānā I Ke Kumu, NKK1 pp.28–29

'anai (Hw) *Lit.* to curse; a curse; to place a curse on someone; a Hawaiian term for a curse intended to bring disease, difficulties, or even death into a person's life:

In the old Hawaiian culture, putting a curse or *'anai* on someone was done in a very direct manner. The curse was said directly *to* another person in a phrase that might be as simple as, "Be forever accursed for your wrongdoing." The *'anai* was not directed by devious means or through a third person. It did not require a sorcerer as did *'anā'anā,* the 'spell' which doomed a person to trouble or even death.

If the recipient of *'anai* was innocent of the wrongdoing, he could refuse the curse and send it back to its originator. The phrase of refusal went, *"Ho'i no kau me 'oe"* or "What you have just given me, so (I return) to you." The whole significance lay in the innocence of the cursed one. A guilty victim could not send the curse back; the phrase was then useless mechanistic ritual.

If the cursed one was indeed guilty, there were ways to have the curse lifted. One was to go directly to the sender of the curse, give evidence of sincere repentance and of righting the wrong, and ask him to *'oki* the curse. (Literally, *'oki* means to cut or sever; the curse is 'severed' from its victim.) Here, tradition demanded that forgiveness be granted and the curse lifted.

"'anai," Nānā I Ke Kumu, NKK1 p.31

See also: **'anā'anā**.

aṇiman, **aṇimā** (S) *Lit.* minuteness, fineness, thinness; like an atom *(aṇu);* the power to shrink, to become as minute as an atom; to become so small that things of the minutest size, even an atom, can be seen. See **siddhi**.

anūrmimattva (S) *Lit.* power *(mattva)* of no disturbance *(anūrmi);* being undisturbed by hunger, thirst, and other bodily feelings. See **siddhi**.

anuvyañjana (S/Pa), **anubyañjana** (Pa), **dpe byad** (T) *Lit.* smaller *(aṇu)* attribute *(vyañjana);* minor or secondary characteristic; the eighty minor signs or marks (S. *ashīti-anuvyañjana,* C. *bāshí zhǒnghǎo,* J. *hachijisshu gō*) on the body of a *buddha* that are in addition to the thirty-two marks of a great man *(dvātriṃsha mahāpurusha-lakshaṇa,* C. *sānshíèr xiàng,* J. *sanjūni sō);* common to all Buddhist traditions. In esoteric Buddhist traditions, the thirty-two greater and eighty lesser marks are regarded as subtle aspects of the *sambhoga-kāya* (body of enjoyment, body of reward), the subtle body in which a *buddha* manifests himself at spiritual levels or in the celestial paradises.[1]

Complete lists of the eighty secondary marks appear in only a few texts,[2] and there are variations in the order and among the individual characteristics. In the Pali literature, they are referred to in the *Apadāna*[3] and the *Questions of King Milinda,* which are probably the earliest instances of use. They are also mentioned frequently in later texts, although these references may themselves have been added at a later date during the course of their transmission.[4]

In the *Questions of King Milinda,* the king asks the Buddhist sage Nāgasena about these marks:

> The king said: "Is it true, Nāgasena, that the Buddha was endowed with the thirty-two bodily marks of a great man *(dvattiṃsa-mahāpurisa-lakkhaṇa),* and graced with the eighty subsidiary characteristics *(asīti-anubyañjana);* that he was golden in colour with a skin like gold, and that there spread around him a glorious halo of a fathom's length?"
>
> (Nāgasena replied,) "Such, O king, was the Blessed One."
>
> *Questions of King Milinda 3:6.3, PTSQ p.75, SBE35 p.116*

The eighty minor marks appear to be an elaboration of the thirty-two marks. They include perfect, shiny, copper-coloured nails on his hands and feet; auspicious marks on his hands and feet; long, slender fingers; lips the colour of a red gourd; emitting a pleasant fragrance; veins that have no knots and are concealed; a youthful appearance; a beautiful, graceful, upright and elegant gait like that of a lion, an elephant or a flying swan, and always like a leader; soft, beautiful, fragrant, well-ordered and black hair; a face as bright and clear as the full moon; flawless eyes and vision; and so on. A *buddha*'s eyebrows, ears, nose, tongue, teeth, voice, hands, palms, main body characteristics and waist are similarly perfectly formed and well proportioned. Finally, his conduct in body, mind and speech is always pure; his behaviour is a delight to everyone; and he is attractive to all who see him. In a similar vein are the sixty aspects of a *buddha*'s speech, which is inspiring, appealing, melodic, articulate and without hesitation, never rushed, calming, appropriate and relevant, logical, without flattery, without rigidity, of pure motivation, and which causes a state of bliss, dispels incorrect views, conveys understanding, amplifies qualities already attained and adds new ones, and is able to communicate any point by drawing on analogies from the material world.[5]

The *Mahāvastu* lists the eighty minor marks in full:

> Exalted *buddhas* have eighty secondary characteristics *(anuvyañjana).* They have their nails long, copper-coloured, and glossy. Their fingers are rounded, beautiful, and regular. Their veins have no knots and are concealed. Their ankles are concealed and compactly formed. They have even and level feet. Exalted *buddhas* have perfect sexual organs. Their radiance extends all around them. Their limbs are soft, flawless, superb, well shaped, and well knit, and all are well proportioned. Their bodies are unimpaired and unmarred. Their limbs are free from freckles and curly hair. Exalted *buddhas* have hands soft as cotton. The lines on their hands are deep, unbroken, and uninterrupted. Their lips are red. Their voices do not carry too far. Their tongues are soft, slender and red. Exalted *buddhas* have voices like the sound of an elephant's cry, well toned and pleasant. Their gait is like the movement of an elephant, a bull, or a lion, always bearing to the right.
>
> Their protuberances are equal, and they are lovely in all parts. Their behaviour is clean. The hair of their bodies is perfectly clean and pure. Their radiance is all around them, undimmed. Exalted *buddhas* have straight, soft, and regular limbs. Their bellies curve like a bow, are lovely, large, and regular. Their navels are deep, regular, unimpaired, and turning to the right. Their kneecaps are curved. Exalted *buddhas* have round, sharp, regular, unbroken, and even teeth. Their noses are high, but not too large. Their eyes are dark like the dark-white lotus. Exalted *buddhas* have dark, glossy eyebrows and large equal ears without defect. Exalted *buddhas* have their faculties unimpaired, unmarred, and well controlled. They have most excellently proportioned foreheads. Their hair is dark, thick, shiny, carefully combed, growing without a break or interruption, soft, glossy and fragrant, with its tips curled. They have well-shaped heads and their hair bears the figures of the *svastika, nandyāvarta,* and *muktika* signs.
>
> These are the eighty secondary marks *(anuvyañjana)* on the body of the infinitely wise *buddha,* and with these the body of the *deva* who is above all *devas,* the supreme Man, is always adorned.
>
> Since there are on his body the thirty-two praiseworthy marks and the eighty secondary characteristics *(anuvyañjana),* and since his radiance extends a full fathom, how, verily, can the wise not have faith in him as the conqueror?
>
> If an ordinary man were to have the merits of all beings a hundredfold, he would not acquire for his body a single one of these characteristics.
>
> *Mahāvastu 2:43–45, MHVA, MVJ2 pp.40–42*

Despite the evident praise being heaped upon the nature of the Buddha's physical form, there are passages in the Pali texts suggesting that the Buddha's physical appearance was actually nothing out of the ordinary. In the *Dhātuvibhanga Sutta,* for instance, the young Pukkusāti, having adopted the life of a homeless monk, meets the Buddha and ends up sharing a shed with him in the grove of the potter Bhaggava. They spend much of the night meditating together, followed by a lengthy conversation before Pukkusāti realizes to whom he has been speaking.[6] Perhaps, however, these incidents demonstrate that a *buddha* can only be recognized when he wants to be.

See also: **dvātriṃshadvara-lakshaṇa**.

1. Chökyi Nyima Rinpoche, *Union of Mahamudra and Dzogchen, UMDC* p.57.
2. *E.g. Abhinishkramaṇa Sūtra, T190* 3:696a–697a; *Vaipulya-Mahāvyūha Sūtra, T190* 3:557b–c.
3. *Apadāna, AKN1* p.156.
4. Guang Xing, *Concept of the Buddha, CBET* pp.32–33.
5. See Khenpo Choga, on Khenpo Kunpal, on *Bodhisattva-Charyāvatāra* 51–60, *DNK1* pp.307–16.
6. *Majjhima Nikāya* 140, *Dhātuvibhanga Sutta, PTSM3* pp.237–47.

aparājaya (S) *Lit.* beyond *(apara)* defeat *(ajaya);* the power to suffer no defeat in any undertaking; not being vanquished by others. See **siddhi**.

aparānta-jñāna (S) *Lit.* knowledge *(jñāna)* of the final end *(aparānta).* See **siddhi**.

āsavakkhaya (Pa) *Lit.* cessation *(khaya)* of all mental effluents *(āsava);* the elimination of defilements; one of the six supernormal forms of knowledge *(abhiññā).* See **abhijñā**, **āsrava** (▸4).

atishaya (S) *Lit.* pre-eminence, eminence; pre-eminent, supreme, extreme, excessive, extravagant; blessed; superiority in quality or quantity; used in a variety of contexts; in Jainism, the thirty-four supramundane characteristics or attributes credited to *arhats* (worthy ones, realized souls) and *Tīrthankaras* (ascended masters). The Jain *atishayas* correspond to the thirty-two physical marks *(dvātriṃshadvara-lakshaṇa)* of a *mahāpurusha* (great man), the eighty minor marks of a *buddha,* and the eighteen characteristics that express the inner perfection of a Buddha. A *mahāpurusha* generally refers either to a *buddha* or a *chakravartin* (universal monarch). A Jain pilgrimage place *(tīrtha)* that is associated with miraculous events is known as a *atishaya kshetra* (blessed land).

Four primary *atishayas* are listed: omniscience *(kevala-jñāna);* the delivery of extraordinarily powerful and penetrating discourses that benefit humanity by reminding them of the spiritual purpose of life; being worshipped by ordinary souls throughout the universe; and the absence of calamity or disease in their vicinity.

A further eight *atishayas* are also listed: a divine seat from which a *Tīrthankara* delivers his sermons (*siṃhāsana,* lion's seat); a halo behind his head *(bhāmaṇḍala);* a retinue of angels waving whisks of yak hair *(camara),* a common insignia of royalty and magnificence; a three-tiered divine parasol *(chhatra)* above the head, symbolizing his spiritual sovereignty over the three regions *(triloka)* of heaven, earth, and the nether regions; an *ashoka* tree *(ashoka-vṛiksha)* under which he sits to deliver discourses; the continuous showering of fragrant flowers *(pushpa-varsha)* upon him, as in the celebrations surrounding any great hero; a divine drum *(deva-dundubhi)* announcing his presence and his discourses; and celestial music or divine sound *(divya-dhvāni)* heard when he delivers his discourses.

When further elaborated, these twelve become the thirty-four *atishayas.* Like those already enumerated, many of these are also regarded as characteristic of a *buddha:*

1. His body is beautiful, powerful, and proportionally built, with 1,008 auspicious birthmarks. For example, no hair grows upon his body.
2. He has no bodily ailments.
3. His blood and flesh are milky white.
4. His breath has the fragrance of a lotus bloom.
5. His food intake and excretion are invisible.
6. He has a three-tiered parasol above his head, symbolic of heaven, hell, and the material world.
7. A magical wheel *(dharmachakra),* symbolizing religion and spirituality, moves above, in front, and behind him.
8. Angels wave white fans above him and on both sides.
9. He sits on a throne of quartz crystal.
10. *Indra*'s flag goes before him.
11. An *ashoka* tree is present wherever he stays.
12. He is surrounded by a divine aura.
13. The country around him is pleasing.
14. In his vicinity, thorns turn in on themselves,
15. the seasons are pleasant and favourable,
16. a pleasant wind blows,
17. dust is settled by light rain or moisture,

18. heaps of flowers of five kinds surround him.
19. No unpleasant sensory input is experienced in his vicinity, whether of sight, sound, smell, taste, or touch.
20–21. He has a calm, soothing, and serene voice that can be heard with the same volume and clarity up to a distance of one *yojana* (a mythical unit of measurement, variously calculated at between two and twenty miles).
22. He speaks in the Ardha-Māgadhī language, the language of Jain sacred literature.
23. All beings in the audience understand his discourse in their own language, even the animals and birds.
24. Enemies forget their animosity in his presence.
25. His opponents become amiable.
26. His dissenters become speechless.
27–28. There is no epidemic or death for a distance of twenty-five *yojanas* around him.
29–33. Wherever he goes, there are no afflictions or calamities, such as floods, drought and disease, either self-inflicted or brought about by other causes.
34. The touch of his feet brings peace to all earlier disturbances in the area.[1]

These idealized signs represent the human attempt to understand something of what a truly holy or divine person might be like. Some are symbolic, like the *dharmachakra,* the wheel of religion or spirituality that accompanies him everywhere, or the magnificent throne signifying the natural kingliness of his bearing. Others are indicative of the powerful effect the purity of his presence has upon all living beings. Others, such as the absence of disease and calamity and the pleasant weather, point to his power over nature. Others are an externalization of an inner experience, such as the divine music that is heard in his presence.

See also: **Buddha** (7.1), **tīrtha** (▸3), **Tīrthankara** (7.1).

1. See *Illustrated Tirthankar Charitra, ITCT; Jain Philosophy and Practice* 2, *JPP2.*

avadhi-jñāna (S) *Lit.* knowledge *(jñāna)* with limit *(avadhi);* limited knowledge; variously described as knowledge of what lies within the limits of the physical universe, and hence, perception extending to the furthest limits of the physical world, including that which is beyond the reach of the senses, such as extrasensory knowledge or perception, clairvoyance, psychic knowledge, and so on; or, knowledge innate to heavenly beings *(devas)* and beings of hell *(nārakis),* but only acquired by animals and human beings through the merit of good deeds and (in the case of human beings) spiritual practice; in a higher form, a kind of knowledge possessed solely by spiritually realized souls;[1] the third of the five basic forms of knowledge identified by Jain philosophy and epistemology.

The five fundamental forms of *jñāna* in Jainism are: *mati-jñāna* (sense knowledge), knowledge acquired through the senses; *shruta-jñāna* (knowledge that is heard), knowledge derived from reading, especially scriptures; *avadhi-jñāna* (limited knowledge); *manaḥ-paryāya-jñāna* (knowledge of another's mind), awareness of the thinking processes of others; and *kevala-jñāna* (absolute knowledge), knowledge of the Absolute, omniscience. *Avadhi-jñāna* is said to be limited either because it is limited to the material universe (gross and subtle) or by comparison to the two higher forms of knowledge.

Avadhi-jñāna is analysed and categorized in a variety of ways. Sometimes there are said to be six forms: that which is constant; that which goes with a soul when it leaves the place of origin, and that which does not; that which increases, and that which decreases; and that which has been lost.[2] Much of the discussion of *avadhi-jñāna* in Jain texts and commentaries centres around its comparison with *manaḥ-paryāya-jñāna,* and the nature and scope of the various forms of knowledge.

See also: **manaḥ-paryāya-jñāna**.

1. See Ramjee Singh, *Jaina Perspective in Philosophy and Religion, JPPR* pp.164–66.
2. See Shri Bhuvanbhanijsoorishwarji, *A Handbook of Jainology, HJBB* pp.183–84.

āveṇika-buddhadharma, **asādhāraṇa-dharma** (S), **āveṇika-buddhadhammā**, **asādhāraṇa-dhammā** (Pa), **bùgòng fǎ** (C), **fugu hō** (J) *Lit.* special or uncommon *(āveṇika, asādhāraṇa, bùgòng, fugu)* characteristics *(dharma, fǎ, hō)* of a *buddha;* the eighteen *(ashṭādashan)* attributes or attainments commonly listed as being especially associated with the physical form or *nirmāṇa-kāya* of a *buddha* or *tathāgata,* which distinguish him from others of lesser attainment. The eighteen special characteristics do not appear in the older, canonical Pali *sūtras,* but are mentioned in the later Pali texts and *Mahāyāna sūtras.* There are three distinct lists of the eighteen characteristics, two originating in the *Sarvāstivāda* monastic school or its *Vaibhāshika* branch, and one from the *Mahāyāna* tradition.[1]

The first *Sarvāstivāda* list understands the eighteen characteristics as a grouping of the ten powers *(dashabalas),* the four fearlessnesses *(chatvāri-vaishāradyāni),* the three (usually listed as four) foundations of mindfulness *(smṛityupasthāna),* together with *mahākaruṇa* (great compassion). All these are regarded as characteristics of a *buddha,* and appear in the canonical Pali texts. The Buddhist philosopher, Nāgārjuna, also details (and refutes) a second *Sarvāstivāda* list, independent of other lists and groups of characteristics, which seems to have originated with a group of *Sarvāstivāda* or *Vaibhāshika* scholars, but is not mentioned elsewhere in Buddhist literature.

The third list is the one that is more commonly known. Though adopted by the *Mahāyāna sūtras,* it is known to all Buddhist groups, whatever their persuasion. The eighteen special characteristics as listed in the *Prajñāpāramitā* group of *sūtras* are:

1. The *tathāgata* has no bodily defect.
2–4. He has no vocal defect, no failure of memory, no notion of variety.
5–6. He does not have an unconcentrated mind nor does he exhibit thoughtless indifference.
7–12. He has no loss of zealousness, exertion, mindfulness, wisdom, liberation, or loss of the knowledge and vision of deliverance.
13–15. Every bodily, vocal and mental action of the *tathāgata* is preceded and accompanied by knowledge.
16–18. He has non-attached and unobstructed knowledge of the past, the future, and the present.[2]

A deeper understanding of this somewhat sparse list can be gained by a study of the observations of various commentators and in other texts. They say, in summary, that the eighteen qualities express a *buddha*'s inner perfection, and relate to his behaviour, his realization, and his enlightened consciousness. The first six are associated with his outer behaviour: he moves gracefully and his conduct is never founded upon delusion of any kind; his speech is neither garrulous, loud, or ill-considered; he possesses an unfailing memory and intelligence; he is always composed and at peace; he is free of conceptual thinking, not clinging to ideas; and he is diligent in all matters, free from indifference or carelessness.

The second group of six are associated with his inner spiritual realization: he gives unwavering attention to his work of spreading the message of the *Dharma* for the benefit of all beings; he is indefatigable, never losing his energy and vigour; he is always focused, mindful, and aware, seeing things for exactly what they are, never losing interest in his mission; he has unfailing wisdom, discernment, and understanding; he lives in a state of constant meditation *(jhāna, samādhi);* and he is permanently liberated.

The third group of six are associated with this state of consciousness and permanent meditative awareness: his deeds, his speech, and his mind are all informed and permeated by his state of constant meditation; as a consequence, whatever he does, says or thinks is meaningful. Likewise, his all-pervading awareness gives him an unobscured vision and wisdom concerning the past, the present, and the future; as a result, he knows everything.[3]

Nāgārjuna himself elaborates on why these eighteen characteristics are unique to a *buddha,* and also why other characteristics are possessed by *shrāvakas* (novices) and *pratyeka-buddhas* (those who attain enlightenment for themselves alone).[4] Some texts also describe eighteen characteristics possessed by *bodhisattvas.*[5]

A *buddha* is also said to bear the thirty-two physical marks *(dvātriṃshadvara-lakshaṇa)* of a great man *(mahāpurusha),* according to *brāhmaṇ* belief,[6] together with eighty minor marks *(ashīti-anuvyañjana).*

See also: **dashabala**, **dvātriṃshadvara-lakshaṇa**, **vaishāradya**.

1. Nāgārjuna, *Mahāprajñāpāramitā Shāstra* 41:2.1–2, *TVW3* pp.1389–92; Étienne Lamotte, *TVW3* pp.1331–33.
2. *Pañchaviṃshati* 1:17–212, 1:7, *Shatasāhasrikā* 1:22–1450, 1:14; in Nāgārjuna, *Mahāprajñāpāramitā Shāstra* 41:1.1, *TVW3* pp.1335–36.
3. See Garma Chang, *Buddhist Teaching of Totality, BTOT* pp.54–55 (n.27); Khenpo Chöga, *Drops of Nectar* 56–61, *DNK1* pp.322–23; *Ratnagotra-vibhāga* 3:15.3.9–15, *SRVU* pp.341–42.
4. Nāgārjuna, *Mahāprajñāpāramitā Shāstra* 41:1.2.1–18, *TVW3* pp.1336–61, 1383–84.
5. *Mahāvyutpatti* 787–804, *MBST,* in *TVW3* pp.1334–35.
6. *E.g. Dīgha Nikāya* 3 *(Ambaṭṭha Sutta),* 4 *(Soṇadaṇḍa Sutta),* 14 *(Mahāpadāna Sutta),* 30 *(Lakkhaṇa Sutta), PTSD1* pp.88–89, 105–6, 116, *PTSD2* pp.16–19, *PTSD3* pp.142–45.

bhūcharī-siddhi (S) *Lit.* moving on the earth *(bhūcharī)* power *(siddhi);* the power to move at will all over the world. See **siddhi**.

bhūta-jaya (S) *Lit.* conquest *(jaya)* of the elements *(bhūtas).* See **siddhi**.

biànxíng, **biànyàng** (C) *Lit.* to change shape *(biànxíng, biànyàng);* to morph *(biànxíng);* to change appearance *(biànyàng);* hence, shapeshifting – a common theme in Chinese mythology, folklore, fairy tales and modern science fiction, in which a person or being has the ability to change or morph their physical form at will. Daoist writings and hagiographies contain several stories in which masters change their outer form.

Gě Hóng's *Shénxiān zhuàn* ('Biographies of Spirit Immortals'), originally written in the fourth century CE and reworked in the sixth, records that the early Daoist sage Tàixuánnǚ ('Lady of Great Mystery') could "change *(huà)* her appearance at will: one moment she was an old man *(lǎowēng),* the next a small child *(ér).*"[1]

The *Shénxiān zhuàn* also relates the story of the visit paid to King Liú Ān of Huáinán (C2nd BCE) by the *bāgōng* – the eight worthies or immortals *(xiān)* who possessed various supernatural powers. At their first meeting, a member of their group tells the king that one of them could not only become invisible, but could also transform his body; and that another could change into the shape of anything he pleased – grass, tree, bird or beast, *etc.*[2]

A fourteenth-century historical work records that the physical form of twelfth-century Daoist master Wáng Zhé, as seen by ordinary people even when they were awake and under normal circumstances, changed continually. His left eye would turn clockwise, whilst his right eye would turn anticlockwise. Sometimes he would appear youthful, at others elderly; sometimes he would appear fat, at others thin. This made it difficult for anyone to make a reliable portrait of him![3]

See also: **huà** (▸4), **shéntōng, xiàn** (7.2).

1. Gě Hóng, *Shénxiān zhuàn* 7:27a, *TEAK* p.292.
2. *Cf. Gě Hóng, Shénxiān zhuàn* 4:14a–15a, *TEAK* pp.295–96.
3. Liú Zhìxuán and Xiè Xīchán, *Jīnlián xiàngzhuàn* 21b, *TPEQ* p.232 (n.26).

bindu-siddhi, bindu-jaya (S) *Lit.* power *(siddhi)* over semen *(bindu);* conquest *(jaya)* of the semen. See **siddhi**.

chalabhiññā (Pa) *Lit.* six *(cha)* kinds of super-knowledge *(abhiññā).* See **abhijñā**.

chetaḥ-paryāya-jñāna, para-chitta-jñāna (S), **parassa ceto-pariya-ñāṇa** (Pa) *Lit.* penetrating *(pariya)* knowledge *(ñāṇa, jñāna)* of another's *(para, parassa, paryāya)* thoughts *(ceta, chitta);* penetration of others' minds; awareness of the thinking processes of others; acquired, according to Patañjali's *Yoga Sūtras,* by focused attention *(saṃyama)* upon the mental processes of others;[1] one of the six supernormal forms of knowledge *(abhiññā)* in Buddhism; also called *manaḥ-paryāya-jñāna,* knowledge of another's mind *(manas),* especially in Jainism.

See also: **abhijñā, siddhi**.

1. Patañjali, *Yoga Sūtras* 3:19.

clairaudience The ability to hear sounds outside the range of normal human hearing, especially the spirits of the dead *etc.*

See also: **clairvoyance**.

clairvoyance The ability to see or know things beyond the range of the physical senses, such as extrasensory perception or the power to foretell future events; an ability mentioned in ancient literature, and present in most if not all cultures; from the French *clairvoyance* (clear seeing).

From a mystical perspective, the events of material existence come about as a result of the outworking of the karmic law of cause and effect. The architect and administrator of this law is the universal mind, from which all the patterns and diversity of the lower creation come into being. As a person evolves spiritually, the soul ascends the ladder of being, so to speak, finding itself in the realms of the higher mind, otherwise known as the astral and causal realms. Just as physical causes can be obvious in this world, so too are higher causes obvious when the consciousness is active in these higher realms of being. In practice, since the concentration of mind comes and goes, ascending and descending without much control, many individuals only receive glimpses or strong intuitions of future events, without really knowing where the information is coming from or how accurate it is. Such people are called clairvoyants, seers, soothsayers, psychics, and so on. Sometimes they get it right; sometimes they do not.

ʿInāyat Khān is speaking of the higher processes of *karma* and the higher mind, when he describes how "thoughts and feelings" ultimately become actions in the external world, and how these subtle, mental seeds of action can be seen – though not without uncertainty – on the inner planes:

> All things that manifest before the mind, such as thoughts and feelings, are in time born on the surface in the world of action, where they are called deeds. And those who cannot see them are sometimes quite unaware of the totally different form they take in their outward manifestation.
>
> Sometimes they come before a person's eyes, and sometimes they manifest far from his notice. Those who dive deep within themselves can, when they touch the plane of the Abstract, perceive things that are preparing to manifest through the mind onto the surface. But the primitive state of these things is so indistinct, even to the seer, that unless he knows the language of that sphere, he cannot understand what his experiences convey, though they are undoubtedly true in their effect. It is just as difficult as to read a line of fate.

> In Sufi terms, such experiences are called *anwār* and *anẓār*. In them lies the secret of prophecy. The first experience is perceived by the ears of the soul, so to speak, for the first experience is audible, while the second experience is visible. And yet it is not audible to the ears nor is it visible to the eyes. The audible experience is called clairaudience, and the visible, clairvoyance, although these words are misused by those who falsely claim these experiences.
>
> *'Ināyat Khān, Sufi Message, SMIK5 p.246*

Scientific experiments designed to test the reality of clairvoyance are likely to produce negative results for a number of reasons. (1) Clairvoyants do not usually have control over their ability; it comes and goes. (2) The information conveyed in clairvoyance comes from higher levels of the mind. Unless the mind is tuned in, so to speak, the subject is unlikely to be able to demonstrate clairvoyance. The psychological atmosphere of a scientific experiment, even if supportive, is unlikely to be conducive to clairvoyance. Even the desire to demonstrate clairvoyance, through egotism or for other reasons, would be sufficient to block the natural processes leading to clairvoyance. (3) Clairvoyance is often spontaneous, in response to emotional or environmental triggers, which cannot be reproduced in a laboratory. For example, experiments such as reading symbols on cards, which have no personal meaning to the subjects and generate no emotion or mental energy, are less likely to demonstrate telepathy than experiments designed to engender some mental or emotional interest. (4) It is a rule among the higher mystical traditions that psychic or miraculous powers are not to be used. They are regarded as highway robbers on the spiritual path. Their use is a waste of spiritual energy, and generates egotism, both of which prevent further spiritual progress. Consequently, those with genuine and controlled clairvoyant ability are extremely unlikely to make themselves available for experimentation. They may not even have told their family or close friends that they have developed such power. They would know that little or nothing would be achieved by a demonstration, spiritually speaking, however astounding it may appear. Spiritual evolution is internal and does not result from witnessing external events. In any case, hardened nonbelievers will always suspect trickery.

Outside the realm of scientific experiment, mystics may sometimes use their clairvoyant ability in order to help generate faith in a disciple, by reading their minds or foretelling some future event. But this is always done in a spontaneous manner, takes place at the right psychological moment, and is personal to that disciple.

See also: **psychic experience** (7.3), **visionary** (7.1).

clairvoyance (in Vodou) Fantastical stories are often told concerning the powers of Haitian *hungan* or *mambo,* male and female *Vodou* priests. It is said they can change people into animals or remain several days under water. Among their commonly attributed powers is clairvoyance or second sight:

> The gift most prized in a priest is second sight. To some *hungan* it has brought fame which merely increased after their deaths. A certain Nan Gommier acquired such a reputation that even today a soothsayer will say as a boast, "What I see for you, Antoine Nan Gommier himself would not have seen." This *hungan* is reputed to have known a long time in advance who was going to come and consult him and if it were a person of importance he sent a horse to meet him. With Nan Gommier questions and explanations were superfluous. He read people's thoughts and replied before being asked.
>
> *Alfred Métraux, Voodoo in Haiti, VHAM p.63*

See also: **hungan** (7.1).

cutūpapāta-ñāṇa (Pa) *Lit.* knowledge *(ñāṇa)* of disappearance and reappearance *(cutūpapāta);* knowledge *(ñāṇa)* according to *(yathā)* the result of *(upaga)* actions *(kamma);* knowledge of the death and rebirth of all sentient beings, in accordance with their good and bad deeds *(kamma),* also called *yathākammūpaga-ñāṇa;* also described as the divine eye *(dibba-cakkhu)* or universal vision that sees all that is happening in heaven and earth, whether near or far, including the *kamma* of all beings; one of the six supernormal forms of knowledge *(abhiññā)* in Buddhism.

See also: **abhijñā**, **yathākammūpaga-ñāṇa**.

dārduri-siddhi (S) *Lit.* froglike *(dārduri) siddhi;* frog-jump *siddhi;* the power to rise briefly and automatically off the ground while seated in the lotus (cross-legged) posture, practising *haṭha yoga, prāṇāyāma,* and the raising of the *kuṇḍalinī, etc.* See **siddhi**.

dashabala (S), **dasabala** (Pa), **stobs bcu** (T), **shílì** (C), **jūriki** (J) *Lit.* ten *(dasha, bcu, shí, jū)* powers *(bala, stobs, lì, riki);* the ten powers of penetrating wisdom and awareness possessed by a *buddha* or *tathāgata,* frequently mentioned in Buddhist texts; often as *dasa tathāgata-balāni* (Pa. ten powers of a *tathāgata*). *Dashabala* (endowed with ten powers) is sometimes used as an epithet of a *buddha,* as in the *Mahāvastu.*[1]

It is also said that the ten powers are possessed by a *bodhisattva* who has reached the eighth or ninth of the ten stages on the *bodhisattva*'s path to enlightenment, although a *bodhisattva*'s powers are not regarded as equal to those of a *buddha.* Some texts, however, ascribe a different set of ten powers to *bodhisattvas.*

The ten powers of a *buddha,* enumerated in a number of texts,[2] relate to a *buddha*'s inner knowledge and wisdom, of knowing things the way they actually are. As generally acknowledged by all mystical traditions, such knowledge is essentially mystical rather than conceptual. It is interior and experiential rather than intellectual.

A *buddha*'s ten powers are a part of a collection of attributes frequently mentioned together. These include the four kinds of fearlessness *(chatvāri-vaishāradyāni),* the four foundations of mindfulness *(chatvāri-smṛityupasthānāni),* the five awarenesses *(pañcha-jñāna),* the eight million billion kinds of *samādhi* (concentrations, states of inner absorption), eighteen characteristics *(ashṭādashan-āveṇika-buddhadharma),* the thirty-two major signs of perfection *(dvātriṃshadvara-lakshaṇa),* the eighty minor distinguishing marks *(ashīti-anuvyañjana),* together with the universal qualities of lovingkindness (S. *maitrī,* Pa. *mettā*) and great compassion *(mahākaruṇa).* The ten powers are commonly listed as:

1. The power to know what is possible and what is impossible; to know what is true and what is untrue; to know the difference between right and wrong; to know what is proper and what is improper.

2. The power to see the law of *karma* at work, and hence to know the way in which causality determines the past, the present, and the future; the power to know the result of actions.

3. The power to know the different dispositions and inclinations of people and all sentient beings, together with their aspirations, and their various ways of understanding.

4. The power to know the better and the worse qualities of people, and their potential; the power to fully understand people.

5. The power to know everything concerning the universe, and its many realms, constituents, and components.

6. The power to know and understand the many spiritual paths and practices, together with the consequences of following them and their different destinations, such as rebirth as a human being, a stay in a heavenly realm, enlightenment, and so on.

7. The power to know all the stages of the various meditative concentrations *(samādhis),* liberations, states of meditative absorption *(jhānas),* and other such inner attainments.

8. The power to know one's many previous lives, ranging back not just through a few past births, but encompassing the last hundred thousand lives, and far beyond that, including the many expansions and contractions of the universe:

> "There I was so named, of such a clan, with such an appearance, such was my nutriment, such my experience of pleasure and pain, such my life-term; and passing away from there, I reappeared elsewhere; and there too I was so named, of such a clan, with such an appearance, such was my nutriment, such my experience of pleasure and pain, such my life-term; and passing away from there, I reappeared here." Thus with their aspects and particulars, he recollects his manifold past lives. That too is a *tathāgata*'s power *(tathāgata-bala).*
>
> *Majjhima Nikāya 12, Mahāsīhanāda Sutta, PTSM1 p.70, MNNB*

9. The power to know, through the exercise of his divine eye *(dibba-cakkhu),* the death, the rebirth and the future lives of all sentient beings, all happening according to the fruition of their actions *(karma):*

> With the divine eye *(dibba-cakkhu),* which is purified and surpasses the human, the *tathāgata* sees beings passing away and reappearing, inferior and superior, fair and ugly, fortunate and unfortunate, and he understands how beings pass on according to their actions thus: "Those worthy beings who were ill-conducted in body, speech and mind, revilers of noble ones, wrong in their views and expressing wrong views in their actions, upon the dissolution of the body, after death, have reappeared in a state of deprivation, in a bad destination, in perdition, even in hell.
>
> "But these worthy beings who were well conducted in body, speech and mind, not revilers of noble ones, right in their views and expressing right views in their actions, upon the dissolution of the body, after death, have reappeared in a good destination, even in the heavenly world." ... That (knowledge), too, is a *tathāgata*'s power *(tathāgata-bala).*
>
> *Majjhima Nikāya 12, Mahāsīhanāda Sutta, PTSM1 pp.70–71; cf. MNNB*

10. The power to eliminate all taints or impurities (S. *āsrava,* Pa. *āsava*) and all illusions, thereby attaining the state of *nirvāṇa* and liberation *(moksha):*

> By realizing it for himself with direct knowledge, the *tathāgata* here and now enters upon and abides in the 'deliverance of mind' and 'deliverance by wisdom' that are taintless with the destruction of the taints *(āsava)*. That too is a *tathāgata*'s power *(tathāgata-bala)*.
>
> *Majjhima Nikāya 12, Mahāsīhanāda Sutta, PTSM1 p.71, MNNB*

There are variations on this theme in different texts, with differences in both order and content. Although the essential theme remains the same, some Tibetan sources list an alternative selection:[3]

1. Power over life; the ability to prolong life.

2. Power over the mind; the ability to enter states of deep meditative absorption *(samādhi, jhāna)* at will.

3. Power over necessities; the ability to provide sentient beings with the necessities of life.

4. Power over *karma;* the ability to choose the place, time, and manner of one's birth, *etc.*

5. Power over rebirth; the ability to be reborn in a sensual realm without losing inner concentration.

6. Power over creative imagination; the ability to perform the eight miraculous powers *(siddhis)*.

7. Power over intention and desire; the ability to fulfil the wishes of oneself and others.

8. Power over miracles; the ability to inspire other beings by performing miracles.

9. Power over knowledge; perfect understanding of all spiritual paths *(dharmas)*.

10. Power over presentation; the ability to inspire all beings with a single discourse.

These ten powers are also credited to *bodhisattvas* who have reached the eighth stage *(bhūmi)*, and they are not too dissimilar to more general enumerations of the ten powers attributed to all *bodhisattvas*. Since *bodhisattvas* are at various stages on the path to enlightenment, it may be presumed that not all *bodhisattvas* possess all ten powers in equal measure. With some variations between texts, and some crossover between the items, the ten powers of *bodhisattvas* are listed as:

1. The power of a profound mind; firm resolve, devotion and intention to attain enlightenment and not get entangled in worldly attachments; to have a mind turned away from the world.

2. The power of a higher profound mind; willpower; steadfastness and an ever-increasing faith on the path to enlightenment.

3. The power of means; bringing whatever they set out to achieve to a successful conclusion; the power of discipline on the *bodhisattva*'s path.

4. The power of wisdom; understanding the content of the minds of all sentient beings.

5. The power of vows; commitment; the ability to fulfil all prayers, vows, and aspirations.

6. The power of practice; constant endurance; continuing on the path until the end of time.

7. The power of the vehicles (paths) of liberation; the ability to understand and be inclusive of all spiritual paths, without ever abandoning the great universal vehicle *(Mahāyāna).*

8. The power of miraculous transformations; the power to manifest all the *buddhas* and all the pure lands (paradises) in every pore of the skin. (Understood metaphorically, the meaning of this power is perhaps akin to perceiving the divine presence in all things.)

9. The power of enlightenment or awakening; the ability to continuously inspire all sentient beings to seek enlightenment and to become *buddhas;* the power to turn the wheel of *Dharma* and bring all beings to enlightenment.

10. The power of turning the wheel of the *Dharma;* the ability to teach the *Dharma* – to explain the *Dharma* according to the faculties, temperaments, and inclinations of all sentient beings; the power to speak in such a manner that it simultaneously appeals to the hearts of all beings; to satisfy all beings with just a single phrase.

By acquiring these powers, says the *Avataṃsaka Sūtra,* "*bodhisattvas* can attain the *buddhas'* ten powers *(shílì)* of omniscience".[4] Describing these powers in a general way, the *sūtra* says:

> They have perfect discrimination of things;
> They possess the ten powers *(shílì);*
> They are free, unhampered by bodily *karma;*
> They know all there is to know about reaching the perfect abode.
> This is the path travelled
> by those with such virtuous attainments.
>
> Guided at all times by wisdom,
> they fully understand the consequences of the *karma*
> of countless and unlimited past, present, and future lives.
> This is the path travelled
> by those with such complete understanding.
>
> With astute insight into the right and the wrong moments in this world,
> always choosing a suitable and opportune moment,
> they never lose an opportunity to awaken living beings.
> This is the path travelled
> by those with such clear-sighted understanding.
>
> Well-disciplined in body, mind and speech,
> always putting the teachings into practice,
> they relinquish attachment to everything, overcoming all demons.
> This is the path travelled
> by those of such a wise mind.
>
> Through accomplished practice of the teachings,
> they realize the true character
> and the universal nature of all existence –
> which they tirelessly and eloquently expound.
> This is the path travelled
> by those who engage in the *buddhadharma*. . . .
>
> All *buddhas* of the past, present and future
> are of the same mind and the same wisdom.
> They are of one form and one nature:
> there is no difference between them.
> This is the path travelled
> by those who are unfettered.

Avataṃsaka Sūtra 21, T10 279:109b14–15, 110a16–27

Speaking more specifically of *bodhisattvas,* the same *sūtra* says:

> Through the changing things of the world,
> they gain full knowledge of the Unchanging.
> When there is no change, there is no place:
> when there is no place, there is extinction *(i.e. nirvāṇa).*
> Their mind free of defiling attachment,
> they vow to save all living beings.
> With a one-pointed mind remembering the *buddhadharma,*
> they are never scattered or perturbed.
> With compassion, they teach the world
> the most expedient means (to liberation).
> Assiduously seeking the ten powers *(shílì),*
> they live in the world, yet remain unattached.
> Without coming or going,
> they expound the *Dharma* by expedient means *(fāngbiàn).*
>
> *Avataṃsaka Sūtra 29, T10 279:235b8–14*

Bodhisattvas are working towards enlightenment, but have not yet attained it:

> They understand:
> what is and what is not,
> all *karmas* and all roots (causes),
> all realms and all explanations,
> all meditation (C. *chán,* S. *dhyāna*),
> all paths and where they lead.
> They know all past and future lives.
> They know how to extinguish all delusion.
>
> They possess the ten powers *(shílì)* of the *buddhas,*
> yet have not fully attained them. . . .
> They entertain neither passions nor delusions,
> yet they have not completely eliminated impurity.
>
> They possess full knowledge of the path to emancipation,
> yet they use that knowledge to liberate sentient beings.
> Such is their courage, demonstrated by their relentless practice.
>
> They neither err nor do they deviate from the path,
> nor do they lose right mindfulness.
> Their diligence, determination, wisdom
> and desire for meditation *(samādhi)* never diminish.

Pure in their practice of the precepts,
they fully understand the past, present, and future.
They have great compassion for living beings,
and are not limited in any way.

Avataṃsaka Sūtra 38, T10 279:316c27–317a9

See also: **abhijñā, iddhi, ṛiddhi, ṛiddhipāda**.

1. *Mahāvastu, MHVA, MVJ1–3, passim.*
2. *E.g. Anguttara Nikāya* 10:21, *Sīhanāda Sutta, PTSA5* pp.33–36; *Majjhima Nikāya* 12, *Mahāsīhanāda Sutta, PTSM1* pp.69–71; *Paṭisambhidāmagga* 2, *PTSP1* pp.174–76; *Pratyutpanna Samādhi Sūtra* 12, *T13* 418:917a–b, *PSSL* p.88; "Ten powers," *Treasury of Mahāyāna Sūtras, TMSC* p.494; "Juriki," *Japanese-English Buddhist Dictionary, JEDS.*
3. *E.g.* "Ten Powers," *Handbook of Tibetan Buddhist Symbols, HTBS* pp.256–57.
4. *Avataṃsaka Sūtra* 38, *T10* 279:295b29–c10; *Shūrangama-Samādhi Sūtra, T15* 642:643a–b, *SSSK* pp.75–76; "Juriki," *Japanese-English Buddhist Dictionary, JEDS;* "Ten powers," *Treasury of Mahāyāna Sūtras, TMSC* p.494.

dathā saṃkalpa saṃsiddhi (S) *Lit.* complete fulfilment *(saṃsiddhi)* of one's *(yathā)* intention *(saṃkalpa);* the power to fulfil all one's desires; the power to accomplish whatever one sets out to achieve. See **siddhi**.

devānām saha-krīḍā anudarshana (S) *Lit.* witnessing *(anudarshana)* and participating *(saha)* in the play *(krīḍā)* of the gods *(devānām)*. See **siddhi**.

divya-saṃvid (S) *Lit.* divine *(divya)* perception *(saṃvid)*. See **siddhi**.

dūra-darshana, dūra-dṛishṭi (S) *Lit.* remote *(dūra)* vision *(darshana, dṛishṭi);* seeing things from far away. See **siddhi**.

dūra-shravaṇa, dūra-shruti (S) *Lit.* remote *(dūra)* hearing *(shravaṇa);* hearing things from far away. See **siddhi**.

dvātriṃshadvara-lakshaṇa (S), **dvattiṃsa-lakkhaṇa** (Pa), **mtshan bzang po sum cu rtsa gnyis** (T), **sānshíèr dàrén xiàng** (C), **sanjūni dainin sō** (J) *Lit.*

thirty-two *(dvātriṃshat, sum cu rtsa gnyis, sānshíèr, sanjūni)* excellent *(vara, bzang)* marks *(lakshaṇa, mtshan, xiàng, sō);* thirty-two marks of excellence; thirty-two auspicious marks; the thirty-two bodily marks or characteristics of a fully enlightened *buddha,* traditionally understood to be possessed by a great man *(mahāpurusha, dàrén, dainin),* as also by a *chakravartin* (universal monarch); almost certainly of pre-Buddhist origin and adopted into Buddhism from *brāhmaṇ* lore. In *Mahāyāna* Buddhist texts, the thirty-two marks are often said to be present on the heavenly bodies (*sambhoga-kāya,* body of delight) of celestial *buddhas.*

The thirty-two marks of a *buddha* or *tathāgata* are listed with some small variations in a number of Pali texts, including the *Lakkhaṇa* and *Mahāpadāna Suttas* of the *Dīgha Nikāya,*[1] and the *Brahmāyu Sutta* of the *Majjhima Nikāya.*[2] They are also mentioned and listed in many later Buddhist texts.

Later texts contain other lists that differ from each other and from earlier lists in many minor ways. The thirty-two marks also make an appearance in Buddhist art, the earliest of which date from the second century BCE. The *ūrṇā* (Pa. *uṇṇa*) – a whorl of hair or a mark between the eyebrows – is an especially common feature, representing the *buddha* eye or divine eye, also found in many images of Hindu deities. The thirty-two characteristics are also supplemented by a further eighty minor marks (S. *ashīti-anuvyañjana,* Pa. *asīti-anubyañjana*).

The marks are entirely physical in nature, and include such things as tender hands and feet; a skin the colour of gold, pure, fair, and shining attractively; an upper body that is broad like that of a lion; a symmetrical body, the span of whose outstretched arms is equal to its height; a long and beautiful tongue that can reach every part of his face, but does not fill his mouth; a voice that has the sixty aspects of the melodious speech of the deity *Brahmā;* forty beautiful, completely white teeth of equal length and width, with no spaces between; and beautiful eyes, blue like a jewel, with black pupils, white eyeballs, a red hue in the corners, and irises blue on the periphery and yellow towards the centre. According to the *Lakkhaṇa Sutta:*

> Once the Lord was staying at Sāvatthī, in Jetavana, Anāthapiṇḍika's park. "Monks!" he said, and the monks replied: "Lord." The Lord said: "There are, monks, these thirty-two marks peculiar to a great man *(dvattiṃsa-mahāpurisa-lakkhaṇa),* and for that great man who possesses them, only two careers are open. If he lives the household life, he will become a ruler, a wheel-turning righteous monarch *(cakkavattī)* of the law, conqueror of the four quarters, who has established the security of his realm and is possessed of the seven treasures.... But if he goes forth from the household life into homelessness, he will become an *arahanta,* a fully enlightened *buddha (sammā-sambuddha),* who has drawn back the veil from the world.

> "And what are these thirty-two marks? (1) He has feet with level tread. This is one of the marks of a great man *(mahāpurisa-lakkhaṇa).* (2) On the soles of his feet are wheels with a thousand spokes, complete with felloe and hub. (3) He has projecting heels. (4) He has long fingers and toes. (5) He has soft and tender hands and feet. (6) His hands and feet are net-like. (7) He has high-raised ankles. (8) His legs are like an antelope's. (9) Standing and without bending, he can touch and rub his knees with either hand. (10) His male organs are enclosed in a sheath. (11) His complexion is bright, the colour of gold. (12) His skin is delicate and so smooth that no dust can adhere to his body. (13) His body hairs are separate, one to each pore. (14) His body hairs grow upwards, each one bluish-black like collyrium, curling in rings to the right. (15) His body is divinely straight. (16) He has the seven convex surfaces. (17) The front part of his body is like a lion's. (18) There is no hollow between his shoulders. (19) He is proportioned like a banyan tree: the height of his body is the same as the span of his outstretched arms, and conversely. (20) His bust is evenly rounded. (21) He has a perfect sense of taste. (22) He has jaws like a lion's. (23) He has forty teeth. (24) His teeth are even. (25) There are no spaces between his teeth. (26) His canine teeth are very bright. (27) His tongue is very long. (28) He has a *Brahmā*-like voice, like that of the *karavīka*-bird (the Indian cuckoo). (29) His eyes are deep blue. (30) He has eyelashes like a cow's. (31) The hair between his eyes is white and soft like cotton down. (32) His head is like a royal turban. This is one of the marks of a great man *(mahāpurisa-lakkhaṇa).*"
>
> *Dīgha Nikāya 30, Lakkhaṇa Sutta, PTSD3 pp.142–45, TBLD pp.441–42*

It must be presumed that the marks on the body of a great man are to be understood as a mythological extension regarding the natural grace and beauty of a perfected and enlightened human being. In some instances, they may have a symbolic significance. The *Mahāyāna* Buddhist philosopher Nāgārjuna expands on the meaning of each of these marks in a section in which he relates the story of the Buddha's previous births as a *bodhisattva,* and his final birth – still a *bodhisattva,* yet to be enlightened – as the son of King Shuddhodana. After the birth of his son, the king asks the "experts in marks *(lakshaṇa-pratigrāhaka)*" to check whether his son has the "thirty-two marks of a great man *(dvātriṃsha mahāpurusha-lakshaṇa)*". They duly examine the boy, and proclaim that he does indeed possess the thirty-two marks, and – following the traditional belief – that he would become a *chakravartin* (universal monarch) or a *buddha.* When the king asks, "What are the thirty-two marks?", and experts enumerate them, to which Nāgārjuna in relating the story, adds his own further observations:

1. "The soles of his feet are well set down." The soles of his feet are set down on the ground without a gap – not even a needle could be inserted.

2. "On the soles of his feet are two wheels with a thousand spokes, a hub and a rim and having three perfections." He has obtained this mark spontaneously; it was not made by an artisan. The divine artists like Vishvakarman are not able to make such a perfect mark. . . .

3. "He has long fingers." His fingers are slender and straight; their arrangement is harmonious and the joints are accentuated.

4. "He has a broad heel."

5. "The digits of his hands and feet are webbed." He is like the king of the swans *(haṃsa):* when he spreads his fingers, the webs show, when he does not spread his fingers, the webs do not show. (In fact, the Sanskrit *jāla* means a 'net', not a 'web', and a number of scholars are of the opinion that the original meaning refers to the lines on the hands and feet. It has also been suggested that the notion of webbed digits arose from an observation of early sculptures, where it was necessary to retain some material between the fingers and toes so that they should not easily break off).[3]

6. "His hands and feet are soft and delicate." Like fine cotton cloth, these members surpass the other parts of his body.

7. "He has a prominent instep." When he treads on the ground, his foot neither widens nor retracts. The soles of his feet are like a red lotus in colour; between the toes there is a membrane; the ends of his feet are the colour of real coral; the toenails have the colour of polished red copper; the upper side of his feet are golden in colour and the hairs covering it are the azure of lapis lazuli. These colours are marvellous; one would say an assortment of jewels, a varicoloured necklace.

8. "He has the limbs of an antelope." His legs taper gradually as in Aiṇeya, the king of the antelopes.

9. "Standing upright without bending over, his arms reach down to his knees." Without bending or straightening up again, he can touch his knees with the palms (of his hands).

10. "The secret part of his abdomen is concealed within a sheath" as in an elephant of good birth or a high-bred horse....

11. Like the *nyagrodha* (banyan) tree, the *buddha*'s body is rounded, and is of the same size on all four sides.

12. "His hair rises up." On his body his hair curls upwards.

13. From each of his pores there arises a single hair; his hairs are not disarranged; they are blue-black, of the colour of lapis lazuli, curved to the right, and standing up.

14. "He is golden in colour." What is this golden colour?... (Nāgārjuna now compares the increasing brilliance of the golden colour of various mythological rivers, oceans, mountains and deities, concluding that the brilliance of the golden colour of a *bodhisattva*'s body is greater than anything else.) Such is this mark of the golden colour.

15. "He has an aura the breadth of an arm-span." He has an aura the breath of an arm-span on all four sides. In the centre of this aura the *buddha* has supreme beauty; his splendour is equal to that of the king of the gods. (This is in keeping with a number of *Mahāyāna* texts, such as the *Avataṃsaka* and *Lotus Sūtras,* which maintain that the body of a *buddha,* especially in the higher heavens, emits powerful rays of light.)

16. "He has fine skin." Dust does not adhere to his body; he is like the lotus leaf that holds neither dust nor water. When the *bodhisattva* climbs a huge pile of dry earth, the earth does not stick to his feet. When the wind blows up a storm to destroy the pile, which becomes dispersed as dust, not a single grain of dust sticks to the *buddha*'s body.

17. "The seven parts of his body are well developed." Seven parts of the body: the two hands, the two feet, the two shoulders and the nape of his neck are rounded, of fine colour, and surpass those of all other bodies.

18. "The bottom of his armpits are well developed." They are without bumps or hollows.

19. "The front part of his body is like that of a lion."

20. "His body is broad and straight." Of all men, his body is the broadest and the straightest.

21. "His shoulders are completely rounded." He has no peer amongst those who straighten their shoulders.

22. "He has forty teeth," neither more nor less. Other men have thirty-two teeth; their body consists of more than three hundred bones and the bones of their skull are nine in number. The *bodhisattva* has forty teeth and his skull is a single bone. In him, the teeth are numerous but the bones of the skull are few; among other men, the teeth are few but the skull bones are numerous. This is how the *bodhisattva* differs from other men.

23. "His teeth are closely spaced." No coarse or fine material can get in between his teeth. People who do not know the secret mark of his teeth say that he has but one single tooth. One could not introduce a single hair between them.

24. "His teeth are white"; they surpass the brightness of king Himavat.

25. "He has the jaw of a lion." Like a lion, king of the beasts, his jaw is straight and broad.

26. "He has the best of all tastes." Some say that when the *buddha* puts food into his mouth, all foods take on an exquisite flavour. Why? Because in all these foods there is the essence of exquisite flavour. People who do not possess this mark cannot give off this essence and, as a consequence, do not have this exquisite taste. Others say that when the *buddha* takes food and puts it in his mouth, the ends of his throat secrete ambrosia (food of the gods) which concentrates all flavours. As this food is pure, we say that he possesses the best of all tastes. (Other texts say that all the food that enters his mouth is transformed into ambrosia.)

27. "He has a broad tongue." When the *buddha* sticks his great tongue out of his mouth, it covers all the parts of his face up to the top of his hair. But when he puts it back in, his mouth is not filled up.

28. "He has the voice of *Brahmā*." Five kinds of sounds come from the mouth of *Brahmā,* king of the gods: (1) deep as thunder; (2) pure and clear, able to be heard from afar and delighting the listeners; (3) penetrating and inspiring respect; (4) truthful and easy to understand; (5) never tiring the listeners. These are also the five intonations from the mouth of the *bodhisattva.* (Other marks): "He has the voice of a *kalavinka*" – his voice is pleasant like the song of the *kalavinka* bird (the Indian cuckoo; also, a mythological bird that dwells in paradise). "He has the voice of a drum" – his voice is deep and powerful like that of a great drum.

29. "His eyes are deep blue" like a beautiful blue lotus.

30. "His eyelashes are like those of an ox." Like the king of the oxen, his eyelashes are long, beautiful, and well arranged.

31. "His head is crowned with a protuberance." The *bodhisattva* has a bony chignon like a fist on his head.

32. "He has a tuft of white hairs." A tuft of white hair grows between his eyebrows, neither too high nor too low. It is white, whorled to the right, growing easily and at the height of five feet.

Nāgārjuna, Mahāprajñāpāramitā Shāstra 8:6.1–32; cf. TVW1 pp.229–33

Continuing the story of the Buddha's birth, the "experts in marks" then add: "In earth and heaven, the young prince possesses the thirty-two marks of the great man *(mahāpurusha-lakshaṇa)* that all *bodhisattvas* possess." Nāgārjuna then concludes that the *chakravartin* also

> possesses these thirty-two marks,... the marks of the *bodhisattva* prevail over those of the *chakravartin* king in seven ways: they are (1) very pure, (2) very distinct, (3) ineffaceable, (4) perfect, (5) deeply marked, (6) conforming with the practice of wisdom and not conforming to the world, (7) lasting. The marks of a *chakravartin* king do not have these qualities.
>
> *Nāgārjuna, Mahāprajñāpāramitā Shāstra 8:6, TVW1 pp.233–34*

He also adds that they are called "marks *(lakshaṇa)*... because they are easy to recognize", just as "water, which is different from fire, is recognized by its marks."

See also: **buddha** (7.1), **chakravartin** (7.1).

1. *E.g. Dīgha Nikāya* 3 *(Ambaṭṭha Sutta),* 4 *(Soṇadaṇḍa Sutta),* 14 *(Mahāpadāna Sutta),* 30 *(Lakkhaṇa Sutta), PTSD1* pp.88–89, 105–6, 116, *PTSD2* pp.16–19, *PTSD3* pp.142–45.
2. *Majjhima Nikāya* 91, *Brahmāyu Sutta, PTSM2* pp.134–37.

3. Étienne Lamotte, *Treatise on the Great Virtue of Wisdom of Nāgārjuna, TVW1* p.229 (n.476).

extrasensory perception ESP, perception of things in this world that takes place independently of normal sensory processes; includes telepathy, clairvoyance, precognition, *etc.;* a form of mental intuition or knowing; also called cryptaesthesia; a faculty associated with the awareness of subtle mind energies, as well as the subtle energy vibration and atmosphere of places *etc.*

It is possible that some of these subtle energies or vibrations may have a presence in the energy field that comprises so-called 'empty' space, which underlies all matter and material phenomena. This would explain why places retain an atmosphere long after people have left. A vibration or residue, so to speak, is left in the energy of space itself, to which the brain/mind is sensitive. Since the brain is the link between physical perception and the higher energies of the mind, it is possible that the brain has activity in the energies of space itself, which underlies all its biochemical and electrical activity. Of course, the details of this activity – as well as the manner by which mind energies, the energy of space, and the brain make up a functioning unit – remain uncertain.

Scientific studies of ESP date from the late nineteenth century, and include laboratory-controlled experiments in which subjects attempt to demonstrate a better-than-chance ability to determine the nature of symbols on hidden cards. Although many scientists remain sceptical of such faculties, people claiming such abilities are sometimes used successfully by the police and other investigative organizations seeking missing persons or things *etc.*

See also: **clairvoyance**.

firāsah (A), **firāsat** (P) *Lit.* insight, sagacity, discernment, perspicacity, especially awareness or intuition concerning the hidden side of things, events, and people; discernment between truth and falsehood, discernment of people's thoughts and hidden motives; a mystic's capacity to read the hearts and minds of others; hence also, second sight, clairvoyance, thought-reading, soul-reading; psychic knowledge of events and people.

According to a frequently quoted *ḥadīth* (traditional saying), Muḥammad says, "Beware the discernment *(firāsah)* of the man of faith, for he sees by the light of *Allāh.*"[1] *Firāsah* is thus understood to be a result of the light that God manifests in a pure heart. It is regarded as proceeding from a divine source, to be among the gifts given to a saint, and to be evidence of holiness. In his *Meccan Revelations,* in a chapter on *firāsah,* Ibn al-ʿArabī recalls this *ḥadīth,* following it with an explanation of the nature of "perspicacity through faith" *(al-firāsat al-īmānīyah)*":

Perspicacity through faith *(al-firāsat al-īmānīyah)* is a divine light which God gives to the person of faith in the eye of his insight, just like the light which belongs to the eye of sight. When a person has this perspicacity *(firāsah),* its mark is like the light of the sun through which sensory objects appear to sight. When the light of the sun is unveiled, sight differentiates among the sensory objects. It discerns the large from the small, the beautiful from the ugly, the white from the black, red, and yellow, the moving from the still, the far from the near, and the high from the low. In the same way, the light of perspicacity through faith *(al-firāsat al-īmānīyah)* discerns the praiseworthy from the blameworthy.

The reason that the light of perspicacity *(firāsah)* is attributed to the name *Allāh,* which is the name which brings together the properties of all the Names, is that this light unveils both the praiseworthy and the blameworthy, both the movements of felicity pertaining to the next abode and the movements of wretchedness.

Ibn al-'Arabī, Meccan Revelations 2:235.35, FMIA3 (2:148) p.355, SPK p.304

Alluding to the same *ḥadīth,* Rūmī writes, "If the true believer was not seeing by the light of God, how would things unseen appear plainly revealed to the true believer?"[2] And in the same vein:

Why should the illuminated souls in the world
  be unaware of our hidden state?…
Though you yourself may be palsied and lame and blind and deaf,
  do not hold this opinion of the great souls…
Be ashamed and do not utter idle words, do not torment yourself,
  for there are many spies (observing you) beyond the body.

Rūmī, Maśnavī IV:1787, 1792–93; cf. MJR4 p.371

And likewise, referring specifically to the *shaykh* or spiritual master:

Anyone that is the lion and prince of spiritual mysteries,
  he will know all that the conscience thinks.
Beware! Guard yourself, O heart disposed to thinking,
  from any evil thought in his presence.

Rūmī, Maśnavī I:3028–29; cf. MJR2 p.165

He goes on to counsel that the only way to develop the discernment *(firāsah)* to perceive the gap between external acts and inner feelings is to develop the inner faculty of vision by which a person can "see by the light of God":

That hypocrite is assiduous in fasting and prayer,
in order that it may be supposed
that he is drunk with devotion.
In short, external acts are different from internal feelings:
but they indicate that which is hidden.
O Lord, grant us according to our desire such discernment *(tamyīz)*
that we may know the false indication from the true.
Do you know how perception *(ḥiss)* becomes discernment?
In this way: that perception *(ḥiss)* should see by the light of God....
When the light of God becomes the means of perception,
then you will no longer be a slave to cause or effect....
There are detailed explanations I could give to complete this subject:
but seek them for yourself, and now farewell.

Rūmī, Maśnavī I:2631–36, 2639; cf. MJR2 p.143

This also explains why Sufis and mystics place little stock in outward displays of any kind.

Many of the hagiographic legends and biographies of the Sufis concern their *firāsah,* particularly seeing into the hearts and minds of those who visited them. Many such stories, for instance, are related of Abū Saʿīd al-Khayr:

There were two friends, a tailor and a weaver, who obstinately asserted that Abū Saʿīd was an impostor. One day they said, "This man pretends to have the gift of miracles *(karāmāt).* Let us go to him, and if he knows what trade each of us follows, we shall then know that his claim is true." They disguised themselves, and went to the *shaykh.* As soon as his eye fell on them, he said:[3]

"On the rack are two craftsmen,
one a tailor, one a weaver."
Then he said, pointing to the tailor:
"This one fashions robes for princes."
And pointing to the weaver:
"This one weaves black woollens only."
Both were covered with confusion and fell at the *shaykh*'s feet
and repented of their disbelief.

Abū Saʿīd al-Khayr, in Asrār al-Tawḥīd, ATS1 pp.184–85, in SIM p.68

See also: **karāmāt**.

1. *Ḥādīth, AMBF* 33.
2. Rūmī, *Maśnavī* I:1331; *cf. MJR2* p.73.
3. Retold by R.A. Nicholson, *Studies in Islamic Mysticism, SIM* p.68.

gariman, **garimā** (S) *Lit.* heaviness, weight; probably from *guru* (heavy); the power to assume extraordinary heaviness, such that one cannot be moved.

See also: **siddhi**.

healing The restoration of health; spiritually, the forgiveness of sins through the mediation of a saviour, leading to the restoration of the soul's innate spirituality through realization and spiritual uplift; part of a family of metaphors from the ancient Middle East, in which the saviour, also known as the divine healer or physician, applies the healing medicine of the Word, which clears the debt of sin, eventually culminating in the soul's return to its natural state with God.

In Christianity, the healing miracles of Jesus are regarded with considerable significance. Yet a greater, though less visible, miracle was Jesus' forgiveness of sins. Indeed, the stories of Jesus' miracles are sometimes accompanied by his explicit linking of illness or infirmity to past sins and his forgiveness of them.[1]

From the many allusions to the miracles of Jesus in ancient Christian and gnostic literature, it is clear that many of the mystically minded in the ancient world understood the stories of Jesus' physical miracles to be literalizations of spiritual healing, understood as a healing of the spirit or soul, not the body. Healing and the forgiveness of sins are clearly equated in ancient Christian literature, as in early writings from Syria:

> Blessed be the Son of the Good, who atoned our debts!
> Blessed is the physician of the Height, who healed our disease.
>
> *Early Christian Liturgy, BDB (5) p.37, MEM p.160*

Likewise, in the early Christian revelational writing, the *Shepherd of Hermas,* an 'angel' says:

> You who are suffering for the Name ought to glorify God
> that God deemed you worthy to bear this Name
> and that all your sins should be healed.
>
> *Shepherd of Hermas 9:28.5, AF2 pp.286–87*

And:

> I bid you keep these commandments,
> and you shall have healing for your sins.
>
> *Shepherd of Hermas 10:2.4; cf. AF2 pp.300–1*

Christian writers have also understood that the healing of a person's spiritual ills – pride and other human imperfections – is a more profound healing than the healing of bodily ailments. As St Augustine says, "It is pride that is the cause of all our sickness, which the Son of God came to heal."[2] Hence, Thomas à Kempis prays to be healed of human imperfection so that he may be able to love God more purely:

> Set me free from all evil passions, and heal my sick heart from all earthly inclinations; so that, inwardly healed and cleansed in spirit, I may be made able to love You, strong to endure, and steadfast in perseverance.
>
> *Thomas à Kempis, Imitation of Christ 3:5; cf. IC p.110, ICTK p.97*

The author of the *Cloud of Unknowing* adds that something has to be done to become worthy of this forgiveness. It is loving contemplation, he says, which cuts at the roots of sin. With patience and practice, the divine grace of forgiveness will be felt:

> For the contemplative work of love by itself will eventually heal you of all the roots of sin.... He who patiently abides in this darkness will be comforted and feel again a confidence about his destiny, for gradually he will see his past sins healed by grace.
>
> *Cloud of Unknowing 12, 69, CU pp.55, 125*

The same author also refers to the faith of the woman in the gospel story who felt that, if she could only touch the hem of Jesus' garment, she would be healed.[3] The final healing, he says, is union of the soul with God:

> She was healed physically; but even more shall you be healed of your spiritual illness by this lofty, sublime work in which your desire reaches out to touch the very being of God, beloved in Himself.
>
> Step up bravely, then, and take this medicine. Lift up your sick self, just as you are, to the gracious God, just as He is. Leave behind all enquiry and profound speculation into your being or His. Forget all these qualities and everything about them, whether they be pure or defiled, natural or grace-given, divine or human. Nothing matters now except that you willingly offer to God that blind awareness of your naked being in joyful love, so that grace can bind you and make you spiritually one with the precious being of God, simply as He is in Himself.
>
> *Book of Privy Counselling 2, CU pp.141–42*

Gnostic writers have also understood the saviour's healing to be the forgiveness of sins. The spiritual healing granted by the divine healer or physician is a recurrent theme in Mandaean writings:

Physician, the healer of his friends,
heal us from our sins and do not condemn us!
Physician, the healer of souls,
heal us and do not condemn us!
Mandaean Ginzā (Treasury); cf. GSBM p.55, MEM p.161

The means of healing is also explicitly said to be the divine Word:

Let healing be theirs
by virtue of the Word of Truth.
Mandaean Prayer Book 20, CPM p.15

This Word is also depicted as the Tree of Life, the Vine from which the true healing of the soul arises. It is

the Vine which is all-life
and the great Tree which is all-healing.
Mandaean Prayer Book 77; cf. CPM p.84

In one instance, all forms of healing are attributed to this Tree:

This is a tree which is a Tree of Life,
and a Vine, a Vine of Life!
Satisfying fare that is superior to all means of healing
is that which you have brought, revealed,
and given to these souls!
Blessed is this pure oblation
which goes before its giver....

It is a deliverer of the bound,
it cheers those who are in affliction,
causes sucklings to flourish,
is the sight of the blind,
and the hearing and pleasure of the deaf.

It establishes speech in the mouths of the stammering,
and the deaf and the dumb.
Its presence is praised,
for thereby souls are held together.
And it provides the means of ascent
to the great place of light and the everlasting abode.
Mandaean Prayer Book 375; cf. CPM pp.269–70

Like Jesus, the third-century Iranian mystic Mānī was also credited with numerous healing miracles of a bodily nature. Even so, throughout the Manichaean hymns, his healing is commonly understood to be the healing of the soul, effected by the divine physician with his Medicine of Life. Equating salvation from this world with spiritual wholeness, a Manichaean psalmist asks rhetorically:

> Who shall lead me to that land without tremors?…
> Who shall answer me with pity?…
> Who shall make me whole?…
> Who shall take off from me this … body,
> and clothe me in a new body?
>
> *Manichaean Hymns, Angād Rōshnān IIIc:3, 11–13, MHCP pp.134–37*

The writer is of course referring to the saviour, in his case, Mānī. In a Manichaean prayer, a devotee naturally equates healing with the forgiveness of sins. The "gift" is divine grace, and specifically the gift of the divine Word or Wisdom:

> My God! My bright, strong, beneficent, just God!
> Have mercy upon me now!
> From now on I shall sin no more….
> You are loving, complete Wisdom:
> deign to heal me now, my God!
> Forgive my sins, grant me dispensation from my offences,
> wash away my misdeeds;
> Grant me now my blessed reward, by your gift of grace.
>
> *Manichaean Prayer, TMC3 p.25; cf. GSR p.296*

The same metaphor was prevalent prior to the time of Jesus and the gnostics. Although the words were later taken as a prophecy of Jesus, Isaiah is speaking of himself when he says:

> The Spirit of the Lord is upon me;…
> He has sent me to heal the brokenhearted,
> to preach deliverance to the captives,
> and recovering of sight to the blind,
> to set at liberty them that are bruised.
>
> *Isaiah 61:1, in Luke 4:18; cf. KJV*

The same imagery appears in the hymns of praise among the Dead Sea Scrolls. The unknown mystic writes:

I have been a snare for transgressors,
but healing for those who repented;
Prudence for the simple,
and steadfastness for the fearful of heart.
Thanksgiving Hymns 6:5–10; cf. CDSV p.262, DSSM p.401

See also: **blindness** (6.2), **deafness** (6.2), **disease** (6.2), **dumbness** (6.2), **good Samaritan** (7.1), **king of healing** (7.1), **Medicine of Life** (3.1), **miracles**, **miracles of Jesus and the apostles**, **paralysis** (6.2), **physician** (7.1), **wounds** (6.2).

1. *Mark* 2:5–12; *Matthew* 9:2–6; *Luke* 5:20–24, 7:47–50; *John* 9:1–41.
2. St Augustine, *On John* 25:16, in *OCM* p.155.
3. *Matthew* 9:20–22.

himmah (A), **himmat** (P) (pl. *himam*) *Lit.* aspiration, ambition, fervour, resolve, courage, fixity of purpose, willpower, volition; spiritually, maintaining a focus on the spiritual goal; concentrated attention towards God; hence also, meditation, concentration, focused thought, attention; also, spiritual power, the mental power that comes with deep concentration and elevated consciousness, which makes it possible to exert control over material and higher levels of existence, and hence over various forces and energies, resulting in apparent miracles at the physical level.

Ibn al-ʿArabī says of one of the Andalusian Sufis he sketches in his *Rūḥ al-Quds:* "By means of his power of *himmah* he was able to control men's thoughts."[1]

Himmah is used along with several other such terms for the miraculous power possessed by advanced Sufis. These include *karāmāt* (gifts, favours), *kharq al-ʿādah* (breaking of habit, going contrary to nature), *taṣarruf* (power, control), *taḥakkum* (governing control), *takwīn* (bringing things into created existence), and *al-fiʿl bi al-himmah* (action with resolve, action with focused intent).[2] Ibn al-ʿArabī says of those who experience mystical "states" *(aṣḥāb al-ḥāl):*

> The possessors of states make things happen through their focused attention *(himmah),* discarding secondary causes far from themselves.
> *Ibn al-ʿArabī, Meccan Revelations 2:573.32, FMIA4 (4:270) p.304; cf. SPK p.265*

Ibn al-ʿArabī gives no importance to miracles, since they are not an indicator of a person's spiritual stature. They can even be performed by magicians and practitioners of the occult. However, a true Sufi, with his concentrated attention, can manipulate the laws of creation if he so desires, but he would only do so under exceptional circumstances and in obedience to the divine command. A Sufi is more concerned with the 'fittingness *(adab)*' of things – that everything should happen at its proper time and place, through the medium of the "secondary causes" of creation. His desire is to be a servant of the Divine, not a competitor.

This attitude regarding miracles has been expressed by many of the great mystics. However, this has rarely diminished the interest seekers have shown in miracles. Hujwīrī relates a number of such stories in his *Kashf al-Maḥjūb,* as for instance:

> In Farghānah, at a village called Ashlātak, there was an old man, one of the *Awtād* (pillars, supports) of the earth. His name was Bāb 'Umar – all the dervishes in that country give the title of *Bāb* to their great *shaykhs* – and he had an old wife called Fāṭimah. I went from Uzkand to see him. When I entered his presence he said: "Why have you come?"
>
> I replied: "In order that I might see the *shaykh* in person and that he might look on me with kindness."
>
> He said: "I have been seeing you continually since such and such a day, and I wish to see you as long as you are not removed from my sight."
>
> I computed the day and the year – it was the very day on which my conversion had begun. The *shaykh* said: "To traverse distance *(sipardan-i masāfat)* is child's play: henceforth pay visits by means of concentrated thought *(himmat);* it is not worthwhile to visit any person, and there is no virtue in bodily presence *(ḥużūr-i ashbāḥ).*" Then he bade Fāṭimah bring something to eat. She brought a dish of new grapes, although it was not the season for them, and some fresh ripe dates, which cannot possibly be procured in Farghānah.
>
> *Hujwīrī, Kashf al-Maḥjūb XIV:7, KMM p.301; cf. KM pp.234–35*

See also: **himmah** (▸4).

1. Ibn al-'Arabī, *Sufis of Andalusia, SOA* p.63.
2. W.C. Chittick, *Sufi Path of Knowledge, SPK* p.265.

hiringa (Mo) *Lit.* energy, power, vitality; perseverance, determination; spiritual power, also called *mana* (power); the mental energy of remembrance; mental alertness, focused attention, diligence; a mind assiduous in the quest for knowledge; also, an honorific for the sun as a symbol of intelligence and knowledge:[1]

To set yourself free of the physical world is to acknowledge *Io* as the highest Being. This is very positive. We rise above the elements and the lesser *atua* (deities) and above this earthly domain. The *akoako* (disciple) was told to do this often so that his personal balance would remain intact. Gradually, the exercises would take the *tohunga* (priestly adept) far up to the higher realm of *Io* just as (the deity) *Tāne* obtained the baskets *(kete)* of knowledge. This is nothing new to the *tohunga* tradition, for a chant from the Ngāi Tara says:

> Listen, O son! There was only one spiritual energy *(hiringa)*
> that transported *Tāne* to the uppermost realm;
> It was the spiritual power *(hiringa)* of the mind *(mahara)*.
> Nothing is seen there but *Io*-the-Parentless (supreme Being) –
> Source of all authority, Source of all.[2]

Samuel Timoti Robinson, Tohunga; cf. TRAK p.104

1. Elsdon Best, "Maori Personifications," *MPAS* p.118.
2. *Ngāi Tara Chant; cf.* in *RTHM* p.174, *TRAK* p.104.

hoa (Mo) *Lit.* recitation of a spell or charm; influencing something by means of a spell or charm; the power to work miracles; a spell or charm of any kind; miraculous healing.

The inner power to work miracles was credited to the *tohunga ahurewa,* Māori priestly adepts who had been initiated into the knowledge and hidden truths of creation and of *Io* the supreme Being. Such adepts had reached the level of *pouwhitu,* the highest level in the *whare wānanga* (school of sacred learning):

> The *pouwhitu* was educated in the highest prize of Māori, the knowledge of *Io* the supreme Being and the hidden truths of creation. In this order, the student was trained in *hoa,* the power to work miracles. All of the teachings in this order were projected on a higher plane of thought. The goal of the *pouwhitu* was achievement of spiritual oneness and service to the people. On graduation, a student became a *tohunga ahurewa,* meaning 'master of the high altar'. This *tohunga* was the most multitalented and excelled in all areas including navigation, healing, public ceremonies, divination, and prayers.

Samuel Timoti Robinson, Tohunga, TRAK p.90

The *tohunga* of the darker arts of *mākutu* (magic) were also well equipped with miraculous spells of destruction. Traditional Māori firmly believed that an unsuspecting person could be slain by a magical *hoa karakia* (incantation charm) recited from a distance, provided that the *tohunga* possessed the necessary *mana* (personal power):

> The many acts, rites and spells that come under the heading of *hoa* are mostly concerned with destructive forces. The tests made of the powers of learners of black magic, the slaying of persons, birds, *etc.*, the blasting of trees, the shattering of stone (powers that enable the warlock to destroy inanimate objects or to endow them with destructive power) are all included in the term *hoa*. Charms or spells termed *hoa* are employed whereby to energize, to strengthen, to render persons or inanimate objects effective. The *hoa tapuwae* (footprint charm) is a charm designed to render a person fleet of foot (and was commonly employed in war, both by pursued and pursuer); the *hoa rākau* (weapons charm) is another formula that renders weapons extremely effective. Also, the word is employed as a verb *(hoaia)*.... Any object, a stone or stick, might be *hoaia*, so that it would serve as a suitable medium in a divinatory rite. *Hoa* is employed also when a spell is recited for the purpose of affecting some distant object....
>
> The *hoa tapuwae* is a charm that was much relied on by both pursued and pursuers during fighting operations, and doubtless this item should be included under the head of white magic.
>
> *Elsdon Best, Maori Religion and Mythology, MRM2 p.164*

Hoa were also used for healing. Speaking of the various parts of a human being as 'souls', Samuel Robinson observes that the *tohunga* heals by removing "blockages", hindrances or disharmonies in the flow of the life force to the various parts of the body. This is the basis of a *tohunga*'s miraculous power *(hoa)* to heal:

> Health relies on the relationship of the souls, as it was taught that *mauri,* or the life force emanating from the *hamano* (highest soul), must transmit from its source in the *hamano,* through the *manawa* (heart, thoughts, human consciousness), through to the *ata* (shadow, pattern image), and into the body. It was when this transmission was disturbed in some way that a person became physically ill. Here we see that the *manawa* and *ata* may interfere with the life-force current by causing blockages. Westerners call blockages of the *manawa* 'mental imbalances', which thus restrict the vitality of the body as it fails to receive the entire *mauri* (life force). This is an old Māori concept... and accounts for the miraculous healing powers of the *tohunga.* He seeks to bring the souls 'into communication with one another properly' with his incantations.
>
> *Samuel Timoti Robinson, Tohunga, TRAK p.222*

Māori symbolism and mythology sees a human being as a receptacle for the *aka,* the cosmic vine that symbolizes the process by which the stages of the heavens and all creation unfold. Man himself, as the microcosm of creation, contains the reflection of *aka* within himself. The *aka* is also a part of the higher pattern or blueprint from which the physical body is formed. Miraculous healing takes place either by adjusting this subtle pattern so that the corresponding part of the body is healed, or by manipulating the body itself so that it correctly receives the life energy:

> Each of the shoots of the vine *(aka)*... has a different role in *tohunga* healing. They each have to be understood, and the *tohunga* has to learn how to manipulate them but also how to handle them safely without disrupting the natural balance of the body.
>
> Knowing the parts of the body – and understanding them as seats in which the soul seats itself into the individual – is the key formula to *tohunga* healing. On one side, the healing is technical; on another it is spiritually miraculous *(hoa).* These seats, being the physical receptors of the *aka* or vine, are manipulated by the *tohunga* with methods such as energy direction, massage, and *karakia* (incantations, prayer).
>
> *Samuel Timoti Robinson, Tohunga, TRAK p.226*

It is by the flow of life energy into this blueprint of *aka,* modulated by the *ahua,* a stepped-down aspect of the higher energy blueprint, that healing takes place:

> The healing... can then be seen as having two stages. One is the opening of the channels to let *mauri* run its course; thus power, or life force, is able to heal. The second is the *aka* or vine, the blueprint by which the *ahua* (semblance, image, form) transforms this potential energy into correctional vitality. How these two stages are brought into action is by *karakia.* The prayers of the *tohunga* possess *mana* or spiritual fire....
>
> The *tohunga* believes that the *ahua* is a mould of every cell of the body. The *tohunga* mends the broken bone in the *ahua,* which the *kiko* (physical body) copies after its higher counterpart. *Mana* comes from the higher self, or *wairua,* and mends the *ahua* once the channels are opened. Both the *mana* of the *tohunga* and that of the patient are at work here. The power of true miraculous *(hoa)* healing is in the hands of the *tohunga ahurewa* and those few elders who are able to wield the *mana.*
>
> *Samuel Timoti Robinson, Tohunga, TRAK pp.229–30*

iddhi, **iddhi-vidha** (Pa), **rdzu 'phrul** (T) *Lit.* success, accomplishment, prowess, power *(iddhi);* well-being, prosperity; anything capable of promoting success, material or mental; from the verb *ijjhati* (to prosper, to flourish, to succeed); thus also, spiritual success or power; hence, specifically, supernatural power; forms of *(vidha)* spiritual power *(iddhi);* one of the six supernormal forms of intuitive awareness or knowledge *(abhiññā)* developed by means of deep meditation and contemplation *(jhāna),* and attributed to *buddhas, bodhisattvas* and advanced spiritual practitioners of all faiths and belief systems, as well as many kinds of *deva* (gods) and other heavenly beings;[1] equivalent to the Sanskrit *ṛiddhi.*

Supernatural *iddhis* are not regarded as unique to Buddhists, but as powers available to all who have attained some success in concentration of the mind. In common with many other spiritual traditions, Buddhist texts generally advise that such powers are not to be used for personal benefit.

Iddhi is used in both its general as well as specific senses. In the *Mahāsudassana Sutta,* the Buddha tells his disciple Ānanda of a previous birth in which he (the Buddha) had been King Mahāsudassana ('Great Glory'), king of Kushāvatī. At that time, Mahāsudassana was said to have been gifted with four blessings or qualities *(iddhis):*

> King Mahāsudassana was endowed with four qualities *(iddhis)*.... Firstly, he was graceful in figure, handsome in appearance, pleasing in manner, with a complexion like the finest lotus, surpassing other men.... Secondly, he was long-lived, outliving other men.... Thirdly, he was free from disease, free from bodily suffering; and his internal fire was neither too hot nor too cold, but such as to promote good digestion, beyond that of other men.... Lastly, he was beloved and popular with *brāhmaṇs* and with householders alike – just as a father is beloved by his children.
>
> *Dīgha Nikāya 17, Mahāsudassana Sutta, PTSD2 pp.177–78; cf. SBE11 pp.259–61, TBLD p.283*

In a similar vein, the refined luxuries of the Buddha's princely childhood are described as *iddhis.* These included beautiful gardens, garments of fine fabrics, a different palace for each season, sweet music, and excellent food.[2]

Commonly included among Buddhist lists of the supernormal *iddhis* are the ability to walk on water; to levitate; to fly in the air; to pass through solid objects; to touch the sun and moon (inwardly); to ascend through the lower heavens to the highest heaven (the heaven of *Brahmā*); to project bodily replicas of oneself (*adhiṭṭhānā-iddhi,* power of determination); to adopt another form (*vikubbanā-iddhi,* power of transformation); to create other bodies through mental power (*manomayā-iddhi,* made-of-mind power); to perceive the otherwise hidden reasons and causes of things through mental purification, which leads to penetrating awareness and concentration (*ñāṇa-vipphārā-iddhi,* power of penetrating knowledge; *samādhi-vipphārā-iddhi,* power of penetrating concentration);[3] and to control one's thoughts such that something abhorrent is perceived as not abhorrent and *vice versa* (*ariyā-iddhi,* power of the noble ones), thus bestowing equanimity and serenity:

> If a *bhikkhu* should desire to exercise each of the different *iddhis,* one by one; being one to become many and being many to become one; to become visible and to become invisible; to go without hindrance through a wall, or a fence, or a mountain, as if through space; to penetrate in and out of solid ground, as if through water; to walk on the water without sinking, as if on solid ground; to travel cross-legged through the sky, like the birds on the wing; to touch and feel the sun and the moon (experience the light within), mighty and powerful though they be; and to reach in the body even up to the heaven of *Brahmā* – then let him then fulfil all the precepts.[4]
>
> *Majjhima Nikāya 6, Ākankheyya Sutta, PTSM1 p.34; cf. SBE11 p.214, MDBB p.116*

Sometimes, the other five forms of supernormal knowledge *(abhiññās)* are also categorized as *iddhis.* Although detailed descriptions of these powers are present in the older texts, the terms used for them are absent. The control of one's thoughts such that the abhorrent becomes non-abhorrent and *vice versa,* for instance, is often mentioned in the Pali *suttas,*[5] but only in one *sutta* does it say that this power *(iddhi)* is called that of the noble ones *(ariya).*[6] In the *Paṭisambhidāmagga,* however, the *iddhis* are listed in order and carefully explained.[7] Of the *ariyā-iddhi,* it is said:

> To abide perceiving the unrepulsive in the repulsive, one pervades a repulsive being with lovingkindness, or one attends to a repulsive object (either animate or inanimate) as a mere assemblage of impersonal elements. To abide perceiving the repulsive in the unrepulsive, one pervades a (sensually) attractive person with the idea of the foulness of the body, or one attends to an attractive object (either animate or inanimate) as impermanent. The third and fourth methods involve the application of the first and second contemplations to both repulsive and unrepulsive objects, without discrimination. The fifth method involves the avoidance of joy and sorrow in response to the six sense objects, thus enabling one to abide in equanimity, mindful and fully aware.
>
> *Paṭisambhidāmagga 22, PTSP2 p.212, in MDBB p.1367 (n.1360)*

According to the *Mahāparinirvāṇa Sūtra,* the Buddha adds extreme longevity to the list of miracles:

> There may be among the monks, nuns, laymen and laywomen, or even among the *tīrthikas* (C. *wàidào,* followers or leaders of another creed), a person who possesses the five divine powers or the unlimited power of a *ṛishi.* He may live for a *kalpa* or less than a *kalpa;* he may be able to fly through the air, and be unconstrained whether reclining or sitting. He emits fire from the left side of his body or water from his right side. His body emits smoke and flames like a fire ball. If he desires to live long, he can do as he wills. He can freely lengthen or shorten his life. With such divine power, he has such freedom of power.
>
> *Mahāparinirvāṇa Sūtra 3, T12 374:381c11–16; cf. MMSY (4) p.38*

And he adds that a *tathāgata* can live for as many *kalpas* (ages) as he desires, for his reality is eternal:

> And how could this not be possible with the *tathāgata* (C. *rúlái*) who possesses unlimited power *(C. zìzàilì,* S. *aishvarya)* in all things? How could it not be that he can live for half a *kalpa,* a *kalpa,* 100 *kalpas,* 100,000 *kalpas,* or innumerable *kalpas?* On account of this, know that the *tathāgata* is an eternal and unchanging existence.
>
> *Mahāparinirvāṇa Sūtra 3, T12 374:381c16–18; cf. MMSY (4) pp.38–39*

Although supernatural powers are regarded as attributes of all *buddhas,* the open display of such knowledge or power is generally discouraged, not only in Buddhism, but in all mystical traditions. Nevertheless, Buddhist texts contain many stories in which the Buddha demonstrates his possession of miraculous powers, and where he also praises his disciples for such attainment. The point is made, however, that not only should such powers be used with discrimination, but that their possession is no proof of true spirituality and wisdom. The real miracle, he says, is the miracle of instruction *(anusāsanī-pāṭihāriya)* by which a true spiritual teacher is able to transform a disciple. If these texts accurately represent the Buddha's teaching rather that that of his later followers, the Buddha seems to be giving credence to the miraculous powers so esteemed in the yogic tradition of his times, while simultaneously pointing out the nature of the true miracle performed by a *buddha* or perfect spiritual teacher.

In the *Kevaḍḍha Sutta,* the young householder Kevaḍḍha suggests to the Buddha that he should enable one of the assembled monks to perform "superhuman feats of miraculous power *(uttarimanussadhammā iddhi-pāṭihāriya)*", so that the crowd of lay devotees will be impressed, resulting in a strengthening of their faith and devotion. The Buddha explains, however, that were a monk to display such powers, the people would not benefit, but would simply explain away the miracles as magic tricks:

Thus have I heard. Once, the Exalted One was staying at Nālandā, in Pāvārika's mango grove. And the householder Kevaḍḍha came to the Exalted One, prostrated himself before him, and sat down to one side. He then said: "Sir, this Nālandā of ours is rich, prosperous, populous, and full of people who are devoted to the Exalted One. It would be well if the Exalted One were to command some monk to perform superhuman feats of miraculous power *(uttarimanussadhammā iddhi-pāṭihāriya).* Thus would this Nālandā of ours come to be even more devoted to the Exalted One."

The Exalted One replied: "Kevaḍḍha, this is not the way I teach the *Dhamma* (Way) to the monks, saying, 'Come now, my monks, go and perform superhuman feats of miraculous power *(uttarimanussadhammā iddhi-pāṭihāriya)* for the white-robed laity!'"

For a second time Kevaḍḍha said: "Exalted One, I would not be importunate, but still I say: This Nālandā of ours is rich, prosperous, ... *etc.*" And the Exalted One made the same reply.

When Kevaḍḍha repeated the same request a third time, the Exalted One said: "Kevaḍḍha, there are three kinds of miracle *(pāṭihāriya)* that I, having myself understood and realized them, have made known to others. What are these three? The miracle of supernatural power *(iddhi-pāṭihāriya),* the miracle of mind reading *(ādesanā-pāṭihāriya),* and the miracle of instruction *(anusāsanī-pāṭihāriya).*[8]

"What is the miracle of supernatural power *(iddhi-pāṭihāriya)?* Here, Kevaḍḍha, suppose that a monk displays various psychic powers *(iddhi-vidha)* in different ways. From being one he becomes many, from being many he becomes one; ... *etc.*

"Then, should some believer of trusting heart see him doing so, and he should tell this to someone who is sceptical and unbelieving, saying: 'It is wonderful, sir, it is marvellous, the great power and skill of that *samaṇa* (holy man)....' Then might that man say: 'Sir, there is something called the *gandhārī* charm. It is by means of this that that monk becomes many, from being many becomes one; ... *etc.*'"

"What do you think, Kevaḍḍha, might not a sceptic so say?"

"Yes, Sir, he might."

"Well Kevaḍḍha, that is why, seeing the danger of such miracles, I dislike, reject, and despise them."

"And what is the miracle of mind reading *(ādesanā-pāṭihāriya)?*"

"Here, a monk reads the minds of other beings, of other people, reads their feelings, their thoughts and ponderings, and says: 'So-and-so is in your mind. You are thinking of such and such a matter. Thus and thus are your emotions.'

> "Then, should some believer of trusting heart see him doing so, and he should tell this to someone who is sceptical and unbelieving, saying, ... *etc.*"
>
> *Dīgha Nikāya 11, Kevaḍḍha Sutta, PTSD1 pp.211–13; cf. DBRD pp.276–78, TBLD pp.175–76*

The Buddha makes a similar reply, and in this case the imaginary sceptic maintains that it is the *maṇikā* charm by which the feat is performed. Finally, the Buddha explains the miracle of instruction is the means by which a *buddha* or *tathāgata* can really convey his message:

> "'Consider in this way, do not consider in that way. Reason thus, and not thus. Get rid of that, acquire this, persevere in that.' This, Kevaḍḍha, is what is called 'the miracle of instruction *(anusāsanī-pāṭihāriya)*'."
>
> *Dīgha Nikāya 11, Kevaḍḍha Sutta, PTSD1 p.214; cf. DBRD p.279, TBLD p.176*

The Buddha goes on to elaborate the teaching of the *Dhamma* that is given by a fully enlightened *buddha,* "which is lovely in its beginning, lovely in its middle, lovely in its ending, in the spirit and in the letter, and displays the fully perfected and purified holy life". This includes the teaching of a *buddha;* the awakening of a seeker and his renunciation of the world; his training in morality and ethics; his growing confidence and fearlessness; his guarding of the sensory outlets and the increasing poise he thus acquires; his contentment with little and understanding of the power of simplicity; his emancipation from the passions and all human imperfection and the resulting joy obtained; his training in the four *jhānas* (states of meditative absorption); his insights regarding the entanglement of consciousness with the impermanent body; and his realization of the four noble truths and final assurance of enlightenment. To each of which the Buddha adds as a refrain, "That, Kevaḍḍha, is what is called the miracle of instruction." His message is that the true miracle is the way in which a *buddha* turns a disciple away from absorption in the world towards absorption in the higher path to enlightenment.[9]

The performance of miracles before the laity is one of the offences laid down in the *Vinaya Piṭaka* (monastic code). A story is related of the *Seṭṭhi* (wealthy man) of Rājagaha, who had a bowl made out of precious sandalwood and, having had it positioned on the very top of a succession of bamboo poles lashed together, announces, "If any *samaṇa* or *brāhmaṇ* (sage) be an *arhat,* and possessed of *iddhi,* let him bring down the bowl. It will be a gift to him." The challenge is met by the monk Piṇḍola Bhāradvāja, who rises into the air and takes the bowl. To make known his victory, the monk goes on to circle Rājagaha three times,[10] creating a considerable commotion. The Buddha, on coming to hear of the incident, is not impressed:

The blessed Buddha rebuked him, saying, "This is improper, Bhāradvāja, not according to rule, unsuitable, unworthy of a *samaṇa,* unbecoming, and ought not to be done. How can you, Bhāradvāja, for the sake of a miserable wooden pot, display superhuman miraculous power *(uttarimanussadhammā iddhi-pāṭihāriya)* before the laity? Just, Bhāradvāja, like a woman who displays herself for the sake of a miserable bit of money, have you, for the sake of a miserable wooden pot displayed superhuman miraculous power *(uttarimanussadhammā iddhi-pāṭihāriya)* before the laity. This will not be conducive, Bhāradvāja, either to the conversion of the unconverted, or to the increase (in faith) of the converted. Rather it will result in those who have not been converted remaining unconverted, and the turning back of those who have been converted."

And when he had rebuked him, and had delivered a spiritual discourse, he addressed the *bhikkhus,* and said: "You are not, O *bhikkhus,* to display before the laity the superhuman power of *iddhi.* Whosoever does so, shall be guilty of a *dukkaṭa* (wrong action). So break that wooden bowl to pieces, O *bhikkhus;* and when you have ground it to powder, give it to the *bhikkhus* as perfume for their eye ointments."

Vinaya Piṭaka 5:8.2; cf. VTP3 pp.80–81

Despite such strictures against the display of miracles, people have always been fascinated by them, and *bodhisattvas* and *buddhas,* as well as Buddhist tantric *gurus,* and even the Buddha himself, are commonly portrayed as possessing and using supernormal powers. Likewise, Buddhist cults, such as those centred around the Buddha's disciples Mahākāshyapa and Upagupta, generally attribute the possession such powers to their chosen figureheads.

See also: **abhijñā**, **ṛiddhipāda**, **siddhi**.

1. *E.g. Dīgha Nikāya* 20, *Mahāsamaya Sutta, PTSD2* pp.259–62.
2. *Anguttara Nikāya* 3:38, *Sukhamāla Sutta, PTSA1* p.145.
3. *E.g.* Buddhaghosa, *Atthasālinī* 256–7, *ABCD* p.91; *Visuddhimagga* 12:2, *PTSV* p.373, *PPVM* p.369.
4. *Cf. Dīgha Nikāya* 2, *Sāmaññaphala Sutta, PTSD1* pp.77–84; *Saṃyutta Nikāya* 51:11, *Hetu Sutta, PTSS5* pp.263–66.
5. *E.g. Majjhima Nikāya* 152, *Indriya-bhāvanā Sutta, PTSM3* pp.298–302.
6. *Dīgha Nikāya* 28, *Sampasādaniya Sutta, PTSD3* pp.112–13.
7. *Paṭisambhidāmagga* 22, *PTSP2* pp.205–14.
8. *Cf. Anguttara Nikāya* 3:60, *Sangārava Sutta, PTSA1* p.170.

9. *Dīgha Nikāya* 11, *Kevaḍḍha Sutta, PTSD1* pp.214–15; *cf. DBRD* pp.279–80, *TBLD* pp.176–77; *cf.* also *Dīgha Nikāya* 2, *Sāmaññaphala Sutta, PTSD1* pp.62–84; *cf. DBRD* pp.78–93, *TBLD* pp.99–108.
10. *Vinaya Piṭaka* 5:8.1–2; *cf. VTP3* pp.78–80.

iʿjāz (A/P) *Lit.* miracle, wonder, astonishment, amazement, surprise; a miracle performed by a prophet; sometimes used synonymously with *muʿjizāt.*

See also: **muʿjizāt**.

ʻike pāpālua (Hw) *Lit.* double *(pāpālua)* knowing *(ʻike),* twice seeing; double knowledge or understanding; a Hawaiian term for second sight, extrasensory perception, psi, intuitive communication, and so on.

The ability to predict the future and to gain an awareness of events that were yet to happen was brought about in several ways, most notably by communication with *ʻaumakua* (ancestor deities). It was believed that spirit ancestors would warn of impending trouble by taking the form of an owl or shark, and would communicate through sounds or actions. This is said to have been fairly common in the old days, when the people lived in harmony with nature.

There were also a few who could see what was happening to someone at another location. This was regarded as a special gift, and an indication that they had unusual *mana* (personal power):

> "One morning, Aunty got up, bathed, dressed in the *holokū* she kept for special occasions, did her hair up beautifully, added her prized Spanish comb, and sent for all the nearby relatives to come and visit her for the last time. After they had come and everybody had talked, then Aunty laid herself down on the *pūneʻe* (couch) and died."
>
> Not all examples of precognition concern inevitable death or disaster. Sometimes, the foreknowledge is one of warning and prevention. We turn again to our *kumu* (teacher) who tells a personal experience. With a companion, Mrs Pukui was on Maui, tape-recording reminiscences of old Hawaiians. Then:
>
> "We were just through recording, but the machine was still on. The old lady said, 'Wait. I must pray for you.' And then she prayed that we would be protected from the accident that would happen on our way back to Wailuku. On the way back, a school bus hit our car. It banged us in the rear. I was in the back seat. My head was hit and I got a headache. When we played the tape back, we heard the old lady's prayer. *ʻEʻepa!* It was strange! The old lady had *ʻike pāpālua.*"
>
> *"Precognition," Nānā I Ke Kumu, NKK2 pp.280–81*

īshitva (S) *Lit.* lord *(īsha)*-ship; overlordship; complete supremacy, superiority or greatness; absolute mastery over all things, animate and inanimate; the attainment of divine power; complete control over nature; the power to become a powerful leader, to have dominion over others and to become great in the eyes of others; the power to become godlike, even including the creation and destruction of creatures.

See also: **siddhi**.

istidrāj (A/P) *Lit.* leading on; etymologically, seeking to move by degrees or step by step, gradually winning over; hence also, deception; derived from the Quranic, "*Sanastadrijuhum* (We shall lead them on)",[1] where the meaning is to be distanced from divine mercy, and gradually led on towards punishment and perdition; being led on by Satan to a high spiritual level before being allowed to fall;[2] also, a miracle performed by an unbeliever, especially magicians, sorcerers and so on, or by debased people, "subject to their passions".[3]

Sufis and Muslim theologians have distinguished four kinds of miracle, the other three being *mu'jizāt* (miracles of prophets), *karāmāt* (miracles of saints), and *ma'ūnat* (miracles of ecstatics, *majānīn*):

> There are four kinds of miracles *(karāmāt)*. They are: *mu'jizāt, karāmāt, ma'ūnat,* and *istidrāj*.... *Istidrāj* pertains to a group of people who are not believers, such as magicians and others like them, and when they cause something unusual to happen, that is called *istidrāj*.
>
> *Niẓām al-Dīn Awliyā', Morals for the Heart 2:23, FFNA pp.116–17, MHN p.160*

Karāmāt and *istidrāj* arise from different motives:

> *Karāmāt* differ from leading on *(istidrāj)* in that one who indulges in leading on *(istidrāj)* and deception *(makr)* is proud and confident in doing so, while the one who is a friend of God flees from the display of powers *(karāmāt),* fearing the use of them.
>
> *Khulāṣah-'i Sharḥ-i Ta'arruf, KSTK p.197, in SSE8 p.65*

See also: **istidrāj** (▸4).

1. *Qur'ān* 7:182.
2. Jurjānī, *Ta'rīfāt, KTJ* p.24, *KTA* p.33, in *SSE8* p.63.
3. Tahānawī, *Kashshāf Iṣṭilāḥāt al-Funūn, KIFT2* p.87, in *SSE8* p.63.

kāmachāra (S) *Lit.* pleasure *(kāma)* by will *(ichchhā);* following one's own inclinations. See **siddhi**.

kāma-rūpa (S) *Lit.* form *(rūpa)* at will *(kāma);* the power to assume any form at will. See **siddhi**.

kāmāvasāyitā (S) *Lit.* the power to fulfil all one's desires *(kāma);* the power to suppress or control desire. See **siddhi**.

karāmāt (A/P) (sg. A. *karāmah,* P. *karāmat) Lit.* gifts, favours; acts of generosity; especially, divine gifts, favours, or graces; commonly implies miracles, wonders, marvels; hence, miraculous powers, charismatic powers; from the same root as *karam* (grace, kindness, munificence) and *karīm* (generous) as in the name of God, *al-Karīm* (the Generous). In the plural, *karāmāt* usually means 'miracles'; in the singular, *karāmah* means generosity, munificence, nobility, honour, favour, kindness, grace, or miracle.

That prophets *(anbiyā')* and saints *(awliyā')* perform miracles might be understood to place them both on the same spiritual platform. Therefore, in order to maintain the superiority of the prophets, Muslim theology carefully distinguishes between the miracles of prophets *(muʻjizāt)* and those of saints *(karāmāt). Muʻjizāt* – sometimes called evidentiary or manifest miracles – are regarded as public, performed by the prophets with the intention of impressing people and awakening them to spiritual realities, to make them take notice of the prophets and their message. Since it would be heresy to suggest that a saint had performed *muʻjizāt* (sg. *muʻjizah*), the miracles of saints are known as divine gifts or favours *(karāmāt),* and are generally understood to be performed personally or in a hidden manner. They are regarded as the blessings or favours of God that happen spontaneously around saints. In fact:

> It is a very common notion that a saint *(walī),* to whom extra-ordinary miracles *(karāmāt)* are continually vouchsafed, does not know himself to be a saint *(walī),* or these miracles *(karāmāt)* to be miracles *(karāmāt).*
>
> *Hujwīrī, Kashf al-Maḥjūb XIV, KMM p.270, KM pp.214–15*

Among the general population, the performance of miracles is often regarded as essential proof of sainthood. Like the saints of all religious traditions, the legends surrounding saints are replete with miracle stories, the majority being of dubious historical authenticity. The miracle stories associated with Rābiʻah of Baṣrah, for instance, include how a swarm of locusts descended upon her corn crop. She prayed, "O my Lord, this is my provision, upon which I have spent money. But if it is Your will, I will give it as food to Your enemies or Your friends." At this, the locusts all flew away. Likewise, while on pilgrimage to Mecca, Rābiʿah's camel died. On asking God to restore it to life, the animal recovered, and lived until she returned home.[1]

Such 'miracles' could, of course, be an exaggerated elaboration of actual events into the realm of the miraculous. On the other hand, it is commonly believed that those who truly put their faith in God are indeed cared for by divine providence.

Many of the miracles performed by saints involve a knowledge of the thoughts and lives of their disciples that could not have been known by normal human means. Such events are common in the lives of evolved souls and their disciples, and are one of the ways by which a saint imbues his disciples with faith.

Both Sufi and orthodox Muslim scholars have been at considerable pains to find suitable intellectual distinctions between the miracles of prophets and those of saints. Consequently, various schools of thought have developed. Hujwīrī, for instance, writes at some length, seeking to prove intellectually the veracity of the *karāmāt* of the saints without undermining the superiority of the *muʿjizāt* of the prophets.

Firstly, he says, only those who adhere to the *sharīʿat* (external religious observances) are deemed capable of performing true *karāmāt.* Secondly, in Muslim thought, unbelievers and imposters cannot perform *karāmāt.* However, since it is generally acknowledged that unbelievers do perform miracles, Hujwīrī argues, somewhat unconvincingly, that if miracles happen around unbelievers, they are intended as signs or warnings to them or others that they are in error:

> *Muʿjizāt* involve publicity and *karāmāt* secrecy, because the result of the former is to affect others, while the latter are peculiar to the person by whom they are performed. Again, the doer of *muʿjizāt* is quite sure that he has wrought an extra-ordinary miracle, whereas the doer of *karāmāt* cannot be sure whether he has really wrought a miracle or whether he has been unknowingly deceived *(istidrāj).*
>
> He who performs *muʿjizāt* has authority over the (religious) law and, in arranging it, denies or affirms, according as God commands him. On the other hand, he who performs *karāmāt* has no choice but to resign himself (to God's will), and to accept the ordinances that are laid upon him, because the *karāmāt* of a saint *(walī)* are never in any way incompatible with the law laid down by a prophet....
>
> You must know that miracles *(karāmāt)* may be vouchsafed to a saint *(walī)* so long as he does not infringe the obligations of the religious law.... Orthodox Muslims agree on this point, nor is it

> intellectually impossible, because such miracles *(karāmāt)* are of a kind that is predestined by God, and their manifestation does not contradict any principle of the religious law; nor, on the other hand, is it repugnant to the mind to conceive of them *(i.e. karāmāt)* as a distinct category (distinguishing them from *muʿjizāt*).
>
> A miracle *(karāmat)* is a token of a saint's *(walī)* veracity, and it cannot be manifested by an impostor except as a sign that his pretensions are false. It is an extra-ordinary act, performed while he (the saint) is still subject to the obligations of religion....
>
> All orthodox Muslims are agreed that an extra-ordinary act resembling a prophetic miracle *(muʿjizat)* may be performed by an unbeliever, in order that by means of his performance he may be shown beyond doubt to be an impostor.
>
> *Hujwīrī, Kashf al-Maḥjūb XIV, KMM pp.276, 278–79, 282; cf. KM pp.218, 220–21, 224*

To support this point, Hujwīrī continues by recounting the legendary story of Pharaoh who "lived four hundred years without falling ill, and who was always followed by water, whenever he climbed onto high ground". Pharaoh, however, claimed to be God Himself, incarnate in a body. Reasonable people, says Hujwīrī, realize that such a claim is false. Therefore, he argues – and one struggles to grasp his reasoning – Pharaoh's miracles were signs of his being an imposter.[2]

Hujwīrī also tries to explain the miracles performed by a manifestly imperfect person who claims to be a saint, but who nonetheless follows the *sharīʿat* without fault. These miracles happen as long as the individual perceives them as emanating from the grace of God:

> It is possible, moreover, that something of the same kind as a miracle *(karāmat)* may be performed by a pretender to saintship who, although his conduct is bad, is blameless in his religion – as long as, by that miraculous act, he confirms the truth of the Messenger (Muḥammad), and manifests the grace of God vouchsafed to him, and does not attribute the act in question to his own power.
>
> *Hujwīrī, Kashf al-Maḥjūb XIV, KMM pp.283–84; cf. KM pp.224–25*

The correct observance of all aspects of external Muslim religious practice is deemed of great significance in determining the status of a saint. Al-Qushayrī quotes Abū Yazīd as saying:

> If you see a man who has been given such divine favours *(karāmāt)* that he rises into the air, do not be deceived. Watch and see how you find

> him with the command *(amr)* and prohibition *(nahy),* the guarding of the boundaries *(ḥifẓ al-ḥudūd),* and the carrying out of the *sharī'ah.*
>
> *Abū Yazīd, in RQQQ p.15, in EIM p.241*

Hujwīrī also maintains that prophets are always composed and in a state of spiritual 'sobriety'. While in that state, they perform miracles with a clear intention in view. Saints, on the other hand, only perform miracles while in a state of intoxication or rapture:

> It is most important, however, that you should know with certainty in what state this miraculous grace is manifested to the saint: in sobriety *(ṣaḥw)* or intoxication *(sukr),* in composure *(tamkīn)* or rapture *(ghalabat).* Dhū al-Nūn the Egyptian and Muḥammad ibn Khafīf and Ḥusayn ibn Manṣūr (al-Ḥallāj) and Yaḥyá ibn Mu'ādh Rāzī and others hold that miracles *(karāmāt)* are not vouchsafed to a saint except when he is in the state of intoxication *(sukr),* whereas the miracles *(mu'jizāt)* of the prophets are wrought in the state of sobriety *(ṣaḥw).* Hence, according to their doctrine, this is a clear distinction between *mu'jizāt* and *karāmāt;* for the saint, being enraptured, pays no heed to the people and does not call upon them to follow him. But the prophet, on the other hand, being sober, exerts himself to attain his object and challenges the people to rival what he has done.
>
> Moreover, the prophet may choose whether he will manifest or conceal his extra-ordinary powers, but the saints have no such choice; sometimes a miracle *(karāmat)* is not granted to them when they desire it, and sometimes it is bestowed when they do not desire it. . . .
>
> The prophet is a man of law *(ṣāḥib-shar'),* and the saint is a man of the innermost consciousness *(ṣāḥib-sirr).* Accordingly, a miracle *(karāmat)* will not be manifested to a saint unless he is in a state of absence from himself and bewilderment, and unless his faculties are entirely under the control of God. While saints are with their selves and dwell in a human state, they are veiled. But when the veil is lifted, they are bewildered and amazed through realizing the bounties of God.
>
> A miracle *(karāmat)* cannot be manifested except in the state of unveiledness *(kashf),* . . . and whoever is in that state, to him worthless stones appear even as gold. This is the state of intoxication *(sukr)* with which no human being, the prophets alone excepted, is permanently endowed.
>
> *Hujwīrī, Kashf al-Maḥjūb XIV, KMM pp.285–86; cf. KM pp.226–27*

Sufis distinguish both *mu'jizāt* and *karāmāt* from psychic and other similar powers:

> There are four kinds of miracles *(karāmāt)*. They are: *mu'jizat, karāmat, ma'ūnat,* and *istidrāj*. *Mu'jizāt* are linked to the prophets *(anbiyā')*, since they have been given perfect knowledge. As conduits of revelation, what they cause to appear are known as *mu'jizāt*. As for *karāmāt,* such miracles are distinctive to saints *(awliyā')*. They also have perfect knowledge and can perform sinless acts. Saints differ from prophets, however, because the former, unlike the latter, are overcome, that is, they are directed by God only in particular moments, and hence what they make appear are *karāmāt*.
>
> As for *ma'ūnat,* they are the property of ecstatic beings *(majānīn)* who exhibit neither perfect knowledge nor sinless actions. From time to time they can cause a contravention of nature, and when they do, that is known as *ma'ūnat*.
>
> As for *istidrāj,* that pertains to a group of people who are not believers, such as magicians and others like them, and when they cause something unusual to happen, that is called *istidrāj*.
>
> *Niẓām al-Dīn Awliyā', Morals for the Heart 2:23, FFNA p.117, MHN p.160*

The majority of Sufis have placed little value on the ability to perform miracles. In fact, they generally regard the performance of miracles as a pitfall:

> Disclosing divine secrets and performing miracles *(karāmāt)* are actually a hindrance on the Path. For true devotees, the real task is to be steadfast in the pursuit of love.
>
> *Niẓām al-Dīn Awliyā', Morals for the Heart 1:29, FFNA p.55; cf. MHN p.117*

The performance of miracles is regarded as disobedience to the divine will:

> Since anyone who performs a miracle *(karāmat)* is disobeying God. What sort of work is that?... There are one hundred stages on the spiritual path. The seventeenth stage provides divine inspiration to perform miraculous acts. Now, if the traveller stops at this stage, how will he reach the other eighty-three?
>
> *Niẓām al-Dīn Awliyā', Morals for the Heart 4:3, FFNA p.202; cf. MHN p.216*

The power to manipulate physical phenomena is one of the first results of the increased mental concentration experienced as the soul rises up from the body. It is a temptation to be overcome:

> There are a thousand stages on the way to God, and the first is miraculous powers *(karāmāt)*. If the wayfarer's aspiration falls short, he will not proceed to any other station.
>
> *Kharaqānī, in Tadhkirat al-Awliyā' 2, TAN2 p.236; cf. in SSE8 p.59*

> The highest on the Path do not desire nor are they attached to miracles *(karāmāt),* for the desire to attain miraculous power holds the risk of deception and self-beguilement.
>
> *Maybudī, Kashf al-Asrār, KA7 pp.234–35; cf. in SSE8 p.59*

Rūmī relates a story to this effect:

> Some of those who are perfected in travelling the mystic path *(ṭarīqat)* and drink at the Salsabīl (Fountain) of Truth (in paradise), take it as a duty to avoid and to shun, with complete aversion, the open performance of miracles *(karāmāt).* Nay, they even consider being engaged in it to be the essence of veiling. Thus, they related the following to Junayd,... "Such and such a dervish, after spreading out his prayer rug alongside the Tigris, performs the prayers and flies in the air, and utters wondrous words."
>
> The *shaykh* (Junayd) said: "Alas that he occupies himself with a trivial game and, being satisfied with it, is content with his present state!" Junayd then summoned the dervish. He raised his awareness, turned him away from all of that, and changed his attitude so as to make known to him how far away the halting-stations really are of the perfect who have obtained perfection."
>
> *Aḥmad al-Aflākī, Manāqib al-'Ārifīn 3:294, MASA1 pp.358–59; cf. FKG (3:293) p.248*

Every level of spiritual evolution has its own temptations. Rūzbihān quotes al-Ḥallāj as identifying the passions of the *nafs* (lower human mind) as the temptations of this world, and the power to perform miracles *(karāmāt)* as the temptations of the next higher level, the *qalb* (heart).[3]

The existence of the desire to perform miracles indicates where the attention is focused. When a person's attention is focused upon himself, then he entertains the thought of performing miracles, because his ego is still active. When the attention is truly focused on God, the power to perform miracles is ignored:

> Whoever seeks to please his *nafs* (lower mind) through combat (with the *nafs*) will gain miraculous powers *(karāmāt),* while he who combats the *nafs* for the sake of God attains God.
>
> *Ja'far al-Ṣādiq, in Tadhkirat al-Awliyā' 1, TAN1 p.14; cf. in SSE8 p.59*

In fact, since people are easily sidetracked by the performance of miracles, the saints are constrained to conceal their miracles:

> God requires that His prophets *(payāmbarān)* manifest miraculous power *(āyāt)* and perform miracles *(mu'jizāt),* but He requires His

saints *(awliyā')* to conceal these things, so that people may not be deceived thereby.

Abū 'Umar Dimishqī, in Ṭabaqāt al-Ṣūfīyah, KTS p.274, in FNI8 p.233; cf. in SSE8 p.58

If miracles do happen, says Kalābādhī, they should increase the humility of the one performing them. The power to perform miracles should be inwardly digested, giving added impetus to their onward progress:

Kalābādhī has said that the humility of the friends of God *(awliyā')* only increases when their miraculous power *(karāmat)* is manifested, for they become humble and more fearful, abasing themselves and acknowledging God's power over them all the more. The greater their miraculous power *(karāmat),* the greater their service to God, which, in turn, brings increased strength to their spiritual endeavours.

Khulāṣah-'i Sharḥ-i Ta'arruf, KSTK p.197; cf. in SSE8 p.61

Maghribī says that he has gone beyond the stage where miraculous powers are first encountered:

Talk not of miracles *(karāmāt),*
for we have passed beyond that stage.

Maghribī, Dīvān 136:1312, DSMR p.170; cf. in SSE8 p.60

Karāmāt is related to the name of God, *al-Karīm* (the Generous, the Giver). Hence, Abū Sa'īd remarks:

Abū Sa'īd said, "Whoever belongs entirely to the Giver *(al-Karīm),* all his actions become miracles *(karāmāt).*" . . .

When God makes a man pure and separates him from his selfhood, all that he does or abstains from doing, all that he says and all that he feels becomes a wondrous gift *(karāmāt).*

Abū Sa'īd al-Khayr, Asrār al-Tawḥīd, ATS1 pp.281–82; cf. in SIM pp.66–67

Rūmī explains that the miracles of prophets come about by manipulating and transforming the subtle essences or energies that lie behind the manifestation of the external phenomena of this world. The *karāmāt* of the saints, on the other hand, arise from their internal illumination and mystical clairvoyance:

The difference between *mu'jizāt* and *karāmāt* is that *mu'jizāt* are acts and customary practices of the prophets, whereas *karāmāt* are effects *(āthār)* and lights *(anvār)* of the friends of God. *Mu'jizāt* consist of bringing forth something out of nothingness and transmuting essences *(aʿyān). Karāmāt* are an attribute of the lights *(anvār)* of the interior of the friends of God.

Aḥmad al-Aflākī, Manāqib al-ʿĀrifīn 3:294, MASA1 p.358; cf. FKG (3:293) p.247

Rūmī also points out that the *karāmāt* of a master *(pīr)* lie in his unseen spiritual influence, which transforms the "heart of a disciple". Such miracles are performed directly upon the heart. Even with *muʿjizāt,* if they have an inner effect upon a soul, it is because there is a hidden connection between the prophet and the individual. The outward effect is "incidental". Their purpose is to touch the "inmost heart":

Secret miracles *(karāmāt-i khafī)* and graces *(muʿjizāt),*
emanating from the *pīr,* transform the heart of a disciple;
For within them are innumerable spiritual resurrections,
the least being that all who are close to them become intoxicated.
Hence, that fortunate one who has brought his burden
to such a blessed one has become the companion of God.

The manifest miracle *(muʿjizat)* that produces
an effect upon something inanimate
is like the rod (of Moses) or (his parting of) the sea
or the splitting of the moon (by Muḥammad).
If it produces an immediate effect upon the soul,
it is because there is a hidden link connecting
(the soul and the miracle worker).
The effects produced upon inanimate objects are incidental:
they are really for the sake of the fair invisible spirit,
so that the inmost heart may be touched
by means of that inanimate object....

Miracles *(muʿjizāt)* from the soul of a perfect one *(kāmil)*
bring life to the soul of the seeker.
The miracle *(muʿjizat)* is the sea,
and the heedless man is a land bird,
unlike the water bird, which is safe from harm.
It (the miracle) brings infirmity to anyone who is uninitiated,
but power to the soul of an intimate *(hamdam).*

Rūmī, Maśnavī VI:1300–6, 1308–10; cf. MJR6 p.331

The greatest miracle performed by the masters is that the attention of their disciples is turned towards God. The orientation of their inner life is changed around, and they feel their master's spiritual influence flooding their being. They become like water birds in water – the spiritual influence of their master and their own inner being have a natural kinship. The "heedless" or worldly man, on the other hand, feels uncomfortable and out of his element when he comes under the spiritual influence of a master:

> What is a true miracle *(karāmāt)* is this: that God should bring you from a lowly estate to a high estate; that you should travel from there to here, from ignorance to reason... from the inanimate to life.... These are the true miracles *(karāmāt).*
>
> *Rūmī, Fīhi mā Fīhi 26:6–10, KFF p.118; cf. DRA p.129*

See also: **muʿjizāt**.

1. Al-Munāwī, *al-Kawākib al-Durrīyah* 1:95, *KDT1* p.269, *KDRM fol.*51b; *cf.* in *RM* p.35.
2. Hujwīrī, *Kashf al-Maḥjūb* XIV, *KMM* p.282; *cf. KM* p.224.
3. Rūzbihān, *Mashrab al-Arwāḥ* 4:43, *MARB* p.90, in *SSE11* p.36.

kāya-indriya-siddhi (S) *Lit.* perfection *(siddhi)* of the body *(kāya)* and senses *(indriya);* a body fit for the practice of *yoga,* with the senses under control. See **siddhi**.

kharq al-ʿādah (A) *Lit.* breaking *(kharq)* of habit *(ʿādah);* contrary to the habitual, going contrary to nature; a miracle, something that breaks the 'habit' of the way created things exist and change.

Etymologically, *ʿādah* means 'that which returns'. Ibn al-ʿArabī, however, points out that nothing really 'returns': the creation is forever new, and nothing is truly habitual. Only the "possessor of this vicegerency", the mystic, is able to change things through his inner attunement to God, who is the source of all change and action:

> The possessor of this vicegerency *(niyābah)* constantly has the power to change the way things are *(taṣarruf).* The common people name this *karāmāt* (miracles), *āyāt* (signs), and *kharq al-ʿādah* (the breaking of habits). For the realized ones *(al-muḥaqqiqūn),* these acts are not the 'breaking of habit', but rather the bringing into existence of created things. The reason is that, in reality, there are no habits, since there is no repetition. So nothing returns.
>
> This is referred to in God's words concerning the people of habits, "No indeed, but they are in confusion as to a new creation."[1] He says, "They do not know that in every instant they are in a new creation, so what they see in the first instant is not identical to what they see in the second instant. They are in confusion about this."

Hence there is no return, so there is no breaking. This is how the situation is perceived by the realized ones *(al-muḥaqqiqūn)* from among the folk of *Allāh.*

Ibn al-ʿArabī, Meccan Revelations 3:288.14, FMIA5 (3:360) p.425; cf. SPK p.99

In Ibn al-ʿArabī's terminology, actual external miracles are called *karāmāt* (gifts, favours, miracles) and breaking of habit *(kharq al-ʿādah).* The internal power by which the external effects are brought about is known as *taṣarruf* (freedom to transform, power to change things), *taḥakkum* (governing control), *takwīn* (bringing things into created existence), and *al-fiʿl bi al-himmah* (action with resolve).[2]

See also: **taṣarruf**.

1. *Qur'ān* 50:15.
2. W.C. Chittick, *Sufi Path of Knowledge, SPK* p.265.

kuni (Hw) *Lit.* to burn; a Hawaiian counter-ritual designed to take revenge for a black-magic killing, in which the murder victim was cremated and their ashes used to kill the *kahuna ʻanāʻanā* who had started the black magic. The ashes of a victim's hair or clothing were spread on the path where the *kahuna ʻanāʻanā* usually walked. This was believed to return the curse to its origin, thereby killing the perpetrator.

See also: **ʻanāʻanā**.

laghiman, laghimā (S) *Lit.* light *(laghu)*-ness; levity, lack of weight, subtleness; the power to assume excessive lightness, to become as light as cotton down, to become almost weightless, to levitate, and to move about at fantastic speed.

See also: **siddhi**.

levitation Rising or causing to rise and float in the air above the ground; a miraculous power normally attributed to supernatural causes, often associated with the yogis of India.

It is also well known from the writings of Teresa of Ávila that her raptures and ecstasies were sometimes accompanied by the raising of her whole body above the ground. When the raptures took place in public, she was greatly distressed, and prayed for them to stop:

> So forceful is this enrapturing that very many times I wanted to resist, and used all my energy, especially sometimes when it happened in public or other times when in secret, and I was afraid of being deceived. At times, I was able to accomplish something, but with a great loss of energy, as when someone fights with a giant and afterwards is worn out. At other times, it was impossible for me to resist, but it carried off my soul and usually, too, my head along with it, without my being able to hold back – and sometimes the whole body, until it was raised from the ground.
>
> This latter has happened rarely. Once it happened when we were together in the choir ready to go up to receive communion, and while I was kneeling. I was very distressed because the experience seemed to me to be something most extraordinary, and it would then become widely known. So I ordered the nuns – for this happened recently while I held the office of prioress – not to say anything about it. But at other times, when I began to see the Lord was going to do the same (and once when there were some ladies of nobility present in order to hear a sermon, for it was our titular feast),[1] I stretched out on the floor and the nuns came and held me down; nonetheless, this was seen. I begged the Lord very much not to give me any more favours that would involve any outward show, for I was tired of being considered so important – and His Majesty could grant me that favour without it being known. It seems, in His goodness, He was pleased to hear me because up to the present I have never had this experience again; true, I made this petition not so long ago.
>
> *Teresa of Ávila, Life 20:4–5, CWT1 pp.173–74*

In fact, from her later writings, it is clear that St Teresa did experience further public raptures and levitations,[2] though her cousin Mother Maria de San Jerónimo writes that they eventually ceased:

> It happened once that her body was raised above the ground. She was just going up to take communion at the time, and as soon as she felt that this was happening she grasped the rails with both hands so as to control herself. She was greatly distressed when such outward manifestations took place, and she used to say that she had striven long with the Lord in prayer for them to cease, as in time they did. She used also to be distressed when she was enraptured in our presence, though eventually she learned to endure that. But for it to happen before people from outside was a terrible trial to her, and she would dissemble by saying that it was caused by heart weakness; so, whenever this happened in anyone's presence, she would ask for something to eat and drink in order to support the idea that it was due to illness.
>
> *Maria de San Jerónimo, On St Teresa; cf. CWTA3 p.341*

Father Pedro Ibanez observes in his testimony to St Teresa's sincerity and holiness that some "devotees" desire that their ecstasies should be seen in public:

> We have also seen people who, after a few revelations and visions, have desired that these things should come to them in some place where they could be seen and admired – during Mass, for example, before an important and aristocratic congregation, so that it should be seen how they were raised above the ground and transported in ecstasy – but have had no desire for them to be seen by poor and ordinary people. The reason for this is that the proud always wish to be thought much of and talked about, and to have men marvelling at the great and extraordinary things that happen to them and not to others; and the world sets store by people like this, but love and humility and the spirit of God flee from all this and desire only to be generally despised.
>
> *Pedro Ibanez, On Saint Teresa, CWTA3 pp.320–21*

See also: **miracles**, **siddhi**.

1. The feast of St Joseph.
2. Teresa of Ávila, *Testimonies* 2:2, 9, *CWT1* pp.380, 388.

mahiman, **mahimā** (S) *Lit.* huge *(mahā)*-ness; magnitude, grandeur, majesty, glory, might, power, high rank; the power to expand, to assume extensive size at will, to become of vast proportions, to touch any object at a distance, to expand into space and become as vast as the cosmos, having a single vision encompassing the entire universe.

See also: **siddhi**.

mana (Hawaiian) (Hw) *Lit.* supernatural or divine power; miraculous power; charisma, personal magnetism, an aura of personal power; a power that emanates from within a person and is regarded as being received from the gods or from some other supernatural source. A Hawaiian chief or *kahuna,* for instance, with a powerful presence or charisma, was said to have great *mana. Mana* is said to be

> the life force itself emanating from a great universal source. This sense of a higher power flowing through all living things, a force which could be harnessed by man for his own use, was the basic concept underlying all thought in pre-Christian Polynesia.
>
> *Kristin Zambucka, Ano Ano the Seed, Introduction, AASZ*

When a chief or *kahuna* enjoyed a concentrated amount of *mana,* he was raised up in the eyes of the commoners to the status of a deity. Many kings in the Kamehameha dynasty, for example, were regarded as gods. Kamehameha I, who brought all the Hawaiian islands under a single rule, founded the dynasty in 1795, which lasted until the death of Kamehameha V in 1872.

See also: **mana (Māori)**.

mana (Māori) (Mo) *Lit.* power, will, influence, prestige, control, authority; charisma, personal magnetism; psychic force, spiritual fire, personal life force; at the deepest level of spirit, the power of love; the spiritual fire and mystic force of *Io* the supreme Being, the- source and welfare of all things. The Māori of ancient times maintained that love comes from within the self, and human beings must '*tuku a Mana ko atu* (surrender to the Power beyond)', to the inner love.

In everyday human experience, the Māori conceive *mana* as being of three main types – *mana whenua, mana tāngata,* and *mana atua:*

> *Mana whenua* is the 'power of the land'. It embraces the earth, all nature, the environment and all living creatures upon mother earth. As people of the land, Māori seek to preserve the *mana whenua.*
>
> *Mana tāngata* is the 'power of the human person'. This comes from ancestral lineage, but should not be restricted to such. Personal power also comes in the form of accomplishment and generosity. One can obtain *mana tāngata* by looking after *mana whenua.* We obtain personal power by showing kindness and hospitality towards others, and by also doing great deeds. Some persons may see a fourth category called *mana tūpuna* or 'ancestral power', but in reality this falls within *mana tāngata.* The person may obtain spiritual power by the work of their ancestors, and this power flows through the veins.
>
> *Mana atua* means 'power of the gods'. This power dwells with spirits, gods, and angels. It also empowers the *mana tāngata* and the *mana whenua.* The person is empowered by the aid of the gods. The land is empowered because manifestations of nature such as the ocean, trees and mountains also have their *mana* in an *atua* such as *Tāne* and *Tangaroa.*
>
> You may take part in each type of *mana* by living with them in your lives. Do something for the land. Take part in preservation projects. When people come together, we have the *mana tāngata* or 'power of the people'. Learn to encourage your peers. In numbers, we can protect the *mana whenua,* and then we gain empowerment by the *atua.*

> We can take part in the *mana atua* by praying to them and by taking care of the self and the land as best we can.
>
> *Samuel Timoti Robinson, Tohunga, TRAK pp.99–100*

Māori creation myths tell the story of how the *mana* (power) of *Io* passed to the *atua* (ancestral deities, elemental gods), and thence to all living beings. According to the story,[1] from *Io* the supreme Diety emerged *Rangi* and *Papatūānuku,* the Sky Father and Earth Mother, the male-female duality who gave birth to the *atua* and all living things. Initially, they all remained bound together until the god *Tāne* separated the dualities of creation, fulfilling the declaration of *Io-Tapu* (*Io* the Most Sacred) that light should break forth, eventually resulting in *te ao mārama* (the world of light), which is this world. At this cosmic event, the *mana tapu* (sacred power) was passed from *Io* to *Tāne.*

The *atua,* however, began to fight among themselves, until *Io* eventually declared:

> *"Io* Most Supreme! I am *Io* Most Supreme! Fall in order before *Io-Io-Whenua."* This was the sound of the Mighty as the supreme Voice roared from above. There came the Mighty, and the universe in its reverence before the Magnificent fell into order. The gods stopped fighting and, by the supreme Being *Io-Io-Whenua,* peace was brought to the firmament. All the *atua* were appointed over the elements. All of them were assigned different tasks.... Each of them had *mana* over the elements and had dominion in equal portions.
>
> *Samuel Timoti Robinson, Tohunga, TRAK p.33*

Some time later in the unfolding of the creation by means of this same *mana, Tāne* climbed the cosmic vine *(aka)* of creation and ascended through the heavens back into the presence of *Io-Tapu* to receive the three sacred baskets *(kete)* of knowledge for humanity, at the same time charting the way for all souls to return to the presence of *Io.*

Since all knowledge of *Io* was highly secret and reserved for the nobility, the uninitiated Māori looked upon the *atua* as manifesting the *mana* – the intrinsic power, potency, essence and vitality within the creation, and within the universe and man:

> The *atua* are full of *mana,* and their origin is in *Te Pō* (the Darkness, the Void), the Darkness where life was ever potential. *Io* is the source of their *mana,* yet each of them came from this source. The *mana* of the *atua* is the divided *mana* of *Io* as they each have their own potential, just as *Io* appointed them separately over the elements.

> The *mana* of *Io* is apportioned between them, yet *Io* has the greatest *mana,* and the *karakia* (incantations, prayers of remembrance) for *Io* are the most *tapu* (restricted, sacred).
>
> *Samuel Timoti Robinson, Tohunga, TRAK p.108*

The first human beings (man and woman) were moulded out of clay by the god *Tāne* (or *Tū* according to some tribes) and brought to life with *mana ora,* the life-giving power of *Io,* through the combined focus of the *atua.* The *atua* later consorted with humanity, and hence the Māori believe that human beings have the *mana* of the *atua* within them. This inherited power *(mana whakaheke)* is handed down through the firstborn male of a family, and great care was taken to remember their genealogy *(whakapapa),* to trace and record their lines of descent from the *atua.*

In the attempt to understand and express something of the nature of *mana,* it is often portrayed in Māori mythology as an unquenchable spiritual fire that has existed since the world began. Māori leader and scholar Teone Taare Tikao (*c.*1850–1927), in talks with Herries Beattie during the 1920s, describes it as a supernatural 'fire' or force that manifests in many ways. At the material level, it is, for example, the power that gives rise to storms and lightning:

> *Mana* is only a word, but no one can wash it out. In one way, I might say it is God – whose power no one can stop. The power of God – that is the *pākehā* (European settlers) side of *mana.*
>
> But to the ancient Māori, *mana* was a fire which no one could put out. There are three kinds of lightning – *uira,* striking down; *kohara,* zigzagging all over; and *kapo,* flashing here and there round the horizon until it gets strongest at one point, and a storm comes from there. The *kapo* (lightning) round the other quarters has given in, and let the strongest *kapo* have the wind to hurl on the earth. This victorious *kapo* is *mana.* It is a fire.
>
> *Teone Taare Tikao, Tikao Talks, TTTT p.95*

It is also the power – controlled and administered by the *atua* – that results in earthquakes, the weather, and all natural events. It is the power by which the world remains in existence:

> From the beginning of the world, it goes on – it cannot be rubbed out. The earthquake is fire – you cannot see it, but you feel the shake, and if it broke out through the earth's surface it would be a fire. *Mana* is all round the world, and *Tāwhiri-mātea* (god of wind god), *Rūaimoko* (god of earthquakes), *Māui* (a demigod) and others are in the centre of the circle, and get hold of this *mana,* and direct the elements, and make the weather. The *Hine* (female *atua*) family hold the winds by *mana.*

> No one can rub it out. *Māui* is not dead, but *Hine-nui-te-pō* (goddess or guardian of death) took his *mana,* and it still exists. The gods stand back to back doing the work of the world – good or bad – and doing it by *mana,* which cannot be put out or overcome. *Mana* holds from the beginning to the end of the world, and keeps it going. Personal *mana* can be overcome and annihilated, but that of the gods cannot.
>
> *Teone Taare Tikao, Tikao Talks, TTTT pp.95–96*

The essence of *mana* is primarily spiritual. In his book *Tohunga,* first published in 2005, South-Island Māori Samuel Timoti Robinson also describes *mana* as a sacred 'fire' in the spirit. Describing something of the Māori creation myth, he says that it originates in *Io,* and descends to earth through the *atua,* empowering human beings and giving rise to all natural phenomena. 'Fire' – as a potent, natural, and penetrating force – is being used metaphorically to describe the processes by which creation comes about. These processes and sub-powers, portrayed in myth and metaphor, include 'Mind', the 'Seed Word', the 'Void', the 'Darkness', and various stepped-down forms of the primal 'Fire' – the primordial power or *mana.* Like all mythology, the details rarely conform to a logical consistency:

> Fire is an *atua* or protecting god itself, in that it lives and it contains a guardian *wairua* (spirit) for the people. Our ancestors are present in fire. When we light it, they are invoked. Humankind descended from *Tāne* (god of primordial light), and he has his birth in *Rangi* and *Papa* (Sky Father and Earth Mother, primordial aspects of duality). The parents have their origin in *Io* the supreme Being, and the entire *mana* of the human race is traced back to *Io.* This line of *mana* burns in the *ahi taitai* (sacred fire of the *tohunga*), providing the *tohunga* with all-powerful *mana* and *tapu.*. . .
>
> The *tohunga* (priestly adept) notion of fire as divinity goes beyond physical fire, for the priest is speaking of fire in the spirit, the invisible fire, the incorruptible spirit of fire, creative fire, the fire of Mind. This fire is creative; Mind has its power *(mana)* in fire, Mind is fire and the power *(mana)* of thought is Intellectual Fire. There were several degrees of fire in the *tohunga* tradition. I have spent several hours in conversation with my teacher, if not years, trying to understand this concept. This was the best explanation given to me on fire and *mana:*
>
>> *Io* is the first great fire. The Intellectual Fire of Mind roars forth in the expansive fire of the Seed Word. The Word of creation is yet another fire consuming the vastness in its way, filling the Void of the *Kore* or Nothingness, entering into the *Pō* or Darkness. Darkness is a fire after the Void has been filled;

> the fire has consumed itself upon the space. We are asked: to where did the fire go? And the answer is: to *Rangi,* to *Papa,* the Sky Father and Earth Mother. The creative fire did not remain in Mind alone, nor in the Seed Word of *Io,* but found its place in *Rangi* and *Papa,* the divine parents; they are an expression of the sacred fire and they are fires.
>
> How did it find its way to *Rangi* and *Papa?* It was Mind that expressed itself in the Word; it was the Word that said, "Night succeeding Night! Let there be creation!" And Mind saw Darkness, where fire consumed the Void. In the *whakapapa* (genealogy) of creation, it was this Mind that brought forth creation, it was Intellectual Fire that gave the commands. All the movements of *Io* in creation are called Active Fire. Here, *Io* began its motion by going over and under the waters, revealing *Rangi* and *Papa,* this was Conceived Fire. *Rangi* and *Papa* are filled with fire and mated where fire met fire, male met female; they are both spiritual fires, and gave birth to seventy gods, each of the many of them, who are living fires themselves.
>
> The Active Fire existed for many millions of aeons as the seventy children dwelt in Darkness. Active Fire ended in the *Pō* when *Tāne* uplifted his father *(Rangi)* to produce the revealed world. Active Fire at last became Manifested Fire. This Manifested Fire is the last stage of fire. This is the *mana* of the Māori, as our blood is tied to the *atua* (gods), and why we are a powerful race. What Fire is to the Māori is pure willpower and heart. It comes from *Io,* the *Pō,* the *atua.* It is fire existent taking form in *te ao mārama,* the world of light and the world of humankind.
>
> *Samuel Timoti Robinson, Tohunga, TRAK pp.95, 281–82*

Traditionally, the *tohunga* was trained to tap into the ancestral line of *mana* and psychic 'fire' or power that burns in the *ahi taitai* (sacred fire of the *tohunga*), providing the *tohunga* with *mana* and *tapu.* Special *karakia* were associated with the *mana* of a particular *atua,* so that the intention of the *karakia* may be manifest. With one-pointed attention and focused repetition of *karakia,* the skilled *tohunga* was able to open himself to become a channel or medium for the *mana* of the inner spiritual powers of *Io,* the *atua,* and the ancestors. By this means, *mana* was used for meditation or, by directing *mana* by means of *karakia,* for healing, protection of the individual or community, or to control the outcome of war. The skilled *tohunga* also used *mana* and *tapu* to control the elements, to ensure good crops, in the conduct of ceremonies, and in other daily activities. Being imbued with such *mana* renders the *tohunga,* the people and objects *tapu,* and strict protocols were observed to restrict the infringement of this *tapu,* to prevent any harm being caused by its powerful *mana:*

> The *tohunga* ascends the macrocosm by *karakia,* and contacts the higher powers *(mana atua)* by naming the *atua,* ancestors, or Hawaiki (spiritual homeland) in his rites. At any time when we call on the aid of the *wairua* (spirit), we ascend the macrocosm. Our minds transcend our mundane level and reach out towards superior powers that are beyond our reckoning. Then, when we apply this *karakia* to the physical level, such as when calling *Rangi* to bless a child, these heavenly powers *(mana)* are brought down into our level in *te ao mārama* (the world of light).
>
> *Samuel Timoti Robinson, Tohunga, TRAK p.109*

Many of these rites and practices took place at the *tūāhu* or sacred altar, the location of the *ahi taitai* or sacred fire used by the *tohunga* in order to tap into the esoteric fire of *mana.* At the end of certain Māori ceremonies, the resounding of thunder in the heavens was proof of the acquisition of *mana.*

The wielding of such power, however, was not without danger. Tikao describes the great *mana* and the inherent danger of the sacred fire used by the *tohunga:*

> The *mana* of the Māori was nothing but sacred fire.... The *tohunga* would make a fire and (chant) *karakia....* When such a fire was covered, no one could uncover it but the *tohunga,* or even step over it – if he did, he would fall stone dead. Its *mana* would kill him instantly.... The people knew the sacred spots where such fires were made and avoided them. If a man dug one up, even a century later, its *mana* would kill that person.... I wish to make it clear that the fire for cooking food or for warmth, the common fires, had no *mana.* If you put your hand in one of these you would be burnt and that was all. It was the sacred fires that had the *mana.*
>
> *Teone Taare Tikao, Tikao Talks, TTTT p.96*

At the physical level, through the mental intention of the *tohunga* and his use of *karakia,* anything, animate or inanimate, could be imbued with *mana. Mana* or power can be increased or decreased, transferred from person to person, handed down from father to son, teacher to pupil, and used to heal the sick. It can be imparted to a *kumara* (sweet potato) that is to be used as the talisman for the first planting of the season, or imparted to other objects such as weapons, ornaments, whale bones, stones, and especially greenstone (New Zealand jade). By means of the *rāhui* ritual, the energy or *mana* of the owners and *tohunga* was transmitted into markers such as trees or stones that marked land boundaries *(pou rāhui).* This had the effect of making the land *tapu* (sacred, out of bounds) to trespassers. Cases have been recorded of people dying or becoming ill through coming in contact with land or objects imbued with *mana.*[2]

The *mana* wielded by the *tohunga* is limited only to those affairs in which the *atua* are deemed to be involved:

> The *mana* of the Māori priest is circumscribed, and only extends to those matters in which the interference of the gods may be recognized, as in the many internal arrangements of the tribe in times of war, or in specific acts in agriculture. In war,... the *mana* of the priest is seen in every movement of the tribe, being guided by him; this does not only include his own tribe or *hapū,* of which he may be a member, but includes all men of other tribes who may join them.
>
> *Thomas Gudgeon, History and Doings of the Maoris, HDMG pp.217–18*

With the passage of time, the *tohunga* themselves became increasingly imbued with this sacred power, which constantly increased their own personal power and proficiency. Eventually, the *mana* would become so much a part of them that they themselves became exceedingly *tapu,* and it was dangerous for ordinary *(noa)* mortals to touch them:

> His food, raiment, house, and all belonging to him are sacred or *tapu,* and his *mana* is inherent in them; that is, if touched by any common person, that *mana* or influence of the gods... will cause death to that person. It is therefore the influence of the gods – or the superstitious dread in which they are held by the people – and not human influence, that gave the *mana* to a priest.
>
> *Thomas Gudgeon, History and Doings of the Maoris, HDMG p.219*

Anything or anyone coming into contact with *mana* becomes *tapu.* The *tapu* must therefore be lifted and the person or object made *noa* (common), before it can be used safely once again in ordinary life. Some effective controls were therefore necessary. This is the origin of the notion of *tapu.* Once something had been imbued with *mana,* it became restricted as well as sacred, so that no harm should come to others:

> *Mana* is a supernatural force said to be in a person, place, object, or spirit. It is commonly understood as prestige, status, or authority – although status is derived from possessing *mana. Mana* can be diminished or lost, and so requires protective devices. *Mana* is a dangerous power both to the possessor and to those who come into contact with it; thus, certain ritual observances are necessary to prevent harm coming to a community or individual.

> *Mana,* as a supernatural power, carries with it certain problems. The 'power' of *mana* is undifferentiated and dangerous unless it has some controls. Just as a nuclear pile requires insulation to protect the experts, the unwary and the ignorant from radiation, so *mana* has its protective shield to prevent illness or death arising from the dangerous force of *mana.* This system of controls, or shielding, is termed *tapu.*
>
> *James Irwin, Introduction to Maori Religion, IMRI p.23*

In present times, the understanding of *mana* includes personal power, charisma; the power of prestige and social position; the power of authority and control; power through ancestry *(mana tūpuna);* the power inherited by those of high birth *(mana ariki);* the power of ancestors and the gods *(mana atua);* and the power of love, the deepest mystical power of all. *Mana* can be inherited – transferred from one person to another – sometimes at the time of death, by performance of the *whakahā* ('breathing') ceremony.

Writers of the last hundred years have tried to summarize in simple language something of the nature of *mana:*

> The *mauri* (life principle) is imparted at birth and *mana* (power) is gained by the *tohi karakia* (birth incantations).... This *mana* is imparted to the person when, at his birth, the father or *tohunga* recites the appropriate *karakia* to a particular *atua* (god, ancestral spirit) to endue the child with *mana* for the course in life the child will follow. Thus, the *karakia* might be addressed to *Tangaroa* (*atua* of the sea and fish) if the child is to be a fisherman or sea traveller.... If it is desired that he be a mighty warrior and leader, then the priest of *Tūmatauenga* (*atua* of war) will be asked to invoke that *atua* to impart his *mana.... Mana,* then, could be a gift of the *atua....* It could come by transference from father to son, or from teacher to pupil. In the latter case, a special rite known as *whakahā* was carried out. In this rite, the *tohunga*-teacher took the toe of the pupil into his own mouth and breathed into it the *ha* (breath) that conveyed his own *mana.*
>
> *James Irwin, Introduction to Maori Religion, IMRI pp.21–22*

> *Mana* is power to act, delegated by the *atua.* The delegation occurs firstly at birth, inherited through the descent lines and this may be extended or reduced during life, depending on how effectively the person uses that power or status. The importance of *mana* provides a strong incentive to live one's life effectively and behave correctly. Even if, inadvertently, the power is not used appropriately, this effectively reduces the capacity for power.
>
> *Rosemary Madden, Dynamic and Different, DDMW p.17*

Tare Tikao speaks of *mana* as a primal activating power:

> The *mana* of the native (Māori) has existed for a very long time – indeed for the thousands of years since the start of the world. If they had not possessed that *mana,* they could not have crossed the wide and often stormy seas in their old canoes.
>
> *Tare Tikao, Tikao Talks, TTTT p.97*

Mana may seem to be a mysterious force, even the product of a superstitious imagination. In fact, it is not so much mysterious as hidden from normal human perception. Mitaki Ra, a contemporary New Zealand writer, explains that the essential aspect of *mana* is the universal and omnipresent *wairua* (spirit). He also counters the common opinion that ancestry and personal achievements are an insufficient source of *mana.* Humility is also required:

> *Mana* is that spiritual energy and charisma shared by *Io* and the gods with those chosen to lead the people home. When the flames of the spiritual fire of *mana* absorb such ones, the presence of *Io* and the gods holds commanding stature in all that they do, opening the doors of the inner spiritual worlds that all might enter.
>
> In the physical world, *mana* is manifested in conduct by the presence of humility in all undertakings, for the benefit of all people as a whole. Where *mana* is not used in this way, the support of *Io* and the gods withdraws, leaving considerable disruption in its wake.
>
> Contrary to belief, *mana* is not gained by entitlement of ancestral line, nor by the achievements of personal ego. Only in the actions of 'humility' is it given by the gods. That is why today many leaders need to re-examine their understanding.
>
> The underpinning plank of *mana* is *wairua* (spirit). Without these two being in complete unison one with the other, nothing of lasting advantage and benefit can be achieved.
>
> *Wairua* means 'spiritual river of light'. It flows as the directing agent in all that we do, from mountain to ocean, absorbing all in its path, and influencing all that is beyond. As water quenches the thirst of the land and gives it life, so too does *wairua* quench the thirst of man and give life to all that is in the physical universe which surrounds us. There is nowhere it is not present; such is the nature of *wairua.*
>
> So that as the *mana* of *Io* is shared with all, so *wairua* makes itself known to all, and that which is desired is achieved. Wherever such unity of desire and purpose coexists, there *mana* and *wairua* stand as a firm foundation upon which the people may advance with confidence and in the complete absence of fear.
>
> *Mitaki Ra, Ancestral Recordings of Tainui, ARTM pp.15–16*

Many believe that since the colonization of New Zealand by the British and European missionaries, the *mana* of the Māori has diminished. The *whare wānanga* (school of sacred learning) of the *tohunga* was closed and outlawed, and many Māori people aligned themselves with the *mana* of Christianity. In addition, it is believed that cooked food and water boiled in pots renders the protecting *tapu* or restriction on *mana* common or *noa*. Nowadays, the *tohunga ahurewa* (highest rank of priest) imbued with powerful *mana* are rare and remain withdrawn, and the common usage of the term *mana* now pertains more to leadership, charisma, prestige or social status, self esteem, and personal power:

> *Mana* is open to a variety of interpretations, depending upon the context in which it is used. Sometimes, as in modern Māori society, it is equated with prestige and status, for no one can hold a place of importance unless he have *mana*. However, this is understood today as the accord and respect given by the community to one who manifests the gifts of leadership and ability.
>
> *James Irwin, Introduction to Maori Religion, IMRI p.21*

See also: **ahi taitai**, **atua** (▸1), **tapu**, **tohunga**.

1. Samuel Timoti Robinson, *Tohunga, TRAK* pp.20–71.
2. James Irwin, *Introduction to Maori Religion, IMRI* pp.23, 29, 41.

manaḥ-java (S) *Lit.* impulse *(javah)* of the mind *(manas);* moving the body at the speed of thought. See **siddhi**.

manaḥ-paryāya-jñāna (S) *Lit.* knowledge *(jñāna)* of another's *(paryāya)* mind *(manas);* awareness of the thinking processes of others; mental telepathy; the ability to read the minds of others without the aid of the physical sense organs, and whether or not the subject of such mind reading is physically present; the fourth of the five primary forms of knowledge identified by Jain philosophy and epistemology; a power credited to *Tīrthankaras, arhats,* and spiritually evolving souls, arising naturally as a result of spiritual practice; synonymous with *chetaḥ-paryāya-jñāna,* the term more frequently found in Buddhist texts.

The other four fundamental forms of *jñāna* in Jainism are *mati-jñāna* (sense knowledge), which is knowledge acquired through the senses; *shruta-jñāna* (knowledge that is heard), which is knowledge derived from reading, especially scriptures; *avadhi-jñāna* (limited knowledge), extrasensory knowledge acquired by human beings or the innate knowledge of heavenly and hellish beings; and *kevala-jñāna* (absolute knowledge), knowledge of the Absolute, omniscience. *Avadhi-jñāna* (limited) is so-called by comparison to the two higher forms of knowledge.

Jainism, like other Eastern mystical philosophies, understands mind to be a real 'substance' or energy. *Avadhi-jñāna* and *manaḥ-paryāya-jñāna* are hence regarded as perceptual, but in a higher and more refined sphere than the gross physical. The mind energies of the observer are perceiving the mind energies of the subject. Such knowledge is not inferred or deduced by a process of reasoning; it is perceived directly. The development of this natural faculty requires purity, self-control, and stillness of mind. Nonetheless, according to Jain descriptions, both these two modes of perception are limited to the perception of forms. They are not modes of pure cognition or awareness. In this context, 'forms' refer to changes of 'shape' in the subtle patterns or vibrations of the mind or other subtle energies.

Since the mental spheres or realms are vast in comparison to the physical realm, the scope for variety in such perception or understanding is also correspondingly vast, beyond the imagination of a human being whose experience is limited to the material realm, and who is hardly aware of his own thoughts and mental processes.

Although *manaḥ-paryāya-jñāna* and *avadhi-jñāna* are both of the same essentially non-physical nature, the former is understood to be a clearer and purer perception than the latter. Other differences between *manaḥ-paryāya-jñāna* and *avadhi-jñāna* are that the latter has a wider spatial range and range of subject, but the former is able to perceive greater detail in a far smaller aspect of the subject; beings from all four classes (heavenly and hellish beings, human beings, and animals) are able to acquire *avadhi-jñāna,* but only human beings who have practised the required spiritual disciplines are able to acquire *manaḥ-paryāya-jñāna;* and while *avadhi-jñāna* is able to perceive a wide spectrum of subtle forms and energies, *manaḥ-paryāya-jñāna* is restricted to the perception of mind energies alone.[1]

Two kinds of *manaḥ-paryāya-jñāna* are identified: *ṛiju-mati* (of honest mind, sincere, personal, simple) and *vipula-mati* (of extensive mind, of great understanding, of complex mind).[2] *Ṛiju-mati* refers to awareness of the personal thoughts and feelings of others, such as, "This person is thinking of a pair of shoes." *Vipula-mati* implies a more complex awareness of the minds of others, such as, "This person is thinking of a pair of shoes designed by so-and-so, and manufactured at such a time and such a place." Basically, the *vipula-mati* form is able to perceive greater detail.

According to Jain philosophy, *manaḥ-paryāya-jñāna* is made difficult by the accumulation of the veils *(āvaraṇa)* of obstructing *karma.* The mind is inherently pure, and faculties such as telepathy and clairvoyance are innate. But the coverings of *karma* stand in the way. *Vipula-mati* implies a purer mind, free of more obstructing *karma* than *ṛiju-mati*. Likewise, *ṛiju-mati* is the faculty of a purer mind than one who has only *avadhi-jñāna*. Five kinds of *karma* and five kinds of covering are identified that prevent the manifestation of the five kinds of knowledge.

Jain texts vary, however, in their more detailed descriptions and discussions of the nature of *avadhi-jñāna* and of the two degrees of *manaḥ-paryāya-jñāna*, and how they each differ from each other – which beings can possess them (animals, heavenly and hellish beings, human beings, or only saints); what can be known; the distance over which things can be known; the degree of subtlety inherent in and the mental purity required for each kind of knowledge; their degree of fallibility; whether things are known by perception, intuitively or by inference; who can possess them, and so on.[3]

See also: **chetaḥ-paryāya-jñāna**, **jñāna** (▸3).

1. See Pandit Sukhalalji, *Commentary on Tattvārtha Sūtra, CTSU* pp.42–50.
2. *E.g.* Āchārya Umāswāmī, *Tattvārtha Sūtra* 1:23.
3. *E.g.* Āchārya Umāswāmī, *Tattvārtha Sūtra* 1:22–29; Akalanka, *Tattvārtha-Vārttika* 1:3.2, 1:23.4; *Āvashyaka Niryukti* 76; Hemachandra, *Pramāṇa-Mīmāṃsā* 1:1.18; Jinabhadra, *Visheshāvashyaka Bhāshya* 569, 669, 814; *Nandī Sūtra* 15, 39–40, 63; Nemichandra, *Gommaṭasāra, Jīvakāṇḍa* 441; Pūjyapāda, *Sarvārtha-Siddhi* on *Tattvārtha Sūtra* 1:24–28; Siddhasena Divākara, *Nyāyāvatāra* 16; *Sthānānga* 71–72; see *Jainism in Buddhist Literature, JBLB* pp.145–46; *Jaina View of Life, JVLK* pp.83–87; *Jain Theory of Perception, JTPB* pp.108–9.

manitou (Ojibwa) *Lit.* spirit power, supernatural force. The Ojibwas of eastern and central Canada believe that power, which they call *manitou,* is an all-pervasive force that is embodied in supernatural beings and sacred objects. *Manitou* makes objects holy. Like the Ojibwas, the Kwakiutls also believe that spirit beings and forces are constantly in motion and are shapeshifters, becoming visible as animals, humans, or material objects. Objects that are inhabited by spirit power are all knowing and can be used by humans for curing disease and providing protection, or conversely for causing disease and misfortune. In Ojibwa religion, power itself is neutral; it is in its application that it becomes good or evil:

> Since the Ojibwas believe that power is constantly changing its shape, it is not always possible to know whether any particular object contains power. An Ojibwa man, when asked by researcher A. Irving Hallowell whether all stones are alive, answered "No! But *some* are."

The only way to discover if an object has power is to observe and test it carefully – for example, if a stone behaves like a living being, it is alive and contains power.

The Ojibwa man interviewed by Hallowell reported that his father had once performed a ritual cure using a large round stone. At the beginning of the healing ceremony, the father walked twice around the stone and then started to sing. According to the man interviewed, the stone began "following the trail of the old man around the tent, rolling over and over, I saw it happen several times and others saw it too." The stone had demonstrated by its actions that it had power and was alive. Since the stone was (literally) powerful, the man's father could tap its power and use it in a healing ritual.

Nancy Bonvillain, Native American Religion, NARB p.16

manojavitva (S) *Lit.* fleetness *(javitva)* of the mind *(manas);* moving about at the speed of the mind, *i.e.* instantaneously; perception without the need of any vehicle or instrument (body or physical senses). See **siddhi**.

mantra-siddhi (S) *Lit. mantra* power *(siddhi),* a *mantra* being a verbal formula used to concentrate the mind by its constant repetition; the effect of a *mantra;* the power gained by the successful practice of a *mantra;* complete mastery of a *mantra* and fulfilment of its purpose. Yogic and tantric texts prescribe particular *mantras* for the attainment of particular *siddhis,* the *mantras* in these cases being used more or less as magic spells. The desired *siddhi* is known as the *mantra-siddhi* of that particular *mantra.*

See also: **mantra** (▸3), **siddhi**.

maraṇa-siddhi (S) *Lit.* death *(maraṇa)* power *(siddhi);* the power to kill by thought alone.[1] See **siddhi**.

1. *Kaula-Jñāna-Nirṇaya* 4:14.

mātāpou (Mo) *Lit.* to repeat incantations; to cast a spell; to create an effect by means of a spell or charm; the spell or charm itself.

The use of such spells appears in Māori mythology. In one such story, *Io* (the supreme Being), while travelling in the company of *Rehua* – an *atua* (spirit, deity) associated with kindness, enjoyment, and entertainment – notices that they are being accompanied by *Io*'s *ata* (shadow):

> *Io* called to *Rehua:* "Follow our companion and send him back to the entrance to the uppermost heaven." Even so *Rehua Nui Atua* ('Great Spirit *Rehua*') followed the *ata* of *Io*-the-Parent that he might overtake it. On arriving at *Tahekeroa* (the descent to the underworld), the *ata* at once descended, and so the path of the *ata* of *Io* was lost by *Rehua.* Then *Rehua* commenced the recital of a form of charm known as *mātāpou,* in order to arrest the advance of the *ata* of *Io,* so that he might have speech with that *ata* of *Io*-the-Parent.
>
> *Elsdon Best, Maori Religion and Mythology, MRM2 p.34*

A *mātāpou* was repeated by a *tohunga* (priestly adept) to create a paralysing effect. Such a chant could be used, for example, to bring a canoe to a halt and remain motionless, regardless of any paddling efforts on the part of the crew, thus preventing a vessel from landing on shore. This spell could also be used for petrification, used to turn people and animals into stone. Many such instances are recorded in Māori folk tales:

> The account of the destruction by magic arts of the armed force that came to slay Taewha and Māhu in order to avenge the death of Taewha's daughter is given with much detail.[1] In this case, the probable method employed was to bury – under the surface of the track by which the force would approach the village – certain objects served as connecting links, mediums between the active spells of the warlock and the persons to be destroyed. Or there may have been no such material links employed, simply a small hole made in the pathway, over or into which the magic spell would be uttered, after which the hole would be carefully filled in, lest it be noticed by travellers it was intended to slay. When a wayfarer traversed a patch so bedevilled, he perished as he attempted to pass over the charmed spot.... We are told that the persons slain are still to be seen in the form of stones; spells having such an effect are termed *karakia mātāpou.* In describing such an act as Māhu's bewitching the path, a Māori would say *"Ka whakauohoia ko mea atua ki taua huanui"* – such a god was located at that path.
>
> *Elsdon Best, Maori Religion and Mythology, MRM2 p.143*

See also: **karakia**.

1. Elsdon Best, "Legend of Mahu and Taewha," *LMTB* p.103.

mateh (He) *Lit.* rod, branch, sceptre, staff; the shepherd's crook; also, in biblical texts, the shoot or branch of a tree; a symbol of power and authority, both mundane and spiritual; identified symbolically with both the divine creative power and the prophet or spiritual master. The true prophet is a 'branch' from the Tree of Life, a common Middle Eastern symbol for the divine power.

According to the prophet Micah (C8th BCE), the prophet, symbolized by the rod *(mateh),* is appointed by God:

> The Lord's voice cries to the city,
> and the man of wisdom shall see your name:
> "Hear the rod *(mateh),* and Who has appointed it."
>
> *Micah 6:9, JCL*

In one of the more obscure psalms, possibly addressed to King David as the king-messiah, the "mighty sceptre *(mateh)*" appears to symbolize the power invested in him by God:

> The Lord says to my master,
> "Sit at my right hand,
> until I make your enemies your footstool.
> The Lord shall send your mighty sceptre *(mateh)* out of Zion:
> rule therefore in the midst of your enemies.
> Your people offered themselves willingly
> in the majesty of their holiness, on the day of your battle,
> when still the dew of youth was upon you,
> fresh from the womb of dawn.
> The Lord has sworn and will not change his mind,
> you shall be a priest forever,
> after the manner of Melchizedek ('My Righteous King')."
>
> *Psalms 110:1–4; cf. KB*

In a mythological extension to the *Genesis* story, it is related that ten miraculous things,[1] mentioned in various biblical texts, were also established by God during His six days of creation.[2] Among these ancient signs and wonders was the staff of Moses and Aaron. Moses was the humble prophet, leader of the Israelites; Aaron was the more articulate of the brothers, the first priest and spokesman for Moses.[3]

The staff, as a legacy inherited by Moses from the earliest patriarchs and used on behalf of the Israelites, is explained symbolically in a well-known medieval prayer book, the *Maḥzor Vitry,* compiled in the eleventh and twelfth centuries by Rabbi Simḥah ben Samuel of Vitry (*d.*1105) and other pupils of the great commentator Rashi (1040–1105) of Provence.[4] According to the *Maḥzor Vitry,* which summarizes the legend recounted in many *midrashim,* the spiritual knowledge – God's unpronounceable Name – was symbolically 'engraved' on a *mateh* that had been handed down by Adam to his son Seth, and subsequently passed down the generations until it came to Moses. Some legends say the staff was made of sapphire, weighed over 400 pounds, and bore an inscription composed of an acronym of the Hebrew letters of the names of the ten plagues that God visited upon the Egyptians before the Exodus.[5] Mystically, the sapphire stone is associated with the light of the heavens and with the *sefirot,* the emanations or qualities of the primal divine Light. Other texts say that the *mateh* was wood, a branch from the Tree of Knowledge.[6] Either way, the staff symbolizes the spiritual power, the divine Name of God invoked by Moses and Aaron as prophets to the Israelites. It is this staff with which Moses parted the Red Sea when the Israelites were fleeing from slavery in Egypt, their erstwhile masters in pursuit. The *Zohar* comments that when God told Moses to lift his staff and divide the sea, it signified: "Lift up your rod, on which is engraved the Holy Name; stretch out your hand with the side bearing this Holy Name, so that the waters, on beholding it, may flee before the power that is in its letters."[7]

In a similar demonstration of the divine power of the *mateh,* when the Israelites lacked water in the wilderness, Moses struck a rock with his *mateh* and water gushed forth.[8] Understood symbolically, it refers to the flow of the Water of Life, the divine knowledge and grace that is concealed within the aridity of material creation.

The rod of Aaron is also associated with miracles. According to *Exodus,* Aaron was sent to Pharaoh as a spokesman to beg for the release of the Hebrews. As a sign, he threw his *mateh* to the ground, and it was transformed into a serpent. Pharaoh called for his magicians who performed a similar feat. But the staff or serpent of Aaron ate the staff or serpent of Pharaoh, indicating the superior power of Aaron's staff. Symbolically, it signifies the greater power of the Israelite God *Yahweh* over the god of the Egyptians.[9]

During the wanderings of the Israelites, Aaron's rod was kept in the ark of the covenant, in the portable sanctuary, where it miraculously sprouted buds and almonds perennially. Symbolically, it represents the perpetual divine nourishment of the divine Name. When the Jerusalem Temple was built, the *mateh* was kept in the ark in the Holy of Holies. The *Maḥzor Vitry* mentions some of these legends:

> The rod of Moses, with which Moses split the Red Sea – there was nothing like it in the world, for on it was engraved the ineffable Name of God. This rod Adam handed on to Seth, and it was handed on from one generation to the next until Jacob, our father, went down to Egypt and handed it on to Joseph. Now when Joseph died, Pharaoh's servants searched through everything in his house, and they deposited the rod in Pharaoh's treasury.
>
> In Pharaoh's household was Jethro, the father-in-law of Moses; Jethro was one of Pharaoh's astrologers and he learned of the importance of this rod by means of astrology. He took it and planted it in

his garden, and it took root in the earth. By means of astrology, Jethro discovered that whoever would be able to uproot this rod would be the saviour of Israel. He therefore used to put people to the test, and when Moses came to his household and then rose and uprooted it, Jethro threw him into the dungeon he had in his courtyard. Ẓippora (Jethro's daughter) fell in love with Moses and demanded from her father that he be given her as husband. Thereupon Jethro married her off to Moses. Another interpretation we have come upon is this: that 'the rod' refers to Aaron's rod which (put forth buds and) bore ripe almonds,[10] ... and it was decreed that by means of it should Moses achieve all the signs and wonders.

Maḥzor Vitry, in LTJG p.195

Such legends point to Moses as a mystic, inheritor of the divine wisdom passed down from the beginning of time. The rod symbolizes the divine authority of God, whose mission Moses undertakes.

See also: **mishʿan** (▸4), **shevet**.

1. *Pirkei Avot* 5:6.
2. *Genesis* 1:1–31.
3. *Exodus* 4:10–17.
4. Simḥah ben Samuel of Vitry, *Maḥzor Vitry,* in *LTJG* p.195.
5. *Midrash Tanḥuma, Va'era* 8, *MTSB,* in "Aaron's Rod," *Jewish Encyclopedia, JE.*
6. See "Tree of Knowledge," *Jewish Encyclopedia, JE.*
7. *Zohar* 2:48a, *ZSS3* p.147.
8. *Exodus* 17:6; *Numbers* 20:8–11.
9. *Exodus* 4:1–4, 7:8–12.
10. *Numbers* 17:23, *JCL.*

medicine (Native North American) *(nanasuigaint, orenda, wakan)* Spiritual power inherent in all creation, in human and spirit beings as well as inanimate things; a term used by Europeans for the almost indefinable natural, spiritual energy infusing all things and all beings, as understood by Native Americans. Some people or objects possess or were believed to possess more 'medicine' than others. Holy men were said to possess great medicine when they manifested supernatural powers as a result of contact with spirit guides. In the Native American context, 'medicine' could also refer to a herbal healing remedy.

'Medicine' translates a number of terms used among the many Native American tribes. *Wakan* (Lakota), for instance, meaning 'sacred' or 'powerful', is a holy energy obtained from *wakan* (spiritual) beings to help humanity and cure the sick. The Iroquois *orenda* implies a belief in an impersonal supernatural power distributed among various spirit beings. The Shoshoni tribe calls it *nanasuigaint,* meaning 'holy' or 'something at which to marvel'.

'Medicine' is an attempt to express in English what cannot truly be conveyed. This native power gleaned from communication with spirit beings had no reference in European lexicons. Consequently, when the early settlers in North America encountered the awesome power of shamans to heal the sick and to perform extraordinary feats of magic and spirituality, they described it in a way that conformed to their own culture. The sacred mysteries and powerful events (*taku wakan,* 'something sacred or holy') that included complete mastery over the natural world were equated by the settlers to a mundane event such as going to a pharmacy to buy medicine.

'Medicine' is the all-pervasive power or energy that is automatically perceived and understood by those who are aware of a supernatural aspect to or a divine presence in all things. To the Native American, as to many other indigenous peoples, this was encompassed in a world view in which the physical, the supernatural, and the spiritual were integrated:

> The Indian religious perspective centres around the supernatural world, populated by gods and spirits but also by human beings, animals, plants, and inanimate objects, for the supernatural breaks through into the everyday world. Its foremost means of expression is supernatural power, at times perceived as a specific, defined potency, at times merely experienced as a psychological reality underlying supernatural occurrences.
>
> *Ake Hultkrantz, Religions of the American Indians, RAIH p.14*

As time passed and European culture smothered the Native American's way of life, the tribes began to use English words to describe their waning power. A *kahnigapi* (chosen one) or *wichasha wakan* (holy man), names used for Native American shamans, were eventually referred to as 'medicine men', even by the Native Americans themselves, and 'medicine' became a term for the inherent spiritual power in all things. The great 'wheel of life' or the 'sacred hoop' became known as the 'medicine wheel'. The small sachets of power that each Native American wore around his neck to remind him of his personal path towards the spirit became known as his 'medicine bundle' or 'medicine bag'.

During the occupation of Wounded Knee in the early 1970s, American doctor Russell Buss was allowed into the war zone to treat wounded Native Americans. He relates how he received his medicine bag from the Lakota shaman Wallace Black Elk:

> After I finished with security, I went back to the hospital and one of the warriors said, "Let's go over to Black Elk's, and he's going to give us your medicine" – because anyone who was in there had to have a medicine bag on. The people who had been shot and killed either knew that they were going to be shot or had not had medicine on when it happened. So it was very important to have medicine from Black Elk. Buddy Lamont was talking about how he was going to die the night he went out on patrol. He just felt it. He knew it. He was shot by sniper fire.
>
> Black Elk was incredibly strong and powerful, and you sensed that right away. He had a lot of knowledge and a lot of humour. But it wasn't like being around someone who was aloof and distant from you. You came in, and you sat down on his couch. If he had anything to eat, he shared it with you. He just gave it to you. He said, "Here, it's time to eat." He never had much, but whatever he had, he gave to you. When he gave me the medicine bag he said, "Here, this has powerful medicine in it. You should wear it at all times." I had a feeling of incredible strength that he put on me. It was just a little leather bag, the size of a large marble. I didn't know what was in it, and I hardly knew the guy. I had read *Black Elk Speaks,* and I just felt very powerful.
>
> *Russell Buss, in "The Occupation of Wounded Knee," OWKG*

It made no difference what was in the medicine bag. The power came from the person giving the medicine. Wallace Black Elk himself explains how his power or medicine was obtained – and it was not from the local pharmacy! –

> To get to these sacred powers you have to go through four stages. When you reach the top, the spirit will come and communicate with you. He will give you your instructions. That's the first power, and it takes four years to acquire it. Then you go another four stages to get the second power. And there's a third power and a fourth power, see? Each of them requires four years. So that is four times four years, or sixteen years, before you reach all the way through and obtain the real power. That is the first level of power. Then there is a second level of power. That also takes sixteen years. Then there is a third and fourth level of power. So you have to go on vision after vision quest. The spirit will give you instructions. As you go, you go deeper and deeper. Eventually, you will be there with them. When you pass the fourth level of power you will be in the hands of the Creator, and you'll be back in Grandmother's arms again.
>
> So a lot of people come to me and want this power right now. But it's not that way. I have one more vision quest to perform, and then I will have the fourth and final power. That is the impenetrable medicine.

> It can cure any disease known to man. So you have to have a lot of patience for this.
>
> *Black Elk, Sacred Ways of a Lakota, BESW pp.43–44*

See also: **shaman** (7.1), **wakan** (▸1).

miracle(s) An event contrary to natural physical laws and to normal expectations, attributed to a supernatural or divine cause; an extra-ordinary happening whose causes are hidden. Miracles are commonly associated with the lives of prophets, mystics, saints, and holy people of the past. Miracles are associated with the biblical prophets, with Jesus, Simon Magus, Apollonius of Tyana, Mānī, the Sufis of Islam, and many of the yogis, mystics, and *sants* of India.

In Christianity, miracles are understood to be acts of God whose purpose is generally believed either to confer faith upon the subject or witnesses of the miracle, or to attest to the sanctity of the miracle worker, or to bear witness to the validity of the divine mission of the miracle worker, or as a divine favour in reward for virtue. Proven reports of miracles figure largely in the process by which a person is canonized as a saint in the Catholic Church, since miracles are supposed to indicate the special love God has for the individual. The eighteenth-century Jesuit Jean-Pierre de Caussade, on the other hand, writes that true faith requires no signs or miracles, for faith in itself is a sufficient miracle:

> The miracle of the saints lies in their life of continuing faith in all things. Without it, all the rest of their visions and the voices they hear would all fall short of that holiness which consists in the loving faith that makes them rejoice in God and see Him in all things. This does not require miracles; they are only for the benefit of those who need such testimonies and signs. Faithful souls do not rely on them. Content in their unknowing, they leave them to be a light for others, and accept for themselves all that is most ordinary: God's order.… Faith needs no proofs. Those who need them have little faith, but those who live by faith receive proof, not as such, but through God's purpose. In this sense, miracles are not inconsistent with perfect faith, for it happens that in the many saints whom God creates for the salvation of souls, there exist proofs to enlighten the feeblest.
>
> *J.-P. de Caussade, Sacrament of the Present Moment 9, SPM pp.89–90*

Christians and others also speak of experiencing the miracle of love, the miracle of grace, or the miracle of mercy, and so on, implying that divine love, grace and mercy transcend the natural laws of the material universe:

> My first taste of the divine was miracle enough for a lifetime. I was carried upwards by the current of primal life and energy, swept out of my little self into an ecstasy, a triumph, an astonishment that nothing in previous experience or imagination could have prepared me for.
>
> *Nancy Mayorga, Hunger of the Soul, HSDM p.22*

Some have seen the wonders of nature and the creation of the world itself as a miracle:

> The manner of its making is as hidden from man and as incomprehensible to man as is He who made it. And so although the miracles of the visible world of nature have lost their value for us, because we see them continually, still, if we observe them wisely they will be found to be greater miracles than the most extraordinary and unusual events. For man himself is a greater miracle than any miracle effected by human agency.
>
> *St Augustine, City of God 10:12; cf. CGAP p.390*

Even with the insights of science into the workings of nature, the fundamental question of how everything came into being remains unanswered.

According to a more general viewpoint, everyone has the potential to perform miracles. Those who support this notion usually invoke the hidden powers of the mind as the means. Mystics agree. They say that this world is a world governed by the mind, and that a person who is able to control or concentrate his mind to a greater or lesser extent gains corresponding power over the physical universe. 'Ināyat Khān describes the power to perform miracles simply as a question of attitude or acceptance:

> It is not the heat which kills a person, but the acceptance of the heat. It is the same with food and medicine; for behind everything there is thought. Even now there are *yogīs* who could jump into the fire and not be burnt. One will find that intolerant souls are the most unhappy in the world, because everything hurts them. Why should they be so – uncomfortable in the house and restless outside? Because of this tendency of disliking, of rejecting, of prejudice. It is this tendency which must be conquered; and when it is conquered, great mastery is achieved.
>
> *'Ināyat Khān, Sufi Message, SMIK4 pp.151–52*

Many mystics have said that the performance of miracles requires considerable mental and spiritual energy, as well as a diversion of the attention downwards. For this reason, they advise that this energy be used for spiritual ascent, and counsel against its use in the performance of miracles. Masters have often decried the performance of miracles by pointing out that what is a miracle to one creature is commonplace to the next. The real miracle is that a person turns his attention towards the Divine:

> When it was related to the master (Abū Saʿīd al-Khayr) that so-and-so had walked on water, he replied, "That is easy; frogs and waterfowl also walk on water." When it was said that so-and-so flew in the air, he replied, "Crows and flies also fly in the air." When it was said that so-and-so travelled from one city to another in an instant, he replied, "Satan, too, can travel from east to west in an instant. These things have no value. The real accomplishment is for a person to be among others, rising and sleeping, interacting and mixing with them, and yet not be heedless of God for a moment."
>
> *Asrār al-Tawḥīd, ATS1 p.199, in SSE7 p.6*

Following a similar line of thought, Richard Rolle, who himself had taken up a hermit's life when still a young man, regards it as nothing short of a miracle if a young man should remain pure when surrounded by temptation:

> No young man who is surrounded by feminine beauty and flattery and sweet nothings and an abundance of luxury can possibly become holy, unless it be by the unimaginable greatness of grace.... I reckon it a major miracle when a man, through God's grace and the love of Christ, completely spurns these allurements, and out of the midst of them all – although they seem pleasant to the flesh – rises like a man to the high holiness of heavenly contemplation.
>
> *Richard Rolle, Fire of Love 8; cf. FLML (1:8) pp.40–4, FLRR pp.67–68*

See also: **miracles of Jesus and the apostles**.

miracles of Jesus and the apostles[1] According to the four gospels and *Acts,* Jesus and his apostles performed many miracles, largely centred around healing the sick and feeding the hungry. The miracles of Jesus have figured prominently in later Christian teaching. Even so, many Christians have pointed out that there are greater miracles than the purely physical, since all things connected with the body will one day pass away. Moreover, there is a higher healing – the healing of the soul, which survives bodily death:

> Why do you marvel at his cures of the body
> which are ended by dissolution (death)?
> Especially when you know that healing of his,
> which passes not away....

And why do you look to this temporal life,
and have no thought of that which is eternal?

Acts of Thomas 78; cf. AAA p.205, ANT p.400

Though it is human nature to marvel at the inexplicable and the seemingly miraculous, the greatest miracle of all must surely be that God comes into the physical creation in the form of a man, a living Son of God, to give spiritual enlightenment to those who live in darkness. Yet, being in darkness, human beings have a tendency to marvel at the miraculous only when it is reduced to material things.

Miracle stories are a common aspect of the cults and religions that form around the teachings of past mystics. In many instances, such stories are even shared, the one being borrowed from the other. The miracle story remains the same – only the name of the central character changes.

Being fathered by God or by gods, virgin births, healing of sickness and infirmity of various kinds, miraculous provision of food and drink, control of the weather and the elements – these are not at all unusual in the folklore and legends that surround the mystics of the past. It seems to be a part of the way in which the mind diverts its attention from what is really important in a mystic's teachings, absorbing it in glamour and in non-essentials.

Mystics are able to perform miracles of a physical and material nature. If they are one with God and one with His creative power, then the 'secrets' of creation are no longer a secret; they are an open book. If mystics can take birth in this world by their own will and organize their life according to the work they have to do, then it is true enough to say that there is nothing about such a mystic that is not miraculous. Their consciousness is one with the supreme consciousness or being of God. Everything lies within themselves and within their power. They have the power of God within them.

In fact, even an individual who can concentrate his mind to some extent, withdrawing it from the senses through ascetic or spiritual practice, develops the power to perform miracles. As Jesus said:

If you had faith as a grain of mustard seed,
you might say to this sycamine (mulberry) tree,
"Be plucked up by the root, and be planted in the sea,
and it would obey you." …

If you have faith as a grain of mustard seed,
you shall say to this mountain,
"Move hence to yonder place," and it shall move,
and nothing shall be impossible unto you.

Luke 17:6, Matthew 17:20; cf. KJV

The material world is a fabrication of the higher mind. Even sensory phenomena are only aspects or experiences of the mind, as is the body itself. When the mind is sufficiently controlled and concentrated, the sensory world can be increasingly manipulated at will. Control of the mind and an increase in faith develop naturally together.

Mystics point out that the performance of miracles is a path of egotism, of setting up one's own will in opposition to the divine will, and those of a higher order do not indulge in such displays. They refer to them as party tricks, distractions or seductions to waylay seekers on their inner journey, catching them by their curiosity and pulling them from the narrow path that leads to God.

According to Mark, Matthew and Luke

Yet the gospels record that Jesus performed not just one or two miracles, but hundreds and thousands of them. Mark, Matthew and Luke, in particular, record in a number of separate places that he healed *all* those who were brought to him, from all the surrounding areas and countries. The gatherings must have been multinational as well as multilingual:

> And Jesus went about all Galilee, teaching in their synagogues, and preaching the gospel of the kingdom, and healing all manner of sickness and all manner of disease among the people. And his fame went throughout all Syria; and they brought unto him all the sick people who were afflicted with various diseases and torments, and those who were possessed with devils, and those who were mad, and those who were paralysed; and he healed them. And there followed him great multitudes of people from Galilee, and from Decapolis, and from Jerusalem, and from Judaea, and from beyond Jordan.
>
> *Matthew 4:23–25; cf. KJV*

And again:

> And when they had passed over (the Sea of Galilee), they came to the land of Gennesaret, and drew close to the shore. And when they had disembarked, the people immediately recognized him, and ran through the whole area, and began to bring sick people on their pallets to him, to any place where they heard that he was.
>
> And wherever he went – into villages, or cities, or country – they laid the sick in the streets, and besought him that they might touch if it were but the border of his garment; and as many as touched him were made whole.
>
> *Mark 6:53–56; cf. KJV, RSV*

The gospels contain a number of other similar assertions concerning the many miracles of Jesus. It is noteworthy, however, that a high proportion of the specific miracles related by the three synoptic writers are to be found in Mark's gospel, which is almost certainly the primary written source of these particular tales. The healing of "Simon's wife's mother" who "lay sick of a fever",[2] of a "leper... beseeching him",[3] of "one sick of the palsy",[4] of a man "which had a withered hand",[5] Jesus asleep in the boat and awakening to calm a "great storm of wind",[6] the healing of the Gadarene demoniac,[7] the raising from the dead of the daughter of Jairus, one of the "rulers of the synagogue" (*i.e.* a synagogue official), into which is inserted the healing of a "woman with an issue of blood twelve years",[8] of an epileptic "who foams, and gnashes with his teeth",[9] and of a blind man at Jericho[10] – all these occur in *Mark, Matthew,* and *Luke.*

The major variations are *Matthew*'s omission of the escapade of the four men who make a hole in the roof of a house in order to lower a paralytic man into Jesus' presence,[11] and the one blind man and one demoniac of *Mark* and *Luke* who become two apiece in *Matthew.*[12] Additionally, *Mark* and *Matthew* tell the stories of the cursing of the barren fig tree,[13] include a second "loaves and fishes" story in the feeding of the four thousand,[14] and relate that Jesus cast out a devil from the "young daughter" of "a Greek, a Syro-Phoenician" woman.[15]

Luke does not follow them. Perhaps he thought that the spurious cursing and killing of a fig tree because it failed to provide out-of-season fruit for Jesus to be too far-fetched. Jesus, he must have thought, would never have been so petulant nor so ignorant of the seasons. His omission of the second and almost identical feeding of the multitude was probably on grounds of space which, from his frequent paraphrasing and shortening, he was clearly anxious to conserve. And considering the story of the Syro-Phoenician woman's daughter, where Jesus at first refuses to heal the girl because the woman is not a Jew, Luke, with his gospel for the gentiles, must have felt the story not only to be inappropriate for his purposes but also uncharacteristic of the unprejudiced and all-loving Jesus.

Blindness, deafness, dumbness, paralysis, leprosy and so on require no medical skill to diagnose and name, and the synoptic writers seem eager to include stories of healing from all such conspicuous conditions. Mark also includes stories of the healing of a deaf man[16] and a blind man at Bethsaida.[17] Matthew and Luke relate stories concerning the healing of a dumb man[18] and the healing of the paralysed servant of a Roman centurion.[19] Luke tells the tale of how Jesus healed ten lepers[20] at one time, and raised from death the only son of a widow,[21] while Matthew adds a second story concerning the healing of two more blind men.[22]

Mark, then, is the foremost recorder of miracle stories in the synoptic gospels. Nine out of his fourteen miracle stories are related almost verbatim by Matthew and Luke, and a further three are copied across by Matthew. Matthew and Luke between them supply only five further stories, all of which are repeats to one extent or another of Mark's prior pattern.

Who, then, was Mark? How much reliance can be placed upon his narration? And what was the source of his stories? The honest answer is that nobody really knows. All that can be said is that the compiler of Mark's gospel seems to have been far more interested in miracle stories than in Jesus' actual teachings. It is one of his primary rationales for belief in Jesus as the Son of God, who would soon be returning to this world.

Whoever Mark was, the last thing he expected is that his gospel would become the focus of belief for the next two thousand years. So far as he was concerned, the last times were at hand, and he did not expect there to be another two thousand years. One can only surmise what his reaction would have been if he had known that future scholars and others would pore over his words, trying to extract from them the last trace of meaning and information.

According to John

The compiler of John's gospel has a different approach to Jesus' miracles. To begin with he relates only seven miracles, each one having been very obviously selected. As in *Mark,* they are also depicted as signs that Jesus is the Son of God. However, although he does suggest in passing that Jesus performed "many miracles"[23] (unless this is a later interpolation), at no point does he say that Jesus went about healing everybody of all and every kind of disease. On the contrary, when Jesus comes to the pool of Bethesda, he sees a "great multitude of invalids, of blind, lame, and paralysed people". But while there is little doubt that Mark would have had them all cry out to Jesus for help, followed by his healing them all, in John's story, Jesus singles out one man only and *asks* him if he would like to be made well again:

> Now there is at Jerusalem by the sheep market a pool, which is called in the Hebrew tongue Bethesda, having five porticos. In these lay a great multitude of invalids, of blind, lame, and paralysed people, waiting for the moving of the water. For an angel went down at a certain time into the pool, and disturbed the water; and the first person to enter after this disturbing of the water was cured of whatever ailment he had.
>
> And a certain man was there, who had been ill for thirty-eight years. When Jesus saw him lying there, and knew that he had been there a long time in that condition, he said to him, "Do you want to be made whole?"
>
> *John 5:2–5; cf. KJV, NJB*

The man is subsequently healed, and the reader is left to presume that the others were left just as they were.

John is also aware that one good story beats by far a myriad loose ones. He therefore makes each of his seven carefully chosen stories into a cameo, thereby heightening the 'wonder' element of each miracle. The man at the pool of Bethesda, for instance, had been there thirty-eight years without improvement and without – apparently – ever getting down to the water in time.

Similarly, John's 'raising from the dead' story outdoes all the others. Lazarus has not just died, he has been dead four days and, as his sister Martha points out, "Lord, by this time he stinketh."[24] John is nothing if not graphic, for at Jesus' command Lazarus then "came forth, bound hand and foot with graveclothes: and his face was bound about with a napkin".[25] The scene is worthy of the grizzliest horror story.

Again, when John has Jesus heal a blind man, it is not just someone who has recently suffered a deterioration of sight. It is the most difficult of all cases, a man "which was blind from his birth".[26]

But perhaps the most significant of all the differences in John's approach to Jesus' miracles is that he uses three out of his seven parables as a means of giving Jesus' teachings. While in the synoptic gospels, Jesus only upbraids the people for their lack of faith or praises them for the faith which has resulted in their being healed, John makes the story of the feeding of the five thousand into the starting point for a discourse on the true "Bread from heaven".[27] Similarly, the man who was blind from birth becomes the focus of a discourse on spiritual blindness, while the raising of Lazarus is at the centre of a discussion on death and resurrection. Additionally, a comment from a certain Nicodemus concerning Jesus' ability to perform miracles being proof that he is a "teacher come from God", leads – by one of those odd *non sequiturs* so characteristic of John's gospel – into a short discourse on being spiritually "born again".[28]

Furthermore, characteristic of his style, John's remaining miracle stories all possess a symbolic significance, as with many of the incidents related in his gospel. The story of the Samaritan woman at the well is an integral part of a short discourse on Living Water.[29] The man at the pool of Bethesda[30] is chosen by Jesus for healing out of a multitude of sick people, which symbolizes the small number of souls that are drawn to a master out of the many spiritually sick people of this world, who have been here for so long a time. Even the place of his healing, "having five porches" may be symbolic of the "five trees" or mansions of the Word mentioned in the *Gospel of Thomas* and the *Second Book of Jeu*,[31] where true healing takes place. Likewise, the miracle of turning water into wine at a marriage feast symbolizes the transformation of the water of worldliness into the wine of spirituality.

Only three of John's seven miracles appear in the synoptic gospels and, of these, two are modified. The paralysed servant of a Roman centurion of Capernaum in *Matthew* and *Luke* becomes the fevered son of a nobleman in *John*,[32] though other elements of the story are identifiably the same, and in

John's version of the feeding of the five thousand, the "loaves" gain a touch of character, becoming "barley loaves".[33] Only John's story of Jesus' walking on the water remains essentially the same.[34]

Altogether, the author of John's gospel brings in his miracles with great circumspection, and they are told more as allegories or parables than as raw miracle stories to be wondered at. By no means does he spread them around liberally and gratuitously in the manner of Mark, Matthew, and Luke. In the total structure of his gospel, each miracle is made to play a definite part aimed at conveying spiritual teachings. In fact, according to John, Jesus himself decries the importance of miracles. The nobleman, for instance, is rebuked for wanting a sign:

> Then said Jesus unto him, "Except you see signs and wonders, you will not believe."
>
> *John 4:48; cf. KJV*

Similarly, in *Mark,* Jesus comments adversely about those who want to gain faith through witnessing miracles, as in his response to the man with an epileptic son:

> O faithless generation, how long shall I be with you?
> How long shall I suffer you? Bring him unto me.
>
> *Mark 9:19, KJV*

And to the Pharisees:

> And the Pharisees came forth, and began to question him, seeking of him a sign from heaven, testing him. And he sighed deeply in his spirit, and said, "Why does this generation look for a sign? Verily I say unto you, there shall no sign be given unto this generation."
>
> *Mark 8:11–12; cf. KJV*

On the other hand, in *Matthew* and *Luke,* the centurion of Capernaum – who had requested Jesus to simply say the word so that his servant should be healed – is praised for his faith:

> When Jesus heard it, he marvelled, and said to them that followed, "Verily I say unto you, I have not found such great faith, no, not in Israel."
>
> *Matthew 8:10; cf. KJV*

All in all, despite Mark's multiple miracle stories, Jesus seems to have had an aversion to performing miracles. He also did not like them being made public. In many places, he specifically instructs the fortunate recipients of his favour to tell no one about it, though the reverse is usually the result:

> And he charged them that they should tell no man; but the more he charged them, the more widely they published it.
>
> *Mark 7:36; cf. KJV*

In fact, the compilers of *Mark, Matthew,* and *Luke* – by relating the miracle stories – took no account of Jesus' feelings on the matter, presumably because they assumed that it did not apply to them.

As fascinating as it may be to witness physical miracles, it is difficult to conceive how miracles in themselves can confer spirituality or even faith. Spirituality and faith develop through spiritual practice, through purification of the mind, cleansing of its innumerable impure tendencies, and elimination of the ego. How can simply being a witness to a miracle cleanse the mind or engender faith?

What helps a person is personal experience. Sometimes, a master may perform what might be called a miracle on behalf of a disciple, but that miracle is personal and is tailored exactly to that individual's need. It matches their stage of development and trend of mind so precisely that the personal message of the miracle is driven firmly home. This can help to generate faith in that individual. But it is a special and personal grace from master to disciple, and is meant to be kept private. As soon as a person begins to talk about it, then the ego comes into play, and the individual starts to lose whatever has been given. This is why Jesus never wanted people to broadcast what he had done for them. Perhaps, it was not so much his own humility as his desire for those so helped to reap the maximum benefit.

The help given by a master is always both spiritual and lasting. After all, even those that Jesus cured – if indeed he did so – must all have died within a few decades. And the world still had, and still has, no dearth of illness and suffering. But those particular souls, if the message was understood spiritually, would have benefited immensely – spiritually.

And as for miracle stories that are passed from one person to another, changing as time goes by, it is difficult to see how any spiritual benefit can be gained from them. They are more likely to attract attention to the physical world, turning the mind away from God. It is the impact of the miracle upon the individual concerned at that particular point in his spiritual evolution which constitutes the reason why a master performs a miracle. And not even the recipient himself can convey the nature of that personal impact, should he ever wish to do so.

It does seem most likely, therefore, that the miracle stories concerning Jesus are greatly exaggerated. He may have performed some miracles, but not as many as are attributed to him and not in such an obvious manner. Even from an analysis of the stories themselves, one becomes dubious of their authenticity, for the narratives do not hang together convincingly. Moreover, masters are great artists of subtlety and never make a public exhibition of themselves, nor do they try to generate faith by such displays. But miracle stories do get told and passed on, becoming amplified and externalized in the process. This is in the nature of the human mind.

Apostolic Miracles

Mark, followed by Matthew and Luke, reports that not only did Jesus himself perform miracles, but that so did his disciples. When Jesus sends his apostles to go and give spiritual discourses, Mark claims that he also gave them the power to effect cures, cast out devils and so on. John, however, makes no such comment. In fact, he says that even John the Baptist "did no miracle".[35]

No specific apostolic miracles are described in the gospels, but in *Acts,* as well as in practically all the apocryphal writings concerning the apostles, the apostles continue in the synoptic tradition of Jesus by healing all and everybody. Moreover, their miracles and those of Jesus become one of the key factors in proving that their preaching was correct and that Jesus was the Son of God. The writer of *Acts,* for example, claims:

> By the hands of the apostles were many signs and wonders wrought among the people.... And the number of those who came to believe in the Lord steadily increased, multitudes of both men and women. So much so that they brought forth the sick into the streets, and laid them on beds and couches, that at the least the shadow of Peter passing by might overshadow some of them. And a large number of people came from the cities around Jerusalem, bringing with them their sick folks, and those who were tormented by unclean spirits; and they were healed, every one.
>
> *Acts 5:12, 14–16; cf. KJV*

Among the many miracles related in the apocryphal writings, perhaps one of the most entertaining is Peter's raising from the dead of a sardine that he happened to see hanging in a shop window. Such stories exemplify the extent to which imagination can take over:

> And Peter turned and saw a herring (sardine) hung in a window, and taking it, he said to the people: "If you were to see this swimming in the water like a fish, would you be able to believe in him whom I preach?" And they said with one voice: "Verily, we would believe you."
>
> Then he said – now there was a bath for swimming at hand: "In your name, O Jesu Christ, forasmuch as hitherto it is not believed in, in the sight of all these, live and swim like a fish." And he cast the herring

> into the bath, and it lived and began to swim. And all the people saw the fish swimming; and it did so not only at that hour: lest it should be said that it was a delusion (phantasm), he made it swim for a long time, so that they brought many people from all quarters and showed them the herring that was made a living fish, so that certain of the people even cast bread to it: and they saw that it was alive. And seeing this, many followed Peter and believed in the Lord.
>
> *Acts of Peter 13; cf. ANT p.316*

Paul, too, who is really the central character of *Acts,* is credited with many miracles. In fact, the writer declares that Paul had special gifts of healing:

> God wrought special miracles by the hands of Paul, such that handkerchiefs or aprons were taken from his body and were brought to the sick, and their diseases departed from them, and the evil spirits went out of them.
>
> *Acts 19:11–12; cf. KJV*

Paul also heals a man who had been a cripple since birth,[36] cures the son of a chief of his fever,[37] remains unaffected by the bite of a viper,[38] and raises a young man from the dead who, having fallen asleep during one of Paul's discourses, had fallen out of a third storey window and been killed.[39]

This all makes for entertaining and romantic reading. But its authenticity is doubtful, for turning to Paul's letters for some verification of these miracles, absolutely none can be discovered. He does speak, it is true, of those among his groups of converts who have the power to perform miracles, but he mentions it as one of a number of psychic 'gifts', such as talking with tongues, prophecy, and so on. He certainly makes no claim to possessing such powers himself, and the gift of miracles, as he describes, it seems to be more in the line of what people these days call a laying on of hands. It is certainly not in the same class as the miracles described in the synoptic gospels and in *Acts,* where everybody gets healed, regardless.

In fact, there is a significant contrast between the style of Paul's letters and that of *Acts.* His letters come across as the writings of a real person, writing to real people about real problems, trying to convince them of things he most fervently believed in. They ring true as genuine letters.

But much of *Acts,* like the narrative elements of the gospels, reads for the most part like fiction. Everything is too over the top and is worked up into something that seems more like romance than a genuine report of real events. Certainly, although Paul describes many things in his letters which he has said and done, he never mentions having performed any miracles. Indeed, quite apart from the sick being healed by his handkerchief or any other item of his clothing, Paul speaks quite candidly of his own serious illness and even those of his companions. If Paul had the power to perform miracles, he certainly did not use it on himself or his friends.

In *2 Corinthians,* for instance, he speaks of a particular chronic complaint – a "thorn in the flesh", of which he cannot rid himself, despite his prayer before God:

> And lest I should be exalted above measure through the abundance of the revelations, there was given to me a thorn in the flesh, the messenger of Satan to buffet me, lest I should be exalted above measure. For this thing I besought the Lord three times, that it might depart from me.
>
> *2 Corinthians 12:7–8; cf. KJV*

He takes his illness in a positive spirit as part of the Lord's means of keeping him humble because of all his "revelations", but he is clearly unable to shift the problem, whatever it may have been.

Likewise, he seems to have extended his stay among the Galatians due to illness, probably this same complaint, taking the opportunity to preach to them, though at the time of writing his letter, he seems to have fallen out of favour with them:

> You have never treated me in an unfriendly way before; indeed, you remember that it was an illness that first gave me the opportunity to preach the gospel to you, but though my illness was a trial to you, you did not show any distaste or revulsion; instead, you welcomed me as a messenger of God, as if I were Christ Jesus himself. What has happened to the utter contentment you had then? For I can testify to you that you would have plucked your eyes out, were that possible, and given them to me.
>
> *Galatians 4:12–15; cf. JB, NJB*

Again, he speaks of a friend who "nearly died":

> I thought it essential to send to you Epaphroditus, my brother and fellow-worker and companion-in-arms, since he came as your representative to look after my needs; because he was missing you all and was worrying because you had heard that he was ill. Indeed he was seriously ill and nearly died; but God took pity on him – and not only on him but also on me, to spare me one grief on top of another.
>
> So I am sending him back as promptly as I can, so that you will have the joy of seeing him again, and that will be some comfort to me in my distress. Welcome him in the Lord, then, with all joy; hold

> people like him in honour, because it was for Christ's work that he came so near to dying, risking his life to do the duty to me which you could not do yourselves.
>
> *Philippians 2:25–30, NJB*

These letters are clearly different from the hyperbole of *Acts* and the gospels. Again, a reader is led to the conclusion that – at best – the miracle stories are the result of some fact plus a great deal of imagination and later elaboration.

Metaphors for Spiritual Truths

The point of greatest significance in a study of these miracles is that practically all of them, whether in *John* or in the synoptic gospels, are also used by the mystical writers of the time – and often by Jesus, too – as metaphors for spiritual truths. All souls in this world are spiritually blind, deaf, and dumb. Practically everyone is crippled and has forgotten how to walk straight. People are carrying a heavy burden of weaknesses and sins from which they need to be healed. Their willpower is paralysed and withered by attraction to the world of the senses. In fact, the souls here have become spiritually dead and full of darkness, needing to be raised from the dead, to come out of the tomb of the body, not after four days but after many ages. Spiritually, everybody "stinketh" with the accumulated sins of many lifetimes!

To accomplish this, a spiritual physician is required to help overcome the feverish activities of the mind, to learn how to walk upon the stormy waters of this world, to cast out the devils and demons of human weakness from within and to overcome the Devil himself. With the help of a Son of God, the soul must bathe in the pool of Living Water and come up healed after many years of infirmity without anyone previously giving a helping hand in the taking of that dip. The hungry and thirsty souls of this world need to eat the true Bread of Life and to drink the wine of divine love. The insipidness of their water needs to be converted into the first quality wine of spirituality.

Masters come and give their pure and spiritual teachings, but soon after their departure and even during their lifetime, the human mind takes over, externalizing and literalizing the mystic truths they teach. It would come as no surprise, then, if many of Jesus' supposed miracles turned out to be externalizations of spiritual realities should the real history of the New Testament writings ever be discovered.

See also: **blindness** (6.2), **deafness** (6.2), **disease** (6.2), **dumbness** (6.2), **healing**, **miracles**, **paralysis** (6.2), **physician** (7.1), **wounds** (6.2).

1. Much of the material for this entry is taken from *The Gospel of Jesus, GJ* pp.580–632.
2. *Mark* 1:29–31, *KJV; cf. Matthew* 8:14–15, *Luke* 4:38–39.

3. *Mark* 1:40–45, *KJV; cf. Matthew* 8:2–4, *Luke* 5:12–16.
4. *Mark* 2:1–12, *KJV; cf. Matthew* 9:1–8, *Luke* 5:17–26.
5. *Mark* 3:1–6, *KJV; cf. Matthew* 12:9–14, *Luke* 6:6–11.
6. *Mark* 4:35–41, *KJV; cf. Matthew* 8:18,23–27, *Luke* 8:22–25.
7. *Mark* 5:1–20, *Matthew* 8:28–34, *Luke* 8:26–39.
8. *Mark* 5:21–43, *KJV; cf. Matthew* 9:18–26, *Luke* 8:40–56.
9. *Mark* 9:14–29; *cf. KJV; cf. Matthew* 17:14–21, *Luke* 9:37–42.
10. *Mark* 10:46–52, *Matthew* 20:29–34, *Luke* 18:35–43.
11. *Mark* 2:1–5.
12. *Matthew* 8:28–34, 9:27–31; *Mark* 5:1–17, 10:46–52; *Luke* 8:26–39, 18:35–43.
13. *Mark* 11:12–14, 20–25, *Matthew* 21:18–19, 20–22.
14. *Mark* 8:1–10, *Matthew* 15:32–39.
15. *Mark* 7:24–30, *Matthew* 15:21–28.
16. *Mark* 7:31–37.
17. *Mark* 8:22–26.
18. *Matthew* 12:43–45, *Luke* 11:24–26.
19. *Matthew* 8:5–13, *Luke* 7:1–10.
20. *Luke* 17:12–19.
21. *Luke* 7:11–16.
22. *Matthew* 9:27–31.
23. *John* 11:47.
24. *John* 11:39.
25. *John* 11:44.
26. *John* 9:1.
27. *John* 6:31–58.
28. *John* 3:1*ff.*
29. *John* 4:1–15.
30. *John* 5:1–15.
31. *Gospel of Thomas* 36:19, *NHS20* pp.60–61; *Second Book of Jeu* 119:50, *BC* pp.166–67.
32. *John* 4:43–54, *Matthew* 8:5–13, *Luke* 7:1–10.
33. *John* 6:1–15.
34. *John* 6:16–21.
35. *John* 10:41.
36. *Acts* 14:8–11.
37. *Acts* 28:7–8.
38. *Acts* 28:3–6.
39. *Acts* 20:9–10.

mu'jizāt (A/P) (sg. A. *mu'jizah,* P. *mu'jizat*) *Lit.* miracles; specifically, evidentiary or manifest miracles performed by a prophet *(nabī),* rather than the *karāmāt* (gifts, favours, miracles) of a saint *(walī). Muʿjizāt* are understood as public demonstrations by a prophet of his power, performed to convince people of the veracity of his message. *Karāmāt* are understood as the miracles of a saint.

Both the *Qur'ān* and the *ḥadīth* speak of the miracles of past prophets. Islam therefore accepts miracles as a reality, for to deny them would be to deny the authority of the sacred texts. However, no miracles *(muʿjizāt)* are explicitly attributed to Muḥammad in the *Qur'ān,* nor does the Prophet make any claims to the possession of miraculous powers. In explanation of this, tradition records Muḥammad as saying:

> Every prophet was given miracles *(āyāt)* because of which, people believed. But what I have been given is divine inspiration *(waḥy)* which *Allāh* has revealed to me. So I hope that my followers will outnumber the followers of the other prophets on the Day of Resurrection.
>
> *Ḥadīth Ṣaḥīḥ al-Bukhārī 6:61.504, HSB*[1]

Despite this comment, there are a number of miracles attributed to Muḥammad in the *ḥadīth.* When the Prophet and his companions have insufficient water for the ritual ablution, Muḥammad puts his hands in a bowl and water runs from his fingers.[2] When they have little or no drinking water, he makes a spring flow in abundance.[3] When Medina is suffering from a drought, he makes it rain profusely, and when it rains too much, he clears the clouds from above Medina itself, but not from the surrounding countryside.[4] He provides butter and barley; foretells a storm; avoids harm from a sword-wielding, would-be assassin;[5] and sends a pair of lights to guide two companions in the dark.[6] And in two well-known miracle stories, often interpreted mystically and based upon enigmatic passages in the *Qur'ān,* Muḥammad splits the moon in two *(shaqq al-qamar),*[7] and travels from Mecca to Jerusalem and back in one night *(al-Isrá', al-Miʿrāj).*[8]

Unlike the *karāmāt* of saints or friends of God, it is always said that *muʿjizāt* of prophets are performed with the express intention of attracting people:

> It is incumbent upon a prophet *(payghambar)* to make his prophetic appeal in a thoroughgoing manner by calling people to his religion and performing miracles *(muʿjizāt).* In his turn, the friend of God *(walī)* must carry out his mission of friendship with God in an equally definitive way by not calling people to himself and by concealing his miraculous powers *(karāmāt).* It is permitted for him to let people believe that what he does is a divine deception. The one exception is that he is allowed on occasion to display his powers *(karāmāt)* to his followers.
>
> These powers *(karāmāt),* of course, are not always at the disposal of the friend of God *(walī).* They sometimes occur spontaneously and involuntarily, and sometimes arise out of prayer. In contrast, miracles

> *(muʿjizāt)* are always at the disposal of a prophet *(payghambar)* and occur at his request. It is not possible for a prophet to be unaware of his position, while it is often the case that a friend of God is unaware that he is a friend of God.
>
> A prophet has no choice but to be involved with miracles *(muʿjizāt)* for he has been delegated by God to lead people, and people need to be aware of the gnosis and sincerity of his prophecy, for the very sincerity of his prophecy is a miracle *(muʿjizat)*. The friend of God, however, has no such obligation to people, for he is not so delegated. Indeed, others need not be aware that he is a friend of God, nor is it necessary that he himself should be aware of it.
>
> *Maybudī, Kashf al-Asrār, KA7 p.232; cf. in SSE8 p.61*

Although the purpose of *muʿjizāt* is to generate faith, things do not always work out that way. In the *Qur'ān,* as in the Bible, the "signs" of the prophets are often ridiculed:

> But when Our signs were shown to them, they said: "This is plain sorcery!" And although their souls were convinced by them, through iniquity and arrogance, they rejected them.
>
> *Qur'ān 27:13–14; cf. AYA, KPA, MGK*

Ibn al-ʿArabī refers to this passage when pointing out that faith in the prophets does not come "by the furnishing of proofs", but by the casting of divine "light" into the heart:

> It may happen that a messenger brings about a miracle *(muʿjizah),* that it is known that it is a miracle *(muʿjizah),* and that the observers acquire knowledge of the truthfulness of the messenger, but that they are not given faith in him. "They denied them, though their souls acknowledged them, wrongfully and out of pride." Hence you come to know that faith is not given by the furnishings of proofs. On the contrary, it is a divine "light which God throws into the heart of whomsoever He will of His servants." It may come after proofs, and it may come after no proof whatsoever.
>
> *Ibn al-ʿArabī, Meccan Revelations 2:374.24, FMIA4 (2:187) p.6, SPK p.194*

Rūmī draws the same meaning when he allegorizes the story of David and Goliath as a spiritual miracle. Goliath is the "wicked man", the essence of negativity in human beings, that is killed by a single 'stone' from the 'sling' of the prophet or master. Then the "Breath" of the master, the creative power, opens the "spiritual eyes" and "bestows . . . everlasting life" on the spiritually "dead" souls of this world, and they rediscover their true relationship with the Divine. This, says Rūmī, is the "essence of all miracles *(muʿjizāt)*". He is addressing David, as a prophet:

> Hundreds of thousands of spiritual eyes were opened,
> and through your Breath were made ready for the Unseen;
> And that (miracle) is stronger than all those (external miracles),
> for this one is lasting:
> You bestow the life that endures forever.
> This indeed is the essence of all miracles *(muʿjizāt),*
> that it should bestow everlasting life on the dead.
> The wicked man was killed
> and a whole world was quickened with life:
> Everyone once again became a devoted servant of God.
>
> *Rūmī, Maśnavī III:2500–3; cf. MJR4 p.140*

Rūmī also explains that miracles do not run counter to the laws of causality. The prophets simply use higher causes than those accessible to people whose consciousness is limited to the phenomenal world:

> This (external) cause is produced by that (spiritual) cause:
> when did a cause ever proceed from itself without a cause?
> Those causes that guide the prophets on their way
> are higher than these (external) causes.
> That (spiritual) cause makes this (external) cause operative,
> sometimes, again, it makes it fruitless and ineffectual.
> Ordinary minds are familiar with this (external) cause,
> but the prophets are familiar with those (higher) causes.
>
> *Rūmī, Maśnavī I:843–46; cf. MJR2 p.47*

Many Sufis, however, have set small store by miracles. They say that the greatest miracle is to control one's own mind:

> If you can walk on water,
> you are no better than a straw.
> If you can fly in the air,
> you are no better than a fly.
> Conquer your heart,
> that you may become somebody.
>
> *Anṣārī, Song of the Dervish; cf. PMA p.36*

Rūmī observes that masters do not perform miracles and create an outward show to attract seekers to themselves. Nor do miracles in themselves create faith. Those who are meant to follow a master are drawn to him automatically, by an inner "affinity":

> Miracles *(muʿjizāt)* are not the cause of faith *(īmān);*
> It is the scent of affinity *(jinsīyat)*
> that attracts to itself qualities of the same kind.
> Miracles *(muʿjizāt)* are wrought
> for the purpose of subjugating the foe:
> The scent of affinity is only for the winning of hearts.
> A foe is subjugated, but not a friend:
> how should a friend have his neck bound?
>
> *Rūmī, Maśnavī VI:1176–78; cf. MJR6 p.324*

See also: **karāmāt**.

1. *Cf. Ḥadīth Ṣaḥīḥ al-Bukhārī* 9:92.379, *HSB.*
2. *E.g. Ḥadīth Ṣaḥīḥ al-Bukhārī* 1:4.170, 190, 4:56.779, *HSB; Ḥadīth Ṣaḥīḥ Muslim* 30:5656–59, *HSM.*
3. *E.g. Ḥadīth Ṣaḥīḥ al-Bukhārī* 1:7.340, *HSB; Ḥadīth Ṣaḥīḥ Muslim* 30:5662, *HSM.*
4. *E.g. Ḥadīth Ṣaḥīḥ al-Bukhārī* 8:73.115, *HSB.*
5. *E.g. Ḥadīth Ṣaḥīḥ Muslim* 30:5661–67, *HSM.*
6. *E.g. Ḥadīth Ṣaḥīḥ al-Bukhārī* 1:8.454, 4:56.833, *HSB.*
7. *E.g. Ḥadīth Ṣaḥīḥ al-Bukhārī* 4:56.831, *HSB; Ḥadīth Ṣaḥīḥ Muslim* 39:6724–30, *HSM; cf. Qur'ān* 54:1.
8. *E.g. Ḥadīth Ṣaḥīḥ al-Bukhārī* 4:55.606–7, 640, 647–48, 5:58.226–28, 6:60.232–33, 240, 7:69.482, 8:77.610, *HSB; Ḥadīth Ṣaḥīḥ Muslim* 1:309–22, 30:5859, *HSM; cf. Qur'ān* 17:1, 53:13–18.

ñāṇa-vipphārā-iddhi (Pa) *Lit.* power *(iddhi)* of penetrating *(vipphāra)* knowledge *(ñāṇa);* the power of intervention *(vipphāra)* by knowledge; the power of deep, discriminating insight and awareness, enabling one to perceive the otherwise hidden causes of things; hence, interpreting *vipphāra* as 'intervention', the power to intervene in and to change bodily or other natural processes and events as a result of a higher knowledge and awareness; thus, a protective power that enables one to remain unhurt in danger;[1] one of the commonly listed *iddhis* (powers); synonymous with *samādhi-vipphārā-iddhi* (power of penetrating concentration).

This power of intervention by knowledge is discussed in the *Paṭisambhidā-magga,*[2] the *Vibhanga,* and the *Visuddhimagga.*[3] According to an anecdote in the *Visuddhimagga,* when a certain Bakkula, the baby son of a councillor of Kosambī, was being bathed in the river Yamunā, he slipped into the water due to the negligence of the nurse, and was swallowed by a fish:

> When the Venerable Bakkula as an infant was being bathed in the river on an auspicious day, he fell into the stream through the negligence of his nurse. A fish swallowed him, and eventually came to the bathing place at Vārāṇasī. Where it was caught by a fisherman and sold to a rich man's wife. The fish interested her, and thinking to cook it herself, she slit it open. When she did so, she saw the child like a golden image in the fish's stomach. She was overjoyed, thinking, "At last I have got a son." The Venerable Bakkula's safe survival in a fish's stomach in his last existence is called power of intervention of knowledge *(ñāṇa-vipphārā-iddhi)* because it was brought about by the influence of the *arahanta*-path knowledge due to be obtained by him in that life.
>
> *Buddhaghosa, Visuddhimagga 12:27, PTSV p.379; cf. PPVM p.374*

According to the more complete story, the rich man whose wife had found the baby looked after the child as though he was her own. Her husband was also a councillor, and later on, when the true parents of the child were discovered, the king decided that the boy should be raised by both the families. He hence became known as Bakkula (two families, *bi* + *kula*). His safety was brought about by the holiness of his past lives, which manifested as *ñāṇa-vipphārā-iddhi.* The *Bakkula Sutta* records that Bakkula lived a prosperous life until the age of eighty, when he attended a discourse by the Buddha. Renouncing the world, it took him only eight days to reach enlightenment, following which he lived as a monk for eighty years,[4] dying at the age of one hundred and sixty.[5]

The *Visuddhimagga* refers to two further stories in which children in dangerous circumstances are saved as a result of their possessing *ñāṇa-vipphārā-iddhi,* arising automatically from the advanced state of holiness they had attained as a result of spiritual practice in previous lives. In one instance, a baby is saved from his mother's womb on the funeral pyre, after the mother had died. The baby cries out when slightly wounded by a stake that pierces his mother's body. In the other story, a child is inadvertently left outside the city gates when they are locked at night, but survives the presence of numerous "wild beasts and spirits".[6]

See also: **iddhi**.

1. See "Human world," *Buddhist Dictionary, PBD.*
2. *Paṭisambhidāmagga* 22, *PTSP2* p.211, *PDPM* p.382.
3. Buddhaghosa, *Visuddhimagga* 12:22, 26–29, *PTSV* pp.378–79, *PPVM* pp.374–75.
4. *Majjhima Nikāya* 124, *Bakkula Sutta, PTSM3* pp.124–28.

5. *Sumangala Vilāsinī, SVD2* p.413.
6. Buddhaghosa, *Visuddhimagga* 12:28–29, *PTSV* pp.374–75, *PPVM* p.375.

oho rangi (Mo) *Lit.* awakening *(oho)* the sky *(rangi),* arousing the heavens; thunder rousing; manifestation of the sound of thunder by controlling the elements and the forces of nature with inner personal power *(mana)* and a high level of magic *(mākutu).*

Thunder rousing is an important traditional Māori rite performed by powerful *tohunga* (priestly adepts) of the highest order. Through focused concentration, repetition of *karakia* (sacred incantations) and striking stones together, thunder is caused to resound in the heavens, thereby imparting *mana* or sacred power to a gathering of people. *Tohunga* of the highest order also had the power to banish thunder.

One form of thunder, known as *puoro rangi* (singing sky), produces a rumbling sound, while *te rangi whakararā* (the rattling sky) is marked by sharp claps of thunder. According to the old Māori priestly tradition, the manifesting of thunder did not fall into the lower category of *mākutu* or magic. Elsdon Best describes this ritual, performed at an end-of-term ceremony at the *whare wānanga* (school of sacred learning) of New Zealand's Kahungunu tribe:

> One of the teaching experts now proceeded to generate fire by friction in the well-known Polynesian manner. This was an *ahi tapu* (sacred fire), and all such ceremonial fires had to be so generated. New, unsullied fire was essential; no brands from another fire might be utilized. As this act was being performed, another of the priestly experts busied himself in intoning a *tapu* (sacred) chant appropriate to the occasion. The prominent feature of this final function was the performance by the principal expert of the highly important, not to say marvellous, rite of *oho rangi.* This act, which was nothing less than causing thunder to resound, was viewed as the culminating performance of the session, inasmuch as it not only proved the *mana* (power) of the performer, but also imparted the same necessary quality to the whole of the proceedings of the session. This implied power over the forces of nature, as possessed by high-class *tohunga,* was a matter of abiding faith in the Māori mind, and apparently still is in many cases.... One of the two forms of thunder, known as *puoro rangi* and *te rangi whakararā,* was called upon in these necromantic rites. The former has a rumbling sound, while the latter is marked by sharp detonations.
>
> *Elsdon Best, Maori School of Learning, MSLB*

In another instance, Elsdon Best records the rite being performed over an infant:

> When the *oho rangi* divinatory rite was performed over an infant, and thunder resounded in the east or north, then the welfare of the infant was assured; but if in the south or west, then the result was a luckless child.
>
> *Elsdon Best, Maori Religion and Mythology, MRM2 p.616*

Whaitiri pakapaka (dry thunder) is thunder unaccompanied by rain; however, according to some tribes, both thunder and rain could be produced:

> When certain calamities befell a community, then tears were demanded from *Rangi,* the Sky Parent, and so a thunderstorm with rain was summoned by the powers of magic; thus were the highborn dead wept for.
>
> *Elsdon Best, Maori Religion and Mythology, MRM2 p.118*

A modern witness to *oho rangi* describes an experience of this thunder:

> I believe I have witnessed this at a funeral – the most incredible, continuous, constant rumbling thunder and some loud outbursts that started the moment the family headed off from the funeral to the crematorium, and it continued for at least the next two to three hours until the wake ended. Such prolonged thunder is quite infrequent in New Zealand. It felt quite wonderful. Even Africa with its numerous thunderstorms never equalled it.
>
> *Janine Archer, Unpublished Note*

parakāya-pravesha, **paradeha-pravesha**, **parasharīra-āvesha** (S) *Lit.* entering *(pravesha, āvesha)* the body *(kāya, deha, sharīra)* of another *(para);* entering the body of another being. See **siddhi**.

pavan(a)-āhārī (S/H) *Lit.* eater *(āhārī)* of air *(pavana);* from *āhāra* (food); consumer of air; one who lives on *prāṇa,* meaning the subtle life energy in the body. The human body derives energy and sustenance from two sources: externally from food and drink, and internally from the *prāṇa* or life force. Most people eat far more than they need, with the result that much energy is unnecessarily consumed in digestion and storage of the excess. Eating less, within reason, actually gives a person more energy, rather than less.

As a person advances in meditation, contact with the inner source of all energy increases, and the need for external food diminishes. Some yogis and others have found that they can sustain themselves on the subtle life force or *prāṇa* itself.

See also: **siddhi**.

pradhāna-jaya (S) *Lit.* mastery *(jaya)* of nature *(pradhāna)*. See **siddhi**.

prākāmya (S) *Lit.* freedom of will, wilfulness; irresistible willpower or command; complete freedom of will; the power by which all impediments to one's will can be removed; the power to obtain anything merely by willing it to be so; the power to obtain anything desired.

See also: **siddhi**.

prāpti (S) *Lit.* advent, reach, range, occurrence; the power to enter or penetrate everywhere; the power to transport oneself anywhere one desires, even to distant places.

See also: **siddhi**.

prātihārya (S), **pāṭihāriya** (Pa) *Lit.* miracle, marvel, wonder, extra-ordinary event; transformation, metamorphosis; supernormal or miraculous power; the working of miracles.

Pali texts ascribe three kinds of miracle to the Buddha: the miracle of magic or psychic power *(iddhi-pāṭihāriya),* the miracle of mind reading *(ādesanā-pāṭihāriya),* and the miracle of teaching or instruction *(anusāsanī-pāṭihāriya).* By mind reading is meant actual awareness of the mental content of others, rather than guessing another's thoughts *(manesikā),* as mentioned in the *Dīgha Nikāya.*[1] Teaching or giving instruction in the *Dhamma* – of discrimination between right and wrong, and how to live properly; of the cycle of birth and death, and liberation from it; of enlightenment and tranquillity; of the practice of meditation; and so on – is regarded as a miracle because of the seemingly miraculous transformation it can have on a person's life.

After providing the standard description of *pāṭihāriya* given in the Pali *suttas,* the *Paṭisambhidāmagga* ('Path of Discrimination') goes on to maintain that success *(iddhi)* in renunciation, conquest of all impurities, attainment of the four states of meditative absorption *(jhānas),* and so forth, are also *pāṭihāriya* – miracles or transformations.[2]

According to the *Kevaḍḍha Sutta,* the Buddha disapproved of the first two kinds of miracle because they were generally used as a means of showing off or to impress the credulous. According to the story, Kevaḍḍha had asked the Buddha three times to instruct one of his monks to perform a miracle so that the people of the prosperous and populous city of Nālandā would have more faith in the Buddha. But the Buddha points out that miracles will not change a person's beliefs. If they are nonbelievers, they will simply find a way of explaining away a miracle:

> "Kevaḍḍha, there are these three miracles *(pāṭihāriya)* that I have declared, having directly known and realized them for myself. Which three? The miracle of psychic power *(iddhi-pāṭihāriya),* the miracle of mind reading *(ādesanā-pāṭihāriya),* and the miracle of instruction *(anusāsanī-pāṭihāriya).*
>
> "And what is the miracle of psychic power *(iddhi-pāṭihāriya)?* There is the case where a monk wields manifold psychic powers *(iddhi).* Having been one, he becomes many; having been many, he becomes one. He appears; he vanishes. He goes unimpeded through walls, ramparts, and mountains as if through space. He dives in and out of the earth as if it were water. He walks on water without sinking as if it were dry land. Sitting cross-legged, he flies through the air like a winged bird. With his hand, he touches and strokes even the sun and moon, so mighty and powerful. He exercises influence with his body, even as far as the *Brahmā* worlds.
>
> "Then someone who has faith and conviction in him sees him wielding manifold psychic powers,... exercising influence with his body even as far as the *Brahmā* worlds. He reports this to someone who has no faith and no conviction, telling him, 'Isn't it awesome. Isn't it astounding, how great the power, how great the prowess of this contemplative. Just now I saw him wielding manifold psychic powers,... exercising influence with his body even as far as the *Brahmā* worlds.'
>
> "Then the person without faith, without conviction, would say to the person with faith and with conviction: 'Sir, there is a charm called the *gandhārī* charm by which the monk wielded manifold psychic powers *(iddhi),*... exercising influence with his body even as far as the *Brahmā* worlds.' What do you think, Kevaḍḍha – isn't that what the man without faith, without conviction, would say to the man with faith and with conviction?"
>
> "Yes, lord, that's just what he would say."
>
> "Seeing this drawback to the miracle of psychic power *(iddhi-pāṭihāriya),* Kevaḍḍha, I feel horrified, humiliated, and disgusted with the miracle of psychic power *(iddhi-pāṭihāriya).*"
>
> *Dīgha Nikāya 11, Kevaḍḍha Sutta, PTSD1 pp.212–13, DNTB*

The Buddha likewise discusses mind reading:

> "And what is the miracle of mind reading *(ādesanā-pāṭihāriya)?* There is the case where a monk reads the minds, the mental events, the thoughts, the ponderings of other beings, other individuals, (saying), 'Such is your thinking, here is where your thinking is, thus is your mind.'"
>
> *Dīgha Nikāya 11, Kevaḍḍha Sutta, PTSD1 p.213, DNTB*

And again, the person with faith feels the miracles to be "awesome", and so on, while the sceptic suspects that it has been brought about by the "*maṇikā* charm", by which it was believed that the thoughts of others could be read. However, the miracle of transformation brought about through the teaching of the *Dhamma* is an altogether different matter:

> "And what is the miracle of instruction *(anusāsanī-pāṭihāriya)?* There is the case where a monk gives instruction in this way: 'Direct your thought in this way, don't direct it in that. Attend to things in this way, don't attend to them in that. Let go of this, enter and remain in that.' This, Kevaḍḍha, is called the miracle of instruction *(anusāsanī-pāṭihāriya).*
>
> "Furthermore, there is the case where a *tathāgata* appears in the world, worthy and rightly self-awakened. He teaches the *Dhamma* admirable in its beginning, admirable in its middle, admirable in its end. He proclaims the holy life both in its particulars and in its essence, entirely perfect, surpassingly pure.
>
> "A householder or householder's son, hearing the *Dhamma,* gains conviction in the *tathāgata* and reflects: 'Household life is confining, a dusty path. The life gone forth is like the open air. It is not easy living at home to practise the holy life totally perfect, totally pure, like a polished shell. What if I were to shave off my hair and beard, put on the ochre robes, and go forth from the household life into homelessness?'
>
> "So after some time he abandons his mass of wealth, large or small; leaves his circle of relatives, large or small; shaves off his hair and beard, puts on the ochre robes, and goes forth from the household life into homelessness.
>
> "When he has thus gone forth, he lives restrained by the rules of the monastic code, seeing danger in the slightest faults. Consummate in his virtue, he guards the doors of his senses, is possessed of mindfulness and alertness, and is content.... This, Kevaḍḍha, is called the miracle of instruction *(anusāsanī-pāṭihāriya).*"
>
> *Dīgha Nikāya 11, Kevaḍḍha Sutta, PTSD1 pp.214–15, DNTB*

The story is also told of a financier of Rājagaha who having arranged for a very expensive, carved sandalwood bowl to be placed on the top of a very high pole, promises to give it to any *brāhmaṇ* or *samaṇa* (holy man) who can fetch it down by using his psychic power *(pāṭihāriya)*. But when the Buddha's disciple Bhāradvāja accomplishes the feat, the Buddha rebukes him harshly.

> The Awakened One, the Blessed One, rebuked him: "It's not appropriate, Bhāradvāja, not fitting for a contemplative, improper, and not to be done. How can you display a superior human state, a wonder of psychic power *(pāṭihāriya)*, to lay people for the sake of a miserable wooden bowl?"
>
> *Vinaya Piṭaka, Cūlavagga 5:8, PTSV2 p.111, BMC2*

Given such stories, it is generally accepted in the *Theravāda* Pali texts that the Buddha discouraged the use of miracles. Later *Mahāyāna* texts, on the other hand, look more positively on the use of miracles. In fact, the *Mahāvastu* ('Great Story'), an early Buddhist text that is something of a missing link between the *Theravāda* and *Mahāyāna* traditions, relates a story in which the Buddha Dīpaṃkāra performs a miracle by suspending around his head a number of lotuses that had been thrown at his feet. The *Mahāvastu* then maintains:

> Exalted *buddhas* convince people by means of three miracles *(prātihārya)*: the miracle of magic power *(ṛiddhi-prātihārya)*, the miracle of mind reading *(ādeshanā-prātihārya)*, and the miracle of instruction *(anushāsanī-prātihārya)*. The five lotuses thrown at the exalted Dīpaṃkāra by the young *brāhmaṇ* Megha, those thrown by the young *brāhmaṇ* girl Prakṛiti, and those thrown by other people, stood over the Exalted One as a canopy of flowers so as to win power over men ready to be trained, and to bring joy and gladness to the young *brāhmaṇ* Megha. It was a canopy lovely and fair to behold, with four props, four entrances, and draped with festoons of fine cloth.
>
> *Mahāvastu 1:238, MHVA, MVJ1 pp.193–94*

See also: **abhijñā**, **iddhi**, **ṛiddhi**, **yamaka-pāṭihāriya**.

1. *Dīgha Nikāya* 1, *Brahmajāla Sutta* 19, *PTSD1* p.7.
2. *Paṭisambhidāmagga* 26, *PTSP2* pp.227–29, *PDPM* pp.395–96.

precognition The ability to foretell future events. See **clairvoyance**.

prophecy See **prophet** (7.1).

psychic experience, psychic phenomena Any experience of the paranormal, such as telepathy, the atmosphere of places, the subtle vibration of people, seeing auras, ghosts, *etc.;* any experience of things beyond the realm of the physical senses, yet below that of the astral and causal planes. Psychic experiences include the experience of anything in the realms of subtle material energies. Practices such as *haṭha yoga* (as practised in the West), *chigong, t'ai chi ch'uan,* acupuncture, and the like, all deal with the body's subtle energy system, and as such are likely to enhance a person's perception of subtle energy phenomena.

Individual psychic experience can sometimes be for the benefit of other human beings. George Fox (1624–1691), founder of the Society of Friends (Quakers), writes in his journal that he was the recipient of an experience ("I was come up in the spirit . . . into the paradise of God") during the course of which the hidden properties ("nature and virtues") of plants and all things in creation were revealed to him, such that he wondered momentarily whether he should take up the practice of medicine ("physic").[1] It can be presumed that it is from experiences of this nature that many of the herbal medicines used by the different cultures of the world have come into being, a significant proportion of which have been shown by scientific analysis to be of medicinal value. This particular psychic gift, given only to a few, must be a part of the natural economy, as indeed is the very existence of such naturally occurring plant substances. The substances in these plants are useful to the plants, to human beings, and to other creatures.

Psychic experiences can also be of the subtle emanations or vibrations of deeply spiritual people. In a diary entry for August 6th, 1958, Nancy Mayorga relates two experiences concerning her *guru* Swami Prabhavananda:

> I have always been sceptical of psychic phenomena or spiritual phenomena manifesting in the physical world. The young men of Calcutta were rational, sceptical, scientifically oriented, like me. They had greater experiences, but mine carry just as much conviction for me as theirs did for them. One night, when Swami Prabhavananda was lecturing on the *Bhagavad Gītā,* his robe had slipped back on his shoulders, and suddenly I saw that his whole body was glowing with light. It came from inside and it was all through him, as an iron bar glows with fire. I was absolutely stunned, and almost overwhelmed with bliss. The same thing happened once again on another evening. Later I told him. I asked him if others had told him that. He said not. He made no comment, but he laughed a little. I would give anything to see it again, but no effort of mine can bring it about. One night, someone asked him the meaning of the light that artists paint around the heads of holy people. He said, "People of high spirituality have a light that glows in and around them, and there are other people who

> are sensitive to that light and can actually see it." Then he added, smiling a little, "I have known American women who could see that light." Everyone laughed.
>
> This other experience may seem a little less spectacular, but it was no less impressive and moving to me. One Sunday morning when he was lecturing, his hands, which are good-looking hands, took on a tremendous, unearthly beauty for me. Without thought or will, I said to myself, "The hands of Kṛishṇa." The vision lasted for ten minutes or so, during which I looked away several times and each time, when I looked back, found the same unutterable beauty and fascination, not only in the appearance of them but in every move they made, which seemed incredibly graceful and charming. After a while, they became Prabhavananda's hands again, but the memory of them fills me even now with joy and wonder.
>
> *Nancy Mayorga, Hunger of the Soul, HSDM pp.69–70*

The word 'psychic' is also used in psychology, in expressions such as 'psychic realm', 'psychic process', 'psychic energy', and so on. These refer to the unconscious or subconscious mental energy from which arise the unconscious motivations and impulses that influence the actions of every human being. Though not necessarily understood by psychologists as subtle energy, the conscious and subconscious processes of the mind – including reason, intuition, and so on – take place in a level of subtle psychic energy, expressed or manifested outwardly as neurological activity in the brain.

Christian mystics have sometimes used the word to refer to the realm of thought and emotion, which can become the arena of considerable struggle, as well as blissful meditative experiences. Translators have used the word in a variety of contexts, which adds further confusion to the melting pot. Such is the nature of words and meanings. In general, something psychic is intermediate between the spirit and the body, and thus corresponds to the mind.

See also: **clairvoyance**, **seer** (7.1).

1. George Fox, *Journal* 1:2, *JGF1* p.66; *An Autobiography, GFAJ* pp.97–98.

pubbe-nivāsānussati, **pubbe-nivāsa-ñāṇa** (Pa), **pūrva-nivāsa-anusmṛiti** (S) *Lit.* knowledge *(ñāṇa)* of former *(pubba)* abodes or living *(nivāsa);* remembrance of one's own past lives, previous existences, or former births; one of the six supernormal forms of knowledge *(abhiññā)* in Buddhism.

See also: **abhijñā**.

qīng (C) *Lit.* of little weight, light (in weight); hence also, weightless. Stories and fables abound of Daoist *xiān* (immortals) whose bodies are so light that they do not leave footprints; or that they rise into the air, float on clouds, or fly without wings from mountain to mountain. A Buddhist *arhat* (S), is said to have the same supernatural powers – they are so light that not even insects beneath their feet are killed:

> The ability of the enlightened ones *(shèngshī)* of all times to shed the mundane, become spiritually transformed *(shénhuà),* and adapt to changes endlessly, comes from their having purified *(jìng jié)* themselves beforehand; thus at the end they rose *(jǔ)* lightly *(qīng).*
>
> *Lǐ Dàochún, Zhōnghé jí, BBH p.72*

Present-day translator and Daoist teacher Stuart Olson explains why the body of a *xiān* (immortal) becomes lighter:

> In Daoist thought, the *pò* (earthly soul) presides over the physical body, and the nature of *pò* is to descend, not ascend. Whatever keeps the body heavy and subject to gravity is supported by the *pò.* The *hún* (heavenly soul) presides over the spiritual body. Its nature is to ascend and not descend, and whatever causes the body to be light and not be subject to gravity is supported by the *hún.* When the golden court is illuminated by the sacred sun and moon, the *hún* then rules over the *pò.* The physical body naturally becomes lighter and not subject to gravity.
>
> The new immortal can now begin living off the wind and dew for nourishment, not food – and especially not grains and meats, which only make the *pò* stronger. For this reason, Daoists in their initial training usually subsist on a pure vegetarian diet and/or herbal remedies.
>
> *Stuart Olson, Mind Seal Classic, JEMS pp.148–49*

The golden court *(jīntíng)* is one of numerous Daoist metaphors for a point in the forehead that equates to what is often called the third eye. The "sun and moon" refer to the light that is seen within when the mind is focused at this inner centre. The "wind" is a Daoist metaphor for the subtle life energies *(qì)* that can be mastered through control of the breathing, and "dew" refers to the saliva *(jīn, tuò).*

Dietary control regimens, together with both breathing exercises and the swallowing of saliva, which is believed to lessen hunger, are practised by some Daoists with aims that include physical well-being and longevity, both of which are intended to support the primary task of spiritual development:

> If you want the body to become light and agile *(qīngkuài),* you should practise the methods *(dào)* of cultivating the generative, vital, and spirit energies *(jīng, qì, shén).*
>
> *Tàixuán bǎodiǎn 2:3.3, NEL p.102*

When a Daoist practitioner has attained enlightenment ("supreme harmony is replete"), it is believed that his bones become infused with *qì* and thus become as light as "powdered jade", resulting in the overall body becoming pure and light:

> Once attained, it is attained forever,
> and then the body will become naturally light *(qīng).*
> Supreme harmony is replete,
> and the bones will become like powdered jade.
>
> *Xīnyìn jīng; cf. TTEP p.67, JEMS p.115*

Lightness of being and the lightness associated with the spirit are not exclusive to advanced Daoist adepts. A feeling of lightness is believed to be enjoyed by all who make inner progress in spiritual practice. The mind's preoccupation with the world is like the ropes holding down a hot-air balloon; the more the mind is emptied of thoughts and emotions, the easier it becomes for the spirit to ascend. This feeling of lightness, though spiritual, is also felt or sensed physically and mentally:

> When you reach this stage of cultivation, no illness will arise. Your body will become light *(qīng),* and with time it will be bathed in a pure light *(qīng guāng).* Your gait will be swift (*rú fēi,* as if flying), and you will be able to run up the mountain paths. Nothing can stop you, because you are now protected by the bright spirit *(shénmíng xiāng yòu).*
>
> *Tàixuán bǎodiǎn 2:2.6, NEL p.99*

And:

> Once your physical posture is steady and your breathing is tuned, relax your abdomen and do not think of good or bad at all. When a thought arises, notice it; once you become aware of it, it is not there. Eventually you forget mental objects and spontaneously *(zì)* become unified *(yīpiàn).* If you get this, you will naturally *(zìrán)* feel light *(qīng)* and fresh *(shuǎng);* this is what is called the method of comfort *(ānlè fǎmén).*
>
> *Yáng Dàoshēng, Zhēnquán, TCC2 p.527*

And again:

> As long as the mind does not stick to things, and you can remain unmoved, this is the correct foundation for genuine stabilization *(zhēn dìng).* If you stabilize *(dìng)* the mind by this means, your mood will become harmonious *(tiáohé);* the longer you do so, the lighter *(qīng)* and fresher *(shuǎng)* you feel.
>
> *Sīmǎ Chéngzhēn, Zuòwànglùn 3:3b, TMED p.86*

When a stage of complete mental emptiness is reached, a vast inner space is perceived or experienced within. At the same time, the "whole body" (body, mind, and spirit) no longer feels restrained:

> Inside one's own primordial chamber *(yuán gōng)* is an immeasurable cosmos *(tàixū).* Feeling mysteriously light *(qīng),* one's whole body yearns to soar *(yù téng).* This is known as "clouds filling the thousand mountains *(yún mǎn qiān shān)*".
>
> *Jīnhuá zōngzhǐ 8, ZW334, JH94*

There is a saying, "healthy body, healthy mind, healthy spirit". Spiritual practitioners take care of the physical body, because a healthy body promotes a healthy mind, and a healthy mind promotes a healthy spirit. Similarly, Daoists progressively refine or transmute the generative energy *(jīng)* into subtle life energy *(qì),* and the subtle life energy into spirit *(shén),* until all three are "joined as one". As a result of this progressive refinement, physical energy becomes subtly lighter, mental energy becomes calm and peaceful; and eventually the "great peace" of the *Dào* is attained and experienced:

> To pursue long life you must guard energy *(qì)* and harmonize spirit *(shén)* and essence *(jīng).* Never let them leave your body, but continue to think of them as joined in one. With prolonged practice your perception will become finer and subtler. Quite naturally *(zì),* you will be able to see within your body.
>
> The physical body will become gradually lighter *(qīng),* the essence *(jīng)* more brilliant, and the light more concentrated. In your mind, you will feel greatly restful, delighted, and full of joy. You will go along with the energy of great peace *(tàipíng).*
>
> By so cultivating yourself, you can turn around and go along with all without. Within, there will be perfect longevity; without, there will be perfect accordance with the order of the universe. Without the exertion of any muscle, you naturally *(zìrán)* attain great peace *(tàipíng).*
>
> *Tàipíng jīng shèngjūn mìzhǐ 1:a–b; cf. TEAK p.195*

When physical and mental energies are refined into spiritual energy, the joyful experience is likened to that of a bird that is lifted upwards by a thermal:

> Your (real) nature is spirit *(shén)*. Your life is *qì*. When nature meets life, it is like a bird that gets a (gust of) wind. It wafts up lightly *(qīng)*, accomplishing its task with decreased effort. (When) the *Yīnfú jīng* says "the control of the bird is in the *qì* (or air)," this is (what it means to say).
>
> *Wáng Zhé, Chóngyáng lìjiào shíwǔ lùn 4b, TPEQ p.38*

Heaviness and density are associated with earth and the physical, whereas lightness and clarity are associated with heaven and the spirit. Daoism holds that when the soul or spirit descends to the material planes from the spiritual planes, the soul divides:

> After descending to the celestial chamber *(qián gōng)*, the soul divides into higher and lower souls *(hún pò)*. The higher (immortal) soul *(hún)* resides in the celestial mind and is *yáng* – its energy is light *(qīng)* and clear *(qīng)*. This is obtained from the great emptiness *(tàixū)* and has the same form as it had in the primordial beginning *(yuán shǐ)*. The lower (mortal) soul *(pò)* is *yīn* – its energy is heavy and turbid. This attaches to the material, temporal mind.
>
> *Jīnhuá zōngzhǐ 2, ZW334, JH94*

See also: **xiān** (7.1).

ṛiddhi (S/H), **riddhi** (Pu), **rdzu 'phrul** (T) *Lit.* growth, prosperity, good fortune, wealth, riches, abundance; accomplishment, perfection; from the root *ṛidh* (to grow, to prosper, to increase, to succeed); esoterically, supernatural or miraculous power arising from spiritual practice or as a natural ability of *devas* (gods) and other celestial beings; the name of the consort of *Kubera,* god of wealth, and an alternative name for *Pārvatī,* consort of *Shiva;* the Sanskrit equivalent of the Pali *iddhi,* which is commonly used in Buddhist texts; appears in the expression *ṛiddhi-siddhi,* which can mean either prosperity and success or miraculous powers, depending on the context. The term more commonly used for supernatural powers in Sanskrit and Hindi is *siddhi.*

See also: **iddhi**, **siddhi**.

ṛiddhipāda (S), **iddhipāda** (Pa), **rdzu 'phrul gyi rkang pa** (T), **shénzú**, **rúyì zú** (C), **jinsoku**, **nyoi soku** (J) *Lit.* footing or base *(pāda)* of supernormal or supernatural power *(ṛiddhi, iddhi);* the legs *(rkang pa)* of supernormal powers *(rdzu 'phrul);* supernormal or miraculous *(shén, jin)* + foot or leg *(zú, soku);* the foundation, basis, bases or fundamentals of (spiritual) attainment or power; the roads or pathways to (spiritual) power; the four fundamental attitudes or qualities of mind required for the development of spiritual power and enlightenment or, more specifically, for the attainment of supernormal powers; often preceded by *chatur* (S), *catu* (Pa), *sì* (C) or *shi* (J), all meaning 'four'. Likewise, the Tibetan term may end with *bhzi* (four).

The four fundamentals are determination, effort, perseverance, and self-examination. It is apparent that none of these four can stand on their own, the existence of each being dependent on the others, though one or other may at times seem to predominate. The four *iddhipāda* are listed among the seven categories of attributes that comprise the thirty-seven ways to enlightenment *(bodhi)*[1] and the long list of qualities and attributes that should characterize a forest-dwelling monk *(araṇyavāsin)*.[2] The four *iddhipāda* are discussed at length in the *Iddhipāda Saṃyutta* of the *Saṃyutta Nikāya*.[3] They are:

1. *Chanda-samādhi* (Pa), *chhanda-samādhi* (S). *Lit.* concentration *(samādhi)* of intention or desire *(chanda),* accompanied by an effort of will *(padhāna-saṃkhāra-samannāgata);* mental determination to control the mind and to lead a life according to the *Dhamma.*

2. *Viriya-samādhi* (Pa), *vīrya-samādhi* (S). *Lit.* concentration of energy *(viriya);* making the effort in life and in spiritual practices.

3. *Citta-samādhi* (Pa), *chitta-samādhi* (S). *Lit.* concentration of mind *(citta);* focusing the mind, and remaining on track whatever pitfalls and difficulties may be encountered.

4. *Vīmaṃsā-samādhi* (Pa), *mīmāṃsā-samādhi* (S). *Lit.* concentration of investigation *(vīmaṃsā),* accompanied by effort of will; awareness through introspection of one's strengths and weaknesses.

As a part of the progression towards enlightenment, these four are regarded as dependent upon other aspects of the Buddhist path, such as the noble eightfold path. Thus, according to *Saṃyutta Nikāya,* the Buddha says to his disciples:

> *Bhikkhus* (monks), those who have neglected the four bases of spiritual power *(iddhipāda)* have neglected the noble path leading to the complete destruction of suffering. Those who have undertaken the four bases of spiritual power *(iddhipāda)* have undertaken the noble path leading to the complete destruction of suffering.

> *Bhikkhus,* these four bases of spiritual power *(iddhipāda),* when developed and cultivated, are noble and emancipating; they lead the one who acts upon them to the complete destruction of suffering.
>
> *Bhikkhus,* these four bases of spiritual power *(iddhipāda),* when developed and cultivated, lead to utter revulsion, to dispassion, to cessation, to peace, to direct knowledge, to enlightenment, to *nibbāna.*
>
> *Saṃyutta Nikāya 51, Iddhipāda Saṃyutta 2–4, PTSS5 pp.254–55; cf. CDBB pp.1718–19*

These same spiritual principles apply to all spiritual seekers, past, present, or future:

> *Bhikkhus,* whatever *samaṇas* (holy men) and *brāhmaṇs* in the past, ... future and present have developed and cultivated the four bases of spiritual power *(iddhipāda)* in part ... or completely, have all done so because they have developed and cultivated the four bases of spiritual power *(iddhipāda).*
>
> *Saṃyutta Nikāya 51, Iddhipāda Saṃyutta 5–6, PTSS5 pp.255–56; cf. CDBB pp.1719–20*

Likewise, continues the same text, *bhikkhus* and *buddhas* alike have all overcome the impurities *(āsrava)* and all other obstructions that stand in their way, and have attained enlightenment by adopting the four *iddhipāda* as the basis of their spiritual practice. The Buddha himself confirms that this was the path that he himself has trodden, and by which "arose in me vision, knowledge, wisdom, true knowledge, and light".[4] In fact, *bhikkhus, samaṇas* and *brāhmaṇs* all develop the various supernatural powers *(iddhis),* listed in the standard manner: "because they developed and cultivated the four bases for spiritual power *(iddhipāda)*".[5]

Bhikkhu Moggallāna, on instructions from the Buddha, then performs a miracle in order to shake up a group of lazy, backsliding disciples:

> Thus have I heard. On one occasion, the Blessed One was dwelling at Sāvatthī in the Eastern Park in the mansion of Migāra's mother. Now, on that occasion, a number of *bhikkhus* who dwelt on the ground floor of the mansion were restless, puffed up, personally vain, rough-tongued, rambling in their talk, muddle-minded, without clear comprehension, unconcentrated, scatterbrained, loose in their faculties.
>
> Then the Blessed One addressed the Venerable Moggallāna thus: "Moggallāna, your brothers in the holy life, dwelling on the ground floor of the mansion of Migāra's mother, are restless ... *etc.* Go, Moggallāna, stir up a sense of urgency in those *bhikkhus.*"

> "Yes, venerable sir," the Venerable Moggallāna replied. Then he performed a feat of spiritual power *(iddhi)* with his toe, such that he made the mansion of Migāra's mother shake, quake, and tremble. Then those *bhikkhus,* shocked and terrified, stood to one side and said: "It is wonderful indeed, sir! It is amazing indeed, sir! There is no wind, and this mansion of Migāra's mother has a deep foundation and is securely planted, immobile, unshaking; yet it shook, quaked, and trembled."
>
> *Saṃyutta Nikāya 51:14, Moggallāna Sutta, PTSS5 pp.269–70; cf. CDBB p.1731*

After further stereotypical dialogue, the Buddha then explains to the awe-struck disciples:

> It is because he has developed and cultivated the four bases of spiritual power *(iddhipāda)* that the *bhikkhu* Moggallāna has become so powerful and mighty.
>
> *Saṃyutta Nikāya 51:14, Moggallāna Sutta, PTSS5 p.271, CDBB pp.1731–32*

The Buddha therefore observes:

> *Bhikkhus,* these four bases of spiritual power *(iddhipāda),* when developed and cultivated, are of great fruit and benefit.
>
> *Saṃyutta Nikāya 51:20, Vibhanga Sutta, PTSS5 p.276; cf. CDBB p.1736*

See also: **iddhi**.

1. *Majjhima Nikāya* 77, *Mahāsakuludāyi Sutta, PTSM2* p.11.
2. *Mahāratnakūṭa Sūtra* 44, *T11* 310:644c12–26.
3. *Saṃyutta Nikāya* 51:1–86, *PTSS5* pp.254–93; see also *Paṭisambhidāmagga* 22, *PTSP2* pp.205–14; Buddhaghosa, *Visuddhimagga* 12:20–24, 44, *PTSV* pp.378, 383–84.
4. *Saṃyutta Nikāya* 51, *Iddhipāda Saṃyutta* 7–9, 18, *passim, PTSS5* pp.257–58, 275–76; *cf. CDBB* pp.1721–23, 1735.
5. *Saṃyutta Nikāya* 51, *Iddhipāda Saṃyutta* 11, 16–17, *PTSS5* pp.263–66, 273–75; *cf. Dīgha Nikāya* 2, *Sāmaññaphala Sutta, PTSD1* pp.77–84; *Majjhima Nikāya* 6, *Ākankheyya Sutta, PTSM1* p.34.

ṛiju-mati (S) *Lit.* of simple *(ṛiju)* mind *(mati);* one of the two kinds of *manaḥ-paryāya-jñāna* (knowledge of others' thoughts). See **manaḥ-paryāya-jñāna**.

rotu, **tāmoe** (Mo) *Lit.* overpower, smother, repress; put to sleep, calm; to overpower by magical means; a spell to help defeat an enemy; a spell for putting someone into a deep sleep, or to weaken and unnerve them; a kind of charm employed during times of war or fighting.

A form of *tāmoe* or *rotu* ritual known as *wheawheau* was one of several spells used by the Tūhoe tribe when advancing against an enemy. The *tohunga* (priestly expert) advanced to the front, preceding the fighting men; in his hand he carried a small branch, made powerful by magic spells, which he flourished before the enemy, at the same time reciting an incantation *(karakia)* designed to unnerve them and render them irresolute.[1]

1. Elsdon Best, "Notes on the Art of War," *NAWB* p.66.

samādhi-vipphārā-iddhi (Pa) *Lit.* power *(iddhi)* of penetrating *(vipphāra)* concentration *(samādhi);* the power of deep, discriminating insight and awareness, enabling one to perceive the otherwise hidden causes of things; hence, interpreting *vipphāra* as 'intervention', the power to intervene in and to change bodily or other natural processes and events as a result of a higher knowledge and awareness; thus, as more commonly defined, a protective power that enables one to remain unhurt in danger; one of the commonly listed *iddhis* (powers); synonymous with *ñāṇa-vipphārā-iddhi* (power of penetrating knowledge).

The power of penetrating concentration is discussed in the *Paṭisambhidāmagga,*[1] the *Vibhanga,* and the *Visuddhimagga.*[2] The *Visuddhimagga* mentions a number of stories to illustrate the nature of *samādhi-vipphārā-iddhi.* The recurrent theme in these stories is that because a monk is seated in deep meditation or is otherwise full of lovingkindness, calamities have no adverse effect on him. A detailed version of one of these tales is related in the *Udāna:*

> On one occasion the Venerable Sāriputta and the Venerable Mahā Moggallāna were staying in Pigeon Cave. There, one moonlit night, the Venerable Sāriputta – his head newly shaven – was sitting in the open air, having attained a certain level of concentration *(samādhi).*
>
> Just at that time, two *yakkhas* (spirits), who were companions, were flying from north to south on some business or other, and they saw the Venerable Sāriputta – his head newly shaven – sitting in the open air. Seeing him, the first *yakkha* said to the second, "I'm inspired to give this contemplative *(samaṇa)* a blow on the head."
>
> When this was said, the second *yakkha* said to the first, "Enough of that, my good friend. Don't lay a hand on that contemplative. He's an outstanding contemplative, of great power and great might."
>
> *Udāna 4, Juṇha Sutta, PTSU p.39, KNTB*

The conversation is repeated a second and third time, following which:

> Then the first *yakkha,* ignoring the second *yakkha,* gave the Venerable Sāriputta a blow on the head. And with that blow he might have knocked over an elephant seven or eight cubits tall, or split a great rocky crag. But there and then, the *yakkha* – yelling, "I'm burning!" – fell into the great hell *(mahāniraya).*
>
> Now, Venerable Moggallāna – with his divine eye *(dibba-cakkhu),* pure and surpassing the human – saw the *yakkha* give Venerable Sāriputta a blow on the head. Seeing this, he went to Venerable Sāriputta and, on arrival, said to him, "I hope you are well, friend Sāriputta. I hope you are comfortable. I hope you are feeling no pain."
>
> "I am well, friend Moggallāna. I am comfortable. But I do have a slight headache."
>
> "How amazing, friend Sāriputta! How astounding! How great your power and might! Just now a *yakkha* gave you a blow on the head. So great was that blow that he might have knocked over an elephant seven or eight cubits tall, or split a great rocky crag. But all you say is this: 'I am well, friend Moggallāna. I am comfortable. But I do have a slight headache'!"
>
> "How amazing, friend Moggallāna!" (replied Sāriputta), "How astounding! How great your power and might! Where you saw a *yakkha* just now, I didn't even see a dust devil!"
>
> The Blessed One – with the divine ear *(dibba-sota),* pure and surpassing the human – heard those two great beings conversing in this way. Then, on realizing the significance of that, the Blessed One on that occasion exclaimed:
>
> Whose mind is like rock, steady, unmoved,
> dispassionate about things that spark passion,
> unexcited by things that spark excitement:
> When one's mind is developed like this,
> from where can suffering and stress arise?
>
> *Udāna 4, Juṇha Sutta, PTSU pp.40–41; cf. KNTB*

Concluding the story, the *Visuddhimagga* then observes:

> At the time the blow was given, the elder was absorbed in an attainment; consequently he suffered no harm from the blow. This was the power of penetrating concentration *(samādhi-vipphārā-iddhi)* in that venerable one.
>
> *Buddhaghosa, Visuddhimagga 12:31, PTSV p.380; cf. PPVM p.375*

The *Visuddhimagga* relates three other similar stories as instances of *samādhi-vipphārā-iddhi.* In one, the Venerable Sañjīva had seated himself against a tree one day, and had entered into the final stage of meditation – the cessation *(nirodha)* of perception and feeling. Some cowherds, shepherds and others happened to pass that way, and seeing him so completely motionless, presumed that the recluse had died. Deciding that they ought to cremate him, they piled up grass and sticks around him in a funeral pyre, set alight to it, and went on their way. The following morning, Sañjīva returned to his physical senses, got up, shook his robe, dressed, and went to the village for alms, where the local people were amazed to see him alive and unharmed. Not even a corner of his robe had been burnt.[3] The *Visuddhimagga* observes:

> This was (the effect of) the power of penetrating concentration *(samādhi-vipphārā-iddhi)* in him, because it was brought about by the influence of the serenity that took place in his successive attainments (as he passed through each of the stages of meditation – the *jhānas* – preceding cessation).
>
> *Buddhaghosa, Visuddhimagga 12:32, PTSV p.380; cf. PPVM p.375*

In another story, the Venerable Khāṇu Kondañña was sitting one night in the forest in a state of deep meditative absorption when some robbers came by with their booty. Mistaking him for a tree stump, they piled their five hundred bundles of goods on top of him, while they took some rest. Some while later, as they were about to depart and the first to have laid down his bundle was picking it up, Khāṇu Kondañña returned to his body and moved. The robbers were startled, but the monk calmed their fears. They paid homage to him, and acquired so much confidence in him that they took to the Buddhist Way, and eventually gained enlightenment. The absence of any harm caused by being covered by five hundred bundles was due, says the *Visuddhimagga,* to the power of penetrating concentration *(samādhi-vipphārā-iddhi).*[4]

In another incident, a jealous harlot poured boiling water over a lay devotee who was full of lovingkindness. The oil ran off her like water, leaving her unharmed.[5] And again, a king who had been misinformed that his wife intended to kill him, decided to kill her first. In his fury, he aimed a poisoned arrow at her, but his wife stood her ground, showering him with feelings of lovingkindness, making him unable to shoot. Both the devotee and the king's wife were unharmed, says the *Visuddhimagga,* due to the power of penetrating concentration *(samādhi-vipphārā-iddhi).*[6]

See also: **iddhi**.

1. *Paṭisambhidāmagga* 22, *PTSP* pp.211–12, *PDPM* pp.382–83.
2. Buddhaghosa, *Visuddhimagga* 12:30–35, *PTSV* pp.380–81, *PPVM* pp.375–76.

3. See also *Majjhima Nikāya* 50, *Māratajjaniya Sutta, PTSM1* pp.333–34.
4. Buddhaghosa, *Visuddhimagga* 12:33, *PTSV* pp.380–81, *PPVM* pp.375–76; *Dhammapada Aṭṭhakathā* 2:254.
5. Buddhaghosa, *Visuddhimagga* 12:34, *PTSV* p.381, *PPVM* p.376; *Dhammapada Aṭṭhakathā* 3:310; *Anguttara Nikāya Aṭṭhakathā* 1:451.
6. Buddhaghosa, *Visuddhimagga* 12:35, *PTSV* p.381, *PPVM* p.376; *Dhammapada Aṭṭhakathā* 1:216; *Anguttara Nikāya Aṭṭhakathā* 1:443.

samarth(a) (S/H), **samrath** (H/Pu) *Lit.* all-powerful, omnipotent; competent, suitably powerful; one who can do what needs to be done; one who can do anything. *Samrath* is used in descriptions of God and the spiritual master.

Since his inner being is one with the Divine, Indian *sants* (saints) have often described the *guru* as all-powerful. Swami Shiv Dayal Singh says that the all-powerful *satguru* is able to purify the minds of his disciples so that they can enjoy the bliss of contact with the divine Name *(Nām),* the creative power:

> Those who want to enjoy the bliss of *Nām* in *parmārth* should give up all other practices and firmly take refuge in the *satguru,* who is all-powerful *(samarth)* and will make this *jīva* pure and whole; that is, he will cleanse his *antaḥkaraṇ* (human mind) which is now filled with desires for sensual enjoyments, and soiled with the filth of lust, anger, greed, attachment, and egotism. He will also remove impurities and disease on account of which the *jīva* cannot taste the sweetness of *Nām,* and will also bestow bliss upon him.
>
> *Swami Shiv Dayal Singh, Sār Bachan Prose 2:122, SBAT p.81*

Eknāth praises his all-powerful *sadguru* for his ability to free his disciples from the illusion of this world:

> O all-powerful *(samrath) sadguru,* whose real form is *Aum* –
> O protector of the orphaned! Before you I bow.
> We bow to you, who is our mother, father, teacher, and benefactor!
> Please sever the bonds of illusion and delusion!
> Who can clear this entangling web of delusion but you, O *sadguru!*
> You are the ocean of bliss!
> You are the support of the three worlds!
> You are self-effulgent!
> Before your light, the sun and moon seem pale!
> Your self-effulgent form is unknown even to the *Vedas.*
> Before you I bow. . . .
> Says Eknāth, disciple of Janārdan: the *guru* is the supreme God.
> His Name should be forever on our lips!
>
> *Eknāth, Abhang 1792:1–7, 29, SSG2 p.251; cf. in SSI4 pp.202–3*

Guru Arjun writes that it is "great good fortune" to meet such a *guru:*

> O my friend, remember the Name of the Lord God.
> In the *sādh sangat* (company of saints), He dwells within the mind,
> and one's works (efforts) are brought to perfect fruition.
> The *guru* is all-powerful *(samrath),* the *guru* is infinite:
> by great good fortune, his blessed *darshan* (vision) is obtained.
>
> *Guru Arjun, Ādi Granth 52, AGK*

saṃyama (S) *Lit.* with *(sam)* restraint *(yama);* control, abstention, restriction, self-restraint, as in *indriya-saṃyama* (control of the senses) and *prāṇa-saṃyana* (control of the *prāṇa*); also, a term used by Patañjali for the kind of profound concentration and meditation that leads to the attainment of miraculous powers.

In his *Yoga Sūtras,* Patañjali devotes a section to the effects of and powers gained by meditation and concentration *(saṃyama)* on different aspects of the body, the mind, the inner and outer universes, and so on. He begins by saying that when all the faculties of the mind focus entirely on one thing, with complete forgetfulness of all else such that nothing but the object of concentration remains, then the practitioner gains complete integration with and understanding of the object of such *saṃyama.* There is, he says, a flow of mind energy between the mind and the object of concentration. Like other verses in the *Yoga Sūtras,* this section is echoed in later texts, such as the *Shāṇḍilya* and *Yogashikhā Upanishads.*[1]

Patañjali identifies three states of the mind – fixation or concentration *(dhāraṇā),* visualization or contemplation *(dhyāna),* and superconscious absorption *(samādhi).* These three, he says, brought together in one mind, constitute *saṃyama* or deep meditation:

> Concentration *(dhāraṇā)* is
> confining the mind to one particular thing.
> Contemplation *(dhyāna)* is
> unbroken flow of the mind towards that particular thing.
> The same (practice), with consciousness shining in its own light,
> unaware of its own self, is absorption *(samādhi).*
> The three, working together, constitute deep concentration *(saṃyama).*
>
> As a result of mastering it *(saṃyama),*
> the light of higher consciousness *(prajñā)* arises.
> Its purpose is to discover higher and higher stages (of consciousness).
>
> *Patañjali, Yoga Sūtras 3:1–6*

Patañjali then goes on to identify various powers and perceptions that come to a person who develops the power of *saṃyama:*

By *saṃyama* on the processes underlying change,
a knowledge of the past and future (is acquired).

Sounds, feelings and the intent behind them,
are present together (in the mind), but are normally confused.
(By *saṃyama*) on their meaning, understanding arises
of the sounds uttered by all living beings.

By bringing impressions *(saṃskāras)* into consciousness,
a knowledge of previous births is acquired.
(By *saṃyama*) on the mental energies of others,
a knowledge of the mind of others is acquired....

By *saṃyama* on the form and colour of the body,
another's power to receive that form and colour can be suspended.
There being no contact between the eye of the observer
and light from the body, the power of invisibility is thus acquired.
Similarly, the power by which sound and other sensations
can be made to disappear is acquired.

Karma is of two kinds: active and dormant;
By *saṃyama* on them, knowledge of the time of death
and other extraordinary happenings is acquired.

(By *saṃyama*) on friendliness, compassion, and so on,
strengthening of that quality can be acquired.
(By *saṃyama*) on the strengths of animals,
the strength of an elephant and so on is acquired.

By focusing *(saṃyama)* on shining, radiating and effulgent light,
knowledge is acquired of subtle, hidden, or distant things.
(By *saṃyama*) on the sun,
knowledge of the cosmos is acquired.
(By *saṃyama*) on the moon,
knowledge concerning the motion
and position of the stars is acquired.
(By *saṃyama*) on the pole star,
knowledge of the movement of the stars is acquired.

(By *saṃyama*) at the navel centre,
knowledge of the organization of the body is acquired.
(By *saṃyama*) at the throat centre,
understanding and control of hunger and thirst is acquired....

By *saṃyama* on the relationship between the body and *ākāsha,*
lightness like that of cotton down
and levitation through space are acquired.

Patañjali, Yoga Sūtras 3:16–19, 21–31, 43

Patañjali lists a number of other powers and insights which come to one who focuses his mind in the right way. In fact, he says:

(By *saṃyama*), anything can be understood:
whatever is tried, spontaneous understanding is acquired.

Patañjali, Yoga Sūtras 3:34

But he cautions:

There should be no attachment to or pride
concerning the attainment of this high position.
Otherwise, it will not be possible to maintain that high estate....

They are obstacles to *samādhi;*
But properly used, supernatural power
can be used to combat instinctive natural forces.

Patañjali, Yoga Sūtras 3:52, 38

See also: **saṃyama** (▸3), **saṃyama** (▸4), **siddhi**.

1. *E.g. Shāṇḍilya Upanishad* 1:7.44–52; *Yogashikhā Upanishad* 5:46–55.

sarvajña (S), **sabbaññū**, **sabbavidū** (Pa), **kun mkhyen**, **kun shes** (T), **yīqièzhì** (C), **issai chi** (J) *Lit.* all *(sarva, kun, yīqiè, issai)*-knowing *(jña, mkhyen, shes, zhì, chi);* omniscient; omniscient one; applied to God, to the true nature of the soul *(ātman),* to deities, saints, sages, and even (as flattering hyperbole) to rulers, philosophers, ministers, *etc.;* commonly used throughout Buddhist literature in descriptions of the Buddha. *Sarvajña* is related to *sarvajñātā* (omniscience) and *sarvajña-jñāna,* the all-knowing wisdom, knowledge, consciousness, or awareness of the Buddha.

A true saint, a *buddha,* or any spiritually enlightened person is all-knowing because he knows the path to liberation and final enlightenment, together with the cause and effect of everything that happens in all the worlds – material and heavenly. 'Omniscient one' is one of many epithets used for the Buddha. The *Mahāvyutpatti,* for instance, a classical Sanskrit-Tibetan lexicon, lists eighty.

In Jainism, the natural state of the soul is understood to be omniscience *(kevala-jñāna),* and the *Jinas, Tīrthankaras* and all enlightened souls are hence regarded as omniscient. *Kevalin* is often used in Jainism in preference to *sarvajña,* and *kevala-jñāna* to *sarvajñātā.*

The omniscience of a true saint or Buddha arises from his oneness with the all-pervading mind or consciousness that encompasses and thereby knows all things by direct perception or awareness. His consciousness is one with the supreme Intelligence by which the universe is organized. A *buddha*'s knowledge, however, is not used to criticize, judge or punish his fellow human beings, but is employed for their betterment and spiritual development. He has the *dharma* eye *(dharmachakshu)* that sees the Truth or Reality of things, and the way that human beings can be led to understand it and escape the cycle of otherwise continual death and rebirth.

Omniscience is mentioned in many places in both Pali and Sanskrit texts in reference to the Buddha and other personalities. In the *Sutta Nipāta,* when the good *yakkha* (demon) Hemavata meets the Buddha, he describes him as the great and all-knowing *(sabbavidū) isi* (seer, sage):

> He who is endowed with a profound understanding, seeing what is subtle, possessing nothing, not clinging to sensual pleasures – behold him who is in every respect liberated, the great *isi,* walking the divine path.
>
> He who has got a great name sees what is subtle, imparts understanding, and does not cling to the abode of sensual pleasures – behold him, the all-knowing *(sabbavidū),* the wise, the great *isi,* walking the noble path.
>
> Today we have indeed seen a good sight, a good daybreak, a beautiful rising, for we have seen the perfectly enlightened *(sambuddha),* who has crossed the stream, and is free from passion.
>
> *Sutta Nipāta 1:9, Hemavata Sutta, PTSN pp.30–31, SNVF p.28*

The true sage *(muni)* is also described as all-knowing *(sabbavidū):*

> Overcoming all, knowing all *(sabbavidū),* wise in all things,
> undefiled, abandoning all things,
> liberated through destruction of desire:
> Him the enlightened call a sage *(muni).*
>
> *Sutta Nipāta 1:12, Muni Sutta, PTSN p.36; cf. KNTB, SNVF p.34*

He is likewise called the all-knowing *(sabbaññū) jina* (conqueror) and teacher or mentor *(ācariya):*

The all-knowing *(sabbaññū),* all-seeing conqueror *(jina):*
he is my mentor *(ācariya).*
Greatly compassionate teacher *(satthar),* all the world's healer,
this *Dhamma* is his, unexcelled, leading to ending.
Because of his teachings is this lack of sorrow acquired.

Theragāthā 16, Adhimutta Sutta 722–23, PTST p.72; cf. KNTB

In all instances, an enlightened one is understood to be all-knowing. Again, according to the *Dhammapada,* the Buddha himself reveals:

All-conquering and all-knowing *(sabbavidū)* am I,
unaffected under all circumstances;
I have renounced everything, liberated through elimination of desire.
Having achieved Realization by myself, whom should I call my teacher?

Dhammapada 24:20; cf. DPR

The nature of such omniscience as it manifests at a human level is a common theme in the Pali texts of *Theravāda* Buddhism. There is a recurrent formula that runs:

> (So-and-so) claims to be omniscient *(sabbaññū)* and all-seeing, to have complete knowledge and vision thus: "Whether I am walking or standing or sleeping or awake, knowledge and vision are continuously and uninterruptedly present to me."
>
> *Majjhima Nikāya 76, Sandaka Sutta, PTSM1 p.519, MDBB p.623*

And the questioner goes on to ask whether the Buddha really said such a thing about himself,[1] or whether it can be true in the case of some other individual who is said to have made the claim.[2] The claim of omniscience is especially highlighted if that person subsequently meets with seemingly unforseen misfortunes or simply exhibits the normal range of human ignorance:

> He enters an empty house; he gets no alms food; a dog bites him; he meets with a wild elephant, a wild horse, a wild bull; he asks the name and clan of a woman or a man; he asks the name of a village or a town, and the way to go there.
>
> *Majjhima Nikāya 76, Sandaka Sutta, PTSM1 p.519, MDBB pp.623–24*

And he then justifies the apparent mistake that seems to belie his claim to omniscience by saying that it was ordained that he should do all these things:

> I had to enter an empty house, that is why I entered it. I had to get no alms food, that is why I did not get any. I had to be bitten by a dog, that

> is why I was bitten. I had to meet with a wild elephant, a wild horse, a wild bull, that is why I met with them. I had to ask the name and clan of a woman or a man, that is why I asked. I had to ask the name of a village or a town and the way to go there, that is why I asked.
>
> *Majjhima Nikāya 76, Sandaka Sutta, PTSM1 p.519, MDBB p.624*

The issue of understanding how an enlightened being lives as a human being among other human beings if he (or she) knows everything – including the contents of everybody's minds as well as everything that has happened, is happening, and is going to happen – is a recurrent theme in Buddhist texts. But it is not a subject that is readily amenable to intellectual understanding, and an entirely satisfactory resolution of the issue is never reached.

According to the *Tevijjavacchagotta Sutta,* the Buddha responds to the initial query concerning his simultaneous knowledge of everything by denying that he knows everything at once, but that he can know whatever he needs or wants to know whenever he so desires. That is to say that "knowledge and vision" are not "continuously and uninterruptedly present" with him:

> Those who say thus do not say what has been said by me, but misrepresent me with what is untrue and contrary to fact.... The Samaṇa Gotama has the threefold true knowledge *(tevijja),*... for, insofar as I wish, I can recollect my manifold past lives, that is, one birth, two births, *etc.*... Thus, I can recollect my manifold past lives in all their aspects and details.
>
> And, insofar as I wish, with the divine eye *(dibba-cakkhu),* which is purified and surpasses the human (eye), I see beings passing away and reappearing, inferior and superior, fair and ugly, fortunate and unfortunate, and I understand how beings pass on according to their actions....
>
> And by realizing for myself with direct knowledge, I here and now enter upon and abide in the deliverance of mind and deliverance by wisdom that are taintless with the destruction of the taints.
>
> *Majjhima Nikāya 71, Tevijjavacchagotta Sutta, PTSM1 p.482; cf. MDBB pp.587–88*

In this *Sutta,* the Buddha reinforces his observation by adding, "There is no *samaṇa* (holy man) or *brāhmaṇ* who is simultaneously all-knowing *(sabbaññū)* and all-seeing; that is not possible."[3]

In the *Anguttara Nikāya,* the Buddha answers in an oblique and intellectually confusing manner. He says that he "directly knows" everything in the cosmos, but adds ambiguously that it "has been realized by the Tathāgata, but in the Tathāgata it has not been established." He then adds that he neither knows, nor does he not know, nor does he even recognize a knower (as separate from what is known). He simply knows things as they really are, as "Such *(Tādī)*":

> The Tathāgata – being ever the same among things seen, heard, sensed, and cognized – is 'Such *(Tādī)*'. And I tell you, there is no other 'Such *(Tādī)*' higher or more sublime.... I know, I see – that is just how it is! – the Tathāgata clings to nothing.
>
> *Anguttara Nikāya 4:24, Kālakārāma Sutta, PTSA2 p.25; cf. ANTB, NDBB pp.412–13*

His bottom line seems to be that an enlightened being knows what he knows and how he knows, but his kind of oceanic knowing cannot be confined in or comprehended by the tiny inkwell of human intellectual knowing.

The same conclusions are reached in a dialogue in the *Questions of King Milinda,* in which King Milinda asks the Buddhist sage Nāgasena how it can be that the Buddha is said to have been omniscient when he had to think about something in order to know it. Nāgasena tells the king that "the thinking power of the omniscient *(sabbaññū) buddhas,*... being purified in every respect,... is clear and active in its high quality, and beyond our ken." Their "thinking powers are, on every point, brought quickly into play, and act with ease," as if "a dart well burnished, free from rust, perfectly smooth, with a fine edge, straight, without a crook or a flaw in it, were to be set on a powerful crossbow." The minds of others, on the other hand, are dull, slow and greatly limited by the effects of "lust, ill will, delusion, and wrongdoing". Even the minds of those who have embraced "right views" are held back by traces of the passions that prevent them from entering the "higher regions". Even the minds of those who can enter the higher regions still face impediments that have been overcome by the *buddhas.* The text progressively depicts seven stages on the path to enlightenment, from the dullest and most worldly oriented, through the *sotāpanna* (stream-enterer), *sakadāgāmī* (once-returner), *anāgāmī* (non-returner), *arhat* (worthy one), *pratyeka-buddha* (one who attains enlightenment for himself alone), and so to the final stage of the *samyak-saṃbuddha* (completely awakened one). At each stage there is a higher degree of internal purity, a deeper penetration into the higher regions,[4] and consequently an increasingly encompassing awareness.

The later *Mahāyāna* tradition understands the omniscience of a *buddha* in a more absolute as well as philosophical manner. Everything is understood to be a part of one interconnected whole, and since a fully enlightened *buddha* knows the whole, he automatically knows all the parts thereof. This perspective is apparent in the various *Mahāyāna* texts. In the *Avataṃsaka Sūtra,* a *buddha,* as an all-pervading cosmic being, is said to manifest at a multitude of different levels among the many heavens, known as "pure lands" or "*buddha*-lands". These manifestations of a *buddha* include those called "Honoured Omniscient *(yīqièzhì)* and All-Conquering One", "Omniscient *(yīqièzhì)* Wondrously Awakened to Wisdom", and by other similar epithets, although these are not depicted as the highest levels of wisdom, since there are other *buddha*-lands beyond them:

> Above this, beyond as many worlds as there are tiny specks of dust in a *buddha*-land, there is a world called Flaming-Jewel Ornament; the *buddha* there is named Pure Wisdom of Everything....
>
> Above this, beyond as many worlds as there are tiny specks of dust in a *buddha*-land, there is a world called All-Illuminating Lion Throne; the *buddha* there is named Great Light of Unending Power Awakened to Wisdom....
>
> Above this,... there is a world called Ornament of Travelling Light Beams; the *buddha* there is named Honoured Omniscient *(yīqièzhì)* and All-Conquering One.
>
> Above this,... there is a world called Wheel of Great Stability; the *buddha* there is named Light of the Ocean of Nonregression Merits and Virtues.
>
> Above this,... there is a world called Unending Sound; the *buddha* there is named Omniscient *(yīqièzhì)* Wondrously Awakened to Wisdom.
>
> Above this,... there is a world called Tree Blossom Banner; the *buddha* there is named Sound of the Realm of Unlimited Wisdom.
>
> *Avataṃsaka Sūtra 5, T10 279:46b7–8, 10–11, c16–22*

Later in the same text, all the deities in the *tushita* heaven catch a glimpse of the awesome effulgence of the Buddha, recognizing his unequivocal omniscience:

> Then, by the great spiritual power *(shénlì)* of the Tathāgata *(rúlái)*, by the roots of goodness stemming from his past, and by his inconceivable and unrestrained power, all the gods and goddess in the *tushita* heaven saw the Buddha from afar, as clearly as if he were right before them. And all were of the same thought: "In this world, the manifestation of a *tathāgata (rúlái)* is rarely encountered. Now we have the opportunity to see the omniscient one *(yīqièzhì)*, the one with unlimited, true awareness of everything, the one with the perfect universal consciousness."
>
> *Avataṃsaka Sūtra 23, T10 279:117c7–11*

As an aspect of enlightenment and liberation, omniscience is one of the objectives of the *bodhisattva*'s path. Hence, the *Mahāratnakūṭa Sūtra* speaks in a number of places of the *bodhisattva*'s pursuit of "all-knowing wisdom *(yīqièzhì)*",[5] listing the quest for such understanding as his tenth objective, associated with the *pāramitā* (perfection) of generosity.[6]

See also: **sarvajñāna** (▸3).

1. *E.g. Majjhima Nikāya* 71, *Tevijjavacchagotta Sutta, PTSM1* p.482.

2. *E.g. Majjhima Nikāya* 14, *Cūladukkhakkhandha Sutta, PTSM1* p.92.
3. *Majjhima Nikāya* 90, *Kaṇṇakatthala Sutta, PTSM2* pp.127–28; *cf. MDBB* pp.735–36.
4. *Questions of King Milinda* 4:19–27, *PTSQ* pp.102–7; *cf. SBE35* pp.154–61.
5. *E.g. Mahāratnakūṭa Sūtra* 32, 33, *T11* 310:551b22, 563b19.
6. *Mahāratnakūṭa Sūtra* 45, *T11* 310:648c12.

second sight The ability to foretell the future, perceive distant events, *etc.;* clairvoyance. See **clairvoyance**.

shakti (H/Pu) *Lit.* power, energy; esoterically, a miraculous or supernatural power; more commonly known as a *siddhi.*

See also: **Shakti** (4.2), **siddhi**.

shéngōng (C) *Lit.* a miracle, a remarkable feat. See **supernormal powers (in Daoism)**.

shéntōng (C) *Lit.* remarkable ability; magical power, supernormal power; various extra-ordinary powers acquired by Daoist adepts, masters, and *xiān* (immortals) as a natural consequence of their ascent to spiritual heights. See **supernormal powers (in Daoism)**.

siddhi (S/Pa/H/Pu), **dngos grub** (T) *Lit.* attainment, accomplishment, fulfilment, fruition, success, perfection; power, might, magnificence, splendour, greatness; dignity, exalted rank; riches, prosperity, opulence, wealth; spiritual felicity, bliss, beatitude, emancipation, liberation; spiritual perfection, power or attainment, sometimes referred to as *mahāsiddhi* (great accomplishment, great perfection); esoterically, miraculous power, superhuman power attained by *yoga* or other spiritual practices; from the same root as *siddha* (an accomplished one, an adept, a perfect one, a spiritually liberated one). *Siddhi* appears in the *Mahābhārata* as a proper name, as well as a term for powers attained through yogic practices; in the *Pañcha-tantra,* a *siddhi* is any unusual talent or ability; in the *Manu Smṛiti,* it is a legal term referring to the fulfilment or repayment of a debt.

More generally known in Buddhist Pali texts as *iddhis,* Hindu, Jain and Buddhist literature frequently mention miraculous powers, providing many examples of their use. Buddhist texts differentiate between the mundane *(laukika) siddhis* and the supramundane *siddhi,* which is the attainment of buddhahood or supreme enlightenment *(bodhi).* The mundane *siddhis* are variously listed, and include the *iddhis* of the Pali literature, as well as the six *abhijñās* (Pa. *abhiññā,* knowledges, skills). Many of these, especially in Tibetan texts, are derived from the descriptions found in yogic and tantric literature, but given a Tibetan Buddhist flavour.

Hindu yogic and tantric texts generally say that *siddhis* are acquired through *haṭha yoga, prāṇāyāma* (control of the *prāṇa,* the physical breath as well as the subtle life energy), the raising of the *kuṇḍalinī,* and the repetition of certain *mantras.* The practices involve concentration at the various *chakras* (bodily centres of *prāṇa*) and mastery of the particular subtle element *(bhūta* or *tattva)* predominating at that *chakra.* By controlling the subtle aspects of matter through the power of a concentrated mind, various phenomena can be manifested at the external material level. The many texts enumerate a large number of *siddhis* of which eight (*ashṭa-siddhis,* eight accomplishments or powers), sometimes called the *mahāsiddhis* (great *siddhis*), are listed, with some variations in their description or interpretation from one text to another.[1] They are:

1. *Aṇiman, aṇimā. Lit.* minuteness, fineness, thinness; like an atom *(aṇu);* the power to shrink, to become as minute as an atom; to become so small that things of the minutest size, even an atom, can be seen. In this context, an atom is understood as the smallest possible particle of matter, according to the theories of some ancient philosophers:

> He who meditates on Me (Kṛishṇa) as the subtlest of the subtle, as dwelling in the subtle form of the elements *(tanmātras),* concentrating on that aspect of Me without distraction, is able to reduce himself to the size of an atom – that is the *siddhi* of *aṇimā.*
>
> *Bhāgavata Purāṇa 11:15.10*

According to the *Laghu-Yoga-Vāsishṭha,* powers such as *aṇimā* and the rest come about through the practice of *yoga* – especially *prāṇāyāma* and the awakening of the *kuṇḍalinī* – together with the "exercise of a determined will":

> It is only by the exercise of a determined will that persons, although ignorant, can transform poison into nectar, and the reverse, thus entirely changing the nature of things.... All psychic powers, such as *aṇimā,* and others acquired through meditation, are awakened by this course alone. This will be self-evident only to those who have mastered the *siddhis* of *yoga* through self-illumination.
>
> *Laghu-Yoga-Vāsishṭha 6:9; cf. TYVL p.281*

2. *Mahiman, mahimā. Lit.* huge *(mahā)*-ness; magnitude, grandeur, majesty, glory, might, power, high rank; the power to expand, to assume extensive size at will, to become of vast proportions, to touch any object at a distance, to expand into space and become as vast as the cosmos, with a single vision of the entire universe:

> He who meditates upon Me as the all-pervading supreme Soul, contemplating Me as the essence of everything and as pervading all the elements (*bhūtas, i.e.* earth, water, fire, air, and ether), and expanding his mind in that dimension, acquires the power of magnification, taking on the all-pervading vastness of that element – that is the *siddhi* of *mahimā:*
>
> *Bhāgavata Purāṇa 11:15.11*

This *siddhi,* like many of the others, can be understood both externally and internally. The *Tattva-Vaishāradi* explains *mahiman* in physical terms, as the power to become as big as an elephant, a mountain, or an entire town.[2] The *Mahāprabha,* however, describes it as *vibhutva* (pervasiveness), as the inner capacity for expansion of mind and consciousness.[3]

3. *Laghiman, laghimā. Lit.* light *(laghu)*-ness; levity, lack of weight, subtleness; the power to assume excessive lightness, to become as light as cotton down, to become almost weightless, to levitate, and to move about at fantastic speed by understanding the nature of time:

> He who meditates on Me as the very essence of the elements acquires the power to make himself extremely subtle, by which means he may realize the subtle truths of time – that is the *siddhi* of *laghimā.*
>
> *Bhāgavata Purāṇa 11:15.12*

4. *Gariman, garimā. Lit.* heaviness, weight; probably from *guru* (heavy); the power to assume extraordinary heaviness, such that one cannot be moved.

5. *Prāpti. Lit.* advent, reach, range, occurrence; the power to enter or penetrate everywhere; the power to transport oneself anywhere one desires, even to distant places, like the moon; also called *yatra-kāmāvasāya.* The *Bhāgavata Purāṇa* interprets *prāpti* to mean the ability to enter into the mind and senses of other beings, and perceive things as they are perceiving them:

> He who meditates upon and absorbs himself in Me as the essence of his self *(ahaṃ-tattve),* regarding Me as the indwelling essence of the sense organs, such a *yogin* attains the *siddhi* of *prāpti.*
>
> *Bhāgavata Purāṇa 11:15.13*

According to the *Yoga-Bhāshya,* a yogi with this power can literally touch the moon with his fingertips.[4] A more reasonable perspective may be that such a yogi enjoys an expanded consciousness, such that the nature of the moon is within his understanding. Alternatively, it may be that the moon refers to seeing the inner light, which can appear like that of the moon.

6. *Prākāmya. Lit.* freedom of will, wilfulness; irresistible willpower or command; complete freedom of will; the power by which all impediments to one's will can be removed; the power to obtain anything merely by willing it to be so; the power to obtain anything desired:

> He who meditates upon Me as the all-pervading *mahat-tattva* (cosmic intelligence and energy) can realize all his desires – that is the *siddhi* of *prākāmya.*
>
> *Bhāgavata Purāṇa 11:15.14*

According to the *Yoga-Bhāshya, prākāmya* is "the non-obstruction of desires, whereby a *yogī* can dive into and rise from the surface of the earth, as if in water".[5] *Prākāmya* is also known as *kāmāvasāyitā,* the power to fulfil all one's desires *(kāma).* The *Yoga-Bhāshya,* which lists *kāmāvasāyitā* as a separate *siddhi,* maintains that *kāmāvasāyitā* permits creation, rearrangement, and even dissolution of the primal elements *(bhūtas)* of the material world, although it also observes that this does not mean that the *yogī* can run counter to the divine will, and disturb the natural order of things:

> Though he has the power, he does not change the nature of things. Why? Because they have been determined by the will of the primeval, perfect Being *(Īshvara)* of irresistible will.
>
> *Yoga-Bhāshya 3:45; cf. YDSP p.126, YSPB p.278*

This is contrary to the many stories in yogic and Indian literature where *yogīs* routinely upset the natural order in order to achieve their ends.

7. *Īshitā, īshitva. Lit.* lord *(īsha)*-ship; overlordship; complete supremacy, superiority, or greatness; absolute mastery over all things, animate and inanimate; the attainment of divine power; complete control over nature; the power to become a commanding leader, to have dominion over others and to become great in the eyes of others; the power to become godlike, even including the creation and destruction of creatures:

> He who meditates upon me as *Vishṇu* (pervader of the universe), the controller of *māyā* (illusion), which consists of the three *guṇas*

(attributes) and the essence of time, has control over the bodies of all living beings – that is the *siddhi* of *īshitva.*

Bhāgavata Purāṇa 11:15.15

8. *Vashitā, vashitva.* From *vash* (to will, to command, to subjugate); subjection, subjugation, mastery, control; being one's own master; the power of dominion over one's own self; also, the power to subdue, overpower or command other beings, human or otherwise; the power to tame wild animals and mesmerize human beings by the exercise of one's will; the power to control both animate and inanimate objects:

> He who meditates upon Me as *Nārāyaṇa,* the transcendental and fourth Principle known as *Bhagavān* – who enjoys universal lordship, *dharma,* fame, prosperity, wisdom, and dispassion – shares My nature, mastering the *siddhi* known as *vashitā.*
>
> *Bhāgavata Purāṇa 11:15.16*

In Buddhism, a *bodhisattva* is said to possess ten kinds of *vashitā* (mastery). These consist of control over various aspects of existence: lifespan *(āyur-vashitā),* the mind *(citta-),* adornments or possessions *(parishkāra-),* deeds or actions *(karma-),* vows *(praṇidhāna-),* faith and understanding or liberation *(adhimukti-),* spiritual powers *(ṛiddhi-),* knowledge *(jñāna-),* coming into being or rebirth *(upapatti-),* and *dharma (dharma-vashitā).*[6]

Such then are the eight primary *siddhis.* However, there are variations between the lists of the eight that are found in different texts. In the *Bhāgavata Purāṇa,* for instance, *garimā* is absent, the eighth *siddhi* being *kāmāvasāyitā* (ending of desire), which is interpreted to mean complete contentment and divine bliss:

> He who meditates upon Me as *Brahman* devoid of attributes attains supreme bliss, all desires being fulfilled – this is *kāmāvasāyitā.*
>
> *Bhāgavata Purāṇa 11:15.17*

The *siddhis* are sometimes interpreted metaphorically or symbolically. For example, the power to become minute or huge can be understood as the power to project one's consciousness into the tiniest details of creation and the creative process, or to expand one's consciousness to encompass the entire creation. It is significant that as an integral aspect of attaining the eight *siddhis,* the *Bhāgavata Purāṇa* presumes an increasing expansion of mystical perception or experiential consciousness of the way in which the elements or primary constituents and forces of creation are put together. This is how the *siddhis* arise, and is why they are associated with meditational practice. They arise simultaneously with a mystically expanded consciousness. Thus, the first *siddhi* arises from an internal consciousness of the subtle form of the elements, the *tanmātras,* that comprise the universe; the second *siddhi* arises from a consciousness of the Divine pervading the essential elements *(bhūtas);* the third from consciousness of the Divine as the essence of these elements; and so on, ascending through the essence of individuality, the cosmic intelligence *(mahat),* the realm in which *māyā* is first manifest, and the transcendent Being, finally reaching the absolute, impersonal, and attributeless *Brahman.*

The *Bhāgavata Purāṇa* also lists ten more minor *siddhis:*[7]

1. *Anūrmimattva. Lit.* power *(mattva)* of no disturbance *(anūrmi);* being undisturbed by hunger, thirst, and other bodily feelings.

2. *Dūra-shravaṇa, dūra-shruti. Lit.* remote *(dūra)* hearing *(shravaṇa, shruti);* hearing things from far away; inner hearing.

3. *Dūra-darshana, dūra-dṛishṭi. Lit.* remote *(dūra)* vision *(darshana, dṛishṭi);* seeing things from far away; inner vision.

4. *Manaḥ-java. Lit.* impulse *(javah)* of the mind *(manas);* moving the body at the speed of thought.

5. *Kāma-rūpa. Lit.* form *(rūpa)* at will *(kāma);* assuming any form at will.

6. *Parakāya-pravesha, paradeha-pravesha, parasharīra-āvesha. Lit.* entering *(pravesha, āvesha)* the body *(kāya, deha, sharīra)* of another *(para);* entering the body of another being; a *siddhi* arising from intense concentration at the *ājñā* (eyebrows), *anāhata* (heart), or *mūlādhāra* (rectal) *chakras;* said in the *Laghu-Yoga-Vāsishṭha* to be attained when "the *kuṇḍalinī shakti* rises up the *sushumṇā*. . . . If the *prāṇa* is rendered steady for a long time, flowing to a distance of twelve digits from the face through the practice of *rechaka* (expiration), then entry into other bodies *(pravishati-aparām-purīm)* can be effected."[8]

   The *Shiva Purāṇa* says that *paradeha-pravesha* is used by a master to awaken a disciple's *kuṇḍalinī.*[9]

7. *Svachchhanda mṛityu. Lit.* death *(mṛityu)* by one's own *(sva)* desire *(chhanda);* the power to die according to one's own desire; dying when one wishes to do so; also called *ichchhā-mṛityu* (death by wish).

8. *Devānām saha-krīḍā anudarshana. Lit.* witnessing *(anudarshana)* and participating *(saha)* in the play *(krīḍā)* of the gods *(devānām).*

9. *Yathā-saṃkalpa saṃsiddhi. Lit.* complete fulfilment *(saṃsiddhi)* of one's *(yathā)* intention *(saṃkalpa);* the power to fulfil all one's desires; the power to accomplish whatever one sets out to achieve.

10. *Ājñā apratihatā gati. Lit.* power *(gati)* of unhindered *(apratihatā)* command *(ājñā);* irresistible command; the power to ensure that all one's orders are obeyed.

Following this list, the *Bhāgavata Purāṇa* goes on to mention a further five *siddhis:*[10]

1. *Trikāla-jñāna. Lit.* knowledge *(jñāna)* of the three *(tri-)* times *(kāla);* knowledge of past, present, and future.

2. *Advandva. Lit.* non *(a-)* duality *(dvandva);* release from duality; rising above duality, going beyond the pairs of opposites.

3. *Para-chitta-jñāna. Lit.* knowledge *(jñāna)* of another *(para)* mind *(chitta);* awareness of the thoughts of others; acquired, according to the *Yoga Sūtras,* by focused attention *(saṃyama)* upon the mental processes of others.[11]

4. *Agni-arkāmbu-vishādīnām pratishṭambhaḥ. Lit.* countering the influence *(pratishṭambhaḥ)* of fire *(agni),* sun *(arka),* water *(ambu),* poison *(visha),* and so on *(ādīnām);* the power to neutralize the influence of fire, sun, water, poison, and other material elements.

5. *Aparājaya. Lit.* beyond *(apara)* defeat *(ajaya);* the power to suffer no defeat in any undertaking.

Yogic and tantric texts also mention other *siddhis,* some more or less synonymous with those already listed, others more descriptive of states of inner consciousness. These include:

Ākāsha-gamana. Lit. space *(ākāsha)* moving *(gamana);* moving at will through space, levitation; understood metaphorically, ascent to higher realms; also called *manogati* (mind walking, to travel in mind wherever one desires):

> If, through the practice of *pūraka* (breathing in, inspiration), the *kuṇḍalinī shakti* is replenished and caused to shine with a resplendent light, then the body acquires the stability of Mahāmeru (a mythological mountain), and becomes strong.
>
> Then, if the consciousness pervading this body, filled with *prāṇa* through (the practice of) *pūraka* (inspiration), takes an upward course, it will make that body become a walker of the skies *(vyomagāmin)*. . . .

> Through the intense practice of *yoga, yogīs* rise up into the air, and roam about therein.
>
> *Laghu-Yoga-Vāsishṭha 6:9; cf. TYVL p.280*

Aparānta-jñāna. Lit. knowledge *(jñāna)* of the final end *(aparānta);* prescience concerning the time of one's death; awareness of how and when one's destiny *(prārabdha) karma* will come to an end.

Bhūcharī-siddhi. Lit. moving on the earth *(bhūcharī)* power *(siddhi);* the power to move at will all over the world. The *Yogatattva Upanishad* lists *bhūcharī-siddhi* as one of the results of practising *prāṇāyāma,*[12] while the *Shiva Saṃhitā* maintains that it can be attained through holding the attention in the heart *chakra.*[13]

Bhūta-jaya. Lit. conquest *(jaya)* of the elements *(bhūtas);* according to Patañjali, arises from *saṃyama* (profound concentration) upon the origins of material substance in its gross, subtle, and other forms.[14]

Bindu-siddhi or *bindu-jaya. Lit.* power *(siddhi)* over semen *(bindu);* conquest *(jaya)* of the semen; control over ejaculation and seminal discharge; said by the *Haṭha Yoga Pradīpikā* to be one of the signs of success in *yoga:*

> A slim body, light on the face, manifestation of the Sound *(Nāda),* bright eyes, good health, conquest of the semen *(bindu-jaya),* good digestion, and purification of the *nāḍīs* are indications of success *(siddhi)* in *haṭha yoga.*
>
> *Haṭha Yoga Pradīpikā 2:78; cf. HYP p.27*

Dārduri-siddhi. Lit. froglike *(dārduri) siddhi;* frog-jump *siddhi;* the power to rise briefly and automatically off the ground through the practise of *haṭha yoga, prāṇāyāma* and raising of the *kuṇḍalinī, etc.,* while seated in the lotus (cross-legged) posture; a prelude to full levitation and the ability to move about in space all over the world *(bhūcharī-siddhi);* sometimes interpreted as a leap in consciousness or as the ability to travel in one's astral body.

Divya-chakshu. Lit. divine *(divya)* eye *(chakshu);* the inner eye or true clairvoyance, the ability to see all that is happening in heaven and earth, whether near or far; also called *dūra-dashana* (remote vision); in Buddhism (Pa. *dibba-cakkhu*), this power includes knowledge of the death and rebirth of all sentient beings according to their *karma.*

Divya-saṃvid. Lit. divine *(divya)* perception *(saṃvid);* heightened sensory perception, which is said to arise by concentration of the attention at various places within the head. Thus, concentration on the tip of the tongue leads to supernormal awareness of taste;[15] concentration in the head behind the eyes leads to a supernormal vision of inner light, while "concentration on the Sound Current leads to supernormal consciousness of the Supreme, in which the entire universe of energy seems to be vibrating in supreme Music in the ocean of consciousness."[16]

Divya-shrotra. Lit. divine *(divya)* hearing *(shrotra);* the divine, celestial or heavenly ear, or clairaudience, which can hear all sounds, subtle or gross, far or near; one of the six supernormal powers *(abhijñās)* of Buddhism (Pa. *dibba-sota*). According to Patañjali:

By *saṃyam* (deep concentration) on the relationship
between the ear and space *(ākāsha),*
divine hearing *(divya-shrotra)* is obtained.

Patañjali, Yoga Sūtras 3:42

Kāmachāra. Lit. pleasure *(kāma)* by will *(ichchhā);* following one's own inclinations; the power to move to any place at will.

Kāya-indriya-siddhi. Lit. perfection *(siddhi)* of the body *(kāya)* and senses *(indriya);* a body fit for the practice of *yoga,* with the senses under control. Here, Patañjali uses *siddhi* in the sense of 'perfection':

From self-discipline *(tapas),*
arises perfection *(siddhi)* of the body *(kāya)* and the senses *(indriya).*

Patañjali, Yoga Sūtras 2:43

The *Yoga-Bhāshya* adds that such physical perfection is manifested in mastery of the classic *siddhis* and other paranormal powers, such as remote seeing *(dūra-darshana)* and hearing *(dūra-shravaṇa).*[17]

Manojavitva. Lit. fleetness *(javitva)* of the mind *(manas);* moving about at the speed of the mind, *i.e.* instantaneously; perception without need of any vehicle or instrument (body or physical senses); said in the *Yoga Sūtras* to arise from control *(saṃyama)* of the processes of sensory perception,[18] along with complete mastery of elemental nature *(pradhāna-jaya).*

Mantra-siddhi. Lit. mantra power *(siddhi),* a *mantra* being a verbal formula used to concentrate the mind by its constant repetition; the effect of a *mantra;* the power gained by the successful practice of a *mantra;* complete mastery of a *mantra* and fulfilment of its purpose. Yogic and tantric texts prescribe specific *mantras* for the attainment of particular *siddhis,* the *mantras* in these cases being used more or less as magic spells. The desired *siddhi* is known as the *mantra-siddhi* of that particular *mantra.*

Maraṇa-siddhi. Lit. death *(maraṇa)* power *(siddhi);* the power to kill by thought alone.[19]

Pradhāna-jaya. Lit. mastery *(jaya)* of nature *(pradhāna), pradhāna* (in this context, synonymous with *prakṛiti*) being the subtle blueprint of all the forms that evolve and appear in what is understood as 'nature'; mastery of the elemental forms of nature, from which all other forms are manifested; said in the *Yoga Sūtras* to arise from control *(saṃyama)* of the processes of sensory perception,[20] along with fleetness of mind *(manojavitva);* also called *aishvarya* (lordship, supremacy). According to the *Tattva-Vaishāradi,* a *yogī* with this power has the ability to manifest thousands of bodies for himself, in order to move about at will through heavenly and earthly realms.[21] These 'bodies' will be appropriate to the region through which the *yogī* wishes to travel – an astral body for the astral realm, a causal body for the causal realm, and so on.

Vāk-siddhi, vākya-siddhi. Lit. speech *(vāc, vākya)* power *(siddhi);* the power of prediction or prophecy; the power by which whatever a person says comes to pass; variously said to arise from full realization of and absorption in *satya* (truthfulness, veracity) and/or from the repetition of *mantras.*

Vashīkaraṇa. Lit. act *(kāraṇa)* of subjection *(vash);* the power to subjugate; the supernatural power to control the actions, feelings and desires of other people, and bring them under one's own influence; popularly used to attract the love of a desired one, to control one's boss or other significant people in one's life, *etc.* The means used to exercise this power include a *vashīkaraṇa mantra,* which is a verbal spell or formula designed to bring about the desired objective; and a *vashīkaraṇa yantra,* a *yantra* (in this context) being a diagram or geometric device symbolizing aspects of the body and the cosmos, sometimes with astrological aspects, which is likewise designed to control the feelings *etc.* of another person.

Vāyu-siddhi. Lit. air *(vāyu)* power *(siddhi);* power over the *tattva* (element) of air, enabling levitation:

> When the *yogī,* though remaining in *padmāsana* (lotus posture), can rise in the air and leave the ground, then know that he has gained *vāyu-siddhi,* which destroys the darkness of the world.
>
> *Shiva Saṃhitā 3:42, SSV p.31*

Though numerous, even these are not exhaustive of the *siddhis* mentioned in the voluminous yogic and tantric texts, some seeming more exotic than others. The *Shiva Saṃhitā,* for example, in addition to some of the stock *siddhis,* also speaks of subtle sight *(sūkshma-dṛishṭi),* turning base metals into gold by rubbing them with one's excrement and urine, and becoming invisible *(adṛishya).*[22]

Breezing through a number of *siddhis,* Patañjali explains how they all arise from the power of a deeply concentrated mind, which he calls *saṃyama,* by means of which particular things are brought into consciousness. For example:

> By bringing impressions *(saṃskāras)* into consciousness,
> a knowledge of previous births *(pūrva-jāti-jñāna)* is acquired.
> By *saṃyama* on the mental energies of others,
> a knowledge of the mind of others *(para-chitta-jñāna)* is acquired. . . .

By *saṃyama* on the form and colour of the body,
another's power to receive that form and colour can be suspended.
There being no contact between the eye of the observer
and light from the body,
the power of invisibility *(antardhāna)* is thus acquired.
Similarly, the power by which sound and other sensations
can be made to disappear is acquired....

By *saṃyama* on gross matter, its essential nature *(svarūpa),*
its subtle aspects *(sūkshma),* its derivatives, and their functions,
conquest over the primal elements *(bhūta-jaya)* arises.
Thence arises the manifestation of *aṇiman* and so on, bodily perfection,
and immunity from the domination of these elements.

Patañjali, Yoga Sūtras 3:18–22, 45–46

The *siddhis* are categorized in various ways. Sometimes, they are grouped according to the element *(bhūta)* with which they are associated, and from which the *siddhis* arise when that particular *bhūta* is made the object of focused attention.[23] In a passage reminiscent of the *Yoga Sūtras,* the *Yogashikhā Upanishad* lists the *siddhis* acquired when the "concentration *(dhāraṇā)* of the mind" is focused on the elements and other things:[24]

Now I shall relate, O Lord of the gods, the *siddhis* and the easy way to acquire them by those who have conquered their senses, attained tranquillity, and conquered their breath *(shvāsa)* and their mind. Resting of the mind in the *Nāda* (inner Sound) is the cause of inner hearing *(dūra-shravaṇa).* By resting the mind in its centre *(bindu),* one attains inner vision *(dūra-darshana).* Resting the mind in the *kālātman* (spirit of time) is the origin of the knowledge of the past, present, and future (*trikāla-jñāna,* knowledge of the three times). The riveting of one's mind onto the body and mind of another is what enables entry to other bodies *(parakāya-pravesha)....* Should one perform *dhāraṇā* of his mind on earth, access to the nether world *(pātāla)* is attained,...on water, he will never be vanquished by water,...on fire, he will never be scorched by fire,...on air, he will be able to traverse the sky. Should he perform *dhāraṇā* of his mind on *ākāsha* (ether), he will attain the *siddhis* of attenuation *(aṇimā),* and so on.... Upon whatever the *yogin* – who has succeeded in *yoga* and conquered his senses – shapes his desires, so accordingly will he attain the objects of those desires. In this, the frame of mind alone is the cause.

Yogashikhā Upanishad 5:46–55; cf. YU pp.380–82

The *Yogashikhā Upanishad* differentiates artificial *(kalpita)* from the non-artificial *(akalpita) siddhis.* Artificial *siddhis* are attained by specific means, practised with the intention of developing those particular *siddhis.* The practices employed for the purpose include the use of medicinal herbs *(aushadhi),* alchemical formulae *(rasa),* rites *(kriyā),* magic *(jāla),* and the repetition of *mantras. Siddhis* acquired in this manner are said to be transient, unreliable, and of little value and efficacy.

The non-artificial *siddhis* are those that arise spontaneously and naturally within those who are solely intent on the practice of *yoga* for spiritual realization. The natural outcome of following the spiritual path for a long time, they are permanent, beneficial, efficacious, pleasing to the Lord *(Īshvara),* and are regarded as the distinguishing signs of a true *siddha* (adept):

> *Siddhis* are of two kinds in this world: artificial *(kalpita)* and non-artificial *(akalpita).* Those *siddhis* that are attained by specific means, such as the various ways of employing alchemical formulae *(rasa)* and medicinal herbs *(aushadhi),* the practice of *mantras* and the like, are known as artificial *(kalpita). Siddhis* acquired through such practices are transient, and possess little efficacy.
>
> But those *siddhis* that arise spontaneously, without the employment of such means, within those who are intent on the practice of *yoga* with the sole intention of realizing their own *ātman* (soul) – they are truly acceptable to the Lord *(Īshvara).* The *siddhis* that arise in this manner are known as non-artificial *(akalpita).* Such *siddhis* – which are acquired spontaneously, last forever, are highly efficacious, are born out of longing, and result from one's personal practice of *yoga* – arise after a long time in those that are devoid of (negative) impressions *(vāsanā)* (of previous births). They should be safeguarded by one who is established in the imperishable state of the *Paramātman* through his practice of *mahāyoga.* They should always be kept as profound secrets, when there is no need of using them. This is the common practice adopted by one who has attained success in *yoga.*
>
> *Yogashikhā Upanishad 1:151–56; cf. YU pp.356–57*

The *Upanishad* gives the example that such *siddhis* arise naturally and automatically, just as a person on pilgrimage to Kāshī (Vārāṇasī) passes by several pilgrimage sites *(tīrtha)* on the way. *Siddhis* of this kind are to be regarded as the distinguishing signs of a true *siddha* (adept). Indeed, "One should look upon a person devoid of *siddhis* as in bondage."[25]

In a similar vein, the last section of Patañjali's *Yoga Sūtras,* though it may be a later addition not actually written by Patañjali, maintains that *"siddhis* are obtained by birth *(janman),* herbs *(aushadhi), mantras,* self-discipline *(tapas),* and contemplative absorption *(samādhi)."*[26]

In these instances, herbs *(aushadhi)* probably refers to herbs, fungi and other preparations with hallucinogenic and psychedelic properties, such as the *soma* described in the *Vedas.* The use of such substances to induce out-of-the-body states is common among the shamans and holy men of tribal and indigenous peoples throughout the world. Obtaining *siddhis* by birth *(janman)* refers to those who are born with the gift, having done the necessary practice in previous lives.

The stereotypical Western mind, trained in rationality and external science, generally finds it hard to accept the possibility of the miraculous control of nature. This is because the nature of mind and consciousness and their interaction with the field of sensory perception or experience have not been properly understood.

All seemingly supernatural power stems from inward concentration of the mind. When an individual is able to take his mind and soul to any subtle realm, either of the physical universe or higher up within, he begins to perceive how the manifestation of the so-called external world comes about through the interplay of *karma* and mental forces, of which, in his normal waking consciousness, he is unaware.

Everything without is an expression or manifestation of what lies within. When the mind and soul become aware of this creative process, through an expansion of consciousness, all that lies below can be readily manipulated, resulting in phenomena that people call miracles.

A person standing at the side of a stream can, by physical means, change the colour, character, or even direction of the water as it flows downstream. But they have far less control of what happens further upstream. Similarly with the flow of the creative process. An individual can modify the creative processes only in accordance with the height to which he himself has attained, and can only manipulate things that lie within the scope of his expanded mind and consciousness. Only a soul who has reached the ultimate Source of the creative flow has full control over everything. But since such souls are one with the divine creative will, they have no need to tamper egocentrically with the creative process.

Yogīs and others who conquer the six *chakras* of *piṇḍa* (the physical body and universe) find that the conquest of each *chakra* brings with it various *siddhis* associated with the *tattva* administered at that centre. The rectal or *mūlādhāra chakra,* for example, administers the earth or *pṛithvī tattva,* and the conquest of this *chakra* gives dominion over this *tattva* in its physical expression; similarly with the other *chakras.*

Such powers come automatically to one who attains concentration at the eye centre, which lies above the five lower centres associated with the five *tattvas.* Such a practitioner may thus be able stop a fast moving train through the force of mind and willpower alone, so that it cannot move another inch forward, and without causing a crash.

Though yogic texts may enumerate the many *siddhis,* yet they routinely point out that they are obstacles on the path, and should not be used. Their use or even the consideration thereof engenders a sense of personal power and ego, drawing the attention down into the material world. Patañjali calls them obstacles in the path of true *yogīs:*

> There should be no attachment to
> or pride concerning the attainment of this high position.
> Otherwise, it will not be possible to maintain that high estate....
>
> They are obstacles to *samādhi;*
> But properly used, supernatural power
> can be used to combat instinctive natural forces.
>
> *Patañjali, Yoga Sūtras 3:52, 38*

Patañjali's verse is echoed throughout yogic literature. The *Yogatattva Upanishad,* after listing some of the *siddhis* that arise from concentration *(dhāraṇā)* of the mind, adds:

> The wise *yogin* should regard these powers *(siddhi)* as great obstacles to the attainment of *yoga,* and he should never take delight in them. The *yogī-rāj* (the king of *yogīs*) should not demonstrate his powers to anyone whatever. He should live in the world like an ignorant man or a fool or a deaf man, keeping his powers *(sāmarthya)* concealed. He will no doubt receive many requests from his own disciples, who, out of their own desire, will ask him to demonstrate his powers to them. But distracted by the attempt to comply with them, he will become negligent of his own practice.
>
> *Yogatattva Upanishad 76–78; cf. TMU p.150, YU pp.313–14*

The *Linga Purāṇa* says that as initial obstacles (human weaknesses *etc.*) on the path disappear through devoted practice, they are replaced by new ones – the *siddhis.*[27] Other texts say much the same: "The *siddhis*... cannot in any way help one to attain the seat of *Paramātman* (the supreme Self);"[28] "Knowers of the Self *(ātma-jñānīs)* do not long for these *siddhis;*"[29] "The *yogin* should not, with a fickle mind, allow his mind to dwell upon the *siddhis;*"[30] "Those wise ones, who practise the highest *yoga* in order to realize Me through My grace, regard these *siddhis* as impediments and a waste of time *(kālakshpana);*"[31] and:

> By various methods, some *yogīs* free the body from disease and old age, and keep it perpetually youthful. Thus they engage in *yoga* for the purpose of achieving supernatural powers *(siddhis).* This... is

> not valued very highly by those expert in transcendental knowledge. Indeed, they consider endeavour for such perfection useless, since the soul, like a tree, is permanent, but the body, like a tree's fruit, is subject to destruction.
>
> *Bhāgavata Purāṇa 11:28.41–42; cf. SB17 pp.701–2*

The real purpose of *yoga* is to dive deep within the innermost layers of consciousness, whereas the display of *siddhis* tends to draw the attention outwards and scatter the mind. The practitioner is thereby exposed to many temptations and distractions, leading eventually to their spiritual downfall. Indian mythology contains numerous stories relating the downfall of *yogīs* and *ṛishis* resulting from their use of miraculous powers. If the *siddhis* have a benefit, it is to give the *yogī* greater knowledge and mastery of the inner planes, and thereby to accelerate spiritual progress. The *Tattva-Vaishāradi* observes that although unnecessary for the attainment of emancipation *(kaivalya),* they can have a benefit in that they may strengthen faith *(shraddhā)* by providing convincing evidence of the validity and efficacy of the discipline being followed.[32]

Only a master of a very high order, who is fully conscious of the divine power by which everything in creation is manifested, is able to use his supernatural power without detriment to himself; and when he does so, it is only for the spiritual benefit of his disciples. Although such a master can do anything he wishes, anywhere in creation, he always lives in accordance with the principles of the level of creation at which he is functioning at any particular moment.

For these reasons, the most spiritually elevated mystics or saints have always spoken of the use of miraculous powers as distractions on the path of pure spirituality, liable to increase ego and keep the mind engrossed in the lower phenomena of the creation. They point out that to indulge in the performance of miracles only wastes spiritual power, and encourages a sense of superiority and egotism. One who uses miraculous power to manipulate the forces of nature feels himself, in a subtle manner, to be apart from God, at odds with the divine will, wishing to change it according to his own ideas and will. The will of the highest saints, on the other hand, is perfectly aligned to the Divine, and their vision encompasses the whole of creation.

If such saints or perfect masters do perform miracles, they do so from the context of this all-encompassing vision of God and the creation, and their purpose is always for the spiritual betterment of the recipient. Mostly, such miracles are of a subtle nature and are meaningful only to the disciple at that particular point in their spiritual evolution. In a certain sense, once a perfect master has taken responsibility for a soul, the entire life of that disciple becomes a miracle, though the disciple may be unaware of what is going on, for such a master takes responsibility for the administration and scheduling of the disciple's *karma.* A master may even take on some of the *karma* of the disciple. Even so, the *karma* still has to be accounted for in one way or another. As Maharaj Charan Singh explains:

> The master stands as a ransom for the souls which he takes out of the realm of *Kāl* (negative power, universal mind). The ransom is, that whatever is due to Caesar must be paid to Caesar,[33] whether the master pays on his own body, or he makes the disciple pay. So if saints want to perform miracles, they have to pay for them through their body, they have to share the *karma.* When they share the burden and *karma* of their disciples, if the disciple is weak and cannot pay, they have to pay for it definitely.
>
> But generally, there are hardly one or two instances in a saint's life where so-called miracles are performed. Generally, they do not perform them, because they like to live in the will of the Lord. Miracles come when the lower mind comes in, and at every step Christ says that "I have merged my mind into the will of the Lord; I have no will of my own; I do not do anything for my own fame or glory." One who performs miracles does it for his own fame. But Christ says that "I do what my Father wants me to do; I am happy to live in His will."[34] So when living in the will of the Father, the question of miracles does not arise. The Lord can do whatever He feels like, and saints are happy to live in His will.
>
> *Maharaj Charan Singh, Light on Saint Matthew, LSMC p.109*

In fact, the greatest miracle of all is the salvation of souls and the forgiveness of sins, which is the purpose of the highest saints in coming to this world. In this sense, the entire life of a saint is a miracle and is of an altogether different nature from that of other human beings. Other souls come to this world as a result of their *karma.* They have no freedom, but are constrained to act according to their past *karma.* Saints, on the other hand, have no *karma* of their own and have a truly free hand in everything they do. Their coming and their going, as well as the course of their lives are entirely within their control. *That* is a real miracle. But because it happens in harmony with the divine will, no one but their disciples may ever even begin to glimpse what is really going on. Maharaj Charan Singh again explains:

> What greater miracle can come in a disciple's life than that his whole attitude towards life is changed? What greater miracle can there be than that? He becomes blind to the world and opens his eyes towards his Home. He gets life! When at first he was dead, now he is living; what better miracle can there be than that? People who were running after worldly pursuits and worldly things and desires, now they do not

want to look at them or see them, they have no time to even talk about them. Day and night they are filled with love and devotion for the Father, and now they are running after the Father in the same manner and with the same zeal. Where other people weep and cry and lament, they become contented. Not the slightest sign of sorrow comes to their face when a loved one departs or dies; where other people may even commit suicide if any relation or friend of theirs dies.

So that is the miracle which comes into every man's life when he comes to the path. And there are some other times also, just to convince the disciple that he should remain on the path, and be on the path, that they do a miracle. But when such a thing happens in a disciple's life, he should not broadcast it; he has to digest all those things within himself, because that is a personal experience he is getting. That is a personal miracle for him, a personal grace from the master, or from the Lord, for himself.

Maharaj Charan Singh, Light on Saint Matthew, LSMC p.110

Other Indian saints *(sants)* have said the same. The thirteenth-century Nāmdev is very clear:

Pierce the six *chakras,* and ascend upwards:
listen to the divine Melody arising there.
Through the Melody, the turbulent mind is quieted:
know this to be the only way your practice will bear fruit.

Crossing this stage, supernatural powers *(siddhis)* will confront you:
they try to lure you towards their own way.
Entangled in these, the *yogīs* remain deluded:
what benefit can be achieved by such *yoga?*

Yogīs toil hard and subject their bodies to hardship and penance:
they gain supernatural powers *(siddhis)* that then prove a hindrance.
Making no further progress, the *yogīs* return (to rebirth).

Can air be tied into a bundle? –
yet the fool would not understand this.
Discarding the path of true devotion, O Nāma,
in vain do the foolish try other practices.

Nāmdev, Gāthā 2037, SNG pp.770–71; cf. SNPS p.61

Referring to Indian mythology, the fifteenth- and sixteenth-century Indian mystic Ravidās writes that since God is the author of all powers and treasures, why not pay attention to Him, rather than to lesser things? –

He is the ocean of peace, the miraculous Tree of Life,
the wish-fulfilling jewel,
and the *Kāmadhenu* (wish-fulfilling cow)....
The four great blessings, the eighteen *siddhis,*
and the nine treasures are all in the palm of His hand....
(Why do you) not chant with your (inner) tongue: "God, God, God"?
Abandon involvement in all other words.

Ravidās, Ādi Granth 658, AGK

See also: **iddhi**, **ṛiddhi**, **saṃyama**.

1. *E.g. Bhāgavata Purāṇa* 11:15.4–5; *Yoga-Bhāshya* 3:45.
2. *Tattva-Vaishāradi* 3:45.
3. *Mahāprabha* 3:44.
4. *Yoga-Bhāshya* 3:45.
5. *Yoga-Bhāshya* 3:45; *cf. YDSP* p.126.
6. Nāgārjuna, *Dharma-saṃgraha* 74.
7. *Bhāgavata Purāṇa* 11:15.6–7; see also *Brahmā-Vaivarta Purāṇa* 39.
8. *Laghu-Yoga-Vāsishṭha* 6:9; *cf. TYVL* pp.280–81.
9. *Shiva Purāṇa* 7:2.15.6.
10. *Bhāgavata Purāṇa* 11:15.8–9.
11. Patañjali, *Yoga Sūtras* 3:19.
12. *Yogatattva Upanishad* 59.
13. *Shiva Saṃhitā* 5:88.
14. Patañjali, *Yoga Sūtras* 3:45.
15. *Yoga-Bhāshya* 1:35.
16. R.S. Mishra, *Textbook of Yoga Psychology, TYPY* p.151.
17. *Yoga-Bhāshya* 2:43.
18. Patañjali, *Yoga Sūtras* 3:49.
19. *Kaula-Jñāna-Nirṇaya* 4:14.
20. Patañjali, *Yoga Sūtras* 3:49.
21. *Tattva-Vaishāradi* 3:18.
22. *Shiva Saṃhitā* 3:54.
23. *E.g. Linga Purāṇa* 1:9.30–43.
24. See also, *e.g. Yogatattva Upanishad* 72–81.
25. *Yogashikhā Upanishad* 1:157–60; *cf. YU* pp.357–58.
26. Patañjali, *Yoga Sūtras* 4:1; see also *e.g. Varāha Upanishad* 3:29.
27. *Linga Purāṇa* 1:9.13–15.
28. *Varāha Upanishad* 3:29; *cf. TMU* p.176.
29. *Laghu-Yoga-Vāsishṭha* 6:14.4; *cf. TYVL* p.327.
30. *Yogashikhā Upanishad* 5:62; *cf. YU* p.383.
31. *Bhāgavata Purāṇa* 11:15.33; *cf. SB2* p.122, *BPT5* p.2002, *SBWG* p.246.
32. *Tattva-Vaishāradi* 3:55.

33. *Cf. Matthew* 22:21.
34. *E.g. John* 4:34, 5:30, 6:38–40; *Matthew* 7:21, 12:50.

siḥr (A/P) *Lit.* magic, sorcery; a spell, a charm; witchcraft, black magic, white magic; a broad term covering all forms of magic; the manipulation of subtle forces and energies in order to bring about effects in the physical world; also, the divining of future events.

Sorcery is mentioned throughout the *Qur'ān,* as in the retelling of the biblical story of Moses' confrontation with the magicians of Pharaoh,[1] and the unbelievers' response to being shown "clear signs"[2] concerning the divine presence and intelligence in creation:

> When Our clear signs are shown to them, the unbelievers say, of the truth when it is declared to them: "This is plain sorcery *(siḥr)!*"
>
> *Qur'ān 46:7; cf. AYA, KPA, MGK*

Although sorcery is mentioned in a derogatory light in both the *Qur'ān* and the *ḥadīth,*[3] it is not entirely unlawful in Islam. Magic is categorized as being of two kinds: divine and satanic. Divine magic consists of charms containing verses from the *Qur'ān,* particular combinations of numbers, magical diagrams, and so on, as well as uttering the holy name *(al-'ism al-a'ẓam).* This is regarded as lawful.

Satanic magic – according to legend – was originally taught by the fallen angels *Hārūt* and *Mārūt,* and is commonly believed to be performed with the help of the *jinn* (supernatural or spirit beings). It consists of the formation of magic circles *(mandal),* astrology *('ilm al-nujūm),* palmistry *(qiyāfah),* and the reading of omens *(tafa'ūl)* by various means, including geomancy *(raml),* and from the entrails and movements of birds and animals *(zajr).*

Al-Jīlī writes of the science of high magic *(al-siḥr al-'ālī),* which resembles the miracles of saints, and does not depend upon external aids such as incantations, formulae and so on, but solely on man's internal and natural powers:

> In the Way of divine unity, I have some experience of this, and if I had desired I could have assumed any shape in the world and done any deed, but I knew it to be pernicious and therefore abandoned it. Then God endowed me with the secret potency which He placed between K and N (*i.e. Kun* (Be!), the Creative Word).
>
> *Al-Jīlī, al-Insān al-Kāmil 1:101.13ff., in SIM p.139 (n.3)*

Rūmī writes of the alchemy of the masters, calling them "artful fish" who dwell in the divine "Sea". They know the art of turning land-bound human "snakes" into "fish" who swim in the waters of eternity. For it is the divine "Sea" itself that has taught the masters this "lawful magic *(siḥr-i ḥalāl)*":

> In this Sea are artful fish,
> who by magic turn snakes into fish –
> The fish of the deepest depth of the Sea of (divine) Majesty:
> the Sea has taught them lawful magic *(siḥr-i ḥalāl).*
>
> *Rūmī, Maśnavī III:3598–99; cf. MJR4 p.202*

1. *E.g. Qur'ān* 10:76–81, 27:13, *passim; cf. Exodus* 7:1*ff.*
2. *Qur'ān* 37:15, 43:30, 61:6.
3. *Ḥadīth Ṣaḥīḥ al-Bukhārī* 4:51.28, 8:82.840, *passim, HSB.*

sixth sense A general expression for any means of perception of physical events, present or future, other than the five normal senses; an intuitive faculty of the mind that includes clairvoyance, telepathy, extrasensory perception, awareness of the subtle energy vibrations and atmosphere of places, *etc.;* a faculty associated with perception through awareness of subtle mind energies.

See also: **clairvoyance**, **extrasensory perception**.

spiritual healing The restoration of the physical health of one person by another by means of spiritual or mental power or energy, involving the transfer of the debt of sin or *karma* from the healed to the healer; also, the healing of the soul or spirit through realization of its innate spirituality.

See also: **healing**.

spiritual healing See **healing**.

supernormal powers (in Daoism) (C. *shéngōng, shéntōng*) Human beings have always been fascinated by remarkable events and extra-ordinary abilities. In particular, miracles and miraculous incidents – or claims thereof – have been an accepted aspect of many religious and spiritual traditions. Daoism is no exception. To mystics who are able to raise their consciousness to a level where they can perceive how the energies of the physical universe come into being and can manipulate those energies through the focused attention of their higher mind, such events are both possible and understandable.

According to writings attributed to Daoist immortal Lǚ Dòngbīn (*b.c.*796), miracles occur "at the extreme end of natural law", and "once the great *Dào* is accomplished, . . . (they) are manifested at will."[1] The *Zhuāngzǐ* says much the same:

> He who understands the Way *(Dào)* is certain to have command of basic principles *(lǐ)*. He who has command of basic principles is certain to know how to deal with circumstances. And he who knows how to deal with circumstances will not allow things to do him harm. When a man has perfect virtue *(zhìdé)*, fire cannot burn him, water cannot drown him, cold and heat cannot afflict him, birds and beasts cannot injure him.
>
> *Zhuāngzǐ 17, CWCT p.182*

Although mystics may have the power to perform miracles and may on occasion do so out of compassion, in order to create faith in a disciple's mind, they certainly discourage their performance for the sake of show. They also see no benefit in the repetition of miracle stories that tend to become increasingly exaggerated with every retelling. Twelfth-century Daoist master Mǎ Yù is clear that the mind's preoccupation with outer phenomena is detrimental to spiritual progress. Here, to "purify your mind's ground" means to eliminate confused and impure thinking – including dwelling on stories concerning "supernatural phenomena":

> Because of the lunatics (*fēngkuáng, i.e.* masters),
> you escaped from the bondage of your (worldly) home.
> Having completely escaped your familial attachments,
> you now need to purify your mind's ground.
> Stop speaking of nonexistent supernatural phenomena
> and deceiving good people.
> Do not make light of the spirits *(shén)* and insult the ghosts *(guǐ)*.
>
> *Mǎ Yù, Dòngxuán jīnyù jí 8:22a TPEQ p.116*

Nevertheless, many incidents describing spectacular or miraculous feats are related in Daoist literature, which may be considered under several categories.

Magical Transformations

The magical power of transformation or metamorphosis is characteristically credited to advanced Daoist adepts, including the *xiān* (immortals). Transformations include the assumption of the body of an animal for a specific purpose, disappearance or camouflage by merging with surrounding objects, and 'multiplication' of the physical body in order to be in more than one place at a time.

Among the many transformations that have been related are those of the early Daoist sage Tàixuánnǚ ('Lady of Great Mystery') who, according to fourth-century Daoist master Gě Hóng's *Shénxiān zhuàn* ('Biography of Immortals'), could

> transform (*líng,* make something happen) small things to be suddenly big, and big things to be small. She could spit fire so big it would rise up wildly into heaven and yet in one breath she could extinguish *(miè)* it again.
>
> *Gě Hóng, Shénxiān zhuàn 7:27a, TEAK p.292*

In their first meeting with King Liú Ān (*c.*179–122 BCE), one of the *bāgōng* (eight worthies) describes the miraculous powers possessed by various members of their group:

> One of us, for example, is able to... trace lines across the lands and they become rivers, scoop up soil and make mountains.... The third among us can divide his body and transform his appearance *(biànhuà),* become visible or invisible at will. He can hide away whole armies, and turn midday into night. Yet another of us can perform a myriad transformations. Bird, beast, grass, tree – as the fancy takes him – he can become each and any of the myriad beings. He can move mountains and bring rivers to a halt. He can transport palaces and move houses around as he pleases.
>
> *Gě Hóng, Shénxiān zhuàn 4:14a–15a, TEAK pp.295–96*

As well as the ability to effect magical changes to their own bodies, their transformational powers also included the ability to transform creatures and objects – like turning goats into white rocks, or making food out of inedible objects, and so on.

Hé Xiāngū ('Immortal Woman Hé', *d.c.*707), the only woman among the *bāxiān* (eight immortals), was visited by a spirit when she was barely fourteen years of age. The spirit told her to grind a particular stone to powder and eat it. This 'mother of clouds' powder made her feel light, and she attained immortality. Because she followed these directions and also vowed not to marry, she was able to fly from one mountain peak to another.

Extra-ordinary Physical Attributes and Powers

Because of their highly refined *qì* (life-force energy), some advanced *Dào* adepts may show few or no signs of aging – retaining a youthful complexion, dark hair, and all their teeth. It is said that the complexion of Tàixuánnǚ was

> always that of a young girl *(shào);* her hair stayed always black as a raven *(yā).*
>
> *Gě Hóng, Shénxiān zhuàn 7:27a, TEAK p.292*

Daoist literature also contains many references to advanced adepts who possessed extra-ordinary physical abilities. These include being unaffected by extreme temperatures, having great strength, and being able to run at great speed, or to walk great distances in a single day. It is also related that Tàixuánnǚ could

> travel ten thousand miles *(wàn lǐ),* yet at the same time continue to stay nearby.
>
> *Gě Hóng, Shénxiān zhuàn 7:27a, TEAK p.292*

One of the *bāgōng* (eight worthies) also had control over space and time:

> (One among us) can go in and out of the spaceless and travel a thousand miles in one breath.
>
> *Gě Hóng, Shénxiān zhuàn 4:14a–15a, TEAK p.295*

The *Zhuāngzǐ* mentions some of these extra-ordinary physical abilities as being among the powers of a *zhēnrén* (true man, *i.e.* sage):

> The true sages *(zhēnrén)* of old never avoided want, never flaunted perfection, never worked at schemes. If you're like that, you can... scale the heights without trembling in fear *(bùlì),* dive into deep water without getting wet *(bùrú),* walk into fire without getting burned *(bùrè).* This is how understanding *(zhī)* can ascend delusion *(jiǎ)* into the heights of *Dào.*
>
> *Zhuāngzǐ 6, CTIH p.83*

Such spiritually elevated adepts are said to be able to exceed or even completely transcend normal pain thresholds. Tàixuánnǚ was reputed to be able

> to enter the water *(shuǐ)* and not get wet. Even in the severest cold of winter, she would walk over frozen rivers wearing only a single garment. All the time her expression *(yán)* would not change *(bùbiàn),* and her body would remain comfortably warm for a succession of days.... She was also able to sit in the middle of a blazing fire *(huǒ),* while her clothes would never be even touched by the flames.
>
> *Gě Hóng, Shénxiān zhuàn 7:27a, TEAK pp.291, 292*

The leader of the *bāgōng* (eight worthies) told King Liú Ān that one of their group

> can enter flames *(huǒ)* unscathed and plunge into water *(shuǐ)* without getting wet. He is invulnerable to swords or arrows. He feels no cold in winter frosts, nor sweat in the heat of summer.
>
> *Gě Hóng, Shénxiān zhuàn 4:14a–15a, TEAK p.296*

By harnessing *qì* (life-force energy), advanced *Dào* adepts are also said to be able to control dangerous animals or the evil tendencies of ghosts and mountain spirits; to stop bleeding, restore broken bones, and cure snake bites; and to show no signs of being cut by swords. In addition, they are reputed to be able to create extra-ordinary and indelible writing, relieve drought, and cover great distances in mysterious ways.

Healing Power

In his biographies of the divine immortals, Gě Hóng records that a certain Huánglúzǐ ('Master with Yellow Pupils') possessed the gift of curing and healing:

> Even at a distance of one thousand miles, if he only knew the name *(xìngmíng)* of the sick person, he could cure him. All would get well, even if he never saw the patient's body *(bìngrén shēn).*
>
> *Gě Hóng, Shénxiān zhuàn 10:40b, TEAK pp.290–91*

Mǎ Yù relates that, while staying in Huátíng, "by accident I became poisoned by a fiery poison inside some muddy fluid, vomited blood, and was afflicted with a coughing disease."[2] Declining to take any medicine, he chose instead to attend to his spiritual practice. He goes on to relate how, following this attack of food poisoning, he had a mystical healing encounter with his deceased master Wáng Zhé. Although he had vowed to treat himself through spiritual practice, Mǎ Yù credits his subsequent recovery to his master:

> West of the Huátíng city walls, (he) appeared,
> and cured my miserable disease;
> And *qì* was distributed throughout my body.
>
> *Mǎ Yù, Dòngxuán jīnyù jí 10:15b–16a, TPEQ p.124*

The healing methods referred to in the various texts commonly include acupuncture; the preparation of remedies using talismans *(fú),* talismanic water, and herbs; and moxibustion – the burning of moxa (a herbal preparation) against the skin to treat pain or illness. In some cases, patients are cured from a distance; in other instances, medicines are delivered by spirits. Other miracles mentioned include exorcism, such as the cleansing of temples or districts of evil spirits, and curing disease. There are even some stories regarding the ultimate form of physical healing: bringing the dead back to life.

Prophetic Power

Advanced Daoist adepts are also able to see the future of other people. They can foresee the rise and fall of emperors, dynasties, and great players in the political arena. They also know the time of their own death. According to Daoist master Mǎ Yù, his own master Wáng Zhé (*aka.* Chóngyáng) possessed such powers:

> That true man of compassionate transformations *(zhēnrén mǐnhuà),* Shīfu Chóngyáng,... had a penetrating understanding of all things, and predicted the time of his death. His speech was like the heart's wind, and his prediction came true in the southern capital.
>
> *Mǎ Yù, Dòngxuán jīnyù jí 10:15b; cf. TPEQ p.123*

Transformations of Lǎozǐ

In the Daoist tradition, Lǎozǐ (as the personification of *Dào*) is believed to have transformed into different entities at different times and in different places. Some writings speak of the 'eighty-one transformations of Lord Lǎo'. Present-day Daoism researcher Alan Chan reports that Lǎozǐ

> is thought to have undergone a series of 'transformations *(biàn-huà)*'.... Throughout history he appeared in different guises to selected individuals to initiate them into the mysteries of the *Dào,* to secure cosmic harmony and socio-political order.
>
> *Alan Chan, "Daode jing and Its Tradition," in DHK1 pp.3–4*

A sixth-century scripture of the *Tiānshī* school of Daoism contains an account of the creation of the universe in which Lǎozǐ is said to have related how 'he' (as the personification of *Dào*) had "changed and transformed myriad times":

> At the beginning of the mysterious transformations *(mì huà),*
> I embodied emptiness and nonbeing (*xūwú,* nothingness).
> Passing along through the limitless *(wúqióng),*
> I changed and transformed myriads of times *(qiān biàn wàn huà).*
> Then I first came down
> and was the teacher *(shī)* of the world.
>
> Before the three sovereigns *(sānhuáng),*
> I was the root of all the spirit transformations *(shénhuà).*

Under the three sovereigns *(sānhuáng)* and five emperors *(wǔdì),*[3]
I helped them as their teacher *(shī).*
Thus it went on, down to the three dynasties *(sānwáng).*
I admonished them all to cultivate goodness.

Kāitiān jīng 6a ff., TEAK pp.42–43

"Transformed myriads of times" translates the four Chinese characters *qiān biàn wàn huà,* which literally mean 'countless changes, constant permutation'.

See also: **biànxíng**.

1. Lǚ Dòngbīn, *TCC3* p.109.
2. Mǎ Yù, *Dòngxuán jīnyù jí* 8:15b–16a, *TPEQ* p.76.
3. See **sānhuáng wǔdì** (7.1).

svachchhanda mṛityu (S) *Lit.* death *(mṛityu)* by one's own *(sva)* desire *(chhanda);* the power to die according to one's own desire; dying when one wishes to do so; also called *ichchhā-mṛityu* (death by wish). See **siddhi**.

tāmoe (Mo) See **rotu**.

taṣarruf (A/P) *Lit.* turning, changing; interference, possession, power, authority, control, initiative, seizure, appropriation; authoritative behaviour, full power to act, free disposal, right of disposal, full power of disposal; to bring about (unwarranted) changes in something; a miracle – something that breaks the habit of the way created things normally exist or change; related to the verb *ṣarafa* (to turn, to turn away, to direct); mystically, the supernatural power of saints, specifically the spiritual and mental energy and concentration that can bring about the seemingly miraculous, in both the physical and spiritual spheres. Actual external miracles are called *karāmāt* (gifts, favours, miracles) and breaking of habit *(kharq al-'ādah).* The internal power is known as *taṣarruf, taḥakkum* (governing control), *takwīn* (bringing things into created existence), and *al-fi'l bi al-himmah* (action with resolve).

The internal spiritual power *(taṣarruf)* of a saint touches all his disciples and those he wishes to help spiritually. Even after his departure from this world, his power and grace continue in the hearts and lives of his disciples. Rūmī's biographer Aḥmad al-Aflākī, writing some fifty to seventy years after Rūmī's death, recalls the words of Rūmī's son, Sulṭān Valad:

> One day my father said, "When the friend of God transfers from this world, his journeying is a hundred thousand times more than when he was alive. That is because this journeying is journeying in God. There is no end to it and, until the Day of Resurrection, his power *(taṣarruf)* over the disciples and lovers will continue."
>
> God is present even after they have gone.
> The power *(taṣarruf)* of God over His bondsmen
> will continue for all eternity.
> And this is sufficient!
>
> *Aḥmad al-Aflākī, Manāqib al-ʿĀrifīn 3:215, MASA1 pp.298–99, FKG (3:214) p.207*

Aflākī also recalls:

> Due to this power and great supernatural control *(taṣarruf)*, a hundred thousand arrogant deniers acknowledged (him). They became disciples and believers, and were made into people destined for paradise.
>
> *Aḥmad al-Aflākī, Manāqib al-ʿĀrifīn 3:547, MASA1 p.564, FKG (3:549) p.390*

See also: **kharq al-ʿādah**.

ṭayrān (A/P) *Lit.* flight; mystically, the rise of the soul into the spiritual realms. Rūzbihān takes care to point out that he does not mean levitation of the physical body:

> In the station of flight *(ṭayrān)*, it is the *khulafā'* (caliphs, saints) who fly with the angels in spirit and body, for they are spiritual ones, in whom is the likeness of the angels.… I have not flown in air because of my knowledge, but I found that meaning by which they fly in me.
>
> *Rūzbihān, Mashrab al-Arwāḥ 18:24, MARB p.294, in SBF p.9*

telepathy The communication of thoughts, feelings, desires, *etc.* between people or animals, using non-sensory means, presently beyond the understanding of science; thought transference; a form of extrasensory perception; a natural faculty of the mind associated with perception through the awareness of subtle mind energies, such as the subtle atmosphere and vibrations created by the minds of others *etc.*

See also: **clairvoyance**.

tipua, **tupua** (Mo) *Lit.* strange, supernatural, enchanted, magical, supernormal, abnormal; possessing strange powers; something enchanted or magical; an object of terror, fear, or dislike; a vengeful or destructive being; a strange being, a spirit; a goblin, fairy, demon, or monster; a person versed in magical practices; also, someone strange, a foreigner.

Tipua appears in names and expressions such as *teka tipua,* a magic dart over which magic incantations have been recited, and *Whiro te tipua,* the *atua* (deity) personifying evil, darkness, and death, and who was also the origin of the *Maiki* clan, the personifications of disease and other human afflictions.[1]

Tipua may be applied to things animate or inanimate, material or immaterial – to anything that is possessed by an indwelling spirit. Such a spirit may even enter someone known to possess occult knowledge and power and who is known for the powerful effect of his magical *karakia* or incantations. Such a *tipua* or person would therefore be treated with respect. Lightning is sometimes understood as a supernatural form of fire, known as *ahi tipua* (enchanted fire; also volcano). Trees and stones could also be rendered *tipua* through magic *(mākutu)* rituals, and could also possess strange powers.

Places where healing ceremonies had been performed over the sick, who were suffering from a contagious disease such as leprosy, were treated as *tipua* and people passing the spot would throw a stone at it to prevent the disease from attacking them as they passed by. Alternatively, chants could be repeated as a precautionary measure as one passed something that was *tipua,* and then one had to be careful not to look back. It was considered necessary to placate *tipua* with offerings the first time one passed them by.

Māori folk tales speak of transmigration, the passing of the human soul into the body of an animal, which could then be regarded as *tipua.* A *tipua* could take on the human form as an ogre, for example, or an animal form such as a bird, a dog, an eel, *etc.*

1. Elsdon Best, "Maori Personifications," *MPAS* p.109.

toki (Mo) *Lit.* a hatchet, adze or axe, generally made of stone or sometimes shell; the sharp cutting edge of a tool; a common, traditional Māori tool; also, a sacred ceremonial stone adze steeped in *mana* (power).

While the stone adze or *toki* was used to cut or hew timber for canoe building or as a weapon *etc.,* in the hands of the *tohunga* or priest, a jade stone *toki* became a sacred personal object. *Karakia* (incantations, chants) were frequently recited over a *toki* causing it to become imbued with great *mana* or the power of Hawaiki (the spiritual homeland of the Māoris), the *atua* (the gods controlling the elements), and the ancestors. Such a *toki* became highly *tapu* (restricted, sacred) and dangerous for ordinary mortals to touch.

Therefore, before the adze could be taken up and put to work, necessary rituals were performed to make them *noa* (ordinary) – free from the restrictions of *tapu* – and *karakia* were recited while using the *toki* for cutting.

Tokis of power, which were prized and highly venerated by the Māori, were used during ceremonies, for rituals and during magical incantations, and were sometimes described as *tokis* "waved to the gods":

> We are told that such implements were 'waved' to or towards the gods during ritual performances connected with black magic, war, infant baptism, *etc.*
>
> *Elsdon Best, Maori Religion and Mythology, MRM2 p.183*

Early accounts of the voyage of the Tākitimu (first migration canoe) to the shores of Aotearoa (New Zealand) towards the middle of the fourteenth century, speak of *tohunga* of great powers using their adzes ritualistically to 'hew' a safe passage through rough high seas and surging waves:

> One very singular performance at sea was connected with certain sacred ceremonial stone *toki.* These implements are described as *he toki poipoi ki ngā atua* (adzes waved to the gods). When a rough sea was encountered by voyagers, a priestly expert possessed of such an adze would produce it, intone a long and special *karakia,* and then make a motion with the stone tool as though chopping at the waves. This extraordinary act is said to have been highly efficacious: it subdued the angry waves; it severed them and caused them to break up and be scattered.
>
> *Elsdon Best, Maori Religion and Mythology, MRM1 p.388*

See also: **mana (Hawaiian)**.

ton, **tomvan** (Lakota) *Lit.* possessing *wakan* (power), having spiritual power; usually objects infused with spiritual energy; a term used by the Native American Lakota Sioux.

If a shaman uses an object like a drum in a spiritual ceremony, that drum is said to be *tomvan* or *ton.* It has acquired spiritual power because a shaman has handled it while communicating with *wakan* beings (spirit beings).

trikāla-jñāna (S) *Lit.* knowledge *(jñāna)* of the three *(tri-)* times *(kāla);* knowledge of past, present, and future. See **siddhi**.

trividyā (S), **tevijjā** (Pa) *Lit.* threefold *(tri)* knowledge *(vidyā, vijjā);* three forms or branches of knowledge; in *brāhmaṇ* lore, knowledge of the three *Vedas;* in Buddhism, the three forms of supernatural knowledge (Pa. *abhiññā*), *viz.* the divine eye (Pa. *dibba-cakkhu*) or the knowledge of the past lives of other beings, the recollection of past lives (Pa. *pubbe-nivāsānussati*), and the extinction of all mental impurities (Pa. *āsavakkhaya*); hence, *traividya* (S) and *tevijja* (Pa), familiar with or possessing the threefold knowledge (S. *vidyā,* Pa. *vijjā*). These three forms of knowledge are described in various Buddhist texts.[1]

In the *Tevijja Sutta* of the *Dīgha Nikāya,* the Buddha explains the deficiency of the threefold knowledge of the *brāhmaṇs* to two young *brāhmaṇs.* He says that *brāhmaṇs* speak about knowledge of and union with *Brahmā,* while neither they, nor their teachers, nor the many successive generations of teachers have ever met *Brahmā* face to face.[2]

See also: **abhijñā**.

1. *E.g. Dīgha Nikāya* 2, *Sāmaññaphala Sutta* 72–82, *PTSD1* pp.78–84; *Majjhima Nikāya* 4 *(Bhayabherava Sutta),* 19 *(Dvedhāvitakka Sutta), PTSM1* pp.22–23, 117.
2. *Dīgha Nikāya* 13, *Tevijja Sutta, PTSD1* pp.235–52.

ushṇīsha (S), **gtsug tor** (T), **dǐngjì**, **ròujì** (C), **nikkei** (J) *Lit.* something wound around the head; a turban, a diadem, a crown; in Buddhism, a fleshy protuberance *(ushṇīsha, gtsug tor, nikkei)* on the crown of a *buddha*'s head; a 'topknot' *(jì)* of flesh *(ròu)* on the crown of the head *(dǐng);* also called *ushṇīsha-shīrsha* (protuberance on the head); one of the thirty-two bodily marks *(dvātriṃshadvara-lakshaṇa)* of a great man *(mahāpurusha),* a universal monarch *(chakravartin),* or a *buddha;* commonly found in Buddhist art, sculpture and iconography, where it represents the flame of enlightenment and the highest aspects of buddhahood; in some instances, especially in Thailand, the protuberance is even depicted in the shape of a flame.

The common explanation of the Buddha's *ushṇīsha* is that he acquired it as the result of having touched his head to the ground so many times in past lives, prostrating before his many spiritual teachers:

> The unfathomable crown protuberance *(gtsug tor)* on the Buddha's head comes from his having respectfully prostrated before his teachers (in past lives).
>
> *Patrul Rinpoche, Words of My Perfect Teacher, WMPT p.321*

There is some scholarly debate concerning the relationship between the fleshy protuberance and the topknot of hair. Some interpret the *ushṇīsha* as hair dressed into a topknot, like the *brāhmaṇs* of the Buddha's time who shaved their heads except for a circular patch of hair on the crown, which they twisted into a knot. They point out that the original meaning of the term is 'dressed hair' or 'turban', rather than 'protuberance'.[1]

Monarchs and princes of old in some Eastern traditions would also wear their hair long and bound in a topknot on the crown of the head, adorned with gold, silver, and precious gems. Texts such as the *Lotus Sūtra, Avataṃsaka Sūtra* and others depict the celestial *buddhas* and *bodhisattvas* in the various paradises as having a fabulous gem in their topknot, often the mythical *chintāmaṇi* (wish-fulfilling gem) that fulfils all desires. Commenting on a passage from the *Kshitigarbha Bodhisattva Pūrvapraṇidhāna Sūtra* ('*Sūtra* of the Past Vows of Earth Store Bodhisattva'), twentieth-century Buddhist, Master Hsuan Hua says:

> Empty Space Store Bodhisattva, who comes from a world thousands of millions of worlds systems away, has a jewel in his topknot from which anything one wishes for will come. Should you ever encounter a *bodhisattva* with a wishing gem atop his head, you should recognize him; for if you do, you will be able to have some of the treasures he has, . . . and you will never be poor.
>
> *Master Hsuan Hua, on Kshitigarbha Bodhisattva Pūrvapraṇidhāna Sūtra 13, SVEB*

Some descriptions combine elements of both versions of the description:

> On another occasion, the Buddha was reborn in the land of Sāketa as the son of the king Golden Crest and the queen Joyous Beauty. On top of his head there was a protuberance *(gtsug tor)* consisting of a precious jewel, from which came a nectar with the power to turn iron into gold. For this reason he was called Maṇichūda ('Jewel Crest').
>
> *Patrul Rinpoche, Words of My Perfect Teacher, WMPT p.231*

A description of the thirty-two marks of a *buddha* speaks of the spiritual power of the protuberance:

> *Buddha* has a protuberance on his head *(gtsug tor),* which is round, black, and curled clockwise. It radiates such intense light that it cannot be gazed upon.
>
> *Khenpo Chöga, On Khenpo Kunpal, Bodhisattva-Charyāvatāra 51, DNK1 p.308*

Here, the portrayal of the *ushṇīsha* is barely physical and, in some instances, the *ushṇīsha* is not physical at all, but represents the spirituality and enlightenment hidden within all beings. The eighth-century Buddhist scholar Shāntideva advocates that *bodhisattvas* should pray that all beings may awaken their invisible *ushṇīsha:*

> When placing the left hand on the ground, think and say, "May I gather all beings who adhere to worldly *dharma,* who cling to the wrong direction, or who are difficult to tame, through the four means of attraction." When touching your head or forehead to the ground, think and say, "May all beings, without any arrogance, serve their teachers, achieve the invisible *ushṇīsha (gtsug),* and become exalted in the virtuous *Dharma.*"
>
> *Shāntideva, Bodhisattva-Charyāvatāra 2:138, DNK2 p.67*

Nor is the protuberance necessarily to be found on a shaved head. Praising the Buddha, the *Rāshṭrapālaparipṛichchha Sūtra* says:

> You are stainless, like a mountain of gold; your unctuous, delicate hair turns clockwise on your head. Your cranial protuberance *(ushṇīsha)* rises like Meru, the king (of mountains), and shines as a result of your extensive merit.
>
> *Rāshṭrapālaparipṛichchha Sūtra, Prologue 28, BFFM p.118*

The *Avataṃsaka Sūtra* describes the extreme generosity and the joy of giving known to *bodhisattvas* who are ready to give even their fleshy topknots to beggars:

> When a *bodhisattva-mahāsattva* (great-being *bodhisattva*) blesses seekers, he gives them his fleshy topknot *(liánfū dǐngjì),* like the *bodhisattvas* Jewel Topknot King, Surpassingly Wonderful Body, and numerous others. Overjoyed at seeing a seeker come forward, the *bodhisattva* says to him, "If you need a fleshy topknot *(liánfū dǐngjì),* take it from me. This one is the best in the land of Jambudvīpa."
>
> At the same time, undisturbed in mind, unperturbed by his remaining *karma,* and unattached to the world, he continues in devotion to tranquillity and utmost purity. With perseverance and determination, he is focused on omniscience. Then he takes a sharp knife and cuts off his fleshy topknot *(liánfū dǐngjì),* kneels upon his right knee, and places his palms together. His only thought is that of giving.
>
> Remembering the generosity of all *buddhas* and *bodhisattvas* of the past, present and future, he becomes ever more joyful and steadfast in his determination. Through grace, he enlightens all beings. He expounds the truth of pain and suffering, of the Formless and the Uncreated. He tells them to relinquish attachment to suffering: for suffering comes and goes; it is impermanent.
>
> Then he says, "Therefore, deeply imbued with faith and filled with great joy, in my quest for omniscience, I will practise the greatest generosity of all *bodhisattvas,* past, present and future, never regressing and seeking no support from other knowledge or teachings."

> When a *bodhisattva-mahāsattva* gives, he bestows the merits of the roots of goodness in this manner, "May all living beings reach the peak of towering achievement, like the *bodhisattvas'* tuft of hair *(jì);* may all living beings have hair as purplish blue, indestructible, fine and soft as the Buddha, and extinguish all passions and delusions;... have lustrous hair, thick hair, silken hair not growing on the forehead;... have hair patterns like the right-whirling conch, as did the Buddha, and be forever rid of habituation to afflictions and attachments;... have radiant hair, shining with a light that illumines the worlds in all the ten directions;... have undisturbed hair, wondrously pure, like the Buddha;... develop a tuft of hair *(jì)* like the Buddha, so that when a person sees it, it is as though he is meeting the Buddha himself;... have hair like the Buddha, free from impurity, and be forever free from all darkness and the obscuring defilement of the passions."
>
> This is how a *bodhisattva-mahāsattva* bestows the merits of the roots of goodness when giving his fleshy topknot *(liánfūjì)*. It is through the supreme wisdom and ten powers of a *tathāgata* that all living beings obtain serenity of mind, are able to complete all meditational practices (*dhāraṇī, lit.* sacred formulae), and can bring the *tathāgata*'s wisdom to its fulfilment.
>
> *Avataṃsaka Sūtra 25, T19 279:144b6–c4*

In a similar vein, there is a well-known traditional story in which Prince Siddhārtha, the *buddha*-to-be, after his first encounter with suffering, makes a statement of his intended renunciation of the world by cutting off his long regal topknot, symbol of his royal status, with his charioteer's sword:

> Prince Siddhārtha took from his charioteer Chandaka's side a sword whose hilt was encrusted with the seven precious jewels and other gems. Grasping the sword with his right hand, he drew it from its scabbard. With his left hand, he then took hold of his shell-shaped topknot, which was the deep blue colour of a water lily, and with his right hand he cut it off. Then with his left hand, he dedicated it before discarding it by throwing it into the sky. At that moment, there arose in the celestial Lord *Indra* a great joy, something that he was not accustomed to feeling. He caught hold of the prince's topknot and, not allowing it to touch the ground, he wrapped it in a wondrous celestial robe for safe keeping. Then all manner of celestial beings made their most excellent offerings to it out of respect.
>
> *Eihei Dōgen, Shōbōgenzō, Shukke-kudoku, T2582 82:282a24–b2, STHT (81) pp.918–19*

These stories, texts and commentaries all indicate that the *ushṇīsha* is taken as a symbol of a *buddha's* spiritual enlightenment, although it may often be understood as a simple physical characteristic.

See also: **dvātriṃshadvara-lakshaṇa**.

1. Emil Schlagintweit, *Buddhism in Tibet, BTLD* p.209.

vaishāradya (S), **vesārajja** (Pa) *Lit.* expertise, experience, skill; infallibility, wisdom; fearlessness, intrepidity; self-confidence, freedom from doubt and hesitation; in Buddhism, the complete unselfconscious confidence and fearlessness of a *buddha* or *arhat* (noble one, enlightened one) that arises from a full understanding of the *Dharma* and from complete wisdom regarding everything; generally described as the four fearlessnesses or four grounds of self-confidence (S. *chatvāri-vaishāradyāni,* Pa. *cattāri vesārajjāni,* T. *mi 'jigs pa,* C. *sì wúwèi*) of a *tathāgata* or *buddha,* a further set of four fearlessnesses being listed for *bodhisattvas* in *Mahāyāna* texts; often mentioned together with the ten powers (Pa. *dasabala*), the eighteen special attributes *(āveṇika-dhamma),* and the various other enumerated characteristics of a *buddha;* listed in many Buddhist texts in Pali, Sanskrit, Chinese, and other languages.

There are a number of places where it is said of others that a true disciple of the Buddha "carries out his instruction, responds to his advice, has crossed beyond doubt, has done away with perplexity, has gained fearlessness *(vesārajja),* and has become independent of others in the teacher's *(satthar)* dispensation".[1]

The four fearlessnesses are generally listed as:

1. That which arises from perfect omniscience and enlightenment (Pa. *sammā-sambodhi*), from which nothing is lacking.

2. That which stems from the destruction of all mental impurities (Pa. *āsavas*).

3. That of explaining the *Dhamma* and in recognizing and pointing out the obstacles *(antarāya)* that stand in the way of enlightenment.

4. That of teaching the way to liberation and the end of suffering.

The stock text describing them appears in a number of places in the Pali *suttas,* where they are presented in a roundabout manner:[2]

The *tathāgata* has these four kinds of intrepidity *(cattāri vesārajjāni),* possessing which, he claims the herd-leader's place, roars his lion's roar in the assemblies, and sets rolling the wheel of *Brahmā (brahmacakka).* What are the four?

Here, I see no ground on which any *samaṇa* (holy man), or *brāhmaṇ,* or god, or *māra* (devil), or *Brahmā,* or anyone at all in the world could, in accordance with the *Dhamma,* accuse me thus: "While you claim full enlightenment *(sammā-sambuddha),* you are not fully enlightened in regard to certain things." And seeing no ground for that, I abide in safety *(khema),* fearlessness *(abhaya),* and intrepidity *(vesārajja).*

I see no ground on which any contemplative…or anyone at all could accuse me thus: "While you claim to have destroyed the taints *(khīṇāsava),* these taints are undestroyed by you." And seeing no ground for that, I abide in safety, fearlessness, and intrepidity *(vesārajja).*

I see no ground on which any contemplative…or anyone at all could accuse me thus: "Those things called obstacles *(antarāya)* by you are not able to obstruct one who engages in them." And seeing no ground for that, I abide in safety, fearlessness, and intrepidity *(vesārajja).*

I see no ground on which any contemplative…or anyone at all could accuse me thus: "When you teach the *Dhamma* to someone, it does not lead him, when he practises it, to the complete destruction of suffering." And seeing no ground for that, I abide in safety, fearlessness, and intrepidity *(vesārajja).*

A *tathāgata* has these four kinds of intrepidity *(cattāri vesārajjāni),* possessing which, he claims the herd-leader's place, roars his lion's roar in the assemblies, and sets rolling the wheel of *Brahmā (brahmacakka).*

Majjhima Nikāya 12, Mahāsīhanāda Sutta,
PTSM1 pp.71–72; cf. MDBB pp.167–68

Bodhisattvas also enjoy four fearlessnesses. The Buddhist philosopher Nāgārjuna summarizes:[3]

1. Since he has the power to remember all that he has heard concerning the *Dharma,* he is fearless in teaching it in the great assemblies.

2. Since he has obtained liberation in all things, he is aware of and able to discriminate between all the ways in which the *Dharma* can be taught to remedy the ills of sentient beings; because he is aware of the thoughts, feelings, inclinations and different levels of understanding of all sentient beings, he is confident in his choice of what to teach in the great assemblies.

3. Since he has eliminated all sources of fear and lack of confidence, he is never concerned that anyone could raise some doubt or contrary viewpoint that he would be unable to address and answer, when teaching the *Dharma* in the great assemblies.

4. He is fearless when resolving any queries of the sentient beings to whom he teaches the *Dharma,* and is able to reply without hesitation.

1. *E.g. Majjhima Nikāya* 35 *(Cūlasaccaka Sutta),* 56 *(Upāli Sutta), PTSM1* pp.234–35, 380; *cf. MDBB* pp.329, 485; *Dīgha Nikāya* 3, *Ambaṭṭha Sutta, PTSD1* p.110.
2. See also *e.g. Anguttara Nikāya* 7:55, *Arakkheyya Sutta, PTSA4* pp.83–84.
3. Nāgārjuna, *Mahāprajñāpāramitā Shāstra* 40:2.3, *TVW3* pp.1321–22.

vāk-siddhi, **vākya-siddhi** (S) *Lit.* speech *(vāc, vākya)* power *(siddhi);* the power of prediction or prophecy; power by which whatever a person says comes to pass; variously said to arise from full realization of and absorption in *satya* (truthfulness, veracity) and/or from the repetition of *mantras.*

In its normal state of vacillation, the mind is unable to see things clearly. Hence, the future and the manner of its manifestation remain hidden. Furthermore, the mind's sense of personal ego or identity is so strong that the things of the present are taken personally. All this contributes to a continuously incorrect perception and interpretation of physical reality. It is thus almost impossible for an average human being to be fully honest and express things as they actually are and as they are going to be. In addition, because the mind is obsessed by the passing show, interpreted personally, a human being's natural foresight is clouded, and even the ability to perceive the otherwise obvious outcome of events is obscured. This is why individuals may set out on a course of action that others can clearly see will result in an unfavourable outcome.

Conversely, a person whose mind and inner consciousness are spiritually developed has the power and capacity to be genuinely truthful in all he says. Such a person also has the consciousness to see the future, should he so wish. In the case of a perfect saint, the highest Truth is so firmly established within him that whatever he says is completely imbued with truth. His words and actions reflect the divine will, anticipating and expressing what is to happen in the future.

See also: **siddhi**.

vashīkaraṇ(a) (S/H) *Lit.* act *(kāraṇa)* of subjection *(vash);* the power to subjugate; the supernatural power to control the actions, feelings and desires of other people, and bring them under one's own influence; one of the yogic *siddhis* (powers); popularly used to attract the love of a desired one, to control one's boss or other significant people in one's life, *etc.* The means used to exercise this power include a *vashīkaraṇa mantra,* which is a verbal spell or formula designed to bring about the desired objective; and a *vashīkaraṇa yantra,* a *yantra* (in this context) being a diagram or geometric device symbolizing aspects of the body and the cosmos, sometimes with astrological aspects, and which is likewise designed to control the feelings of the other person.

See also: **siddhi**.

vashitva (S) *Lit.* subjection, subjugation, mastery, control, being one's own master; the power of dominion over one's own self; also, the power to subdue, overpower or command other beings, human or otherwise; the power to tame wild animals and mesmerize human beings by the exercise of one's will; the power to control both animate and inanimate objects; from *vash* (to will, to command, to subjugate).

See also: **siddhi**.

vāyu-siddhi (S) *Lit.* air *(vāyu)* power *(siddhi);* power of the *tattva* (element) of air, enabling levitation. See **siddhi**.

vibhūti (S/H) *Lit.* penetrating, pervading; might, power, superhuman power; splendour, magnificence, greatness; prosperity, wealth, abundance; the manifestation of might and power; used a number of times in chapters ten and eleven of the *Bhagavad Gītā,* where all aspects of the creation are depicted as the glorious and divine manifestation *(vibhūti)* of the divine being of Kṛishṇa, personified as an incarnation of the supreme Being, *Brahman;* also, supernatural powers or *siddhis;* also, ashes of burnt cow dung, and the ashes smeared on their bodies by Shaivite ascetics as an indication of their renunciation.

See also: **siddhi, vibhūti** (4.1).

vikubbanā-iddhi (Pa) *Lit.* power *(iddhi)* of transformation *(vikubbana),* especially the power of miraculous transformation; the power to adopt another form; one of the commonly listed *iddhis* (powers). See **iddhi**.

vipula-mati (S) *Lit.* of complex *(vipula)* mind *(mati);* one of the two kinds of *manaḥ-paryāya-jñāna* (knowledge of others' thoughts). See **manaḥ-paryāya-jñāna**.

walking on water See **miracles of Jesus and the apostles**.

wānana (Hw) *Lit.* prophesy, prediction; a foretelling of future events, making predictions; as made by a *kāula* (prophet). Many Hawaiians like to think that they can make predictions *(wānana),* but very few are authentic. A true *kāula* is said to possess *'ike pāpālua* (second sight, clairvoyance).

See also: **'ike pāpālua**, **kāula** (7.1).

whakaara hau (Mo) *Lit.* rousing *(whakaara)* wind *(hau);* to summon up wind by magical control of the elements. The ritual of wind raising, practised by Māori *tohunga* (priestly adepts), was performed to give spiritual energy or power *(mana)* to the people, to ceremonies, and to rites such as the *oho rangi* (raising sound and thunder).

Elsdon Best relates how the *tohunga* of earlier times sometimes raised wind to cover an attack. However, once recognized as a wind raised magically by a *tohunga* of the enemy, the *tohunga* of the opposing war party would attempt to subdue it by means of more potent charms, and a contest would thus arise between the two *tohunga.* Tribes favoured different winds; thus the wind of the Tamakaimoana clan of the Tūhoe tribe was the south wind called *Tutakangāhau* ('South Wind') while that of the Urewera clan was *Urukāraerae* ('Strong Wind from the Sea'):[1]

> The *Hau-o-Rongomai* ('Wind of Rongomai,' one of the *atua* or spirit-ancestors, symbolized by stars and comets), the *Puaroa-a-Tāiri* ('Suspender of Comets'), the *Whakararā-o-te-Rangi* ('Rattler of the Heavens'), *Hurimoana* ('Churner of the Sea') and *Auru-Whenua* (Eroder of the Land) are said to be names of winds so raised by magic arts. These are not, apparently, ordinary wind names in common use.... A number of these wind names are special terms, honorific, or personificatory.
>
> When the Ngā Maihi clan of Ngāti-Awa of Te Teko (a small inland township in the Bay of Plenty region of New Zealand's North Island) was attacked in its formidable fortified village of Puketapu by Ngāi Tamaoki, the latter folk utilized fire as an aid to attack. The high and massive earthworks prevented them burning the main stockades apparently, but by making a great fire on the windward side of the village and throwing green fern and brush thereon they hoped to enter the place under cover of the dense smoke. But within the fort was the famed *tohunga* Te Hahae, a man of parts, a man possessing powers that demanded obedience from the elements. By calling upon the

> south wind to rise he prevented the entry of the enemy, and the smoke was blown northward to befog the assailants. A fire was then kindled at the southern end of the fort, but Te Hahae raised the *paeroa* wind, and again triumphed. So the contest continued with yet other winds, but the doughty warlock of Ngā Maihi saved his clan from the ovens of the baffled enemy.
>
> *Elsdon Best, Maori Religion and Mythology, MRM2 pp.119–20*

1. Elsdon Best, *Maori Religion and Mythology, MRM2* p.118.

yad al-bayḍā' (A), **yad-i bayżā'** (P) *Lit.* white *(bayḍā')* hand *(yad);* bright hand; the white hand of Moses, said in Muslim legend to have been bright like the sun, and regarded as one of the signs of his prophethood. In the biblical story, Moses meets with Pharaoh, seeking the release of his people from slavery. Asked for a sign of his authority, Moses first turns his staff into a snake; then he withdraws his hand from his bosom, first white with leprosy and then fully healed.[1] The story is retold five times in the *Qur'ān,* where Moses' hand is described as white, but not as leprous.[2]

The white hand of Moses has become a common Sufi symbol, appearing in a variety of contexts. According to a miracle story told about Rābiʿah of Baṣrah:

> One night, Ḥasan of Baṣrah went with some friends to visit Rābiʿah. Rābiʿah had no lantern, and their hearts yearned for light. Rābiʿah blew on her finger, and that night it shone like a lantern until daybreak, and they sat in its radiance.
>
> If anyone asks, "How could this be?" I answer, "Just like the hand of Moses *(dast-i Mūsā),* peace upon him."
>
> *'Aṭṭār, Tadhkirat al-Awliyā' 1, TAN1 p.65; cf. in EIM p.161, MSM pp.45–46*

ʿInāyat Khān describes the healing power of the human hand by reference to the bright hand of Moses:

> Moses is known to have possessed a light in his palm, which the poets call *yad-i bayżā';* and Zoroaster is always pictured with burning fire in his hand. Both suggest the radiance, the battery that can be developed in the human hand. When the power is developed in the palm, it pours out from the tips of the fingers, and it shoots out when it is directed by the will. Then, by magnetic passes and by touch on the painful part, the healer is able to cure diseases.
>
> *'Ināyat Khān, Sufi Message, SMIK4 pp.76–77*

According to the biblical story, retold with elaborations in the *Qur'ān* and Muslim legend, Moses serves the righteous priest Shuʻayb (in *Exodus,* Jethro) for ten years, as a dowry payment for the hand of Shuʻayb's daughter Ṣafūrā' (Zipporah).[3] After he has completed his ten years' service, Moses is appointed by God as a prophet. Sanā'ī relates:

> For ten years he served Shuʻayb, till the door of the Unseen was opened to his soul. His hand became bright as his piercing eye; he became the crown on the head of the men of Sinai.
>
> *Sanā'ī, Ḥadīqat al-Ḥaqīqat 1, HHGP p.15; cf. HHG pp.24–25*

For Saʻdī, the white hand of Moses represents the spiritual power of the prophets. Yet unless it is written by God into a person's destiny, no one can approach Him, even if they meet a master:

> The rust of Pharaoh's heart was inborn,
> for even polishing with the white hand *(yad-i bayżā')* of Moses
> did not cleanse its blackness.
> He (God) summoned the unfortunate wretch,
> but refused him access – so where could he go?
> He bandaged the poor man's eyes,
> and then commanded him to see.
>
> *Saʻdī, Ṭayyibāt 133:3–4, KSSS p.272, TOS p.183*

Nothing is equal to this spiritual power:

> The magic *(siḥr)* of my poetry has pervaded the universe;
> But of what use is it
> compared to your luminous hand *(yad-i bayżā')?*
>
> *Saʻdī, Ṭayyibāt 412:6, KSSS p.339, TOS p.549*

Rūmī also uses the image as symbolic of a master's spiritual power. Speaking of his own master, he is recorded as saying that Shams-i Tabrīz had the spiritual power ("the white hand of Moses") to "subdue" the *nafs* (lower human mind) of both men and *jinn* (supernatural or spirit beings):

> Our Mawlānā Shams al-Dīn had the white hand of Moses *(yad-i bayżā')* to subdue the lower minds *(nufūs)* of the *jinn* and human beings, as well as regarding the secret of the holy Names and the secrets of things.
>
> *Aḥmad al-Aflākī, Manāqib al-ʻĀrifīn 4:18, MASA2 p.625; cf. FKG p.430*

But this power is not given to a soul until he has turned his back on all the pleasures and temptations of materiality:

When the messiah (Jesus) held back his hand from every sour stew,
his hand became the remedy of all the world.
When Moses washed his hands and lips of Pharaoh's bounty,
the Ocean of Generosity gave him the white hand *(yad-i bayżā').*

Rūmī, Dīvān-i Shams-i Tabrīz 96:1075–76, KSD1 p.62, in SPL p.337

Therefore, Rūmī begs the master to use his spiritual power to lift souls out of the "hell" of this world and of the lower mind with the "Breath" of the Holy Spirit, the divine creative power:

Hark, show your white hand *(yad-i bayżā'),* O king:
out of the black nights reveal a new dawn!
A hell has blazed forth; breathe enchantment over it,
O you whose Breath is more excellent
than the breath of the sea.

Rūmī, Maśnavī II:2288–89; cf. MJR2 p.339

1. *Exodus* 4:6–7.
2. *Qur'ān* 7:108, 20:22, 26:33, 27:12, 28:32.
3. *Exodus* 2:11–25, 3:1.

yamaka-pāṭihāriya (Pa) *Lit.* twin *(yamaka)* miracle *(pāṭihāriya);* twin marvel, double miracle, miracle of the pairs, miracle of Shrāvastī (Pa. Sāvatthī); a miracle said to have been performed by the Buddha at Shrāvastī in answer to the challenge of some sceptics, and which was impossible for any of his disciples to perform. Because of the legend of this miracle, Shrāvastī remains one of the most popular sites of Buddhist pilgrimage.

According to the story, the Buddha produced a dazzling display in which a stream of fire and a stream of water sprang simultaneously from either side of his body, running up and down, alternating from left to right. An abbreviated account of the incident is given in the *Paṭisambhidāmagga* ('Path of Discrimination,' part of the *Khuddaka Nikāya* in the Pali canon), which explains that the streams of fire and water symbolize rays of blue, yellow, red, white, pink, and brilliant light.[1] The colourful story and its background are summarized from Buddhaghosa's extensive fifth century (CE) account in his *Dhammapada Aṭṭhakathā:*

A millionaire of Rājagaha found a large piece of red sandalwood while bathing in the Ganges, and had it made into an alms bowl. Then he had it set up on strings between bamboo towers over his house and challenged any *samaṇas* (holy men) to take it down with their psychic powers. The heretics, who had no powers, pretended that they were too modest to exhibit their powers, and tried various schemes to get it given to them. After a week, the elders Moggallāna and Piṇḍola Bhāradvāja overheard some gamblers talking about the bowl and saying that there were no *arahantas* in the world. Piṇḍola Bhāradvāja urged Moggallāna to take it down. Moggallāna told Piṇḍola Bhāradvāja to take it, so the elder used his powers to lift the thirty-mile-wide flat rock to cover the entire city of Rājagaha. The people were terrified, so the elder split the rock with his toe, set it back in its rightful place, then descended onto the roof of the millionaire's house. The man paid homage, had the bowl fetched, and offered alms food. The elder returned with the bowl to the monastery. The people pestered him to perform miracles so that there was an uproar at the monastery.

The Buddha asked the elder Ānanda the reason, and then summoned the elder Piṇḍola Bhāradvāja. The Buddha rebuked the elder Piṇḍola Bhāradvāja severely for exhibiting his powers, had the bowl broken up and pounded into paste, then laid down a training rule prohibiting monks from displaying their powers. Hearing of this, the heretics made the most of it, saying that henceforth they would only exhibit their powers together with the Buddha.

King Bimbisāra told the Buddha about this, and the Buddha said that he had laid down the rule for his disciples, not for himself. He promised to perform a miracle in four months' time at Sāvatthī on the full moon day of Āsālhī. The heretics knew that they were lost, but followed the Buddha to Sāvatthī saying that he was trying to run away from them.

In due course, the teacher arrived at Sāvatthī. The heretics collected money and built a pavilion where they said they would perform miracles. King Pasenadi approached the Blessed One and offered to make him a pavilion. The Buddha declined, saying that Sakka would make him a pavilion. On being asked where he would perform a miracle the Buddha said that he would do it at the foot of the Kaṇḍa mango tree. The heretics had every mango tree for miles around uprooted.

On the day of the full moon, the teacher walked for alms and Kaṇḍa, the king's gardener, offered him a mango. The elder Ānanda made a mango drink for the teacher, and after his meal the teacher asked Kaṇḍa to plant the mango seed right there. When the teacher washed his hand and poured the rinsing water onto that spot, a mango tree fifty cubits high sprang up right away, fully laden with fruit. The monks ate their fill, and other men came to enjoy the fruit, throwing some at the heretics, blaming them for destroying all the mango trees in the district. Then Sakka ordered the wind god to blow, scattering

> the heretics' pavilion, covering them with dust until they looked like red ants, and they fled in all directions. Purāṇa Kassapa committed suicide by drowning himself in the river and was reborn in *Avīci* hell.
>
> Sakka created a jewelled walking path in the sky stretching from the eastern horizon to the western horizon. By the time that the shadows of evening had lengthened, a huge crowd had assembled. The teacher came out of his perfumed chamber and stood on the terrace. Then Gharaṇī, a female lay disciple, asked permission to perform a miracle, but the teacher declined her offer. Other lay disciples, novices, nuns, and monks did likewise, up to the elder Moggallāna, but the teacher, after acknowledging their ability, declined all of their offers saying that this basket of flowers was prepared only for him, and that no one else could bear this burden. Then the teacher stepped onto the jewelled walking path and, pacing up and down, performed the twin miracle, emitting streams of fire and water simultaneously from each pore of his body. Then, as he paced up and down, he taught the *Dhamma* to the assembly, and seeing no one able to ask suitable questions, he created a double to ask questions to which he replied. Two hundred million in the vast crowd gained stream-winning (elimination of the first three *saṃyojanas* or fetters) on that occasion. Then the Buddha reflected on what previous *buddhas* had done after performing the twin miracle, and seeing that they had all ascended to *tāvatiṃsa* to teach the *Abhidhamma,* he did the same.
>
> *Dhammapada Aṭṭhakathā 14:2, PTSDA3 pp.199–230, DCBP pp.117–18; cf. BLD3 pp.35–56*

It is said that, out of his great compassion, the Buddha remained in the paradise of *tāvatiṃsa devaloka* (heaven of the thirty-three deities) for three months, preaching the *Abhidhamma* to his deceased mother and a multitude of *devas* (deities). Interestingly, the account given in the *Cūlavagga* of the *Vinaya Piṭaka* (monastic code) is less elaborate and ends with the admonition of Piṇḍola Bhāradvāja by the Buddha not to make a display of higher powers. It is only in later elaborations of the story that the Buddha's own miracle is added.

1. *Paṭisambhidāmagga* 1, *PTSP1* pp.125–26, *PDPM* pp.126–27.

yathākammūpaga-ñāṇa (Pa) *Lit.* knowledge *(ñāṇa)* according to *(yathā)* the result of *(upaga)* actions *(kamma);* knowledge of the death and rebirth of all sentient beings, in accordance with and as a result of their good and bad deeds *(kamma);* also called *cutūpapāta-ñāṇa* (knowledge of disappearance and reappearance); one of the six supernormal forms of knowledge *(abhiññā)* in Buddhism; also described as the divine eye *(dibba-cakkhu)* or universal vision that sees all that is happening in heaven and earth, whether near or far, including the *kamma* (S. *karma*) of all beings.

See also: **abhijñā**, **cutūpapāta-ñāṇa**.

yogaja (S) *Lit.* born of *(ja) yoga;* intuitive knowledge arising from the practice of *yoga;* specifically, supernatural yogic powers by which a person may perceive the past, present and future, or know things about another person's thoughts and emotions through mind reading, and so on; the third kind of *alaukika pratyaksha* (extra-ordinary perception), according to the *Nyāya* school of Indian philosophy, which is essentially a logical study of the nature of knowledge (*i.e.* epistemology).

According to *Nyāya,* there are only two forms of perception. One is *laukika pratyaksha* (ordinary perception), which refers to perception through the five sense organs and the mind. The other is extra-ordinary perception *(alaukika pratyaksha),* which is of three kinds. The first is *sāmānya-lakshaṇa* (generic attribute), by which one perceives something general or generic from something specific. For instance, one may see an apple and know that it is also a fruit. The second is *jñāna-lakshaṇa* (knowledge attribute), by which one knows something about a thing that is experienced through another sense. For instance, when one *sees* an apple, one may also know that it *tastes* sweet.

Yogaja is the third kind of extra-ordinary perception, involving the use of higher mental faculties, arising only when an extra-ordinary power of inner mental concentration has been developed.

See also: **pratyaksha** (▸3).

7.4 Baptism, Initiation, Mysteries

Entry into a spiritual path is often accompanied by an initiatory or baptismal procedure. The form that this takes varies, depending upon the underlying culture and the particular path. But just as a marriage ceremony is a traditional way of marking a new phase in life, so does an initiation or baptism mark the beginning of a new phase in spiritual life.

Practically all faiths, religions and spiritual groups require new members to undergo some form of instruction and/or ceremony before they are accepted as fully participating members. This may take the form of some external rite of baptism or initiation, together with instruction in the mysteries of the faith.

Whatever the details may be, this kind of initiation is essentially external in character. Mystics say that although external instruction and guidance is necessary, there are other forms of initiation that take place beyond the confines of the external material world.

Terms associated with baptism and initiation, especially where they are related to spiritual life, form the basis of the entries in this section.

abhishek(a) (S/H), **dbang** (T), **guàndǐng** (C), **kanjō** (J) *Lit.* sprinkling *(abhisheka)*, anointment; empowerment *(dbang);* irrigate or pour + crown of head *(guàndǐng);* inauguration, consecration by the sprinkling of water; the inauguration or coronation of a king; religious bathing or ablutions; bathing the idol of a deity or a statue of the Buddha or of a Jain Tīrthankara with fragrant water, as an act of worship; esoterically, an initiation ceremony, based on the coronation ceremony of kings in traditional India, and used particularly in tantric *yoga* and tantric Buddhism; instruction in secret teachings and practices (including the giving of a *mantra*), together with the permission to practise them and the transmission of spiritual energy, given by a qualified *guru, āchārya* (teacher, preceptor) or *lama* who comes from an established and authentic lineage of masters; a ritual of empowerment, a blessing of the disciple's spiritual striving; also, the inauguration of a *guru* or *āchārya* (teacher, preceptor).

The pouring of water from a jug onto the head is the traditional Indian method of bathing in the absence of modern plumbing facilities. *Abhisheka* is sometimes used synonymously with *dīkshā* (initiation), and sometimes refers to an external ceremony held before or after *dīkshā.* Buddhist monasteries generally have a special hall dedicated to the purpose of *abhisheka.*

An *abhisheka* ceremony varies in its details, according to its particular purpose and the practices and beliefs of the particular school. It may be accompanied by ritual and ceremony or it may be a pure transmission of teachings and spiritual energy, without any ceremony. Although the sprinkling of water may be absent from some variations of the ceremony, the notion of purification is always present.

Tantric Buddhist and yogic *abhisheka* ceremonies bear considerable similarities to each other, both in their outward rituals and inner symbolism. Both symbolize a new birth and a new beginning, signified in many ceremonies by the initial blindfolding of the initiate, the removal of the blindfold, and his receiving a new name. The initiate is being brought from the darkness of ignorance into the light of spiritual wisdom. He is empowered by being placed upon the path of liberation from spiritual ignorance, from human impurity, and from the cycle of rebirth.

Tantric Buddhist texts speak of several levels or degrees of *abhisheka* or initiation, especially jug or vase initiation (T. *bum pa'i dbang,* S. *kalashābhisheka*), secret initiation (T. *gsang ba'i dbang,* S. *guhyābhisheka*), knowledge-wisdom (T. *shes rab ye shes kyi dbang,* S. *prajñā-jñānābhisheka*) initiation, and fourth or precious word initiation (T. *tshig dbang rinpoche*). These take place respectively at the level of body, speech, mind, and higher consciousness.

Vase initiation refers to the sprinkling of water on the head of the initiate, symbolizing purification of the body from all negative *karma.* The initiate begins to awaken to the presence and functioning of the *vajra* (energy) body, which is comprised of subtle physical energy (S. *prāṇa*) and its channels *(nāḍīs).* The student is prepared for awakening at the *nirmāṇa-kāya* (created body) level.

Secret initiation involves purification of negative *karma* through the giving of a *mantra,* together with instructions in both human behaviour and spiritual practice. These practices provide the means of controlling the hidden or secret processes of the mind, of quietening the otherwise endless mental chatter of concepts and concerns that occupy the mind, and project an illusory sense both of reality and of one's own identity. The process of rebalancing and unblocking the flow of *prāṇa* continues. Negative *karma* accumulated through speech is purified. The student is prepared for awakening at the subtle or *sambhoga-kāya* (body of bliss) level.

Transcendent knowledge-wisdom initiation takes place at the level of thought or mind. It is an expansion of awareness and understanding that arises as a consequence of an increasing degree of personal mind control and mental concentration. Purification of the higher mind (*vajra* mind) takes place. The student is prepared for awakening at the *dharmakāya* (body of Reality) level.

The fourth initiation is an extension of the same process, a further expansion of consciousness into the state of complete inner unity. The student is prepared for awakening at the level of absolute inner oneness *(svābhāvika-kāya).*

All four of these degrees may be contained within the instructions and symbolism of the *abhisheka* ceremony, and initiates may experience something of them at the time of the ceremony, according to their prior state of spiritual development and the grace and power of the *guru, āchārya,* or *lama.* They are also regarded as a part of the ongoing process of the initiate's spiritual evolution.

Tantric *yoga* texts mention a number of other initiations or blessings received at various stages of spiritual evolution. John Woodroffe, translator of and commentator on various tantric texts, describes eight such initiations, although details of the stages at which they are given are not provided.[1] They begin with the entry-level stage of *shākta-abhisheka,* in which the disciple *(shishya)* sets out upon the spiritual path *(sādhana).* His *guru* reveals to him the *shakti* (energy, consciousness) by which he is to become purified of human imperfection, and make progress to the higher stages. The next and intermediate level of *pūrṇa* (fulfilment) *abhisheka* is given when the disciple has earned it through the success in preliminary practices. It is here that the real spiritual path begins with the various practices of tantric *yoga* and *ashṭānga yoga.* Following this, the *shishya* receives the increasingly advanced initiation of *krama* (progress) *dīkshā-abhisheka,* and by undergoing various ordeals *(parikshā)* receives *sāmrājya* (complete dominion) *abhisheka, mahāsāmrājya* (great complete dominion) *abhisheka,* and at last receives *yoga-dīkshā-abhisheka.* Finally, he becomes qualified to receive *pūrṇadīkshā* (full initiation) *abhisheka* and subsequently *mahāpūrṇadīkshā* (fullest initiation) *abhisheka,* also called *viraja-grahaṇa* (free from captivity) *abhisheka.* Here, the relationship with his *guru* ends, and he ascends on his own until he realizes the truth of the *mahāvākya* (great saying) of the *Upanishads, "So'ham* (I am That)."[2] This is the stage of *jīvanmukti,* and the soul may now be correctly called a *paramahaṃsa* (supreme soul).

In some Chinese and Japanese schools of tantric Buddhism, such as *Zhēnyán* and *Shingon,* during the course of his initiation *(abhisheka),* the disciple stands upon a *maṇḍala* that represents the entire cosmos and its many worlds. The different sectors of the *maṇḍala* are also associated with various *buddhas* and *bodhisattvas.* By dropping or throwing a flower onto the *maṇḍala,* the disciple associates himself with a particular *buddha* or *bodhisattva,* from whom he will receive initiation *(abhisheka)* and protection. Thereafter, the disciple, in his meditation, forms a detailed mental image of his chosen protector, understanding that his protector symbolizes his own inherent buddhahood.

The *Shingon* school generally recognizes two kinds of *kanjō (nishu kanjō): kechien kanjō* and *dembo kanjō. Kechien* (connection) *kanjō* is the ceremony in which a monk makes the connection with his protective *buddha* or *bodhisattva* by tossing a flower onto a *maṇḍala. Dembo* (transmission) *kanjō* is the head-sprinkling ceremony in which a monk is inaugurated as a teacher (J. *ajari,* S. *āchārya*) qualified to instruct others.[3]

Also recognized in Japanese Buddhism are *sanshu kanjō* (three kinds of *kanjō*) and *shishu kanjō* (four kinds of *kanjō*). The three kinds are *machō* (lay-hands-on-top-of-the-head) *kanjō,* in which the Buddha indicates that a person will attain enlightenment by patting him on the head; *juki* (prophecy) *kanjō,* in which the Buddha indicates that a person will attain enlightenment by word of mouth; and *hoko* (light-emitting) *kanjō,* in which the Buddha emits a light for the universal benefit of all sentient beings. The four kinds of *kanjō* are the removal of obstacles, the attainment of wisdom, the attainment of blessings, and inauguration as a teacher *(ajari).*[4] It is believed that the Buddha would also sprinkle water, symbolizing the wisdom of the *buddhas,* on the head of a *bodhisattva* who was approaching enlightenment.

Abhisheka, as a lustration through the sprinkling of scented water, is also performed on a statue of the Buddha, during his birthday celebrations. In Jainism,[5] *abhisheka* refers to the ritual of bathing a consecrated image of a *Tīrthankara* with purified water or with one or more of the *pañcha-amṛita* (five nectars). Water is purified by straining, to avoid causing harm to micro-organisms in accordance with Jain principles, and is then either boiled or 'sterilized' using a substance such as cloves.

Practices vary between the different Jain schools and traditions. In *Digambara* temples in North India, purified water is generally used. The priests of *Digambara Bīsapanthī* temples in South India and a few in North India, on the other hand, perform a more elaborate daily lustration of the *Tīrthankara* image in which (traditionally) water, milk, water, yellow sandalwood water, and again water are successively poured over the image.

In more elaborate rituals, the *pañcha-amṛita* (five nectars) are used. Here, the substances successively used are coconut juice, sugarcane juice, milk, yellow sandalwood water (or milk, curds, water, yellow sandalwood water), and lastly red sandalwood water. There are also other variations that use ghee (clarified butter). On occasions, an *abhisheka* of nine pots or 108 pots may be performed. After the lustration, the image is carefully dried with clean cloths. In modern times, milk and its products are sometimes avoided due to the suffering of cows in modern intensive dairies.

At the periodic *mastaka* (head) *abhisheka,* the head-anointing ceremony of huge statues of Bāhubali, held every twelve years at Shravaṇa Belgola in Karnataka and at a few other locations in India, yellow and red powder, sandalwood paste, milk, pure water and gold coins are poured over the image from scaffolding erected behind it. The tenth-century statue of a naked Bāhubali, carved out of a single block of granite and located on the top of a hill at Shravaṇa Belgola, is seventeen metres (fifty-five feet) high, and can be seen from a distance of twenty miles. The colours used symbolize the degree of purification of Bāhubali in his progress toward *kevala-jñāna* (omniscience). The coloured liquids are poured from 1,008 pots by prominent members of the Jain laity, and tens of thousands of Jain devotees assemble to witness the anointing, which continues for several weeks. Participation in the ceremony is deemed to be of great merit, and to have a purifying effect upon the attendees.

Bāhubali was the second of the hundred sons of Ṛishabha, the first *Tīrthankara* and king of Poḍanpur. According to *Digambara* tradition, Bāhubali was the first in the current world cycle to reach enlightenment. *Shvetāmbara* tradition, however, maintains that Mārudevī; Ṛishabha's mother and thus Bāhubali's paternal grandmother, achieved this exalted status before him. As a consequence, Bāhubali is less venerated by *Shvetāmbaras* than *Digambaras,* although Jains of both traditions join in the *mastaka-abhisheka* festivities. In this ceremony, Bāhubali receives the adoration otherwise preserved for *Tīrthankaras.*

See also: **dīkshā**.

1. See John Woodroffe, *Mahānirvāṇa Tantra, Introduction, MTTL* pp.29–30; *cf. Mahānirvāṇa Tantra* 10, *GLMT* p.299*ff.*
2. *Bṛihadāraṇyaka Upanishad* 5:15.2, *Īshāvāsya Upanishad* 16.
3. See "Dembo-kanjō," "kechien-kanjō," *Japanese-English Buddhist Dictionary, JEDS.*
4. See "Sanshu-kanjō," "shishu-kanjō," *Japanese-English Buddhist Dictionary, JEDS.*
5. See "abhiśeka," "mastakabhiśeka," *A to Z of Jainism, AZJW.*

ankūri (H) *Lit.* one who is sprouting; from *ankur,* a sprout, a seed that has just started to germinate; spiritually, someone within whom the seed of spirituality has been planted in a previous life and who is ready to germinate in this life; hence, one who is destined to receive initiation from a perfect saint:

> When a saint sows the seed in a soul, no one can destroy it:
> in time, the seed will begin to germinate *(ankur).*
> Whenever a saint comes, he who is sprouting *(ankūri)*
> will find his company.
>
> *Swami Shiv Dayal Singh, Sār Bachan Poetry 38:7.31–32, SBP p.344*

anointing The application of oil, often scented, to the head as a sign of consecration, sanctification or – especially in more ancient times – succession to kingship or simply as a greeting; hence also, the inner spiritual anointment with the Holy Spirit of the messiah to his divine appointment, the messiah being regarded in Judaism as both spiritual leader and temporal king; in Christianity and some gnostic groups, baptism, in which consecrated oil and water, or oil and wine, were used; also, mystic baptism or initiation, in the sense of being anointed with the unseen Holy Oil and Living Water of the Spirit or Word – Holy Oil being a common metaphor for the Word in the ancient Middle East.

The practice of anointing with consecrated oil and water, or oil and wine, was a part of the baptism ritual of early Christianity. Paul writes of this anointing in a number of his letters. In *2 Corinthians,* it is linked to that of being "sealed" – another metaphor used for baptism:

> He who has established us with you in Christ, and has anointed us, is God; who has also sealed us, and given the promise of the Spirit in our hearts.
>
> *2 Corinthians 1:21–22; cf. KJV*

The use of the metaphor for baptism is witnessed in many early Christian texts, where the emphasis is often on inner baptism with the Holy Spirit, and may or may not have been accompanied by the outer ritual. Thus, in the *Acts of Thomas,* in a story concerning the baptism of King Gundaphorus and his brother Gad, Judas Thomas prays to Jesus:

> And now, at my supplication and request, receive the king and his brother and join them unto your fold, cleansing them with your washing and anointing them with your Oil from the error (illusion) that encompasses them. And keep them also from the wolves, bearing them into your meadows. And give them to drink out of your immortal

> Fountain which is neither fouled nor dries up. For they entreat and supplicate you and desire to become your servants and ministers.
>
> *Acts of Thomas 25; cf. ANT p.375*

Here, the "Oil" and "Fountain" are metaphors for the divine Word. In the same text, Judas Thomas also prays to God to bless a community of Christians under the care of the deacon Xanthippus. Here, the robbers and wild animals are the human imperfections that undermine the soul's contact with the Holy Spirit. Once again, the "Holy Oil" is entirely spiritual:

> Anoint this flock with Your Oil of Life, and heal it of its disease, and preserve it from wolves and from robbers, that they may not snatch it from his hands.
>
> *Acts of Thomas 67; cf. AAA p.205, ANT p.396*

The souls in the material world have often been portrayed by mystics as spiritually sick and diseased. Consequently, true baptism or initiation and the subsequent purification of the soul through meditation upon the Word, has also been described as a process of healing. Since in ancient times, as with some herbalists of today, oil extracts and spices were used for their therapeutic qualities, it is no surprise to find that such baptism was described as being healed with oil.

According to the gospels, the disciples of Jesus were said to have performed a similar function, though it is likely that the writer of Mark's gospel is misunderstanding and externalizing the meaning of what actually took place when he writes:

> And they (the disciples) cast out many devils, and anointed with oil many that were sick, and healed them.
>
> *Mark 6:13, KJV*

Mystically speaking, the "devils" are imperfections of the mind, the human weaknesses and all the powers that keep souls tied down to this world; and the oil that heals these weaknesses is the Holy Spirit.

In the first epistle of John, baptism by Jesus is specifically described as the "anointing you have received from him":

> But the anointing you have received from him abides in you, and you need no man to teach you. But as the same anointing teaches you all things, and is Truth, and is no lie, and even as it has taught you, you shall abide in him.
>
> *1 John 2:27; cf. KJV*

Here, the "anointing" is explicitly described as being "received from him", and it also "abides in you". Moreover, this "anointing" alone "teaches you all things", since mystic initiation will ultimately bring a soul to the point of supreme mystic experience where "all things" are fully known and understood from the point of view of God Himself. As the same writer says, "You have been anointed by the Holy One and have all received the knowledge."[1]

The gnostics speak even more explicitly of this anointing, also called being "born again":

> We are born again through the Holy Spirit, and we are born of the anointed one through two things. We are anointed by the Spirit; and when we were so born, we were united (with it). No one can see himself either in water or in a mirror without light. Nor again can you see by the light without water or mirror. For this reason, it is necessary to baptize with two things – light and water. And light means chrism.
>
> *Gospel of Philip 69; cf. GS pp.342–43, NHS20 pp.178–81*

Baptism, being anointed or being reborn, is understood mystically. It comes "through the Holy Spirit" and originates from the "anointed one" or Christ. Anointing with the Spirit means being "united" to that Spirit, mystically. Clearly, such an anointing requires an adept who knows how to perform that inner joining or uniting. No outward ritual, however symbolic, can take its place. The writer then mentions two things that are required for such a baptism – "light and water". "Water" symbolizes the Living Water or Word, while "light" refers to the inner light of the Word. "Light" also implies the "chrism" or receptacle for oil – the provider of light in ancient oil lamps.

The author of the *Gospel of Philip* is fond of such cryptic metaphors, and double meanings can confidently be sought in his pithy, enigmatic expressions. In many cases, he goes on to explain himself explicitly. In another passage, he says:

> He who has been anointed has everything: the resurrection, the light, the cross, the Holy Spirit. The Father has given it to that person in the bridal chamber; that person merely received (the gift).
>
> *Gospel of Philip 74; cf. GS p.346, NHS20 pp.190–91*

The initiated or "anointed" person has been given the key to everything. The "resurrection" means that he can learn to rise up in consciousness and leave his body at will. The "light" refers to the experience of divine Light within himself. The "cross" implies the sacrifice of his ego or individual self, so that he can rise up to the single, spiritual eye, which lies between the two physical eyes, at the intersection of the vertical (spiritual) and horizontal (material) ways. The "Holy Spirit" is the Word, the essence of life which takes the soul back to the Father. All this has been given to the soul inwardly, "in the bridal chamber". The initiate is simply the recipient.

In the gnostic *Gospel of Truth,* the "Oil" is explicitly identified with the "mercy of the Father", and once again it is the "anointed one" – the Christ or saviour – who bestows this anointing upon those who "seek" it:

> With the coming of the anointed one, it was said publicly: "Seek, and those who are disturbed will receive restoration, and he will anoint them with Oil." The Oil is the mercy of the Father, who will be merciful to them; and those whom he has anointed are the perfected ones.
>
> *Gospel of Truth 36; cf. GS pp.261–62, NHS22 pp.108–9*

"Those who are disturbed" are the souls in the material world, their minds full of desire and activity. They will be released from the turmoil of the creation and will be taken back to the Father. Mercy is required rather than justice, for the sins of countless lifetimes need to be forgiven. Then they will become the "perfected ones".

In the *Nature of the Rulers,* which concerns the origins of man and those who are ultimately destined to return to God, a fictional dialogue takes place between an angel and a soul in human form. The angel first says:

> "You, together with your offspring, are from the primeval Father; from above, out of the imperishable Light, their souls are come. Thus, the authorities (inner powers) cannot approach them because of the Spirit of Truth present within them; and all who have become acquainted with this way exist deathless in the midst of dying humankind."
>
> *Nature of the Rulers 96; cf. GS p.75, NHS20 pp.256–57*

The dialogue then continues, concerning the length of time that will pass before the bound souls are freed, and the manner by which they are freed. The "true man", says the 'angel', "will anoint them with the Oil of Life Eternal". He means initiation by a saviour into the mystic Word by a saviour:

> Then I said, "Sir, how much longer?"
>
> He said to me, "Until the moment when the true man, within a modelled form (human form), reveals the existence of the Spirit of Truth which the Father has sent. Then he will teach them about everything; and he will anoint them with the Oil of Life Eternal, given to him by the race of the free.
>
> "Then they will be freed from blind thought: and they will trample death under foot.... And they will ascend into the limitless Light, where this sown element (chosen seed) belongs.... Then all the

children of the Light will be truly acquainted with the Truth and their Root, and the Father of the Totality (creation) and the Holy Spirit."

Nature of the Rulers 96–97; cf. GS p.76, NHS20 pp.258–59

The souls will continue to be bound to this world until a "true man", a saviour, comes in a human form and reveals the existence of the Spirit of Truth to his chosen ones. He will teach his disciples about the reality of God, and the creation, and the true purpose of human life. He will teach them how to meditate upon the "Spirit of Truth", and will initiate them into that path. Then these "children of the Light" will be released from the blindness of mind and intellect, will return to the Light of God, and will experience the absolute, mystic Truth and Source of all things.

Among the Mandaeans, a gnostic baptismal sect for whom oil played a significant ritualistic role, and in whose sacred literature the metaphor of oil is found extensively, it again seems clear that the real "Oil" was that of the purifying Word or divine "Name of Truth". In a poem that describes the coming to this world of the mythical saviour *Manda-ḍ-Hiia* ('*Gnōsis* of Life'), the poet speaks of the divine blessings, including forgiveness of sins, that come from the "Oil with which he anointed". "Life" is a Mandaean term for the supreme Being:

This is the Oil with which he anointed,
  the radiance, light and glory,
  which *Manda-ḍ-Hiia* blessed with his pure mouth,
  and bestowed on all who love his Name of Truth.
From all those who are anointed with this Oil,
  every pain, disease, complaint...
  and physical evil will be removed....
Every man anointed with this Oil will be sinless
  and blameless in the place of Life.

Mandaean Prayer Book 24; cf. CPM pp.20–21

Since anointing the head with fragrant oils has a soothing quality, the metaphor also refers more generally to the blessings of divine grace, as in the twenty-third psalm:

Thou preparest a table before me in the presence of mine enemies;
Thou anointest my head with oil, my cup runneth over.

Psalms 23:5, KJV

Many Christian writers have used the metaphor in this context. Often, they also refer to the psalm in which it is said that the messiah is "anointed (by

God) with the Oil of Gladness",[2] themselves longing to be so anointed with the grace of the divine Spirit. Others have found a spiritual meaning in the *Song of Songs,*[3] where the lover says to the beloved, "Your name is an oil poured out, and that is why the maidens love you."[4] But the general understanding is of being anointed with divine grace. Hence, Thomas à Kempis prays, "Send down Your grace from above, and with it anoint my dry heart."[5] And speaking of the soul in whom the fire of love has been lit, Richard Rolle observes:

> So the soul, anointed with heavenly sweetness, and made alive by heavenly joy, longs to set out heavenward, but feels frustrated because she must remain in this mortal flesh. Nevertheless she gladly endures whatever adversity comes her way, for she rests sweetly in the joy of eternal love.
>
> *Richard Rolle, Fire of Love 36; cf. FLML (2:6) p.155, FLRR p.160*

And:

> I would consider the truer prayer and meditation to be when a man's love is great enough to turn his prayer into song, so that he melts into the melody of heavenly sweetness, and produces angelic sounds rather than human, anointed as he is with honeyed fervour.
>
> *Richard Rolle, Fire of Love 40; cf. FLML (2:10) p.181, FLRR p.182*

John of the Cross speaks of the inwardly sweet and subtle blessings that come to the contemplative soul who is anointed by the Holy Spirit:

> The interior blessings that this silent contemplation leaves impressed upon the soul without its perception of them are… inestimable; for they are in fact the most secret and delicate anointings of the Holy Spirit, which secretly fill the soul with spiritual riches and gifts and graces.
>
> *John of the Cross, Living Flame of Love 2:36; cf. CWJC3 p.72*

And again:

> These unctions are so subtle and so delicate in their anointing that they penetrate the inmost substance of the depth of the soul, preparing it and filling it with sweetness in such a way that its suffering and fainting with desire in the boundless emptiness of these caverns is likewise boundless.
>
> *John of the Cross, Living Flame of Love 3:68, CWJC3 p.179*

See also: **mashi´aḥ** (7.1), **Oil** (3.1).

1. *1 John* 2:20, in *ADP* p.104.
2. *Psalms* 45:7, *JB*.
3. *E.g.* Bernard of Clairvaux, *On the Song of Songs* 13:8, *WBC1* p.95, *passim;* Walter Hilton, *Ladder of Perfection* 2:41, *LPH* p.231.
4. *Song of Songs* 1:2, *JB*.
5. Thomas à Kempis, *Imitation of Christ* 3:23, *IC* p.141.

bakhshish (P), **bakhshīs**, **bakhsīs**, **baksīs** (H/Pu), **bakhshash** (Pu) *Lit.* gift, favour; something given for free; spiritually, a gift of divine grace, a gift of God; blessing, benediction; hence also, divine pardon, forgiveness, mercy; in a specific context, the gift of the divine Name or creative power:

> The first giver is the disciple,
> surrendering his body, mind, and head.
> The next giver is the *guru*
> granting the gift *(baksīs)* of the Name.
>
> *Kabīr, Sākhī Sangrah, Gurudev kā Ang16, KSS p.2*

Rūmī speaks of "two intelligences". One is the acquired intelligence *('aql),* the intellect or reason that learns human knowledge. The "other Intelligence *('Aql)*" is the divine creative power, the essence of all being, the "gift of God":

> The other Intelligence *('Aql)* is the gift of God *(bakhshish-i Yazdān):*
> its fountainhead is in the midst of the soul.
>
> *Rūmī, Maśnavī IV:1964, MJR4 p.381*

See also: **bakhshish** (▸4), **gift**.

baptism (Gk. *baptisma*) An experience of initiation, regeneration or dedication, commonly used in reference to the Christian religious rite, though prior to the Christian era, similar sacraments and purificatory ablutions were practised by both Jews and others – gnostic and baptismal sects having flourished in the ancient Middle East; also called anointing, being sealed (on the forehead), being planted in heaven, the sowing of the Seed, the gift of God, gift of the Name, a second birth, being born again, and so on; from the Greek *baptō* or *baptizō* (to wash, to immerse).

Among the Jews, baptism as a sacramental initiation was presaged by circumcision, through which a person was admitted into the children of God. Various ablutions are also prescribed in the Mosaic law, external cleansing being required to wash away an internal blemish. Likewise, external washing to effect internal purification was prevalent among the Babylonians, Assyrians, Egyptians, Greeks, Romans and others, and remains a part of religious practice today in Judaism, Christianity, Islam, Hinduism, Buddhism, and Shintō.

Baptism is the primal sacrament of the Christian church. In its original form, it entailed complete immersion. Later, various forms of sprinkling were also adopted. By the second century, however, the essential components of baptism were the use of water and the invocation of the Trinity. According to a fifteenth-century papal bull:

> Holy baptism holds the first place among the sacraments, because it is the door of the spiritual life; for by it we are made members of Christ, and incorporated with the church. And since, through the first man (Adam), death entered into all, unless we be born again of water and the Holy Ghost, we can not enter into the kingdom of heaven, as Truth himself has told us. The matter of this sacrament is true and natural water; and it is indifferent whether it be cold or hot. The form is: "I baptize you in the name of the Father and of the Son and of the Holy Ghost."
>
> *Eugene IV, Decree for the Armenians, "Baptism"; cf. Catholic Encyclopedia (1907)*

Christianity has always understood that the outer ritual of baptism, although regarded as essential, is only a token of the true spiritual baptism, for by it the soul is believed to have received baptism in the Trinity. According to Christian doctrine, baptism also cleanses the soul of its 'original sin', the first sin committed by Adam, and thus the hereditary stain with which human beings are born on account of their descent from Adam. The contemplative life and true inner love of God are regarded as the flowering of the gift of baptism. As the fifth-century bishop Diadochos of Photiki writes:

> Grace is hidden in the depth of the mind from the moment of baptism, its presence being hidden even from the spiritual sense. But when anyone begins to love God with all his resolution, then by an ineffable communication through the feeling of the mind, it communicates part of its benefits to the soul.
>
> *Diadochos of Photiki, Gnostic Chapters 77 (OSDP), in OCM pp.127–28*

Walter Hilton also speaks of the essentially mystical nature of baptism, and its effects, likening it to the sacrament of penance:

> The church holds that, by the right reception of the sacrament of baptism, the soul of a Jew, a pagan, or a new-born babe is reformed to the likeness of God by the secret and imperceptible working of the Holy Spirit, although bodily temptations will be experienced as strongly

> after baptism as before.... Similarly, by the humble and right reception of the sacrament of penance, the soul of an unworthy Christian, who has lived his whole life in mortal sin, is imperceptibly reformed and his will redirected by the hidden power and gracious action of the Holy Spirit. This power works swiftly, correcting a stubborn soul in a moment, and transforming its spiritual ugliness into invisible beauty. It changes a servant of the devil into a son of joy, and promises a former prisoner of hell a place in the kingdom of heaven, despite all the carnal inclinations fostered by this sinful image within us.
>
> *Walter Hilton, Ladder of Perfection 2:8, LPH p.126*

It has been Christian belief since the very earliest times that all those who profess faith in the tenets of Christianity will be 'saved' and 'go to heaven', as long as they have been baptized. Assertions to this effect are found throughout Christian literature. The long ending to *Mark,* for example, though appended at some uncertain later time, demonstrates the traditional importance of baptism:[1]

> He who believes and is baptized shall be saved,
> but he who does not believe shall be damned.
>
> *Mark 16:16; cf. KJV*

Likewise, in the *Acts of John,* to one who asks, "Command me what I should do, that I may live," John replies:

> Believe in the Name of the Father, the Son,
> and the Holy Ghost, the one God, and be baptized,
> and you shall receive eternal life.
>
> *Acts of John; cf. MAA p.46*

Although external baptism was deemed of great importance in first-century Christianity, it is uncertain whether it was regarded as essential to the new birth or was looked upon merely as an external symbol. The true nature of baptism, as many of the early Christians understood it, was – and still is – essentially mystical. The baptized person is believed to have been incorporated into the mystical Christ. As Judas Thomas describes it in the *Acts of Thomas,* addressing the inner Christ as the mystical Son of God, the divine Word:

> Glory to you, hidden one,
> who is communicated to us in baptism.
> Glory to you, unseen Power that is in baptism.
> Glory to you, renewed ones, who are renewed through baptism,
> and with love take hold on you....

Living Bread, the eaters of which die not –
  bread that fills hungry souls with your blessing:
You are he that confers a gift on us,
  that you may become the remission of sins for us,
  and that they who partake of you may become immortal.

Acts of Thomas 132–33; cf. AAA pp.267–68, ANT p.422

The hidden Power of the Word, the Holy Spirit, is infused into or communicated to a soul at the time of mystic baptism. But this cannot be outwardly observed. It is an "unseen Power" through which the soul is renewed, given a new birth or a new beginning in the spirit, through the awakening of love for God and his divine Power. The "Living Bread", the divine Word, which is the true and natural nourishment of the soul, is a powerful spiritual "blessing", a current from God Himself, which satisfies the craving of "hungry souls", who find eternal life within themselves. This Power, through a saviour, "confers a gift on us" – the gift of baptism – which also confers upon the soul, the "remission of sins".

The belief in the remission of sins through this kind of internal, mystical baptism is reiterated in a number of other places. Again, it is Judas Thomas who says:

This baptism is of the remission of sins:
  it is the bringer forth of new men;
It is the restorer of understandings,...
  and the establisher of the new man in the Trinity,
  making him a partaker in the remission of sins.

Acts of Thomas 132; cf. AAA p.267, ANT p.422

And again, when giving baptism to a group:

In your name, O Jesu Christ,
  let it be to these souls for the remission of sins,
  and for the turning back of the Adversary (the devil),
  and for salvation of their souls.

Acts of Thomas 157; cf. ANT p.433

Likewise, in the *Acts of John,* it is said that John

baptized them in the Name of the Father
and the Son and the Spirit of Holiness,
for the forgiveness of debts and the pardon of sins.

History of John, AAA p.54

As the writer of the gnostic *Gospel of Philip* summarizes it, when speaking of the crop harvested by those who receive this baptism:

> Then the slaves will be free and the captives ransomed.
>
> *Gospel of Philip 85, NHS20 pp.212–13*

The same writer also comments almost scathingly on the baptism that is comprised of no more than immersion in water:

> If one goes down into the water and comes up without having received anything, and says, "I am a Christian," he has borrowed the name at interest. But if he receives the Holy Spirit, he has the gift of the Name. He who has received a gift does not have to give it back, but of him who has borrowed it at interest, payment is demanded.
>
> *Gospel of Philip 64; cf. NHS20 pp.168–69*

It is clear that such a baptism must be more than a simple ritual immersion, or sprinkling with water, or anointing with oil. A baptism that forgives sins, results in the liberation of captive souls, confers eternal life, and is a gift of the Holy Spirit, must be of a special nature, something that only a prophet or mystic of the highest attainment can bestow, and it must be presumed that this was the kind of baptism given by both Jesus and John the Baptist. This is evident from the Christian gospels themselves. Matthew, following Mark, relates Jesus' response when his authority to teach is questioned by the "chief priests and elders". Jesus asks them:

> "The baptism of John, whence was it? From heaven or of men?" And they reasoned with themselves, saying, "If we shall say, 'From heaven,' he will say unto us, 'Why then did you not believe him?' But if we shall say, 'Of men,' we fear the people; for all hold John as a prophet."
>
> *Matthew 21:25–26; cf. KJV*

Not only does he suggest that the authority to teach such things is the same as the authority to baptize, he also indicates that there is a difference between baptism "from heaven" and the baptism "of men". He also presumes that baptism from heaven can only be given by a prophet. For the "chief priests and elders," relates Matthew, were afraid to reply "of men," "for all hold John as a prophet." Evidently, men can be expected to give a human baptism and a true prophet or mystic to give baptism "from heaven". Baptism from heaven means baptism by the Holy Spirit.

In the gospels, the subject is mentioned in only a few places and that unsatisfyingly and unclearly. To begin with, John the Baptist is said to baptize with "water unto repentance" and Jesus with the "Holy Ghost and with fire". According to Matthew, John the Baptist says:

> I indeed baptize you with water unto repentance;
> But he who comes after me is mightier than I,
> whose shoes I am not worthy to bear:
> He shall baptize you with the Holy Ghost, and with fire.
>
> *Matthew 3:11; cf. KJV*

But what does this mean? For it would be unwise to take the images literally. The Holy Ghost is of course the Holy Spirit or Word and "fire" must be a metaphor for the inner Light, since no one ever suggested that Jesus set fire to his disciples. The compiler of John's gospel, however – or perhaps a later editor – is adamant that John the Baptist baptized in real, physical water and the point is made in several places. John the Baptist speaks of "he that sent me to baptize with water"[2] and again, even more specifically:

> And John also was baptizing in Aenon near to Salim, because there was much water there; and they came, and were baptized.
>
> *John 3:23, KJV*

But this is a human baptism, and Jesus has indicated that John's baptism was that of a prophet and was hence, "from heaven". It is likely, therefore, that somewhere along the line, baptism in the Living Water of the Word, the real "water unto repentance" which is capable of washing away sins and turning a soul towards God, became literalized into this kind of anecdote concerning John the Baptist. Indeed, it is probable that these and other gospel passages were designed to put John the Baptist into a lesser place than Jesus, despite Jesus' considerable praises of John in other gospel passages.

Jesus provides other indications in the gospels that the baptism he gave was more than just an immersion in the water. Luke records him as saying:

> But I have a baptism to be baptized with!
>
> *Luke 12:50, KJV*

And Jesus uses a similar expression on another occasion, in a story found in *Mark* and copied across almost verbatim into *Matthew* and *Luke*. Mark relates that Jesus has been asked by James and John for seats on either side of him "in your glory":

> Jesus said unto them, "You know not what you ask. Can you drink of the cup that I drink of, and be baptized with the baptism that I am baptized with?"

> And they said unto him, "We can."
>
> And Jesus said unto them, "You shall indeed drink of the cup that I drink of; and with the baptism that I am baptized with shall you be baptized."
>
> *Mark 10:38–39; cf. KJV*

Jesus is clearly talking of a very special kind of baptism. Not only that, but he indicates that it is the same as that with which he was baptized by John the Baptist. He and his disciples have both received the same kind of baptism, and his disciples obviously expect to reap the same fruits as Jesus: "You shall indeed drink of the cup that I drink of." Although traditionally understood to be referring to Jesus' forthcoming death upon the cross, and the similar deaths of some of his disciples, there is no reason why these passages should not be understood to mean exactly what they say. The baptism which Jesus is describing is a mystic touch of soul to soul, from the soul of the master to the soul of the disciple. It is a retuning of the soul to the Creative Word, present within all, yet heard by very few. It is the acceptance of a soul by a master into his fold.

John's gospel has two further comments concerning the baptism given by Jesus:

> After these things, Jesus and his disciples came into the land of Judaea; and there he tarried with them, and baptized.
>
> *John 3:22; cf. KJV*

And:

> When therefore the Lord knew how the Pharisees had heard that Jesus made and baptized more disciples than John, (though Jesus himself baptized not, but his disciples), he left Judaea, and departed again into Galilee.
>
> *John 4:1–3, KJV*

The parenthetical "though Jesus himself baptized not, but his disciples" is an interesting aside and may perhaps point to a practice in which people were accepted for baptism by Jesus, while the instructions were actually given to them by disciples designated to do so. The passage also suggests that Jesus had far more followers or disciples that his close entourage of twelve.

There is another source that helps shed light upon the mystery of the baptism given by Jesus. The Mandaeans, an intriguing gnostic sect who acknowledge John the Baptist as a saviour and who survived into the twentieth century in the southern marshlands on the borders of Iran and Iraq, also practised baptism in water and with oil. But their sacred writings very clearly reveal that the water they talk about is the Living Water of the Word. Furthermore, one of their terms for *any* stream or river is a 'jordan', a term used frequently in their scriptures for the divine 'stream' of Living Water. In fact, in the earlier years of the twentieth century, many among them did not even know that elsewhere in the Middle East, there was a river called the Jordan.

Being baptized in the 'Jordan', then, did not mean a dip in the muddy waters of a Palestinian river, but a mystic immersion, a washing of the soul and mind in the Living Water. There are many examples from the Mandaean writings that can be given to demonstrate this point. In a poem where the Word is referred to as a "Staff of Water", Hībil (the biblical Abel, son of Adam), one of the pantheon of mythical Mandaean saviours, baptizes or "raises up living souls in the Jordan":

> By it (the power of the Staff of Water),
> Hībil raises up living souls in the Jordan,
> those worthy of the great place of light
> and of the everlasting abode.
>
> By it, they will be established
> and raised up in the house of the mighty Life.
> It will raise those souls
> who go to the Jordan and are baptized:
> They will behold the great place of light
> and the everlasting abode.

Mandaean Prayer Book 14; cf. CPM p.10

The Mandaean usage of the term is intriguing, for the very use of the term 'jordan' as well as the Aramaic character of their language and their references to both Jewish mythical characters together with John the Baptist and Jesus, all point to their origins in Palestine around the time of Jesus and John the Baptist. It seems likely, then, bearing in mind how little is really known of the lives of these two great spiritual teachers, that the gospel stories concerning baptism in water have arisen from a misunderstanding of something far more deeply mystical.

The Mandaean writings clearly demonstrate their belief in the role of a saviour in the giving of baptism. In fact, in their religion as it came to be, they acknowledge a pantheon of saviours including Noah's sons Hībil (Abel) and Shitil (Seth), Enosh (Enoch, descendant of Adam and great-grandfather of Noah), *Manda-ḍ-Hiia,* and two lesser known saviours Shilmai and Nidbai. Most, if not all of these, are mythological rather than historical characters, but their role in Mandaean thought is clearly stated. Shilmai and Nidbai, for instance, are described as:

the two delegates of *Manda-ḍ-Hiia,*
who rule over the great Jordan of Life,
for they baptize with the great baptism of light.

Mandaean Prayer Book 9, CPM p.8

In essence, they are all saviours who can initiate a physically incarnate soul into the mysteries of the Word and take her back to God. In the words of one poem, they are "helpers" of *Manda-ḍ-Hiia,* the divine Word and the archetypal master of the Mandaean pantheon. Says the Word of Life:

I went to the Jordan, but not I alone,
for Shilmai and Nidbai, my helpers, went with me to the Jordan;
Hībil and Shitil and Enosh went with me to the Jordan –
they who baptize with the great baptism of Life....

I go down to those souls whom Life delivers and saves,
and protects these souls from all that is evil....
In your names, Shilmai and Enosh,
secure, seal and guard these souls who enter into the Jordan,
and will be baptized by the great seal of holy *Manda-ḍ-Hiia,*
the healer, whose strength none can attain.

Mandaean Prayer Book 13; cf. CPM pp.9–10

Just as women went down to the river to draw water for their family, so too does the saviour draw from the Jordan of Living Water in order to initiate and satisfy the spiritual thirst of souls. He comes down to the physical universe for the salvation of souls; to baptize them in the Living Water, to protect them from evil, and to return with them to God. Receiving the "seal", an emblem of entry into secret or forbidden places, is a common expression for being baptized in Mandaean, Christian, Manichaean, and other Middle Eastern mystic literature.

Among other gnostic and mystical groups, baptism is commonly portrayed as entirely spiritual, something given to the soul in the inner heavens. In the *Trimorphic Protennoia,* for instance, the aspirant, who is given the "five seals",[3] "stripped off the garments of ignorance and put on a shining light".[4] He is cleansed in the "Water of Life",[5] receives a throne of glory, and is raised to a place of pure spiritual light:

I am inviting you into the exalted, perfect Light.
Moreover, (as for) this (Light), when you enter it,
you will be glorified by those who give glory,
and those who enthrone will enthrone you.
You will accept robes from those who give robes,
and the baptists (masters?) will baptize you,

and you will become gloriously glorious,
the way you first were when you were light.
Trimorphic Protennoia 45, NHS28 pp.422–33

Other gnostic texts, too, such as the *Pistis Sophia* and the *Second Book of Jeu,* make frequent mention of baptisms that take place entirely in the spiritual realms. Likewise, in the revelational *Zostrianos,* the protagonist receives an increasingly higher baptism at each stage of his ascent through the various heavens, until at last he is told, "You have received all the baptisms in which it is fitting to be baptized, and you have become perfect."[6]

In Manichaeism, baptism was also regarded as an inner spiritual event. The Coptic texts, for instance, speak of "holy baptism"[7] or the "baptism of Life"[8] as a "gift".[9] And the Hermetic literature describes how God "filled a mighty bowl with the *Nous* (divine Mind or Intelligence, the creative power)", and sent it down to humankind, "joining a herald (a master) to it" with the message:

> "Those hearts that are able, baptize (*lit.* immerse) yourself with the baptism of this bowl – if you who have faith that you can ascend to Him that has sent down the bowl; and if you who know the purpose for which you have come into being."
>
> Then as many as understood these tidings and were baptized in the *Nous,* became partakers in *gnōsis,* and having received the *Nous,* became perfect men.
>
> *Corpus Hermeticum 4:4; cf. HAG p.61, HGCH p.15, TGH2 p.87*

See also: **anointing, herald** (7.1), **Jordan** (3.1).

1. Much of the material for this entry is taken from *The Gospel of Jesus, GJ* pp.671–76.
2. *John* 1:33, *KJV.*
3. *Trimorphic Protennoia* 48–50, *NHS28* pp.428–33.
4. *Trimorphic Protennoia* 49, *NHS28* pp.430–31.
5. *Trimorphic Protennoia* 37, 41, 48, *NHS28* pp.406–7, 414–15, 428–29.
6. *Zostrianos* 62, *NHS31* pp.138–39.
7. *Manichaean Psalm Book* CCXLIX, *MPB* p.58.
8. *Manichaean Psalm Book, MPB* p.139.
9. *Manichaean Psalm Book* CCXXVII, *MPB* p.22.

bayʻah (A), **bayʻat** (P) *Lit.* pledge, pact, allegiance, bond, oath, undertaking, agreement, promise; homage; an oath of allegiance to Muḥammad, or to the caliph following him; esoterically, initiation by a *shaykh* into a Sufi order; the pledge of allegiance given by a disciple to a *shaykh* upon initiation into a Sufi order. The term appears in such expressions as *bayʻat al-Islām* (pledge to Islam), given at the time of embracing Islam; *bayʻat al-jihād* (pledge to the struggle), given while engaged in some difficult task or, more specifically, the pledge to engage in holy war – understood either materially or spiritually; *bayʻat ṭalab al-asrār* (pledge to the mysteries), being initiated into the Sufi path; *bayʻat al-tawbah* (pledge to repentance); and *ʻahd bayʻatī* or *mubāyaʻah* (oath of allegiance), made either to God, the Prophet, a master, or to a worldly beloved.

According to Muslim history, the *bayʻat al-riḍwān* – variously translated as 'pact of God's good pleasure', 'oath of felicity', 'oath of benediction', 'covenant of fealty', 'pledge of allegiance', and so on – is the name of the renewal of the oath of allegiance exacted by the Prophet from 1,500 of his companions at al-Ḥudaybīyah during the early days (Medinan period), when the Prophet had resolved to conquer Mecca, but the success of their mission was still uncertain. It is said that at the time the Prophet requested the renewal of their faith and their continued willingness to fight with him in battle, while he was leaning against the trunk of a tree. The incident is referred to both in the *ḥadīth*[1] and in the *Qur'ān*:[2]

> Those who swear allegiance *(bayʻah)* to you (Muḥammad) swear allegiance *(bayʻah)* to God Himself. The Hand of God *(Yadullāhi)* is above their hands. Whoever breaks his oath *(nakatha),* harms his own soul, but whoever keeps his covenant *(ʻāhada)* with God, on him will He bestow a rich reward. . . .
>
> God's good pleasure *(raḍiya)* was with the believers when they swore fealty *(yubāyiʻu)* to you under the tree. He knew what was in their hearts, and He sent down tranquillity upon them, and rewarded them with a speedy victory.
>
> *Qur'ān 48:10, 18; cf. AYA, KPA, MGK*

The *bayʻat al-riḍwān,* often abbreviated to *al-riḍwān,* has been used as a pattern for Sufi initiation, including the renewal of allegiance by a disciple to his *shaykh* (master). It is said in the *ḥadīth*[3] that some of Muḥammad's followers had previously renewed their oath, but were willing to renew it once again. In the same way, disciples may renew their allegiance to their *shaykh* many times. According to the diary of one of his disciples, Niẓām al-Dīn Awliyā' once commented:

> If a disciple wants to renew his oath of allegiance *(bayʻat al-riḍwān),* but his *shaykh* is not present, he may take the garment of his *shaykh* and, placing that garment before him, make his oath of allegiance *(bayʻat al-riḍwān)* to it. Don't be surprised that Shaykh al-Islām Farīd

al-Dīn (Shaykh Farīd) – may God sanctify his lofty secret – renewed his allegiance to Shaykh Quṭb al-Dīn many times in this fashion, and I have followed his example.

Niẓām al-Dīn Awliyā', Morals for the Heart 2:16, FFNA pp.98–99, MHN pp.148–49

After the time of Muḥammad, the same oath of allegiance was made by Muslims to the caliph, the head of the Muslim community. Sufi interpreters have understood the verse to refer to initiation by a master, and the "Hand of God" to mean a perfect master. *Bayʿat* therefore implies initiation by a master into the mystic path. Extending the metaphor, Rūmī refers to initiation as placing one's hand in the hand of the master (*pīr, lit.* old man, elder):

Do not surrender your hand *(dast)*
save to the hand *(dast)* of the *pīr*,
for God is the helper of his hand *(dast)*.
The old man *(pīr)* of your intellect
has made a habit of childishness
from being neighbour to the *nafs* (lower mind), which is veiled.
Make your intelligence *(khirad)* the companion
of the *ʿAql-i kāmil* (perfect Intelligence, the divine Word).
so that your understanding may turn back from its bad habits....

When you place your hand *(dast)* in the hand of the *pīr*,
the *pīr* of Wisdom who is knowing and venerable,
who is the prophet of his own time, O disciple,
so that the light of the Prophet is manifested in him –
Then you have been present at Ḥudaybīyah,
and are fellow to those companions
who swore the covenant *(ṣaḥābah-'i bayʿat)*....
so that communion may be made perfect:
For a man becomes one with he whom he has made his friend.

Rūmī, Maśnavī V:736–38, 741–43, 745; cf. MJR6 pp.46–47

Using the same metaphor, he also advises discrimination when seeking a master:

Since there is many a devil with the face of Adam,
do not entrust your hand *(dast)* to every hand *(dast)*.

Rūmī, Maśnavī I:316; cf. MJR2 p.20

The customs associated with Sufi initiation vary from order to order, and according to local circumstances. In some cases, the master of the order gives the initiation. In other instances, one of his disciples is appointed to instruct novitiates and perhaps to give the initiation. There is a Sufi saying that the master attracts and the preparatory master *(pīr-i dalīl)* repels. That is, the seeker is attracted to the path by the grace and lovingkindness of the master, while the *pīr-i dalīl* instructs the seeker in the discipline and rigours of the path, and the correct conduct, duties, and practices. When he considers the seeker ready, he recommends him to the master for initiation.

A period of time for taking stock is generally set aside prior to initiation, often a matter of two or three years, so that seekers may have time to understand the life and spiritual practices they are preparing to follow, and to see whether it is what they really want to do. Both before and after initiation, disciples may continue their lives in the world, meeting with their master on a regular basis. Other disciples may live with their master in the *khānaqāh* (Sufi residence, 'monastery'). Still others may be more loosely associated with the *khānaqāh,* receive blessings from the master and attend meetings, but not wish to fully commit themselves to the order.

'Ināyat Khān, who brought Sufism to the West in the early twentieth century, has much to say concerning initiation. To begin with, the relationship between *murshid* (master) and *murīd* (disciple) is one of trust and confidence:

> Initiation, or in Sufi terms *bay'at,* first of all has to do with the relationship between the pupil and the *murshid.* The *murshid* is understood to be the counsellor on the spiritual path. He does not give anything to, or teach the pupil, the *murīd,* for he cannot give what the latter already has; he cannot teach what his (the disciple's) soul has always known. What he does in the life of the *murīd* is to show him how he can clear his path towards the light within by his own self. This is the only purpose of man's life on earth. One may attain the purpose of life without a personal guide, but to try to do so is to be like a ship traversing the ocean without a compass. To take initiation, then, means entrusting oneself in regard to spiritual matters to a spiritual guide.
>
> *'Ināyat Khān, Sufi Message, SMIK1 p.47*

> What does initiation mean? Initiation means confidence on the part of the teacher and trust on the part of the pupil. Initiation is not given to the one who is curious, who comes to examine the teacher, or who comes to find out if, in this particular culture, in this cult, there is truth or not. If by any chance such a person received an initiation, he would go through it all and come back by the same door that he had entered without having found anything.
>
> *'Ināyat Khān, Sufi Message, SMIK2 p.181*

> By *bay'at,* the initiation which a teacher gives to his pupil, a magnetism is given: the soul of the pupil is charged with a new battery. And if

the pupil knows how to maintain it, how to keep it without wasting it, it will be like yeast, which never spoils and which lives for thousands of years.

ʿInāyat Khān, Sufi Message, SMIK11 p.121

Initiation is a sacred trust, a trust given by the *murshid* to his *murīd* and a trust given by the *murīd* to the *murshid.* There should no longer be a wall from the moment of this initiation; for if there is a wall, then the initiation is not an initiation any more. When the wall between the *murīd* and the *murshid* has been removed, then the next step will be to remove the wall that stands between God and the worshipper.

The Sufi order is an order of mysticism, and there are certain thoughts and considerations that should be observed. One of these is that when once a secret has been entrusted to one, it must be kept as one's most sacred trust. One must also accept all the teaching that may be given to one. Whether it is bitter medicine or sweet, the patient takes it. There is a time for everything, and so illumination has its time. However, progress, the real progress, depends upon the patience of the pupil, together with his eagerness to go forward.

ʿInāyat Khān, Sufi Message, SMIK10 pp.80–81

People make a great many mysteries out of the name initiation, but the simple explanation of initiation is trust on the part of the pupil and confidence on the part of the initiator. I heard from my *murshid,* from my initiator, something which I shall never forget: "This friendship, this relationship which is brought about by initiation between two persons, is something which cannot be broken, it is something which cannot be separated, it is something which cannot be compared with anything else in the world; it belongs to eternity."

When this initiation takes place, it then becomes the responsibility of the initiator to think of the welfare and well-being of his pupil; and it becomes the responsibility of the initiated to be faithful and true, steady and unshaken, through all tests and trials. There are some who will go to one person and be initiated, and then afterwards, they go to another to be initiated, and then to a third. They might go to a hundred persons, but they will become a hundred times less instead of a hundred times more blessed. For the object of friendship is not the making of many friends; the object is to keep friendship steady, unchanged, whole. Of all kinds of friendship, the friendship that is established by initiation is the most sacred and must be considered beyond all other relationships in the world.

ʿInāyat Khān, Sufi Message, SMIK10 p.84

> In the East, a teacher does not give guidance until he has full confidence in the pupil, so as not to allow that which is most sacred to be mocked and laughed at by others. When he gives an initiation the pupil takes an oath that he will not speak about these things before those unaware of their value, importance, and sacredness; and only then is he guided. Also, every individual is guided by the teacher separately.
>
> *'Ināyat Khān, Sufi Message, SMIK4 p.131*

A master does not give his disciples something that they do not already possess. He only helps them to find what has been lost:

> It must be understood that the path of discipleship, the path of initiation, is not such that the teacher gives some knowledge to his pupil, tells him something new which he has not heard before, or shows him some miracle; if he does, he is not a true teacher. Man is really his own teacher; in himself is the secret of his being. The teacher's word is only to help him to find himself.
>
> *'Ināyat Khān, Sufi Message, SMIK4 p.203*

The time of initiation is a turning point in a disciple's life. He makes a pledge to himself and to his master that he will follow the spiritual path and all that that entails:

> The time of initiation is meant to be a time for clearing away all the sins of the past. The cleansing of sins is like a bath in the Ganges. It is the bath of the spirit in the light of knowledge. From this day, the page is turned. The *murīd* makes his vow to the *murshid* that he will treasure the teachings of the masters in the past and keep them secret, that he will make good use of the teachings and of the powers gained by them, and that he will try to crush his *nafs,* his ego. He vows that he will respect all the masters of humanity as the one embodiment of the ideal man and will consider himself the brother not only of all the Sufis in the order to which he belongs, but also outside that order of all those who are Sufis in spirit, although they may call themselves differently; and of all mankind, without distinction of caste, creed, race, nation, or religion.
>
> *'Ināyat Khān, Sufi Message, SMIK10 p.86*

The purpose in receiving initiation should be entirely spiritual:

> The objects one should have in taking initiation under the *murshid* are: to realize the self within and without; to know and communicate with

> God, whom alone the world worships; to kindle the fire of divine love, which alone has any value; to be able to read nature's manuscript and to be able to see in the world unseen; to learn how to control oneself; to light the torch of the soul and kindle the fire of the heart; to journey through this positive existence and arrive in this life at the goal at which every soul is bound in the end to arrive. It is better to arrive in the light than to be only transported through the dark.
>
> *'Ināyat Khān, Sufi Message, SMIK1 pp.48–49*

Other motives for seeking initiation will not lead to spiritual evolution:

> One does not take initiation for the sake of curiosity to see what is going on in a 'secret' order. Such a one will certainly not be able to see what he wishes to, for only the eye of sincerity can see. The eye of curiosity has the cataract of doubt, and is blind already. Neither does one take initiation for the sake of gaining some material advantage in one's occupation. Initiation is not a scientist's process, or an engineer's invention, or a business enterprise; it is not something that can be stolen, nor anything to be bought. It is revelation, which has new offspring at every moment, which can never be stolen by a thief. The only process for gaining it is righteousness, and when its light is covered under a bushel, even the cup *(jām)* of mystery (in which he could view the entire universe) stolen from Jamshed will serve no better than an earthen bowl.
>
> *'Ināyat Khān, Sufi Message, SMIK1 p.49*

Initiation leads to a sense of kinship not only with all other spiritual seekers, but with all human beings, whoever they may be, for the same divinity is present in all:

> The only thing that happens when a person is initiated is that from the hour of initiation one is the brother of all in the Sufi movement, of all other Sufis outside the Sufi movement, of all knowers of truth, whether they call themselves Sufi or not, and of every human being, without distinction of caste, creed, race, nation, or religion. One is the companion of the illuminated souls of the Sufis living on earth and of those who have passed to the other side of life. Thus one is linked with the chain of *murshids* and prophets, and so enabled to receive the light running through this current, through the chain of masters. And one is the confidant to the *murshid* and of the order. Therefore the initiate takes a vow in his heart to make use to the best of his ability of all he receives from the Sufi teaching and practices, not using any parts for selfish purposes. These teachings have been kept secret for

thousands of years, so why should they go out of the order without the *pīr-u murshid*'s authorization?

'Ināyat Khān, Sufi Message, SMIK1 p.50

See also: **muraqqa'** (▸3), **riḍwān** (▸4), **silsilah** (7.5).

1. *E.g. Ḥadīth Ṣaḥīḥ al-Bukhārī* 4:52.207; 5:57.48; 5:59.395, 471, 475, 477, 480–83, *HSB.* The number of companions varies between 1,300, 1,400, and 1,500.
2. See *Qur'ān* 48:1–29.
3. *E.g. Ḥadīth Ṣaḥīḥ al-Bukhārī* 4:52.207, *HSB.*

Book of Life, **Book of the Living** A mythical heavenly book in which are written the names of those destined for salvation, in some contexts, from the beginning of creation; an ancient Middle Eastern myth found in the Hebrew Bible,[1] in the New Testament,[2] in apocryphal Jewish[3] and Christian[4] writings, and among the gnostic texts,[5] the Dead Sea Scrolls,[6] and other literature.

It was said that the names of the chosen or the elect were written in heaven in the Book of Life. Conversely, the names of those who were to be damned were "blotted out" or erased from the Book of Life. Who were deemed the chosen and who the damned depended, of course, upon the beliefs of the individual writers.

The earliest biblical mention is in *Exodus,* when Moses discovers that his people have made themselves "gods of gold". Moses begs God to forgive them:

> Moses returned to the Lord, and said, "This people have sinned a great sin, and have made gods of gold for themselves. Yet now, if You will forgive their sin.... But if not, blot me, I pray You, out of Your Book which You have written."
>
> And the Lord said unto Moses, "Whoever has sinned against Me, him will I blot out of My Book."
>
> *Exodus 32:31–33; cf. KJV*

The writer of psalm 69, on the other hand, prays to God to vent His fury on his enemies, and to "blot them out of the Book of Life".[7]

In the Christian gospels, according to *Luke,* Jesus counsels those whom he has baptized, "Rejoice, because your names are written in heaven."[8] Paul[9] and the unknown writer of *Hebrews*[10] speak of their fellow Christians as being written in the Book of Life, and the author of *Revelations* is also fond of the imagery. Among a series of "He that overcomes" verses, interspersed throughout the book, he writes:

He that overcomes,
the same shall be clothed in white raiment,
and I will not blot out his name out of the Book of Life,
but I will confess his name before my Father,
and before His angels.[11]

Book of Revelation 3:5; cf. KJV

Conversely, the same author predicts an unfortunate end for any whose names are not so recorded:

> And death and hell were cast into the lake of fire. This is the second death. And whoever was not found written in the Book of Life was cast into the lake of fire.[12]

Book of Revelation 20:14–15; cf. KJV

Revelations also ends with the warning:

> If any man shall add unto these things, God shall add unto him the plagues that are written in this book. And if any man shall take away from the words of the book of this prophecy, God shall take away his part out of the Book of Life, and out of the Holy City, and from the things which are written in this book.

Book of Revelation 22:18–19, KJV

In ancient times, every book was hand-copied, and the opportunities for pirating, editing, changing, amalgamating, incorporating and generally making free with other people's material, usually unacknowledged and commonly claimed as the author's own, was so great that – like *Revelations* – it was not unusual for a manuscript to end with the threat that dire consequences would befall any who should change it. In the case of *Revelations,* this is a particularly rich caveat, for scholars are generally agreed that it is itself a composite document, probably based upon a Christianized version of an earlier Jewish apocalypse, with further additions from other sources. Even the terminal threat is unlikely to be completely original!

Many later Christians have echoed the New Testament beliefs concerning the Book of Life. Various writers have also given their own interpretations of its actual nature. To Jean-Pierre de Caussade, it is a record of the "universal Spirit that pervades every heart"; it speaks through the prophets and inspired souls, and, "In it will be written down every thought, word, deed, and suffering of all souls. And that scripture will then be a complete record of divine action."[13] To Walter Hilton, it is "the life of Jesus Christ, which consisted of poverty, humility, sorrow, scorn, grievous pain, and faithful obedience".[14]

To Angela of Foligno, it is "naught else save Jesus Christ, the Son of God, who is the Incarnate Word and the Wisdom of the Father"; it is also the book of the "life and death of Jesus Christ".[15] To Angelus Silesius, the Book of Life is God Himself, in which Angelus is himself inscribed.[16]

To Isaac of Nineveh, it is a record held for the future, the names of the faithful being, "written in the Book of Life until the coming of our Lord".[17] To St Augustine, who has quoted the passage from *Revelations* concerning those whose names are absent from the Book of Life being cast into a lake of fire, the Book is a symbol of God's foreknowledge of those who are predestined for salvation:

> This 'Book' is not an aid to God's memory, to prevent Him from making a mistake through forgetfulness! What is symbolized is the predestination of those to whom eternal life will be given. For God is not unaware of their existence, so that He has to refer to the book to know about them. The fact is that His foreknowledge of them, which is infallible, is itself the Book of Life in which they are written, that is, they are known beforehand.
>
> *St Augustine, City of God 20:15, CGAP pp.926–27*

Turning to gnostic uses of the term, in the allegorical poem, the *Robe of Glory,* found in the *Acts of Thomas,* the soul who has fallen fast asleep in Egypt (the physical universe) is sent a speaking letter, symbolizing the Word. Among the encouraging contents of this mystic letter is found:

> Your name is named in the Book of Life,
> and with your brother, whom you have received,
> you shall return to our kingdom.
>
> *Robe of Glory 47–48, Acts of Thomas IX, in PSW p.191*

In this context, being named in the Book of Life means being destined to return to God in the company of the brother – the saviour or master. Being 'written' implies that the soul is destined – destined to receive Life, to find the source of Life. Likewise, in the story of *Joseph and Aseneth,* probably stemming from the early Christian period, Aseneth is to be married to Joseph which symbolizes initiation into the family of the master's disciples. She, too, is told that her "name is written in the Book of Life". The "Book of Life", "Cup of Immortality", and the "Unction of Incorruption" are all metaphors for the divine Word:

> Take heart, Aseneth,... your name is written in the Book of Life in heaven,... and it will not be blotted out for all eternity. Behold, from today you will be renewed and refashioned, and made alive again, and

> you will eat the blessed Bread of Life and drink the blessed Cup of Immortality, and be anointed with the blessed Unction of Incorruption.
>
> *Joseph and Aseneth 15, DR p.135*

The term was also used to indicate the converse. The names of those who have not received baptism into the Word do not appear in the Book of Life. Metaphorically, they have been erased or "blotted out". In the *Acts of John,* a young man who, according to the story, has just been raised from the dead or lifted up from the death of this world through initiation, recommends to others standing by:

> Nothing else remains for you save to ask the apostle of the Lord that, just as he has raised me to life, he should also raise you from death to salvation, and rescue your souls which now are blotted out of the Book of Life.
>
> *Acts of John 17; cf. ANT p.261*

The author of the Nag Hammadi text, the *Gospel of Truth,* also uses the expression. Writing in metaphors, he not only speaks of the chosen ones, the "little ones", as being "inscribed in the Book of the Living", but he also equates this "Book" with the Word. Talking specifically about Jesus, he says that when Jesus came to this world, at first the clever and self-righteous ones came to him; but they only wished to test him. Then came the chosen ones, the "little children" that "manifested the living Book of the Living" "in their hearts", within themselves, meaning that they had personal, inner experience of this mystic "Book":

> He (Jesus) became a quiet and peaceful guide (*lit.* a pedagogue, a trained slave who supervised the education of children). In a school, he appeared, where he spoke the Word in the capacity of a teacher. And there came to him those who – in their own estimation – were wise, testing him; but he confounded them because they were not truly wise men.
>
> After all these, there came the little children also, those to whom belongs the knowledge *(gnōsis)* of the Father. Having been strengthened (initiated), they learned about the nature of the Father. They gained knowledge *(gnōsis),* and they were known; they were glorified and they glorified. In their hearts was manifested the living Book of the Living – that which is written in the Thought and the Mind of the Father, which from before the foundation of the totality (the creation) was within His incomprehensibility; that which no one can take up without being put to death (coming to this world).

> Had that Book not been manifested (as Jesus), none of those who believe in salvation could have attained it. For this reason, the merciful and faithful Jesus was patient in accepting suffering by taking up that Book; since he knew that his death would mean life for many.
>
> *Gospel of Truth 19–20; cf. GS pp.254–55, GT pp.56–62, NHS22 pp.86–87*

The Book "which is written in the Thought and the Mind of the Father", which existed "from before the foundation of the totality" is the Word. It is the source of creative activity – metaphorically, the "Thought and Mind" of God. To human beings, it is a teaching, a practice, a Way and something to be experienced. But, says the writer, a soul can only "take it up" by "being put to death" – by taking birth as a human being. Speaking specifically of Jesus, but actually of all masters in general, the same author continues:

> He draws himself down to death though clothed in life eternal. Having divested himself of the perishable rags, he put on imperishability, something which no one can take from him. Having entered the empty ways of fear, he escaped the clutches of those who had been stripped naked by forgetfulness – for he was knowledge *(gnōsis)* and perfection (personified) – and read out the contents (of the Book of the Living)....
>
> And those who are to receive the teaching are the living ones who are inscribed in the Book of the Living. It is about their selves that they are given instruction, receiving it from the Father, turning again to Him.... He has brought many back from error.
>
> *Gospel of Truth 20–21, 22; cf. GS pp.255–56, GT pp.66–70,78, NHS22 pp.86–91*

The saviour, though at one with the Eternal, takes on the "perishable rags" of the body and comes to this world. He "enters the empty ways of fear": he is not troubled by its spiritually dead and ignorant inhabitants, stripped of their innate spirituality. And he "reads out the contents" of the Book of the Living: he teaches them about the Word.

But not everyone is destined to hear him. Only "those who are to receive the teaching" are "inscribed in the Book of the Living": only they are tuned to the Word of God. And this "teaching" is "about their selves", it concerns the real nature of the soul or self. It comes from the Father and entails their repentance, their "turning again to Him". And the author adds that the master has "brought many back from error": over the millions of years in which the creation has existed, many have been returned to God from the illusion and "error" of this world.

See also: **baptism**.

1. *Exodus* 32:32–33; *Psalms* 69:28; *cf.* also *Psalms* 40:7, 56:8, 87:6, 139:16; *Isaiah* 34:16; *Daniel* 7:10, 12:1; *Malachi* 3:16.
2. *Book of Revelation* 3:5, 20:14–15, 22:18–19.
3. *E.g. Jubilees* 30:22–23; *1 Enoch* 47:3, 108:3; *Apocalypse of Zephaniah* 3:7, 9:2; *Testament of Jacob* 7.
4. *E.g. Acts of John* 17; *Apocalypse of Peter; Robe of Glory, Acts of Thomas* 10; *Joseph and Aseneth* 15:3.
5. *E.g. Gospel of Truth* 19–22.
6. *E.g. War Scroll* (1QM) XII; *Words of the Heavenly Lights* (4Q504) VI.
7. *Psalms* 69:28.
8. *Luke* 10:20, *KJV.*
9. *Philippians* 4:3.
10. *Hebrews* 12:23.
11. See also *Book of Revelation* 21:27.
12. See also *Book of Revelation* 13:8.
13. J.-P. de Caussade, *Sacrament of the Present Moment* 9, *SPM* p.95.
14. Walter Hilton, *Perfection* 2, *PAS* p.3.
15. Angela of Foligno, *Book of Divine Consolation* 8, 20, *BDC* pp.53, 98–99.
16. Angelus Silesius, *Cherubinic Wanderer* 2:20, *CW* p.58.
17. Isaac of Nineveh, *Treatise* 3, *On Excellence, MTIN* p.27.

born again An expression used in John's gospel for mystic initiation or baptism into the Holy Spirit; probably Jesus' most well-known reference to spiritual baptism; also called second birth, new birth, spiritual birth, being born of the spirit, and so on. Omitting the narrative in which it is set, Jesus says:

> Verily, verily, I say unto you,
> except a man be born again,
> he cannot see the kingdom of God. . . .
> Verily, verily, I say unto you,
> except a man be born of water and of the Spirit,
> he cannot enter into the kingdom of God.
>
> *John 3:3, 5; cf. KJV*

Jesus explains that without this kind of baptism, it is not possible to "enter into" or to "see the kingdom of God", the eternal realm. Being "born of water and of the Spirit" is an allusion to the Living Water of the Word, not to physical water, since physical water cannot enable a person to leave their body and enter the higher regions, let alone reach the kingdom of God. It is also possible that "of water" is a later addition to this saying of Jesus, inserted to justify the external baptismal ceremony, for Jesus goes on to explain what he means, making a clear distinction between physical birth and spiritual birth. And here he speaks only about being "born of the Spirit":

> That which is born of the flesh is flesh,
> and that which is born of the Spirit is spirit.
>
> *John 3:6, KJV*

Physical birth involves the physical body, he says, and spiritual birth involves the spirit or soul. The two are quite distinct. Baptism is called a new birth because it represents a new beginning. The baptism of a master enables a soul to truly repent, to change the inner direction of their mind and soul, and to turn again towards God. Jesus then gives a hint of what being baptized in this way actually means to a soul:

> Marvel not that I said unto you:
> you must be born again.
> The wind blows where it pleases,
> and you hear the sound of it,
> but cannot tell where it comes from,
> nor where it goes:
> So is every one that is born of the Spirit.
>
> *John 3:7–8; cf. KJV*

The word translated as 'wind' is the Greek *pneuma* which means both wind and spirit. So in a double meaning characteristic of John's gospel, Jesus is making a veiled reference to the Sound of the Spirit, the divine Music of the Word, which only those souls baptized into it can hear.

Christian writers have generally interpreted being "born again" as spiritual awakening through the grace and power of the Spirit within. Maximos the Confessor links the passage from *John* with the verse from *Matthew* that relates to baptism "in the Holy Spirit and in fire",[1] taking both of them to refer to the same thing:

> Some are reborn through water and the spirit; others receive baptism in the Holy Spirit and in fire. I take these four things – water, spirit, fire, and Holy Spirit – to mean one and the same Spirit of God. To some, the Holy Spirit is water because he cleanses the external stains of their bodies. To others, he is simply Spirit because he makes them active in the practice of virtue. To others, he is fire because he cleanses the interior defilement which lies deep within their souls – . . . for the single identical Spirit takes his different names from the different ways in which he acts on each person.
>
> *Maximos the Confessor, On Theology 2:63, Philokalia, PCT2 p.152*

Julian of Norwich writes that the "spiritual birth" is of far greater significance than physical birth:

> In comparison with our spiritual birth, our physical birth is a small, unimportant, straightforward sort of thing.... In the matter of our spiritual birth, he (Jesus) preserves us with infinitely greater tenderness, since our soul is so much more valuable in his sight (than our body). He kindles our understanding, he directs our paths, he eases our consciences, he comforts our soul, he lightens our heart. He gives us – partially at least – knowledge and trust in our blessed Godhead.
>
> *Julian of Norwich, Revelations of Divine Love 60–61, RDL pp.170–71*

Once a soul has been "born again", says Jan van Ruysbroek, then the struggle to break free from the body really begins:

> When we are born again of the Spirit of God, spirit and flesh are at odds and strive against each other: the flesh indeed desiring things contrary to God and to the spirit, and the spirit, together with God, desiring things contrary to the flesh.
>
> *Jan van Ruysbroek, Seven Steps 3, SSL p.21*

And John of the Cross says that only with spiritual rebirth can the soul attain the perfection of God:

> He that is not born again in the Holy Spirit will not be able to see this kingdom of God, which is the state of perfection; and to be born again in the Holy Spirit in this life is to have a soul most like to God in purity, having in itself no admixture of imperfection, so that pure transformation can be wrought in it through participation of union.
>
> *John of the Cross, Ascent of Mount Carmel 5:5, CWJC1 p.77*

Among the gnostic texts, in the allegorical *Expository Treatise on the Soul,* being born again through the "brother" or saviour is described as an essential step for the rescue of the soul who has become lost in the material world. In the allegory, the soul is portrayed as a virgin who gives herself to many lovers, none of whom satisfy, until finally a longing for her original state of purity is reawakened by the "brother":

> Then when she becomes young again, she will ascend, praising the Father and her brother by whom she was rescued. Thus it is by being born again that the soul will be saved.
>
> *On the Soul 134, NHS21 pp.160–61*

In the Hermetic literature, the mythical master Hermēs Trismegistos expresses his inability to explain his transcendent state of consciousness to his disciple Tat:

> This thing cannot be taught; nor is it possible for you to see it with any sense fashioned of material elements. I can tell you nothing but this: I see that by God's mercy there has come to be in me a form which is not fashioned of matter, and I have passed forth out of myself, and entered an immortal body, and I am not now what I was before. I have been born again in Mind *(Nous),* and my previous bodily form has been put away from me. I no longer possess colour, touch, or size; I am a stranger to them now. You see me with your eyes, but by gazing with bodily sight you do not understand what I am. To eyes such as yours, my son, I am no longer visible.
>
> *Hermetica 13:3; cf. HAG p.99, HGCH p.50, TGH2 pp.221–22*

Here, to be "born again" refers to an inner awakening to higher consciousness of the *Nous,* the divine Mind or Intelligence, rather than to baptism or initiation *per se.*

See also: **baptism**.

1. *Matthew* 3:11.

born of the Spirit See **born again**.

bound (in heaven) An expression used by Jesus for baptism. According to *Matthew,* Jesus says to Peter:

> You are Peter, and upon this rock I will build my church; and the gates of hell shall not prevail against it. And I will give unto you the keys of the kingdom of heaven: and whoever you shall bind on earth shall be bound in heaven: and whoever you shall loose on earth shall be loosed in heaven.[1]
>
> *Matthew 16:18–19; cf. KJV*

Jesus is instructing Peter to take care of his church – the assembly or community of his disciples. Those who are bound "on earth" – while they are still living as human beings – will be "bound in heaven" – they will be taken back to God. But those who are "loosed on earth", who are not "bound", will not be connected up inside and taken to their spiritual home.

Traditionally, the passage is understood to be Peter's appointment as the first pope. In fact, Jesus may have been appointing Peter as his successor, a supposition reinforced by a passage from the last chapter of *John* (probably an addition to the original text), where Jesus repeats three times to Peter, "Feed my sheep".[2] Although it seems likely that Peter was appointed to be Jesus' successor, there is no historical indication that either Jesus or Peter ever intended the appointment to become crystallized in history, for centuries to come. The Catholic Church argues that, since the permanence of the office is essential to the existence of the church, the intention must have been for Peter to have been successively replaced, throughout all history. Since the sixteenth-century Reformation, the Protestants, of course, have disagreed.

In the gnostic text, *Pistis Sophia,* being "bound in heaven" is linked to the forgiveness of sins, and with another passage from *Matthew,* where Jesus tells his disciples that they are privileged to "know the mysteries of the kingdom of heaven".[3] Here, the giving of the "mysteries" is another expression for mystic baptism:

> Truly I say to you, not only will I purify your sins, but I will also make you worthy of the kingdom of my father. And I will also give to you the mystery of forgiveness of sins upon earth, so that whoever you forgive upon earth will be forgiven in heaven, and whoever you will bind upon earth will be bound in heaven. I will give you the mystery of the kingdom of heaven, so that you yourselves perform them (the mysteries) for men.
>
> *Pistis Sophia 374:141; cf. PS pp.738–39, PSGG p.310*

Similar imagery of baptism by a saviour as being "bound" is also found in the Mandaean texts, as in a poem that describes how the "deliverer", the saviour, rescues the soul from the material world, taking her back to her original spiritual home:

> To her came the deliverer
> who loosed her and bore her away:
> He who had bound her, who had loosed the soul,
> went before her whom he had bound.
> Coming behind him, the soul hastened,
> reached her deliverer, ran after him
> who had bound her to her own home.
>
> *Mandaean Prayer Book 68; cf. CPM p.55*

In another poem, souls who are rescued by "*Bihram* the Great", one of the Mandaean's mythological saviours, are said to be "bound and sealed" in the "Jordan", a metaphor for the river of Living Water or divine Word:

Bound and sealed are these souls who went down to the Jordan,
and were baptized in the name of the Great Life.
They have been baptized with the baptism of *Bihram* the Great.
Their souls have been secured with bonds of righteousness,
and with the bonds of *Zhir,* the great light of Life.

Mandaean Prayer Book 26, CPM pp.22–23

The biblical Isaiah also speaks of binding and sealing his disciples, from which it may be presumed that Isaiah also practised some form of baptism of initiation:

I bind up this testimony,
seal this instruction in the heart of my disciples.

Isaiah 8:16; cf. JB, NJB

See also: **baptism**.

1. *Cf. Matthew* 18:18, *KJV.*
2. *John* 21:15–18, *KJV.*
3. *Matthew* 13:11, *KJV.*

dāt (H/Pu) *Lit.* gift, bounty, liberality, largesse; mystically, the gift of the divine Name, which is eternal:

No one can undo the bounty *(dāt)* of the *guru:*
he whom the Lord forgives – him he ferries across.

Guru Nānak, Ādi Granth 1030, MMS

It is also perfect:

Perfect is the gift *(dāt)* of the Lord,
and it increases day by day.

Guru Arjun, Ādi Granth 783, MMS

It is a limitless gift, given by the *guru:*

O benefactor, remove me from this creation:
your gift *(dāt)* is limitless.

Swami Shiv Dayal Singh, Sār Bachan Poetry 7:2.2, SBP p.70

In fact, ultimately, the gift is God and He Himself is the giver:

Rādhā Swāmī is the one who gives:
and He Himself is the gift *(dāt).*

Swami Shiv Dayal Singh, Sār Bachan Poetry 3:3.46, SBP p.23

See also: **gift**.

dhur karam, dhur bakhsh, dhur likhiā, dhur mastak likhiā (Pu) *Lit.* primal *(dhur)* destiny *(karam);* pre-ordained destiny; primal grace or gift *(bakhsh);* written *(likhiā)* from the beginning; written on the forehead *(mastak)* from the beginning; original destiny, original grace, original gift; written in one's destiny.

According to the Indian *gurus* whose writings are preserved in the *Ādi Granth,* when God first created souls out of His own essence, they were pure and untouched by attachment to the creation. *Dhur karam,* also called *ādi karma* (primal *karma*), is the impelling force given to souls by God to separate them from Himself and project them into the creation, setting in motion the play of *karma* by which souls are held captive in the creation.

The *gurus* indicate that the potential for the return to God is written into this primal *karma.* The implication seems to be that when all the souls were sent out into the creation, not all of them were 'marked' for return through contact with the mystic Name *(Nām)* or divine creative power:

Those who have such pre-ordained destiny *(dhur karam)*
are attached to the Lord's Name.
Says Nānak, they are at peace,
and the unstruck Sound Current vibrates within their homes.

Guru Amardās, Ādi Granth 917, AGK

The Name *(Nām)* is the panacea, the remedy to cure all ills:
singing the glory of God is the embodiment of bliss and emancipation.
It cannot be obtained by any religious rituals.
O Nānak, he alone obtains it
whose *karma* is so pre-ordained *(dhur karam likhiā).*

Guru Arjun, Ādi Granth 274, AGK

Contact with the divine Name is made possible through the *guru,* and that too is predestined:

Those humble servants of the Lord, who have
attained the company of the true *guru,* have such
pre-ordained destiny inscribed on their foreheads *(dhur mastak likhiā).*

Blessed, blessed is the true congregation *(sat sangat),*
where the Lord's essence is obtained.
Meeting with His humble servant,
O Nānak, the light of the *Nām* shines forth.

Guru Rāmdās, Ādi Granth 10, AGK

If such pre-ordained *(dhur)* (destiny)
is written *(likhiā)* upon one's forehead *(mastak),*
then the true *guru* enjoins him to serve him.
O Nānak, then he obtains the jewel, the gem.
Blessed, blessed is that one
who follows the *guru's* teachings, and finds the Lord.

Guru Rāmdās, Ādi Granth 880, AGK

See also: **ādi karma** (6.3).

dīkshā (S/H), **dīkhiā** (Pu) *Lit.* consecration, initiation; instruction; an inaugural religious ceremony; initiation into a religious or spiritual path; also known as *dīkshā-vidhi* (initiation rite).

In Jainism, *dīkshā* implies initiation into any of the various mendicant orders of either the *Digambara* or *Shvetāmbara* traditions. The requirements for *dīkshā* and the various rituals associated with the ceremony vary between the two traditions and the various lineages. However, all would-be mendicants must first serve a probationary period by living with other mendicants. At the time of the ceremony, they shave their heads and take the five great vows *(mahāvratas)* of *ahiṃsā* (non-injury, non-violence), *satya* (truthfulness), *asteya* (not stealing, taking only that which is given), *brahmacharya* (celibacy), and *aparigraha* (non-possession). They vow not to perform any prohibited actions in body, mind or speech, nor to cause others to do so, nor to condone such actions in others. The same vows are taken by laymen *(aṇuvratas),* but are less stringent in their detail.

Jain texts say that the minimum age for initiation is eight, although nowadays some *āchāryas* (leaders) will only initiate children provided parental permission is given, while others set a minimum age of eighteen. Some will give initiation only to merchant castes, others include the agricultural castes. Among *Shvetāmbaras,* any initiated monk *(sādhu)* can perform the actual initiation, although it is often the *āchārya* himself who performs the ceremony. Among *Digambaras,* when no suitable monks *(munis)* have been available, individuals who have fulfilled the probationary requirements have sometimes performed the initiation on themselves, by relinquishing all clothing and manually pulling out the hairs on their head and face, which are the final signs of monkhood.[1]

In Vedic times, *dīkshā* referred to the preparatory consecration of a man and his wife, performed prior to a sacrificial ceremony *(yajña),* which the man (the *yajamāna,* the one paying for the sacrifice) would have requested. It was believed that, without such preparation, no benefit would accrue from the sacrifice. On the day of a sacrifice, therefore, the man and his wife would fast, wear a girdle of *muñja* grass (a kind of rush or sedge), and keep various other preparatory observances:

> Remaining hungry, remaining thirsty, abstaining from pleasures – these are the (preparation for) initiation *(dīkshā).*
>
> *Chhāndogya Upanishad 3:17.1*

Dīkshā is also used for the *upanayana* ceremony in which a *guru* invests boys born in the upper three classes of Hindu society with a sacred thread *(yajñopavīta).* After this ceremony, the boys are considered fit to study the *Vedas* and to participate in Vedic ceremonies. The members of the three upper classes are known as twice-born *(dvija),* since it is held that they take a second birth when they are invested with the sacred thread. According to the Hindu sage Manu, the purpose of the ceremony is purification:

> For twice-born men *(dvijanman),* the ceremony of conception and other sacraments must be performed with the sacred rites *(karma)* prescribed by the *Vedas.* This sanctifies and purifies a man (from sin) both in this life and hereafter.
>
> *Manu Smṛiti 2:26; cf. MCLM p.95, SBE25 p.33*

Dīkshā is a term used throughout the yogic and tantric tradition for initiation of spiritual seekers by a *guru* or *āchārya* (teacher, preceptor).[2] In this sense, it is sometimes depicted as a third birth. The first is from the mother's womb; the second, investiture with the sacred thread; the third, initiation into the spiritual path. Many texts insist that the soul's liberation and enlightenment is unattainable without this latter form of *dīkshā:*

> It is said in the teaching of *Shiva* that there can be no *moksha* (liberation) without *dīkshā* (initiation), and no initiation without a teacher from the lineage *(āchārya-paramparā).*
>
> *Kulārṇava Tantra 14:3, KTAA p.308; cf. KTAA (10) p.101*

Yogic initiation is generally comprised of two parts. Firstly, *mantra-* or *kriyā-dīkshā,* which entails instruction on the techniques of meditational and yogic practice, especially the giving of a *mantra.* The *guru* gives a *mantra* charged with his spiritual power to the disciple. The *mantra* is kept secret and is not divulged to anyone without the *guru*'s approval. Often, the giving of a *mantra* is accompanied by a ceremony *(kriyā)* at which the disciple vows to follow his *guru*'s instructions.

The second part, not necessarily given at the same time as *mantra-dīkshā,* is *shakti-dīkshā. Shakti-dīkshā* is the conveying of spiritual energy and wisdom from *guru* to disciple, which may result in an immediate spiritual experience. Though an expansion of consciousness of this nature may be of brief duration, it can have a lasting effect on the life of the recipient, since it is a powerful and tangible experience of a higher reality. In tantric *yoga,* the conveying of spiritual energy is also known as *shaktipāta,* and involves the awakening or activation of the disciple's *kuṇḍalinī.* The *Shiva Purāṇa* says that this requires the *guru* to enter the student's body, a power known as *paradeha-pravesha* (*lit.* entering the body of another).[3] If a *guru* conveys his spiritual energy by a touch or glance, thereby plunging the disciple into a state of blissful *samādhi,* it is known in the tantric tradition as *Shiva-dīkshā,* although there may be little difference between *Shiva-dīkshā* and *shakti-dīkshā* except in the depth and intensity of the experience. The transmission of spiritual energy from *guru* to disciple is also known in tantrism as *vedha-dīkshā* (penetrating or piercing *dīkshā*)[4] and *Shāmbhavī-dīkshā, Shāmbhavī* being a name of *Shiva.*

Different yogic and tantric schools, past and present, have described several variants on this theme. The *Kulārṇava Tantra* identifies seven kinds of *dīkshā:*

1. *Kriyā-dīkshā.* Initiation at a ceremony *(kriyā).*

2. *Varṇa-dīkshā.* Initiation in which the *guru* awakens the inner sound *(varṇa)* within the body by 'placing' the letters of the Sanskrit alphabet at each of the six *chakras.* This leads to the awakening of consciousness in these centres. It is said that each *chakra* has a particular number of petals or aspects of pranic energy, and that the Sanskrit alphabet was fashioned by *yogīs* of the past by relating individual letters to the sound of each petal.

3. *Kala-dīkshā.* Initiation in which the *guru* places subtle forms of energy *(kala)* in the body, leading as above to an awakening.

4–7. *Sparsha-, vāg-, dṛig-,* and *mana-dīkshā.* Initiation in which the *guru* conveys his power by touch *(sparsha),* speech *(vāc),* glance *(dṛish),* or thought *(manas).*[5]

Of these, the *Shāradā-Tilaka Tantra* describes only four, which it calls: *kriyāvati-dīkshā, varṇamayi-dīkshā, kalātmā-dīkshā,* and *vedhamayi-dīkshā.*[6] In the Kashmiri Shaivite schools, initiation without any external means is known as *anupāya-dīkshā* (without-means initiation), while initiation by means of a ceremony is called *āṇavī-dīkshā,* from the term *aṇu* (minute, atomic), a term used in Kashmiri Shaivism for the individual self.[7]

Through *dīkshā,* the disciple becomes a part of the spiritual family of the *guru* or *āchārya* (preceptor, teacher) and is accepted within the orbit of the *guru's* spiritual influence and heritage – the line of transmission or succession of which a *guru* is generally a part. This is an ancient tradition, dating back at least to the time of the *Vedas:*

> Initiation *(upanaya)* takes place in that the teacher *(āchārya)* carries the pupil within himself so to speak, just as a mother bears the embryo inside her body. After the three-day ceremony, the disciple is born.
>
> *Atharva Veda 11:5.3; cf. "dīkshā," in EDYF p.99*

It is therefore deeply personal, and a part of the long process of spiritual evolution. After *dīkshā,* spiritual effort begins to bear more substantial fruit:

> By self-dedication (*vrata,* vows), one obtains consecration *(dīkshā);*
> By consecration *(dīkshā),* one obtains grace *(dakshiṇā);*
> By grace, one obtains faith *(shraddhā);*
> And by faith, is Truth *(Satya)* obtained.
>
> *Yajur Veda 19:30; cf. CVAB p.55*

Dīkshā is also associated in the *Vedas* with *tapas* (self-discipline, spiritual fervour and effort), as one of the primary principles underlying the world and human existence in it:

> The highest *Satya* (Truth), unyielding Order *(Ṛita), dīkshā, tapas,*
> prayer *(brahma),* and holy ritual *(yajña)* are the foundation of the earth.
> May she (the earth), the ruling mistress of what has been
> and what will come to be, spread wide for us a limitless domain.
>
> *Atharva Veda 12:1.1; cf. VE p.123*

In fact, *dīkshā* is said to be the womb or source from which *tapas* arises.[8] *Dīkshā* is just the beginning; the disciple generally has many years, even lifetimes, of spiritual effort before him. But God and nature conspire to help. The *Atharva Veda* suggests that even the intermediate deities send help to the true seeker:

> The seers *(ṛishis)* in the beginning,
> desiring the excellent and searching the heavens,
> set out with fervour *(tapas)* and consecration *(dīkshā).*
> Thence were born energy, force, and kingship:
> may the gods bestow them upon this man!
>
> *Atharva Veda 19:41.1; cf. VE p.266*

It seems likely that in these Vedic verses the writer is speaking of a truly mystical initiation and consecration, rather than the simple preparation for sacrificial rites.

Many yogic and tantric schools institute a period of probation in which the novitiate serves the *guru* and follows the required lifestyle and code of conduct, without receiving full *dīkshā.* This provides the would-be disciple with an opportunity to assess whether or not they will be able to follow the path laid out by the *guru.* In some schools, the *dīkshā* may include the adoption of certain forms of dress and other customs. For example, initiates of the *Kānphaṭā* order of ascetics – who trace their origins to Gorakhnāth (C11th–12th CE), who is credited as one of the primary developers of tantric *yoga* – in addition to receiving a *mantra* and a particular garb, have their ears pierced. This is believed to stimulate a particular *nāḍī* (channel of life energy or *prāṇa*), leading to the development of miraculous powers *(siddhis).*

According to the teachings of Indian *sants* (saints), the *dīkshā* of a perfect master implies an inner connection or 'tuning' of the soul of the disciple to the divine creative power or *Shabd* (Sound, Word). In a general sense, this initiation is a master's acceptance of a soul, since the real master is the *Shabd* itself. At the time of initiation, the master accepts responsibility for a soul's spiritual welfare, to take the soul back to God. He also takes on the administration and scheduling of the *karma* that is the cause of the soul's separation from God. The twentieth-century Indian mystic Maharaj Sawan Singh explains:

> The master gives his spiritual light to the disciple. He makes him fit to lead a spiritual life.... Initiation *(dīkhiā)* can be had from a living master only, and not from the so-called preceptors who merely whisper a *mantra* in the ears of the disciples. This gift of life or ray of life can be obtained from a living *guru.* The life-giving impulse can be obtained only from a living being; it is impossible to get it from books or scriptures....
>
> At the time of being initiated *(dīkhshat),* the master imparts the secret knowledge of the heart. It then becomes possible to make spiritual progress by following the master's directions. After explaining everything, directions are given which help in repetition *(simran),* contemplation *(dhyān),* and manifestation of the inner *Shabd* or divine Sound. They help the disciple in his inner ascent.
>
> At the time of being initiated *(dīkhshat),* the master gives the ray of life and connects him with the melody of the *Shabd.* He then establishes a subtle link with the disciple, guides him, and takes him to the original home.
>
> However learned, religious-minded, self-disciplined or respected a man may be, he remains deluded by the mind and *māyā* (illusion).

In these circumstances, only a master can connect him with the inner *Shabd*. However virtuous a man may be, he cannot, by his own efforts alone, contact the Sound. Unless the master gives him the gift of the ray of life and initiates him, he cannot contact the divine Sound.

At the time of being initiated *(dīkhshat)* by the master, the soul becomes fit for being connected with the *Shabd*. This moment is considered as the moment of birth in the master's family. After a disciple is connected with the Name by the master, he begins to progress on the spiritual path and to get control over his weaknesses. When the seeker progresses on the spiritual path by following the directions of the master, he does not remain subservient to the body. On the other hand, his soul tends to soar to the spiritual regions, to break off all the ties with the earth, and to dwell more and more in the higher regions within.

This gift of the Name is given to a conscious being, and is meant to awaken him to a new life by its animating impulse. How soon one obtains the benefits of initiation (*jīa dān,* gift of life) depends on the person initiated *(dīkhshat)*. It depends on his inner spiritual condition. The inner condition is different in different persons. Certain persons are fully ready, while others are less so. The master 'injects', as it were, his consciousness and light into the soul of the disciple at the time of initiation *(dīkhshā)*. This injection of His own consciousness and light permeates the disciple like leaven, and produces a new spiritual consciousness and light as the practice of *Nām* is continued. The spiritual light of the master gives a new life to the soul of the disciple and begins to free it. Consequently, the disciple begins to have a feeling of fulfilment. This gift of the master cannot be taken away. Time and *māyā* (illusion) cannot destroy this seed, this ray of life. The disciple, once initiated, will certainly progress, sooner or later. He will one day certainly reach his true home.

Unless one gets initiation *(dīkhiā),* one does not get knowledge and therefore cannot discern the truth....

What is this initiation *(dīkhiā)?* It is a ray of the Name of power of God which can be obtained only from a perfect master....

This initiation *(dīkhiā)* is obtained only by great good fortune. When one gets it, the mind becomes happy and still. We know ourselves and are released from birth and death.

Maharaj Sawan Singh, Philosophy of the Masters 5; cf. PMS5 pp.131–33

Many religious groups have traditionally performed a ritual or ceremony called *dīkshā,* an initiation or baptism when a neophyte is accepted into the fold. But *dīkshā* into the mystic Word can only be had from a genuine master of the Word:

> Initiation *(dīkhiā)* from those who have never gone within serves no purpose whatever.
>
> *Maharaj Sawan Singh, Philosophy of the Masters 5; cf. PMS5 p.133*

The initiation given by a true mystic or *guru* is initiation into the divine Name. To receive such initiation *(dīkhiā)* is written in a person's destiny:

> The *guru* comes to meet those whose destiny is so pre-ordained:
> he blesses them with the *dīkhiā* of the ambrosial Name of the Lord
>
> *Guru Nānak, Ādi Granth 729, AGK*

Without this higher initiation, the highest divine knowledge cannot be experienced, and the soul cannot see God:

> Without the *guru*'s *dīkhiā,* how can anyone obtain spiritual wisdom?
> Without seeing (the Lord) – tell me:
> how can anyone visualize in meditation?
>
> *Guru Arjun, Ādi Granth 1140, AGK*

See also: **dvija**.

1. See "dīkṣā," *A to Z of Jainism, AZJW.*
2. For some of the following details, see "dīkshā," *Encyclopedic Dictionary of Yoga, EDYF.*
3. *Shiva Purāṇa* 7:2.15.6.
4. *E.g. Shāradā-Tilaka Tantra* 5:121–32.
5. *Kulārṇava Tantra* 14:39*ff.; cf. TPEF* p.284 (n.14).
6. *Shāradā-Tilaka Tantra* 4:3*ff.; cf. TPEF* p.107.
7. See Georg Feuerstein, *Tantra, TPEF* p.284 (n.14).
8. *Āpastambīya Shrauta Sūtra* 10:6.5.

dù, **guò**, **guòdù** (C) *Lit.* to cross (a river or sea), to ferry (across), to pass through; a Daoist a term for salvation generally and, more specifically, for the initiation of a disciple by a Daoist master and ordination into a Daoist monastic order.

The term *dù* is used in both religious and mystical Daoist traditions. In translations of Daoist writings, *dù* has been rendered as either 'initiation' or 'ordination', and in some of the literature these two terms are used synonymously, since they are closely related. In general, however, initiation is of new *dìzǐ* (disciples) and ordination is of either new *chūjiārén* (monks or nuns) or new *dàoshì* (priests). Both cases involve a transmission from master to initiate or master to ordinand. In the case of initiation, the transmission is of spiritual techniques; in the case of ordination, it is the transmission of *jiè* (precepts) and *lù* (registers – of the names, titles, and physical descriptions of gods to be invoked).

Broadly speaking, *dù* may include procedures, rites and ceremonies (usually conducted discreetly, away from the public eye), in which knowledge of the inner spiritual journey is imparted to new initiates or ordinands. Bestowal of this knowledge is accompanied by practical instruction on how to put this knowledge into practice in order to attain personal realization of *Dào*. The various techniques include chanting the names of inner powers, breathing and other specific physical exercises, and meditation. Particular precepts *(jiè),* including moral principles and lifestyle habits, such as diet and abstinence from drugs and alcohol, may also be advocated.[1]

Initiation of the Disciple

According to tradition, Lǎozǐ transmitted his teachings to Yǐn Xǐ only after Yǐn Xǐ had proved his ability, determination, and loyalty – and had also requested instruction. Lǎozǐ passed on the formal precepts and practical instructions orally and in stages. According to some records, after each stage, time was allowed for Yǐn Xǐ to practise and fully absorb the ideas before the next level was transmitted. Eventually Yǐn Xǐ, dressed in the proper ceremonial clothing, was given the formal title of 'Master of the Beginning of the Scripture', and Lǎozǐ initiated or ordained him to the elevated rank of 'Highest Perfected'.

Outer initiation and inner transmission have existed in one form or another from the time of the earliest *wū* (shamans). The *wū* probably performed a ritual of some sort when they selected or accepted apprentices to whom they would pass on their own methods and accomplishments. This is attested by the archaeological discovery of charms, talismans, and sacred inscriptions from antiquity.

In mystical Daoism, initiation marks the beginning of a path or way that leads the initiate to ultimate reunion with *Dào*. Through initiation, the master transmits the traditions and knowledge needed to cultivate the *Dào*. Initiation by a master may be given all at one time, or it may be bestowed gradually over time, according to the spiritual fitness of the disciple. From the time of initiation, the relationship between master and disciple develops progressively and spontaneously, not necessarily dependent upon their being in each other's company. The level of spiritual development of the master and the spiritual efforts of the disciple together define the latter's progress in attaining ultimate illumination and transformation.

In Daoism, serious seekers are advised to look for a *míngshī* (enlightened master) from whom they can learn the mysteries of *Dào,* and be initiated into the method of attaining the *Dào*. There are ample records in Daoist writings – both within and outside the *Dàozàng* (Daoist canon) – of Daoist masters initiating disciples, many of whom became masters themselves.

It is also apparent from Daoist literature that all *dùshī* (masters of initiation) received similar initiation, guidance and inward training from their own masters. It therefore appears that in the Daoist mystical tradition, initiation by a personal, living guide has always been a prerequisite for attaining *Dào*.

The subtle, unseen influence of the master acts like a mirror, exposing inherent weaknesses within the disciple, while facilitating opportunities for further transformation and progress. Even though the commitment of a disciple may wax and wane, that of the master remains abiding and absolute.

An important facet of Daoism is the promotion of equality of men and women in all aspects of society. Historically, women have shared in the leadership, either individually or as partners with their husbands. Many women have also reached the status of master, such as Wèi Huácún (251–334), an aristocrat and married mother of two children, and Sūn Bù'èr (*c.*1119–1182), who had been the wife of Daoist master Mǎ Yù (1123–1183) before they both became masters.

Ordination

Some seekers of the spiritual leave their worldly life to live in a Daoist monastery, where they are initiated by a master into the mysteries of *Dào* through ordination as a monk *(dàoshì)* or a nun *(dàogū)*.

The purpose of priestly ordination is to grant a degree of religious or ministerial authority, having the effect of setting them apart so that they can perform various religious rites and ceremonies in their communities.

Ordination practices developed as Daoism moved from the world of the *wū* (shaman) into a world where politics and an increasing population asserted their respective influences. By the fifth century (CE), the various schools of religious Daoism had reorganized and elaborated their rituals, including those for ordination.

Ordination ceremonies increasingly began to focus on the transmission of *lù* (registers of the names, descriptions *etc.* of the gods being invoked), presenting the new initiate with *fú* (talismans), and the recitation of specific invocations (to the gods). Outward practices now included incense burning and the wearing of ceremonial vestments.

Various grades or ranks of ordination through which the initiate passes are present in the more formalized religious schools. Progress through the religious hierarchy is made either by acquiring merit or upon reaching a particular age. These various grades are characterized by the transmission of additional sets of *jiè* (precepts), the transmission of increasingly esoteric *jīng* (scriptures), and the receipt of more comprehensive *lù* (registers). Ordination at the different levels is granted once the ordinand has performed certain tests or has undergone certain ordeals. Such ordinations are accompanied by different types of rituals, which are intended to emphasize the monk's or nun's place in the hierarchy of Daoist religious authority.

See also: **chūjiārén** (7.1), **dìzǐ** (▸4), **fú** (▸3), **lù** (▸3).

1. See *e.g.* Livia Kohn, *Cosmos and Community, CCED, passim.*

dvija (S), **dojanmā** (H) *Lit.* twice *(do)* -born *(janmā);* a Hindu man who has undergone the sacred-thread ceremony *(upanayana* or *yajñopavīta),* generally as a child, and is thus considered to have secured a second birth. At this time, he receives religious *mantras* from the *paṇḍits* and is initiated into brahmanical rites and rituals. The terms *dvija* or *dojanmā* can be applied to any member of the three higher castes *(brāhmaṇ, kshatriya, vaishya)* of Hindu society who have undergone the thread ceremony. The observance and significance of the custom is greatly reduced in present times.

Traditionally, the thread ceremony marked the acceptance of a boy or adolescent by his *guru.* It was the time when his formal education would begin, following which he would live for some years in his *guru*'s *āshrama,* receiving an education, both spiritual and mundane. The initiation entitled him to life as a student, and entering the first of the four phases of life, he became a *brahmachārin* (celibate) until his marriage, according to the social rules laid down in the *Manu Smṛiti.* He received the sacred *gāyatrī updesh* (initiation), and the *gāyatrī mantra* was also given to him, after which he was expected to perform *sandhyā* twice daily (*brāhmaṇ* prayers at dawn and dusk). He was also made aware that the purpose of life is realization of *Brahman,* the ultimate Reality. After receiving this initiation, the individual is said to be twice-born. The custom is very ancient, dating back to Aryan times. After fulfilling the duties of the first three stages *(āshramas)* of life – as a student or celibate young man *(brahmachārin),* householder *(gṛihastha),* and forest dweller *(vānaprastha)* – the *dojanmā* becomes entitled to enter the fourth stage (renunciation, *sannyāsa*), and completely renounce worldly life in the quest for God.

In times past, since the adoption of a *guru* was a part of the educational system, very few people among the higher (and educated) classes were without a *guru,* and the *brāhmaṇs, kshatriyas,* and *vaishyas* were all known as *dojanmā.* Nowadays, the thread ceremony is only a part of religious education, not of formal school education, and few *gurukulas* (residence of a *guru*) have survived that teach the *Vedas.* Even so, the importance of the place held by the custom in Hindu society is still indicated by the strength and prevalence, even in modern times, of the Indian belief in initiation by a *guru.*

See also: **dīkshā**, **upadesha**, **upanayana** (▸3).

Eleusinian mysteries See **mysteries**.

five seals A metaphor for a particular form of mystic baptism or initiation (also known as 'receiving the seal' or being 'sealed'), found in some gnostic tractates from early Christian times. The five seals were perhaps related to the Five Trees, also mentioned in gnostic texts,[1] and which probably represented five major aspects of the Word as it descends into the creation.

A few gnostic tractates, all of them associated with Jesus' teachings, mention receiving the "five seals". Although in some instances the full context is confused, it would seem that some teacher or teachers, around Jesus' era, baptized souls with the "five seals". This was regarded as the highest kind of baptism and, in the minds of the writers of these texts, the one who gave this baptism was Jesus.

The *Gospel of the Egyptians* speaks of the "five seals which the Father brought forth from his bosom",[2] and which are intimately associated with the "Father, the Mother, the Son, and the whole *plērōma*",[3] the *plērōma* being a vast and eternal archetype from which the rest of creation comes into being.

In the revelational *Apocryphon of John,* Jesus describes how he came from the light of God, down into the darkness of this world, taking his abode in the "prison of the body". Here, he gives the mystic Call, and those who hear the sound of his Call are awakened. They are sealed with the "five seals" so that they can escape from this world, the realm of death:

> And I raised him up and sealed him
> in the Light of the Water with five seals,
> in order that death might have no power over him from this time on.
>
> *Apocryphon of John 31; cf. NHS33 pp.173, 175*

The "Light of the Water with five seals" is the Living Water, the divine Word, with its five principle stations or "trees" that have to be conquered during the inner ascent.

In the *Trimorphic Protennoia,* another revelational description is given of how Christ, who is the divine Word or *Logos,* receives his divine appointment to act as saviour in this world. He remains concealed until the time comes to reveal himself to his chosen ones ("the sons of light"). He then teaches them about the "ineffable Ordinances . . . of the Father", which are the "five seals" – aspects of God's primary Ordinance, the divine "Word" by which the soul receives salvation. But the "five seals" are available only to the "sons of light", not to any of the many powers in the hierarchy of creation. In this passage, it is the saviour who is speaking:

> I hid myself within them all,
> until I revealed myself among my members which are mine.
> And I taught them about the ineffable Ordinances. . . .

That they (these Ordinances) cannot be invoked
by any of the realms and ruling powers,
but only by the sons of light.
For they are the Ordinances of the Father:
They are the glories that are higher than every glory;
They are the five seals that are perfect through the *Nous.*

Trimorphic Protennoia 49; cf. GS p.100, NHS28 pp.430–31

Later, the saviour says that he will not leave this world

until I have revealed myself to all the brethren,
and until I have gathered together all the brethren,
within my eternal kingdom.

And I proclaimed to them the five ineffable seals
in order that I might dwell in them,
and they also might dwell in me.

Trimorphic Protennoia 50; cf. GS p.100, NHS28 pp.432–33

As the saviour gathers each soul to himself, he gives them the "five ineffable seals" so that he may take up his place within each of his chosen "brethren" and that they may live with him, spiritually and inwardly. Hence, he also says, describing the salvation of a particular soul:

And he received the five seals
from the light of the Mother, *Protennoia,*
and it was granted him to partake of the mystery of knowledge,
and he became a light in Light.

Trimorphic Protennoia 48, NHS28 pp.428–29

So close an association does the soul develop with these "five seals" that the two become one, light merging into the divine Light.

See also: **Five Trees** (3.1), **seal**.

1. *Gospel of Thomas* 36:19, *NHS20* pp.60–61; *Second Book of Jeu* 119:50, *BC* pp.166–67.
2. *Gospel of the Egyptians* 58–59, *NHS4* p.83.
3. *Gospel of the Egyptians* 58, *NHS4* p.81.

gift, gift of Christ, gift of God, gift of the Holy Ghost, gift of Wisdom, heavenly gift The gift of mystic baptism into the Holy Spirit or Word of God; a group of terms commonly encountered in early Christian writings. It is a gift because a master takes absolutely nothing in return, neither financially, nor by way of emotional dependence, nor personal fame and acclaim. A perfect master, like God with whom he is one, is always a giver.

It is a gift of God because no one can give it except a master, a saviour, or a true Christ – one who has been anointed or appointed by God to do so. The purpose of the gift is so that a soul may return to God.

It is the gift of the Holy Ghost because that is what true baptism entails. The soul is tuned to the Holy Ghost or Word, is brought into the family of souls who are connected to the Word, and are thereby being taken back to God.

The expression appears in John's gospel, where Jesus, meeting a Samaritan lady at a well, asks her for a drink. She asks him why a Jew should ask a Samaritan for water, to which he responds:

> If you knew (the meaning of) the gift of God, and who it is that is asking you, "Give me a drink," you would have asked of him, and he would have given you Living Water.
>
> *John 4:10; cf. KJV*

The "Living Water" is the water of the divine Word, and the anecdote is typical of John's gospel where stories are used as allegories and as the basis for the explanation of spiritual truths. Whether such incidents actually happened is not relevant to the writer's purpose.

In a similar vein, again in *John,* when asked about the baptism of Jesus, John the Baptist responds enigmatically, "A man can receive nothing, except it be given him from heaven."[1] Jesus himself also says, "No man can come unto me, except it were given unto him of my Father,"[2] which implies that the gift is essentially the gift of God, and that certain souls are intended by God for salvation. As Jesus reiterates, he himself has no choice in the matter. He baptizes only those souls who are given to him by God:

> All that the Father gives me shall come to me; and him that comes to me I will in no wise cast out.
>
> *John 6:37; cf. KJV*

In the New Testament letter attributed to James the brother of Jesus, the writer repeats that this gift comes from God, which he equates with being born of the "Word of Truth":

> Every good gift and every perfect gift is from above,
> and comes down from the Father of Lights,
> with whom is no alteration or hint of change.

Of His own will, He brought us forth with the Word of Truth,
that we should be a kind of firstfruits of His creatures.

James 1:17–18; cf. KJV

The expression is little used for baptism in later Christianity, but there are many examples of its use in some of the early literature, especially in some of the early liturgy[3] and among the apocryphal writings. Speaking of baptism in the *Acts of Peter,* Peter relates that Jesus "did them good and gave them the gift of God".[4] In the *Acts of John,* John, giving baptism to a young man, prays to Jesus: "Now also let your gift be accomplished in this young man."[5] In the *Acts of Thomas,* Judas Thomas speaks of the "gift of the Holy Ghost"[6] and of "your heavenly gift". At one place, he expresses his gratitude to Jesus, saying:

Our souls give praise and thanks unto you, O Lord,
for they are yours.
Our bodies give thanks to you,
which you have accounted worthy to become
the dwelling place of your heavenly gift.

Acts of Thomas 94; cf. ANT p.405

In the *Story of St James,* a crowd of people beg the apostles to give them the "gift of Christ":

We entreat you, O good servants of God, to give us the gift of God, which you have given to our friend.... We entreat you, O disciples of the Christ, that you would make us fit for the gift of the Christ.

Story of St James; cf. MAA p.33

In the *Gospel of the Twelve Apostles,* this "gift that is from Yourself" is equated with the grace, mercy and compassion of God, together with the *gnōsis,* knowledge or mystic experience that comes from Him and from the indwelling of the Holy Spirit. This "gift" brings the soul to perfection:

We beseech You, our Lord and God,
not to deprive us of Your grace,
but establish us in that grace,
and enrich us in the knowledge that comes from You,
and cause Your Holy Spirit to dwell in us,
and give us the mercies and compassion that come from Yourself:
And perfect with us the gift that is from Yourself.

Gospel of the Twelve Apostles; cf. G12A p.28

The devotional writer of the *Odes of Solomon* attributes everything he has attained to this "gift", including the "ascent of my soul" and the return to God:

> And I grew strong through His gift,
> and rested in His perfection.
> And I spread out my hands in the ascent of my soul,
> and turned myself towards the Most High,
> and was redeemed by Him.
>
> *Odes of Solomon 35:6–7, OSD p.150*

It is the source of all spiritual riches:

> I abandoned selfhood,
> and turned towards the Most High, my God,
> and was enriched by His gift.
>
> *Odes of Solomon 11:8–9, OSD p.50*

Baptism was also described as receiving the "Wisdom of Jesus Christ". In the *Acts of Paul,* in a passage clearly intended to reflect the canonical beatitudes, Paul says:

> Blessed are they that receive the Wisdom of Jesus Christ,
> for they shall be called sons of the Most High.
> Blessed are they that have kept their baptism pure,
> for they shall rest with the Father and with the Son.
> Blessed are they that have compassed
> the understanding of Jesus Christ,
> for they shall be in light.
>
> *Acts of Paul 2:6, ANT p.273*

Here, the gift of the Wisdom of Jesus Christ is equated by juxtaposition with a baptism or initiation that makes the recipients the sons of God.

The Manichaeans also spoke of the supreme gift that takes a soul back to God. As it says in one of the Coptic psalms:

> God it is who teaches whom He pleases, and gives to him
> the gift that surpasses all gifts, as a seal.
>
> *Manichaean Psalm Book CCXXV, MPB p.16*

Since God is the creator of all things, anything may be regarded as His gift. Christian writers, and those of other traditions too, for that matter, have commonly spoken of the gift of the Holy Spirit, the gift of His love, the gift of divine grace, the gift of faith, the gift of prayer, the gift of contemplation, and so on. Thus, the early-nineteenth-century Russian Orthodox bishop Ignatius Brianchaninov writes of the great gift of the Jesus Prayer, as a key to unlocking the priceless treasure of the continuous remembrance of God:

> O giver of a priceless, incorruptible gift! How can we sinful mortals receive the gift? Neither our hands, nor our mind, nor our heart are capable of receiving it. Teach us to know, as far as we are able, the greatness of the gift, and its significance, and the ways of receiving it, and the ways of using it, that we may not approach the gift in a sinful manner, that we may not be punished for indiscretion and audacity, but that, for the right understanding and use of the gift, we may receive other gifts from You, promised by You, known only to You.
>
> *Ignatius Brianchaninov, On the Prayer of Jesus 1; cf. OPJ p.4*

See also: **baptism**, **gift of the mysteries**, **mysteries**.

1. *John* 3:27, *KJV.*
2. *John* 6:65, *KJV.*
3. *E.g. Nestorian Liturgy, NR2* pp.110, 156, *passim.*
4. *Acts of Peter, Fragment, ANT* p.302.
5. *Acts of John* 75; *cf. ANT* p.246.
6. *Acts of Thomas* 52, *ANT* p.389.

gift of the mysteries, receiving the mystery of the forgiveness of sins The mysteries were the secret teachings and practices imparted to initiates of any of the many esoteric and religious movements of ancient Egypt, the Middle East, and the Graeco-Roman world. In early gnostic Christianity, the gift of the mysteries implied receiving baptism into the mystic Word. In the *Acts of Thomas,* for example, Judas Thomas is described as the "receiver of the secret mysteries of the Son of God"[1] and "sharer in the holy mysteries of God".[2] To one who had recently been baptized, he says, "May our Lord make you worthy of his divine mysteries."[3] He also prays that certain souls "be confirmed by your glorious mysteries", calling this confirmation or baptism, the "gifts of gifts":

> Let them therefore have boldness in you,
> and be confirmed by your glorious mysteries,
> and receive your gifts of gifts.
>
> *Acts of Thomas II; cf. AAA p.165*

The same expression is used in the *Acts of John* when a group of people ask for initiation, saying:

> We beg of you, servant of the Living God, do what pleases you,
> and let us participate in the living mystery,
> that we may live and not die: and this in haste.
>
> *History of John; cf. AAA p.38*

Likewise, in the *Pistis Sophia,* Jesus is said to speak of the "gift of the great mystery and its exceedingly great glory".[4] In fact, in the *Pistis Sophia* and the two *Books of Jeu,* the expression is used repeatedly. Souls are said to have "received the mysteries of the Light" and the "mysteries of purification". When leaving the realm of the counterfeit spirit (the universal mind), the soul "says the mystery of the releasing of the seals and all the bonds of the counterfeit spirit". Jesus is also said to be one that has brought these "mysteries" to the world:

> I have brought the mysteries into the world because all are under sin, and they all are in need of the gift of the mysteries.
>
> *Pistis Sophia 350:134; cf. PS pp.700–1, PSGG pp.292–93*

There are many places throughout the *Pistis Sophia* which refer to Jesus saying that the only escape from the domain of Satan and the grip of sin is through this "gift of the mysteries", for it brings with it the complete forgiveness of God, through the saviour:

> I tell you that every man who receives the mysteries of the Ineffable, not only if he transgresses once, and again turns and repents, will he be forgiven; but every time he transgresses, while he is still living, if he turns again and repents, without hypocrisy, . . . he will be forgiven every time, because he has received the gift of the mysteries of the Ineffable, and also because those mysteries are merciful and forgiving at all times.
>
> *Pistis Sophia 305:119; cf. PS pp.610–11, PSGG p.254*

He says that even if an initiate continues to act sinfully after "receiving the mysteries", all the same, as long as he sincerely continues struggling towards the light, he will be forgiven again and again, because he has "received the gift of the mysteries".

The *Second Book of Jeu* recounts how, having just initiated a group of disciples, described as "giving to them all these mysteries", Jesus speaks of their receiving the "mystery of the forgiveness of sins":

> It is necessary that you should receive the mystery of the forgiveness of sins, so that you may become sons of the Light, and completed in all the mysteries.
>
> *Second Book of Jeu 126:51, BC pp.180–81*

Elsewhere in this book, the "mystery of the forgiveness of sins" is also called the "great mystery":

> But when you reach the six aeons, they will restrain you until you receive the mystery of the forgiveness of sins, because that is the great mystery, which is in the Treasury of the Innermost of the Innermost. It is the whole salvation of the soul, and all those who receive that mystery will surpass all gods and all rulerships of all these aeons.... For this is the great mystery of the Unapproachable One, which is in the Treasury of the Innermost of the Innermost.
>
> *Second Book of Jeu 117:49, BC pp.162–63*

In other words, the "great mystery", the mystic blessing that grants salvation to the soul, permitting it to enter the realm of God ("the Innermost of the Innermost"), is the forgiveness of sins.

See also: **First Mystery** (2.1), **gift**, **mysteries**.

1. *Acts of Thomas* IV, *AAA* p.180.
2. *Acts of Thomas* V, *AAA* p.185.
3. *Acts of Thomas* VIII, *AAA* p.223.
4. *Pistis Sophia* 187:84; *cf. PS* pp.374–75, *PSGG* p.251.

heavenly gift See **gift**.

holy seal See **seal**.

hungan apprenticeship The training of a Haitian *Vodou* priest *(hungan)* or priestess *(mambo)*. See **hungan** (7.1).

initiation (Gk. *mystagōgia*) A rite, ritual, experience, or conveyance of instructions – often secret – by which an individual is inducted into a particular community, tribe, or organization; induction into any of the mystery religions or societies of ancient Egypt, the Middle East and the Graeco-Roman world, whether esoteric or exoteric in nature; practical instruction given by a mystic into the techniques of meditation, together with an inner mystic connection or re-tuning of the soul to the Divine and to the mystic who has accepted responsibility for the initiate's spiritual evolution.

Initiation can range from the entirely external and ritualistic to the highest form of spiritual initiation – initiation into the divine Word – which can ultimately take a soul back to God. A mystic can only take a soul to the spiritual height that he himself has reached. Consequently, different mystics may initiate souls to different stages on the spiritual journey, but only a perfect mystic or perfect master, by definition, can initiate and take a soul back to God Himself.

At the time of initiation, such a master comes to dwell, so to speak, within his disciple, in a spiritual form. From that time onwards, the administration of the future destiny of the soul, its release from the many realms of creation, and its return to God are all in the hands of the master. In fact, such initiation is essentially the acceptance of a soul by the master, which normally takes place before any outward instructions are actually conveyed to the initiate – perhaps before an individual has even come to know about the master.

Initiation, however, has been understood in a variety of ways by different writers, by different mystics, and in different traditions. The external rites of some of the mystery religions were not regarded by the more mystically inclined as effecting the purification of the soul. In this regard, St Augustine quotes the Neo-Platonist Porphyry:

> Porphyry also says that, according to the reply of the divine oracles, the initiatory rites of the sun and of the moon cannot purify us. The purpose of this reply, he says, is to make it clear that a man cannot be purified by the initiatory rites of any god. For where is the god whose rites can effect our purification, if those of the sun and the moon are of no avail? For they are regarded as the chief divinities among the gods of heaven.
>
> *St Augustine, City of God 10:3; cf. CGAP p.403*

In early Christian times, it is clear from the garbled and prejudiced accounts of the anti-'heresy' writers, such as Irenaeus and others, that initiation in various forms was an essential aspect of the life of the many gnostic groups that flourished in the first three centuries of Christianity. Some clearly followed a ritual using water, or oil and water, not dissimilar to Christian baptism. Some included a repetition or *mantra* of Hebrew or other names.[1] Eusebius and Epiphanius intimate that the gnostics Basilidēs in Egypt and Saturninus in Syria received initiation from Menander.[2] Though no details are known, since they were gnostic teachers of good standing, each with considerable followings, it is likely that the initiation included details of spiritual practice.

Among the Mandaeans, a gnostic group who survived more or less intact into the late twentieth century, a secret initiation, with secret texts given only to initiates, and performed in a small building set aside for the purpose, was an essential aspect of Mandaean life.

The first-century Philo Judaeus, speaking of the *Therapeutai,* a contemporary community of the spiritually minded who had settled on the shores of Lake Mareotis near Alexandria, says that, "In each house, there is a sacred room, which is called a sanctuary, in which they retire by themselves and practise the mysteries of the holy life."[3] In conformity with his interpretation of the Bible in the light of Greek philosophy, Philo also speaks of Moses as initiating people into the sacred mysteries.[4]

To some later Christian writers, initiation into the Holy Spirit meant mystical revelation or mystical experience *per se.* The language of these Greek-speaking fathers is often that of the Greek mysteries, applied to Christian belief:

> Revelations occur when the purified and illumined soul is able to contemplate in a way that transcends normal sense perception. They have the force of things and thoughts, miraculous and divine, initiating us into the hidden mysteries of God.
>
> *Nikitas Stithatos, On the Inner Nature of Things 61, Philokalia, PCT4 p.124*

Thus, Paul's heavenly vision ("I knew a man in Christ, . . . caught up to the third heaven, . . . caught up into paradise")[5] is understood by Gregory of Nyssa as Paul's "mystical initiation in paradise".[6]

A person who was the recipient of divine revelations was often deemed capable of initiating others. As Gregory of Nyssa writes of Gregory Thaumaturgus (Gregory the Wonderworker): "He received – and all those who were initiated by him – a revelation of the mysteries."[7]

In the Orthodox Church, there is a long tradition of adopting a spiritual guide, and seeking initiation from him:

> We have, as a natural criterion, the law of nature. This teaches us that, before we can acquire the wisdom that lies in all things, we must through mystical initiation seek their Maker.
>
> *Maximos the Confessor, On Theology, 2:28, Philokalia, PCT2 p.193*

> No one can learn the art of virtue by himself, though some have taken experience as their teacher. For to act on one's own and not on the advice of those who have gone before us is overweening presumption – or, rather, it engenders such presumption. If the Son does nothing of his own accord, but does only what the Father has taught him,[8] and the Spirit will not speak of his own accord,[9] who can think he has attained such heights of virtue that he does not need anyone to initiate

him into the mysteries? Such a person is deluded and out of his mind rather than virtuous.

Gregory of Sinai, On Stillness 15, Philokalia, PCT4 p.274

St John Cassian maintains that Paul, according to the story in *Acts,* received initiation from Ananias:

> When Christ himself spoke to Paul and called him, he could have opened his eyes at once and made known to him the way of perfection. Instead, he sent him to Ananias, and told him to learn from him the Way of Truth, saying: "Arise and go into the city, and there you will be told what you must do."[10] In this manner, he teaches us to be guided by those who are advanced on the Way, so that the vision rightly given to Paul should not be wrongly interpreted. Otherwise, it might lead later generations presumptuously to suppose that each individual must be initiated into the Truth directly by God, as Paul was, and not by the fathers.

St John Cassian, On the Holy Fathers of Sketis, Philokalia, PCT1 p.107

Ultimately, however, though a human guide was deemed essential, the real initiation was of and by the Holy Spirit:

> In the presence of Christ, you will feel the Holy Spirit spring up within your soul. It is the Spirit who initiates man's spirit *(nous),* so that it can see with 'unveiled face'.[11] ... In other words, it is the Spirit who mystically confirms Christ's presence in us.

Hesychios the Priest, On Watchfulness and Holiness 29, Philokalia; cf. PCT1 p.167

And to receive this kind of initiation requires divine grace:

> When our Lord (*i.e.* Christ) desires to give us initiation into the spiritual mysteries, he opens in our mind the ocean of faith.

Isaac of Nineveh, Treatise 43, On Wisdom, MTIN p.210

See also: **gift of the mysteries**, **hierophant** (7.1), **mysteries**, **Therapeutai** (7.1).

1. Irenaeus, *Against Heresies* I:21.3–4, *AH1* pp.82–83.
2. Eusebius, *History of the Church* 4:7, *HC* p.158; Epiphanius, *Panarion* 2:22–24, *PES* p.55.
3. Philo Judaeus, *On the Contemplative Life* 3; *cf. PCW9* pp.126–27, *WPJ4* p.6.

4. *E.g.* Philo Judaeus, *Allegorical Interpretation* 3:33; *On the Life of Moses* 2:30; *On the Virtues* 33.
5. *2 Corinthians* 12:1–4, *KJV.*
6. Gregory of Nyssa, *On Canticles* 8, *GGG* p.211.
7. Gregory of Nyssa, *Life of Gregory Thaumaturgus, PG46 col.*913c, in *GGG* p.28.
8. *John* 5:19–20.
9. *John* 16:13.
10. *Acts* 9:6.
11. *1 Corinthians* 13:12, *2 Corinthians* 3:18.

initiation (in Māori tradition) The sacred lore of the Māori *tohunga* (priestly adept or expert) was learned through the *whare wānanga* (school of sacred learning).

Contemporary Māori Samuel Timoti Robinson writes of his own childhood training and of the practices, beliefs and mythology according to his own tribe *(iwi),* the Ngāi Tahu or (in the southern dialect) Kāi Tahu, the principal Māori tribe of New Zealand's South Island. He says that the complete course could take seven years, with seven degrees, courses or stages of learning through which the *akoako* (student) had to pass. Acceptance into each degree was subject to the passing of rigorous tests, a ritual cleansing, and then an initiation into that specific stage or year of study. *Akoako* were hand picked by the *tohunga,* and only accepted after passing a variety of such tests to determine discipline, obedience, memory, bravery, survival skills, and dedication. A sequence of tests had to be undergone before entering even the first degree of learning:

> Before the *akoako* began any training, they first had to be accepted as a student by a master *tohunga.* The adolescent was selected firstly on their birthright by family genealogy; however, today this criterion has been relaxed for the purpose of providing *tohunga* for the new era. The second criterion for selection was obedience and listening, while the third requirement was a good memory. Without a good memory the teaching was for naught, thus before any initiation was performed it was decided by trial who would enter the house of learning.
>
> I learnt that the pupil was taken aside and tested in the Kāi Tahu way by various means, and the student was expected to recall such details as ancestral names and place names, and the meanings behind them after some history had been explained. The student was also tested and caught off-guard when he least expected it. One *tohunga* would say, "I'm in a bit of a hurry. Go and tell so-and-so that I need six of this for our fishing trip, eight of that, and eleven of this, and tell

him I only have four hooks left, and that the other five went missing. You'll need to tell him now because he's waiting." The second crafty *tohunga,* waiting at some distance, knew the details of the list and observed how keen the mind of the student was in recalling each item.

In my understanding of student selection, students were quite well known by the *tohunga.* For the most part, the tests were given on a daily basis, and included how receptive the youths were to suggestion, and how productive they were in day-to-day chores. The student underwent two more similar trials: one testing bravery and honesty, and another to test survival skills. The student passed or failed the trials and was never told fully of the tests to take place, because they were a part of the initiation procedure.

Samuel Timoti Robinson, Tohunga, TRAK p.96

Some of the tests were of a seemingly repugnant nature:

> On the day of initiation, the *tohunga* would take the student towards the shrine. On the way, they stopped for another test and cleansing ceremony at a riverside. At this point, the *tohunga* wrapped *tūtae* or human dung in wild cabbage leaves. In this part of the trial, the student was expected to eat the teacher's dung. Many people are perplexed by this part of the initiation process, but in a recent conversation I was told:
>
> > *Tāne* (progenitor of humanity) established the first *whare wānanga* in Hawaiki (spiritual homeland). Our ancestors ate of the fish from within the knowledge baskets and received knowledge by eating those fish. And so their students ate their *tūtae* to eat what has been eaten. This is how the knowledge is passed on. The students of *tohunga* lore have forever eaten the *tūtae* of their teachers, and what knowledge was known shall always be known. This line has never been broken since Hawaiki.
>
> Also related to this part of the initiation process was the South Island proverb which said, "He is one who would even eat *tūtae.*" Among learned people of my tribe this was said of someone ambitious, or ruthless and determined. It meant 'he would do anything to get what he wants', referring to the test of a student who will show if he really wants to learn the knowledge or not.
>
> *Samuel Timoti Robinson, Tohunga, TRAK pp.96–97*

According to Māori lore, three "knowledge baskets *(kete)*" were given by *Io* the supreme Being to *Tāne,* the progenitor of humanity, as knowledge to be given to humankind. Following these initial trials, the student's moral and ethical stature was assessed, and he underwent certain purificatory rituals:

> After the *tūtae* trial, the Kāi Tahu method next had a cleansing ritual to free the student's mind. Now the student was taken into the river and asked, "Are you an *ahurangi* or a *whiro?*" meaning, "Are you of a good or bad character?" (This relates to *Tāne* being tested by the winds of the *Pō* (the Void) before obtaining the baskets of knowledge.) Then the heart of the student was cleansed spiritually.
>
> The student was instructed to confess to the *tohunga* any immoral wrongdoings such as theft, lies, trickery or the like, and then the adolescent was placed into the stream to let the bad things wash away. A *karakia* (incantation) or prayer was said over the adolescent while water was at the same time splashed over the torso. This cleansing of 'sins' prepared the candidate for the next part of the initiation.
>
> The student was then led towards the *tūāhu* (shrine) but, before they reached it, the *tohunga* stopped the student for a second cleansing ceremony to take place. A branch with healthy green leaves was taken as a symbol of *ihi* or light and the uplifting power of *Tāne*. This was brushed over the student's whole body so as to wipe away any further negativity. The brushing was also done in the shadowy parts of the body where the sun does not shine, including under the arms, under the feet, and beneath the groin area. The student was now ready to be taken to the *tūāhu* or shrine of the *tohunga*.
>
> *Samuel Timoti Robinson, Tohunga, TRAK p.98*

A ceremony was then performed in which the student was infused with spiritual power before being prepared for re-entry into the flow of everyday life:

> At the shrine, *karakia* were recited over the head of the student, asking for protection from the higher self, or the student's personal *atua* (deity), and requesting that the mind of the student would always be strong and able to retain the knowledge. The most important part of this ceremony now occurred, in which the spiritual powers were bound to the student. They were called to give him *mana* and for protection.
>
> After this, the student was taken away from the *tūāhu* and cleansed once more with water at a pool near the *tūāhu* called 'the tranquil waters of *Rongo* (god of peace)'. This was to remove the *tapu* (sacred energy) created by the *tūāhu,* and also to ground the pupil back into the world away from the spiritual. The sacred waters of *Rongo* are located near the *tūāhu* in my area, in a small spring for purifications. Special initiation prayers were said while water was sprinkled upon the student's head. These prayers are said to have 'opened the ears' of the student so he

> would 'hear the knowledge and listen'. Then prayers were said so his 'mind will retain the knowledge learnt' and to 'open the throat so that the knowledge will pass therefrom onto the next generation'.
>
> All of this marked the beginning of training to allow the student to enter the *whare kura.* He had been tested, purified, and empowered at the *tūāhu.* Now the newly initiated *akoako* was ready for training.
>
> *Samuel Timoti Robinson, Tohunga, TRAK pp.98–99*

Having passed the initial tests, the student was permitted to enter the first school or degree, that of the *whare kura* (school of learning, house of learning). Following this, he passed through the *whare mauri* (school of the life principle) to the *whare wānanga* (school of sacred learning). Of the seven degrees, the first was in the foundational *whare kura,* the second to sixth degrees were a part of the *whare mauri,* and only the seventh degree was in the culminating *whare wānanga:*

> Initiation into each division came after completing several tests undertaken within each grade. The students were called *akoako* in each of the grades and received an extra title upon graduation. The first *akoako* were trained in the *whare kura.* The students then left the *whare kura* and were placed into *whare mauri* instruction. Later, if the student went far enough they were admitted into the *whare wānanga.* Each grade presented a different skill to learn, which had a specific role in the Māori community. The course itself took seven years of study.
>
> *Samuel Timoti Robinson, Tohunga, TRAK p.89*

Having completed the first six degrees of training, the *akoako,* if he was deemed a suitable candidate, then entered the seventh degree required if he was to become *tohunga ahurewa,* training to become a priest of the high altar in the sacred school of the *whare wānanga.* The last initiation rite is to bind the most sacred *karakia* or chants together. As an aid to learning, the *tohunga* and their students made use of a *tokotauwaka* or learning stick. A *tokotauwaka* is a stick about eighteen to twenty-four inches long, with five holes at one end and eighteen notches or grooves carved horizontally down its length. Students would often make their own *tokotauwaka,* which were generally quite basic and less ornate than those of the *tohunga.* The holes symbolize names of *Io* and the grooves represent the unfolding of the universe as portrayed in ancient *karakia.* They are used by students and *tohunga* during recitals as an *aide-mémoire* for teaching and recalling the successive stages of the creative process:[1]

> Training nears its end for the *tohunga ahurewa* when he is ready for *Te Uru ō te Karakia* ('Binding the Chants'). Here the chants are 'bound together' in the last initiation rite.

An *uru* is a group of 'trees' or 'rods' (such as a group of *tokotauwaka*).... 'To *uru* the chants' means to bind them together in a group like the trees and to strike out several of them with the 'rod' of the *tokotauwaka.* Here the *tohunga* was ready for what I think are the most wonderful teachings in the *whare wānanga.*

When the student was ready, two teachers took the disciple away to a quiet place and they sat down together. The student and teachers each had their own *tokotauwaka* as an emblem of their priesthood. It marked out their status and was a symbol of light. They all had a common commitment to the path of spirituality, and so the student was ready.

Finally, one of them would say, "Today you will recite the *Karakia kā Ikoa Tau* ('Recital of the Ages of Creation')," and the student recited the chant, naming the ages to his teachers. And the master *tohunga* would say, "Now recite the *Karakia kā Ikoa a Iho* ('Recital of the Names of *Io*')," and the student recited the names of *Io*. "Now recite the chant *Te Aka Rangi* ('Recital of the Cosmic Vine')," and the student was required to recite the chant of the vine, learnt as an *akoako* in the *whare mauri.*

Now the old men demonstrated how to recite them all together in a certain way with each of them taking part. The old men sat before the student sitting to the left and right in front of him. One of them said, "I will say the first stage of the *kā Ikoa Tau* recital and then he will say the first stage of the *kā Ikoa a Iho* chant. We will take turns at saying our stages. He will say a stage and I will say a stage, and so on. Then, when we get past the holes, onto the first groove of the *tokotauwaka,* you will join in with the *Te Aka* chant after he says the name of *Io*. Listen carefully."

And so the elderly man said, "*Ko te kore* (the Void without anything)," and the second *tohunga* said, "*Io-Mata-Moe* (*Io* the Slumbering Countenance)," and they continued taking turns at reciting the stages of their designated *karakia:*

> "*Te Kore te whiwhia* (the Void without understanding) – *Io-Kore-te-Whiwhia* (*Io* the One Without)."
>
> "*Te Kore te kerekere* (the Void without identification) – *Io-Mata-Ngaro* (*Io* of the Unseen Face)."
>
> "*Te Kore te taumaua* (the Void without time or space limits) – *Io-Roa* (*Io* the Eternal One)."
>
> "*Te Kore te matua* (the Void without parental origin) – *Io-Matua-Kore* (*Io* the Parentless One)."

The priests continued to say their *karakia,* taking turns after one another. When both teachers reached the first groove on the *tokotauwaka,* the

> first *tohunga* said, "*Te Pō Tipu* ('the Night of Growth')" from the *kā Ikoa Tau* recital. Then the second said, "*Io-Taketake* (*Io* the Origin)" from the *kā Ikoa a Iho* chant. Then the student joined in with them by saying, "*Ko Maku* (the Darkness)" from the vine chant of the *whare mauri.* And so the three of them continued, each saying a part from their own chant, one after the other, until they each reached the end, saying, *"Tihei, mauri ora!"* or "Sneeze, living soul!"
>
> *Samuel Timoti Robinson, Tohunga, TRAK pp.289–90*

The teachers now begin to impart the meaning of the combined chants to the student, going through the stages of process by which creation came into being. The details are perhaps hard to follow, but the general import is clear:

> When the *karakia* had been joined together in the ceremony of *Te Uru ō te Karakia,* the student was ready to learn the higher secrets of creation from the *Io* priesthood. Now the two men recited their *karakia* over the holes (in the *tokotauwaka*) once more, and in doing so stopped at each point to disclose the knowledge of *Io.* "*Ko te kore – Io-Mata-Moe* – In the beginning, there was just nothingness, just nothing because *Io* lay in slumber." For the duration of this part of the ritual, the tutors explained the beginning of the creation as I learnt it.
>
> On the first point of the *tokotauwaka,* the student would join in with them again when they said, *"Te Pō-Tipu – Io-Taketake – Ko Maku."* And then the teacher stopped and explained this knowledge along the lines of: "There was the time of *Te Pō-Tipu* ('It was the Night of Growth'). It came from *Io-Taketake,* so called because *Io* is the root and begins positive creation. *Io* the Origin recognized the first night out of nothingness, and *Maku* ('the Darkness') was identified thereof, and *Maku* reigned here for a time." And then they continued with their chants; when one said, *"Te Pō-Rea,"* the second said, *"Io-Mata-Wai."* The student followed with *"Te Timu."* Here the *tohunga* said to his student, "And so there was *Te Pō-Rea* ('The Night of Development'). *Io* found water in the Darkness becoming *Io-Mata-Wai* ('*Io* the Watery Countenance'), begetting *Te Timu,* the waters of the first cause." (Please note: this is a simplified version of the ritual used by me to explain the process of initiation. In reality, the ritual was conducted only in Māori.)
>
> Now they said, *"Te Pō tahuri atu – Io-Whatatata – Te Tiketike."* Here the teacher said, "And so there was *Te Pō tahuri atu* ('The Night of Extension or Rolling Over'). *Io* became *Io-Whatatata* ('*Io* going that way'), as *Io* went over the waters. As *Io* went over the waters, there came *Te Tiketike* ('The Height'), as height was found in the darkness as *Io* rolled over the waters." The three of them continued this process until they finished their chants. The *karakia* were now tied together.

> The master *tohunga* had completed the education of his disciple, and the student was expected to meditate on the meanings and come to understand them. In the process of undergoing *Te Uru ō te Karakia,* the three chants in their entirety were explained. The teaching of the beginnings of life was explained, starting with the marriage of *Tangaroa* (god of fish and the sea) to the Great Deluge, or waters of the first cause, begetting fish life in the darkness. The mythology of *Tāne* revealing the world of light is also bound up in the genealogy. *Te Uru ō te Karakia,* as the process, is quite a long one, but one that cannot be forgotten, seeing that all its knowledge is bound up in the *karakia* in relationship to one another.
>
> *Samuel Timoti Robinson, Tohunga, TRAK pp.290–91*

Secrecy is generally maintained regarding Māori lore and ceremonies of this nature; but, although the foregoing is only one individual's account of the customs of his tribe, it is likely that those of other tribes followed a similar pattern.

See also: **tohunga** (7.1).

1. Samuel Timoti Robinson, *Tohunga, TRAK* pp.111–13.

jīvandān (S/H/Pu), **jīa dān** (Pu) *Lit.* gift *(dān)* of life *(jīvan, jīa);* gift of true life, gift of spiritual life; used in the *Ādi Granth* for initiation or baptism by a perfect master into the divine Name or creative power. In this context, life means the eternal or immortal life of the soul. The physical world has commonly been described by mystics as the 'realm of the dead', the 'valley of death', and so on. Initiation is a touch of soul to soul – the soul of a master to the soul of the disciple. It brings a soul into contact with the Fountain or Stream of Life, the divine Name, the divine outpouring of creative energy. It is the key to realizing the immortal life of the soul. Hence, Guru Arjun describes the masters:

> Your saints are very fortunate:
> their homes are filled with the wealth of the Lord's Name.
> Their birth is approved, and their actions are fruitful.
> Those generous, humble beings are above both birth and death:
> they give the *jīa dān* (gift of life), and practise devotional worship;
> They inspire others to meet the Lord.
>
> *Guru Arjun, Ādi Granth 749, AGK*

And likewise:

My boat was sinking under the weight of greed and corruption,
but it was uplifted when the true *guru*
implanted the Name of the Lord within me.
The perfect *guru* has given me the gift of (spiritual) life *(jīa dān),*
and I centre my consciousness on the Lord's Name.
The merciful Lord Himself has mercifully given this gift to me:
O Nānak, I take to the sanctuary of the *guru.*

Guru Rāmdās, Ādi Granth 443, AGK

See also: **gift**.

kaidan (J), **jiètán** (C) *Lit.* vow, precept *(jiè, kai)* altar, platform *(tán, dan);* precepts dais or platform; ordination platform; place of ordination; the raised dais or altar where the ceremony of ordination of new Buddhist monks and nuns and the transmission of the code of monastic discipline (the precepts) takes place. By extension, a *kaidanin* (C. *jiètányuàn*) is an ordination temple or monastery in which there is a *kaidando* (C. *jiètándiàn*), an ordination hall, in which is housed the *kaidan.*

In India, the earliest Buddhist ordinations were generally conducted at places regarded as sacred. Only later were special platforms constructed for the purpose.

In China, the first *jiètán* is believed to have been constructed at Luòyáng during the mid-third century CE. Tradition has it that early Chinese ordination platforms were built to emulate those at the Jetavana and Nālandā monasteries in India.

In 742, the Chinese monk Jiànzhēn (688–763) was invited by the Japanese government to go to Japan to teach Buddhism and to help with the establishment of an ordination platform. On the order of the retired Emperor Shōmu, himself a devout Buddhist, the first *kaidan* was built in 754 CE at the Tōdaiji temple complex of the *Risshū (Ritsu)* school in the city of Nara, where Jiànzhēn (J. Ganjin) had taken up residence a year before.

This first *kaidan* was a temporary structure, but a year later in 755 CE a permanent ordination hall was built on the same site in the Tōdaiji temple complex. In 756, Jiànzhēn conferred the precepts upon around eighty monks and four hundred lay aspirants. Among these ordinands were the retired Emperor Shōmu himself, together with his consort, Empress Kōken, who had received their initial ordination in 754.

This and two other replacement *kaidans* were destroyed by fire in the twelfth, fifteenth, and sixteenth centuries. The building that is seen today, and which is known as the Kaidanin, was built in 1732; however, it is no longer used for ordinations.

For some time, all ordinations were conducted at the Tōdaiji temple complex. However, in 761, two more *Risshū kaidans* were constructed, one within the temple complex of Kanzeonji on the island of Kyūshū and one within the temple complex of Yakushiji in the Tochigi prefecture. Together with the *kaidan* in Tōdaiji, these became known as the 'three *kaidans* of the nation'.

Since these three temples had their roots in the *Theravāda* tradition, the *Tendai* school of the later *Mahāyāna* Buddhism believed that they, too, should have their own ordination platform. Despite opposition from the *Risshū* priests at Nara, the school's founder, the Japanese monk Saichō (767–822), repeatedly petitioned the Emperor Kanmu until imperial permission was finally granted – seven days after Saichō's death. This platform, the first in *Mahāyāna* history, was built in 827 at the *Tendai* headquarters at the Enryakuji temple complex on Mount Hiei, where the monks received the *bodhisattva* precepts *(bosatsukai)*. During the fourteenth century, four more *Tendai* ordination platforms were built, but they were later destroyed by fire and were never rebuilt.

Most of the temples housing these early *kaidan* have been designated and are presently preserved either as National Heritage sites by the Japanese Government or as World Heritage sites by UNESCO. Many of these sites do not retain the original buildings but replacements that have been built following destruction by fire, earthquake, or war – in some cases many centuries later. While all of these temples remain popular tourist locations, some are no longer active.

The use of *kaidans* appears to have been prevalent between the seventh and ninth centuries, particularly in China and in Japan, peaking with the large ordination in Tōdaiji in 756. There is little evidence of their specific use in the present day. In fact some present-day ordinations are known to be conducted in open spaces, even in public streets, albeit with the presence of some form of altar.

leaven A metaphor used by Jesus in one of his analogies in which he explains the greatness of spiritual baptism into the divine Word. He says that the Word is like the leaven or yeast that is used to raise bread. Only a very small quantity is required to make a large amount of dough rise:

> The kingdom of heaven is like unto leaven,
> which a woman took, and hid in three measures of flour,
> till the whole of it was leavened.
>
> *Matthew 13:33; cf. KJV*

The gift of the divine Word may seem like something of little significance, but when hidden in the body, it can ultimately raise a soul to God, just as a little leaven can raise heavy dough. The term used here for a "measure" is *seah,* three of which make something in the order of ten gallons, by volume. In other words, a little leaven serves to raise a lot of bread. The example appears in *Matthew* along with the parables of the sower, the tares, and the mustard seed, which, Jesus explains, refer to the sowing of the Seed of the Word in a human heart.[1]

Alluding to the analogy, Ephraim Syrus writes of God's "leaven in our souls",[2] adding, "It is leaven of the Lord that enters into a slave, raising him to freedom."[3] Here, the "slave" is the soul enmeshed in and enslaved by this world. Elsewhere, he writes that the gnostic Bar Daisan says that "the Word is the strange leaven that is hidden in the soul."[4] Irenaeus similarly observes that the gnostic Valentinus maintained that the "leaven" in Jesus' saying refers to the saviour himself.[5] But here again, the real Christ is the Word.

The imagery of a little leaven spreading throughout the whole of something and changing its nature is used in a variety of other contexts. Paul, for instance, uses what was perhaps a common proverb of the times, "A little leaven leavens the whole lump."[6] In *1 Corinthians,* he goes on to speak of purging the "leaven of malice and wickedness", replacing it with the "unleavened bread of sincerity and truth".[7]

See also: **baptism**.

1. *Matthew* 13:3–32.
2. Ephraim Syrus, *Hymns on the Nativity* 2, *HEDA* p.227.
3. Ephraim Syrus, *Hymns for the Epiphany* 4:6; *cf. HEDA* p.271.
4. Ephraim Syrus, *Against Bar Desain* 59; *cf. EPR2* p.lxiii.
5. Irenaeus, *Against Heresies* I:8.3, *AH1* p.34.
6. *1 Corinthians* 5:6–8, *Galatians* 5:9, *RSV.*
7. *1 Corinthians* 5:6–8, *KJV.*

mark of God, **mark of destruction**, **mark of the beast** A family of metaphorical terms designating souls who are destined or marked for salvation and those who are not, according to the beliefs of the writer; also described as 'receiving the sign' or as 'being sealed', especially as being 'sealed on the forehead'.

The terms appear frequently in *Revelations,* where it is said that those who receive the "mark of the beast", either on their foreheads or on their right hands, are destined to experience the "wrath of God":

> If any man worship the beast and his image,
> and receive its mark in his forehead, or on his hand,
> the same shall drink of the wine of the wrath of God,
> which is poured without mixing into the cup of his anger;

And he shall be tormented with fire and brimstone
  in the presence of the holy angels, and in the presence of the Lamb.

Book of Revelation 14:9–10; cf. KJV, RSV

And:

There fell dreadful and evil sores
  upon the men which had the mark of the beast,
  and upon those who worshipped his image.

Book of Revelation 16:2; cf. KJV

This is standard apocalyptic material: the good will be saved and the rest are doomed to damnation. To distinguish the two, the chosen ones will receive the "seal of God in their foreheads",[1] or will have "his (Jesus') Father's name written in their foreheads".[2]

Similar expressions are also found in the *Psalms of Solomon,* a group of psalms whose origin is obscure, though they bear some interesting similarities to the *Thanksgiving Hymns* found among the Dead Sea Scrolls.

Like the *Book of Revelation,* one of these psalms also speaks of the "mark... upon the foreheads", specifically the "mark of destruction... upon the foreheads" of "sinners", as opposed to the "mark of God... upon the righteous for salvation". Speaking of the man with a "holy and righteous heart", who has "a new psalm with song in gladness of heart", he continues:

The flame of fire and wrath against the unrighteous
  will not touch him, when it goes forth
  from the presence of the Lord against sinners,
  to destroy all the substance of sinners;
For the mark of God is upon the righteous for salvation.

Famine and sword and death will be far from the righteous,
  for they will flee from the holy, as men pursued in war;
But they will pursue sinners and overtake them,
  for those who act lawlessly will not escape the Lord's judgment.
They will be overtaken, as by enemies skilled in war,
  for the mark of destruction is upon their forehead.

And the inheritance of sinners is destruction and darkness,
  and their iniquities shall pursue them to *Sheol* (hell) below.
Their inheritance will not be found by their children,
  for sins shall devastate the homes of sinners;
And sinners shall perish forever on the Lord's Judgment Day,
  when God oversees the earth at His judgment.

But those who fear the Lord will find mercy on it,
    and will live by the compassion of their God;
But sinners will perish for all eternity.

Psalms of Solomon 15:1–13; cf. AOT pp.673–74, OTP2 p.664

The soul who has the "mark of God ... for salvation", maintains the psalmist, will be saved on the Day of Judgment, while those who bear the "mark of destruction ... upon their forehead" will be "pursued" by their sin, suffering extinction on Judgment Day. As in *Revelation,* a distinction is being made between the ultimate fate of the sinners and of the holy – according to the writer's perspective.

See also: **seal**, **sign**.

1. *Book of Revelation* 9:4, *KJV;* see also *Book of Revelation* 7:3–5.
2. *Book of Revelation* 14:1, *KJV.*

mysteries (Gk. *mystēria,* sg. *mystērion*) The secret teachings and practices imparted to initiates of any of the many esoteric and religious cults (mystery religions) of the ancient Egyptian, Chaldaean, and Graeco-Roman world; sometimes divided into the lesser mysteries and the greater mysteries; from the Greek *myein* (to close the eyes or lips, to initiate into the mysteries; hence, to keep a secret by not disclosing the contents of one's initiation), and related to *mystēs* (initiate), *mystagōgeō* (to initiate), and *mystagōgos* (one who initiates, leader of the *mystēs*). Among the leaders were those known as *hierophantēs* (revealer of holy things) and *diadochos* (torchbearer).

The origin of the mystery religions is uncertain. Some probably had their origins in tribal communities, where every clan or village member would have received initiation. Some of the rites were adopted from earlier seasonal and fertility festivals. Other groups may have formed around the teachings of particular mystical teachers. Present in early Egyptian civilization, over 4,000 years ago, they were enthusiastically embraced first by the ancient Greeks, and later by the Romans, their popularity peaking during the first three centuries of the Common Era. In ancient Egypt, the cults of *Isis* and *Osiris* were well known, though few details have survived. In the Roman world, the cult of the Iranian deity *Mithras* achieved considerable popularity, especially among the Roman military.

Among the more exoteric groups and mystery religions, like those associated with *Dionysus, Demeter, Isis* and *Mithras,* the mysteries included rites, rituals and pageants, often seasonal. Members of such groups shared common meals, dances, ceremonies, initiation rites, and so on. Some of these cults had an inner as well as an outer aspect, and the secret mysteries were jealously guarded, imparted only to those deemed sufficiently worthy or advanced to receive them. Some groups, on the other hand, relinquished religious connections altogether, becoming more like secretive secular societies, some of which, especially those with an aristocratic membership, wielded considerable political power. In 415 BCE, a number of such societies conspired unsuccessfully to overthrow the Athenian democracy. The conspirators, however, were ultimately unmasked, put on trial, and sent into exile.

Most famous among the ancient Greek mysteries were the Eleusinian, which took place at the village of Eleusis near Athens, in honour of the gods *Demeter* and *Persephonē,* according to a myth related in Homer's *Hymn to Demeter.* These annual mysteries, also known as the greater mysteries, were held in the month of *Bōēdromion* (September–October), and opened with a procession of the *mystai* (initiates) from Athens to Eleusis. The rites, preceded by ritual bathing in the sea and fasting for three days, were performed in the *Telestērion* or Hall of Initiation, and included the revelation of secret teachings, recitation, and various ritual acts. Their actual content, however, remained a secret and are now unknown, though it is believed that initiates were promised various benefits in the afterlife. Neophytes were initiated in stages, beginning with purification rites (the lesser mysteries) held in the month of *Anthestērion* (February–March) by the stream of Ilissos, at Agrai, outside Athens.

A spectrum of practices, from the sublime to the gross, were no doubt encompassed within the many mystery religions and cults of ancient times. Leaving details to his reader's imagination, Heraclitus (*c.*535–475 BCE) is scathing of some of the so-called "mysteries" as they were practised in his day:

> Night-walkers, magicians, *bacchantēs,* revellers, and participants in the mysteries.... What are regarded as mysteries *(mystēria)* among men are unholy rituals.
>
> *Heraclitus, Fragment 76 (14), HCPF*

Genuine mystics (in the modern sense of the word), like Heraclitus and Plato, denounced the exploitations of priests who initiated people into the mystery religions, promising salvation after death for a substantial fee. Plato spoke with indignation of charlatans equipped with "a bushel of books of Musaios and Orphēus" who sold salvation to the rich. Although Plato himself was greatly influenced by the spiritual side of Orphism, he felt nothing but indignation and contempt for the degrading superstitions and practices connected with some of the Orphic initiatory rituals and private mysteries. He denounced the idea that sin could be expiated by external means:

> Mendicant priests and soothsayers visit rich men's doors and persuade them that, by means of sacrifices and incantations, they have acquired

> from the gods the power to heal and expiate, by means of amusements and festal rites, whatever sin has been committed by a man himself or by his ancestors.... And they persuade not only ordinary individuals, but whole cities, that there are ways of absolution and purification from sin by means of sacrifices and amusements that fill a vacant hour, and are equally efficacious for the living or the dead; and that those special rites, which they call the mysteries, deliver us from pains of hell, while dreadful things await those who have been negligent in sacrifice.
>
> *Plato, Republic 2:364b–c, 364e–365a; cf. CDP pp.611–12, DP2 pp.205–6*

A papyrus, discovered in 1962 in a nobleman's grave at Derveni in northern Greece and dating to around 340 BCE, reveals the writings of another philosopher, believed to have been Diagoras of Melos, who tried to expose the fate of initiates into the mysteries who were being led blindly and exploited unscrupulously. The teachings of Diagoras became so influential that he was condemned to death at the instigation of the powerful priests of the Eleusinian mysteries for divulging the secrets of both the Orphic scriptures and the Eleusinian mysteries. Yet Diagoras had only tried to explain the deeper esoteric and allegorical meaning of the mystery rites, and the superficiality of many of the practices. His direct and critical approach earned him more than a few enemies, and the survival of his writings is only due to the discovery of this ancient papyrus:

> But those who have been initiated by someone who makes a profession of the rites are worthy of amazement and pity: amazement, because, although they suppose, before they perform the rite, that they will have knowledge, they go away after they have performed it without gaining knowledge and (yet) they make no further enquiries, as if they know something about what they saw, heard, or learned; and pity, because it does not suffice them that they have wasted the fee which they paid beforehand, but they also go away bereft of their judgment too.
>
> *Derveni Papyrus, col.20, CSRK p.51*

Although Plato and other philosophers raised their voices against the abuses that occurred in the mysteries, they referred abundantly to the practices of the mysteries to describe spiritual experiences. They even relied on the authority of the mysteries to convey their teachings, and make them more credible. In fact, when Socratēs introduces the topic of reincarnation in Plato's dialogue *Meno,* he says that he learned this teaching from "men and women who are wise about things divine" and who "are able to give an account of what they are doing".[1] It may be concluded, therefore, that not all mystagogues involved in the mysteries led their clients blindly, with an eye on their purse. In the *Symposium,* Socratēs claims to have learned the secrets of divine love from

Diotima, a priestess in the Eleusinian mysteries. Even if Diotima was a fiction, as many presume, the scenario of someone like Socratēs receiving spiritual instruction and guidance from a priestess of the mysteries must have served as a credible framework for Socratēs' praise of love as the path to the Divine.[2]

Some priests were indeed practising philosophers, as in the case of Plutarch (*c.*46–120), a Platonist who served at the temple of Apollo at Delphi. He advocated that people should take the *Logos,* the divine Word, as their guide for a deeper understanding of the mysteries:

> In the study of these matters, it is especially necessary that we adopt the *Logos* of philosophy as our guide *(mystagōgos),* and meditate reverently upon each one of the things said and done.
>
> *Plutarch, On Isis and Osiris (68) 378b; cf. PMB5 pp.156–57, TGH1 p.348*

If the mysteries themselves encompassed a broad spectrum of practices, the term itself developed an even wider spread of meaning. Among the more esoteric mystery groups, like the Orphics and Pythagoreans, the mysteries included secret teachings such as reincarnation, as well as the cosmogony of the inner realms of creation and instructions on spiritual practice. In Christianity and Mandaeism, the sacraments and rituals were known as the mysteries.

The mysteries were also the mystical understanding and inner experiences of the inner realities where the mysteries of God and His creation are revealed. Often, the inner realities, powers, patterns, and archetypes were themselves described as mysteries. In fact, anything of the world unseen could be, and often was, described as a mystery. Christians, for example, talk of the mysteries of God, of the Trinity, of the Incarnation, of the Word, of Christ, of love, and so on. On occasion, the heavenly realms themselves were also designated as succeeding mysteries, one above or within the other.

The highest mystery was the experience of God Himself who was thus sometimes known in gnostic writings as the Great Mystery or the First Mystery, as in the *Pistis Sophia,* which has Jesus say:

> I forgive and I will forgive: for this reason has the First Mystery *(Mystērion)* sent me, that I may forgive all men their sins.
>
> *Pistis Sophia 253:100; cf. PS pp.506–7, PSGG p.210*

And likewise, in the *First Book of Jeu:*

> Hear me as I sing praises to You, O First Mystery *(Mystērion),*
> who has shone in Your mystery *(mystērion),*
> and has established all the *archons* (rulers).
>
> *First Book of Jeu 82:32; cf. BC pp.90–91*

The mystic "Name" or divine Word was also called a mystery, as in the *Pistis Sophia:*

> For the sake of the mystery *(mystērion)* of Your Name, O Light, forgive my transgression, for it is great.
>
> *Pistis Sophia 80:46; cf. PS pp.160–61, PSGG p.65*

Among the Manichaean texts, the Coptic *Kephalaia* speaks of the "mystery of the Light and the Darkness", the "mystery of the creation of Adam, the first man", and the "mystery of the Tree of Knowledge from which Adam ate, by which his eyes were opened".[3]

For the Mandaeans, the mysteries covered everything from the "Great Mystery", which was seemingly a part of the Godhead from which the creative power of the "mystic Word",[4] the "Living Water" or *Manda-ḍ-Hiia* (*'Gnōsis* of Life', the archetypal Mandaean saviour), flowed forth, creating all lower mysteries. "Great Life" and "First Life" are names of God:

> Strengthened and enhanced is the Great Mystery of radiance,
> light and glory, which rests on the mouth of the Great Life!
> For from it, *Manda-ḍ-Hiia* came into being,
> and was manifest, knew, and interpreted
> the thoughts of the First Life, which are wondrous.
>
> *Mandaean Prayer Book 7; cf. CPM p.5*

In their religious life, the mysteries included the sacraments and rites of the Mandaean religion. These included everything from everyday religious observances to rites for the departed soul to ensure a happy rebirth in the heavenly realms.

Mandaean texts speak continuously of innumerable hidden or secret mysteries, both of the body and the material world, as well as the higher creation. These scrolls held secrets never to be divulged to outsiders. As E.S. Drower relates:

> When the head priests of the community learned some years ago that two of their number had permitted certain scrolls to pass into my possession, they showed resentment and anger. These scrolls, they said, contained 'secrets', knowledge imparted only to priests at ordination, and never to laymen or to outsiders. Their attitude is understandable. When I was advanced enough in their language to read these documents, I found at intervals stern insistence on secrecy. Only "one in a thousand and in two thousand, two" would be found worthy of initiation into certain mysteries, and any initiate who

> permitted them to become public was doomed to punishment in this world and next.
>
> *E.S. Drower, Secret Adam, SA pp.ix–x*

As a well-known expression, the term would have been familiar to Jesus, and it is to this that he refers when comparing his disciples with other people:

> It is given unto you to know the mysteries *(mystēria)* of the kingdom of heaven, but to them it is not given.... Therefore speak I to them in parables.
>
> *Matthew 13:11, 13, KJV*

By which he means that his disciples have been instructed in the correct path to follow in order to reach the kingdom of heaven and to experience the mysteries at first hand. Such experience was also known as 'revelation', as in the *Apocalypse of Peter:*

> And he (Jesus) said to me, "Be strong, for you are the one to whom these mysteries have been given, to know them through revelation."
>
> *Apocalypse of Peter 82, NHS30 pp.243–44*

The mysteries were quintessentially secret. Hence the saying attributed to Jesus and quoted in a few places by the writers of antiquity. Both Clement of Alexandria and the *Clementine Homilies* have it as, "Keep my mystery *(mystērion)* for me and for the sons of my house."[5] And a variant of the same saying appears in the *Acts of John,* where Jesus says, "Keep silence about my mysteries."[6]

The meaning is twofold. Firstly, it means that disciples should keep quiet and not talk about their inner revelations or experiences. Secondly, even certain of the teachings and instructions that they have been given should be kept secret.

Paul, too, speaks of teachings concerning the "hidden Wisdom of God" (the creative power) which were taught in the Christian baptismal mysteries of those times:

> The Wisdom of God *(Theou Sophia),* which we teach in our mysteries *(mystērion),* is the hidden Wisdom that God ordained for our glory before the world began.
>
> *1 Corinthians 2:7; cf. JB, KJV*

The understanding that the mysteries of the inner path were to be kept secret was prevalent throughout the ancient world. Plotinus writes:

> This, therefore, is manifested by the mandate of the mysteries *(mystēria)*, which orders that they shall not be divulged to those who are uninitiated. For as that which is divine cannot be unfolded to the multitude, this mandate forbids the attempt to elucidate it to anyone but him who is fortunately able to perceive it.
>
> *Plotinus, Enneads 6:9.11, SWP p.320*

The tradition of a secret teaching conveyed by Jesus is also evident in the writings of one of the earliest Christian teachers, Clement of Alexandria, who refers to Jesus' metaphor concerning pearls and swine when explaining why spiritual matters are often veiled in obscure parables:

> It is requisite, therefore, to hide in a mystery *(mystērion)* the wisdom spoken, which the Son of God taught.... Such were the impediments in the way of my writing. And even now I fear, as it is said, "to cast pearls before swine, lest they tread them under foot, and turn and rend us".[7] For it is difficult to express the really pure and transparent words respecting the true light, to swine-ish and untrained hearers. For scarcely could anything that they could hear be more ludicrous than these to the multitude; nor any subjects on the other hand more admirable or more inspiring to those of noble nature. "But the natural (worldly) man receives not the things of the Spirit of God; for they are foolishness to him."[8]
>
> *Clement of Alexandria, Miscellanies 1:12; cf. WCA2 p.388*

Part of the reason for keeping certain aspects of the mystic teachings secret is made clear in an introductory letter at the start of the *Clementine Homilies,* where James the brother of Jesus explains Peter's request that the books of his teachings should not be handed out to everyone indiscriminately:

> If we should give the books to all indiscriminately, and they should be corrupted by any daring men, or be perverted by interpretations as you have heard that some have already done, it will remain even for those who really seek the truth, always to wander in error. Wherefore it is better that they should be with us, and that we should communicate them with all the forementioned care to those who wish to live piously, and to save others. But if any one, after taking this adjuration, shall act otherwise, he shall with good reason incur eternal punishment.
>
> *Epistle of Peter to James 5, CH p.5*

How much of the *Clementine Homilies* is based upon fact is a question that will remain a matter of debate, for it is clear that much of the story is quite purposefully intended to be fictitious, as a means of conveying spiritual truths as the author understood them. Nevertheless, the traditions conveyed are, evidently, to some extent authentic.

That the mysteries also referred to the inner revelations of mystic experience is brought out in many of the early Christian texts. In the *Acts of Thomas,* the Holy Spirit, the "compassionate Mother", is depicted as "she that reveals the hidden mysteries",[9] and Jesus is described as the

> revealer of the mysteries of the Exalted (One),...
> utterer of hidden things,
> and shower of the works of our God,...
> giver of life in secret.
>
> *Acts of Thomas III, AAA p.189*

The source of all revelation is the "good Father", who reveals the mystery of His "Firstborn (the Son, the Word)" to the prophets, by means of the Holy Spirit. And the same Spirit reveals these mysteries to the devotees ("His saints") by the "hearing of Your Word":

> Glory to You, good Father,
> who has revealed the mystery of Your Firstborn
> to the prophets by the Spirit of Holiness....
> Glory to You, the Father giving life to all,
> who has revealed the mysteries of Your Son
> by the Spirit to His saints, in tranquillity and rest....
> Glory to You, benign Father,
> who has given us peace by the hand of our Life-giver,
> and has revealed unto us Your glorious and holy mysteries,
> by the hearing of Your Word.
>
> *Acts of Thomas VIII; cf. AAA pp.246–47, 250*

Jesus himself is called the "hidden mystery" who reveals "many mysteries" by means of "one Word" which consumes and is yet unrepeatable:

> Jesu, the hidden mystery that has been revealed to us,
> you are he who has shown unto us many mysteries.
> You that called me apart from my fellows,
> and spoke to me one Word with which I am inflamed,
> and am unable to speak it to others.
>
> *Acts of Thomas 47; cf. ANT p.387*

Some Jewish writers also wrote about the mysteries within the context of their own faith. The first-century Alexandrian Philo Judaeus, interpreting Judaism with an eye on Greek mystical philosophy, portrayed Moses as a hierophant, an initiator of his followers into the divine mysteries:

> There is also a more perfect and more highly purified mind, which has been initiated into the great mysteries *(mystēria);* a mind that gains its knowledge of the First Cause not from created things, ... but, having risen above creation, obtains a clear vision of the Uncreated One. The mind of which I speak is Moses, who says (to God), "Show Yourself to me; let me see You that I may know You."[10]
>
> *Philo Judaeus, Allegorical Interpretation 3:33; cf. PCW1 pp.368–69, WPJ1 pp.100–1*

Elsewhere, interpreting a passage from *Leviticus,*[11] Philo again depicts Moses as one who initiated others into the mysteries:

> After other additional sacrifices had been brought, some by the priests on behalf of themselves, and others by the body of elders on behalf of the whole nation, Moses entered the tabernacle, leading his brother by the hand – this was on the eighth and last day of the celebration, for the seven previous days had been devoted to the initiation of the hierophants – and he now initiated both his brother and his nephews. And when he had entered in, he taught his brother the way in which the high priest should perform the rites of the inner shrine.
>
> *Philo Judaeus, On the Life of Moses 2:30, PCW6 pp.524–25, WPJ3 p.106*

And like many others, Philo repeats the doctrine that the "sacred mysteries" are not to be divulged to the unworthy:

> It is not lawful to divulge the sacred mysteries *(mystēria)* to the uninitiated until they are purified by a perfect purification; for the man who is not initiated, or who is of moderate capacity, being unable either to hear or to see that nature which is incorporeal and appreciable only by the intellect, being deceived by the visible sight, will blame what ought not to be blamed. Now, to divulge sacred mysteries *(mystēria)* to uninitiated people, is the act of a person who violates the laws of the privileges belonging to the priesthood.
>
> *Philo Judaeus, Fragments in John of Damascus (Sacred Parallels), WPJ4 p.255*

Earlier Jewish mystics also spoke of the mysteries in an expressly mystic fashion. The wonderful psalms from among the Dead Sea Scrolls often speak of the mysteries in a manner that clearly refers to mystic revelation or experience:

These things I know
by the Wisdom which comes from Thee;
For Thou hast unstopped my ears
to marvellous mysteries.

Thanksgiving Hymns 6:20–25; cf. CDSV p.260

And I have loved Thee freely
and with all my heart;
Contemplating the mysteries of Thy Wisdom,
I have sought Thee.

Thanksgiving Hymns 5:25ff., CDSV p.255

Thou hast made known to me the Counsel of Thy Truth
and hast taught me Thy marvellous mysteries;...
and hast revealed Thy wonders to me.

Thanksgiving Hymns 22:15–20, CDSV p.294

In Thy goodness is much forgiveness
and Thy mercy is towards the sons of Thy goodwill.
For Thou hast made known to them
the Counsel of Thy Truth,
and hast taught them Thy marvellous mysteries.

Thanksgiving Hymns 21:5–10, CDSV p.293

But to the elect of righteousness
Thou hast made me a banner,
and a discerning interpreter of wonderful mysteries.

Thanksgiving Hymns 6:10–15, CDSV p.262

In Thy marvellous mysteries,
and in Thy lovingkindness to a man of vanity,
and in the greatness of Thy mercy to a perverse heart
Thou hast granted me knowledge.

Thanksgiving Hymns 16:25–30, CDSV p.282

In these, it appears that "Wisdom" and the "Counsel of Thy Truth" both refer to the creative power of God. These mysteries are heard, they are contemplated, they are marvellous and wonderful, they bring mystic knowledge, and they are made known only by the mercy and grace of God to the "sons of Thy goodwill" – to the seekers of God.

See also: **First Mystery** (3.1), **gift of the mysteries**.

1. Plato, *Meno* 81a.
2. Plato, *Symposium* 201d–212c.
3. *Kephalaia* 1; *cf. GSR* pp.3–4, *KOT* pp.20–21.
4. *Mandaean Prayer Book* 173, *CPM* p.157.
5. Clement of Alexandria, *Miscellanies* 5:10, *cf. WCA2* p.259; *Clementine Homilies* 19:20, *cf. CH* p.305.
6. *Acts of John* 96, *ANT* p.254.
7. *Matthew* 7:6.
8. *1 Corinthians* 2:14; *cf. KJV.*
9. *Acts of Thomas* 27; *cf. ANT* p.376.
10. *Exodus* 33:13.
11. *Leviticus* 9:1*ff.*

Nām dān (H/Pu) *Lit.* gift *(dān)* of the Name *(Nām);* initiation by a perfect *satguru* into the divine Name or creative power of God. The expression is used by the *gurus* whose writings are collected together in the *Ādi Granth:*

> I am a trader in the Name of the Lord of the universe:
> He has given it to me as my supplies, to carry with me.
> I have forgotten and forsaken other things:
> the perfect *guru* has given me the gift of the Name *(Nām dān),*
> this alone is my support....
> I contemplate him while I walk along the path.
> The *guru* has implanted the *Nām* within my mind,
> and my thirst has been quenched.
>
> *Guru Arjun, Ādi Granth 401, AGK*

> O my mind, meditate on the Lord, the Lord God!
> He blesses His servant with the gift of the Name *(Nām dān),*
> he is the destroyer of pain and suffering.
>
> *Guru Arjun, Ādi Granth 639, AGK*

See also: **gift**.

nayā janam (H/Pu) *Lit.* new *(nayā)* birth *(janam);* a Christian term used in India for the concept of being born again.

See also: **born again**.

new birth See **born again**.

planted in heaven, planting Planting means setting a plant firmly in the ground with the intention that it should grow; metaphorically, baptism or initiation; from the same family of agricultural metaphors as the sowing of the Seed (the Word), a metaphor that became current in Christianity from Jesus' well-known parables of the sower, the tares, the mustard seed,[1] the barren fig tree,[2] and the labourers in the vineyard.[3]

According to a story related in *Matthew,* Jesus is commenting upon the uselessness of the rituals performed by the Jewish religious authorities of the time, when someone observes that the Pharisees are offended at his remarks. Jesus responds somewhat enigmatically:

> Every plant that my heavenly Father has not planted shall be rooted up.
>
> *Matthew 15:13; cf. KJV*

The response is something of a *non sequitur,* but assuming that the anecdotal setting of this saying is relevant, even if not a precise record of fact, Jesus seems to be saying that the feelings of the Pharisees will not alter the reality. What people may believe to be the value of rituals and ceremonies has no effect upon their efficacy. Simply following the external observances of a particular religion entitles no one to return to God. Only those who are "planted" by the "heavenly Father" from heaven are truly on the path that leads back to Him. Others "shall be rooted up" – they will bear no fruit. Unless souls are planted in heaven or baptized into the Word, they will be unable to bear the fruit of salvation.

There are many places in the literature of the period where the metaphor is used with the same meaning. Clement of Alexandria (*c.*150–215), for instance, speaks of his fellow baptized Christians as "those who have been planted by the Word".[4] In the Nag Hammadi tractate, the *Gospel of Truth,* the writer speaks of the initiates as the "plantings" of Christ:

> He (Christ) is good. He knows his plantings, because it is he who planted them in his paradise.
>
> *Gospel of Truth 36, NHS22 pp.108–9*

In the *Acts of Thomas,* Judas Thomas refers to Jesus as the "planter of the Good Tree".[5] Here, the "Good Tree" is the "Tree of Life", the Word planted in the soul by the saviour. In the *Odes of Solomon,* the odist is expanding on the imagery of the disciple as planted by the saviour, when he says:

> And I said, "Blessed, O Lord, are they
> who are planted in Thy land,
> and who have a place in Thy paradise,

and who thrive in the growth of Thy Trees,
and have passed from darkness into light.

"Behold all Thy labourers are fair,
who work good works (or 'practise spiritual practice'),
and turn away from wickedness
to the kindness that is Thine.
For they turned themselves away
from the bitterness of the (evil) trees,
when they were planted in Thy land."

Odes of Solomon 11:18–21, OSD pp.52, 54

Another of these *Odes* explicitly explores the imagery of being planted "by the Hand of the Lord", the "Hand" being a metaphor for the divine creative power. The devotee is full of gratitude for the spiritual blessings that have been showered upon him:

My foundations were laid by the Hand of the Lord,
for He planted me.
He dug in the root and watered it,
and made it firm and blessed it,
and its fruits will be forever.

And it rooted deeply, and sprang up tall,
and spread out its branches,
and became fully grown.

And the Lord alone is to be praised for His planting,
and for His skill in cultivation:
For His care, for the blessing of His lips,
for the beautiful planting made by His Right Hand –
And for the existence of His planting,
and for the Thought of His Mind.

Odes of Solomon 38:16–21, OSD p.162

In a Mandaean poem, the souls baptized in the Living Water of the 'Jordan' are depicted as "plants":

How lovely are the plants which the Jordan
has planted and raised up!
Pure fruit have they borne,
and on their heads they set living garlands.

Yawar Ziwa (Dazzling Radiance) rejoices in the good plants,
which the Jordan has planted and raised.
The plants rejoice and flourish
in the Perfume of *Manda-ḍ-Hiia* ('*Gnōsis* of Life'),
which breathes upon them.

Mandaean Prayer Book 83; cf. CPM pp.90–91

Yawar Ziwa and *Manda-ḍ-Hiia* are two of the mythical saviours of Mandaean literature. The "Perfume of *Manda-ḍ-Hiia*" is the sweet emanation of God – a reference to the Word, often termed the Fragrance or Perfume. It is "breathed upon" the "plants", which "rejoice and flourish", the breathing once again being a further allusion to the Word as the Breath of Life.

In a passage from the Mandaean *John-Book,* where the "Water" which heals the soul and makes it grow spiritually is the Living Water that the master brings to his plants, the saviour says to the mythical devotee Miryai:

I have come to heal Miryai,
(come) to bring water to the good beloved plants,
to the vines who stand at the mouth of the Euphrates.
In a (pure) white pail I draw water,
and bring it to my plants.
I bear and I hold it on arms of splendour,
which are my own.
I bear and I hold it, and give them to drink.
Well for him who has drunk of my water.
He drinks, finds healing, and is made whole,
and grows to twice (his stature).

Mandaean John-Book, JMM p.135; cf. GJB p.66, JM pp.132–33, MEM p.153

In the Manichaean psalms, alluding to Jesus' parable of the sower and speaking of the chosen ones as "his elect" and "his men of knowledge", the psalmist writes of the saviour who plants the "Shoots" and the "Seed" of the Word in those who seek divine Wisdom:

He planted his Shoots in the field of his elect.
He sowed the Seed in the soil of his men of knowledge.

Psalms of Heracleidēs, Manichaean Psalm Book, MPB p.194

Similar expressions are found in the revelational text, the *Apocalypse of Baruch,* probably dating from the second half of the first century CE, where the chosen ones are described as being "justified in My Law" or having the "root of Wisdom" "planted in their heart". Both "Law" and "Wisdom" are terms for the divine Word:

> As for the glory of those who have lived righteously in My Law, who have had understanding in their life, and who have planted in their heart the root of Wisdom – their splendour shall be glorified by transformation, and the form of their face shall be turned into the light of their beauty, so that they may acquire and receive the world that does not die, which is promised to them.
>
> *2 Baruch 51:3; cf. ABC p.68, OTP1 p.638*

Such souls will be transformed. They will be able to leave their bodies and experience the "light of their beauty" in the higher regions. They will "acquire and receive the world which does not die" – they will return to the eternal realm, the kingdom of God, which has been "promised to them" by virtue of having been planted.

Metaphors associated with planting have found favour among writers of all ages. In the Hebrew Bible, the Garden-of-Eden creation allegory is fundamentally one of planting.[6] The nation of Israel is also commonly depicted as a vine planted by God.[7] Of the virtuous or spiritual man, Jeremiah writes:

> He is like a tree by the waterside
> that thrusts its roots into the stream:
> When the heat comes, it has nothing to fear,
> its foliage stays green;
> Untroubled in a year of drought,
> and never ceases to bear fruit.
>
> *Jeremiah 17:8; cf. JB, NJB*

The same imagery is echoed among the *Psalms* when the psalmist likens a virtuous man to "a tree that is planted by water streams, yielding its fruit in season, its leaves never fading".[8] Or as another psalm has it:

> The virtuous flourish like palm trees
> and grow as tall as the cedars of Lebanon.
> Planted in the house of *Yahweh,*
> they will flourish in the courts of our God,
> still bearing fruit in old age,
> still remaining fresh and green,
> to proclaim that *Yahweh* is righteous:
> My rock in whom no fault is to be found!
>
> *Psalms 92:12–15, JB*

In later Christian literature, 'planting' imagery is often derived from the parables of Jesus and other biblical sources. God is said to have planted His love, or faith, or various virtues in the heart, and so on. The first-century

Jewish writer Philo Judaeus also says that God "plants in the garden of our souls the valuable trees of right instruction".[9] Like the nation of Israel, the church is also described as being planted by God in this world.

See also: **gardener** (7.1), **Living Water** (3.1), **sowing of the Seed**, **Tree of Life** (3.1).

1. *Matthew* 13:3–32.
2. *Luke* 13:6–9.
3. *Matthew* 21:33–41.
4. Clement of Alexandria, *Instructor* 2:1, *WCA1* p.195.
5. *Acts of Thomas* 10, *ANT* p.369.
6. *Genesis* 2:8*ff.*
7. *E.g. Isaiah* 5:1–7; *Jeremiah* 11:17; *Amos* 9:15; *Psalms* 80:8, 15.
8. *Psalms* 1:3, *JB.*
9. Philo Judaeus, *On Drunkenness* 53; *cf. WPJ1* p.500.

pravrajya (S), **pabbajjā** (Pa), **rab tu byung ba** (T) *Lit.* going forth, going abroad; more fully, "going forth from home to homelessness *(agārasmā anagāriyaṃ pabbajjā)*"; the act of leaving the world, cutting all family and social ties, and adopting the pure life of a renunciate in order to attain the goal of enlightenment and liberation from the otherwise continuous suffering of *saṃsāra* (cycle of birth and death); renunciation; the lower of the two degrees of ordination or initiation into the life of a Buddhist monk, the higher being known as *upasaṃpadā;* a term appearing throughout the Pali scriptures and other Buddhist texts; related to the terms *parivrājaka* (S. religious mendicant) and *parivrājya* or *prāvrājya* (S. life of a religious mendicant).

A monk or nun who has received *pravrajya* is known as a *shrāmaṇera* (novice, *fem. shrāmaṇerī* or *shrāmaṇerikā*), and a fully fledged monk who has received *upasaṃpadā* is a *bhikshu* (Pa. *bhikkhu*) or, in the case of nuns, a *bhikshuṇī* (Pa. *bhikkhuṇī*). Although there are differences between countries, the minimum age for *pravrajya* is generally eight, and twenty for *upasaṃpadā* (dated from the time of conception). A novitiate desiring the full *upasaṃpadā* must also have parental permission, be free of debt and contagious diseases, and – where applicable – be exempt from military service.

The ordination of monks is said to have been started by the Buddha himself. According to tradition, the Buddha conferred ordination upon those who asked for it and whom he perceived were ready with the simple comment, "*Ehi bhikkhu!* (Come monk!)", "*Ehi bhikkhuṇī!* (Come nun!)" or, more fully, "Come monk, the *Dharma* is well proclaimed; live the holy life for the complete ending of suffering."[1]

With this simple formula, a person was admitted to the *sangha* (community), where he was given the necessary instructions. As the number of his followers grew, and the Buddha started to travel more in order to spread his teachings, it became increasingly difficult for him to personally give ordination to those who wished it. This task was therefore taken on by appointed disciples. It was not until after his death that the two-part ordination came into being, and a more formal ordination ceremony was introduced.

The requirements for both levels of ordination have evolved over time, together with the code of conduct (S. *prātimoksha,* Pa. *pātimokkha*), which is laid down in more extensive detail in the *Vinaya Piṭaka* of the Pali canon. As well as the rules of conduct concerning monastic life, the *pātimokkha* includes rules of etiquette, dress and demeanour to be observed that are intended to be conducive to harmony both within the monastery and in relationships with the laity.

The rules are arranged in categories according to the penalties incurred for various infringements. The *pātimokkha* is made up of a core of around 150 primary rules, but the diversification of Buddhism into various schools and ordination lineages has led to differences between the minor rules. In Southeast Asia, there are 227 rules for *Theravāda* monks and, before the decline of women's lineages, there were 311 for nuns. Tibetan monks observe the 258 rules (354 for nuns) rules laid down in the *Mūlasarvāstivāda Vinaya,* while the *Dharmaguptaka Vinaya,* observed by Chinese and Korean monks, lays down 250 rules for monks (348 for nuns). Fully ordained monks and nuns come together from two to six times during the month (depending on the school and the culture) on *uposatha* days to recite the *pātimokkha.* Since the rules are different for men and women, they do this separately.

Ordination is essentially the same in both *Theravāda* and *Mahāyāna* Buddhism. In the East Asian *Mahāyāna* tradition, however, a monk or nun follows the higher ordination *(upasaṃpadā)* by taking the *bodhisattva* vows detailed in the *Brahmā Net Sūtra,* in which the *bodhisattva* vows to postpone his own entry into *nirvāṇa* until all other sentient beings have attained enlightenment. This is known as *bodhisattva-upasaṃpadā.* In Japan, the *bodhisattva* vows have completely supplanted the *pātimokkha.*

The rules of the *pātimokkha* are only observed by monks and nuns who have received the higher ordination. For the *pravrajya,* the novice repeats the formula of the triple gem *(triratna)* or three refuges *(trisharaṇa)* three times, and vows to follow the ten precepts of good conduct *(dasha-shīla).* His (or her) head is shaved and the novitiate is presented with three robes *(chīvara)* and a begging bowl *(piṇḍapātra)* as the outward symbols of the new status. The ten precepts are:

1. Not to harm living beings.
2. Not to take what is not given.
3. Not to be unchaste.

4. Not to lie or speak ill.
5. Not to permit the mind to become clouded by intoxicants.
6. Not to sing, dance, play music, or attend entertainment programmes.
7. Not to wear perfume, cosmetics, ornaments, *etc.* to beautify the body.
8. Not to sit on raised chairs or to sleep on luxurious beds.
9. Not to eat at the wrong time (*i.e.* after midday).
10. Not to handle gold, silver, precious objects, or money.

Originally, *pravrajya* was understood literally, and the novitiate 'went forth' as a mendicant: but with the passage of time the practice has been abandoned. After his ordination, he or she is assigned a teacher *(āchārya)* and a preceptor *(upādhyāya),* but continues to live a normal daily life, although some choose to live in the monastery for some time. The purpose of 'going forth' is to turn the mind away from thoughts of the world of the material senses, and to focus it on the quest for enlightenment. It may not be an easy life, but neither is so-called normal life. As the Buddha says:

> Renunciation *(pabbajjā)* is difficult: it is difficult to enjoy it;
> Difficult, too, is the life of a householder;
> It is painful to live with those who are unsympathetic.
> Suffering befalls the wanderer (in *saṃsāra*).
> Therefore, be not such a wanderer, be not a pursuer of suffering.
>
> *Dhammapada 21:13; cf. DPN, DPR*

It is only those who receive *upasampadā* who are obliged to be bound by the *pātimokkha* rules. Although the monks of some Buddhist schools are permitted to marry in some countries (especially Japan, Korea, Taiwan, and China), the general rule is that a monk who has received *upasaṃpadā* should remain celibate. However, Buddhist ordination and vows are not regarded as a lifelong commitment, and a person can decide at any time to relinquish their life as a monk, a nun or a novitiate, and return to normal society. They may also return to monastic life, starting once again with the first level of ordination. Theoretically, leaving the order should be without any sense of betraying a religious obligation, but in practice human feelings are likely to be evident in both the one who is leaving and the remaining members of the order. However, there is less stigma attached to a *Theravāda* monk or nun who leaves the order than there is in the *Mahāyāna* tradition.

The simple ceremony is similar in all Buddhist traditions:

> Ordination, in Buddhism, is initiation into the Buddhist order *(sangha)* in the presence of witnesses *(i.e.* members of the *sangha),* and self-dedication to monastic life.... It is not necessarily lifelong or unrepeatable. There are two kinds of Buddhist ordination: the lower,

by which a man becomes a *sāmaṇera* or novice; the higher, by which a novice becomes a monk *(bhikkhu)*. The more formal ceremony for admission of a novice who intends to become a monk subsequently consists of a candidate being brought before a chapter of at least ten monks, headed by an abbot or senior monk of at least ten years' standing, and taking part in a set form for the ordaining of novices and monks. This is held in the sanctuary *(vihāra)*.

The candidate kneels, and asks for admission as a novice, handing to the abbot two yellow robes in which he is to be ordained. The abbot then formally presents these robes to him, reminding him of the frailty and impermanence of the human body which they are to cover. The candidate receives them, and retires to put them on; as he does so he recites a formula reminding himself that his robes are worn as protection against cold and heat and to cover nakedness, and that he wears them in all humility, for use and not for ornament. He then returns, makes obeisance, and asks to have administered to him the three refuges and ten precepts. Having received them from the abbot, repeating them sentence by sentence, he makes obeisance, seeks forgiveness by his brethren of all faults, and declares his wish to share with his brethren any merit he has gained.

The *sāmaṇera* spends his time in a monastery learning the life of the *sangha,* helping with daily chores, *etc.* He does not attend recitation, twice monthly, of *pātimokkha;* this is attended only by *bhikkhus.*

When a novice subsequently seeks higher ordination *(upasampadā)* as a monk, he first goes through the form for the ordination of a novice again; this is then followed by a further and longer ceremony of ordination in the course of which a candidate must be able to answer satisfactorily a list of questions concerning his status and condition (whether he is free from disease, debt, obligation to serve in the military, is twenty years of age, *etc.*). He is presented by one of his two tutors. On this occasion, the three robes, including a stole, are presented. These are then ceremonially returned to him by the abbot. An address is then given by the abbot or president, in which the new *bhikkhu* is reminded of the glory of the life of a *bhikkhu,* and of the high moral standards which must now be his, and the chaste, honest, peaceable, and humble life he must live.

Ordinations are held at any time of the year except the three months of *Vassa* (the rainy season retreat). The actual date is agreed upon in consultation with the abbot of the monastery where the ordination is to be carried out, which is usually in the man's home village. A favourite time is just before *Vassa,* since it is the *Vassa* period alone which is reckoned in counting years of service as a monk.

"Ordination," Dictionary of Buddhism, DBGT p.200

The going forth of the Buddha has been subject to the accretions of legend, and there is little or no historical evidence as to what actually happened. Later versions of the story tend to be more ornate than the earlier. A poetic account of his going forth is related in the *Pabbajjā Sutta* of the *Sutta Nipāta:*

> I will describe the going forth *(pabbajjā):*
> how he, the one-with-vision, went forth,
> how he reasoned and chose the going forth *(pabbajjā).*
> "Household life is crowded, a realm of dust,
> while going forth *(pabbajjā)* is the open air."
> Seeing this, he went forth.
>
> On going forth *(pabbajjā),* he avoided evil deeds in body.
> Abandoning verbal misconduct,
> he purified his livelihood.
> Then he, the Buddha, went to Rājagaha,
> the mountain fortress of the Magadhāns,
> and wandered for alms,
> endowed with all the foremost marks.
> King Bimbisāra, standing in his palace, saw him,
> and on seeing him, consummate in marks, said:
> "Look at this one, sirs.
> How handsome, stately, pure!
> How consummate his demeanour!
> Mindful, his eyes downcast,
> looking only a plough-length before him,
> as one who's not from a lowly lineage:
> Send the royal messengers at once
> to see where this monk will go."
>
> They – the messengers dispatched –
> followed behind him.
> "Where will this monk go?
> Where will his dwelling place be?"
> As he went from house to house –
> well restrained, his sense doors guarded,
> mindful, alert – his bowl filled quickly.
> Then he, the sage, completing his alms round,
> left the city, headed for Mount Pāṇḍava.
>
> "That's where his dwelling will be."
> Seeing him go to his dwelling place,
> three messengers sat down,
> while one returned to tell the king.

"That monk, your majesty, on the flank of Pāṇḍava,
sits like a tiger, a bull, a lion in a mountain cleft."

Hearing the messenger's words, the noble warrior king
straight away went by royal coach, out to Mount Pāṇḍava.
Going as far as the coach would go,
he got down, went up on foot, and on arrival sat down.
Sitting there, he exchanged courteous greetings, then said:
"You are young, youthful, in the first stage of youth,
endowed with the stature and colouring of a noble warrior.
You would look glorious in the vanguard of an army,
arrayed with an elephant squadron.
I offer you wealth: enjoy it.
I ask your birth: inform me."

"Straight ahead, your majesty, by the foothills of the Himalayas,
is a country consummate in energy and wealth,
inhabited by Kosalans – solar by clan, Shakyans by birth.
It is from that lineage that I have gone forth,
but not in search of sensual pleasures.
Seeing misery in sensual pleasures,
and happiness in renunciation,
I will go and exert myself.
That's where my heart delights."

Sutta Nipāta 3:1, Pabbajjā Sutta, PTSN pp.72–74, KNTB

See also: **bhikshu** (7.1), **parivrāja** (7.1), **pravrajita** (7.1), **upasaṃpadā**.

1. *Vinaya Piṭaka, Mahāvagga* 1:6, in *LBBN* p.45.

sachchā saudā (H/Pu) *Lit.* true *(sachchā)* merchandise *(saudā);* true bargain, true trade; mystically, exchanging attachment to the world for attachment to the divine Name or creative power within. Metaphorically, the soul is understood as a trader who comes to this world to buy goods or merchandise. Some 'buy' things of the world; but only the 'merchandise' of the creative power is of lasting, eternal value, all else is transitory:

How rare are those who obtain the true merchandise *(sachchā saudā):*
meeting the perfect true *guru,* one meets with the Lord.

Guru Nānak, Ādi Granth 1036, AGK

The true merchandise *(sachchā saudā)* is the Lord's Name:
this is the true trade.

Under *guru*'s instruction, we trade in the Lord's Name:
its value is very great.
The value of this true trade is very great:
those who are engaged in the true trade *(sachchā saudā)*
are very fortunate.

Guru Amardās, Ādi Granth 570, AGK

The perfect masters are also known as merchants who deal in the true merchandise of the divine Name.

According to a traditional Sikh story, the father of the future Guru Nānak gave his son a sum of money to make a good bargain. His son, however, spent the money in the service of *sādhus* (holy men). In return, his father, not realizing the greatness of his son, administered a few slaps, unaware that the true bargain in this world is to serve the saints in whatever way is possible. By this means, true spiritual benefit is acquired. The actions of the young *guru*-to-be are known as the *sachchā saudā,* the true bargain.

See also: **banjārā** (7.1), **merchant** (7.1).

seal, seal of baptism, seal of Christ, seal of God, seal of Truth (Gk. *sphragis*) A mark or a stamp impressed on wax and used to seal a letter or document, especially in ancient times, and acting as a mark of personal endorsement, authentication and authority; a metallic finger ring or an arm bracelet, engraved with a personal design, with which an individual could seal a letter, a container or any other document with wax, and stamp it with his or her own personal mark or sign; metaphorically, baptism, initiation or acceptance of a disciple by a prophet or spiritual master; also used in various other metaphorical contexts.

The term is used in early Middle Eastern literature from both pre- and post-Christian times, as in *Isaiah:*

I bind up this testimony,
seal this instruction in the heart of my disciples.

Isaiah 8:16; cf. JB, NJB

The first-century Alexandrian Jew Philo Judaeus speaks of the divine Word as the "seal of God" that gives the soul its being:

> Our great Moses likened the nature of the noetic soul to no created thing, but has pronounced it to be genuine coinage of that divine and invisible Being, stamped and impressed with the seal *(sphragis)* of God, the stamp of which is the eternal Word *(Logos).*
>
> *Philo Judaeus, On Planting 2:5; cf. PCW3 pp.222–23, WPJ1 p.420*

He also says that the "Word *(Logos)* of the Creator is the seal *(sphragis)* by which every existent thing has received its form".[1]

In early Christian literature, being "sealed" or receiving the gift of the "seal" referred to baptism "in the name of the Father, Son, and Holy Ghost", and many writers have made use of the metaphor. Paul speaks of being "sealed with the Holy Spirit":[2]

> After you believed, you were sealed with that Holy Spirit of promise, which is the guarantee of our inheritance.
>
> *Ephesians 1:13–14; cf. KJV*

The late-first-century Clement of Rome instructs the recipients of his letters to "keep the seal of baptism pure".[3] A mid-second-century text, the *Shepherd of Hermas,* speaks throughout of those who had "received the seal *(sphragis)*".[4] Clement of Alexandria (*c.*150–215) writes of the "mystery of the seal *(sphragis)*".[5] The fourth-century Ephraim Syrus frequently uses the expression in his hymns,[6] often in reference to Jesus' observations in *John* that the shepherd (the saviour) knows his sheep (the disciples),[7] because of the mark or seal upon them. The custom of marking animals with the owner's seal is an ancient custom, as the gnostic Theodotus observes:

> Dumb animals show by a seal whose property each is, and are claimed from the seal. Thus also the faithful soul receives the seal of Truth, and bears upon it the marks of Christ.
>
> *Excerpts from Theodotus, ETCA pp.90–91*

Although baptism was a gift that was highly sought after, it was not conferred simply by the asking. In the *Acts of Paul,* a devotee, eager to receive the "seal of Christ", is told to be patient:

> Thecla said, "Only give me the seal of Christ, and temptation shall not touch me."
>
> And Paul said, "Have patience, Thecla, and you will receive the water."
>
> *Acts of Paul 2:25; cf. ANT p.277*

Receiving the "water" presumably refers to immersion or sprinkling with water, a symbol of the Living Water of the Word. Again in the *Acts of Paul,* the writer describes the baptism of a certain Hermocratēs, saying:

> And in that hour he (Hermocratēs) was whole, and received the grace of the seal in the Lord, he and his wife.
>
> *Acts of Paul 3; cf. ANT p.282*

Likewise, in the *Acts of Peter,* the author tells the story of the eagerness for baptism of a certain Theon:

> Now when there was a calm upon the ship in Hadria (the Adriatic), Theon pointed it out to Peter, saying unto him: "If you consider me worthy, whom you might baptize with the seal of the Lord, you have an opportunity now."
>
> *Acts of Peter 3:5; cf. ANT p.308*

In the *Acts of Thomas,* a woman begs Judas Thomas for baptism, with the further observation that this baptism or "seal" will protect her from the "Enemy (devil)":

> And the woman besought him, saying: "O apostle of the Most High, give me the seal, that the Enemy should not return again to me." Then he caused her to come near him, and laid his hands upon her and sealed her in the name of the Father and the Son and the Holy Ghost, and many others also were sealed with her.
>
> *Acts of Thomas 49, ANT p.388*

The indication of group baptisms is not infrequent in the apocryphal literature. In the *Clementine Homilies,*[8] which concerns the mission of Peter, the apostle takes several days to baptize applicants in groups, suggesting that baptism included instruction and consisted of more than a simple ritual.

Compared to other gnostic and apocryphal texts, the *Acts of Thomas* probably has more references than any other to the receiving of the seal, and the details of these stories and the discourses of Judas Thomas at those times also reveal something of the true nature of baptism. There is, for example, a long story concerning the yearning of a certain Mygdonia for baptism. Mygdonia is the wife of Charisius, a "kinsman of the king" Misdaeus. Early on in the story, having heard the teaching of Judas Thomas, she comes and prostrates herself before the apostle, begging that, through baptism, God "may dwell in me". She prays

> that the compassion of the God whom you preach may come upon me, and I may become His dwelling place and be joined in prayer and hope and faith in Him, and I also may receive the seal, and become a holy temple, and He may dwell in me.
>
> *Acts of Thomas 87; cf. ANT p.403*

Later on, Judas is imprisoned by king Misdaeus and is awaiting execution, but Mygdonia has not yet received her baptism. She is beginning to get frantic and to make matters worse, Charisius is not at all sympathetic to his wife's spiritual aspirations. She therefore has to wait until her husband is asleep at night before she can go to Judas Thomas.

By bribing the guards, visitors are able to see the apostle, but while Mygdonia is on her way to the jail, Judas Thomas appears before her in "great light" – in a spiritual form. In the story, she does not recognize him, taking him for one of the "rulers" of the inner heavens, and turning aside, she feels that she has now lost her chance of receiving initiation:

> Charisius ... went to sleep: but she (Mygdonia) took ten denarii to give them to the jailers that she might gain access to the apostle. But on the way Judas Thomas came and met her, and she saw him and was afraid, for she thought that he was one of the rulers: for a great light went before him. And she said to herself as she fled: "I have lost you, O my unhappy soul! For you will not again see Judas, the apostle of Jesus, the living God, and you have not yet received the holy seal."
>
> *Acts of Thomas 118; cf. ANT p.417*

Judas Thomas, however, in his physical form, then comes to her and she falls upon the ground in fright. But the apostle takes her by the hand, lifts her up, and comforts her.[9] The story, like many others in the *Acts of Thomas,* is full of allegorical meanings. Mygdonia is raised from the earth; Jesus has released Judas Thomas from prison (this world), and so on. Mygdonia then asks for the gift of baptism:

> And Mygdonia said: "Give me the seal of Jesus Christ and let me receive the gift by your hands before you depart from life."
>
> *Acts of Thomas 120; cf. ANT p.417*

And the apostle obliges, saying: "You have received your seal: receive for yourself eternal life."[10] The attainment of eternity is thus specifically linked to the receipt of the "seal" of initiation. Mygdonia is naturally overjoyed to receive the gift and later, at her home, Charisius comes to Mygdonia's room to find her giving thanks to

> God, who for love of man and for pity
> came down to our littleness;
> God who sought us out when we knew Him not;
> God who dwells in the heights
> and from whom the depths are not hid.
>
> *Acts of Thomas 123; cf. ANT p.419*

The "seal" is that of baptism or initiation from God "who came down to our littleness" in the form of the saviour, who "sought us out when we knew him not".

Gnostic literature also contains many references to spiritual baptism or initiation as the seal. Speaking of those who have been "regenerated by Christ", the gnostic Theodotus writes that he who has been "sealed" is beyond the scope of all lesser powers in creation:

> They die to the world but live to God.... For he who has been sealed by Father, Son and Holy Spirit is beyond the threats of every other power, and by these three Names has been released from... mortality.
>
> *Excerpts from Theodotus; cf. ETCA pp.88–89*

Some texts, such as the *Pistis Sophia* and the two *Books of Jeu,* speak of multiple seals received by an initiate. These seals are generally depicted as mystic passwords, so to speak, that permit the soul access to the various heavenly realms. In the *Second Book of Jeu,* the "living Jesus" associates this "great seal" and the "great Name" with the "Five Trees". From them, the soul will receive the "mystery" or divine knowledge which they possess, "which is the great mystery" – the greatest knowledge and initiation of all:

> You will go into their interior
> to the rank of the Five Trees of the treasury of the Light,
> which are the unmoved (eternal) Trees.
> They will give to you their mystery,
> which is the great mystery, and their great seal,
> and the great Name of the treasury of the Light,
> which is ruler (king) over the treasury of the Light.
>
> *Second Book of Jeu 119:50, BC pp.166–67*

The soul will receive the "great seal" of the "great Name", the Word of the "treasury of light", the eternal realm of God.

The term is again found among the Manichaean texts, especially the Coptic. The Coptic *Kephalaia* mentions the "seal of Truth" that is given to novices.[11] One of the Coptic psalms speaks of the "seals" that build a spiritual "treasure in the heavens" with God, and which protect the soul from the "demons" of the mind that constitute the "goad of error", the beguiling web of illusion. The psalmist speaks of

> these sure seals that are upon you are your kin, O soul,
> by reason of which no demon can touch you;
> For you have rightly worshipped
> him who has broken the goad of error;
> You have laid up your treasure in the heavens.
>
> *Manichaean Psalm Book CCXLV; cf. MPB p.52*

Another psalm describes the cosmic master, the "perfect man", as having come "into the midst of the world" so that the soul may become part of him, sealed with the seal of spiritual baptism and drawn to the Light:

> Lo, the perfect man is stretched out in the midst of the world
> that you may walk in him and receive your unfading garlands. . . .
> Lo, the righteous one will enlighten you. . . .
> Walk, therefore, in joy, drawn to the land of light,
> sealed with your seal and with your unfading garlands.
> Walk also in gladness: your sufferings have passed today;
> Lo, the harbour of peace – you have moored in it.
>
> *Manichaean Psalm Book; cf. MPB p.163*

In another psalm, the soul is called back to God by the mediator – the cosmic or inner master – after having received the "holy seal" from the *Nous,* the divine Intelligence in creation:

> Jesus the dawn and the paraclete-spirit –
> they have summoned you, O soul,
> that you may ascend by it to the Height.
> Receive the holy seal from the *Nous,* . . .
> and fulfil the commandments.
>
> *Manichaean Psalm Book CCXXVII; cf. MPB p.22*

Being "sealed" with the "seal" are very common metaphors for baptism in the Mandaean literature. Here, the "Jordan" is the "Living Water" of the divine Word:

> I am secured and sealed, . . .
> I . . . and these souls who enter into the Jordan
> will be sealed by the seal of the mighty sublime Life.
>
> *Mandaean Prayer Book 15; cf. CPM p.11*

Just as bundles of letters or ancient documents were "bound and sealed", so too, says another poem, are souls sealed by and bound to the Divine. *Bihram* the Great, elsewhere described as "Son of the Mighty One",[12] is one of the mythical saviours of the Mandaean pantheon:

> Bound and sealed are these souls who went down to the Jordan,
> and were baptized in the name of the Great Life (God).
> They have been baptized with the baptism of *Bihram* the Great.
> Their souls have been secured with bonds of righteousness,
> and with the bonds of *Zhir,* the great light of Life.
>
> *Mandaean Prayer Book 26, CPM pp.22–23*

The metaphor of a seal has been used in a variety of other contexts. In a verse commonly quoted by later writers, Christian and Jewish, the writer of the *Song of Songs* uses the expression in the concluding poem when the Beloved urges the soul to engrave his love and presence in her whole being:

> Set me like a seal *(ḥotam)* on your heart,
> like a seal *(ḥotam)* on your arm.
>
> *Song of Songs 8:6, JB*

In John's gospel, Jesus also uses the expression for his appointment by God:

> Labour not for the meat that perishes, but for that meat which endures unto eternal life, which the Son of Man shall give unto you: for him has God the Father sealed.
>
> *John 6:27; cf. KJV*

See also: **five seals, sealed on the forehead**.

1. Philo Judaeus, *On Flight and Finding* 2; *cf. PCW5* pp.16–17, *WPJ2* p.196.
2. See also *2 Corinthians* 1:22; *Ephesians* 4:30.
3. *2 Clement* 7:6, 8:6; *cf. AF1* pp.138–41.
4. *Shepherd of Hermas* 8:6.3, 9:16.3–7, 9:17.4, 9:31.1, 4, *AF2* pp.204–5, 262–65, 292–93.
5. Clement of Alexandria, *Miscellanies* 5:11, *WCA2* p.265.
6. Ephraim Syrus, *Hymns on the Nativity* 18:6; *For the Epiphany* 3:1*ff.*, 4:1, 5:2, *passim, HEDA* pp.259, 269–72.
7. *John* 10:3–5, 15–16.
8. *Clementine Homilies* III:73, *CH* p.89.
9. *Acts of Thomas* 119; *cf. ANT* p.417.
10. *Acts of Thomas* 121; *cf. ANT* p.418.
11. *Kephalaia* 56, 90, *KOT* pp.150, 233.
12. *Mandaean Prayer Book* 18, 22, 24, 104; *cf. CPM* pp.14, 18, 21, 103.

sealed on the forehead An extension of the term 'seal', which is a metaphor for baptism and initiation; also called the gift, the mark, and the sign. Since it is commonly said that a person's destiny is written on their forehead, being sealed on the forehead implies that baptism is pre-ordained. It may also imply that baptism is an essentially spiritual affair, the soul or spirit being 'located' in the head, especially in the forehead.

The expression is used primarily in Christian literature. The fourth-century Ephraim Syrus writes in a baptismal exhortation:

> You have been baptized in water; you have put on the name of Christ; the seal of the Lord is upon your person, and His stamp is upon your forehead. See that you do not become another's, for you have no other Lord.
>
> *Ephraim Syrus, Homilies 2:2; cf. HEDA p.330*

In the *Acts of John,* when about to perform a baptism in Jesus' name, the apostle says: "I will place a seal upon (what is) between your eyes."[1] Likewise, the *Second Book of Jeu* relates:

> Jesus... baptized all his disciples with the baptism of the Holy Spirit. And he gave to them the gift. He sealed their foreheads with the seal... which made them to be numbered within the inheritance of the kingdom of the light.
>
> And the disciples rejoiced with very great joy because they had received the baptism of the Holy Spirit, and the seal that forgave sins and purified iniquities and made them to be numbered among the inheritance of the kingdom of the Light.
>
> *Second Book of Jeu 113–14:47; cf. BC pp.154–57*

Here, sealing their foreheads is specifically equated with "baptism of the Holy Spirit", the "gift", the "seal which forgave sins and which purified", and "being numbered among the inheritance of the kingdom of the light". All these expressions are used in reference to spiritual baptism.

The expression is found even in clearly mythological texts. The *Acts of Andrew and Matthias,* for example, relates a story in which some of the apostles are attacked by devils:

> And one of the devils said: "Now we will kill you like your master, whom Herod slew."... But they saw the seal on his forehead and were afraid.
>
> *Acts of Andrew and Matthias 26–27; cf. ANT p.457*

The expression does not always refer to baptism *per se.* In the *Odes of Solomon,* the saviour indicates that his chosen souls are sealed on their foreheads even before they came into existence. This would imply that such souls were 'sealed' or marked for this destiny even before they received baptism:

> For I turn not my face away from those that are mine,
> because I know them.
> Before they came into being, I knew them,
> and on their foreheads, I set my seal.
>
> *Odes of Solomon 8:14–15, OSD p.40*

The same implication of the saviour coming for his chosen ones appears in another verse:

And I heard their voices,
and I treasured their faith in my heart,
and I sealed my Name upon their foreheads.
For they are free (or 'noble') men, and they are mine.

Odes of Solomon 42:19–20, OSD p.178

Likewise, in the *Book of Revelation,* in a passage purporting to foretell the end of the world, although baptism would again be implied, the expression refers to those who will be saved:

I saw four angels standing at the four corners of the earth,
restraining the four winds of the earth,
that the wind should not blow upon the earth,
nor upon the sea, nor against any tree.
And I saw another angel ascending from rising of the sun,
having the seal of the living God:
And he cried with a loud voice to the four angels,
to whom was given power over the earth and the sea,
saying, "Harm not the earth, neither the sea, nor the trees,
till we have sealed the servants of our God on their foreheads."
And I heard the number of those who were sealed:
a hundred and forty-four thousand
out of all the tribes of the children of Israel;
And from the tribe of Judah were sealed twelve thousand.

Book of Revelation 7:1–5; cf. KJV

The writer goes on in a similar vein to list the "sealing" of twelve thousand souls from each of the twelve tribes of Israel – a belief prevalent among some of the early Judaic Christians. Elsewhere, he again speaks of this "hundred and forty-four thousand having his Father's Name written in their foreheads".[2]

The expression is greatly favoured by the author of *Revelations.* Later on, he describes with some relish the horrors to be meted out to the unbaptized on the expected Day of Judgment – to "those men who do not have the seal of God on their foreheads":

And the sun and the air were darkened
by reason of the smoke of the pit.
And there came out of the smoke locusts upon the earth:
and unto them was given power,
as the scorpions of the earth have power.

And they were commanded not to hurt
the grass of the earth, nor any green thing, nor any tree,
But only those men who do not have
the seal of God on their foreheads.

Book of Revelation 9:2–4; cf. KJV

Vividly painted apocalypses of this nature are fairly commonplace in the ancient literature, especially of Judaism, and the tradition was carried forward for some time into early Christianity. The recipe of torture, fire, plagues and destruction all follow a similar pattern, repeating and copying each other in apocalyptic zeal.

See also: **dhur karam, five seals, seal.**

1. *Acts of John, AAA* p.37.
2. *Book of Revelation* 14:1; *cf. KJV.*

second birth See **born again.**

shaktipāt(a) (S/H) *Lit.* alighting *(pāta)* of spiritual energy *(shakti);* the descent of power, the descent of spiritual energy; the transmission of spiritual energy from *guru* to disciple by means of a look, thought or touch, and generally including the giving of a *mantra;* initiation into the *siddha* tradition, at which time *shakti kuṇḍalinī* is said to be infused into a disciple by the *guru.* At that time, the *kuṇḍalinī* is awakened in the *mūlādhāra chakra* at the base of the spine, and rises up the spine in the *sushumṇā,* the central *nāḍī* (channel) of *prāṇa* (subtle life energy). This awakening of the *kuṇḍalinī* is experienced by disciples in a variety of ways, both in experiences within their own consciousness, as well as in the spontaneous adoption of physical *āsanas* and *mudrās* (postures).

Shaktipāta is bestowed by the grace of the *guru,* and cannot be demanded. It can be transmitted in person, at a distance, or even through an object such as a flower, a letter, or even a telephone call.[1] When Ramakrishna initiated Narendranāth Datta (later to be Swami Vivekananda), he placed his foot upon him, plunging his young disciple into deep *samādhi* (blissful inner absorption).

The disciple must also be receptive to the inflow of spiritual energy, since it cannot be forcibly imposed. By this means, the initiate is accepted into the spiritual family of the *guru.* A number of recent *gurus,* such as Swami Muktananda (1908–1982), Osho (1931–1990), and Swami Lakshman Jee Raina (1907–1991), have used the expression for their form of initiation.

These paths are all associated with various kinds of tantric *yoga* involving the raising of the *kuṇḍalinī.* They are also associated with Kashmir Shaivism, a tantric system dating back to at least the early ninth century CE, in which everything is regarded as a manifestation of consciousness, and the goal is union with the divine Power *(Shiva).*

Swami Muktananda describes the experience of his initiation by his *guru,* Swami Nityananda:

> August 15th 1947.... He (Nityananda) stood directly in front of me. He looked into my eyes once more. I watched him very attentively. A ray of light was coming from his pupils and going right inside me. Its touch was searing, red hot, and its brilliance dazzled my eyes like a high-powered bulb. As this ray flowed from Bhagawān Nityananda's eyes into my own, the very hair on my body rose in wonder, awe, ecstasy, and fear. I went on repeating his *mantra "Guru Aum",* watching the colours of this ray. It was an unbroken stream of divine radiance. Sometimes it was the colour of molten gold, sometimes saffron, sometimes a deep blue, more lustrous than a shining star. I stood there, stunned, watching the brilliant rays passing into me. My body was completely motionless.... He sat down and, in his aphoristic way, said, "All *mantras* are one.... All are *Aum. Aum Namah Shivāya Aum* – should be *Shivo'ham* (I am *Shiva*). *Shiva, Shiva* should be *Shivo'ham.* It should be repeated inside. Inside is much better than outside."
>
> *Swami Muktananda, Play of Consciousness, PCCV pp.73–75*

In his book, *Kashmir Shaivism,* Swami Lakshman Jee speaks of seven degrees of *shaktipāta* that are received by disciples depending upon the intensity of their spiritual aspiration and the grace of *Shiva* and the *guru.* Here, *shaktipāta* is understood as divine grace. The seven degrees range from *tīvra-tīvra-shaktipāta* (super-supreme *shaktipāta*), which is the grace of *Shiva,* which is bestowed without the intervention of a *guru,* and results in immediate liberation of the soul and union with *Shiva.* The intensity of the grace is such that the physical body dies, and soul becomes a *siddha,* dwelling in *siddhaloka,* from where he bestows grace directly into the heart of deserving aspirants in the material world.

Madhya-tīvra-shaktipāta (medium supreme *shaktipāta*) is the grace received by someone who desires, seeks and finds an enlightened *guru,* receiving initiation and instruction from him. In time, he reaches enlightenment, but during his life in this world he is not totally absorbed in that higher state. Only after death does he attain permanent union with *Shiva.*

Tīvra-manda-shaktipāta (supreme inferior *shaktipāta*) is the grace received by a person who yearns to meet a realized and enlightened *guru.* Instruction is not required – a touch, a look or simply being in the presence of the *guru* is sufficient to trigger an intense spiritual awakening and state of illumination.

Other degrees of *shaktipāta* are received by disciples who seek a *guru,* but retain some worldly desires after initiation. They find liberation only after a post-death period in some heavenly realm, or in their next incarnation, or after many future incarnations.[2]

See also: **siddha** (7.1).

1. John Dupuche, *Abhinavagupta, AKRT* pp.131, 154–55.
2. Swami Lakshman Jee, *Kashmir Shaivism, KSSL* pp.66–70.

shinpyu (Burmese) *Lit.* to make one *(pyu)* a novice *(shin);* a Burmese term for a ceremony common in Southeast Asian *Theravāda* Buddhism for ordaining or initiating a boy who is younger than twenty years old, marking his transition into manhood; also transliterated as *shinbyu.* The ordination is not binding, and since comparatively few go on to become monks in adult life, *shinpyu* is also known as temporary ordination.

Customs vary from country to country, but in all cases it must happen before marriage, and in Myanmar, the age of the boy can be anywhere between five and fifteen, though normally between nine and twelve. According to common belief, the entire family of a boy who receives *shinpyu* earns great merit. The occasion, marked by significant festivities, fanfare and ritual, is cause for great celebration and family pride, and the initial festivities are generally held in a public place, often preceded by a parade through the streets on decorated horses or cars. Some *shinpyus* may be associated with charity feasts.

After these celebrations, the boys return home, change into simpler clothes, and in the late afternoon they go to the monastery. Here, they make their request (in the ancient Pali language) to be accepted as novitiates. Their heads are then shaved, and the religious part of the ceremony is performed. After the ceremony, they remain in the monastery for seven days, following the monastic rules and studying Buddhist scriptures under the care of the monks. Although the ceremony is primarily for boys, girls (usually sisters of the boys) have their own ceremony in which they have their ears pierced while the boys are at the monastery.

In Thailand, where a similar custom is followed, the young novitiate is normally required to spend at least one rainy season in the monastery. Allowing the boy to spend this time in a monastery is regarded as the greatest religious gift that parents can give to their child, and it is thought to have a lasting effect on the boy's life.

Because of the merit and social status associated with the ceremony, parents like at least one boy to receive *shinpyu.* Those who have no boys of their own will often arrange the ordination of a boy from a family who cannot afford the ceremony. Sometimes as many as a thousand wealthy people will group together to sponsor the ordination of a number of such boys.

The tradition is said to be based on the story of Rāhula, son of the Buddha, who received novice ordination from his father at the age of seven. According to legend, the Buddha visited his home at the request of his father King Shuddhodana. Taking advantage of the opportunity, Yashodharā, the Buddha's wife before his enlightenment, sent her son to his father in order to claim his worldly inheritance. But instead of giving the boy material wealth, the Buddha gave him temporary ordination.

shŏudù (C) *Lit.* first *(shŏu)* time *(dù);* ordination as a Daoist monk. See **dù**.

sign, sign of Life, sign of the Jordan Mystic baptism into the divine Word; also, in Christianity, the cross. Baptism as "receiving the (pure) sign", being "signed with the sign of Life" or the "sign of the Jordan" are commonly used expressions in Mandaean literature. The "sign" would seem to refer to the Word itself, though it is generally used only in the context of baptism, and often carries the connotation of receiving an identifiable 'mark' or 'seal', other expressions used for baptism.

A Mandaean prayer, for instance, speaks of being baptized and receiving the pure sign by entering the "Jordan", which symbolizes the Living Water of the Word:

> Let every man whose strength enables him
> and who loves his soul, come and enter the Jordan
> and be baptized and receive the pure sign,
> put on robes of radiant light.
>
> *Mandaean Prayer Book 18; cf. CPM p.13*

Another prayer maintains that the sins of those who have received such baptism are also forgiven by the saviour, who is the "forgiver of sins". The "Name of Truth" or True Name is a term for the divine Word:

> On the day that light arises,
> darkness returns to its place.
> The forgiver of sins, trespasses, follies,
> stumblings and mistakes will remit them,
> for those who love his Name of Truth,

and for those souls who went down to the Jordan,
were baptized and received the pure sign.

Mandaean Prayer Book 31; cf. CPM p.28

In another prayer, the saviour directly addresses the baptized souls as "men who have received the sign", advising them not to be influenced by the desires and the ways of worldly folk:

To you do I call, and you do I teach:
men who have received the sign.
Hearken not to the talk of all peoples and generations;
Let not their stumblings cause you to stumble,
stumble not because of their stumblings!

Mandaean Prayer Book 89, CPM p.92

In another, the saviour says that he will collect all the souls of his spiritual family, the "sons of my sign", and return with them to eternity. Here, "Life" is a Mandaean term for God:

Betimes I will come and will fly
and will reach the sons of my Name, the sons of my sign,
and the sons of the great family of Life.
I will bind you together into the bundle of Life,
and I will build you into a great building of Truth,
and will bring you forth to the great place of light,
and to the everlasting abode.

Mandaean Prayer Book 76, CPM p.80

Other prayers speak of those who have been "signed with the sign of Life":

The souls of our fathers were signed with the sign of Life, and the Name of the Life, and the Name of *Manda-ḍ-Hiia* ('*Gnōsis* of Life') was pronounced over them.

Mandaean Prayer Book 49, CPM p.45

The *Alma Rishaia Rba* speaks of how the soul "looks yearningly towards its baptism so that it can breathe the Breath of Life and (be signed) with the sign of the Jordan".[1] Like the Living Water, the Breath of Life is again the divine creative power.

The *Alf Trisar Šuialia* ('Thousand and Twelve Questions') describes how souls leave this world, but, on reaching the boundaries of *mshunia kushṭa,* can proceed no further unless they have been initiated or "signed with the sign of the Jordan". *Mshunia kushṭa* is the Mandaean world of spiritual realities, *kushṭa* meaning 'truth' or 'reality', and *mshunia* meaning something like 'double', 'counterpart', or 'equivalent':

> As they depart, set forth and fly into the sky, traversing the road, they behold the gate of mercies which is opened in the midst of *mshunia kushṭa* and then they move onwards and sit at the boundary that bounds *mshunia kushṭa,* which no earthly being may cross unless signed with the sign of the Jordan, in which is Truth *(Kushṭa).* So there they wait, the spirit and soul, until they are taken up into worlds of light.
>
> *Thousand and Twelve Questions I:283; cf. TTQ p.189*

In Christian writings, the 'sign' generally refers to the sign of the cross, as a symbol of Christ's suffering for the forgiveness of human sin. By extension, in the early apocryphal texts, this became the sign of baptism, the mark or seal of Christ upon the soul, 'sign', 'seal' and even 'cross' sometimes being used interchangeably in translations. As Judas Thomas says in the *Acts of Thomas:*

> Come forth from the darkness,
> that the light may receive you!
> Come to him that is indeed good,
> that you may receive his grace,
> and implant his sign (cross) in your souls.
>
> *Acts of Thomas 28; cf. AAA p.168, ANT p.377*

See also: **seal**.

1. *Alma Rishaia Rba* 7:504–5; *cf. SA* p.78, *PNC* p.38.

sowing of the Seed An expression drawn from Jesus' parables of the sower, the tares, and the mustard seed. As Jesus himself explains, "The Seed is the Word of God,"[1] sown in the hearts of his followers. The sowing of the seed, therefore, refers to baptism in the divine Word. The remainder of the parable relates to the different kinds of disciple who are drawn to a master and receive the Seed of the Word. The parable is preserved in *Mark* and retold in *Matthew* and *Luke*. Jesus says:

> Behold, a sower went forth to sow; and when he sowed, some seeds fell by the wayside, and the fowls came and devoured them up. Some fell upon stony places, where they had not much earth; and forthwith they sprang up, because they had no depth of earth. And when the sun was up, they were scorched; and because they had no root, they

> withered away. And some fell among thorns; and the thorns sprang up and choked them. But other fell into good ground, and brought forth fruit, some a hundredfold, some sixtyfold, some thirtyfold. Whoever has ears to hear, let him hear.
>
> *Matthew 13:3–9; cf. KJV*

The story is a simple agricultural one, told to people who lived close to the land. The scene Jesus depicts would have been the common experience of any farmer at that time, perhaps even nowadays. When a farmer goes to sow, his main intention is to sow his seed in fertile, well-prepared land. Nevertheless, by the very nature of things, he has so much seed in his bundle that some of it falls in other places. Jesus then explains his parable:

> Hear therefore the parable of the sower. When anyone hears the Word of the kingdom, and understands it not, then comes the Wicked One, and catches away that which was sown in his heart. This is he who received seed by the wayside. And he who received the seed into stony places, the same is he who hears the Word, and anon with joy receives it. Yet he has no root in himself, but holds fast only for a while: for when tribulation or persecution arises because of the Word, by and by he is offended. He also who received seed among the thorns is he who hears the Word, but the concerns of this world, and the deceitfulness of riches, choke the Word, and he becomes unfruitful. But he who received seed into good ground is he who hears the Word, and understands it, and who also bears fruit, bringing forth, some a hundredfold, some sixty, some thirty.
>
> *Matthew 13:18–23; cf. KJV*

The seed is the Word, implying both the outer teachings as well as baptism in the divine Word, the sowing of the Word within the soul of the disciple. Jesus points out that many kinds of people come to a master and receive this baptism or initiation. Some hear the teachings but "understand it not" – they receive initiation almost incidentally, through the influence of relatives or friends, perhaps, but they do not really understand what has been given to them or what they have to do to make that seed bear fruit. And hardly have they been initiated than the "Wicked One" – Satan, in the form of all their negative tendencies – tempts them in various ways, and they are unable to resist. They go on living their lives as they always have done, and are swept away by the activities of physical existence and material pleasures.

The disciple whose seed falls on stony ground is immediately attracted and enthusiastic. But his sincerity is only superficial, and he remains on the path, practising his meditation only for so long as he is not put to the test.

As soon as troubles come, such as ridicule or antagonism from his family or community, he gives up the struggle. His sense of spiritual direction is easily deflected, and he falls away.

The one whose seed falls among thorns understands the mystic path and may even be in touch with the music of the Word within himself. Yet, he also has many material tendencies, perhaps lying dormant in his subconscious mind. Consequently, he is still deluded by wealth and by other concerns of this world, and even if he continues with his spiritual practice, his progress is hampered by his worldly and sensual desires. He therefore becomes unfruitful: he does not attain the spiritual treasure in this life.

But, naturally, the main purpose of the sower is to sow his seed in fertile ground where it will bear fruit. This is the disciple who hears the Word, and understands the spiritual path. Such disciples know what is required of them, are not overly distracted by their life in the world, and learn, increasingly, to keep everything in balance. They are the ones who get some results in their spiritual practice.

But even among these, they do not all bear the same fruit. Every disciple is carrying a different burden of sin, and it is the clearing of this load that determines their individual progress. Some have a lighter load, some a heavier load. Some may have been initiated in past lives and are just picking up the threads from their previous incarnation as a disciple. Others are just starting out upon the path, and may thus have more of a burden to clear.

As a result of these differences in their background, some will progress all the way back to God: they achieve a one hundred percent result. Some gain access to the heavenly regions, to a greater or lesser extent, but still have further to go before they can reach home. This they will slowly accomplish after death. Others lead a spiritual life, but have no experience of the heavenly realms during the course of their lives.

So although the majority of disciples may not need to take another birth in this world, there is still a difference in their spiritual progress, due to the differences in their burden of past sins. This is the meaning of Jesus' famous saying which he uses to summarize both this and other parables with a similar meaning:

> So the last shall be first, and the first last:
> for many be called, but few chosen.[2]
>
> *Matthew 20:16, KJV*

What he means is that there is no seniority among disciples. Those who are baptized or initiated into the spiritual path early in life may not make such good progress as those who come during their later years. Those who are initiated first may be the last to return to God. "Many be called" to follow the path, "but few are chosen" to return to Him in this life.

Some may have to take further lives before sufficient of their burden is cleared for them to have no further inclination to return here, and nothing is strong enough to bring them back. Every disciple will ultimately be taken back to God, but they will not all go at the same speed, nor will they be all taken at once.

Similar agricultural imagery is used by Jesus in his parable of the tares, which begins:

> The kingdom of heaven is likened unto a man who sowed good seed in his field. But while men slept, his enemy came and sowed tares among the wheat, and went his way.
>
> *Matthew 13:24–25; cf. KJV*

When the seed sprouts, it is accompanied by the weeds. The labourers therefore ask the landowner whether they should pull up the weeds, but he says:

> No, lest while you gather up the tares, you also root up the wheat with them. Let both grow together until the harvest.
>
> *Matthew 13:29–30; cf. KJV*

At the time of harvest, the wheat can be separated from the weeds, and weeds can be 'burnt', presumably by the meditation and devotion of the disciple at the time of death. As Jesus explains:

> He who sows the good seed is the Son of Man; the field is the world; the good seed are the children of the kingdom; but the tares are the children of the Wicked One. The enemy that sowed them is the devil; the harvest is the end of the world; and the reapers are the angels.
>
> *Matthew 13:37–39; cf. KJV*

The sower of the seed is the master, the Son of Man. The seed is the Word, and the place where the seed has to be sown is the world, meaning that both the master and the disciple have to be in human form. The parable of the tares only appears in *Matthew,* and it is probably the writer's fondness for eschatology that has turned his retelling of the parable into an end-of-the-world scenario.

The imagery of spiritual baptism as the sowing of a seed is appropriate. Everything in a seed is hidden as potential. The oak tree lies in the acorn, but in potential or essential form. Similarly, every human being has the inner potential to become or to realize God, but this is only attained by inner spiritual growth. Hence, as Jesus says in another 'sowing' parable:

> The kingdom of heaven is like a grain of mustard seed, which a man took and sowed in his field, and which indeed is the smallest of

> all seeds; but when it is grown, it is the greatest among herbs, and becomes a tree, so that the birds of the air come and lodge in its the branches.
>
> *Matthew 13:31–32; cf. KJV*

God is within, and every soul has the potential to become God, but the seed has to grow. The soul becomes God through having the seed of the Word sown in him. He is spiritually baptized, and when that seed grows to its full stature, he has become God. So spiritual baptism may appear to have been no more than an outer formality or ritual, but the real baptism takes place beyond human perception, and when it germinates and grows to its full potential, the soul has realized its essential divinity.

Understandably, metaphors concerning sowing of the seed are commonplace in Christian literature. In some instances, the meaning is understood evangelically as proselytization, as sowing the word or message of Jesus in the hearts of listeners. In other cases, especially among the mystically minded, it refers to baptism, to the sowing of the Seed of the Word in the soul.

Interestingly, among later Christian writers, sowing is only rarely understood as sowing the Seed of the Word. Among these was Angelus Silesius:

> God is a husbandman, His seed His only Word;
> The ploughshare is His Spirit, my heart the sowing ground.
>
> *Angelus Silesius, Cherubinic Wanderer 1:64, CW p.42*

Among the early writings, especially among the so-called apocryphal texts, sowing is more commonly understood as sowing the Seed of the Word. In the *Clementine Homilies,* for instance, Peter says of the soul: "Being sown with the true prophet's whole Word of Truth, he is enlightened in his understanding."[3] In the Arabic *Death of Saint John,* John addresses Jesus as he who "has sown your life-giving Word in our hearts".[4]

The author of the *Acts of Thomas* is also fond of the metaphor. Having received baptism through Judas Thomas, a devotee says, "I have received the living Seed of the Word;"[5] another says that he has "sown life in me",[6] while one who is anxious for initiation pleads:

> I beg of you, apostle of God, sow in me your Word of Life, so that I may again hear perfectly the Voice of him who delivered me to you, and said to you, "This is one of those who shall live through you, and henceforth let him be with you."
>
> *Acts of Thomas III; cf. AAA p.176*

Speaking of his own initiation and the protection of his master, Judas Thomas himself thanks Jesus, saying, "You are he who from childhood has sown life in me, and protected me from sin,"[7] and "you showed me my remissness, and sowed in me your heavenly love."[8]

In the *Odes of Solomon,* writing in the name of the master, the poet links release from the captivity of this creation with baptism, here called the sowing of his "fruits":

> And I sowed my fruits in their hearts,
> and transformed them into myself.
> And they received my blessing,
> and lived;
> And they were gathered to me,
> and were saved;
> Because they were to me as my own members,
> and I was their head.
>
> *Odes of Solomon 17:13–15, OSD p.80*

In the gnostic *Tripartite Tractate* the saviour is said to sow the Word "in an invisible way", pointing to the hidden, mystic nature of true baptism. And this sowing will grow into divine *gnōsis,* direct knowledge or personal experience of God:

> And he sowed in him, in an invisible way, a Word which is destined to be knowledge.
>
> *Tripartite Tractate 88, NHS22 pp.252–53*

In *Marsanēs,* bearing fruit from the "imperishable Seed" is linked with self-control and detachment from the world, as it is in Jesus' parable of the sower:

> Control yourselves, receive the imperishable Seed,
> bear fruit, and do not become attached to your possessions.
>
> *Marsanēs 26, NHS15 pp.294–95*

The parables of Jesus were also current among the Manichaeans, where the analogy of sowing is understood as both the sowing of the Seed of the Word, as well as the sowing of the spiritual message in human hearts. Sometimes, it is unclear which meaning is implied: it could indeed have been both. As one of the Coptic psalms says of Jesus: "He sowed the Seed in the soil of his men of knowledge."[9] In the Pahlavi texts, Mānī is described as "a sower of the Seed of Truth",[10] while in the Coptic *Kephalaia,* Mānī himself says that he has "sown the Seed of Life" and "sown the Truth in every land, far and near".[11]

The Manichaean writings from Chinese Turkestan, which exhibit some interesting cross-cultural expressions with terminology borrowed from Daoism, Buddhism and Christianity, also contain allusions to Jesus' parables of the sower and the tares. Here, where the "Law (C. *fǎ*, S. *Dharma*)" and the "Commandments" are synonyms for the Word, the disciple expresses humility before his master, praying for help against the forces of the mind, using a number of agricultural metaphors:

> I am . . . the bright and sweet-scented seed of the great saint *(dàshèng)*,
> thrown into the dense forest and thorny shrubs.
> Bestow great mercy: pray take and adopt me,
> convey me to the vault of light in the field of the Law *(fǎ)*.
>
> I am also the vine branch of the great saint *(dàshèng)*,
> once planted in the garden of the Law *(fǎ)*, the clean and pure park,
> suddenly strangled by creepers and entwined by climbers,
> extracting my wonderful strength,
> and leaving me to languish and wither.
>
> I am also the fertile soil of the great saint *(dàshèng)*,
> on which have been grown the five poisonous trees by the devils;
> I only hope that the great hoe of the Law *(fǎ)*,
> the sharp knife and sickle, will hew down and cut them,
> burn them out, and make me clean and pure.
> All the rest of the evil weeds and the thorny shrubs,
> pray destroy all of them with the fire of your Commandments *(jiè)*.
>
> *Móníjiào xiàbù zàn, T54 2140:1272a4–11; cf. LSMH (67–70) p.182*

The devotee is the sweet-scented "seed", the "vine branch" and the "fertile soil" who has been overtaken by the entanglements of physical life and the strength of the human passions – the "dense forest", the "thorny shrubs", the "creepers", the "climbers", the "five poisonous devils", and the "evil weeds". He is, however, one of the master's initiates and, consequently, despite his condition, he has the hope and the master's personal assurance that he will be able to surmount all his problems.

Even among the Sufis, the parables of Jesus are not unknown. Rūmī is probably alluding to the parable of the sower when he concludes a story concerning ʿUmar (the "spiritual guide") and a seeker:

> When that spiritual guide perceived
> that he possessed the potential for guidance,
> he sowed the good Seed in the good soil.
>
> *Rūmī, Maśnavī I:1445; cf. MJR2 p.80*

Elsewhere among the mystical writings of the ancient world, the analogy of spiritual teachings or human virtues being sown in the soul are not uncommon.

Among the Hermetic texts, the fictional master Poimandrēs ('Shepherd-Man') says that he came as a teacher to humankind:

> And some of them mocked me, and stood aloof; for they had given themselves up to the way of death. But others who desired to be taught, cast themselves at my feet. And I, bidding them rise, made myself a guide to mankind, teaching them the doctrine, and how and in what manner they might be saved. And I sowed in them the teachings of wisdom; and that which I sowed was watered with the Water of Immortal Life.
>
> *Hermetica (Poimandrēs) 1:29; cf. HAG p.54, HGCH p.6, TGH2 p.18*

Philo Judaeus also maintains in a number of places[12] that all virtues are sown in the soul by God as a reflection of higher spiritual qualities:

> God therefore sows and plants earthly virtues in the human race, as an imitation and representation of the heavenly.
>
> *Philo Judaeus, Allegorical Interpretation 1:14; cf. PCW1 pp.174–75, WPJ1 p.63*

He also adds that the "selfish and atheistic mind, thinking itself God's equal" imagines that it is the doer, and is "guilty of impiety" when it thinks, "I am planting." For in reality, "God sows and plants noble qualities in the soul."[13]

See also: **planting, Seed** (3.1), **sower** (7.1).

1. *Luke* 8:11, *KJV*.
2. *Cf. Matthew* 19:30.
3. *Clementine Homilies* III:27, *CH* p.68.
4. *Death of Saint John; cf. MAA* p.56.
5. *Acts of Thomas* VIII; *cf. AAA* p.226.
6. *Acts of Thomas* 15, *ANT* p.370.
7. *Acts of Thomas* 144; *cf. ANT* p.427.
8. *Acts of Thomas* III; *cf. AAA* p.174.
9. *Psalms of Heracleidēs, Manichaean Psalm Book, MPB* p.194.
10. *Manichaean Text, MH* p.27*ff.*, *HMV* p.344, *ML* p.12.
11. *Kephalaia* 1, 38, *KOT* pp.21, 105.
12. See also Philo Judaeus, *On the Cherubim* 13, *PCW2* pp.34–37; *On the Posterity of Cain* 49, *PCW2* pp.428–31.
13. Philo Judaeus, *Allegorical Interpretation* 1:15; *cf. PCW1* pp.176–77.

spiritual birth See **born again**.

tikanga ā Io (Mo) *Lit.* method *(tikanga)* of belonging to *(ā)* the supreme Being *(Io);* the Māori tradition of *Io;* initiation into the mysteries of *Io* the supreme Being.

Only the elect few who were initiated into the priesthood and mysteries of *Io* knew of His existence. Such intense sacredness *(tapu)* pertained to *Io* that it prevented any familiar description of Him, even His name being considered too sacred to be uttered aloud. Only initiates and priests of the *Io* tradition could mention Him by name, and then only in the privacy of a secluded spot, away from buildings, food, and people. These elite few, most of whom were of noble birth, were custodians of the secret knowledge of the Creator and were entrusted with the highly secret chants, prayers and incantations *(karakia),* rituals, and sacred practices of worship:

> The number of men initiated into the cult of *Io* was but small; only members of the higher grade of priestly experts *(tohunga)* and men of high-class families were allowed to learn the ritual pertaining to it. The common folk apparently had no part in it; and it is doubtful if they were even allowed to know the name of the supreme Being. This cult of *Io* was an esoteric one; that of the lower tribal gods may be termed exoteric. All ritual and ceremonial pertaining to *Io* was retained in the hands of the superior priesthood, by no means a numerous body.
>
> *Elsdon Best, Some Aspects of Maori Myth and Religion, AMMB p.20*

While going about their daily routine, initiates endeavoured to remember *Io* and the lesser gods *(atua)* at all times, and recited *karakia* before commencing most activities. A sense of what these old priests longed for is conveyed in a *karakia* in which the poet prays for knowledge of *Io,* and that that knowledge may also be given to other initiates:

> Here am I, begging that the great knowledge,
> the enduring effort, may come to me –
> The supreme and complete knowledge,
> such as possessed by Thee, O *Io* the all Parent,
> foundation of the Waters of Life.
> That they may come to Thy son, O *Io* the Exalted of Heaven!
> rest on me Thy great and enduring skill – Thy godlike knowledge.
> Give to these Thy sons,
> that they may possess the ancient and occult powers,
> like Thy godlike sons, O *Io* the All-Knowing, the Origin of all.
> Give freely to these sons, *e-i!*
>
> *Traditional Karakia; cf. in LWKT p.200*

Although rituals and offerings were often addressed to the *atua* (elemental and ancestral deities) and their assistance was frequently called upon, "It is interesting to note that no form of offering or sacrifice was made to *Io,* that no image of Him was ever made, and that He had no *aria,* or form of incarnation, such as inferior gods had."[1]

1. Elsdon Best, "Some Aspects of Maori Myth and Religion," *AMMB* p.20.

tohi (Mo) *Lit.* to cut, to divide, to separate; dedication ritual, baptism; a power-giving blessing or consecratory 'baptism rite'; a sacred ceremony in which a child is dedicated to an *atua* (ancestral deity, elemental spirit) or to *Io* the supreme Being; a ceremony, the details varying according to individual tribal customs, in which an infant is immersed in or sprinkled with water from a twig dipped in the flowing water of a sacred stream, while a petition is made to a particular *atua* to endow the child with *mana* (inner power) and with particular physical and mental talents and attributes, according to the wishes of the parents:[1]

> *Mana* is the gift from the *atua.* The *mauri* (life principle) is imparted at birth, and *mana* is gained by the *tohi karakia* (birth incantations).... This *mana* is imparted to the person when, at his birth, the father or *tohunga* (priest) recites the appropriate *karakia* to a particular *atua* to imbue the child with *mana* for the course in life the child will follow. Thus, the *karakia* might be addressed to *Tangaroa* (*atua* of the sea and fish) if the child is to be a fisherman or sea traveller,... or *Tūmatauenga* (*atua* of war), if the child is meant to be a mighty warrior or leader.
>
> *James Irwin, Introduction to Maori Religion, IMRI p.22*

An initial invocation ceremony *(tāngaengaetanga)* is performed when the first breath is drawn and the umbilical cord *(iho)* has been cut.[2] The *tohi* ritual or ceremony is performed ten days later at dawn or dusk in the *wai tapu* (sacred waters) of a flowing stream. Since *tohi* also means 'to cut, to divide', it is perhaps in reference to the cutting of the umbilical cord that the rite has been named. The birth and baptism are understood symbolically as a portrayal of Māori creation mythology:

> Of all the ceremonies of the Māori *tohunga,* baptizing a newborn baby is the most sacred and holy. The unborn child represented *Tāne* (the deity who brought light) in the womb of its mother dwelling in *Te Pō* (the Darkness). The child also represents the unfolding of the universe, the struggle out of darkness, and breaking forth of the day....
>
> The actual ceremony itself is simple. The *tohunga* performed a ceremony *(tāngaengaetanga)* at the birth, welcoming the child to the world of light. The *tohunga* took the afterbirth and umbilical cord for

safekeeping instead of burning them, as is the modern norm. These parts are an *ohonga* or link to the child, and the *tohunga ahurewa* (highest class of priest) used them to secure a good life and *mana* for the infant. The remains were buried at the base of a pole at the *tūāhu* (altar, sacred place). It represented the pole by which *Tāne* lifted his father (*Rangi,* Sky Father) to the sky. In mythology, the pole held *Rangi* in place while the heavens were being created. In the ritual, it served to protect the child during the ten days of waiting before the child was baptized. Prayers were said at the pole and over the *ahi taitai* or sacred fire to empower the child's *mana* in order to link him or her to their godly lineage. The *karakia* (prayers, incantations) were said for ten days at each sunrise, symbolizing the establishment of the ten heavens (some tribes ascribed to twelve heavens)....

On the tenth day, the child was finally baptized with a twig dipped in holy water *(wai tapu).* The blade of grass or twig was lightly brushed onto the head of the child. Fresh water was used for the blessing *(tohi),* and the child was dedicated to *Io* with *karakia.* Then several *atua* (lesser gods) were named to watch over the child throughout his or her life. Two small stones were furthermore thrust down the throat of the baby. The small stones were named *Rehutai* and *Hukatai* (representing the knowledge and intuition within). (Today we do not need to insert the stones, rather they are placed with the umbilical cord when buried.) They gave the child the power to choose wisely, and would also make his heart as hard as stone and his emotions as cold as stone, making him brave in battle. Finally, the baby was held high up to dedicate this one to the heavens, showing that our child was a person belonging to the Supreme Parent *Io-Matua* – as we all are.

Samuel Timoti Robinson, Tohunga, TRAK pp.311–13

The *tohi* ceremony originates with the traditional mythology concerning the primordial *atua* in the upper heavens. When the god *Tāne* ascended *te aka* (the cosmic vine leading up to the heavens) in order to obtain the three baskets *(kete)* of knowledge for humankind, he was compelled to undergo the *tohi* ceremony in *tapu* water twice before being admitted to the palace and the presence of *Io* the supreme Being

Depending on individual tribal beliefs, the deities *Tāne* and *Tū* (god of war) are both credited with the creation of man. As Walter Gudgeon (1841–1920) describes it, *Tū* is said to have planted two green branches of *koromiko (Hebe elliptica)* on a mound of earth at his *tūāhu* (sacred place, altar). With his right hand he planted the branch on the right, representing *Oromatau* (Tree of Life); and with his left hand the branch on the left, representing *Oromania* (Tree of Death). This traditional story is reflected in the *tāngaengaetanga* invocation, when the baby has drawn its first breath, and at the baptism *(tohi),* ten days later. Holding the baby's head in his right hand and its body in his left, the *tohunga* lifts the infant and places it on the branches on the altar, while at the same time dedicating the child to the type of work chosen by the parents. This is done to ensure the child's ability and proficiency. If the *koromiko* branch of the Tree of Life takes root and flourishes, it is seen as a good omen and an indication that the child will have much *mana* or inner power. According to the myth:

> *Tūmatauenga (Tū)* had seen reason to believe that the godlike race of beings, who at that period inhabited the earth, were unfit for the positions they occupied. He therefore resolved to make a man after his own image, using the clay of the earth as the material wherewith to carry out his purpose. To effect this project, he built an altar *(tūāhu)* at Te One-potaka, a place situated in Hawaiki, that mythical home of the Māori people. The altar was a very rude affair, merely a mound of earth roughly scraped together. When it was finished, the site was called Te Kauhanga Nui, and the altar itself Te Oropuke.
>
> In the mound of earth so made, *Tū* planted two green branches of the *koromiko,* both of which had the leaves and branches intact. The right-hand branch, he placed in the ground with his right hand and the left-hand branch with his left hand. This was a matter of the utmost importance since these branches represented life and death, and even to this day bright are the prospects of a child who, after the *tohi* ceremony, finds that his Tree of Life has taken root and is growing vigorously The great *Ngā Puhi* chief, Tāmati Wāka Nene, was an instance in point, for it is said that his Tree of Life grew, and hence his *mana* was very great.
>
> *Tū* called the right hand branch, or Tree of Life, *Oromatau;* the other he called *Oromania.* He then took *para-uku* (riverside clay) and mixed it, kneading it into the shape of a man, in other words into the image of *Tū* himself and, having done these things, he lifted the clay, the head of the image in his right hand, and the lower part of the body in his left hand, and placed it on the branches of *Oromatau* and *Oromania.* This ceremony is still followed by *tohungas* when they perform the *tohi* rite over a newly born child, after the ceremony of the *tāngaengaetanga....* It is then that the *tohunga* lifts the child on to the altar, holding ... the head in his right hand, and repeats the *tohi,* dedicating the infant to such work as the parents shall think fit and proper. Be it understood that until this ceremony has been performed the child cannot be relied on to carry out any work however simple without making many mistakes.
>
> *Walter Gudgeon, Maori Religion, MRG p.125*

A Māori Christian baptism is known as *iriiri.*

1. See "Tohi," *Māori Dictionary, AMEI;* Walter Gudgeon, *Maori Religion, MRG* p.125.
2. Walter Gudgeon, *Maori Religion, MRG* p.125.

upadesh(a) (S/H), **updesh**, **updes** (H/Pu), **man-ngag** (T) *Lit.* instruction, teaching, information, dialogue, discussion, advice, admonition, preaching, sermon, exhortation; spiritual instruction or direction; also, initiation into a spiritual path, which includes advice and instruction on how to meditate and follow that particular path, and which varies in content and intention between different spiritual schools and traditions. Since the term can mean both teaching as well as initiation, it is sometimes difficult to be certain of the meaning intended by the original writer.

Depending upon the context, *upadesha* is used to mean both teachings and initiation. Even in present and relatively recent times, there are spiritual paths whose *gurus* have spoken of their initiation as *upadesha.* According to the contemporary Loka Ksema Yagna Trust, "*Upadesha* is an initiation from the *guru* on a specific *mantra* or a *pūjā* (form of worship)."[1] The term also appears to have been used by Ramana Maharshi (1879–1950), or at least by his followers, in both a general and specific sense.[2] Kabīr (*c.*1398–1518), a medieval Indian *sant,* also seems specific as to his meaning, though much depends upon the translation. Kabīr's message is that liberation from the cycle of birth and death and the return of the soul to its native home with God is only possible through the teaching and initiation *(updes)* of a *satguru:*

> Listen to this one thought
> on the value of initiation *(updes)* by a perfect master *(satguru):*
> Were you without a master,
> you'd be dragged to the door of the angel of death.
>
> At the door of the angel of death,
> his minions would tear you to pieces.
> From them, indeed, you would never be freed –
> you'd be hurled again into the wheel of birth and death.
>
> Without a master you'd wander hopelessly
> within the cruel wheel of transmigration –
> Never would you find escape.
> But, through the grace of your *satguru,*
> you have been rescued from that dreadful wheel.

I pray you, Kabīr, come to that country
  where old age and death can never distress you,
  where death is unheard of –
Where your attentive doctor, the master,
  protects you from disease and death.

Only with initiation *(updes)* by a perfect master
  may you go across, stepping on the head of *Kāl* (Death).
The Lord himself will then stretch out His hands,
  and take you safely to His own abode.

Kabīr, Sākhī Sangrah, Gurudev kā Ang 70–74, KSS pp.6–7; cf. KGME p.228

He also says that mystics have always been coming to this world to give this initiation:

Age after age, we have come to give initiation *(updes)*
  into the essential Melody.

Kabīr, Shabdāvalī 3, Mahimā Ādi Dhām, Shabd 8:1, KSS3 p.6

Baba Jaimal Singh (1839–1903) writes that as a direct result of the *updesh* given by a perfect master, all the *karma* relating to the physical, astral *(sahans dal kanwal)* and causal *(trikuṭī)* spheres is erased:

Those *jīvas* who have taken refuge in a perfect *satguru* and have received from Him the *updesh* of the five *shabds* . . . – if they have such love and faith that the *satguru* is not merely a human being but has assumed the human form for the good of others, and never think that he is a human being – all the *karmas* belonging to the material bodies of such people are wiped off. The *karmas* pertaining to the *sukshm* (astral) body will be cancelled in *sahans dal kanwal.* On reaching *trikuṭī,* the *karmas* referring to *kāraṇ* (causal) *māyā,* out of which *Īshwar* and *jīva* have sprung and which is the source of *daivi samprada* (good qualities) will also be wiped off.

Then the *surat,* that is *jīvātmā* (living soul, incarnate soul), being purified, will hold fast to *Shabd Dhun* and merge into it. Then the *Shabd Dhun* (Melody of the Word) which comes from *sach khanḍ* will take the *jīvātmā* to *sach khanḍ* (true region, eternity), and it will merge into *sach khanḍ.* Then there is nothing to fear. That is our home. Now you have not to take another birth. Everything will be finished in this life.

Baba Jaimal Singh, Letter 11, SLO p.26

The same dual meaning is present in the writings of the *gurus* recorded in the *Ādi Granth.* Here, *updesh* is used more or less synonymously with the *guru's bachan* (words) and the *guru's mat* (path, teaching); but there is no doubt that this teaching included initiation into the inner secret of the mystic Name *(Nām)* or Word *(Shabd),* the creative power. Souls who receive such *updesh* are blessed:

> In the *sat sangat* (company of the saints), God's praise is sung:
> by associating with the saints, the Beloved is met.
> Amongst men, blessed is that mortal being
> who imparts instruction *(updes)* for the good of others.
>
> *Guru Rāmdās, Ādi Granth 311, MMS*

This *updesh* is the same, whatever the social background of the individual:

> The four castes – the *khatris* (warriors), *brāhmaṇs,*
> *sudras* (menials) and *vaishas* (traders) –
> Are equal partners in divine instruction *(updes).*
>
> Nānak, he who utters the Name of God
> who abides in all hearts,
> is saved in the *kaliyuga* (age of darkness).
>
> *Guru Arjun, Ādi Granth 747, MMS*

The *updesh* of a saint is true:

> True are the words *(bachan)* and instructions *(updes)* of the saint.
> True are the persons into whose minds the Lord enters.
>
> *Guru Arjun, Ādi Granth 284, MMS*

The *updesh* of a *satguru* is to meditate on the divine Name. Here, *gurbāṇī* can refer either to the divine and mystic Word *(Bāṇī)* imparted by a *guru* or to his teachings written in poetic form and later compiled as the *Ādi Granth:*

> He, who calls himself a *sikh* (disciple) of the great *satguru,*
> should rise early and meditate on God's Name. . . .
> By repeating Lord God's Name under the *guru's* instruction *(updes),*
> all his sins, misdeeds, and accusations are wiped off.
> Afterwards, at sunrise, he sings *gurbāṇī,*
> and whilst sitting or standing, he meditates on God's Name.
>
> The *guru's* disciple, who with every breath and morsel
> contemplates my Lord God,
> he becomes pleasing to the *guru's* mind.

He unto whom my master becomes merciful,
to that disciple of his, the *guru* imparts his instruction *(updes).*
Servant Nānak asks for the dust of the feet of that *sikh* of the *guru,*
who himself contemplates on God's Name,
and makes others contemplate thereon.

Guru Rāmdās, Ādi Granth 305–6, MMS

Keep the *(guru's)* instruction *(updes)* in your heart:
and gather the fruit of your mind's desire.

Guru Arjun, Ādi Granth 293, AGG

The *updesh* of a *satguru* opens the inner eye, and brings about an understanding of what this world really is:

A sacrifice am I to the true *guru,*
by meeting whom the Lord is remembered:
And who, through his instruction *(updes),*
blessed me with the collyrium of wisdom
with which I beheld the world.

Guru Nānak, Ādi Granth 470, AGG

The *updesh* of a saint leads to control of the wayward mind, to contact with the divine Water of Life, and to the soul's discovery of its own innate immortality:

Rare is the one who realizes the essence of the Lord:
he tastes nectar and becomes immortal.
He, to whose heart is revealed the treasure of good,
for him there is no death: he lives eternally.
He calls on his Lord, the God, night and day,
and gives true instruction *(updes)* to the devotees of the Lord.
He is attached neither to *māyā* (illusion) nor *moh* (attachment),
and keeps the one Lord eternally in his mind.
And the utter darkness of his mind is illumined,
and, he casts away his doubt, and attachment, and pain.

Guru Arjun, Ādi Granth 287, AGG

Happiness ensues, pain departs,
and the fear of birth and death is dispelled
by the perfect teachings *(updes)* of the holy saint.
Fear is lifted, and one abides in fearlessness:
all evils are dispelled from the mind.

Guru Arjun, Ādi Granth 287, AGK

By following the *guru's* *updesh,* the soul becomes aware of the divine presence, and worldly inclinations slip away:

> Listen to the *updes* (instruction) of the perfect *guru:*
> see the supreme Lord God near you.
> With each and every breath,
> meditate in remembrance on the Lord of the universe,
> and the anxiety within your mind shall depart.
> Abandon the waves of fleeting desire,
> and pray for the dust of the feet of the saints.
>
> *Guru Arjun, Ādi Granth 295, AGK*

Among other *sants,* Kabīr is characteristically forthright concerning the significance of *updesh:*

> Listen to this one thought
> on the value of initiation *(updes)* from a perfect master *(satguru):*
> You'd be dragged to the door of the angel of death
> were you without a master *(satguru).*
>
> At the door of the angel of death, his minions would tear you to pieces:
> From them, indeed, you would never be freed –
> you'd be hurled again into the wheel of birth and death.
> You'd wander hopelessly within the cruel wheel of transmigration.
> Never would you find escape.
> But through the grace of your master *(satguru),*
> you have been rescued from that dreadful wheel.
>
> I pray you, Kabīr, come to that country
> where old age and death can never distress you,
> where death is unheard of –
> Where your attentive doctor, the true master *(satguru),*
> protects you from disease and death.
>
> Only with initiation *(updes)* by a true master *(satguru)*
> may you go across, stepping on *Kāl's* (Death's) head.
> The Lord himself will then stretch out His hands,
> and take you safely to His own abode.
>
> *Kabīr, Sākhī Sangrah, Gurudev kā Ang 70–74, KSS pp.6–7; cf. KGME p.228*

See also: **upadesha** (7.5).

1. Loka Ksema Yagna Trust, www.lokakshemayagna.org/mantra-diksha-updesa, ret. June 2012.
2. *Path of Self-Knowledge,* bhagavan-ramana.org/ramana_maharshi/private/pos/, ret. December 2014.

upasaṃpadā (S), **upasampadā** (Pa), **bsnyen par rdzogs pa** (T) *Lit.* acceptance, acquisition; the higher of the two degrees of ordination into becoming a Buddhist monk (S. *bhikshu,* Pa. *bhikkhu*); full admission into a Buddhist monastic order. See **pravrajya**.

written in heaven See **Book of Life**.

xuán zhī yòu xuán (C) *Lit.* mystery *(xuán)* and again *(yòu)* mystery *(xuán)* + *zhī* (possessive particle); mystery within a mystery; the mysteries of the *Dào.*

The term appears in the first chapter of the *Dàodé jīng,* where it is used to describe the two aspects of *Dào* – the Nameless as the subtle origin of the creation and the Named as the mother of all manifested things – the mystery (the 'Named') that lies within the deeper mystery (the 'Nameless'):

> The *Dào* that can be spoken is not the eternal *Dào;*
> The name that can be named is not the eternal Name;
> The Nameless is the origin of heaven and earth;
> The Named is the mother of myriad things.
> Thus, constantly without desire, one observes its essence;
> Constantly with desire, one observes its manifestations.
> These two emerge together but differ in name.
> The unity is said to be the mystery –
> Mystery of mysteries *(xuán zhī yòu xuán),*
> the door to all wonders.
>
> *Lǎozǐ, Dàodé jīng 1, TCVC p.3*

In a question-and-answer *(wèndá)* exchange with his disciple Zhào Dàokě (*aka.* Dìng'ān), thirteenth-century Daoist master Lǐ Dàochún refers to the *Dào* as the "mystery of mysteries *(xuán zhī yòu xuán)*" because there are simply no other words to describe it:

> Dìng'ān said, "I have just entered the mystic school *(xuán mén)* and am completely ignorant. I am very fortunate to have been taken on as a disciple (*shī shōulù,* admitted by a teacher). I really do not know the *Dào* of supreme true Reality, and hope you will teach me."

> The teacher *(shī)* said, "The *Dào* of supreme true Reality has no limit that can be surpassed. It is the mystery of mysteries *(xuán zhī yòu xuán);* no image can describe it. It is so without affirmation. It refers to the ultimate, supreme Wonder. Sages *(shèngrén)* have called it the *Dào.*"
>
> *Lǐ Dàochún, Zhōnghé jí, BBH p.45*

7.5 Spiritual Association

Spirituality is more easily caught than taught, and the spiritual presence of an advanced being can have an indescribable effect upon a receptive heart. Teachers of spiritual paths have therefore recommended association with the holy, and with fellow travellers on the spiritual path. It is, after all, an old adage that human beings are affected by the company they keep.

Established spiritual paths also have a heritage or tradition by which one teacher or master passes on the mantle of mastership to a successor.

Terms pertaining to both of these two topics are to be found in the entries collected together in this section.

ācariyamuṭṭhi (Pa) *Lit.* teacher's *(ācariya)* fist *(muṭṭhi);* the close-fistedness or secrecy of a teacher who holds things back, declining to reveal all he knows or reserving them for only favoured students; the secret knowledge of a teacher. According to the Buddhist Pali texts, the Buddha never held back anything that would have been helpful to his disciples in their quest for liberation and enlightenment. There was no inner and outer circle of followers who each received different teachings.

According to the *Mahāparinibbāna Sutta,* shortly before the Buddha passed away, Ānanda, one of his most trusted disciples, requested him to give some last instructions to the community of *bhikkhus* (monks). But the Buddha replied that he had already helped them in every possible way. He had never held anything back:[1]

> What more does the community of *bhikkhus (bhikkhu-sangha)* expect of me, Ānanda? I have set forth the *Dhamma* making no distinction of inner and outer *(anantaraṃ abāhiraṃ, i.e.* secret and public) doctrine. Regarding doctrines, the Tathāgata has no teacher's fist *(ācariyamuṭṭhi).* If someone thinks, "I should lead the community of *bhikkhus,*" or "the community of *bhikkhus* should be under my direction," let him make some statement concerning the community of *bhikkhus.* But, Ānanda, the Tathāgata has no such thought. So what instructions should the Tathāgata have regarding the community of *bhikkhus?*
>
> Ānanda, I am frail now, old, aged, far gone in years, and have travelled life's journey. This is my eightieth year, and my life is spent. Even as an old cart, Ānanda, is held together by a combination of straps, so the body of the Tathāgata is kept going only by being strapped together. Ānanda, it is only when the Tathāgata, withdrawing his attention from all outer phenomena and through the cessation of mundane sensations, enters into the mental concentration beyond phenomena, that his body is more comfortable.
>
> Therefore, Ānanda, be islands unto yourselves, refuges unto yourselves, seeking no external refuge; with the *Dhamma* as your island, the *Dhamma* as your refuge, seeking no other refuge.
>
> *Dīgha Nikāya 16, Mahāparinibbāna Sutta, PTSD2 pp.100–1; cf. TBLD p.245, DNVS*

1. See also *Saṃyutta Nikāya* 47:8, *Gilāna Sutta, PTSS5* pp.153–54.

ān dam (P) *Lit.* that *(ān)* moment *(dam);* a special or particular moment; in Sufism, a moment of grace, a moment of supreme blessing from the beloved:

> When you receive a moment *(dam)* from the beloved,
> you will profit from that moment *(ān dam)* throughout your life.

Beware that you do not waste that moment *(ān dam),*
for you will find few other moments *(dam-i dīgar)* like that.

Rūmī, Dīvān-i Shams-i Tabrīz, Rubā'īyāt 1667, KSD8 p.280; cf. DDRR p.147, in FKG p.128

See also: **drishti**.

anjuman (P) *Lit.* assembly, meeting, company, party, crowd; society, club, association; sometimes used for the assembly of the Sufi disciples with their spiritual master. Rūmī makes an interesting comment concerning the effect that people in an audience have on him:

If I find in the assembly *(anjuman),*
he who draws the discourse from me,
I, like a garden, grow hundreds of thousands of roses;
And if at that time I find there a base person,
who kills the discourse,
the deep sayings flee, like a thief, from my heart.
Everyone moves towards the Drawer:
the true drawing is not like the false drawing.

Rūmī, Maśnavī IV:1319–21; cf. MJR4 p.345

See also: **khalwah** (▸3).

ānupubbi-kathā (Pa) *Lit.* graduated *(anupubba)* discourse *(kathā);* step-by-step discourse; gradual instruction, progressive training; a method used by the Buddha in his discourses to explain the basic principles of the Way (S. *Dharma,* Pa. *Dhamma*) to newcomers:

1. Generosity *(dāna).*
2. Virtue *(sīla).*
3. Heaven *(sagga).*
4. Danger of sensual pleasure *(kāmānaṃ ādīnava).*
5. Renunciation *(nekkhamma).*
6. The four noble truths *(cattāri ariya-saccāni)* – there is suffering; its origin is desire; suffering can end; there is a path that leads to its cessation.

The various topics guide the listener in a steady progression through the basic principles of a human life founded upon goodness and virtue, together with the implications of good and bad *kamma* (S. *karma*); to the rewards of a virtuous life to be experienced both here and hereafter, together with an understanding that this world is only a small part of the entire cosmos; to the consequent desire to become detached from this world; and so to an understanding of the four noble truths; and ultimately to their fulfilment in the realization of *nibbāna* (enlightenment). By this means, the Buddha was able to cover the basics of living as a decent human being, before broaching the subject of suffering and its escape in a way that would make it seem relevant. The standard text, found in a number of places in the Pali texts, reads:

> Then the Blessed One gave the householder Upāli gradual instruction *(ānupubbi-kathā)* – that is to say, he spoke on giving *(dāna),* on virtue *(sīla),* and on the heavens *(sagga);* he explained the danger, the vanity and the defilement of sensual pleasures, and the blessing of renunciation. When the Blessed One perceived that the listener's mind was prepared, receptive, free from obstacles, elevated, and lucid, then he explained to him that Teaching *(Dhamma)* special to the *buddhas,* that is: suffering *(dukkha),* its cause, its cessation, and the Path.
>
> *Majjhima Nikāya 56, Upāli Sutta, PTSM1 pp.379–80; cf. MDBB p.485*

Modern monk Thanissaro Bhikkhu explains the process in more detail:

> The Buddha would describe good actions under two main categories: generosity and virtue. Together, the two categories could be stretched to cover almost any type of good physical, verbal, or mental deed. For example, generosity covers not only the giving of material gifts, but also generosity with one's time, knowledge, gratitude, and forgiveness. Virtue begins with the five precepts – against killing, stealing, illicit sex, lying, and taking intoxicants – includes prohibitions against five forms of wrong livelihood – selling slaves, intoxicants, poisons, weapons, and animals to be killed for food – and goes on to cover abstention from all forms of harmful behaviour. Thus, good behaviour, taken under the categories of generosity and virtue, means both refraining from harmful behaviour and performing actions that are beneficial.
>
> Having described good actions, the Buddha would describe their rewards, as results of the cosmic principle of *kamma.* The rewards here include both those visible in this world and those to be anticipated in the next. The Buddhist texts contain glowing descriptions both of the sense of well-being in the immediate present that results from good actions, and of the exquisite pleasures that rebirth in heaven entails. Implicit in these descriptions is the dark side of the principle of *kamma:* the inherent punishments that come from bad behaviour, again both in this world and in the next: in the various levels of hell and other lower births – such as a common animal – and again in this world on one's return to the human state.

However – because finite actions can't produce infinite results – the rewards of *kamma,* good or bad, are not eternal. This point led naturally to the next topic in the discourse: the drawbacks of the cycle of rebirth as a whole. No happiness within the cycle is permanent; even the most refined heavenly pleasures must end when the force of one's good *kamma* ends, and one is forced to return to the rough and tumble of lower realms of being. The changeability of the mind lying behind the creation of *kamma* means that the course of an individual's life through the realms of rebirth is not necessarily ever upward. In fact, as the Buddha saw from his remembrance of his own lives, the course leading from one rebirth to another is filled with aimless ups and downs, like a stick thrown into the air: sometimes landing on this end, sometimes on the other end, sometimes in the middle. The amount of suffering and stress suffered in the course of these many throws is more than can be measured.

These considerations led naturally to the next topic of the discourse: renunciation. Having realized the fleeting nature of even the most refined pleasures in the round of rebirth, the sensitive listener would be prepared to look favourably on the idea of renouncing any aspiration for happiness within the round, and cultivating the path to release. The texts compare this mental preparation to the act of washing a cloth so that it would be ready to take dye. This was when the Buddha would take the listener beyond the level of mundane right view and broach the transcendent level.

The texts describing the steps of the graduated discourse describe this step simply as "the Teaching *(Dhamma)* special to the *buddhas:* suffering, its cause, its cessation, and the Path," *i.e.* the four noble truths.

Thanissaro Bhikkhu, Refuge, RBDS pp.71–72

A similar term, *anupubba-sikkhā* (gradual training) is used in the Pali texts for the steady progress of a disciple towards enlightenment.

See also: **anupubba-sikkhā** (▸4).

ārya-saṃgha (S), **ariya-sangha** (Pa) *Lit.* noble *(ārya)* community *(saṃgha, sangha);* the community comprised of those noble persons *(ariya-puggala)* – lay or otherwise – who have at least reached the level of *sotāpanna* (stream-enterer), the 'stream' being the noble Path *(ariya-magga)* that leads to enlightenment.

See also: **saṃgha**.

āshram(a) (S/H) *Lit.* place or stage of exertion; from the Sanskrit root *shram* to exert oneself, to toil, especially in spiritual life; hence, dwelling, abode, residence, hermitage, monastery; a spiritual centre associated with a particular *guru* or spiritual school; a place of residence normally available free of charge, attached to a temple, where *sādhus* (wandering holy men) can stay for a few days; also, the four stages or *āshramas* of traditional Hindu life, according to the sage Manu: *brahmacharya* (celibacy, childhood, youth), *gṛihasthya* (domestic life, householding), *vānaprasthya* (forest dwelling, retirement, contemplation), and *sannyāsa* (renunciation).

Many Indian *āshrams* have been built by wealthy people with the intention of earning 'merit'. Others have been built from the group donations of followers of the school or the *guru.* The purpose of an *āshram* is to provide a refuge away from worldly concerns, where people may establish themselves in meditation. Some may stay at the *āshram* for a long time, or even make their life there. Others come to recharge their spiritual batteries and renew their spiritual awareness, before returning to their everyday lives. Ramakrishna describes something of the simple and focused lives of the ancient *ṛishis:*

> The *ṛishis* attained *Brahma-jñāna* (knowledge of *Brahman*). But if you have the slightest desire for worldly things, you cannot attain the knowledge of *Brahman.* What an effort the *ṛishis* made! They would leave their *āshram* in the morning to meditate and contemplate on God alone throughout the day. And then they ate only roots and fruit at night when they returned to their *āshram.* They would guard themselves from seeing, hearing, and touching other worldly things. Only then did they realize *Brahman* as their own inner Self.
>
> *Ramakrishna, in Kathāmṛita 3:1.4, SRK3*

See also: **āshrama** (▸4).

avyākṛita-vastu (S), **avyākata-vatthu** (Pa) *Lit.* unexplained things; undeclared, undecided, or indeterminate things; the four questions that the Buddha intentionally left unanswered because no adequate answer can be given in words and the attempt to do so is a waste of time and energy. Time spent in doing so is regarded as 'unskilful' and better spent in following the *Dhamma* (Way). The four questions are:

1. Whether the world is eternal, or not, or both, or neither.
2. Whether the world is infinite in space, or not, or both, or neither.
3. Whether the *tathāgata* exists after death, or not, or both, or neither.
4. Whether the soul (or life in the body) is identical with the body or different from it.

The four questions are enumerated at several places in the Pali texts.[1] When the Buddha is challenged by the Venerable Mālunkyaputta for being evasive, he replies:

> Mālunkyaputta, remember what I have left undeclared *(avyākata)* as undeclared, and remember what I have declared *(vyākata)* as declared. And what have I left undeclared? 'The cosmos is eternal' – I have left undeclared. 'The cosmos is not eternal,' … 'The world is finite,' … 'The world is infinite,' … 'The soul (*jīva,* life) is the same as the body,' 'The soul (*jīva,* life) is one thing and body another,' … 'After death a *tathāgata* exists,' … 'After death a *tathāgata* does not exist,' … 'After death a *tathāgata* both exists and does not exist,' … 'After death a *tathāgata* neither exists nor does not exist' – I have left undeclared.
>
> Why have I left that undeclared? Because it is unbeneficial; it does not belong to the fundamentals of the holy life; it does not lead to disenchantment, to dispassion, to cessation, to peace, to direct knowledge, to enlightenment, to *nibbāna.* That is why I have left it undeclared.
>
> And what have I declared? 'This is suffering *(dukkha)*' … 'This is the origin of suffering,' … 'This is the cessation of suffering,' … 'This is the way leading to the cessation of suffering' – I have declared.
>
> Why have I declared that? Because it is beneficial; it belongs to the fundamentals of the holy life; it leads to disenchantment, to dispassion, to cessation, to peace, to direct knowledge, to enlightenment, to *nibbāna.* That is why I have declared it.
>
> *Majjhima Nikāya 63, Cūlamālunkya Sutta, PTSM1 p.431; cf. MDBB p.536*

The Buddha also relates a story to explain the futility of such questions:

> Mālunkyaputta, if anyone were to say, "I will not live the holy life under the Blessed One as long as he does not declare to me that 'The cosmos is eternal,' … or that 'After death a *tathāgata* neither exists nor does not exist'" – the man would die and those things would still remain undeclared by the *tathāgata.*
>
> It is as though a man were wounded with an arrow thickly smeared with poison. His friends and companions, kinsmen and relatives brought a surgeon to treat him, but the man would say, "I will not have this arrow removed until I know whether the man who wounded me was a noble warrior, a *brāhmaṇ,* a merchant, or a worker." He would say, "I will not have this arrow removed until I know the given name and clan name of the man who wounded me, … until I know whether he was tall, short, or of medium height, … until I know whether he was dark, ruddy brown, or golden coloured, … until I know his home village, town, or city, … until I know whether the bow that wounded

me was a long bow or a crossbow,... until I know whether the bowstring that wounded me was fibre, bamboo threads, sinew, hemp, or bark,... until I know whether the shaft that wounded me was wild or cultivated,... until I know whether the feathers of the shaft that wounded me were those of a vulture, a heron, a hawk, a peacock, or a stork,... until I know whether the shaft that wounded me was bound with the sinew of an ox, a water buffalo, a langur, or a monkey." He would say, "I will not have this arrow removed until I know whether the shaft that wounded me was that of a common arrow, a curved arrow, a barbed, a calf-toothed, or an oleander arrow." The man would die and those things would still remain unknown to him.

Majjhima Nikāya 63, Cūlamālunkya Sutta, PTSM1 pp.428–29; cf. MDBB pp.534–36

The discussion relates to the Buddha's historical context. There are numerous references in the Pali texts to the many varying viewpoints propounded by the *samaṇas* (holy men) and *brāhmaṇs* of the different schools, many of whom deferred to no particular scriptural authority, who were part of the religious and spiritual landscape of his time. Although Buddhist texts such as the *Abhidhamma* are intensely analytical and intellectual, the view of the Buddha as propounded in the Pali texts is that such views are speculation, and that he declines to be drawn into the debate.

See also: **shramaṇa** (7.1).

1. *E.g. Majjhima Nikāya* 25, *Nivāpa Sutta, PTSM1* p.157; *Dīgha Nikāya* 9, *Poṭṭhapāda Sutta, PTSD1* pp.187–90.

'ayn al-kamāl (A), **'ayn-i kamāl** (P) *Lit.* the eye of perfection; the eye of the perfect master; the fatal eye, the glance that kills; an expression used by Rūmī for the glance of the perfect saint, which has the capacity to annihilate the ego of the recipient. Rūmī tells the story of a prince (the disciple) who devotes himself to the service of his father, the emperor (the master). Even so it was not because of his human relationship with the emperor that he was admitted to the court of divine union, but because of his master's glance of grace:

Although he laid hold of the emperor's saddle strap,
in the end he was admitted by the glance that kills *('ayn al-kamāl).*

Rūmī, Maśnavī VI:4875; cf. MJR6 p.527

bahār (P) *Lit.* spring; the season of springtime; metaphorically, a flourishing and joyful state of being, as in a disciple's happiness at seeing his master, within or without:

The spring *(bahār)* has come, the spring *(bahār)* has come,
the spring *(bahār)* with loads of musk has come:
The friend *(nigār)* has come, the friend has come,
the burden-bearing friend has come.

Rūmī, Dīvān-i Shams-i Tabrīz 569:6043, KSD2 p.26, in TSR p.53

Have you heard that the soul has become drunk
from the cup of spring *(bahār),*
and gone off gay and dancing into the *sulṭān*'s sanctuary?

Rūmī, Dīvān-i Shams-i Tabrīz 782:8160, KSD2 p.137, MP1 (98:5) p.84

Joyous spring *(bahār)* has arrived
and the beloved's message has come;
We are drunk with love and intoxicated,
and cannot be still.

Rūmī, Dīvān-i Shams-i Tabrīz 1121:11824, KSD3 p.23, MP1 (141:1) p.118

The advent of the inner beloved is heralded by the "zephyr *(ṣabā)*" of the divine Spirit:

Rejoice, O heart, that a new spring *(bahār)* has come!
The zephyr *(ṣabā)* has brought the scent of the beloved's tresses.

'Irāqī, Kullīyāt 143, KHI p.73, in SSE4 p.82

For souls imprisoned ("frozen") in a human body ("water and clay"), the beloved heralds a springtime of spiritual awakening:

For those things frozen in water and clay:
you are a spring *(bahār)* within spring *(bahār).*

Sanā'ī, Dīvān 386, AMM p.1030, in SSE4 p.82

The "seed" of initiation sown in the "heart" by a master becomes a "tree" as the spirit awakens:

The seed of the heart sown in such water and clay
will not become a tree until the coming of your spring *(bahār).*

Rūmī, Dīvān-i Shams-i Tabrīz 545:5811, KSD2 p.14, in SSE4 p.82

I am like a seed under the soil,
I am waiting upon the signal of spring *(bahār),*
That without my own breath, I may breathe sweetly,
that without my own head, I may scratch a head.

Rūmī, Dīvān-i Shams-i Tabrīz 1562:16416–17, KSD3 p.272, MP1 (192:8–9) p.159

barakah (A), **barakat** (P) (pl. *barakāt*) *Lit.* increase, prosperity, blessing, benediction; spiritual power, spiritual blessing, blessed influence; the blessing power of the Prophet's name; the blessing of a saint; also used in everyday Muslim life when invoking the blessings or grace of *Allāh* and His Prophet, as in the greeting, "*Al-salām ʿalaykum* (peace be upon you)", to which are often added, "*Raḥmat Allāh wa barakatuh* (and the mercy of *Allāh* and His blessings)".

Barakah is a well-known concept in both Islam generally, as well as Sufism. Muḥammad is said to have brought his blessing and spiritual power – his *barakah* – to the world:

> God on high sent a Prophet to transform the abode of unbelief into the abode of *Islām* through his blessing *(barakah),* and to bring development and prosperity to the world through justice and equitable rule. The king of that epoch was Nūshirwān, who surpassed the kings who had been before him in justice, equity, and discipline. This was due to the blessings *(barakāt)* of the Apostle, God bless him, because he (the king) was born during his (the Prophet's) lifetime.
>
> *Al-Ghazālī, Counsel for Kings 2:1; cf. GCK p.55*

The name Muḥammad is believed to have *barakah,* and is a common choice among parents, though it is sometimes pronounced differently out of respect. *Sayyids,* who trace their family origins to the Prophet, regard themselves as enveloped by a particular sanctity, disseminating a *barakah.* The Muslim world contains many local shrines or tombs of saints, each still believed to retain something of the saint's *barakah.* Those wanting children or seeking fulfilment of worldly ambitions, children taking exams, sick people, those in search of spiritual illumination, and many others, all visit these shrines, hoping to invoke the saint's *barakah.* Despite the efforts of some reformers to eliminate the practice as un-Islamic, it continues as a characteristic aspect of Muslim life.

A Sufi *shaykh* confers his *barakah* on novitiates at the time of their initiation, and continues to bless them with his *barakah* to aid their spiritual evolution. Sometimes, he may put his own cloak *(khirqah* or *muraqqaʿ)* around them, as a means of conferring his *barakah.* It is believed that the *barakah* or blessed influence of the founding *shaykh* of a Sufi order is transmitted via his successors to all succeeding generations. Hence, the chain *(silsilah)* of human transmission is of great importance in Sufi orders, many tracing their descent to Muḥammad himself. Before a *shaykh* dies, he may divide up the regions where his disciples live between various successors, each being given his *barakah* for a specific geographical area only. Among Sufi orders, in addition to the initiated followers, there are often many lay members who wish to benefit from the *barakah* of the order and its *shaykh,* without making a full commitment. Many believe that the spiritual influence or *barakah* of some of the greatest Sufi mystics, like Rūmī, still exists at the present time.

Many have experienced the aura of blessedness that surrounds a master during his lifetime, and which is conveyed to others – according to their receptivity – simply by their coming into his presence. He also confers particular blessings on individuals, as he deems appropriate. A preface to the verses of Ibn al-Fāriḍ (1181–1235) contains a description given by his son Kamāl al-Dīn Muḥammad (*d.* 1290) concerning the spiritual atmosphere that surrounded his father, which characterizes such saints:

> He had a light, a diffidence, a splendour, and a venerableness. When he attended a session, there would appear over the people there a dignified silence and tranquillity. I saw attending his teaching session a group including respected jurisprudents, mendicants, and judges, and great men of state, including amirs, viziers, and the leaders of the people, and they treated him with the utmost respect and humbleness; when they addressed him, it was as if they were addressing a great king. Further, when he walked in the city, people would crowd around him seeking from him spiritual blessings *(barakah)* and benedictions, while trying to kiss his hand. But he would not allow anyone to do that; rather he shook hands with them.
>
> *Kamāl al-Dīn, Dībājat al-Dīwān, in SVSL pp.303–4*

bāxiàng chéngdào (C), **hassō jōdō** (J) *Lit.* eight *(bā, hachi)* aspects *(xiàng, sō)* to attaining the *Dào (chéngdào)* or to becoming *(jōdō)* a *buddha;* eight acts, scenes or events in the life of the Buddha, described in East Asian Buddhism, of which there are some variations, by which the Buddha revealed his teachings and brought liberation to other beings;[1] abbreviated as *bāxiàng* (C) or *hassō* (J):

1. Descent from the *tushita* paradise.
2. Entry into the womb.
3. Gestation.
4. Birth.
5. Renunciation of the householder life.
6. Attainment of enlightenment *(bodhi).*
7. Setting in motion the wheel of *Dharma.*
8. Final *nirvāṇa (parinirvāṇa).*

Some lists, especially that of the *Tendai* (C. *Tiāntái*) school, omit gestation and add (after renunciation) the Buddha's suppression of *Māra* (the Evil One) or subjugation of demons.

1. See "Hassō," *Oxford Dictionary of Buddhism, ODB.*

bhṛingī (H), **bhringī** (Pu) A parasitic wasp, which, according to Indian folklore, catches and stings a caterpillar or grub, takes it to its nest and, by making a loud humming sound, transforms it into another *bhṛingī* like itself. The apparent transformation of the caterpillar into a *bhṛingī* is used in mystical and devotional literature as a metaphor for the transformative power either of divine love or of a *guru.*

This description of the *bhṛingī* seems to identify it as a generic name for any of a number of solitary parasitic mason wasps of the genus *Odynerus,* which excavate nests in sand or in the mortar of old walls. The wasps construct nests of mud, consisting of several cells in each of which they lay a single egg suspended from the cell wall by a fine filament. They then catch and paralyse caterpillars or grubs, placing them in the mud cells before sealing the entrance. Some species place as many as thirty small grubs in each cell. Upon hatching, the wasp larvae consume the grubs before undergoing metamorphosis, and emerging from the chamber as adult wasps, giving the impression that the caterpillars have been transformed into wasps.

This popular folkloric account of the *bhṛingī* has been used by some Indian *sants* as an example of how a *guru* can turn lowly and ordinary human beings ('caterpillars') into beings like himself through the power of his care, attention, and love. In some instances, several similar metaphors are used:

> There are four kinds of *guru,* each with his own quality:
> the touchstone, the lamp, the Malaya-mountain,
> and the *bhṛingī guru.* . . .
> As soon as the touchstone *guru* touches iron, it turns to gold.
> As soon as the Malaya-mountain *guru*
> touches the *shīsham* and *ḍhāk* trees,
> they turn completely to sandalwood.
>
> When the disciple becomes like a caterpillar *(kīṭ),*
> the *bhṛingī guru* turns him into his teacher's form.
> When the *guru,* who is a lamp burning without a flame,
> sees the disciple and reaches out brightly towards him,
> light shines in the middle of the house.

Sahajobāī, Bānī, Satguru Mahimā kā Ang 6, Dohā Chaupāī 8, SBB p.2, SPBS pp.6–9

> Iron turns into gold by the touch of a philosopher's stone –
> so does one meet the Lord by contact with a saint.
> A caterpillar becomes a *bhṛingī* in the company of a *bhṛingī* –
> so does one meet the Lord by association with a saint.
> A tree in the neighbourhood of sandalwood takes on its fragrance –
> so does one meet the Lord in the company of a saint.

Whatever goes into fire becomes fire –
so does one meet the Lord by contact with a saint.

Nāmdev, Gāthā 863, SNG p.319; cf. SNPS p.28

A devoted disciple is deeply influenced by his *guru*. The mind takes on the character of whatever it dwells upon; and the *guru* himself, by his spiritual power, slowly transforms the disciple:

Just as the caterpillar *(kīṭ)* finds its transforming *guru* in the *bhṛingī,*
so is the disciple transformed by the *guru*'s wisdom.
It is the contemplation of the *satguru*'s lotus feet
by which a human being is transformed....
This secret is known to a wise one, or is spoken of by some poets.

Dariyā Sāhib, Sahasrānī, UHMD p.13; cf. DSSK p.298

A *guru* is a personification of the divine Name, the creative power that purifies the mind:

Abandoning my evil ways, I have counselled my mind:
adopting the Name, I have overcome lust;
Purity and forgiveness are now firmly planted in my heart,
and my mind has soared like a bird into the inner sky.
Like a *bhṛingī,* my *guru* has transformed the caterpillar *(kīṭ)* of my soul.

Swami Shiv Dayal Singh, Sār Bachan Poetry 5:5.23–25,
SBP p.48; cf. SBPS pp.33–35

I am restless, O Lord, for a glimpse of You.
You are the lamp, I am a moth:
in Your flame I have burnt my mind to ashes.
I have met the perfect adept in You, *Rādhā Swāmī,*
You have transformed this helpless caterpillar *(kīṭ),* as does a *bhṛingī*....
You are the ocean, I am a wave,
from You I arose, in You I am finally merged.
You are the sun, I am a ray of light,
from You I emerged, to You I have returned.
You are the pearl, I am the string,
never am I really separate from You....
I am a little child, You are the father,
You are the mother, day and night I play in Your lap.

Swami Shiv Dayal Singh, Sār Bachan Poetry 6:5.4–6, 8–10, 13,
SBP p.54, SBPS pp.43–45

The creative power is experienced as both sound and light. Hence, says Ravidās:

> When the mind becomes completely absorbed in the light,
> only then will the caterpillar *(kīṭ)* become a *bhṛingī.*
>
> *Ravidās, Vāṇī 49, SGRV p.90*

Just as the caterpillar does not know what has happened to it, so is the disciple unaware of the power of the *guru* to transform him:

> The caterpillar *(kīṭ)* knows not the *bhṛingī,*
> who converts it into his own form.
>
> *Kabīr, Sākhī Sangrah, Gurudev kā Ang 1, KSS p.1*

See also: **ḍhāk**, **kūnj**, **nimba**.

bī-murshid (P), **bemurshid** (U) *Lit.* without *(be)* a master *(murshid);* synonymous with *nigurā* (without a *guru*); one who has no master or *guru.* The tradition of having a *guru* is so strong in India and among the Sufis, that to call a person *bemurshid* or *nigurā* was – at least until modern times – a significant insult. Spiritual progress was considered impossible without a competent master:

> Do not utter the name of one without a *murshid (bī-murshid):*
> a perfect *murshid* gives you signs from the Lord.
>
> *Bhā'ī Nand Lāl Goyā, Kullīyāt, KNLG p.103, in SBU p.136, SBE p.70*

See also: **guru** (7.1), **murshid** (7.1), **nigurā**.

brahmachakra (S), **brahmacakka** (Pa) *Lit.* wheel *(chakra)* of *Brahmā* or the wheel of *Brahma;* either the wheel of *Brahma (Brahman)* or of the Hindu deity *Brahmā;* used more or less synonymously in Buddhism with *dharmachakra,* the wheel of *Dharma.*

There is some ambiguity in Buddhist usage because *Dharma* (Pa. *Dhamma*) is sometimes used synonymously with *Brahma* or *Brahman,* the supreme Reality of the *Upanishads.* Hence, *brahmachakra* can mean either the wheel of *Brahman* or the wheel of the deity *Brahmā.* A verse in the *Dīgha Nikāya,* for example, says that one who has risen above craving *(nicchāta)* lives in bliss, having "become as *Brahma (brahmabhūta)*",[1] while another verse says that the Tathāgata (the Buddha) is characterized by the expressions: "The 'body of *Dhamma (dhammakāya)*', that is, the 'body of *Brahma (brahmakāya)*'; or 'become as the *Dhamma (dhammabhūta)*', that is, 'become as *Brahma (brahmabhūta)*'".[2] In this instance, the Buddha was speaking to *brāhmaṇs,* telling them that the *Dhamma,* being the term used by the Buddha for the highest Reality, is the same as the *Brahma* or *Brahman* of *brāhmaṇ* philosophy.

In Hindu literature such as the *Upanishads, brahmachakra* refers to the universe in which all the souls "flutter about" in the cycle of birth and death, thinking that it is separate from the divine Doer. Here again, *Brahma* is commonly interpreted to mean *Brahman,* the divine Reality, rather than the Hindu deity *Brahmā.*[3]

Brahmachakra is also a synonym for the *mūlādhāra chakra,* the lowest centre of *prāṇa* (life energy) in the human body, which is associated with the deity *Brahmā.*

See also: **dharmachakra**.

1. *Dīgha Nikāya* 33, *Sangīti Sutta, PTSD3* p.233, *TBLD* p.494.
2. *Dīgha Nikāya* 27, *Aggañña Sutta, PTSD3* p.84; *cf. TBLD* p.409.
3. *E.g. Shvetāshvatara Upanishad* 1:6, 6:1.

buddhavachana (S), **buddhavacana** (Pa) *Lit.* word *(vachana)* of the Buddha; the texts accepted within a particular Buddhist tradition as being the words of the Buddha, either literally or as an accurate expression of the Buddha's teachings, which includes those texts that make no claim to being the Buddha's actual words; also called *pravachana* (foremost words, a spiritual discourse, a sermon).

There are two interpretations of *buddhavacana* – the literal and the liberal. According to the literal interpretation, the *tipiṭaka* (basket) of canonical Pali texts were committed to memory at the First Council, held soon after the Buddha's death. The *tipiṭaka* is said to contain the entire teachings of the Buddha, including everything he said from the time of his enlightenment until the day of his death.

The more liberal view maintains that the discourses and teachings of the Buddha, his disciples, *ṛishis* and *devas* can all be regarded as *buddhavacana.* If a text was not believed to be the actual words of the Buddha, the process of establishing it as *buddhavacana* involved comparison with accepted texts and teachings, and ratification by a *buddha,* a gathering of the *sangha* (a Buddhist community), or a group of wise monks. These criteria are laid down in the *tipiṭaka* itself, in the *Mahāpadesa Sutta* of the *Dīgha Nikāya.*

The different Buddhist traditions each have their own canon of accepted teachings or *buddhavacana.*

See also: **vachana**.

bùlì wénzì (C), **furyū monji** (J) *Lit.* not established *(bùlì, furyū)* by written language *(wénzì, monji)*; an expression embodying the *Chán* and *Zen* concept that understanding is non-verbal, that spiritual awakening can occur through intuitive discernment and may be transmitted from the mind of the master to the mind of the disciple. It does not consist of intellectually understanding the words of either the master or Buddhist scriptures. It is a realization of the inner Truth, as expressed in the *Xuèmài lùn* (J. *Ketsumyaku ron*), a text attributed to Bodhidharma, who is credited with bringing Buddhism to China, whence it spread to Japan:

> The three worlds arise from and return to One Mind. From *buddhas* of the past to succeeding *buddhas,* (the *Dharma*) is transmitted from mind to mind, without reliance on words and letters *(bùlì wénzì).*
>
> *Xuèmài lùn, T48 2009:373b13–14, in IEZB p.156*

See also: **ishin denshin**, **menju shihō**.

bùyán zhī jiào (C) *Lit.* teaching *(jiào)* without words *(bùyán)* + *zhī* (possessive particle); unspoken teaching.

Mentioned several times in the *Dàodé jīng,* teaching without words has three aspects:

1. The *shī* (teacher) does not want to 'lord it' over his disciples; he prefers to emulate the primary characteristics of *Dào,* which are *wúwéi* (noncontrivance, noncontention), *zìrán* (naturalness, spontaneity), and *pǔ* (plainness, simplicity). The disciples then learn by the example of their master.

2. The *shī* chooses to use the fewest words to convey his teachings – keeping them simple and to the point, without prevarication.

3. The *shī* explains that practice is better than precept; meaning that his teachings will convey the concepts of Reality, but the disciple will only realize the truth of the teachings when, by following the teacher's instructions, the disciple actually experiences the Reality for himself.

According to the *Daode jing:*

> The sage *(shèngrén)* carries on his business
> without (contrived) action *(wúwéi),*
> and gives his teaching without words *(bùyán zhī jiào)*
>
> *Lǎozǐ, Dàodé jīng 2, TTCT p.13*

A later chapter confirms that *bùyán zhī jiào* is on an equal footing with the teaching of *wúwéi* (noncontrivance, noncontention) as regards a person's behaviour:

> The teaching without words *(bùyán zhī jiào)*
> and the benefit of taking no action *(wúwéi)*
> are without compare in the universe.
>
> *Lǎozǐ, Dàodé jīng 43, WLT p.216*

Transmission of the teachings may occur by just a touch or a look from an enlightened master. Such a true master has the power to transmit the teachings without words, in such a way that those who are meant to absorb them will do so:

> When pure sincerity forms within, it is outwardly realized in other people's hearts. This is the Way *(Dào)* that is not transmitted *(búchuán)*. When sages *(shèngrén)* are in high positions, they embrace the Way and do not speak *(bùyán)*, yet the benefit extends to all the people. Therefore, the unspoken teaching *(bùyán zhī jiào)* is very great indeed.
>
> *Wénzǐ 2, TCC1 pp.170–71*

It is said metaphorically that a lime tree, if planted in close proximity to a sandalwood tree, will absorb the fragrance of the sandalwood; whereas a bamboo does not have the capacity to absorb any fragrance at all. Similarly, the aura of spiritual energy surrounding an enlightened teacher may be sufficient to transform a deserving disciple by awakening the spirit to the *Dào,* elevating it to higher levels of consciousness. This is reflected in a story in the *Zhuāngzǐ* (C4th BCE), in which Huángdì (the Yellow Emperor) quotes an ancient scripture:

> (As it is said), "Those who know *(Dào)* do not speak of it; those who speak of it do not know it;"[1] and, "Hence the sage *(shèngrén)* conveys his instructions without the use of speech *(bùyán zhī jiào)*."[2]
>
> *Zhuāngzǐ 22, TT2 p.58*

1. Lǎozǐ, *Dàodé jīng* 56.
2. Lǎozǐ, *Dàodé jīng* 3; *cf. Dàodé jīng* 43.

chashm-i nargis (P) *Lit.* narcissus *(nargis)* eye *(chashm)*. See **nargis**.

chatuḥ-saṃgraha-vastu, **chatvāri-saṃgraha-vastu** (S), **bsdu ba'i dngos po bzhi** (T), **sì shèfǎ**, **sì shèshì** (C), **shi shōhō**, **shi shōji** (J) *Lit.* four *(chatuḥ, bzhi, sì, shi)* all-embracing *(saṃgraha, shè, shō)* principles *(fǎ, hō)* or things *(vastu, dngos po, shì, ji);* four persuasive or inducing things; four methods of winning people over; four means by which to assemble (seekers); four means of conversion; a term from *Mahāyāna* Buddhism for the four means used by *bodhisattvas* to attract other beings; the four methods or stratagems to be developed by *bodhisattvas* for inducing their fellow beings to follow the path of liberation; the four all-embracing virtues by which a desire for enlightenment (*bodhichitta,* 'wisdom-mind') is engendered in the minds of others; listed by the Buddhist philosopher Nāgārjuna as one of the thirty-two *dharmas* (virtues) of a *bodhisattva.*[1] The four means, mentioned in a number of *Mahāyāna* texts, are:

1. Unstinting giving or generosity (S. *dāna-saṃgraha*), both spiritually and materially.

2. Kind, loving, and pleasant words (S. *priya-vādita-saṃgraha*); giving discourses on the *Dharma* in an attractive manner.

3. Beneficence and helping others (S. *artha-charya-saṃgraha*), by body, mind, and words.

4. Sympathy, empathy, comradeship, and accommodation (S. *samānārthatā-saṃgraha,* Pa. *samānattatā,* T. *don mthun pa*). *Samānārtha* means 'equivalence' or 'having a common object or intention'. In this instance, it refers to the development of a mutual spiritual purpose, co-operation with and adaptation to others' viewpoints with the intention of guiding them towards a clearer understanding concerning the nature of things and of Reality; also, coming to the same level and taking on the same form as the particular sentient beings that are to be helped.

By this kind of compassionate and kindly conduct, a *bodhisattva* is able to influence those who might not otherwise be attracted to the *buddhadharma* (teachings of the Buddha). In the process, according to the Buddhist way of thinking, a *bodhisattva* acquires great merit, which brings him closer to buddhahood.

The four means of inducement are mentioned in a number of *sūtras,* along with other attributes and virtues to be found in a *bodhisattva.* In the *Mahāratnakūṭa Sūtra,* King Prasenajit meets Bodhisattva Surata, who informs the king that because of his insatiable greed, he is the poorest man in his kingdom. Fortunately for the *bodhisattva,* the king takes the criticism in the spirit with which it is intended. Filled with shame and remorse, he asks Surata to take him to meet the Buddha:

> Bodhisattva Surata told him, "Be aware, Your Majesty, that it is most uncommon to meet a *buddha* and to listen to (an exposition of) the

true *Dharma.* Your Majesty, do not go alone. Rather, as a good friend to sentient beings, order everyone in the city of Shrāvastī to accompany you there. Decree that anyone who disobeys your order will be punished according to the law of the land."

King Prasenajit enquired of the *bodhisattva,* "What is a *bodhisattva*'s retinue?"

Surata replied, "To inspire a mind that seeks enlightenment *(bodhichitta)* is the retinue of a *bodhisattva,* because it leads to enlightenment *(bodhi).*

"To raise the consciousness and encourage a meeting with the *tathāgata* is the retinue of a *bodhisattva,* because it leads to a rejection of what is unreal.

"To encourage listening to (a discourse on) the true *Dharma* is the retinue of a *bodhisattva,* because it results in great understanding.

"To encourage association with spiritually minded people *(i.e.* the *sangha)* is the retinue of a *bodhisattva,* because it fosters the habit of keeping good company.

"The four inducements *(sì shèshì)* are the retinue of a *bodhisattva,* because all sentient beings are attracted thereby (to the *buddhadharma*)."

Mahāratnakūṭa Sūtra 30, T11 310:540a1–11

Again, in the *Mahāratnakūṭa Sūtra,* the Buddha includes the practice of "the four inducements" as one of four effective means of accumulating the roots of goodness *(kushala-mūla)* that will further the spiritual evolution of a *bodhisattva:*

A *bodhisattva* has four means of accumulating the roots of goodness *(kushala-mūla).* What are these four?

1. To avoid idleness, flattery, and fawning.
2. To practise the four inducements *(sì shèfǎ)* among sentient beings with no expectation of a reward.
3. To seek the *Dharma* enthusiastically, with little regard for body or life.
4. To cultivate the roots of goodness *(kushala-mūla)* tirelessly.

Mahāratnakūṭa Sūtra 43, T11 310:632c20–22

1. Nāgārjuna, *Dashabhūmika Vibhāshā, T26* 1521:94a11.

chatvāri-pratisaṃvidaḥ (S), **sì wúài jiě** (C) *Lit.* fourfold *(chatvāri)* reasoned or analytical knowledge *(pratisaṃvid);* fourfold *(sì)* unimpeded *(wúài)* understanding *(jiě);* also as *sì wúài zhì* (*zhì* means 'knowledge') or *sì wúài biàn* (*biàn* means 'reasoning and interpretation'); four forms of unlimited knowledge of the *Dharma* (Way, teachings); a *Mahāyāna* Buddhist term for the source of the teaching power of *buddhas* and *bodhisattvas,* and their ability to convey understanding of the *Dharma.* The unimpeded or unrestrained aspect of such understanding is an addition made to the term by Chinese Buddhism.

The four forms of unimpeded understanding are explained at length in the *Mahāparinirvāṇa Sūtra*[1] and a number of other texts. In summary, they are:

1. *Dharma-pratisaṃvid.* Complete understanding of the *Dharma;* full knowledge concerning the intrinsic nature of all phenomena and its essential unreality, together with the names of everything, without any attachment or clinging to that understanding. It is because a *bodhisattva* remains unattached to all aspects of his knowledge and eloquence that it is said to be "unhindered" and "unimpeded". The *bodhisattva* also understands that all the various Buddhist schools are essentially one school – the various outer Ways, with their apparent doctrinal divergences, meet together in one inner Way.

2. *Artha-pratisaṃvid.* Complete mastery of the meanings inherent in the *Dharma;* full understanding of the detailed meaning and characteristics of all phenomena, past and future, their beginning and their end, including which names belong to which meaning, without any attachment or clinging to that understanding. A *bodhisattva* knows the divisions and differences between all things, including all the basic elements that comprise the material world and the sense organs that perceive them, the various spiritual paths and Buddhist schools, and the ten stages *(bhūmis)* passed through by *bodhisattvas.* He knows all the characteristics and ruling principles governing the myriad different kinds of being; and he understands the teachings of the Buddha.

3. *Nirukti-pratisaṃvid.* Full understanding of all the languages spoken in different countries; mastery of both languages and oratory, giving rise to complete freedom in expressing the *Dharma* in various languages and dialects; a knowledge of the names and associated etymology of all things regarding all aspects of their existence, without any attachment or clinging to them. A *bodhisattva* knows how to teach the pure *Dharma,* without confusing the past, present, and future. He does not confuse the relative truth concerning phenomena with the experience of true knowledge. His language is accessible to everyone, and everyone finds him pleasant to listen to. He teaches according to all spiritual paths without distinguishing between them. He teaches the stages of perfection, the Way, and meditative

concentration. He teaches the word of the Buddha, and the duties incumbent upon the different living beings. He also comes to know the means of communication used by celestial beings such as *devas, nāgas, yakshas, gandharvas, asuras, garuḍas, kinnaras,* and *mahoragas.*

4. *Pratibhāna-pratisaṃvid.* Understanding supported by complete confidence, courage, and fundamental intelligence. *Pratibhāna* implies quick-wittedness, presence of mind, intelligence, understanding, confidence, self-reliance, courage, boldness. From this inner focus of complete integrity and presence of mind arises the ability to discourse to all people with great ease and eloquence. A *bodhisattva* can speak about all ideas and all teachings *(dharmas)* to all people, and he goes on doing so for innumerable *kalpas* (ages), without any attachment or clinging to these ideas and teachings. He speaks truth, not falsehood; righteousness not unrighteousness; he encourages beings to seek liberation and escape from the cycle of transmigration. *Pratibhāna* in an enlightened being is inspiring, pleasing, and breeds confidence in the listeners.

The four unlimited understandings and unhindered eloquences are commonly enumerated along with the ten powers *(dashabala),* the four fearlessnesses *(chatvāri-vaishāradyāni),* the eighteen attributes *(āveṇika-dharma),* and so on, of a *buddha.*[2] Their nature is further explained in the *Mahāratnakūṭa Sūtra.* Here, "phenomena" refers to everything in the realms of apparent duality:

> What is a *bodhisattva*'s hidden treasure of *dharma?* It means that the *bodhisattva* sees all phenomena for what they really are. He knows that they originate from the unborn, the innately pure. Because the *bodhisattva* has acquired the ability to see through (the appearance of) phenomena, he is able to realize the four kinds of unimpeded understanding *(sì wúài biàn).* What are these four? They are the unimpeded understanding of meaning, the unimpeded knowledge of *dharmas,* the unimpeded use of language, and the unimpeded ability to discourse.
>
> The unimpeded understanding of meaning is the unobstructed and unattached understanding of all phenomena. To understand the meaning of all phenomena is to find the ultimate Truth. Why is it called the ultimate Truth? Because of the unreality of phenomena. Realization of such understanding is supreme wisdom. So it is called the unimpeded understanding of meaning.
>
> The unimpeded knowledge of *dharmas* is to gain knowledge of the Truth. It arises from the complete understanding of phenomena.
>
> The unimpeded use of language is the skilful use of any kind of language or expression to describe phenomena in every possible way, with unobstructed wisdom.

The unimpeded ability to discourse is to elucidate and discourse upon all phenomena to living beings according to their various dispositions, without any attachment or effect upon oneself.

Such are the unimpeded eloquences, the effortless wisdom attained by a *bodhisattva.* He enlightens deluded beings who cling to phenomena. With his wisdom of non-action, he expounds the *Dharma* consistent with their natural tendencies and desires. He holds no dualistic view concerning *dharmadhātu* (the essence of existence). He also explains this view to those deluded beings who are attached to sounds, scents, tastes, textures, and *dharmas* (*i.e.* various doctrines).

Mahāratnakūṭa Sūtra 20, T11 310:485c14–27

1. See *Mahāparinirvāṇa Sūtra* 17, *T12* 374:462c22–463c5, *MMSY* (22) pp.225–27; see also Har Dayal, *Bodhisattva Doctrine, BDBS* pp.263–67.
2. *E.g. Mahāratnakūṭa Sūtra* 21, *T11* 310:486b29–c7.

church (Gk. *ekklēsia, kyriakos*) From *kyriakon doma* (Gk. Lord's house), from *kyros* (Gk. power); related to *cirice* (Old English); a building used for public Christian worship; also, a particular Christian community or branch of Christianity. Although the origin of the word is from the Greek *kyriakos,* it is used to translate the Greek *ekklēsia* (assembly, congregation, community). *Kyriakos* came into Christian usage during the third century, especially among the Teutonic races, and was used along with *ekklēsia* for places of Christian worship. The French and Spanish words for church *(église, iglesia)* are both derived from *ekklēsia,* but also have the double meaning of both building and community. The Scottish 'kirk' (from Old Norse, *kirkja*) also has the same double meaning, referring to both the building and the Presbyterian Church of Scotland.

The history of the Christian church from its earliest times, with its various schisms and divisions, development of doctrine, ecclesiastical hierarchy, and so on, is a long and complex story, and there is no intention here of entering upon that extensive territory. A brief consideration of the early usage of the term will suffice.

In Christianity's earliest days, before the construction of churches, a Christian community was known as a church *(ekklēsia).* Hence, the King James Version of *Acts* speaks of the "church *(ekklēsia)* that was at Antioch",[1] while other translations speak of the "community"[2] or "congregation".[3] Paul also addresses letters to the "church *(ekklēsia)* of God which is at Corinth",[4] the "church *(ekklēsia)* of the Thessalonians",[5] and the "churches of Galatia *(ekklēsiai)*".[6] In fact, the term appears throughout *Acts,* the letters of Paul and others, and continuously throughout the literature of early Christianity.

In the four gospels, however, the term only appears in *Matthew,* where Jesus says that he will build his church upon a rock (Gk. *petra*), meaning Peter (Gk. *petros*);[7] and also where *Matthew* has Jesus advise – when dealing with brotherly transgressions – first try to clear things personally with the individual; then if that fails, in the presence of "two or three witnesses"; and if that does not work, before the "church *(ekklēsia)*".[8] Bearing in mind its earlier occurrence in Paul's letters, it is likely that the term was adopted into Christianity at an early stage. It was a common Greek word, and was also the Greek term, along with *synagōgē* (gathering), used for Jewish communities.

According to Irenaeus, some of the gnostics posited a higher spiritual church, which is an archetype or pattern of the earthly church below. This would be in keeping with the gnostic principle that everything below is a representation of something that lies above. Ptolemy, disciple of Valentinus, spoke of eight primal powers or divine entities (the *Ogdoad*) forming the *plērōma* (fullness), the higher Essence from which all creation below came into being. The eight are: the Father, *Charis* (Grace), *Monogenēs* (Only-begotten), *Aletheia* (Truth), the *Logos* (Word), *Zōē* (Life), *Anthrōpos* (Man), and *Ekklēsia* (Church). The spiritual *Ekklēsia* in the higher world is the archetype or pattern of the earthly church. Within the *plērōma,* the higher gives rise to the lower. The Father is hence the origin of all, who gives birth to the *Monogenēs,* from whom the *Logos* comes into being; and the conjunction of *Logos* and *Zōē* give rise to *Anthrōpos* and *Ekklēsia.*[9] Ptolemy, following Valentinus, derives this cosmogony from the opening of John's gospel,[10] where all the above are mentioned.

In the Nag Hammadi text *On the Origin of the World* the writer speaks of the creation of a host of angels as an *ekklēsia,* created as a reflection of a higher heaven by a lesser ruler *(Sabaoth)* in the 'administration' of the demiurge *Yaldabaoth:*

> Thereafter, he *(Sabaoth,* son of *Yaldabaoth)* created a congregation *(ekklēsia)* of angels, thousands and myriads, numberless, which resembled the congregation *(ekklēsia)* in the eighth heaven.
>
> *Origin of the World 105, NHS21 pp.44–45*

Various terms for church or religion, in different languages, were also used among the Manichaeans. Here, the various terms refer to both the congregation of followers or devotees as well as the religion or spiritual path itself. In Manichaean literature, the church is led and inspired by the "Great *Nous*", the *Vahman* (Pv), or *Nom Quti* (Turkish) – the primal Intelligence or Mind of God, the divine active Principle in creation, the divine Word or *Logos.*

The *Nous, Vahman* or *Nom Quti* is also the essence of the saviour. In his day, Jesus was the saviour; later, it was Mānī. Mānī also taught that in their own times, Buddha, Zarathushtra and others had all been saviours, incarnations of the divine *Nous* or *Vahman.* In Manichaean texts, the "*Vahman* of Light" or the "valiant *Vahman*" is described as the "ruler of the holy church". One of the Pahlavi terms commonly translated as 'church' is *dīn,* which also means 'religion'. Mānī, too, is described as the "king",[11] "lord", or "ruler of the church":[12]

> You have come in peace, giver of life to souls,
>   Lord Mānī, Messenger of Light!...
> You have come in peace, lord of the church!
>
> *Manichaean Hymns, HMV p.304ff.; cf. GSR p.84, ML p.11*

The equivalent term appears frequently in the Coptic psalms. Speaking of the saviour as a cosmic power who takes various human forms over the course of time, the unknown psalmist says:

> You left your great glory,
>   you came and gave yourself for souls.
> You assumed different forms
>   until you had visited all races:
> For the sake of your loved ones,
>   until you had chosen them out of their midst....
> You sought out your beloved, your church,
>   until you had found her.
>
> *Manichaean Psalm Book CCXLI; cf. MPB pp.42–43*

Here, the implication is that a saviour comes for a particular preordained group of disciples whom he "seeks out" or draws to himself in a variety of ways. Another psalm reflects the geographical extent of Mānī's church – from China to Rome:

> Lo, your holy churches have spread out
>   to the four corners of the world.
> Lo, your vine trees have filled every place.
> Lo, your sons have become famous in all lands.
>
> *Manichaean Psalm Book CCXXIV; cf. MPB p.13*

Indicating that this "church" as a spiritual path is always present, though different saviours bring the revelation, another psalm says:

> Lo, the church has been revealed again, even as it is;
> But it is renewed from time to time.
>
> *Manichaean Psalm Book, MPB p.162*

Another psalm speaks significantly of

> the Power that supports the universe,
> the holy Wisdom *(Sophia)* that is in the church.
>
> *Manichaean Psalm Book, MPB p.134*

Here, Power and Wisdom are both terms for the divine Word, the *Vahman* or Great *Nous*. That it is the individuals who comprise a church, not a building, is evident from another psalm, where the saviour is Jesus:

> Holy hearts, holy minds,
> may we build into a church....
> The bride is the church,
> the bridegroom is the *Nous* of light.
> The bride is the soul,
> the bridegroom is Jesus.
>
> *Manichaean Psalm Book, MPB pp.153–54*

See also: **congregation, early Christian communities, ekklēsia**.

1. *Acts* 13:1, *KJV*.
2. *E.g. ANTH*.
3. *E.g. New English Bible, NEB*.
4. *1 Corinthians* 1:2, *2 Corinthians* 1:1, *KJV*.
5. *1 Thessalonians* 1:1, *2 Thessalonians* 1:1, *KJV*.
6. *Galatians* 1:2, *KJV*.
7. *Matthew* 16:18, *KJV*.
8. *Matthew* 18:15–17, *KJV*.
9. Irenaeus, *Against Heresies* I:8.5, *AH1* pp.35–38.
10. *John* 1:1–14.
11. *E.g. Manichaean Hymns, MBB* p.18*ff.*, *GSR* pp.134.
12. *E.g. Manichaean Hymns, MDT* p.556*ff.*, *RMP* cn, *GSR* p.93; *MDT* p.599*ff.*, *RMP* cd, *GSR* p.80.

congregation (in Daoism) (C. *huì, huìzhòng*) The origins of Daoism are uncertain, but it is commonly assumed in Daoist literature to have evolved from human closeness to nature in ancient times, and from the consequent state of simplicity in which human beings lived. Later, people were attracted to the writings of the *Yìjīng* (*c.*1000 BCE) and, from the sixth century BCE, to the *Dàodé jīng*. Both of these ancient scriptures prescribed naturalness and spontaneity *(zìrán)*, as a means of finding peace of mind and happiness. By combining a life of simplicity and naturalness with a harmonious attitude towards nature and its benevolence, it was believed and hoped that both rulers and their people would embody the *dé* (nature, characteristics, virtue) of *Dào*.

During the Warring States period (475–221 BCE), withdrawal from the divisive world of war and politics, and the life of a recluse was advocated by the *Lièzĭ* and the *Zhuāngzĭ* in order to cultivate physical longevity and spiritual immortality. These two primary Daoist texts are named respectively after Daoist philosophers Lièzĭ (*fl.c.*400 BCE) and Zhuāngzĭ (*c.*370–301 BCE).

The establishment of various Daoist schools began during the early centuries of the Common Era (CE). Congregations developed, and religious writings appeared, many of which became holy scriptures. Around the year 142, Daoist master Zhāng Dàolíng founded the *Tiānshī* school of Daoism, which, among other things, encouraged the formation of congregations as a means of mutual support.

The mid-fourth century saw the formation of the *Shàngqīng* mystical school of Daoism. Its principle tenets included the doctrine that the human body is both the meeting place of 'heaven and earth' and home to various deities. The school established practices to realize these deities within.

The *Língbăo* school of Daoism, which later became the foundation of organized Daoist religion, came into being during the late fourth century. Many of the *Língbăo* rituals from this period are still practised today.

During the late fifth century, seekers were drawn to the teachings of the *Tiānshī* school of Daoism. Lù Xiūjìng established congregations in southern China, while Kòu Qiānzhī established congregations in northern China. The *Tiānshī* school continues in the present day under its alternative name of *Zhèngyī*.

In the late sixth century, Táo Hóngjĭng took the *Máoshān Shàngqīng* school of Daoism (established fourth century) to a higher level of prominence with the establishment of a major Daoist centre on the mountain of Máoshān. During the seventh to ninth centuries, the school established temples throughout the country, and became the dominant school in China. However, the school eventually declined in popularity and, in the early tenth century, was absorbed into the *Tiānshī (Zhèngyī)* school.

Around 1160, Daoist master Wáng Zhé founded the *Quánzhēn* school of Daoism in northern China, which incorporated various Confucian and Buddhist influences into Daoism. Members of this school lived a strict monastic lifestyle. *Quánzhēn* survives today as one of the two major schools of Daoism, with its headquarters in Běijīng.

Since the early first century (CE), therefore, associations of various sizes have existed, all possessing a common interest in the *Dào*. These ranged from small rural and village groups to large urban associations, with varying degrees of organization and structure. To this day, Daoist congregations meet together to perform religious ceremonies, rites, and rituals.

Daoist congregations are associations of people who have a common interest in cultivating the *Dào* within themselves. Members range from seekers and disciples to adepts and sages. Many also engage in charitable works in their communities. Tolerance, harmony and acceptance are aspirations of Daoist individuals and communities everywhere.

It has been a common practice for these associations to distinguish the headquarters of their association from others by giving them a unique name. Examples include Lóuguàn ('Lookout Tower Monastery') in Zhōngnán, and Báiyún Guàn ('White Cloud Monastery') in Běijīng.

Many disciples join monasteries to further dedicate themselves to *Dào* and to associate with others of like mind. Adepts and sages, having a permanent and natural association with *Dào,* share their spiritual knowledge with students and disciples by teaching them the benefits and methods of reading, self-cultivation, and meditation.

In a mystical and spiritual context, the term 'association' may be used to describe something linked to *Dào* in the imagination or memory, or to the process of forming mental connections to, or bonds with *Dào.*

congregation, council of the holy An assembly of people who gather together for worship of a particular kind; in Judaism, especially throughout the Hebrew Bible, the "congregation of Israel", meaning the entire Jewish community; in Christianity, a group who collect together in a church, or who habitually attend a particular church; in Manichaeism, the community of disciples and later followers of the Manichaean religion; in Mandaeism, the community of followers; also, the community of disciples who congregate around a mystic; used somewhat synonymously with church, in the sense of 'community'.

The followers of the Jewish group responsible for the Dead Sea Scrolls describe themselves as the "congregation of His elect", "congregation of the Poor",[1] the "holy congregation", or simply as "the Congregation".[2] Some translators have used the alternative word 'council'.

In the translations of the psalms from the Dead Sea Scrolls, the "congregation", "all those who are gathered in Thy Covenant" and the "council of the holy" are the souls who are gathered together under the care of a master, in this case – it is presumed – the teacher of righteousness, who is presumed to have been the leader of the Qumran community that lived at the settlement near the caves where the Dead Sea Scrolls were discovered. The "way of Thy heart" is the inner path that leads back to God. The psalmist writes:

> Thou hast revealed Thyself to me in Thy Power as perfect Light,
> and Thou has not covered my face with shame.
> All those who are gathered in Thy Covenant enquire of me;

And they hearken to me who walk in the way of Thy heart,
who array themselves for Thee in the council of the holy....

Through me Thou hast illumined the face of the congregation
and hast shown Thine infinite Power.
For Thou hast given me knowledge through Thy marvellous mysteries,
and hast shown Thyself mighty within me
in the midst of Thy marvellous council.
Thou hast done wonders before the congregation
for the sake of Thy glory,
that they may make known Thy mighty deeds to all the living.

Thanksgiving Hymns 12:20–30, CDSV pp.270–71

In language and imagery consonant with the Hebrew Bible and Jewish apocryphal literature, the same writer also speaks of the heavenly host, the angels of heaven, as the "host of the holy ones" and the "congregation of the sons of heaven":

Thou hast cleansed a perverse spirit of great sin
that it may stand with the host of the holy ones;
And that it may enter into community
with the congregation of the sons of heaven.
Thou hast allotted to man an everlasting destiny
amidst the spirits of knowledge,
that he may praise Thy Name in a common rejoicing
and recount Thy marvels before all Thy works.

Thanksgiving Hymns 10:20–25, CDSV pp.266–67

A recurrent theme among the Mandaean texts is the coming of a saviour, sent by "Life (God)" to the "congregation of souls" in this world, to take some of them back to their eternal home ("the house of perfection"). "Came to their end" can mean either the end of human life or the end of the spiritual journey. Some souls accept the message of the saviour; others do not:

I came to the congregation of souls,
for Life sent me, sent me forth.
Some there were who bought my wares,
there were those who came to their end and lay down.
There were those who bought my wares:
their eyes were filled with light;
Filled with light were their eyes,
beholding the Great One in the house of perfection.

> Some there were who did not buy my wares:
> they went on, reached their end and lay down.
> They were blind and saw not,
> their ears were stopped and they heard not;
> And their hearts were not awakened
> to behold the Great One in the house of perfection.
>
> *Mandaean Prayer Book 90, CPM p.94*

In a number of places, the "congregation of souls" refers more specifically to the Mandaeans themselves. Again, it is the saviour who is speaking:

> To the earth they sent me to voice the Call of Life....
> To deliver the whole congregation of souls,
> (the souls) of Naṣoraeans and Mandaeans,
> so that the Sinner (the Evil One, the devil)
> may have no power over them.
> I set forth – with my radiance that is great
> I came to this world:
> I called with the Voice of Life.
>
> *Mandaean Prayer Book 161, CPM pp.138–39*

See also: **church**, **ekklēsia**.

1. *E.g. Commentary on Psalm 37, CDSV* p.520.
2. *E.g. Community Rule, passim; cf. DSSE.*

daishū (J), **dàzhòng** (C), **mahāsaṃgha** (S) *Lit.* big *(tai, dà, mahā)* mass of people, congregation *(shū, zhòng, saṃgha);* great assembly, large gathering; a formal *dharma* talk and subsequent discussion given by the abbot of a *Zen* or *Chán* monastery or temple, and attended by the entire monastic community. In Indian Buddhism, especially in the early centuries, a *mahāsaṃgha* was an assembly of Buddhist monks, often convened for political reasons associated with Buddhist organization and principles.

In a modern *Zen* context, the talk or discourse delivered by the abbot, seated in the *dharma* chair *(hōza)* on a central dais in the *dharma* hall *(hattō)*. The content is generally based upon one of the classical *Zen* texts. It is said that, at that time, the abbot represents the Buddha and the *Zen* patriarchs who taught the *Dharma* before him. The formal discourse part of the *daishū* is known as a *teishō*. Traditionally and according to the monastic code, *daishū* should be held every five days. In modern times, they are held mostly during the summer and winter retreats.[1]

See also: **saṃgha**, **shōsan**.

1. See "Daisan," *Illustrated Encyclopedia of Zen Buddhism, IEZB.*

darbār (P/U/H/Pu) (pl. *darbārān*) *Lit.* court, especially a royal court; hall of audience, meeting hall; anglicized as 'durbar'; from the Persian *dar* (door) + *bār* (entrance); metaphorically, the presence of God or a master, both being described as kings. The devotee takes refuge in the master's court, inner and outer. In many instances, no distinction is made between the *darbār* of God and the *darbār* of the master:

> I will stand in your court *(darbār)*
> as if I were a slave in your house.
> *Malūkdās, Bānī, Prem 2:2, MDB p.6*

> Among courts *(darbārān),* yours is the (true) court *(darbār):*
> yours is the most sublime of sanctuaries.
> *Guru Arjun, Ādi Granth 507, AGK*

The devotee longs to see the master, inside and out:

> I am forever a sacrifice,
> to my friend and intimate, the divine *guru.*
> When I could not be with you for just one moment,
> the dark age of *kaliyuga* dawned for me.
> When will I meet you, O my beloved Lord?
> I cannot endure the night, and sleep does not come,
> without the sight of the beloved *guru*'s court *(darbār).*
> I am a sacrifice, my soul is a sacrifice,
> to that true court *(darbār)* of the beloved *guru.*
> *Guru Arjun, Ādi Granth 96–97, AGK*

The mystical, inner *darbār* of the master is beyond the realms of the mind:

> The fourth region is the saint's *darbār* –
> only those beloved of saints can reach there.
> *Swami Shiv Dayal Singh, Sār Bachan Poetry 24:7.110, SBP p.205*

> Become acquainted with the real path –
> the current of the unrepeatable Name *(ajapā Nām).*
> Become engrossed in it and reach the *guru*'s court *(darbār).*
> *Jagjīvan Sāhib, Bānī 2, Updesh kā Ang 49:3, JSB2 p.29*

The *darbār* of the Divine is eternity, where the soul is absorbed in peace:

> In the court *(darbār)* of *sat Purush* (true Being),
> I have forgotten all other places.
> *Swami Shiv Dayal Singh, Sār Bachan Poetry 22:2.5, SBP p.188*

Celebrations in memory of a Muslim holy man, held at his tomb, where music is played together with other festivities, is also known as a *darbār.*

See also: **darbār** (2.1).

dargāh (P) *Lit.* doorway, threshold, portal; thus, household; also, the arched portal or gateway to a palace courtyard; hence, a royal court or palace itself; also, a visit to such a court; a sacred place; in Sufism, a Sufi centre, especially in Turkey, the 'court' of a Sufi master, a meeting place for Sufis, a Sufi monastery; in India, a visit to the tomb or shrine of a saint; in North Africa, a small cupolated mosque erected over the tomb of a Muslim saint, with teaching facilities and a hospice attached; appears in such expressions as *ahl-i dargāh* (people of the household), the disciples of a Sufi master.

Mystically, the portal or threshold of God or the master symbolizes the humility and obedience of the disciple who comes as a spiritual beggar before his master, knocking on his master's door for grace and blessings. This threshold can be external, implying the physical place where a master is teaching; or it can be internal, referring to the inner realms and ultimately to God Himself:

> For the one who finds himself distanced from God's portal *(dargāh),*
> the veil of darkness befits him more than light.
> *Mir'āt-i 'Ushshāq, in TAT p.195, in SSE4 p.89*

> O bird of auspicious face, be my guide on the way.
> For my eye brims with tears in yearning
> for the dust of that threshold *(dargāh).*
> *Ḥāfiẓ, Dīvān, DHA p.226, DIH p.364; cf. DHWC (483:2) p.798*

> Shattered, I came to your threshold *(dargāh),*
> where the physician administered the medicine of your grace.
> *Ḥāfiẓ, Dīvān, DHA p.56, DIH p.127; cf. DHWC (269:3) p.475*

Alluding to a story told in the *Qur'ān,* in which Solomon marches his "host of *jinns* and men and birds" through the "valley of ants", and meets the ant queen,[1] Sa'dī points out that the seeker is nothing and has done nothing, and yet he desires everything at the "palace gate" of the "divine Majesty":

You have not given up (material) life,
and yet you long for the beloved.
You have not severed the infidel's thread,
and yet you desire the true faith.

At the palace gate *(dargāh),*
where the kettledrums of inaccessibility are beaten,
you are less than an ant.
Yet still you yearn for the kingdom of Solomon....

O Saʿdī! Be like an atom in this world in which you dwell,
if your heart desires closeness to the divine Majesty.

Saʿdī, Ṭayyibāt 42:1–2, 10, KSSS p.251; cf. TOS pp.59–61

See also: **khānaqāh**.

1. *Qur'ān* 27:17*ff.*

darshan(a) (S/H), **dassana** (Pa), **daras** (H/Pu), **darsan** (Pu) *Lit.* seeing, looking at, observing, noticing; vision, sight; audience, meeting; observation, perception, insight; viewpoint, opinion, perspective, philosophy; inner, spiritual, or mystical vision; from the root *d-ṛi-sh* (to see, to look at, to know, to discern); the vision of a deity or God; audience with or sight of a *guru* or holy person, within or without; the sight of an image or idol of a deity in a temple; looking at a holy man or idol with devotion and reverence, and with such absorption that everything else, even one's own body, is forgotten, and the sense of a separate existence is lost.

Darshana has a spectrum of associated meanings, broadly focussed around three main topics. Firstly, it means perception and vision; secondly, it refers to philosophy, opinion, or viewpoint; and thirdly, it is devotional gazing at a holy man, or at an idol or image of a holy man or deity. The latter meaning is prevalent in Hindu and Jain traditions, but not in Buddhism.

In Jainism, a *jīva* (embodied soul) is said to consist of *chaitanya* (consciousness) and *upayoga*, which is the impulse and drive to apprehend things, and which consists of perception *(darshana)* and knowledge *(jñāna).* Pure perception without any analysis comes first, followed by the desire to acquire knowledge of whatever is perceived. In this context, *darshana* is perception *per se,* without any cogitation thereon or consideration of the attributes of the thing perceived. But *darshana* also means 'philosophy', as in *Jaina darshana* (Jain philosophy), as well as 'viewpoint', 'belief', and 'faith'; hence, the term *samyag-darshana* (right view, right belief, right faith), which implies full acceptance and understanding of the path and teachings laid down by the

Jain *Tīrthankaras.* Lastly, *darshana* refers to gazing at the image or idol of a *Tīrthankara,* as well as having the *darshana* of a holy man.

In Buddhism, in addition to its general meaning as vision or perception, *darshana* refers to insight into Reality or into the various formulations of Buddhist doctrine, such as the well-known noble eightfold path *(āryāshṭānga-mārga)* or the four noble truths *(ārya-satya)* of early Buddhism. Pre-*Mahāyāna* Buddhism generally speaks of the five paths *(pañcha-mārga)* to buddhahood that are traversed by an aspiring seeker. Of these, *darshana-mārga* (path of seeing) is the third *mārga,* the stage at which uncertainty *(vichikitsā),* false views or opinions *(dṛishṭi),* and impurities *(kleshas)* are eliminated. *Jñāna-darshana* (knowledge-insight) refers to direct mystical perception and understanding of Buddhist truths, especially that of *nirvāṇa.*

The same distinctions apply in other branches of Indian philosophy. The six schools of Indian philosophy are known as the *shaḍ-darshanas* – the six viewpoints: *Nyāya, Vaisheshika, Sāṃkhya, Yoga, Mīmāṃsā,* and *Vedānta. Darshana* also appears in a variety of expressions. *Ātma-darshana* (vision of the self) is used synonymously with *ātma-jñāna* (self-knowledge, self-realization).[1] Patañjali lists *bhranti-darshana* (false vision, incorrect understanding, erroneous perception, illusion) as one of the nine inner obstacles *(antarāya)* that disturb the mind on the path of *yoga,*[2] and there are many other such uses.

Darshan, meaning the *darshan* of images, idols, and relics of deities or holy men, is a traditional aspect of devotional Hindu religion and mysticism. In the language of Indian *sants,* yogis and holy men, however, *darshan* refers more specifically either to the vision of God, or to the *darshan* of a living *guru* or *sant:*

> O Lord, may our speech be engaged in recounting Your qualities,
> our ears in hearing Your stories, our hands in serving You,
> our mind in the remembrance of Your feet,
> our head in bowing to this world, which is Your dwelling place,
> and our sight *(dṛishṭi)* in gazing at *(darshana)* the saints,
> who come from You.
>
> *Bhāgavata Purāṇa 10:10.38; cf. in PU pp.137–38*

The *darshan* of a saint or genuine holy person implies more than simply looking. It involves gazing or looking intently with one-pointed attention and a deep feeling of respect, love, and devotion. This means that the inner attitude and devotional feeling are an essential aspect of truly spiritual *darshan.* For the disciple of a *guru, darshan* means seeing the physical *guru* face to face. This is outer *darshan,* which brings instant blessing, depending upon the receptivity of the disciple and the grace of the *guru.* Seeing the spiritual, radiant or astral form of the *guru* within is inner *darshan.* In practice, since blessings only come or are felt by a disciple when the *guru* so wishes, *darshan* – inner or outer – is always a gift of the *guru,* and cannot be had by the disciple simply by looking.

The *darshan* of a *guru* or holy man that the mystics generally talk about – and the one that elevates the soul to higher levels of consciousness – is inner *darshan,* that is, the *darshan* of the inner spiritual form of the *guru,* which is attained through the practice of deep inner contemplation. To the true mystic, inner *darshan* is regarded as of greater significance than external *darshan.* The external *darshan* helps a disciple to experience the inner *darshan* of the *guru* within himself. It is a means to an end. The disciple comes to long for the internal *darshan* of the *guru,* since that is the focus of his love and the form that will always be within him, guiding him through the heavenly realms, back to the divine Source.

The twentieth-century Indian mystic Maharaj Sawan Singh has written concerning the effects of the *darshan* and company of a master on a loving disciple:

> By sitting near a perfect master and contemplating on him, the mind is inclined to get under control and is stilled to some extent.... Rays of purity constantly radiate from him. He is full of wonderful light and kindness. He has an indescribable influence on others. He has magnetic attraction. By his words, which are full of mystical meaning, he pulls the soul upwards. He produces an experience of bliss that defies description.
>
> One finds a strange radiance and attraction in his eyes and forehead when one gazes at them, even for a moment. One feels a pull, and one's attention gathers together and seems to ascend to the higher subtle regions from the gross regions. One's consciousness expands and is elevated.
>
> There is peace and evenness within a perfect master. As a result of being in his company, a current of bliss runs through us. We feel happy on meeting him. All our doubts are removed and we feel certain that our ultimate destination will be attained....
>
> He is full of the elixir of life. His face is bright and radiant. His voice is attractive and the light in his eyes is both alluring and piercing. Powerful currents of life energy emanate from a saint and surcharge the surrounding atmosphere. His words have a strange influence. They penetrate the hearts of the listeners. The mere presence of a saint awakens souls and redeems them.... When one begins to visit a perfect master, his good days begin.
>
> *Maharaj Sawan Singh, Philosophy of the Masters 5; cf. PMS5 pp.283–85*

Everything that a perfect master teaches is intended to lead a disciple from the outer to the inner. Longing for outer *darshan* leads to experience of the inner. Maharaj Charan Singh, an initiate of Maharaj Sawan Singh, writes to a disciple:

> You will get the inner *darshan* only when you have longing for the outer *darshan.* The outer *darshan* is a means to an end, because longing for the outer *darshan* will lead you to longing for the inner *darshan.* Christ says that they are the blessed ones who mourn, for they will be comforted.[3] . . . We mourn when we can't bear the separation from the beloved. They are the fortunate ones or blessed ones who mourn, who feel the separation from the Father, and who have that real longing to go back to the Father: they will be comforted. Ultimately, they will be able to reach back to the Father.
>
> Christ referred to the inner and outer *darshan* in an indirect way when he said: "It is expedient, it is in your interest, that I leave you now, for then I'll be able to send you the Comforter."[4] How can it be in the interest of a disciple for the master to leave him physically? The master, by his physical presence, creates love and devotion in the heart of the disciple, but the master cannot stay physically with the disciple forever. He eventually separates himself from the disciple, who then has no option but to seek his master within.
>
> In separation, the disciple will direct all his devotion and longing within to find the master, and ultimately he will find the Comforter. That is why it is in the interest of the disciple for the master to leave him. No doubt the disciples are in love with the master's physical form, they are running after him – but how long can the disciples be with the physical form of the master? When the master leaves the disciples and they want to be with the master, they have no option but to turn within to find him. The purpose of the physical presence of the master is to create that love and devotion in us, and ultimately to convert it into the real inner *darshan,* which is the end, which is the real love, the real devotion.
>
> *Maharaj Charan Singh, Die to Live 289, DTL pp.230–31*

Outer *darshan* imprints the form of the master on the mind of a disciple, which helps inner contemplation *(dhyān).* This in turn leads to a longing for *darshan,* which again draws a disciple closer to the inner master:

> Physical *darshan* of the master is very helpful for the purpose of *dhyān.* The ancient saints attached great importance to having the *darshan* of saints and masters, the source of the flow of love and light which makes an irresistible appeal to the inner being of the *satsangi* (disciple). . . .

> The effect of the *darshan* is dependent upon the receptivity of the seeker, whose reach is determined by his own *sanskāras* and past connections.... To derive bliss from mere *darshan* of the master is a great thing because it indicates that the seeker has love – essential for spiritual life. Having had the *darshan* of the beloved, the lover naturally desires nothing except to have more and more *darshan.* He is always anxious to have as much *darshan* of the master as possible, which results in drawing the lover closer to the master on the inner plane.
>
> *Maharaj Charan Singh, Divine Light, Letter 434, DL p.372*

As a disciple progresses inwardly, he realizes that the reality of the inner form is the divine Word or *Shabd.* Baba Jaimal Singh writes to his successor-to-be Maharaj Sawan Singh that the longing for outer *darshan* will continue until the end of of the spiritual journey, and for as long as a soul is in the body:

> You write that your mind keeps hankering after the outer form because you have not been able to have *darshan* of the inner *Shabd* form. That is right; it will remain so until the outer form has become fully imprinted and the *Anāmī* Lord and Creator has taken a permanent abode in the inner self.
>
> *Baba Jaimal Singh, Spiritual Letters 38, SL p.63*

It is the impurities in the disciple's mind that stand in the way of inner *darshan,* but listening to the *Shabd* purifies the mind:

> If the form of the *satguru*'s (true *guru*) image appears at that place (behind the eyes), his *darshan* will be enjoyed every day. Because the being is very weak, totally unclean, and surrounded by *māyā* (illusion), he becomes pure through the *darshan* of the *satguru*'s form and by following his teachings. The *satguru*'s intrinsic form is *Shabd Dhun.* The disciple becomes very pure by listening to it, and exceedingly pure when he receives the *satguru*'s full *darshan* within.
>
> *Baba Jaimal Singh, Spiritual Letters 34, SL pp.56–57*

The yearning for *darshan,* inner and outer, also purifies the mind. Imperfections are burnt in the intense fire of love and longing. This results in liberation from the cycle of birth and death:

> You write that for *darshan* you are writhing like a fish out of water. His will is like that. When true love for the *satguru* is felt inwardly, only then does true yearning for *darshan* develop. Please understand that even with hundreds of years of *bhajan* (meditation) one does not become so pure as one does with true yearning for the *satguru*'s

darshan. That is why the disciple is separated from the physical form of the *satguru:* because he does not become pure so quickly through doing *bhajan* as through true love for the *satguru* and true longing for his *darshan.*

In fact, *sat Purush* (true Lord) himself is the *satguru.* So, in the *Shabd* form,... I am always by your side. The disciple, however, cannot discern the *satguru's Shabd* form. And why can't he do so? Because he is unclean, his intellect is also unclean, and highly unclean is his mind as well. In this age, my son, to attain liberation, to meet the Lord, to become pure in a short time, the only way is to have true love and faith for the *satguru* and never to regard him as merely human. True yearning for *darshan* is the key for meeting the Lord. The mind's dirt is shed only when these means become fully ingrained in the mind. Only then can the disciple perceive the *Shabd Dhun* form of the *satguru.* So please try to listen to the *Shabd Dhun* – then the *Dhun* itself will take you to your home. He who has true longing for the *satguru* in his mind has accomplished everything. The *satguru* has the authority to take him at once to *sach khanḍ,* the land of saints. Please do not feel apprehensive; he who attaches himself to the *Shabd Dhun* will not be born again.

Baba Jaimal Singh, Spiritual Letters 16, SL p.29

Many other Indian saints have also spoken lovingly of *darshan,* generally implying both its outer and inner aspects. Such *darshan* is said to bring about multiple benefits. It purifies the mind and body, induces a state of love and bliss, washes away past *karma,* ends the cycle of rebirth, brings the benefit of countless good deeds and religious observances, and fulfils the purpose of human life:

Sahajo's *guru* is a dyer, he colours us all with his dyes:
Whether our cloth be dirty, shiny or white,
he dips it in his dye, and it comes out right.
Sahajo's *guru* gave her his *darshan,* the whole world was hers:
she saw him everywhere she looked – saw him and no one else.
On seeing him, she was filled with bliss;
She took refuge in the *satguru:*
he saved her from the sorrow of the ocean of existence.

Sahajobāī, Bānī, Guru Mahimā 71–73, SBB p.11, SPBS pp.54–55

Sahajo says, in the company of the holy *(sādh),* all afflictions fall away:
evil inclinations and sins disappear.
Saints *(sādh)* are like trees, their verses like buds,
their conversation like flowers;

Sahajo says, in the garden of the company of truth,
the trees are covered with fruits.
Sahajo says, when you have the *darshan* of a saint,
use both your eyes:
It will destroy your burning passions and cool your body.
Sahajo says, when you have the *darshan* of a saint,
see truly and be prepared to lay down your life.
When he bestows his kindness upon you,
all fear will flee and you will be worthy of *nirvāṇa.*

Sahajobāī, Bānī, Sādh Mahimā 14–17, SBB pp.12–13; cf. SPBS pp.62–65

Narsī Mehtā (1414–1480), well-known poet-saint of Gujarat and devotee of Kṛishṇa, sings of the attributes of a "man of God", and repeats the traditional Hindu belief that the *darshan* of a holy man brings blessings upon past family members:

He is called a man of God who understands the pain of others;
Helping others in trouble, he feels no pride in it;
He is polite to all people and does not condemn or criticize anyone;
He is pure in speech, deed and thought, and everyone blesses his mother;
He is at peace, relinquished all desires,
and looks upon women as mothers;
He speaks no untruth,
neither does he covet the wealth of others;
Delusion and desire never dominate him:
his mind is firm in detachment;
He is continuously engaged in the repetition of God's Name;
All places of pilgrimage are within his body;
He has no greed and no deceit; he has overcome lust and anger.
Says Narsī, the *darshan* of such a person
sanctifies the entire family lineage.

Narsī Mehtā, Songs; cf. in SSI2 pp.108–9

Shyāma Shāstri (1762–1827), whose family had been devotees of *Kāmakshi,* the divine Mother, for many generations, is speaking of an inner vision of the goddess, when he writes:

This form of yours is radiant!
You are the embodiment of all virtues!
Can this glorious form of yours
be seen anywhere else in the three worlds?
I have had the *darshan* of your lotus feet several times
due to spiritual practice in previous births!

I feel blessed and grateful!
Protect me, and heed my pleading!
Shyāma Shāstri, Songs; cf. in SSI2 pp.208–9

The *gurus* whose writings are collected together in the *Ādi Granth* write extensively of the blessings of *darshan,* inner and outer:

As a lamp gives light in darkness,
so does the soul bloom on beholding the *guru*'s *darsan.*
As the man finds his way in a great wilderness,
so is his light burnished by *sādhū sang* (the company of saints).
Of the feet of those saints, I desire the dust:
fulfil Nānak's desire, O God.
Guru Arjun, Ādi Granth 282, MMS

Having the *darshan* of my *guru,*
all sins are eradicated, and he unites me with my Lord.
My *guru*-God is the giver of peace:
he implants the supreme Lord's Name in me,
and shall be my helper in the end (at death).
Applying the dust of the saints' feet to my face,
the seat of all pains within me is destroyed.
Guru Arjun, Ādi Granth 915, MMS

O mother, the *guru*'s feet are so sweet:
by great good fortune, the transcendent Lord
has blessed me with them.
Millions of rewards come from the blessed *darsan* of the *guru.*
Guru Arjun, Ādi Granth 717, AGK

Beholding the *darsan* of the *guru,*
departs the pain of birth and death.
Swayyās Guru Angad, Ādi Granth 1392, MSS

O my *guru,* I live by seeing your *darsan:*
like this my destiny (life's purpose) is completed.
Guru Arjun, Ādi Granth 741, MMS

In fact, through *darshan,* God Himself is revealed to the devotee:

To see the sight *(daras)* of the *guru*
amounts to beholding the primal Lord.
Guru Nānak, Ādi Granth 416, MMS

The medieval mystic Kabīr takes up the theme:

Do not ask for supernatural powers *(ṛiddhi siddhi):*
ask only for one boon – for the *darshan* of a saint every day.
Give me that *darshan,* prays Kabīr. . . .

Your greatest moment is when, by good fortune,
you receive the *darshan* of a saint.
For this, it is not too much to sacrifice your whole life,
for it is the saint who gives you Truth, and through his power
transforms you from sin to sinlessness, from folly to wisdom.

Kabīr, Sākhī Sangrah, Satsang kā Ang 6, 15, KSS pp.49–50; cf. KGME p.188

He speaks of the master coming to his "house", by which he means the body, the temporary abode of the soul:

Today my Lord has come to my house:
my eyes met with his – I received his *darshan.*
All sorrow has gone, I have repeated
the true Name *(satya Nām)* of the Lord of all,
the treasure house of mercy.

Kabīr, Āj more ghar sāhib āy; cf. in SS11 pp.170–71

Blessed is that day, that hour, that propitious moment,
when the man of God came and graced my home.
Such was the effect of his *darshan* that the veil fell from my eyes:
I heard the divine Melody within and duality came to an end.
The gates that blocked my hearing were hard as granite,
yet they broke to pieces when the man of God
came and blessed my home.
One touch from my master remoulded the ill-shaped pot of my being;
The chains of *karma* fell from my body
when the man of God came and graced my home.
Says Kabīr: I love, I adore the saint:
through his grace I found the supreme One,
the diadem of all, within my own body.

Kabīr, Granthāvalī, Pad 395, KG p.165, KWGN p.195

Writing in the nineteenth century, Swami Shiv Dayal Singh is specific. The inner master is met at the "third eye", the centre of attention behind the eyes. Such *darshan* is an experience of great bliss:

Establish your base at the third eye
and have *darshan (daras)* of the inner master.

Always listen to the voice of the *Shabd guru,*
burn to ashes the low cravings of your mind and merge into him.
This form of the master is of unsurpassed beauty –
it will light up your inner being, like the radiant glow of the sun.
Like the black bee on a lotus in full bloom,
your soul will revel in the master's love.
Dismal are the hearts which have not received
the light of knowledge from the master, O friend!
They have not met a true master,
they constantly wander around in the maze of the creation.

As for myself, I have found a true master,
and I sacrifice myself to him in humble adoration.
Like a moonbird lost in watching the moon,
I lose myself in contemplation of his sublime form *(rūp nihār).*

Swami Shiv Dayal Singh, Sār Bachan Poetry 4:8.1–8, SBP pp.41–42, SBPS pp.20–21

True longing for the inner master requires a completely one-pointed mind, and cannot exist alongside desire for material things:

Take refuge in the master, dear soul,
and he will pay your karmic toll....
The magnificence of this state is beyond words –
only a rare *gurmukh* can realize it.
Having lost interest in all else,
he stays absorbed in the bliss of his *guru*'s feet.
Fully engrossed in his *guru*'s *darshan,*
he has become oblivious of his own body –
let alone his home and the world about him!
There is nothing I can say
about the state of a soul so drenched in the colours of love.

Swami Shiv Dayal Singh, Sār Bachan Poetry 8:13.1, 5–8, SBP pp.82–83, SBPS p.71

He also warns against hypocrisy, and outlines the human imperfections that stand in the way of enjoying the inner *darshan* of the master:

Superficially, you sing the praises of the *guru,*
but you never bring the *guru* into your heart.
You have his *darshan* outside,
yet you never hold his form within.
With so casual a relationship with the *guru,*
how can you hope to attain anything, friend?

Your heart pines for wealth and honour,
while outwardly you display humility and meekness.
Deep down in your heart, you harbour lust and anger,
while on the outside, you feign purity and forgiveness.

Inwardly you have not cultivated love for the *guru,*
but what can outward love achieve, O foolish one?
How can the master come to your help
when you have no love for the *Shabd* within?
I have tried to explain this to you in many ways,
but perhaps your destiny stands in your way.
You are overcome by *tamoguṇ* (darkness, inertia) within,
while *satoguṇ* (harmony, peace) has not touched your heart.
You never meditate with sincerity
and your surrender to the *guru* is only half-hearted.

You will not bear with even a mild rebuke,
yet you severely reprimand others.
When threatened by misery, you apply yourself to meditation,
but when the misery ends, you go straight back to your old ways.
You have not received the elixir of the imperishable Name *(Nām),*
nor have you ever detached yourself from the world.
Now you are at a loss to know what to do –
without the master's grace, how can you possibly attain anything?

Swami Shiv Dayal Singh, Sār Bachan Poetry 31:8.1–14,
SBP pp.257–58; cf. SBPS pp.298–99

Longing for inner *darshan* is the essence of the matter. It is the force that detaches the mind from material things. Many mystics have written of this. Ravidās pleads with his *satguru* (true *guru,* perfect master):

O Lord, grant me your *darshan!*
Make no delay, grant me your *darshan!*
Your *darshan* is what I live for!
How can the *chakor* (moonbird) live without seeing the moon?
The Lord is the *satguru,* the whole world His disciple;
If I remain separated this time, it will be hard to be united again.
False is the hope of wealth and youth;
Ravidās speaks the truth.

Ravidās, Vāṇī 109, SGRV p.114

Dādū does not differentiate between the inner *darshan* of his *guru* and that of God. The door at which he longingly waits is the third eye or eye centre:

O omniscient one!
You are the master of all nations, a powerful creator!
As God, you play with the creation, show me your vision *(dīdār)!*
I am penitent, I shall obey your every command!
Dādū is waiting at the door and calling you:
why don't you give me your *darshan?*

Dādū, Rāg Todī, Shabd 276:2–3, DDB2 p.118; cf. in SSI5 pp.134–35

Mīrābāī, too, expresses her longing:

Pray come, O master, illumined and wise:
a glimpse of your face has enchanted me.
When you come my way, enquire for the one
who, pining for you, is frenzied with pain.
Day and night I have neither peace nor respite,
and I writhe like a fish out of water.
Save for your *darshan (daras)* nothing can soothe me:
in constant anguish, I'm nearing my end.
Mīrā is ever a slave at your feet:
hear her prayer, O bestower of bliss.

Mīrābāī, Sadguru Mahimā ke Pad 8, MSS p.843; cf. MDLS p.161

Likewise, Swami Shiv Dayal Singh, who – out of compassion – first identifies himself with the enfeebled state of the devotee who struggles with the lower mind, and then, at the end, encourages the devotee to keep going:

My helpless mind now cries for *darshan (daras)* –
it has no patience, it knows no peace.
I can neither eat, nor sleep, nor stay awake,
for every moment I am beside myself with grief.
In separation from you, my love, I am restless with pain –
worry eats at my heart and bites me like a snake.
What can I do now, my friend,
to swim across the ocean of existence?
One thought consumes me every day –
that my condition gets worse by the moment, O friend,
and no one is there to help.

My beloved lives in the fourth plane,
while I languish here, in the world of mortality.
Away from the beloved I suffer intense pain,
and, though I try, I cannot follow the path leading to him.
Dark and fearsome is the uphill path,
and no one is there to hear my cries of pain.

I do not know what else to do:
  I feel demoralized, for I cannot win my beloved's heart.
My beloved can call me to him at a moment's notice,
  should he so desire –
  he can pull me up in an instant by handing me the rope of *Shabd.*

How unfortunate I am – I haven't caught the melody of *Shabd!*
I am in the grip of lust, anger, and *māyā* (illusion).
I cannot even practise the path of *surat Shabd*
  that has been granted to me:
Unclean of mind, corrupt of spirit,
  I am helpless and debased in every way.
You are all-powerful, O Lord, and all-knowing,
  while I writhe in pain without you, like a fish out of water.

Help me now, O Lord! Accomplish my task for me!
  I surrender myself, I sacrifice myself to you.
I lie at your door, weary and defeated,
  for who but you will protect me?

The Lord then spoke, saying: "Accept My will and stay calm.
Have patience, have faith, I shall bring to fruition your heart's desire."
Hearing His words I feel calm:
  I have taken permanent refuge in the Lord's feet.

Swami Shiv Dayal Singh, Sār Bachan Poetry 33:1.1–19, SBP p.262, SBPS pp.308–11

In another poem, he again writes of the great longing of the soul for inner *darshan* of the master; and again, at the end, he speaks of the fulfilment of his longing:

An intense longing for *darshan* has entered my burning heart.
Ever since I put my mind into *satsang,*
  worldly pleasures seem like afflictions.
I understand that your status is beyond comprehension,
  but without your *darshan (daras)* I cannot be content.
I am unable to achieve the state of true discipleship –
  how can I make myself worthy to be in your presence?
You are not far away,
  you are with all your souls, yet hidden from them,
  for, without the grace of a perfect master,
  you never reveal your true form.

I writhe in pain, I am restless and tantalized
  because you are close at hand, yet out of reach.

You are the all-powerful giver to everyone,
please pull me as well to yourself.
How else am I to see you? –
no amount of effort on my part will do.
Open the window of my heart, O beloved –
it can't be that hard for you.
Should you so will, you can do it in an instant,
without putting me through this struggle, life after life.

Please bless me with your *darshan (daras)* soon,
for without it I stay withered and dispirited.
Bestow on me such grace that I stay attached to your feet,
that I hold you in my embrace and think of none but you.
I have now sung that unique song of devotion –
my soul has now merged in *Shabd.*

Swami Shiv Dayal Singh, Sār Bachan Poetry 33:21.1–15,
SBP pp.277–78, SBPS pp.334–35

Many are the mystics who have written of this longing. Guru Arjun Dev, during his days of discipleship, was physically separated from his master Guru Rāmdās. His lyrics, a spontaneous outcome of deep love and intense longing for the *darshan* of his *satguru,* are regarded as some of the most beautiful poems on longing:

My mind longs for *darsan* of the *guru:*
it cries out like the thirsty *chātrik* (rainbird).
My thirst is not quenched, and I can find no peace
without the *darsan* of the beloved saint.
I am a sacrifice, my soul is a sacrifice,
to the *darsan* of the beloved saint-*guru.*
Your face is so beautiful, and the sound of your words
imparts intuitive wisdom (spiritual awareness).
It is so long since this rainbird has had even a glimpse of water.
Blessed is that land where you dwell,
O my friend and intimate divine *guru.*

I am a sacrifice, I am forever a sacrifice,
to my friend and intimate, the divine *guru.*
When I could not be with you for just one moment,
the dark age of *kaliyuga* dawned for me.
When will I meet you, O my beloved Lord?
I cannot endure the night, and sleep does not come,
without the sight of the beloved *guru*'s court *(darbār).*

I am a sacrifice, my soul is a sacrifice,
to that true court *(darbār)* of the beloved *guru.*

Guru Arjun, Ādi Granth 96–97, AGK

Kabīr summarizes the benefits of a *satguru's darshan* in his characteristically pithy manner. He is speaking of both the inner and outer *darshan:*

Like a monsoon rain, the *darshan* of a *satguru*
showers countless blessings:
Run for the *darshan* of the *satguru,* therefore, as often as you can.

The *darshan* of a *satguru* protects you
from *Kāl's* (Death) ever-present, terrible deceits:
If you cannot have *darshan* many times,
have it, Kabīr, at least twice each day.
If you cannot have *darshan* twice a day,
have it, Kabīr, at least once each day:
The *darshan* of a *satguru* takes you safe and sound
across the ocean of great dread.

If you cannot enjoy *darshan* once a day,
have it, Kabīr, at least every other day:
Mere *darshan* of a *satguru* can give you human birth again,
and this will lead to salvation.
If you cannot have *darshan* every other day,
have it, Kabīr, at least every third day:
The *darshan* of a *satguru* gives permanent salvation.
If you cannot have *darshan* every third day,
have it at least once every week:
Do not delay, Kabīr advises –
the *darshan* of a *satguru* is precious beyond words.

If you cannot enjoy *darshan* once a week,
have it, Kabīr, at least once every fortnight.
Kabīr tells devotees: thus you make your life fruitful.
If you cannot have *darshan* once a fortnight,
have it, Kabīr, at least once each month:
Never be lazy in your efforts to obtain the *darshan* of a perfect *satguru.*
If you cannot have *darshan* at least once a month,
be sure, Kabīr, to meet him every six months.
Never neglect the *darshan* of a *satguru.*

If you cannot have *darshan* once every six months,
have it, Kabīr, at least once every year.

The *darshan* of a *satguru* will save you
from the dreadful struggle with the eagle of death.

Those who forego a *satguru*'s *darshan* through one full year, says Kabīr,
are making a mistake, a sad mistake –
They will not be carried across the fearsome ocean of dread....

Listen, Kabīr reveals this secret now:
between the saint and the almighty Lord, there is no difference.
In thought, word and deed, the saint *(sādhu)* and Lord *(Sāhib)* are one....

Beware, ignore the caste, race, and religion of a saint:
enquire of his spiritual stature alone.
Value the sword and ignore the sheath, value his knowledge –
judge not by appearance....

Hurry, hurry to have the *darshan* of a saint,
for this will give you wealth imperishable.
Listen! Laziness brings you eternal harm:
wealth is earned through hard work alone.

Kabīr, only that time will go to your credit
that you spend in the *darshan* of a saint,
for know that the Lord and the saint are one.
The rest of your life is an utter waste....

How can that disciple be saved, O Kabīr, who is hard-hearted –
Who doesn't dance with joy when the saint arrives,
and doesn't weep with sorrow when he leaves?

Kabīr, Sākhī Sangrah, Sādh kā Ang 46–56, 41, 43, 33–34, 22,
KSS pp.118–21, KGME pp.184–86

See also: **darshana** (▸3), **dṛishṭi**.

1. Patañjali, *Yoga Sūtras* 2:41.
2. Patañjali, *Yoga Sūtras* 1:30.
3. *Matthew* 5:4.
4. *Cf. John* 16:7.

dastār bandī (P/U/Pu) *Lit.* tying *(bandī)* of the turban *(dastār);* a ceremony in which a turban is tied onto a person's head; commonly performed to mark the inauguration of the new head of an organization (which may be of spiritual, religious, or entirely material nature) or the initiation of a Sikh boy into the *Khālsā* branch of the Sikh religion, generally between the ages of eleven to sixteen. The latter ceremony is performed at a *gurdwāra,* after which the young man is expected to incorporate the five symbols (*panj kakkā,* five Ks) of the *Khālsā* into his outward appearance. The five symbols are uncut hair and beard *(kesh);* a comb *(kanghā)* to keep the hair tidy; a pair of knee-length breeches *(kachh);* a steel bracelet *(kaṛā)* on the right wrist (perhaps as protection in battle); and a sword *(kirpān),* so as to be always ready for battle.

See also: **panj kakkā** (▸3).

derā (H/Pu) *Lit.* residence, house, home, abode, dwelling, camp, tent; also used as a proper noun, as a part of the name of a place, *e.g.* Derā Ghazī Khān, Derā Ishmail Khān, Derā Nawala, and so on; commonly anglicized as 'Dera'. Residents or those associated with that place commonly refer to it as 'the Dera'. Mystically and metaphorically, *derā* is also used for the original home or permanent and eternal abode of the soul.

From a spiritual perspective, the purpose of a spiritual centre away from the busy-ness of worldly life is to provide a place to recharge the inner batteries – to listen to spiritual discourses, to serve the community, to renew spiritual awareness, and above all to establish oneself in meditation. Speaking of his own centre in the Punjab, Dera Baba Jaimal Singh, Maharaj Charan Singh used to say that the real Dera is inside. To be of lasting benefit, the atmosphere of the outer Dera is to be carried within, wherever a person may be:

> Baba Ji Maharaj (Baba Jaimal Singh) and Huzur Maharaj Ji (Maharaj Sawan Singh) have laid the foundation of the Dera on love, humility, *sevā* (service), and meditation. That is the foundation of this Dera. Everybody's equal here, irrespective of country, caste, creed, or colour. And if we feel we have not been able to come to that level yet, we try to improve ourselves. That is the atmosphere of the Dera, and that is the atmosphere which we take with ourselves wherever we may go. The Dera is not built of mortar and bricks. It is built on *sevā* and love and devotion and humility and meditation. And we have to build our whole life on these principles. Only this foundation will take us back to the Father....
>
> You see, we have certain obligations, responsibilities in life, and destiny has placed us at certain places to discharge those responsibilities and obligations, and we have to attend to them. And we also have to meditate, which is the main purpose of life. So we cannot always remain in the presence of the master. We have to build our own atmosphere of devotion and love within us, in which the master is always

there with us. Ultimately, we have to leave this body. Ultimately, the master has to leave this body. It is a relationship of the soul with the inner master, the divine master, the *Shabd*. And that has to be developed while being in the body. That relationship of the soul and the *Shabd* has to be strengthened while we have the privilege of being in this human form. Then we are always with our master. As Christ said, "You have come unto me, and I have come unto you."[1]

That is the merging of the soul into the *Shabd*. So we have to prepare for that.

Maharaj Charan Singh, Spiritual Perspectives, Question 139–40, SP3 pp.94–95

See also: **āshrama**, **maṭha**.

1. *Cf. John* 14:21–23.

deshanā (S), **desanā** (Pa) *Lit.* direction, instruction, teaching; discourse, talk, exposition, sermon; prevalent in Buddhism and Jainism; especially as *dhamma-desanā* (an exposition of the *Dharma*, a *dharma* talk), given by the Buddha or by a suitably qualified monk.

All the discourses delivered by the Buddha are regarded as *desanā*, which are said by later commentators to fall into two categories. Talks concerning things that are true in the highest sense are known as *paramattha-desanā*, while talks that are true but only in the relative, mundane and impermanent sphere are called *vohāra-desanā*. *Paramattha* means the highest Truth; *vohāra* is simply mundane expression. *Vohāra-desanā* is sometimes called *sammuti-sacca* (conventional truth, general opinion).

According to the *Abhidhamma Piṭaka*, which is a collection of later analytical commentaries and intellectual expansions on the earlier Pali *suttas*, the language of the *Abhidhamma* can be regarded as solely *paramattha-desanā*. Although the distinction does not appear in the *suttas*, the Buddha himself is said to have used both forms of expression. When using everyday language, he was speaking *vohāra-desanā*; when using philosophical language to speak of the higher Reality, he was employing *paramattha-desanā*. What the Buddha would have said concerning the distinction is uncertain, but what he does say is that words are an unreliable means of communicating the nature of the higher Reality:

These are the world's names, the world's expressions, the world's ways of speaking, the world's descriptions, with which the Tathāgata expresses himself, but without misapprehending them.

Dīgha Nikāya 9, Poṭṭhapāda Sutta, PTSD1 p.202

This is understandable, and there is little or no reason to presume that philosophical analysis of the higher Reality is any less liable to misapprehension or error. The Buddha himself puts it simply:

> Blessed is the birth of the *buddhas;*
> Blessed is the teaching of the true *Dhamma (dhamma-desanā);*
> Blessed is harmony in the *sangha* (community);
> Blessed is the discipline of those who live in harmony.
>
> *Dhammapada 14:17; cf. DPN, DPR*

Enmeshed in the world of phenomena, the mind needs constant inspiration and reminders of the higher purpose of life. In addition to daily meditation, *dharma* talks have therefore remained a significant aspect of Buddhist life, for the nature of the human mind is essentially the same now as it was in days of the Buddha, and human problems also remain fundamentally the same.

The term is used in other Buddhist expressions such as *pāpa-desanā* (confession of sins), and *Desanā-Mahājāti.* The *Desanā-Mahājāti* is a ritualized discourse on the *Mahājāti* ('Great Birth'), also called the *Vessantara Jātaka.* The *Mahājāti* is one of the most popular birth stories. It tells of the Buddha's past life as a compassionate prince, in which he gives away all his possessions, even his children, thereby demonstrating his perfect charity.

The Pali *suttas* also speak of three fundamentals for acquiring merit *(puñña-kiriyā-vatthu).* These are *dāna* (generosity), *sīla* (morality, good conduct), and *bhāvanā* (meditation), which the *Abhidhamma* elaborates into ten, of which the eighth or ninth is *desanā* – expounding the *Dhamma.*

See also: **dharma talk**.

ḍhāk (H) The *Butea frondosa* or *Butea monosperma* tree; known in English as the flame of the forest, bastard teak, or parrot tree; also called the *palāsh, kingshuk, keshū, plash,* and by a variety of other names in various parts of India; a tree used in ayurveda (traditional Indian medicine), known for the acrid and bitter taste of its bark. Like some other trees, such as the neem *(nīm),* the *ḍhāk* has been used as a metaphor by Indian mystics to describe the effect of association with a mystic. It is said that when these bitter-tasting trees grow in the vicinity of sandalwood, they absorb the sandalwood's fragrance:

> A *ḍhāk* tree growing in the vicinity of a sandalwood tree takes on the fragrance of sandalwood. The effect of association is indeed great. The tree that grows near a sandalwood tree is indeed fortunate.... The ever-merciful Lord abides within the master. By following his precepts, we are released from the cycle of birth and rebirth. Such is the greatness

> of *satsang* (association with a saint) that, like the philosopher's stone, it transforms the iron-like sinner into a gold-like being of virtue. The lowly is raised on high. One who is worthless becomes precious. Go to *satsang* and lovingly contemplate upon the master and the Lord. Your thoughts, words and deeds will automatically become pure. You will find that, through *satsang,* the spiritual wealth that can be obtained as a result of following the various kinds of *yoga* will come your way without any effort on your part.
>
> *Maharaj Sawan Singh, Philosophy of the Masters 1, PMS1 p.121*

Likewise, Kabīr says:

> The sandalwood tree is good,
> even if entangled with the *ḍhāk* or *palāsh* –
> That which grows near the sandalwood tree
> also becomes (like) sandalwood.
>
> *Kabīr, Sākhī Sangrah, Satsang kā Ang 21, KSS p.50*

See also: **bhṛingī**, **kūnj**, **nimba**.

dharmachakra (S), **dhammacakka** (Pa), **chos kyi 'khor lo** (T), **fălún** (C), **hōrin** (J) *Lit.* wheel *(chakra, kyi 'khor lo, rin, lún)* of the Law *(Dharma, chos, fă, hō);* wheel of *Dharma,* wheel of Truth, wheel of the Buddhist Way, wheel of the Buddhist teachings; in a more general context, wheel of religion, wheel of righteousness. *Dharma* (Pa. *Dhamma*) is a term whose wide range of meaning makes it impossible to translate into a single word. The *dharmachakra* is symbolized in the *dharmachakra mudrā,* a gesture in which the index finger and the thumb of each hand are touched together, forming two circles. This *mudrā* is commonly seen in iconographic representations of the celestial *buddha* Vairochana.

In India, there are many iconographic representations of the *dharmachakra,* the oldest dating back to the times of the emperor Ashoka (304–232 BCE). Ashoka was a great patron of Buddhism, and although he never forced Buddhism on his subjects, he promoted its cause throughout his kingdom. As a part of this enterprise, he had massive stone pillars erected engraved with Buddhist teachings, exhorting his people to live a life of morality, tolerance, and non-violence. These pillars generally included at least one lion, as a symbol of his rule, and many had representations of the *dharmachakra* in the form of a wheel with twenty-four spokes. After independence and partition in 1947, the new Indian government chose Ashoka's *dharmachakra* as its official emblem, placing it at the centre of the national flag. The *dharmachakra* is also venerated in Jainism as a sacred symbol of religion and spirituality, as attested by its common presence in Jain sculpture and iconography.

The most prevalent usage of the *dharmachakra,* however, is as a symbol of Buddhist teachings, where it is generally portrayed in the form of an eight-spoked wheel, representing the eightfold Path that summarizes the Buddha's teaching. The eight steps are right understanding, right thought, right speech, right action, right livelihood, right effort, right mindfulness, and right concentration. In early Buddhism, images of the *dharmachakra* became objects of veneration, before they were replaced by representations of the human Buddha and the many celestial *buddhas* and *bodhisattvas.*

The *dharmachakra* is sometimes called the *brahmachakra* (wheel of *Brahmā*), where *Brahmā* is understood to mean 'the highest', 'the most excellent', 'the transcendental'.[1] The Buddhist philosopher Nāgārjuna discusses the meaning of the two terms, stating that there is no essential difference between them, although the contexts in which they are used may sometimes differ. It is the *brahmachakra* when it is meditation and the transcendental that is being taught, and the *dharmachakra* when speaking of the four noble truths and the more human aspects of the Way:

> *Brahma* means vast *(bṛihat),* for the wheel of the Buddha or the wheel of the *Dharma* extends everywhere in the ten directions. Furthermore, it is called the wheel of *Brahmā* because the Buddha teaches the four abodes of *Brahmā (brahmaviharā),* because at the very beginning, when the Buddha attained enlightenment, *Brahmā,* the king of the gods, invited him to turn the wheel of the *Dharma,* because at Vārāṇasī when the Buddha turned the wheel of the *Dharma* and Ājñāta Kauṇḍinya obtained the Path, the Buddha's voice penetrated as far as the *Brahmā*-heaven; or else because there are people who respect the god Brahmā and want to please him....
>
> There is no difference between the wheel of *Brahmā* and the wheel of *Dharma.* However, according to some, we say wheel of *Brahmā* when it discloses the four immeasurables *(paramāṇa-chitta),* and wheel of the *Dharma* when it teaches the four noble truths. Furthermore, we say wheel of *Brahmā* when the Path is acquired thanks to the four immeasurables, and wheel of the *Dharma* when it is acquired thanks to some other thing.
>
> The wheel of *Brahmā* teaches the four *dhyānas,* and the wheel of the *Dharma* teaches the thirty-seven auxiliaries of enlightenment *(bodhi-pākshika-dharma).* The wheel of *Brahmā* teaches the path consisting of the practice of concentration *(samādhi-bhāvanā),* and the wheel of the *Dharma* teaches the path consisting of the cultivation of wisdom *(prajñā-bhāvanā).*

> These are the various distinctions to be made between the wheel of *Brahmā* and the wheel of the *Dharma.*
>
> *Nāgārjuna, Mahāprajñāpāramitā Shāstra (245b) 40:2.6, TVW3 p.1312*

The term appears throughout the texts of all Buddhist schools in the expression "turning the wheel of *Dharma*", which implies the transmission or giving out of the Buddhist teachings – the spreading of spirituality. The *Dharma* is understood to be eternal, true for all time, and is symbolized by a wheel because its circular shape has no beginning or end. There are said to be countless *buddhas* throughout the many 'world-systems', all engaged in 'turning the wheel of *Dharma*'.

The symbolism of the turning wheel originated from the first sermon said to have been given by the Buddha, the *Dhammacakkappavattana Sutta* ('Discourse on Setting in Motion the Wheel of the Law') in which he sets out the four noble truths: human life is full of troubles and suffering of one kind or another; the origin of this suffering is self-centred desire; suffering can come to an end in liberation or true freedom, in a state of consciousness known as *nirvāṇa;* there is a Path that leads to liberation and the cessation of suffering:

> Now when the Blessed One set in motion the wheel of Truth *(dhammacakka),* the earth-dwelling *devas* (deities) proclaimed: "The unsurpassed wheel of Truth *(dhammacakka),* which cannot be stopped by *samaṇa* (holy man), *brāhmaṇ, deva, māra* (devil), *Brahmā,* or anyone in the world, has been set in motion by the Blessed One in the Deer Park at Isipatana, near Vārāṇasī."
>
> *Saṃyutta Nikāya 56:11, Dhammacakkappavattana Sutta, PTSS5 p.423*

This proclamation is then repeated by the *devas* and other celestial beings throughout the higher heavens. The *Dharma* as presented in this discourse is sometimes regarded as the first of the three turnings of the wheel recognized by later Buddhism, the second and the third being the developments of the *Mahāyāna* and *Vajrayāna* traditions. But there are several other symbolic interpretations of the three turnings.

Firstly, it is said that each of the four noble truths taught by the Buddha in the Deer Park can be viewed from three perspectives, aspects, or 'turnings' – as a truth in itself, as a truth to be realized, and as a truth that has been realized. For the first truth, for instance – the existence of suffering – the first turning is to accept and recognize the existence of suffering. The second turning is to study the nature and origin of that suffering. The third turning is complete understanding of suffering. Likewise for each of the three other noble truths.[2]

Then there is the viewpoint of the *Yogāchāra* school, which maintains that the three turnings of the wheel represent three levels of the Buddha's teachings. There is the basic doctrine taught to novices *(shrāvaka);* the doctrine of emptiness *(shūnyatā)* taught in *sūtras* such as the *Prajñāpāramitā Sūtra* group; and the doctrine of the three natures *(tri-svabhāva),* which purports to present the true nature of the Buddha and of Reality. The *Yogāchāra* school identified the second level with that of the *Madhyamaka* school, while the third level and the third turning, was understood to be exemplified by the *Yogāchāra* school. Naturally enough, the *Madhyamaka* school did not share this interpretation. The *Madhyamaka* and *Yogāchāra* schools are two of the main branches of *Mahāyāna* Buddhism.

The *dharmachakra* is also compared to the wheel *(chakra)* of the universal ruler *(chakravartin).* According to the mythology, of which there are several symbolic interpretations, in whatever land a *chakravartin* was able to roll his wheel without challenge, he would be the acknowledged ruler. Many of the characteristics attributed to a *chakravartin* were also attributed to the *buddhas,* a *buddha*'s wheel being the *dharmachakra,* by means of which he became a spiritual ruler, leading people to liberation and *nirvāṇa.* From likening the *dharmachakra* to the *chakravartin*'s wheel has arisen another threefold interpretation. The wheel is round, symbolizing its perfection and completeness; as it rolls, it crushes the illusory views by which human beings are otherwise bound, or it is like a millstone that crushes to powder the grains of illusion as it turns. Moreover, it turns freely, indicating that the *Dharma* can be taught to all human beings wherever they may be, and its turning transports them across this world to the other shore, which is *nirvāṇa:*[3]

> Like a fearless lion, he destroys the heretical systems,
> he turns the peerless wheel of *Dharma (dharmachakra),*
> he saves and delivers the threes worlds.
>
> *Nāgārjuna, Mahāprajñāpāramitā Shāstra (75b–c) 4; cf. TVW1 p.143*

Teaching the *Dharma* is no idle occupation, taught by rote and the unthinking repetition of doctrine; nor should listening to the *Dharma* be a passive activity, if the listeners wish to absorb the message. Tibetan *lama* Khenpo Chöga puts it clearly:

> Turning the wheel of *Dharma* is the antidote to ignorance. The essence of turning the wheel of *Dharma* is knowledge and faith. The function is to dispel the darkness of ignorance. Turning the wheel of *Dharma* is a supreme method to gather the accumulation of merit.
>
> Turning the wheel of *Dharma* only takes place when the listeners understand the value of the teaching being taught. The listeners need to have gained confidence in the *Dharma.* If they lack this quality, then the teaching is not called 'turning the wheel of the *Dharma*'. The first persons who requested the Buddha to turn the wheel of the

Dharma were *Shakra,* the king of the gods, and *Brahmā.* They knew that Buddha had realized a priceless *Dharma.* They understood the value of the *Dharma.*

Dharma means 'the wisdom of inseparable knowledge and compassion'. *Dharma* is the true cause of happiness, as it liberates us from suffering. The great masters of the past, who understood the value of the teachings and methods that they held in their minds, were able to turn the wheel of *Dharma.* Only when both teacher and listeners understand the true value of the *Dharma* are the teachings called 'turning the wheel of *Dharma*'. Only then is something of value being passed on and received. Turning the wheel of *Dharma* requires the knowledge that realizes the wisdom of the teachings as well as the compassion to pass on these teachings to others. Turning the wheel of *Dharma* in this way bears boundless merit.

In most cases, nowadays, teachers pass on the eight worldly concerns. Listeners request what interests them and the teacher teaches what he likes best. A true teacher, however, does not try to please his audience. The *Dharma* is fundamentally opposed to the ways of the world. A *dharma* that is in harmony with the world is not the *buddhadharma.* The *Dharma* should not be an enhancement for worldly life. When one requests a *buddha* to turn the wheel of *Dharma,* one requests him to destroy worldly ways of thinking. You ask the teacher to teach you how to destroy ego-clinging. You ask for teachings on how to free yourself from suffering.

Turning the wheel of the *Dharma* is a method to make a connection between the enlightened mind of the Buddha and the minds of sentient beings. The *Dharma* needs to be communicated. Buddha said:

> I have shown you the methods that lead to liberation. Be diligent, as liberation depends upon yourself.

Beseeching the Buddha to turn the wheel of *Dharma* is an act of faith. As it is said: "If the ring of faith is lacking, the hook of compassion cannot connect." Unless the student is a proper vessel, teaching the *Dharma* is useless. When devotion rises in a student's mind, he becomes a proper vessel for the *Dharma.*

Khenpo Chöga, On Khenpo Kunpal, Bodhisattva-Charyāvatāra 5:50–55, DNK3 pp.79–80

There is a clear purpose in such teaching, he continues, and it is the greatest gift that anyone can receive:

> The request to turn the wheel of the *Dharma* for the sake of sentient beings has the purpose of dispelling the darkness of their ignorance.

> To turn the wheel of *Dharma,* to actually teach the *Dharma,* is the greatest of all meritorious deeds. It is the greatest of all gifts, the most beneficial donation. A donation of food will help the recipient for one or two days, while a gift of *Dharma* will remain in the recipient's mind, benefiting him or her for all lifetimes to come. That is why requesting the Buddha to turn the wheel of the *Dharma* is such a meritorious act.
>
> *Khenpo Chöga, On Khenpo Kunpal, Bodhisattva-Charyāvatāra 5:50–55, DNK3 p.80*

There is also a method of teaching the *Dharma* that attempts to circumvent the common inability of listeners to really take on board what is being said:

> The *Dharma* wheel must be continuously set in motion. This means that during one single teaching session the teacher should address each topic at least three times. When this occurs, the teaching can be called 'setting the *Dharma* wheel in motion'. This manner of teaching also accounts for the repetitive nature of traditional Buddhist discourses and writings. In this way, the teacher ensures that the true meaning of the teaching is actually transmitted to the student.
>
> *Khenpo Chöga, On Khenpo Kunpal, Bodhisattva-Charyāvatāra 5:50–55, DNK3 p.80*

Many of the *sūtras* speak of the millions upon millions of celestial beings who beg the Buddha or other *buddhas* to set the wheel of *Dharma* turning, as a result of which untold millions of beings are enabled to become enlightened and attain liberation. In the *Lotus Sūtra,* the Buddha tells the story of the *buddha* Mahābhijñā-jñānā-bhibhu ('Victorious through Great Universal Wisdom'), who lived "Long ago, beyond incalculable limitless, inconceivable and unutterable *asaṃkhyeya-kalpas* (innumerable ages)":[4]

> The *buddha* Victorious through Great Universal Wisdom,
> for ten *kalpas* (ages) sat in the place of practice;
> Yet no *buddhadharma* came to the fore,
> nor was he able to attain (the culmination of) the *buddha* Path.
> Gods, demons, dragon kings, a multitude of *asuras,* and others
> constantly rained down heavenly flowers upon him,
> as offerings to that *buddha.*
> Heavenly beings beat divine drums, making music of many kinds;
> Then a fragrant wind blew away the withered flowers,
> raining down new and lovely ones in their stead.
> When ten minor *kalpas* had passed,
> at last he was able to attain the *buddha* Path,
> and heavenly beings and people of the world
> all danced for joy of heart.

All of that *buddha*'s sixteen sons, in company with their retinues,
a thousand myriads of millions of them gathered round,
all went together before that *buddha.*
With heads bowed in obeisance at the *buddha*'s feet,
they entreated him to turn the *Dharma* wheel *(fălún):*
"Saintly lion, let the *Dharma* rain fall in full upon us and others!"

A world-honoured one is very hard to encounter,
only once in a long time does he appear.
In order to bring enlightenment to all living beings,
he makes the regions all around to shake and tremble.

In the world-spheres to the east,
in five hundred myriads of millions of lands,
the *Brahmā* palaces gleamed in a way they had never done before.
When the *Brahmā*-kings saw this sign,
they went forth in search of the *buddha:*
They made an offering before him of scattered flowers,
also presenting their palaces to him as well.
Praising him with *gāthās* (songs),
they entreated the *buddha* to turn the *Dharma* wheel *(fălún).*
But the *buddha,* knowing that the time had not yet come,
remained seated in silence throughout their entreaties.

In the other three principal directions and the four intermediate ones,
and in the upper and lower regions, the same thing happened:
Scattering flowers as offerings, they presented their palaces,
entreating the *buddha* to turn the *Dharma* wheel *(fălún):*
"A world-honoured one is very hard to encounter.
We beg you, in your great mercy and compassion,
open wide the ambrosial gates
and turn the unsurpassed *Dharma* wheel *(fălún).*"

The World-Honoured One, being of incalculable wisdom,
accepted the entreaties of that multitude,
and for their sakes preached a variety of *dharmas,* saying:
"The four noble truths and the twelve-linked chain of causation –
from spiritual ignorance through to old age and death –
all exist through the cause of birth.
Concerning the multitude of faults and troubles,
you should understand this about them."

When he pronounced this *dharma,*
six hundred myriads of millions of beings

were enabled to overcome the limitations of suffering,
all of them becoming *arhats* (noble ones, enlightened ones).

Lotus Sūtra 7, T9 262:26a26–b26; cf. LBFD pp.149–51

In another chapter, the historical Buddha relates the traditional story of how he himself decided to begin turning the *Dharma* wheel. Having attained enlightenment, the gods and their retinues beg him to "turn the *Dharma* wheel":

At that time the *Brahmā*-kings
and the heavenly king, *Shakra (Indra),*
and the four heavenly kings who protect the world,...
as well as the multitudes of other heavenly beings
and their retinues of hundreds of thousands of myriads,
reverently joining their palms together in obeisance,
begged me to turn the *Dharma* wheel *(fălún).*

Lotus Sūtra 2, T9 262:9c9–12; cf. LBFD p.43

Having considered the matter, this he decides to do, making use of "expedient means", a term also translated as "skilful means", by which he refers to the methods used by the *buddhas* to get their teachings across to human beings who are steeped in spiritual ignorance and suffering. Here, he recalls his first discourse in Vārāṇasī, where his first five disciples came to him:

And then I thought to myself:
"Having come into this impure and evil world,
as the *buddhas* have preached,
so must I too follow that example in my deeds."
And having considered the matter in this way,
I immediately set out for Vārāṇasī.
And since the subtle aspect of the teachings
cannot be proclaimed in words,
I resorted to the power of expedient means,
to preach to the five *bhikshus.*
This is called 'turning the *Dharma* wheel *(fălún)*'....
Since remote *kalpas* (ages),
I have set forth and extolled the *Dharma* of *nirvāṇa,*
and an end to the sufferings of birth and death –
It is thus that I have ever preached.

Lotus Sūtra 2, T9 262:10a1–9; cf. LBFD p.44

But this *Dharma* is nothing new. It is the same teaching that all *buddhas* have given since time out of mind. This time it is the Buddha's disciple Sāriputra who is speaking:

The Buddha said that in ages past
  countless *buddhas,* now passed into extinction *(nirvāṇa),*
  who dwelt securely in the midst of expedient means,
  also preached this *Dharma,* every one of them;
And those *buddhas,* present and future,
  their numbers beyond all reckoning,
  will also resort to expedient means,
  setting forth a *dharma* such as this one –
Just as the present World-Honoured One,
  having been born and later relinquishing the household life,
  in his attainment of the Way and his turning of the *Dharma* wheel,
  also preaches by resorting to expedient means....

When I hear the Buddha's soft and gentle voice – profound,
  far removed from ordinary understanding, and extremely subtle –
Setting forth the pure *Dharma,* my heart is filled with great joy.
My doubts and second thoughts are forever cleared away,
  and I dwell securely in the midst of real wisdom (knowing):
"Of a certainty I will become a *buddha,*
  revered by heavenly and human beings,
  turning the unsurpassed *Dharma* wheel *(fălún),*
  teaching and converting *bodhisattvas.*"

Lotus Sūtra 3, T9 262:11a24–b8; cf. LBFD pp.52–53

See also: **chakravartin** (7.1), **Dharma** (▸4).

1. *E.g. Majjhima Nikāya* 12, *Mahāsīhanāda Sutta, PTSM1* p.69; *Saṃyutta Nikāya* 12:21–22, *Dasabala Sutta, PTSS2* pp.27–28; *Anguttara Nikāya* 4:8, 23, *Vesārajja Sutta, Loka Sutta, PTSA2* pp.9, 24; *Anguttara Nikāya* 5:11, *Tathāgatabala Sutta, PTSA3* pp.10–11; *Anguttara Nikāya* 6:64, 10:21, *Sīhanāda Sutta, PTSA3* pp.417–19, *Dutiya-ariyavāsa Sutta, PTSA5* pp.33–34.
2. *Saṃyutta Nikāya* 56:11, *Dhammacakkappavattana Sutta, PTSS5* p.423; Master Hsuan Hua, on *Prajñāpāramitā Sūtra, HPPS* pp.99–100.
3. Master Hsuan Hua, on *Shūrangama Sūtra, SS1* p.104; "Wheel of the Dharma," *Illustrated Encyclopedia of Zen Buddhism, IEZB.*
4. *Lotus Sūtra* 7, *T9* 262:22a20*ff.*, *LBFD* p.130.

dharmashālā (S), **dharmshālā** (H), **dharamsālā**, **dharmsālā** (Pu) *Lit.* house *(shālā)* of religion *(dharma);* a religious sanctuary; a free guest house, an inn, a resting place for pilgrims; common in Hinduism, Jainism, and Tibetan Buddhism; also, a town in the Indian state of Himachal Pradesh, established by the British in 1849 on vacant land where a *dharamshālā* once stood, and now the home of the fourteenth *Dalai Lama,* spiritual leader of the Tibetans, presently living in exile; often anglicized as 'dharamsala'. In India, *dharmshālās* are built either by individuals or religious institutions for *sādhus* and others to lodge in during their travels. Their purpose is mainly to help poor *sādhus,* and thereby to earn merit for the donors.

See also: **āshrama**.

dharma talk (S. *dharma-deshanā,* Pa. *dhamma-desanā*) A talk or discourse on the Buddhist Way *(Dharma)* by a Buddhist teacher; often as a commentary on a Buddhist text, often scheduled on a daily or twice-daily basis, especially in *Zen* Buddhist monasteries and temples; also called a *teishō* (J). A number of Buddhist teachers have assembled collections of their talks for the benefit of their disciples and for posterity.

Such discourses are often times of elevated consciousness, when the attention focuses both on the meaning of the talk and the inspired character of the giver. Wang K'ai recalls times spent with his own teacher, Grand Master T'an Hsu (1875–1963):

> My master's words were sincere, and there was such a glow, such depth to his purpose, that I immediately visualized a meeting of a great *dharma* assembly *(daishū),* highlighted with my master's lecture, sometime in the near future. The sound of his *dharma* talk is still in my ears, and his kindly face is still in my mind; yet he is gone. I am overwhelmed with grief. I always went to see my master whenever I was free and had a question regarding *Dharma.* Even when I received only one word or one sentence from him in response, my heart was moved and my consciousness felt clear and bright. Later, when he was advanced in years and could not talk for long, he could not complete his answer at times; and I had to leave disappointed. Had I anticipated then that he was going to leave us so soon, I would not have left him for one single moment, my worldly concerns notwithstanding.
>
> *Wang K'ai, Memorial for my Master, in PPHS p.123*

See also: **daishū, shōsan, teishō**.

dīdār (P) *Lit.* witnessing, beholding, seeing, sight (of), vision (of); meeting, visiting; hence also, face; in Sufism, inner vision, mystical vision, either of God or inner realities or of the spiritual form of the master, within or without. Saʿdī speaks of the vision of the divine beloved, either internally or externally.

To "sacrifice" one's "life" means to give up all thought of self. When this happens, then the Divine is seen in everything and in every "face":

> Some day I shall sacrifice my life for a sight *(dīdār)* of you,
> lest I should look at any other face *(dīdār)* again.
>
> *Sa'dī, Ṭayyibāt 366:2, KSSS p.329; cf. TOS p.489*

Maybudī quotes an otherwise unattributed *pīr-i ṭarīqat* (master of the path), who says that when the beloved is seen, then the joy of it wipes away all worldly suffering and all the agony of separation:

> What is a hundred years of suffering,
> when you have had sight *(dīdār)* of the beloved for a day?
>
> *Pīr-i Ṭarīqat, in Kashf al-Asrār, KA7 p.513; cf. in SSE2 p.52*

Attributed to the same source is a dialogue between *mihr* (love) and *dīdār* (beholding), in which *mihr* is portrayed as a bringer of the anguish of separation and testing, while *dīdār* is the gift of fulfilment and the bringer of joy:

> Love *(mihr)* and Beholding *(dīdār)* once encountered one another. Love said, "Beholding *(dīdār)*, you are like the light that illumines the world."
>
> Beholding *(dīdār)* said, "Love, you are like a fire that consumes the world. When I unveil, I root out all sadness from the heart."
>
> Love said, "I cultivate the heart in which I take up residence."
>
> Beholding *(dīdār)* said, "I am the gift to those who are tested."
>
> Love said, "I agitate the world."
>
> *Pīr-i Ṭarīqat, in Kashf al-Asrār, KA3 p.639; cf. in SSE2 p.52*

Ḥāfiẓ prays that grace may once more descend upon him, for he has temporarily lost his vision of the inner beloved and his spiritual progress appears to have come to a standstill:

> Our ship is becalmed: spring up, O favourable breeze,
> that we may have sight *(dīdār)* of the beloved once again!
>
> *Ḥāfiẓ, Dīvān, DHA p.3, DHHM p.11; cf. DHWC (6:2) p.30, in SSE2 p.52*

Sulṭān Bāhū, a seventeenth-century Indian Sufi, says explicitly that nothing compares with the *dīdār* of his *murshid* (master). Again, he is speaking of both outer and inner *dīdār:*

> Were my whole body festooned with eyes *(chashmān),*
> I would gaze at my *murshid* with untiring zeal.

Oh, how I wish that every pore of my body
would turn into a million eyes *(chashmān):*
Then, as some closed to blink, others would open to see!
But even then my thirst to see him might remain unquenched.
What else can I do?
To me, O Bāhū, one glimpse *(dīdār)* of my *murshid*
is worth millions of pilgrimages to the holy *Kaʻbah!*

Sulṭān Bāhū, Bait 11, SBU p.339; cf. SBE pp.234–35

See also: **darshan, dīdah** (▸3).

dokusan nyūshitsu (J), **dúsān rùshì** (C) *Lit.* alone *(dú)* visiting *(sān)* + enter *(rù)* room *(shì) i.e.* of the master or abbot; going alone to the master; a private audience or consultation; a private interview of a disciple with a *Zen* master *(rōshi),* especially in the *Rinzai* and *Ōbaku Zen* traditions; used synonymously with *sanzen* in the *Rinzai* tradition.

Both *dokusan* and *nyūshitsu* are individually used as abbreviations for *dokusan nyūshitsu,* while *nyūshitsu* – more specifically, 'entering the (abbot's) room' – carries the additional connotation of 'studying under a Buddhist teacher'. Although voluntary, *dokusan* is regarded as an essential aspect of life in a *Zen* monastery. The first interview of a disciple with his master, at which he or she is officially accepted, is known as a *shōken* ('seeing one another', 'mutual seeing').

The purpose of such meetings is to enable the master to evaluate a disciple's progress, check the profundity of the disciple's understanding, and give necessary advice. Disciples can also relate their meditation experiences, and the master can validate them or not, as the case may be. Disciples are generally counselled to discuss only aspects of their spiritual practice with their master, and are discouraged from raising personal issues. They are also advised against talking about the content of their meeting with other disciples, part of the reason being that the replies given to one disciple may not be applicable to another, and might cause confusion. Moreover, meetings are intended to be private, and some of the mind-to-mind blessings and understanding that may flow in such meetings are liable to dissipation if the contents are broadcast to others.

The meetings take place in a *Zen* monastery during the course of the morning and evening meditation sessions. Traditionally, the master sits on a cushion in a darkened room, illuminated from behind by a single candle, and the experience can be somewhat daunting. Disciples await their turn outside the master's room. When their turn comes, they announce their presence by striking a small bell *(kanshō)* with a mallet (provided there is no possibility of disturbing the neighbours), enter the room, and bow before the master.

The master signals the end of the meeting by ringing a small bell, and the disciple bows and makes his exit. During periods known as *sesshin* (intensive meditation, traditionally lasting seven days and seven nights), disciples have the opportunity for *dokusan* at least once during the course of a day.

Rinzai and *Ōbaku Zen* meditation is centred around the contemplation of *kōans* (paradoxes to be resolved). During a *dokusan,* the master may give a *kōan* to a disciple as the subject of his ongoing meditation, encouraging him to make further progress. Sometimes, the master may test a disciple on his progress in understanding the *kōans.* The verbal nature of the answer to these tests is another reason why the substance of a *dokusan* is intended to be private. Although crib sheets containing correct answers are in circulation, an astute master will be able to tell if a disciple is presenting an answer parrot-fashion or has genuinely understood the inner meaning of the *kōan.*[1]

See also: **sanzen**.

1. See "Dokusan," "kanshô," "sesshin," *Illustrated Encyclopedia of Zen Buddhism, IEZB.*

dṛishṭi (S/H), **diṭṭhi** (Pa), **drishṭi**, **drisṭi**, **drisṭ** (Pu) *Lit.* looking, viewing, beholding; look, glance, gaze; vision, sight; insight, perception, wisdom; view, opinion, belief, perspective; regard, reflection; from the Sanskrit root *d-ṛi-sh* (to see, to look at, to know, to discern); also, the focused, contemplative attention that is practised during meditation; a special look or glance from a spiritually evolved soul, conveying spiritual power and uplift to the recipient.

In Hindu, Buddhist and Jain traditions, *dṛishṭi* is often used more or less synonymously with *darshana* (vision, perception, seeing, looking at, observing, noticing, view, opinion, *etc.*). Strictly speaking, *darshana* refers to the opinion or belief *per se; dṛishṭi* to the act of seeing or believing or having such a viewpoint. Also, while *dṛishṭi* can mean both true and false beliefs, *darshana* without qualification never refers to a false belief. In Hindu tradition, *dṛishṭi* is used in expressions such as *divya-dṛishṭi* (divine vision),[1] *dūra-dṛishṭi* (far sightedness), *divya-chakshu* (divine eye), *antar-dṛishṭi* (inner vision), *sūkshma-dṛishṭi* (subtle sight, keen vision, perception of the subtle aspects of the material universe),[2] and *sama-dṛishṭi* or *sama-darshana* (same, equal or even vision; impartiality).

In the *Bhagavad Gītā,* in the chapter in which Arjuna experiences a vision of Kṛishṇa in his cosmic form, Arjuna speaks of seeing *(dṛishṭvā)* the "wondrous, awe-inspiring form" of Kṛishṇa, at which he is "overjoyed", though at the same time he is "also perturbed by fear". Later, on seeing the human form of Kṛishṇa once again, Arjuna becomes "composed, and restored" to his "natural state of mind".[3] Kṛishṇa then tells him:

This form of Mine that you have seen *(ḍrishṭavān)*
is extremely difficult to behold.
Even *devas* themselves are ever eager to see it.
Not by studying the *Vedas,* nor by austerities,
nor by charity, nor by sacrifices,
is it possible for Me to be seen *(ḍrashṭuṃ)*
in the way you have seen *(ḍrishṭavān)* Me.

Bhagavad Gītā 11:52–53; cf. BGT

In the yogic and *sant* traditions, the *ḍrishṭi* of a master or holy man refers to a grace-filled glance by which he transfers spiritual power and bliss to a disciple. In an instant, should he so desire, he can grant even the highest spiritual wealth:

The *guru* is perfect, his teachings are everlasting:
beholding his ambrosial glance *(amrit drisṭ),* one becomes saintly.
Endless are his virtues, his worth cannot be appraised:
O Nānak, one who pleases him is united with him.

Guru Arjun, Ādi Granth 287, AGK

His wisdom is perfect, and his glance *(drisṭ)* is ambrosial,
beholding his *darshan,* the universe is saved.

Guru Arjun, Ādi Granth 293, AGK

You are all-powerful and all-knowing –
what more can I say, O lord *satguru?*
Through your merciful glance *(dayā ḍrishṭi)* and your gracious will,
take away the anguish of my heart.

Swami Shiv Dayal Singh, Sār Bachan Poetry 33:6.8–9, SBP p.268, SBPS p.316

Cast your merciful glance *(mehr kī ḍrishṭi)* on me, master,
for every moment I suffer unrelenting pain.

Swami Shiv Dayal Singh, Sār Bachan Poetry 33:8.1, SBP p.269, SBPS pp.318–19

The master has cast his merciful glance *(kṛipā ḍrishṭi)* on me,
and shattered the wheel of time forever.

Swami Shiv Dayal Singh, Sār Bachan Poetry 4:6.6, SBP p.41, SBPS pp.18–19

Baba Jaimal Singh says that initiation is bestowed by the inner *drishṭi* of a master. He writes in a letter that a certain Hari Rām

will receive the grace and mercy of initiation through the *satguru*'s benign inner glance *(drishṭi).* Even if life now departs from his body, he will again receive a human birth, and will not re-enter the cycle of eighty-four.

Baba Jaimal Singh, Spiritual Letters 14, SL p.26

See also: **darshana, dṛishṭi** (▸3).

1. *E.g. Haṭha Yoga Pradīpikā* 2:30, 3:96, *HYP* pp.17, 43.
2. *Shiva Saṃhitā* 3:54.
3. *Bhagavad Gītā* 11:20, 23–25, 45, 49, 51; *cf. BGT.*

early Christian communities It is popular belief that Jesus had only twelve disciples. There is considerable evidence, however, of the existence of sizeable Christian communities soon after the death of Jesus.[1] Peter, for instance, at the beginning of *Acts,* not long after the death of Jesus, is said to have addressed a group of about 120 disciples at Jerusalem:

> And in those days Peter stood up in the midst of the disciples, and said, (the number of names together were about an hundred and twenty),...
>
> *Acts 1:15, KJV*

A few years later, when Paul writes to the Roman Christians, probably around 57 CE, it is to a community which he has never previously visited, and it seems from what he writes that he is unsure whether any of them there will agree with his doctrinal point of view. *Luke* also mentions disciples in Damascus, Antioch, Joppa, Lydda, Caesarea, Ephesus and in many other places, who seem to have been there before Paul began his missionary activities.[2] Paul himself speaks of places that he has visited where there were already disciples who were not of his calling. Moreover, from comments in his letters, it is clear that communities of his own converts existed alongside other Christian groups and that their relationship was not always harmonious.[3] Paul himself castigates all others as following the wrong path, but one is left wanting to know more about these 'other' groups of Jesus' followers. Were they, in fact, Jesus' original disciples, dating from his lifetime?

The gospel writers themselves certainly speak of large crowds which gathered around both Jesus and John the Baptist, even following them from place to place, and one can only presume that many of these were baptized disciples. They were also drawn from many different localities, no doubt forming their own groups in their own local communities. Matthew, for instance, records that crowds from "Jerusalem, and all Judaea" went out to listen to John the Baptist, who seemed to have his headquarters in the desert:

> Then went out to him Jerusalem, and all Judaea, and all the region round about Jordan.
>
> *Matthew 3:5, KJV*

And John reports that

> Jesus made and baptized more disciples than John.
>
> *John 4:1, KJV*

So if "all Judaea" went out to listen to John the Baptist, then a greater number must have gone out to see Jesus. As John's gospel records elsewhere, "and a great multitude followed him".[4] There are also the well-known stories of the feeding of the five thousand and the four thousand, related by Mark and copied by Luke and Matthew,[5] while multitudes and great numbers of people who flocked to hear the great teacher are often mentioned. People obviously enjoyed being around their master and must have gained great inspiration from it. As Mark records:

> And again he began to teach by the seaside: and such a great multitude gathered around him that he got into a boat, and sat in it on the sea; and the whole multitude was on the land beside the sea.
>
> *Mark 4:1; cf. KJV*

And:

> When he rejoined his disciples, he saw a great multitude around them, and the scribes questioning them. And immediately upon seeing him, all the people were wonderstruck, and ran to greet him.
>
> *Mark 9:14–15; cf. KJV, NJB*

Similarly, Luke writes:

> But so much the more went there a fame of him abroad: and great multitudes gathered together to hear (him).... And one day it came to pass that while he was teaching, there were Pharisees and doctors of the law sitting by, who had come out from every town of Galilee, and Judaea, and Jerusalem.
>
> *Luke 5:15, 17; cf. KJV*

But crowds also came from much further afield, as Mark relates:

> A great multitude from Galilee followed him, and from Judaea, and from Jerusalem, and from Idumaea (south of Judaea), and from beyond

> Jordan; and a great multitude of those who lived near Tyre and Sidon, when they had heard what great things he was doing, came unto him.
>
> *Mark 3:7–8; cf. KJV*

Matthew recasts this passage from Mark, adding that "his fame went throughout all Syria", and that people also came from the Greek-speaking cities of the Decapolis.[6] There are other similar reports, and the conclusion that one reaches is that by the time of Jesus' crucifixion, there were sizeable communities of his disciples, spread throughout the Roman Empire. Places in Palestine, Asia Minor, Greece, various Mediterranean islands, Rome and Italy are all mentioned in this respect, and it is not improbable, considering the crowds that Jesus attracted when he spoke, that he had disciples in all these areas.

One thing is certain, whatever role the twelve apostles may have played, they were not the sole followers of Jesus. In fact, it is likely that the number twelve was an invention of the later gospel writers, possibly to fit in with the idea of the twelve disciples sitting upon twelve thrones judging the twelve tribes of Israel – an altogether odd sort of an idea to the modern mind, but consonant with Jewish thought of those times. Paul, writing in the 50s CE, never mentions anything in his letters concerning twelve disciples. He just speaks of the 'brethren', the 'elders' and so on, among whom he includes James the brother of Jesus,[7] though he is never mentioned in the gospels as a disciple.

There is also the evidence of the gnostic Mandaeans who give allegiance to John the Baptist. If the Baptist's ministry was so short, how could his influence have reached Mesopotamia and Persia? Some passages found in the Slavonic edition of Josephus' *Jewish War*[8] are helpful here, for they indicate that John the Baptist could have had a far longer ministry than is commonly supposed, being active as a teacher during the time of the ethnarch Archelaus (4 BCE – 6 CE), successor to Herod the Great (*d.*4 BCE), king of Judaea.

Both the synoptic gospels and Josephus agree that John the Baptist was beheaded during the ministry of Jesus in the early 30s CE and there is no reason to doubt them. So if the text of the Slavonic Josephus is authentic, it would mean that John the Baptist had a public ministry lasting around thirty years. Such a chronology, of course, is inconsistent with Luke's account that John the Baptist was only six months older than Jesus and was consequently only a child during the reign of Archelaus. But then Luke's historical accuracy is known to be debatable. In fact, there are also historical inaccuracies in Mark's account of the death of John the Baptist. Herod Antipas, for example, had married the ambitious Herodias, wife of his half-brother, not of Philip the tetrarch, as Mark (followed by Matthew and Luke) states.[9]

It is certainly true that many of the communities giving allegiance to Jesus also contained disciples of John the Baptist. Luke mentions Paul's meeting with some disciples of John the Baptist at Ephesus[10] and in a tradition recorded in John's gospel,[11] Peter's brother Andrew (and possibly Peter too), though a disciple of John the Baptist, was happy to accept Jesus as the master in his place. Moreover, it seems unlikely that the teachings of John the Baptist and Jesus would have differed, whatever their later followers may have thought, and the two groups would have had a natural affinity to each other. It is clear, therefore, that the traditional picture of Jesus and his twelve disciples is not supported by the evidence of the New Testament and historical records of the period.

See also: **church**.

1. The material for this entry is taken from *The Gospel of Jesus, GJ* pp.148–51.
2. *Acts passim.*
3. *E.g. 1 Corinthians* 1:11–16.
4. *John* 6:2, *KJV.*
5. *Mark* 6:44, 8:9; *Matthew* 14:21, 15:38, 16:9–10; *Luke* 9:14.
6. *Matthew* 4:24–25.
7. *Galatians* 1:18–19; *1 Corinthians* 15:5–7.
8. Josephus, *Jewish War* (Slavonic), *JWW* pp.397–400, *J3* pp.644–48.
9. *Mark* 6:17*ff.; Matthew* 14:3*ff.; Luke* 3:19*ff.* See also *Luke* 3:1; Josephus, *Antiquities* 18:5; E. Schürer, *History of the Jewish People, HJP1* pp.343–49.
10. *Acts* 19:1*ff.*
11. *John* 1:35*ff.*

ekklēsia (Gk) *Lit.* congregation, assembly, community; often translated as 'church', meaning both the Christian community and buildings constructed for public worship; originally, an assembly of citizens in an ancient Greek city-state; from *ekklētos* (called), from *ekkalēin* (to call out), from *kalein* (to call).

In Athens, a ruling body known as the *ekklēsia* was in place as early as the seventh century BCE. In the process of Solon's codification of the law (*c.*594 BCE), the term was applied to the assembly of adult men over the age of eighteen who had final control over political decisions. Such assemblies continued in most Greek city-states, even into the Roman period, though their powers were gradually diminished.

See also: **church, congregation**.

evaṃ mayā shrutaṃ (S), **evaṃ me sutaṃ** (Pa), **'di skad bdag gis thos pa** (T), **rúshì wǒwén** (C), **nyoze gamon** (J) *Lit.* thus *(evaṃ, rúshì, nyoze)* I *(mayā, wǒ, ga)* heard *(shrutaṃ, wén, mon);* thus have I heard; the stock clause that opens almost all Buddhist *sūtras* (Pa. *suttas*), indicating that the *sūtra* consists of what the one who recorded the *sūtra* had heard the Buddha say.

The earliest Buddhist *suttas* are all in Pali. The words are generally followed by *ekaṃ samayaṃ* (at one time, on one occasion; S. *ekasmin samaye*), after which comes either *Bhagavā* (the Lord, the Blessed One) or the name of a leading disciple. This is followed by an indication of the place where the Buddha was staying *(viharati)* at the time, or where the Buddha delivered his discourse, or where the recorded dialogue took place, such as Rājagaha (S. Rājagṛiha). The full sentence (though there are variations) thus reads:

> *Evaṃ me sutaṃ ekaṃ samayaṃ Bhagavā (Rājagaha) viharati (Pa).*
>
> *Evam mayā shrutam ekasmin samaye Bhagavān (Rājagṛiha) viharati sma (S).*

The 'I' in "Thus have I heard" is traditionally believed to have been Ānanda, the Buddha's first cousin – a devoted disciple and his close attendant for the last thirty years or so of the Buddha's ministry. According to the story, Ānanda had an exceptionally retentive memory, and being in such close and constant company with the Buddha, he committed many of the Buddha's discourses, discussions and sayings to memory, becoming a living repository of the Buddha's oral teachings. At the First Council, held shortly after the Buddha's death (*c.*480 BCE) at the Cave of the Seven Leaves in Rājagaha (now Rajgir in the state of Bihar) and presided over by the disciple Mahākassapa, Ānanda was among the five hundred senior monks who attended in order to recite and verify all that they could recall of the Buddha's teachings. Each discourse or discussion, long or short, is known as a *sutta* (S. *sūtra*). The *suttas* thus collected were divided into two collections or *piṭakas* (baskets). Those specifically associated with the teachings were called the *Sutta Piṭaka* ('Basket of Discourses', 'Collection of Discourses'); those concerned with the conduct and behaviour of the community of monks were known as the *Vinaya Piṭaka* ('Basket of Discipline').

It was decided that only those discourses that could be verified as being the Buddha's words should be included. It became clear, however, that some of the *suttas* were either the words of the Buddha's disciples or that they had come into existence after the Buddha's departure. Nonetheless, since they were regarded as true expressions of the Buddha's teachings, they were also included. After the First Council, the collection was closed and no further texts are supposed to have been added.

Scholars have speculated whether *"evaṃ me sutaṃ"* meant that Ānanda or some other disciple had been present personally, or whether he had heard things from other disciples, or both. That is, they suggest that there is some doubt whether the *suttas* were heard directly from the Buddha or are a report of what had been heard from others. Some maintain that, "Thus I have heard," indicates that the *sutta* rests entirely upon hearsay; others say that it means that the *suttas* are a direct replication of the Buddha's words. There is no normal human way of knowing which is true.

In ancient times, the oral tradition was well recognized as a valid means of preserving scriptures and other literary works. In fact, it was the standard means long before the Buddha's time, and the Pali texts were only committed to written form during the first century BCE. The constant repetition of passages with only minor variations, so characteristic of these *suttas,* is one of the mnemonic aids used to remember the texts. In a modern world, where the ability to read and write are commonplace, the skills required to remember long texts have largely been lost. Indeed, written literacy is one of the reasons for the loss of the required skills, much as the advent of calculators has diminished people's capacity to do mental arithmetic. Even so, the exact content of the *Sutta Piṭaka,* as it was decided at the First Council, is uncertain. It was not written down until four centuries later, and it is not until the time of the first written commentaries on these texts – attributed to Buddhaghosa in the fifth century CE – that a clear idea of the content of the *Sutta Piṭaka* (as it was at that time) emerges, one thousand years after the death of the Buddha. Much could have happened in that time as the various schools and traditions developed.

Tradition accords the same degree of authenticity to the discourses relating to monastic discipline and collected together in the *Vinaya Piṭaka,* as it does to the *Sutta Piṭaka.* However, their origin as a part of the collection of the Buddha's discourses and teachings is dubious, not least because they represent an evolution of the monastic movement that did not exist during the Buddha's lifetime.

There is also a third collection of Pali texts, the *Abhidhamma Piṭaka,* an analytical systematization of and commentary on the *Sutta Piṭaka,* which is necessarily a later development, after the *Sutta Piṭaka* had been formalized, and which is not mentioned anywhere in the *Sutta Piṭaka.* Tradition maintains that *Abhidhamma Piṭaka* came to the Buddha soon after his enlightenment, and that he taught it to the gods some years later. The Buddha then repeated it to his disciple Sāriputta, who handed it on to the community of disciples. Scholars, however, are of the opinion that the *Abhidhamma Piṭaka* was composed at least a century or two after the Buddha's passing, and that it comprises the work of scholars, not the words of the Buddha. Some accounts of the First Council, although mentioning both the *Sutta Piṭaka* and the *Vinaya Piṭaka,* make no mention of the *Abhidhamma Piṭaka.*

Within 250 years of the Buddha's departure, these three collections or baskets, known as the *Tripiṭaka* (three baskets) had become the established canon of Pali scriptures, attributed to the Buddha. The school of early Buddhism that formed around this collection of original teachings, before the development of the major breakaway movements, became known as *Theravāda* (Way of the Elders).

In later times, with the rise of the *Mahāyāna* and *Vajrayāna* schools, further texts were written and added, initially in Sanskrit, and later – with the spread of Buddhism – in Chinese and Tibetan as well. The *Mahāyāna* and *Vajrayāna* perspective was that although these later texts were not actually spoken by the historical Buddha, they were inspired by him and hence deserved a place among the accepted scriptures. Known as *buddhavacana* (words of the Buddha, teachings of the Buddha), they were accepted as part of the *buddhadharma* (teachings of the Buddha). In many instances, as in the case of the *Lotus Sūtra* and *Avataṃsaka Sūtra* ('Flower Garland *Sūtra*'), the teachings are said to have been delivered to an audience of gods and celestial beings, far away in some celestial realm, unrelated to this world and to material time. These later traditions had no defined body of canonical literature. Some sub-schools were focused almost entirely on single *sūtras,* which in themselves were actually an accumulation of texts, put together over a period of time, as with the *Avataṃsaka Sūtra.* In any case, Buddhism had by this time spread to a number of countries outside India, each developing its own particular characteristics and favoured texts.

Over the centuries, the original Sanskrit of many of these texts – if they were not actually written in Chinese or Tibetan or some other language – was lost. Many were destroyed by Muslim depredations in North India, especially during the eleventh and twelfth centuries. Most of the Sanskrit texts that have survived have been found in Nepal. So although many of these later texts begin with the standard *"evaṃ mayā shrutaṃ"* or the equivalent in the various languages, they are not regarded as original discourses or sayings of the historical Buddha. Even the *suttas* comprising the Pali canon have been through a historical process that makes it very difficult to be sure of their authenticity as the actual words of the Buddha.

fǎsì (C), **hassu** (J) *Lit.* transmitted; *dharma (fǎ)* heir *(sì);* a *Chán* and *Zen* Buddhist term denoting a master's appointed successor and legitimate heir; or, one of a number of disciples who has been certified as qualified to accept disciples and to teach the *Dharma;* one who has received the seal of recognition (J. *inka shōmei*) from his master; can be either a monk or a nun. The Japanese *hassu* is a phonetic rendering of the Chinese *fǎsì.*

According to the Chinese and Japanese Buddhist tradition, the *buddhas* and Chinese patriarchs (up to the sixth patriarch) who traced their lineage back to the Buddha himself left only one legitimate successor or *hassu.* But with the passage of time and with the proliferation of various schools and sub-schools, the concept has been diluted, with every school, monastery or temple having its own master and spiritual lineage. Indeed, in modern times, monks may be designated as *dharma* heirs merely in order to authenticate their position in the clerical hierarchy at the local temple of a particular school. It has also become commonplace for the sons of *Sōtō Zen* masters to be designated as *dharma* heirs at any early age in order to legitimize their position as their father's successors.[1]

See also: **inka shōmei**.

1. See "Hassu," *Illustrated Encyclopedia of Zen Buddhism, IEZB.*

fătáng (C), **hōdō**, **hattō** (J) *Lit. Dharma (fă, hō)* hall *(táng, dō);* the main hall in *Zen* and *Chán* Buddhist monasteries; among other things, a preaching or lecture hall *(jiăngtáng);* equivalent to the *kōdō* (lecture hall) of other Japanese Buddhist schools; used for lectures *(teishō),* discussions, questions and answers *(mondō),* and various *Zen* rituals. Contrary to the practice in other Buddhist schools, a *Zen hattō* contains no images of celestial *buddhas* and *bodhisattvas.* When the master or abbot addresses the entire monastic community at the morning assembly *(chōsan)* or on the less frequent *daishū* (great assemblies), he is understood to represent the Buddha and all the *Zen* patriarchs. The focus of the hall is the central dais, approached by three sets of stairs. Located on the dais is the *dharma* chair *(hōza),* from which he delivers his discourse. Many *hattōs* have a high circular ceiling decorated with the painting of a dragon.[1]

See also: **deshanā**.

1. See "Hattô," *Illustrated Encyclopedia of Zen Buddhism, IEZB.*

flock Metaphorically, in a religious or mystical context, any group of people whose care rests with one individual; part of a family of metaphors in which God or a saviour is the shepherd or pastor, and his devotees are the sheep, referred to collectively as his flock; also used for a priest and his congregation.

The imagery is prevalent throughout the Hebrew Bible. In Christianity, its use originates with Jesus' parable of the good shepherd,[1] an imagery that is repeated in his example of the shepherd who rescues the stray sheep, leaving the others safe in the fold.[2] The same imagery is commonly encountered in Manichaean writings.

See also: **sheep** (▸4), **shepherd** (7.1).

1. *John* 10:1–15.
2. *Matthew* 18:11–14.

fold Metaphorically, in a religious or mystical context, the safe haven or protecting power of a master or saviour; also, the protecting 'walls' of the Christian church, or of any religion or spiritual path; also, any group or community who share a way of life or hold the same beliefs; part of a family of metaphors in which God or a saviour is the shepherd or pastor, and his devotees are the sheep, who are protected in the sheepfold.

The imagery is prevalent throughout the Hebrew Bible, in the New Testament,[1] and is widespread in Manichaean literature.

See also: **flock**, **sheep** (▸4), **shepherd** (7.1).

1. *John* 10:1–15; *Matthew* 18:11–14.

fusetsu (J) *Lit.* sermon, talk, lecture, discourse; an informal talk given by a *Zen* master or head abbot of a monastery or temple; a *dharma* talk, less formal than a *daishū* or *teishō*.

See also: **deshanā**, **shōsan**, **teishō**.

gachchha (S) *Lit.* family, race; group, order, monastic tradition; a term used by Jain *Shvetāmbara Mūrtipūjakas* for the main groups within a particular lineage of monks or mendicants; previously known as a *gaṇa* (group, community) or *kula* (family); also used in previous times by *Digambaras* for subdivisions within a lineage.

According to traditional sources as many as eighty-four *gachchhas* existed in medieval times, each with its own lay community. Nowadays, only a few *Mūrtipūjaka gachchhas* remain. In 1999, these were, with their approximate number of members, the *Tapā Gachchha* (6,027), the *Añchala Gachchha* (250), the *Kharatara Gachchha* (229), the *Tristuti* or *Bṛihat Saudharma Tapā Gachchha* (190), the *Pārshvachandra Gachchha* (74), and the *Vimala Gachchha* (41). The last two began as a branch and subbranch of the *Tapā Gachchha,* and are still regarded by some as a part of the *Tapā Gachchha.*

The difference between *gachchhas* has always been more about practices than doctrines. A new *gachchha* generally came into being when a group of monks parted with their *āchārya* (leader) over the need to follow a more rigorous discipline or to practise traditional rites in a different manner. Unlike other *Mūrtipūjaka gachchhas,* for example, lay followers of the *Añchala Gachchha,* among other differences, offer no lamps or solid foods to images of the *Tīrthankaras* and use an alternative wording of the *namaskāra mantra.* Followers of the now extinct *Āgamika Gachchha* of medieval times, reverting to an earlier practice, worshipped neither *kshetrapālas* (protector deities) nor

Sarasvatī (goddess of learning), and therefore omitted three hymns of praise *(tristuti)* addressed to her in their ritual of confession *(pratikramaṇa).* Other differences exist, some past and some present, concerning the clothing worn, the rigour with which the five vows *(mahāvratas)* are followed, the days of the month on which the *pratikramaṇa* should be performed, and so on.

Each *gachchha* is further subdivided into smaller independent groups or sub-lineages, known as *samudāyas* (who may have several *āchāryas*) and smaller groups who travel together, known as *parivāras* (each with their own *āchārya*). Only the *Añchala Gachchha* has one central *āchārya.*[1]

In the past, the Jain mendicant community consisted of lineages, each arising from one prominent *āchārya* of the past, and further divided into a large number of groups and subgroups known as *gaṇas, kulas,* and *shākhās* (branches). However, although these terms are mentioned in various Jain texts, their precise meaning is uncertain. The *Sthānakavāsīs* speak of their main lineages as *sampradāyas* (traditions). Among the *Digambaras,* the term used for basic divisions of the monastic community is *sangha* (community).[2]

See also: **gaṇa**, **saṃgha**.

1. See "gaccha," *A to Z of Jainism, AZJW.*
2. See "mendicant lineages," *A to Z of Jainism, AZJW.*

gaddī (H/Pu) *Lit.* throne, cushion, padded seat, mattress; metaphorically, the seat or position of some eminent personage, such as a sovereign, a *rāja,* a pope, or a bishop; seat of authority or office; in a spiritual context, the position occupied by a spiritual master or leader, as in the expression "when so-and-so came to the *gaddī*", referring to the time when that individual was appointed as the spiritual leader of a particular centre; hence, *gaddī-nishīn* (U) or *gaddī-nashīn* (Pu), the incumbent of such an office, a regent, the present leader or master of a spiritual centre or *āshram.*

gaing (Burmese) *Lit.* monastic group; from the Pali *gaṇa* (group), which refers to a chapter of monks. More of a grouping than a sect, a Burmese *gaing* is distinguished more by differences in monastic lineage, organizational structure, rules, rituals, and practices, rather than by differing doctrines. Local geography and the recognition of governmental authorities also have a part to play.

Burmese Buddhism follows the *Theravāda* tradition, but the history of its growth in the country is uncertain. It is likely that Buddhism got started in Burma on several occasions, but faded out after some time.

gaṇa (S/Pa) *Lit.* troop, band, group, company, assembly; multitude, host; tribe, race; class, category, series; used in expressions such as a host of deities *(gaṇa-devāta),* a multitude of virtues *(guṇa-gaṇa),* a group meal *(gaṇa-bhojana),* and of more or less anything that can come in a group, a multitude, or a category; in Buddhism and Jainism, a group of monks, as few as three and up to the entire *sangha* (community). The term is also used in Buddhism for a secretive group of followers of *Anuttara-Yoga Tantra,* who practise their rituals in lonely places such as graveyards.

In the Jain *Digambara* tradition, a *gaṇa* was a group of monks within a *sangha* (community), who were led by a *gaṇadhara* ('support of a *gaṇa*'), and which consisted of a minimum of three, though there could be many more. A *gaṇa* of monks lived, travelled, and studied the same scriptures together, but could contain disciples of different *āchāryas.* A subgroup within a *gaṇa,* made up of those who have received initiation from the same *āchārya,* was known as a *kula* (family), of which there could be many. In early *Shvetāmbara* times, a *gaṇa* was the largest unit of a lineage, but over time the term was gradually replaced by or sometimes used synonymously with *gachchha* (family, order). *Shvetāmbara Terāpanthīs* refer to their undivided community, which is led by a single *āchārya,* as a *gaṇa.*[1]

See also: **gachchha**, **gaṇin** (7.1), **sthavira** (7.1).

1. See "gaṇa," *A to Z of Jainism, AZJW.*

garanbō (J) *Lit.* temple *(garan)* + *dharma (hō, bō);* temple lineage; the practice, common until the early eighteenth century, of a *Zen* monk changing his lineage *(in'in ekishi),* when he moved from one temple to another, and adopting the lineage of the new temple's founders and abbots. The practice applied to abbots as well as regular monks. Should such a monk subsequently move on to another monastery, he would again change his lineage.

Although *dharma* transmission is generally understood to be founded upon face-to-face transmission of master to disciple, *garanbō* was a method of transmission prevalent within the *Sōtō Zen* school from medieval times (1185–1600) until the reforms of the Tokugawa period (1600–1867) saw a return to the traditional practice of lineage being determined by face-to-face transmission. By retaining a fixed lineage, regardless of the previous lineage of incoming abbots or monks, a temple was able to ensure financial and spiritual support from a network of temples sharing the same the founder and lineage. Despite powerful opposition, the practice was banned by government decree in 1703. *Garanbō* referred to the practice, while the actual change of lineage was called *in'in ekishi.*[1]

See also: **in'in ekishi**.

1. See "Garanbō," *Illustrated Encyclopedia of Zen Buddhism, IEZB;* "garanbō," *Princeton Dictionary of Buddhism, PDB.*

ghamzah (A), **ghamzat** (P) *Lit.* a glance, especially an amorous, coquettish or coy glance, even an ogling; in Sufi symbolism, a transformative glance of grace from the beloved – inner or outer – that confers an inward pull towards God and a spiritual awakening,[1] culminating ultimately in the annihilation *(fanā')* of the lover's sense of individual self.

Many of the Sufi poets, longing for the sight of their own master – inner or outer – have spoken of the power and effect of his glance. As a result of a master's spiritually charged and transforming glance or focus of attention, a devotee's consciousness rises and is flooded with the bliss of divine love and longing:

> Every glance *(ghamzat)* of his is trap and bait:
> through him, every corner is a winehouse....
> With his glance *(ghamzat)*, he plunders our being,
> and with his kisses, in a moment he restores it again.
> *Shabistarī, Gulshan-i Rāz 749–50, SGR pp.570–71; cf. GRSS p.73*

> My heart is entangled in the snare of your tresses.
> Slay it with your glance *(ghamzat)*,
> for this is what it deserves.
> *Ḥāfiẓ, Dīvān, DHA p.16, DIH p.59; cf. DHWC (80:1) p.186*

> Ambushes are taking place everywhere
> due to your bloodthirsty glance *(ghamzat)*:
> Not a night passes
> without this happening in a hundred places.
> *'Irāqī, Kullīyāt 1909, KHI p.167; cf. in SSE2 p.124*

> His enchanting glance *(ghamzat)*
> comes from the eyes of the angel-faced one,
> and steals people's hearts with a hundred spells.
> *Maghribī, Dīvān 35:353, DSMR p.94; cf. in SSE2 p.125*

> How long will the arrows of your glance *(ghamzat)*
> be darted in secret?
> Reason has surrendered to you on account of their murderous fire.
> *Sa'dī, Badāyi' 23:2, KSSS p.348; cf. BOS p.26*

I know not what you require of me, brokenhearted that I am;
You have stolen my heart with your glances *(ghamzat)*.
What else do you want from me?

Sa'dī, Badāyi' 182:1, KSSS p.389; cf. BOS p.198

Without a bow, your arrow-like glances *(tīr-i ghamzat)*
pierce the heart – mercy, mercy, O merciless one!

Rūmī, Maśnavī VI:3764; cf. MJR6 p.465

Such a glance is also known as "murderous glance *(ghamzah-'i khūnkhvār)*" because it slays the ego-self and dissolves the reasoning faculty that stands between the lover and the beloved:

I no longer fear the cruel dart of death: for it is not
more terrible than your murderous glance *(ghamzah-'i khūnkhvār)*.

Sa'dī, Badāyi' 18:2, KSSS p.349; cf. BOS p.21

What anguish has been wrought in the hearts of your kindly lovers
by the mischief of your cruel
and murderous glances *(ghamzah-'i khūnkhvār)!*

Sa'dī, Badāyi' 22:2, KSSS p.350; cf. BOS p.25

You slay a whole army of lovers
with your murderous glances *(ghamzah-'i khūnkhvār)*.
Slay on! For no opponent can stand up against you.

Sa'dī, Badāyi' 24:3, KSSS p.351; cf. BOS p.27

Your eyes, like swords,
flash forth murderous glances *(ghamzah-'i khūnkhvār)*,
so that, all at once, they deprive man of sense and reason.

Sa'dī, Badāyi' 26:1, KSSS p.351; cf. BOS p.29

See also: **'ayn al-kamāl**, **chashm** (7.2), **dṛishṭi**, **kirishmah**, **nargis**, **naẓar**, **nigāh**.

1. Tahānawī, *Kashshāf Iṣṭilāḥāt al-Funūn, KIFT4* p.449.

gurukula (S) *Lit.* family or residence *(kula)* of a master *(guru)*; a *guru*'s dwelling, where pupils receive instruction from their *guru;* also, the circle of disciples around a *guru.* According to Hindu tradition, as laid down in the *Manu Smṛiti,* the idealized life of a twice-born *(dvija)* man of the *brāhmaṇ, kshatriya* or *vaishya* classes is divided into four stages *(āshramas)*. The first is that of the *brahmacharya* (celibate), when the young student is taught secular knowledge, social and family customs, and a knowledge of the *Vedas.* In this context, the *guru* is a teacher, and may not necessarily be a mystic or yogi who teaches the higher spiritual path. However, as a Jain text describes, to pass one's life in the company of a *guru* who teaches the mystic path is matter of great good fortune:

> Blessed are those who reside throughout their whole life in their *guru*'s entourage *(gurukula),* for they acquire knowledge, attaining stability of faith and conduct in particular.
>
> What is the use of residing in the *guru*'s entourage *(gurukula)* for one who has no sense of devotion, respect, reverence, regard and affection, and feels no awe of his *guru?*
>
> *Samansuttam 28–29; cf. SSJV*

In present times, a *gurukula* can also be a school, residential or otherwise, that prepares students for higher education, while at the same time imparting a particular religious or spiritual view of life. A number of such schools exist in India, originating in Hindu and Jain traditions.

See also: **āshrama** (▸4), **dvija** (7.4).

ḥalqah (A), **ḥalqat** (P) (pl. A/P. *ḥalaq, ḥalaqāt, ḥalq'hā*) *Lit.* circle, ring, link; as in *ḥalqah-'i zanjīr* (a door ring, a door knocker), *ḥalqah-'i gūsh* (an earring), *ḥalqah-'i zulf* (a ringlet in tresses of hair), *ḥalqah firangī* (a gold necklet of interlaced rings, worn by European Christians in medieval times), *etc.;* also, a gathering or assembly to hear a preacher in a mosque or to see some public performance, *etc.;* used for the gatherings who came to hear Muḥammad, and later for Sufis sitting together in an assembly in remembrance of God (*ḥalqah-'i ẕikr,* circle of remembrance). A gathering is called a *ḥalqah* because all the links in a chain (the people present) are joined together by a single purpose – to make one unit (a single heart); hence also, a fraternity, a brotherhood, an association.

Sufi poets have been fond of wordplays on the various interlinked meanings of the word. *Ḥalqah rabūdan,* for instance, is a game in which mounted horsemen compete to carry off a ring from a post on the point of a lance. Thus, Saʻdī writes:

> The horsemen carry off rings *(ḥalqat),*
> while our captivating beloved
> snatches away the hearts of the assemblies *(ḥalq'hā).*
>
> *Saʻdī, Ṭayyibāt 181:7, KSSS p.284; cf. TOS p.247*

And in a more complex example:

O Saʿdī, seek words of spiritual wisdom
from the circle of mystics *(ḥalqah-'i darvīshān):*
It would be well to listen to this circle *(ḥalqat).*

Saʿdī, Ṭayyibāt 417:11, KSSS p.340; cf. TOS p.557

Here, the last line reads, *"Az īn ḥalqat dar gūsh kardan."* To wear a ring in the ear *(ḥalqat dar gūsh kardan)* is a mark of slavery in ancient times. *Dar gūsh kardan* means 'to listen to'. Thus, the line may also be rendered, "to wear a ring of this (circle) in your ear", *i.e.* to acknowledge subservience to it.

Rūmī refers to the daily meditation of the circle of devotees as knocking every day on the inner "door":

We are the circle of drunken lovers *(ḥalqah-'i ʿāshiqān):*
Every day we announce our arrival, like a knocker *(ḥalqat)* on the door.

Rūmī, Dīvān-i Shams-i Tabrīz 1554:16335, KSD3 p.267; cf. MP1 (190:12) p.158

Ḥāfiẓ likewise speaks of the meditation *(ẕikr)* that will ultimately untie the "knot" that hides the inner beloved:

The heart is engaged in the circle of remembrance *(ḥalqah-'i ẕikr),*
hoping that this may loosen the knot *(ḥalqat)*
in the tip of the beloved's tresses *(zulf).*

Ḥāfiẓ, Dīvān, DHM p.50, DIH p.120; cf. DHWC (243:4) p.439

Referring to the jangling rings on the circumference of a tambourine, he advises steadfastness on the Path and to the Sufi fraternity, even if the ego takes a "beating" (like a tambourine), before being finally annihilated:

In this circle *(dā'irat),* be ringed *(ḥalqat)* like a tambourine:
though you suffer a beating, do not leave this circle *(dā'irat).*

Ḥāfiẓ, Dīvān, DHA p.224, DIH p.360; cf. DHWC (477:9) p.789

He also exhorts the Sufi who has already "kindled a fire" of love within himself (under his Sufi "cloak") to strive for the highest spiritual goal. The "profligates", here, are the Sufis, intoxicated with divine love:

Now that you have set fire to your cloak *(khirqat),*
O gnostic wayfarer *(sālik),* make an effort and become
chief of the circle of profligates *(sar-i ḥalqah-'i rindān)* of the world.

Ḥāfiẓ, Dīvān, DHA p.144, DIH p.251; cf. DHWC (319:3) p.552

ḥavurah, **ḥevra** (He) (pl. *ḥavurot*) *Lit.* fellowship; an organized brotherhood; a term used during all periods of Jewish history, including kabbalistic fellowships; fellow companions were known as the *ḥaverim* (friends).

Rabbi Ḥayyim Vital, disciple of Rabbi Isaac Luria, writes about the *ḥavurah* of his master's disciples in sixteenth-century Safed, Israel. Their fellowship extended from the mystical to the mundane:

> My teacher, may his memory be for a blessing, cautioned me and all the brethren *(ḥaverim)* who were with him in this fellowship *(ḥavurah)* that before praying the morning service, we should take upon ourselves the positive commandment, "... and thou shalt love thy neighbour as thyself."[1] ... And especially when it comes to the love of our *ḥaverim,* each and every one of us must bind himself to the others as if he were one limb within the body of this fellowship. And if any *ḥaver,* God forbid, was in distress, or if there was any illness in his house or among his children, all should share in his trouble and pray on his behalf; similarly, in all matters, each of the *ḥaverim* should be mindful of his fellows.
>
> *Ḥayyim Vital, Sefer ha-Ḥezyonot, SHHV p.156, in JMKS p.97*

Prior to Luria's arrival in Safed, there had been a number of similar fellowships *(ḥavurot),* centred around previous mystics. Luria therefore found himself in a society in which mystical fellowships were widely accepted:

> Although Kabbalah permeated the air of Safed in the sixteenth century in general, and few could have been left untouched by the powerful currents surrounding them, many chose to associate themselves with one of the several intentional fellowships that emerged there. We presume that such individuals sought to devote themselves to a more disciplined and rigorous style of spiritual life than did others. Most of the individuals whose names appear with any frequency in the kabbalistic literature are likely to have been associated with one or another of the groups we know about.... These fellowships served to institutionalize kabbalistic life to a certain degree, helping to define the direction that piety ought to take and to channel religious energy in a disciplined way....
>
> Some of these circles were under the spiritual guidance of particular personalities, such as Moses Cordovero (1522–1570) and Ele'azar Azikri (1533–1600). The latter, a disciple of Cordovero's in kabbalistic studies, organized two different fellowships in Safed, one under the name *Ḥaverim Makshivim* ('Hearkening Companions'), the other *Sukkat Shalom* ('Tent of Peace'). Others appear to have been more loosely structured around some specialized goal. Thus, the Fellowship

> of Penitents that Abraham Berukhim (*c.*1515–1593) informs us about sought to achieve atonement through certain especially severe ascetic practices.[2] ... Berukhim also tells us about a group whose dedicated purpose seems to have been to rejoice at the conclusion of every Sabbath. An anonymous authority indicated: "There is a group that goes out on the night of the festival of *Simḥat Torah* for the purpose of singing and dancing in the presence of the *Torah* scroll in every synagogue."[3]
>
> *Lawrence Fine, New Approaches, in JMKS pp.95–96*

The earlier *merkavah* (chariot) mystics (*c.*100 BCE – 1000 CE) also referred to themselves as *ḥaverim* (companions) and to their fellowships as *ḥavurah.* The *Hekhalot Rabbati* describes a meeting of such a fellowship at which the first-century (CE) Rabbi Neḥuniah explains the process of ascent and descent, according to the *merkavah* system:

> Then, the (following men) came: Rabban Simon ben Gamaliel, Rabbi Eli'ezer the Great, Rabbi El'azar ben Damah, Rabbi Eli'ezer ben Shamu'a, Rabbi Yoḥanan ben Dahavai, Ḥananya ben Ḥaniḥai, Jonathan ben Uzziel, Rabbi Akiva, and Rabbi Judah ben Baba. We (all) came and sat before him while the mass of companions *(ḥaverim)* stood on their feet, for they saw that globes of fire and torches of light formed a barrier between them and us. Rabbi Neḥuniah ben ha-Kanah sat and set in order for them (the whole group) all the matters of the *merkavah:* the descent to it and the ascent, how to descend, who should descend, how to ascend, and who should ascend.
>
> *Hekhalot Rabbati 16:3, in UJM1 p.60*

Like-minded human beings characteristically come together for mutual support and companionship, and the mystical circles or *ḥavurot* of Judaism are no exception. The same is true of the medieval fellowship that gathered around Rabbi Moses de Leon in thirteenth-century Spain, to whom the writing of the mystical work, the *Zohar,* is credited:

> These tales of Rabbi Simeon and his disciples wandering about Galilee a thousand years before the *Zohar* was written are clearly works of fiction. But to say so is by no means to deny the possibility that a very real mystical brotherhood underlies the *Zohar* and shapes its spiritual character. Anyone who reads the *Zohar* over an extended period will come to see that the interface among companions and the close relationship between the tales of their wanderings and the homilies those wanderings occasion are not the result of fictional imagination alone. Whoever wrote the work knew very well how fellow students respond

to companionship and support, and are inspired by one another's glowing renditions of a text. He (or they) has felt the warm glow of a master's praise, and the shame of being shown up by a stranger in the face of one's peers.

Leaving aside for now the question of who actually penned the words, we can say that the *Zohar reflects the experience* of a kabbalistic circle. It is one of a series of such circles of Jewish mystics, stretching back in time to Qumran, Jerusalem, Provence, and Gerona, and forward in history to Safed, Padua, Miedzybozh, Bratslav, and again to Jerusalem. A small circle of initiates gathered about a master is the way Kabbalah has always happened, and the *Zohar* is no exception. In fact, the collective experience of this group around Rabbi Simeon as 'recorded' in the *Zohar* forms the paradigm for all later Jewish mystical circles.

Arthur Green, A Guide to the Zohar, GZAG p.72

See also: **idra**.

1. *Leviticus* 19:18.
2. Lawrence Fine, *Safed Spirituality, SSRF* pp.47–53.
3. Lawrence Fine, *Safed Spirituality, SSRF* p.11.

hossen (J) *Lit. dharma (hō)* contest *(sen);* an exchange intended to challenge or test an individual's understanding of the *Dharma;* a *Zen* Buddhist term for a verbal exchange between two monks with the intention of deepening their mutual understanding of the *Dharma* (Way) and of the nature of Reality. The term is more metaphorical than descriptive since the encounter is by no means a contest, nor even a debate. Using words and gestures, the two endeavour to convey to each other their understanding of the ultimate Truth, Reality, or enlightenment. The intention is that each should learn from the other. It is somewhat similar in nature to *mondō,* which is a question-and-answer exchange between master and disciple.[1]

See also: **mondō**.

1. See "Hossen," *Oxford Dictionary of Buddhism, ODB.*

huì, **huìzhòng** (C) *Lit.* to assemble, to meet, to gather; a group, an association *(huì);* participants in a meeting, members of a sect or society, a congregation *(huìzhòng);* in Daoism, an association or a congregation of fellow Daoists. See **congregation (in Daoism)**.

ichiji fusetsu (J), **yīzì bùshuō** (C) *Lit.* one word *(yīzì)* not spoken *(bùshuō);* not a word is preached, to say not a word; a Japanese *Zen* saying, transliterated from the Chinese, alluding to the ultimate Reality by indicating that enlightenment or the experience of Reality is far beyond all verbal descriptions. None of the sayings and discourses attributed to the Buddha or indeed to anybody else contain satisfactory words to describe Reality, since it is beyond words. At best, they are only pointers to the wordless experience.

idra (Am/Gk) *Lit.* threshing floor (Am) or sitting in a semicircle (Gk); a term used on occasion for mystical brotherhoods in the Kabbalah.

Idra is the name of one of the most important sections of the *Zohar,* and which is further subdivided into the *Idra Zuta* ('Lesser *Idra*') and *Idra Rabba* ('Greater *Idra*'). The term brings to mind an image of a semicircle of disciples seated around their master. The origin of this use of *idra* arose from a pilgrimage in which Rabbi Isaac Luria took his closest disciples to a place close to the road from Meron to Safed, in Israel. According to his disciple Ḥayyim Vital, the *idra* took place in a cave (*lit.* great rock)[1] although other translators of Vital's text understood the reference to be to a small white building with a dome.[2] Today the cave is an important place of pilgrimage for Jews interested in studying Kabbalah.

Luria and his disciples believed that the second-century mystic Simeon bar Yoḥai (to whom the *Zohar* is traditionally ascribed) assembled his *idra* of disciples around him at this place, and revealed to them what became known as the *Idra Rabba.* Luria believed he was the incarnation of Rabbi Simeon, and he therefore wanted to hold the *idra* with his disciples (whom he believed were incarnations, or at least representations, of Simeon's disciples) at the same place. Thus Luria's pilgrimage with his disciples was seen as an important and special spiritual event. Ḥayyim Vital wrote:

> I once travelled with my master, may his memory be blessed, to the place where Rabbi Simeon bar Yoḥai's disciples assembled when they held the *Idra Rabba.* There, on the eastern side of the road, there is a cave (*lit.* great rock) in which there are two large openings. In the opening on the northern end was the place where Rabbi Simeon bar Yoḥai, peace be upon him, sat on the occasion of the *Idra.* And Rabbi Abba sat in the opening on the southern side. And next to the tree opposite these two openings, to their west, sat Rabbi Ele'azar. And (on the present occasion) my master, may the memory of the righteous be for a blessing, sat in the opening to the north, in the (same) place where Rabbi Simeon bar Yoḥai, peace be upon him, had sat. And I sat, unwittingly, in the opening to the south, in the place of Rabbi Abba. Afterwards, my master, blessed be his memory, explained something to

> me of which I had been unaware, namely, that one of the companions who took part in the *Idra* was part of my soul-ancestry *(gilgul),* that is, Rabbi Abba. I had therefore sat in his place without realizing it. With respect to our positions in these two openings, I am uncertain whether it was not the reverse.[3]
>
> *Ḥayyim Vital, Sefer ha-Ḥezyonot, SHHV p.153, in PSHC p.300*

Another account, in certain ways considered a less reliable version of this event because it was written thirty-five years after Luria's death, is found in the letters of a Moravian Jew named Solomon Shlomi´el of Dresnitz, who emigrated to Safed in the early seventeenth century. He heard about Luria and his teachings from some of Luria's immediate disciples. He writes:

> Occasionally, (Isaac Luria) travelled with his disciples to Meron, where he would have them sit in the place where Rabbi Simeon bar Yoḥai, peace be upon him, revealed the *Idra Rabba.* And he would say: "Here sat Rabbi Ele῾azar, here sat Rabbi Abba, in this spot sat Rabbi Judah, and so on with the rest. And then he would place each one (of his own disciples) in the proper place in accordance with his soul. He himself sat in the place of Rabbi Simeon, and Rabbi Ḥayyim (Vital) sat in Rabbi Ele῾azar's place, and Rabbi Jonathan (Sagis) in Rabbi Abba's place, Rabbi Gedaliah (ha-Levi) in the place of Rabbi Judah, Rabbi Joseph (ibn Tabul) sat in Rabbi Yo´se's place, Rabbi Isaac Kohen Ashkenazi in the place of Rabbi Isaac, and so on with the rest. He would tell them that today the soul of the *tanna* (rabbinic teacher from the period of the *Mishnah*) so-and-so is invested in your soul. He would say that he saw a fire burning around the companions, but that they did not have permission to see it with their own eyes, only he could see it.
>
> *Solomon Shlomi´el, Letter 3, in SAGH p.44, in PSHC pp.300–1*

Although Vital's account is considered more accurate from the point of view of the location and the description of where he sat – since he was a direct disciple of Luria – Shlomi´el's account, despite having been written later, is still illuminating, since it relates the names of Luria's closest disciples and conveys some of the drama of the event.

Kabbalists in later periods often called their fellowships *benei idra* (companions of the *idra*).

See also: **ḥavurah**.

1. Lawrence Fine, *Physician of the Soul, PSHC* pp.300–1; *cf.* Ḥayyim Vital, *Sefer ha-Ḥezyonot, SHHV* p.153.

2. Moshe Hallamish, *Introduction to the Kabbalah, IKMH* p.61; Ḥayyim Vital, *Sha'ar ha-Gilgulim, Introduction* 38, *SGHV* pp.132–33; *Sefer ha-Ḥezyonot, SHHV* p.153.
3. Ḥayyim Vital, *Sefer ha-Ḥezyonot, SHHV* p.153, in *PSHC* p.300.

in'in ekishi (J) *Lit.* changing *(eki)* lineage *(shi)* in accordance *(in)* with one's temple *(in);* the change of lineage when a monk moved from one monastery to another in order to take up the position of abbot, and inherited the lineage of the former abbots of the new monastery. If such an abbot subsequently moved on to another monastery, he would again change his lineage. The practice was known as *garanbō.*

Although the practice became prevalent in the *Sōtō Zen* school (and to a lesser extent in the *Rinzai* school) during medieval times (1185–1600), it is no longer regarded as true to the *Zen* ideal of *dharma* transmission and inheritance *(shihō)* direct from one's own master *(isshi inshō).* According to this tradition, a disciple becomes a part of his master's lineage as soon as he receives authentication *(inka)* of his enlightenment from his own master, and becomes a *dharma* heir (J. *hassu*). This kind of lineage is retained, even if he moves to another temple or monastery.[1]

See also: **garanbō, inka shōmei, isshi inshō.**

1. See "In'in ekishi," *Illustrated Encyclopedia of Zen Buddhism, IEZB.*

inka shōmei (J), **yìnkě zhèngmíng** (C) *Lit.* seal *(inka)* of clearly furnished proof *(shōmei);* seal *(yìn)* can *(kě)* prove *(zhèng)* clearly *(míng);* legitimate proof of transmission; certification of the authenticity of enlightenment; seal of *dharma* transmission; often abbreviated to *inka* or *inshō,* a transliteration of *yìnzhāng* (C. seal); formal recognition given by a master to a disciple in *Zen* Buddhism, authorizing the disciple as a legitimate spiritual descendant of his master, empowered to give his master's teaching and to continue an unbroken lineage of masters as a spiritual 'bloodline (J. *kechimyaku*)', theoretically traceable to Bodhidharma and thence to the Buddha himself; official recognition that a disciple has reached the same degree of enlightenment as his master and is qualified to act as a master; also called *dembōin.* Without receiving *inka* from his master, no disciple can legitimately set himself up as a *Zen* master. *Dharma* transmission is a notion that arose in early Chinese *Chán* Buddhism, lending a degree of authenticity to the lineage.

Bodhidharma is traditionally believed to have brought *Chán* (S. *dhyāna,* J. *Zen*) to China during the fifth or sixth centuries (CE), from where it was transmitted to Japan. The Chinese *yìn* (seal) originates from the tradition of the emperor's or high authority's stamp or seal, used to authenticate documents. Historically, the conferral of a *yìn* upon a disciple has been as significant in *Chán* Buddhism as it became in *Zen,* where a master conferring *inka* on a disciple or a disciple receiving *inka* are common expressions.

In modern Japan, there are about fifty to eighty *inka shōmei* bearers. In ancient times, the *inka* was an actual document, though this is generally no longer the case. The conferral of *inka* may also be accompanied by the gift of a personal religious item from the master, such as a robe, a whisk, his portrait, or a scripture. One who receives the *inka* is known as a *dharma* heir (J. *hassu*), the process is known as *dharma* transmission (J. *shihō*), and the names of the designated successors are recorded in the official records of the temple or sect. They may be men or women.

The certification of a person's experience by his master is a safeguard against a disciple mistakenly thinking that an uplifting spiritual experience was actually enlightenment, when in fact it was only an initial experience along the way. A truly enlightened master knows the inner condition of all his disciples, and is able to assess the nature of the spiritual experiences of his disciples.

The *inka* may be given to more than one disciple. In ancient times, a disciple would normally live either with his master or close by, although this is not necessarily the case nowadays. Once a master is convinced that a disciple has reached the required degree of spiritual understanding, the master will declare the disciple to be a *dharma* successor. The disciple will then be awarded the status of *rōshi* (elder teacher, venerable master), and may stay with his master or may move away in order to start a new centre or monastery. In *Zen* traditions that focus on *kōans,* mastery or full understanding of the *kōans* is a prerequisite for attaining the status of *dharma* successor. A *kōan* is an intellectual paradox that is designed to force the student to give up reliance on reasoning. In those traditions that are more focused on *zazen* (seated meditation), the master must be satisfied that the disciple has reached the required level of inner attainment. When a disciple has received *inka,* he may accept disciples of his own.

See also: **in'in ekishi, isshi inshō, menju shihō, uḍumbara**.

intiqāl al-nisbah (A), **intiqāl-i nisbat** (P) *Lit.* transfer *(intiqāl)* of relationship *(nisbah);* transfer of attribution or affiliation; transfer of spiritual qualities. If a *shaykh* selects as his successor someone who has insufficient spiritual progress to his credit, the *shaykh* can "transfer his lofty qualities to his successor at the moment of his death *(intiqāl al-nisbah),* and thus endow him with the necessary spiritual power."[1]

1. Annmarie Schimmel, *Mystical Dimensions of Islam, MDI* p.236.

ishin denshin (J), **yǐxīn chuán xīn** (C) *Lit.* transmission *(chuán)* by means of *(yǐ)* mind *(xīn)* to mind *(xīn);* mind-to-mind transmission of the *Dharma;* the mind seal of the *buddhas;* used synonymously with *menju shihō* (bestowal of face-to-face transmission); transmission of the *Dharma* from one *Zen* Buddhist master to a disciple, thus appointing the disciple as his successor; *dharma* transmission; the direct transmission of spiritual power from master to disciple, together with the mandate given to the disciple to continue in his master's place. Through this transmission and the formal, authentic recognition *(inka)* of the disciple's enlightenment, the disciple becomes a *dharma* heir, carrying forward the spiritual lineage. *Ishin denshin* is a phonetic Japanese rendering of the Chinese *yǐxīn chuán xīn.*

More generally, *ishin denshin* refers to the direct, mind-to-mind transmission of the *Dharma* or of the enlightenment experience from master to disciple, in the absence of all verbal and intellectual descriptions thereof, including the words of the master or the scriptures; hence the *Zen* expression, *ishin denshin furyu monji* ('transmission from mind to mind without dependence on words or letters'). The expression embodies a *Chán* and *Zen* concept that understanding is non-verbal, that spiritual awakening can occur through intuitive discernment or may be transmitted from the mind of the master to the mind of the disciple. It does not consist of the intellectual understanding of the words, either of the master or of Buddhist scriptures. It is a realization of the inner Truth, as expressed in the *Xuèmài lùn* (J. *Ketsumyaku ron*), a text attributed to Bodhidharma, who is credited with bringing Buddhism to China, whence it spread to Japan:

> The three worlds arise from and return to One Mind. From *buddhas* of the past to succeeding *buddhas,* (the *Dharma*) is transmitted from mind to mind *(yǐxīn chuán xīn),* without reliance on words and letters *(bùlì wénzì).*
>
> *Xuèmài lùn, T48 2009:373b13–14, in IEZB p.156*

Ishin denshin is also a common everyday Japanese expression implying an unspoken understanding between people. In this sense it is translated as 'intuitive communication from mind to mind', 'thought transference', 'heart-to-heart communication', 'being on the same wavelength', 'tacit understanding', 'what the mind thinks, the heart transmits', or sometimes 'telepathy'. The principle of intuitive, implicit understanding is wide-ranging and widely accepted in Japanese culture, where Western modes of upfront and explicit verbal communication are perceived as coarse and unsubtle.

See also: **bùlì wénzì**, **menju shihō**.

ʿishrah (A), **ʿishrat** (P) *Lit.* pleasure, delight, enjoyment, rapture; association, companionship, conviviality, togetherness, intimacy. ʿIrāqī says that *ʿishrat* "signifies the pleasure of intimacy with God, accompanied by the conscious understanding and awareness generated by this joy".[1]

In a couplet with multiple allusions, Ḥāfiẓ speaks of the intimate companionship of the soul with the divine Music within, attained through the company of the *pīr* (master, *lit.* elder). Being old, he is like the "bent harp" (the *chang,* a harp with a curved frame), which plays the perennial music of the mystical teaching that invites the soul to hear the inner symphony:

> A bent harp *(chang-i khamīdah)* beckons you to intimacy *(ʿishrat):*
> Listen to the advice of the masters *(pīrān),*
> for it will never do you harm.
>
> *Ḥāfiẓ, Dīvān, DHA p.61, DIH p.135; cf. DHWC (170:9) p.327*

1. ʿIrāqī, *Iṣṭilāḥāt, RLRI* p.81, in *SSE1* p.177.

isshi inshō (J) *Lit.* one teacher *(isshi)* seal *(inshō)* (of transmission); inheritance of a *dharma* lineage from a single master; the receipt of *dharma* transmission and inheritance *(shihō)* and certification of proof *(inka)* thereof direct from one's master, whose lineage one then inherits, and following which it is not permissible to seek certification from another master; a tradition associated with the *Sōtō Zen* school.

During medieval times (1185–1600), it had become customary for a monk, when he took up the position of abbot in a new monastery, to adopt the lineage of his predecessors at that place, a practice known as *garanbō.* This practice was reversed during the Tokugawa period (1600–1867), when it received particular attention from the *Sōtō Zen* reformer Manzan Dōhaku (1636–1715). Manzan successfully reinstituted the principle of *isshi inshō* and face-to-face *dharma* transmission *(menju shihō)* that he believed to have been the original intention of the *Sōtō* founder Dōgen Kigen (1200–1253).[1]

See also: **in'in ekishi, inka shōmei**.

1. See "Isshi inshô," "Manzan Dôhaku," *Illustrated Encyclopedia of Zen Buddhism, IEZB.*

jamʿ (A/P) *Lit.* collectedness, concentration; union; sum, group, conjunction; concentrated, close, total, gathered together, collected; also, assembly, gathering; assembly of the elect, the community of the saints. In its sense of an assembly, the term appears more commonly as *al-jamāʿah* (the community).

See also: **jamʿ** (▸3), **jamāʿah**.

jamāʿah (A), **jamāʿat** (P) *Lit.* meeting, community, assembly, group, party, society, clan, order, rank, congregation; also, occasionally, as *jamʿ* (union, community); in Islam, from the time of Muḥammad, the community of Muslim believers; in Sufism, the community of disciples gathered around a saint; hence also, *jamāʿat khānah* (assembly room, assembly hall).

Considerable importance is given to the *jamāʿat* in Muslim life generally, as well as in Sufism. According to a *ḥadīth,* the Prophet said, "Whoever among you desires the spacious abode of paradise, let him cleave to the Muslim community (*jamāʿat al-muslimīn, lit.* the community of those who have submitted to God)." Also, "The devil is a wolf to man: like the wolf, he seizes the sheep that remains at a distance from the flock. Beware of schisms and disunion, and adhere to the *jamāʿah.*"

Although the Sufi path is inward in essential character, the world has a strong pull, and an individual is supported by being a part of the community of fellow Sufis. Rūmī therefore advises the seeker to be a part of a united community *(jamʿ).* Alluding to this *ḥadīth,* Rūmī writes:

Whoever the devil separates from the noble *(karīm),*
 he finds with none to support him,
 and he (the devil) devours his head.
To go for a single moment apart from the community *(jamʿ)*
 is the devil's guile.
Listen, and understand it well.

Rūmī, Maśnavī II:2165–66; cf. MJR2 p.333

He says that even if a person experiences enmity among the community of disciples, their company is still better than trying to get along without support, especially since kindness does much to ameliorate enmity. If necessary, he advises, be like a maker of idols, carving "a friend out of stone" – making a friend out of an enemy:

Deem it obligatory to attach
 yourselves to the friends of the Way,
 whosoever he may be, and whether he be footmen or rider.
And if he be an enemy to you, still this kindness is good,
 for by kindness many an enemy has been made a friend;
Even if he does not become a friend, his enmity is lessened,
 because kindness becomes the balm of enmity.
There are many profits besides these,
 but I am afraid of being tedious, good friend.

The gist is this: be a friend of the whole community *(jam')*:
like the idol maker, carve a friend out of stone.
Because the throng and multitude of a caravan
will break the backs and spears of the highwaymen.

Rūmī, Maśnavī II:2146–51; cf. MJR2 p.332

In this way, he says, you will experience a sense of oneness with everyone, and know true happiness:

Become one with the community *(jamā'at)*
that you may feel spiritual joy.

Rūmī, Dīvān-i Shams-i Tabrīz 2577:27361, KSD5 p.280; cf. SDST (XLII) pp.166–67

This, he also observes, is for the benefit of the disciples, not the master, for the master is at a far higher spiritual level than his disciples:

To a king like this, the soldiers are an annoyance,
but he accompanies them:
A united party *(jamā'at)* is a mercy.
A moon like this is disgraced by the stars:
it is among the stars for generosity's sake.

Rūmī, Maśnavī I:3017–18; cf. MJR2 p.164

jikishi tanden (J), **zhízhǐ dānchuán** (C) *Lit.* simple transmission *(tanden, dānchuán)* of direct guidance or direct pointing *(jikishi, zhízhǐ)*; mind-to-mind transmission of the *Dharma,* from the mind of a *Zen* master to the mind of the disciple; synonymous with *ishin denshin* (transmission from mind to mind). See **ishin denshin**.

jinsīyah (A), **jinsīyat** (P) *Lit.* of a kind *(jins)*; affinity, similarity, sameness, homogeneity; an irresistible attraction between one thing and its 'similar' or its 'familiar' – one with whom it has affinity; the principle behind 'like attracts like'. From a cosmic viewpoint, every created thing has a purpose given to it by God. It is the manifestation of an archetype or pattern of it at a higher level in the hierarchy of creation. Consequently, it will always have an affinity with its origin or archetype, and when its purpose is fulfilled, it will return to its archetype.

The notion is commonly used by Rūmī. "Affinity" between human beings, he says, is an empathy between those of like mind, enabling them to see into each other's minds:

What is affinity *(jinsīyat)?*
A kind of insight whereby people gain admission
to the minds and feelings of one another.
When God endows you with the same insight
which He has hidden in another person,
you become his familiar *(jins).*

Rūmī, Maśnavī VI:2992–93, MJR6 p.423

In another place, Rūmī likens the souls in this world to the accidental mixing of the substances displayed in orderly trays in a "druggist's shop". "Good and evil" are mixed together, and in the dark "night" of the world, it has become very difficult to distinguish the one from the other. When the prophets come, they automatically attract the good, and return with them to God:

Look at the trays in the druggist's shop:
he has placed each thing next to its own kind.
Things of one kind are mixed with their own kind,
and a certain beauty is produced by their similarity *(jinsīyat).*
If the sugar and the aloeswood get mixed,
the druggist separates them from each other, piece by piece.
The trays were broken and the souls were spilled:
good and evil ones were mixed together.
God sent the prophets with their teachings
to sort the grains upon the trays.
Before this, we were one community,
none knew whether we were good or bad.
False coin and true, both were current in the world,
since all was night, and we were as night travellers,
Until the sun of the prophets rose and said,
"Begone, base coin! Come, you who are pure!"

Rūmī, Maśnavī II:280–87; cf. MJR2 p.236

It is the affinity of the "good" with the prophets that draws them. In a similar vein, Rūmī also uses the idea to illustrate the need for a human being to have a spiritual teacher who is also alive and accessible in human form. For human beings can only relate to and feel affinity with other human beings, not with spirits or angels or even with God. He tells the story of a woman whose child has got himself into danger on a rooftop. He is clinging to a "water spout", but will not respond to any coaxing from his mother to come down. In fact, he turns his face away from her whenever she offers enticements. The woman seeks advice from ʻAlī, who advises her:

"Take another child up on to the roof,
in order that the boy may see one of his own kind *(jins),*
and come nimbly from the water spout to his own kind *(jins):*
For one of a certain kind *(jins)*
is ever in love with his own kind *(jins).*"

The woman did so, and when her child saw his own kind *(jins),*
he turned his face towards it with delight,
and came from the ridge of the water spout to the roof:
Know that one of a certain kind *(jins)*
attracts every other of same kind *(jins).*
The child came crawling along to the other child:
it was saved from falling to the ground below.

The prophets are human beings for this reason:
so that human beings, through their affinity *(jinsīyat)*
with the prophets, may be saved from the drainpipe.
Therefore, the Prophet called himself "a man like you",[1]
so that you might come to your own kind *(jins)*
and might not get lost;
For similarity *(jinsīyat)* is a wondrous attractor:
Wherever there is a seeker,
his own kind *(jins)* is attracting him.

Rūmī, Maśnavī IV:2664–71; cf. MJR4 pp.419–20

Taking another example to illustrate the same point, Rūmī says that just as a tightly stoppered jar floats on water, always seeking the surface, so too will the *ʿaql* (higher mind) of the good lead them towards the prophets, while the desires of the lower mind *(nafs)* will lead the "enemy of God", the entirely worldly person, towards "the lowest":

When you stop the mouth of an empty pot
and put it in a tank or river,
it will not sink till the Resurrection,
for its heart is empty, and there is nothing in it but wind.
Since the inclination of the wind in it is upwards,
it also draws upward the vessel containing it.

Likewise, souls *(jān'hā)* that have an affinity *(jins)*
with the prophets, move gradually, like shadows, towards them,
because their *ʿaql* is predominant,
and beyond doubt the *ʿaql* has an affinity *(jins)* with the angels;

While in the enemy of God,
the strong desire of the *nafs* is predominant,
the *nafs* has an affinity *(jins)* with the lowest and goes towards it.

Rūmī, Maśnavī IV:2699–704; cf. MJR4 p.421

But "this affinity is spiritual", he says in another place, not of "outer" bodily "form". The soul of the seeker recognizes its affinity with the soul of the saint, regardless of any outward differences of form or race:

It is certain that this affinity *(jinsīyat)* is spiritual in origin,
not from water and clay (the body).
Take heed, do not become a worshipper of form:
do not believe in that.
Seek not the secret of this affinity *(jinsīyat)* in the outer form.
Form resembles minerals and stones:
an inorganic thing has no knowledge of affinity *(jinsīyat)*.

Rūmī, Maśnavī VI:2952–54; cf. MJR6 p.421

1. *Qur'ān* 18:110.

kalyāṇa-mittatā (Pa) *Lit.* noble *(kalyāṇa)* friendship *(mitra);* good friendship; virtuous, admirable, excellent friendship; spiritual friendship; related to *kalyāṇa-mitta* (noble friend, spiritual friend); in Buddhism, the company of a friend who is known for spiritual wisdom, whose company benefits one's understanding and practice of the *Dhamma.* See **kalyāṇa-mitra** (7.1).

kauwhau (Mo) *Lit.* a sermon, a lecture, an address; the ritual recital of a Māori legend or genealogy *(whakapapa);* from the verb *kauwhau* (to recite, to lecture). According to traditional Māori lore, human beings are descended from the *atua* (ancestral spirits or gods), and remembrance and recitals of such genealogies are a significant part of Māori culture and the education of Māori *tohunga* (priestly adept or expert).

See also: **whakapapa**.

kentan (J) *Lit.* inspecting *(ken)* the slip *(tan)* of paper; checking a monk at his assigned sitting place, his name being written on a slip of paper that is hung above his allocated place, which by extension is known as a *tan;* an early morning visit made by the master *(rōshi)* or supervising elder monk *(jikijitsu)* to the meditation hall *(zendō)* during the first period of sitting during a *sesshin* (intensive meditation, traditionally lasting seven days and seven nights), at which time he walks along the rows of monks practising *zazen* in order to check their posture and gauge their mental state.

See also: **zendō** (▸4).

khānaqāh, **khānqāh** (A), **khānagāh**, **khānagah** (P) A Sufi meeting place or place of residence; a monastery, a hospice (for travellers); a building used for spiritual retreat and training; a place where a Sufi *shaykh* would live with a group of his followers; the lodge of a Sufi brotherhood; *khānqāh* and *khānaqāh* are arabicizations of the original Persian word; also known in Arabic as a *ribāṭ* or a *zāwiyah,* and in Turkish as a *tekke* (A. *takīyah,* P. *takyah*).

Early Sufis, such as al-Qushayrī (*c.*817–875) and Junayd (*d.*910) speak of the value of retirement and solitude for the sincere seeker of God. Celibate recluses, both men and women, also appear in the early history of Sufism. In fact, there is evidence that some of the followers of Muḥammad were celibates. The desire to withdraw from worldly life led naturally to the founding of the first monasteries or *khānaqāhs.* The Christian monastic and solitary ascetic tradition, prevalent in the Middle East, would have provided a model. ʿIzz al-Dīn Maḥmūd Qāshānī, however, sees the first *khānaqāhs* as a reflection of the famous *ṣuffah* (veranda) in Madīnah, where the companions of Muḥammad lived a life of poverty after their flight from Mecca.[1]

The founding of dedicated religious establishments appears early in the history of Islam. Al-Ṭabarī (839–923) speaks of

> the house of Saʿd ibn Khaythamah, who was a celibate, without family, and there were celibates among the followers of the Apostle from among those who fled to him, and therefore this house of Saʿd ibn Khaythamah was called the house of the celibates.
>
> *Al-Ṭabarī, Annales I, AJT p.1243, in RM p.171*

Ibn Baṭṭūtah (*d.*1377) also records:

> On the bank of the moat dug by the Apostle of God, when he met with the assembly of the confederates (not far from Madīnah) is a ruined dwelling, known as the abode of the celibates, and it is said that ʿUmar built it for the celibates of Islam.
>
> *Ibn Baṭṭūtah, Tuḥfat al-Nuẓẓār I, TNB1 pp.289–90, in RM p.171*

Writing somewhat later, Jāmī (1414–1492) maintains that the first *khānaqāh* for Sufis was at Ramlah in Syria, and he relates a version of the traditional story of how it came to be built:

> One day, a Christian *amīr* (Amīr Naṣrānī, ruler of the area around Jerusalem) had gone out hunting, and on the road he saw two persons of this sect (Sufis) who had met together and were embracing one another. They then sat down in that same spot, and spreading out what food they had, they ate together. His business brought the Christian *Amīr* there, and their affection for one another pleased him, and he called one of them and asked him who the other was. He replied, "I do not know."
>
> The *Amīr* said, "What relation is he to you?"
>
> The man answered, "None at all."
>
> The *Amīr* asked, "From what place has he come?"
>
> He said, "I do not know."
>
> The *Amīr* said, "Then whence came this affection which you showed to one another?"
>
> The dervish replied, "He belongs to my Way."
>
> The *Amīr* asked, "Have you any place where you meet together?" and when the man said they had not, the *Amīr* said, "I will build you a place where you may meet together," and so he built that monastery in Ramlah.
>
> *Jāmī, Nafaḥāt al-Uns, NUJ pp.31–32; cf. in RM pp.171–72*

Another version of the story relates more simply how Amīr Naṣrānī was generally impressed by the affection, lovingkindness and brotherhood among Sufis, who held to the saying, "Intimacy and lovingkindness in God are our two practices." He therefore built the first *khānaqāh,* where all their basic needs could be accommodated.[2]

The pattern was repeated elsewhere and, in many instances, *khānaqāhs* were built or provided by wealthy patrons. Suyūṭī writes:

> The first *khidīv* (king) to establish a *khānaqāh* in Egypt was Sulṭān Ṣalāḥ al-Dīn Yūsuf, who not only built a *khānaqāh,* but specified daily provisions for the Sufis connected therewith.
>
> *Suyūṭī, Unsourced, in FNI15 p.85, in SSE15 p.80*

The historian Maqrīzī (1364–1442 CE), citing Abū Nu'aym as his source, says that the word *khānaqāh* came into use during the eleventh century, when the growth of Sufism led naturally to the desire to establish residential centres. He relates that the first to build a house for devotees was Zayd ibn Ṣawḥān of Baṣrah. Impressed by their tranquillity and way of life, his intention was to provide food, drink, clothing and shelter for those men who had dedicated themselves to the Sufi Way, but who had no occupation or means by which to support themselves.[3]

Although the majority of the *khānaqāhs* were for men, convents for women also existed from an early date. According to the *Chronicles of Mecca,* containing the writings of ninth- and tenth-century authors, several such convents existed in Mecca. Apparently, there were two near al-Duraybah, one of them known as the convent *(ribāṭ)* of Ibn al-Sawdah:

> Over the door is a stone with an inscription stating that Umm (Mother) Khalīl Khadījah and Umm ʿĪsá Mariam, the two daughters of the Qāʿid Abū Tamar al-Mubārak, that is ʿAbd Allāh al-Qāsimī, founded it for women Sufis desiring to lead a celibate life, who belonged to the *Shāfiʿ* rite, in the year 590 AH (1211 CE), and it is also called the convent *(ribāṭ)* of the Hurrīsh.
>
> *Chronicles of Mecca II, CSM p.115, in RM p.173*

There were other early convents in Mecca and elsewhere. Among the most well known was the Hostel of the Baghdādīs in Cairo, built in 1305 CE for the Shaykhah Zaynab and her "pious women" by Princess Sitt Jalīlah Tadhharīyah, daughter of King al-Ẓāhir Baybars (who ruled Egypt from 1260–1277). Shaykhah Zaynab was the daughter of Abū al-Barakāt, and was known as the daughter of the Baghdādī.[4]

Many *khānaqāhs* were built by rulers to demonstrate to the people that they were the champions and protectors of religion. But like most politicians, their motives were often mixed. Some *shaykhs* in Egypt and Syria gained state recognition, and were given prestigious titles, government stipends, and had imposing *khānaqāhs* built for them. A number of Muslim *sulṭāns* became the disciples of the *shaykhs,* they and their retinues calling on them regularly for advice. But little of this was without ulterior motivation. It was good for public popularity, and helped the rulers keep Sufism under their control. Many Sufi *shaykhs* therefore avoided such *khānaqāhs,* and the web of political intrigue and pressure that came with them, preferring to teach from their own homes or in privately owned buildings.[5]

A number of derivations have been suggested for *khānagāh:*

> *Khānah* (house) + *gāh* (place) = dwelling place, paralleling words such as *manzil-gāh* (station-place) and *qarār-gāh* (site-place).
>
> *Khān* (leader) + *gāh* (place) = place of the leader, place of the master, place where the Sufis live with their master.
>
> *Khān* (worship) + *gāh* (place) = place of worship.
>
> *Khān* (tavern, winehouse) + *gāh* (place) = the place where Sufis drink the cup of divine love.

Khān (caravanserai) + *gāh* (place) = place of transience, where all are travellers, coming and going, symbolizing the world.

Khwān (feast, pron. *khān*) + *gāh* (place) = place where Sufis could find food and shelter.[6]

Traditionally, the *khānaqāh* was a place of Sufi residence, where they served each other, and also provided food and board for travelling Sufis. Indeed, accounts reveal that non-Sufis were often accommodated. There was no fixed charge, and poor visitors paid no fee. Those who could afford it made a voluntary donation on departure. They were hospitable to all, tolerant of others, and questioned no one concerning their beliefs.

The residences of the followers of the path of *futuwwat* (chivalry, generosity) were also called *khānaqāhs,* where the members catered to the needs of others, feeding, caring, and providing whatever help they could.

Javād Nūrbakhsh depicts the ideal *khānaqāh:*

> At the present time, the *khānaqāh* serves as both place of retreat and meeting house for the Sufis. It houses the assembly of the people of (mystical) state and the school of the journey to perfection. Wayfarers towards God come there to polish the corrosion of manifested form *(taʿayyun)* from the mirror of the heart. It is the *Kaʿbah* (sacred place) of lovers and the *qiblah* (true direction) of the truthful. It is the sanctum of those who experience mysteries and the *miḥrāb* (prayer niche) of the pure-hearted. It is the refuge of those who are completely absorbed in love and those who have fearlessly abandoned their very selves.
>
> It is the resting place of those pledged in fidelity and of the companions of purity. In its confines, one hears only the melody of the Beloved, and in its atmosphere one scents only the breeze of lovingkindness and fidelity. Its residents are estranged from everything but God. Its accomplished ones have put ego aside, declaring, "I am God *(Anā al-Ḥaqq)!*"
>
> In the *khānaqāh,* their tongues are constantly engaged in litanies of invocation of God, while their hearts are imprinted with remembrance of Him. The lovingkindness of the friend allows no room for animosity of any kind. Tranquillity of heart, contentment and ecstasy are acquired there. The one who keeps silent is engaged in reflection *(tafakkur)* and meditation *(murāqabah),* while the one who speaks has only the Name of the Beloved upon the tongue.
>
> *Javād Nūrbakhsh, Sufi Symbolism, FN115 p.86; cf. SSE15 pp.81–82*

Sanā'ī puts it poetically:

The *khānaqāh* is the nest of the bird of purity,
  the rose garden of relishing, and the bower of fidelity.
The Sufis have elect status in the divine court:
  those who wear the cloak are advanced in God's Way.
They know the subtleties and the nuances,
  they have no outward sign, as they sit with God.
Their work is ascetic discipline and detachment from the world,
  their occupation is fairness, retreat, and detachment from the self.

Sanā'ī, Maśnavī, MSAN pp.109–10, in SSE15 p.82

See also: **ribāṭ**, **zāwiyah**.

1. Maḥmūd Qāshānī, *Miṣbāḥ al-Hidāyah wa-Miftāḥ al-Kifāyah, MHK* p.153, in *SSE15* p.81.
2. Javād Nūrbakhsh, *Sufi Symbolism, SSE15* p.81.
3. Maqrīzī, *al-Khiṭaṭ* 2, *KMA4* pp.281–82, in *RM* p.172.
4. Margaret Smith, in *RM* p.173.
5. W.M. Thackston, *BWIC* pp.17–18.
6. Javād Nūrbakhsh, *Sufi Symbolism, SSE15* pp.79–80.

kirishmah (P) *Lit.* an amorous glance, a loving glance, amorous gesture, a wonder, a miracle; talisman, a charm; in Sufi symbolism, a transformative glance of grace from the master that confers an inward attraction towards God and spiritual awakening, culminating in the annihilation *(fanā')* of the lover's sense of individual self;[1] sometimes described as a manifestation by the beloved of his divine nature; the glance can be understood at the human level or it can be an inner 'glance' – an impulse of divine grace with no external source; more or less synonymous with *ghamzah*.

Aḥmad Ghazālī distinguishes in his *Sawāniḥ* between a glance or manifestation of the divine Beauty *(kirishmah-'i Ḥusn)* Itself and a glance or manifestation of the divine beloved-ness *(kirishmah-'i maʿshūqī)* – of his lovable nature. The former is a favour from the entirely self-sufficient divine Essence, the latter is from the beloved, and implies a need of the beloved to be loved. According to an additional sentence present in one of the manuscripts of *Sawāniḥ,* the two terms convey the meaning of the well-known *ḥadīth,* "I (God) was a hidden treasure, and I wanted to be known, so I created the creation." The first *kirishmah* is implied by "I was a hidden treasure," and the second by "I wanted to be known." Whether or not the difference between the two is anything more than conceptual, only a mystic would know.[2]

Most Sufis seem to have used the term in a more general manner:

With one loving glance *(kirishmah),*
you can set our work aright;
Why don't you help the helpless ones?
Unattributed, in Mir'āt-i 'Ushshāq, in TAT p.224; cf. in SSE2 p.118

Take the reproach of the friend like a lover,
for with one glance *(kirishmah),* he can make amends
for a hundred acts of tyranny.
Ḥāfiẓ, Dīvān, DHA p.73, DIH p.145; cf. DHWC (234:2) p.424

See also: **'ayn al-kamāl**, **chashm** (7.2), **dṛishṭi**, **ghamzah**, **nargis**.

1. 'Irāqī, *Iṣṭilāḥāt, RLRI* p.76; *Mir'āt-i 'Ushshāq,* in *TAT* p.224; Muḥammad al-Dārābī, *Laṭīfah-'i Ghaybī* 2, *LGMD* p.141.
2. Aḥmad Ghazālī, *Sawāniḥ* 12:1, *MAFG* p.122 (n.1–8), *SIS* (11:1) pp.31, 96 (n.1).

kūnj (H/Pu) The demoiselle crane, the Numidian crane *(Anthropoides virgo);* a small migratory crane of central Asia, North Africa and southeastern Europe, with grey plumage, long black breast feathers and white ear tufts; known for flying together in a row with others of their kind, calling continuously to one another, especially if one of them gets separated from its companions; an image used by Oriental poets to convey the idea of comradeship and separation from loved ones; mystical poets have used the imagery in a variety of contexts.[1]

According to Indian folklore, there is a difference between the way a duck, a tortoise, and a *kūnj* care for their eggs and their young. A duck incubates her eggs by the warmth of physical contact and must then feed the chicks; a female tortoise lays her eggs in the sand of the sea shore and keeps them under constant watch while she swims in the water; but a *kūnj* lays her eggs and flies away to distant lands, but always remembers them. If the duck deserted her eggs or a tortoise took its eyes off the beach where her eggs were laid for a prolonged period, their eggs will die. During her long migratory flights, the *kūnj* supposedly hatches her eggs and nurtures her nestlings by means of her focused thought or remembrance. Were she to forget them, they would die. This ability of the *kūnj* has been compared to that of the master who, wherever he may be, sustains his disciples through thought and contemplation, or inner *dṛishṭi,* and whose relationship with his disciples, being spiritual, is not hampered by physical separation.[2]

See also: **bhṛingī**.

1. *E.g.* Bulleh Shāh, *Kullīyāt* 72, *KBS* p.147, *BSPS* p.166; Guru Amardās, *Ādi Granth* 34; Guru Rāmdās *Ādi Granth* 168; Kabīr, *Ādi Granth* 1371.
2. Guru Arjun, *Ādi Granth* 10; Guru Rāmdās, *Ādi Granth* 168.

kuṭīra (S/H) *Lit.* hut, cottage, hovel; the small hermitage of an ascetic or yogi. Following a similar description of a yogi's dwelling in the *Bhagavad Gītā* and other yogic texts,[1] the *Gheraṇḍa Saṃhitā* counsels:

> In a good country whose king is just, where food is easily and abundantly available, where there are no disturbances, let him erect there a small hut, and around it let him raise walls. In the centre of the enclosure, let him sink a well and dig a tank. Let the hut be neither very high nor very low: let it be free from insects. It should be completely, plastered over with cow dung. In a hut *(kuṭīra)* built in such a manner and situated in such a hidden place, let him practice *prāṇāyāma* (control of the breath and *prāṇa*).
>
> *Gheraṇḍa Saṃhitā 5:5–7; cf. GSV pp.37–38*

See also: **āshrama**, **maṭha**.

1. *Bhagavad Gītā* 6:10–14; see also *Darshana Upanishad* 5:3–6; *Haṭha Yoga Pradīpikā* 1:12–14, *HYPM* pp.40, 43, 47; *Shāṇḍilya Upanishad* 31–33; *Yogatattva Upanishad* 32–35.

kū-yi mughān (P) *Lit.* lane *(kū)* of *(yi)* the magi *(mughān);* alley, street, road, *etc.* of the magi; the place where the mystics dwell, either physically or internally, in the inner sanctum. See **mugh** (7.1).

langar (P/Pu) *Lit.* anchor; a Sufi residence; a term used by Sufis in the eastern Iranian regions of Khurāsān and Kirmān for a monastery, known elsewhere in Iran as a *khānaqāh.* The name probably originated from the custom, adopted by many Sufi masters of the past, of travelling with their disciples. Whenever they stopped for a while at one place, it was said that they had cast anchor *(langar andākhtan).* The expression remains in popular usage for someone who stays for a long period in another's house, perhaps overstaying their welcome.[1]

Through the Sufi custom of serving free food at their places of residence, the *langar* came to be associated with free meals. This meaning has come into popular usage in North India and Pakistan, an area deeply influenced by Islamic language and culture, where a free kitchen is commonly known as a *langar.*

Many North Indian saints have maintained a free *langar* to serve not only visiting disciples but everyone who wants a meal. Guru Nānak and his successors (whose line led to the formation of the Sikh religion) held free *langars* at their headquarters, where everyone (at least from the time of Guru Amardās) sat together on the ground, regardless of caste distinctions – a significant innovation in India at that time. This institution became so firmly established that, even in modern times, an essential aspect of a *gurdwāra* is its casteless *langar,* where all sit together in rows on the ground, and eat a communal meal.

See also: **ribāṭ**.

1. Javād Nūrbakhsh, *Sufi Symbolism,* in *SSE15* p.104.

madrasah (A), **madrasat** (P) (pl. *madāris*) *Lit.* place of study, school; from the root *d-r-s* (to learn, to study, to read); a traditional Muslim school or college, where some of the teaching scholars and students also live; in medieval times, generally attached to a mosque in which the actual teaching took place, and hence more a place of residence than of study; a natural development of the teaching that already took place in the mosques from earliest Muslim times; usually specific to a particular school of religious law; especially in the past, often built by pious rulers or wealthy philanthropists, sometimes for a particular teacher whom they wished to support, for whatever reasons; commonly used by travelling scholars, *imāms,* and the like. According to his biographer Aḥmad al-Aflākī, Rūmī – whose profession was that of a religious scholar – lived in a *madrasah,* rather than a traditional Sufi *khānaqāh.*[1]

Although the *madrasahs* were already well established, the development of education was especially introduced by the Fāṭimids (909–1171, descendants of Fāṭimah and ʻAlī) in North Africa, Syria, and Shiʻite countries. They founded the al-Azhar university in Cairo, and schools known as *dār al-ʻilm* (house of knowledge) were established to train students in Fāṭimid theology. *Sunnīs* responded by opening schools to teach their own theology.

In the past, students entering a *madrasah* were presumed to have already learnt the entire *Qur'ān* by heart. Studies, which could last several years, were focused largely on religious matters, but could include traditional mathematics *(abjad),* higher grammar, literature, history, and so on. Sometimes, medicine and agronomy were also taught. Many architecturally fine *madrasahs* still stand, especially those in Morocco and India. During Mongol times, the mother of the ruler Halākū (1217–1265) built two *madrasahs* in Bukhārā, attended daily by a 1,000 students. During the time of the Tīmūrids (C15th–16th), a great many *madrasahs* were built in Central Asia, especially Samarkand. Some important cities had dozens at the same time.

The *madrasahs* became the prototype of the European university, also bequeathing traditions such as the wearing of the scholar's black gown, and the division of education into graduate and undergraduate departments. In modern times, there are *madrasahs* of many types throughout the Muslim world, which do not necessarily have a religious orientation and where students are not required to be Muslims.

See also: **majlis**.

1. Aḥmad al-Aflākī, *Manāqib al-'Ārifīn, passim.*

mahāpurisa-vitakka (Pa) *Lit.* thoughts or reflections *(vitakka)* of a great man *(mahāpurisa);* in Buddhist lore, the eight thoughts of a great person *(aṭṭha-mahāpurisa-vitakka).*

According to a story told in the *Anguttara Nikāya,* the first seven of these thoughts arose in the mind of the Venerable Anuruddha while he was sitting "in seclusion", *i.e.* in meditation. Being aware of Anuruddha's thoughts, the Buddha appeared miraculously before him, commended him on his seven thoughts, and taught him the eighth. The Buddha then returned to his original location, where he taught these eight thoughts to the monks who are gathered around him:

> What are the eight thoughts of a great person *(aṭṭha-mahāpurisa-vitakka)?* This *Dhamma* is for one of few wants, not one of many wants;…for the contented, not the discontented;…for those who live in seclusion, not those who delight in company;…for the energetic, not the lazy;…for one whose mindfulness is established, not one who is scattered;…for one whose mind is collected, not one who is uncollected;…for one with wisdom, not one who is lacking in wisdom;…for one who enjoys simplicity, not one who enjoys complication.[1]
>
> *Anguttara Nikāya 8:30, Anuruddha Sutta, PTSA4 pp.232–33*

The Buddha tells Anuruddha that as a result of thinking these eight thoughts, he will pass through the stages of the four *jhānas* (states of meditative absorption), and subsequently be able to attain them at will. Withdrawn from the world of the senses, with thoughts still and directed, enjoying inner rapture and bliss, and free from elation and distress, pleasure and pain, he will find pure serenity and mindfulness. Then he will find himself contented with the simplest of things. His mendicant's robe of old rags will seem like a householder's chest of clothes; plain alms food, as if full of spices and variety; his dwelling at the foot of a tree, like a mansion; and his bed of grass, like a richly laid bed.[2]

See also: **mahāpurusha** (7.1).

1. See also *Dīgha Nikāya* 34, *Dasuttara Sutta, PTSD3* p.287.
2. *Anguttara Nikāya* 8:30, *Anuruddha Sutta, PTSA4* pp.228–35.

majlis (A/P) *Lit.* place of sitting; assembly room, lecture hall; gathering, assembly, meeting, session; a school associated with a mosque; in Sufism, a gathering of a master or his representative with his disciples, at which the master may give a discourse, answer questions, or generally discuss spiritual matters with his disciples. Sometimes, those present chant a communal *dhikr,* and repeat the litanies *(wird)* peculiar to their order, as well performing the usual ritual prayers of Islam. The litanies and *dhikr* are often said with the help of a rosary of ninety-nine beads, representing the ninety-nine names of *Allāh.* The *dhikr* may be accompanied by music and, in some Sufi orders, by sacred dance. The primary intention of a Sufi *majlis* is that the attention should become focused entirely upon God.

Comparing the encounter with the beloved on the inner and outer planes, Ḥāfiẓ says that the outer lights and fragrances used in the outer *majlis* pale into insignificance alongside their counterparts on the inner realms:

> Bring no candle to this assembly *(bazm),*
> for tonight in our assembly *(majlis),*
> the moon of the friend's face is full.
> Wear no scent to this assembly *(majlis),*
> for his perfumed tresses
> continuously fill the soul with fragrance.
> *Ḥāfiẓ, Dīvān, DHA p.40, DIH p.96; cf. DHWC (34:2, 4) p.91*

See also: **madrasah**.

manṭiq al-ṭayr (A/P) *Lit.* speech *(manṭiq)* of the birds *(ṭayr);* the language of the birds, the discourse of the birds; the title of a well-known allegorical poem by Farīd al-Dīn ʿAṭṭār, commonly translated as *The Conference of the Birds.* The title is taken from the *Qur'ān.* According to mythology, retold in Jewish legend and in the *Qur'ān,* King Solomon had a ring that enabled him to understand the language of animals and birds:

> Solomon was David's heir. He said: "O my people! We have been taught the speech of birds *(manṭiq al-ṭayr),* and have been given everything. Surely this is a manifest grace."
> *Qur'ān 27:16; cf. AYA, KPA, MGK*

Bird imagery is used throughout Sufi literature. The soul is a bird who must learn to fly in the realms of the spirit. Sometimes the bird is caged (in the body), and must find a way of escape. At other times, it is a royal falcon seated on the king's (God's) wrist, and misfortune befalls it when it leaves the protection of the king. Sometimes the bird is the perfect saint, whose 'song' is divine Music and whose 'language' is likewise the Voice or Speech of God.

Solomon is commonly understood to represent the sage or perfect saint. Rūmī says that such a master knows the innermost heart of all his disciples ("birds"). He knows how to relate to them and how to guide them:

Come, O master
  of the speech of birds of Solomon *(manṭiq al-ṭayr-i Sulaymānī),*
  sing the song common to every bird there is.
Since God has sent you to the birds,
  He has instructed you in the song of every bird.
To the fatalist bird speak the language of fatalism;
To the bird whose wings are broken speak of patience:
  keep the patient bird happy and free from harm.
To the *'Anqā*-bird (phoenix)
  relate descriptions of Mount Qāf (its home).
Bid the pigeon beware of the falcon;
To the falcon speak of forbearance
  and of guarding against pride.
As for the bat that is left destitute (in the dark),
  teach it to consort with and be familiar with the Light.
Cause the belligerent partridge to know peace;
To cocks, manifest the signs of dawn.
Proceed like this from the hoopoe to the eagle,
  and show the Way.
And God knows best the right course.

Rūmī, Maśnavī IV:851–58; cf. MJR4 p.319

Rūmī also contrasts the ornate and pompous worldly "speeches" of intellectuals and court poets such as Khāqānī of Shīrwān with the song or "speech of the birds of Solomon", the Speech of the masters, the divine Music. The bird that sings this song is the master, who majestically traverses the 'space' between the divine Essence and this world, and back to God again. The song of this master-bird "thrills" and enraptures the soul. Therefore, he advises the ordinary human-bird to adopt the company of a Solomon – a master – to avoid living in spiritual darkness, like a bat. In Rūmī's poetry, a bat is a night bird! –

The speeches of princely birds *(manṭiq al-ṭayrān-i Khāqānī)*
  are but an echo:

Where is the speech of the birds
  of Solomon (*manṭiq al-ṭayr-i* Sulaymānī)?
How will you understand the songs of those birds,
  when you have never seen Solomon, even for a single moment?
The wings of that bird whose song thrills
  are beyond East and West.
It flies from the footstool of God to the earth;
And from the earth to the throne of God,
  it moves in glory and majesty.

The bird that goes without this Solomon
  is in love with darkness, like a bat.
Make yourself familiar with Solomon, O reprobate bat,
  in order that you may not remain in darkness forever.

Rūmī, Maśnavī II:3758–63; cf. MJR2 p.417

Rūmī also rebukes those who learn the language of spirituality ("the language of the birds"), but only intellectually. They are inflated with ego at their 'success', while unknowingly misleading true seekers:

You have learned the language of the birds *(manṭiq al-ṭayr)*
  by imitation of their sound;
You have invented a hundred analogies and a hundred caprices.
Seeking hearts are wounded by you,
  like an invalid by a deaf man,
  who was intoxicated by the vain notion of his success.

Rūmī, Maśnavī I:3410–11; cf. MJR2 p.185

See also: **hoopoe** (7.1).

maṭh(a) (S/H) *Lit.* the hut or cottage of an ascetic or yogi; hermitage, monastery, convent, seminary, temple; a centre for spiritual, religious or philosophical teaching in Hinduism, generally run on more formal lines than an *āshram;* also, a Jain monastery, which, in the *Digambara* tradition, generally includes a temple, a library, temporary accommodation for monks and guests, and (among *Bīsapanthī Digambaras*) a permanent residence for a *bhaṭṭāraka,* who is responsible for administering the complex.

The oldest surviving Hindu *maṭhs* are those devoted to *Advaita Vedānta* (non-dualism or monism), given prominence by the ninth-century Shankarāchārya (*c.*788–820). Other philosophically oriented *maṭhs* teach *Dvaita Vedānta* (dualism), established by Madhva (*c.*1197–1276), and *Vishishṭa Advaita* (qualified non-dualism), founded by Rāmānuja (*c.*1017–1137). There are other *maṭhs* that teach Vaishnavism *(Vaishṇava,* devoted to the veneration of *Vishṇu),* those that promote the non-sectarian Smartism *(Smārtha Sampradāya),* and so on. Among the *maṭhs* devoted to the various forms of *yoga,* the most well-known present-day *maṭh* is probably the Ramakrishna Math, now an international organization with its headquarters at Belur Math in West Bengal.

The purpose of a centre attended by disciples or students is to create a focus for meditation or study related to the ideals and principles of the founder. In the case of a yogi's dwelling place, the intention is to provide a refuge from worldly concerns, where the individual can focus without distraction on meditation and the spiritual life. The *Bhagavad Gītā* describes the ideal features of such a dwelling:

> Dwelling in solitude, disciplined in mind and body,
> without hopes or expectations, without possessions –
> Let the *yogī* steadfastly practise spiritual communion.
>
> In a clean place *(desha),* neither too high nor too low,
> prepare a seat *(āsana)* out of grass,
> covered with a skin and a cloth.
> Firmly seated thereon, to purify the self *(ātman),*
> practice *yoga,* making the mind one-pointed,
> with the activity of the mind and senses under control.
>
> Holding the body, head and neck
> straight, motionless and firm;
> Gazing at the tip of the nose and not all round;
> Being without fear, serene, controlled in mind,
> and established in a vow of celibacy;
> Meditating upon Me as the highest goal,
> he should sit in communion with Me.
>
> *Bhagavad Gītā 6:10–14*

The passage has been echoed, with variations, through a number of yogic texts:

> Listen, O Sāṃkṛiti! I shall presently relate briefly the method by which the *nāḍīs* (bodily channels of subtle life energy or *prāṇa*) may be purified. With action and conduct properly regulated in accordance with the rules prescribed; devoid of desire and volition; endowed with the eight *angas* (aspects of *yoga*), such as *yama* and the like; tranquil; having the Truth alone as the final refuge, established in one's own self; properly instructed by knowers (of *Brahman*); resorting to a *maṭha* either on the summit of a mountain, or the banks of a river, under a *bilva* tree or in a forest, in a clean and pleasant place; assuming a

posture either facing the east or the north, with neck, head and body kept erect and mouth closed, and utterly motionless, the *yogī* should gaze – with his (inner) eye focused at the root of the nose – at the disc of the moon in the middle of the *bindu* (centre behind the eyes), the *turīyaka* (the fourth state, the transcendental source of all below), which is dripping nectar.[1]

Darshana Upanishad 5:2–6; cf. YU pp.135–36

Having assumed *padmāsana* (lotus posture), after resorting to a *maṭha* with a small entrance and devoid of other apertures; either well cleansed with cow dung water or lime-washed with due effort; carefully made free from bugs, mosquitoes, and lice; specially swept every day with a broom; emitting a sweet smell and perfumed with the smoke of frankincense; neither too elevated nor too low-lying and covered with cloth, deer skin, or grass; seated there, assuming the posture of *padmāsana* (the *yogī* should commence the practice of *prāṇāyāma*).

Yogatattva Upanishad 32–35; cf. YU p.307

The *haṭha yogī* should live alone in a small hermitage *(maṭha)* and practise in a place the length of a bow (one and a half metres), where there is no hazard from rocks, fire or water, and which is in a well-administered and virtuous kingdom (nation or town), where good alms can easily be attained.

This is the description of the *yoga* hermitage *(maṭha)* as prescribed by the *siddhas* (adepts) for *haṭha yoga* practitioners. The room for *sādhana* (practice) should have a small door, without aperture (window), holes or cracks, being neither too high nor too low. It should be spotlessly clean, wiped with cow manure, and free from animals or insects. Outside, there should be an open platform with thatched roof; a well and a surrounding fence. The appearance of the hermitage should be pleasant.

In this manner, dwelling in the hermitage, without too much thinking, *yoga* should be practised in the manner instructed by the *guru*.

Haṭha Yoga Pradīpikā 1:12–14; cf. HYPM pp.40, 43, 47

See also: **āshrama**.

1. See also *Shāṇḍilya Upanishad* 1:32–33; *Varāha Upanishad* 5:32–33.

mathal, mathāl (pl. *amthāl*), **mithāl** (pl. *muthul*) (A), **miśāl** (P) *Lit.* similitude, parable, analogy, metaphor, example, illustration; comparison, likeness, image, pattern, archetype; from *mithal* (to resemble, to look like, to imitate, to appear in the likeness of); an earthly example used to convey spiritual truth. The term and a number of others derived from the same root appear in the *Qur'ān*[1] and the *ḥadīth,* where many things are described using examples or parables *(amthāl).* As the *Qur'ān* itself says:[2]

> We have explained in detail in this *Qur'ān,* for the benefit of mankind, all manner of parables *(mathal).* But man is exceedingly contentious!
>
> *Qur'ān 18:54; cf. AYA, KPA, MGK*

Some Quranic similes possess a wry humour. "The likeness *(mathal)*" of those charged with understanding and conveying the message of the *Torah* (books of Moses) is "as a donkey laden with books", while understanding nothing in them.[3] And when counselling Muḥammad on how to deal with disbelievers, God advises:

> Tell them the story of the man to whom We sent Our revelations, but who shrugged them off, and Satan overtook him, and he went astray. Had it been Our will, We would have elevated him with Our revelations, but he clung to this earthly life, and succumbed to his desires. His likeness *(mathal)* is that of a dog: if you chase him away, he pants with his tongue lolling out; if you leave him alone, he still pants with his tongue lolling out. This is the likeness *(mathal)* of those who reject Our revelations. So tell them this story: maybe they will reflect.
>
> *Qur'ān 7:175–76; cf. AYA, KPA, MGK*

Rūmī distinguishes a *miśāl* (analogy, example, illustration) from a *miśl* (a perfect likeness), when explaining that mystical realities cannot be adequately expressed in words:

> These expressions are not a perfect likeness *(miśl)* of it,
> they are an illustration *(miśāl):*
> Old words fall short of new meaning.
>
> *Rūmī, Maśnavī III:1155, MJR4 p.65*

Similarly, in the *Qur'ān,* the inner light is described as "a lamp".[4] Rūmī explains that there is not really "a lamp" inside. It is just an example to give some idea of the reality:

> God has called the light of the Unseen "a lamp".
> It is not an exact likeness *(miśl),*
> it is an illustration *(miśāl)* thereof,
> so that he who is confused may get a scent.
>
> *Rūmī, Maśnavī III:3406–7; cf. MJR4 p.191*

Rūmī makes the point a number of times because he is aware that people have a tendency to take the metaphors and parables in the scriptures literally:

He (Muḥammad) once compared ʿAlī to a lion,
but the lion is not really like him,
though he used the expression.
O youth, move on from example *(miśāl)* and replica *(miśl)*
and the difference between them.

Rūmī, Maśnavī III:1941–42; cf. MJR4 p.108

Rūmī continues the same theme elsewhere:

Endless are the differences
between the corporeal figure of a lion
and the figure of a courageous son of man;
But at the moment of making the comparison consider,
O you of goodly understanding,
their oneness in respect of hazarding their lives;
For, after all, the courageous man did resemble the lion,
though he is not like the lion in all points of the definition.
This abode (world) does not contain any forms
that are the same (as you will find that world),
so that I might give you a precise example *(miśl)*.
Therefore, I bring to hand an imperfect illustration *(miśāl)*,
that I may rescue your mind from confusion.

Rūmī, Maśnavī IV:420–24; cf. MJR4 p.295

In other words, there is nothing in the physical world from which words or images can be formed to explain the higher realities. This also explains why different mystics have sometimes used widely varying images to convey their experience of the inner realms. Those who have traversed the inner realms and shared the experience can see that the different mystics are describing the same reality, but others fall into discord over what seem to be utterly different descriptions.

The term *miśāl* is also used to convey the nature of the phenomenal world, also called *khayāl* (fantasy). In fact, the physical world is described as an imperfect copy of the realm of patterns *(ʿālam-i miśāl)*, which is also an imperfect copy of the realm above it. Hence, this world has also been called a reflection of a reflection of a reflection.

1. *E.g. Qur'ān* 2:17, 26; 3:59; 7:176; 16:60, 74; 17:89; 18:45, 54; 30:27–28; 47:3; 48:29; 57:20; 59:21; 62:5, *passim.*
2. See also *Qur'ān* 17:89.

3. *Qur'ān* 62:5.
4. *Qur'ān* 24:35.

menju kuketsu (J), **miànshòu kǒujué** (C) *Lit.* face-to-face instruction *(menju, miànshòu),* oral *(ku, kǒu)* transmission *(tsu, jué);* in Buddhism, the secret handing down of teachings orally from master to disciple; sometimes abbreviated, in Japan, to *kuketsu;* also referred to as *kuden.*

See also: **menju shihō**.

menju shihō (J), **miànshòu sìfǎ** (C) *Lit.* face-to-face instruction *(menju, miànshòu)* + to succeed (to a title), to inherit *(shi, sì)* + *dharma* methods *(hō, fǎ)* (of the master); face-to-face bestowal of succession; transmission of the *dharma* from one *Zen* Buddhist master to a disciple, thus appointing the disciple as his successor; *dharma* transmission; often simply as *menju;* the direct transmission of spiritual power directly from master to disciple, together with the mandate given to the disciple to continue in his master's place. Through this transmission together with the formal, authentic recognition *(inka)* of the disciple's enlightenment, the disciple becomes a *dharma* heir, carrying forward the spiritual lineage.

Zen Buddhism traces the origins of the tradition to legends relating how the Buddha appointed his disciple Mahākāshyapa as his successor. There are a number of variants of the story:

> Towards the end of his life, the Buddha took his disciples to a lake on Mount Gṛidhrakūṭa (Vulture Peak), and prepared to give a discourse to the disciples who were gathering there to hear him speak. Customarily, he would then have begun to speak, but he did not. Throughout the entire time that he would normally have given a discourse, he stood in silence. Eventually, he reached down into the lake, and from it he drew out a lotus flower, its roots dripping mud and water, which he showed to his disciples. Coming close to each of them, he asked them in turn what the lotus symbolized. Each in turn did their best to reply. The last to be shown the flower was Mahākāshyapa, who suddenly understood, and started to laugh quietly. Buddha then remarked, "What can be said I have said to you, and what cannot be said, I have given to Mahākāshyapa." From that day forward Mahākāshyapa was Buddha's successor.
>
> *Traditional Zen Story*

Mahākāshyapa's sudden smile or laugh is sometimes taken as an indication that he received enlightenment from the Buddha at that moment; or maybe he was simply laughing at the divine joke his master was playing on him by making him his successor.

The great *Zen* master Dōgen Zenji (1200–1253), who founded the Japanese *Sōtō Zen* school after training in China with the master Rújìng, describes how the *Dharma* was transmitted from the *buddhas* preceding Shākyamuni Buddha to the Buddha himself, and thence to his disciple Mahākāshyapa. From there, the *Dharma* was passed on until it reached Bodhidharma (credited with introducing Buddhism into China), whence, through the Chinese patriarchs, it came to Dōgen Zenji himself:

> Then Shākyamuni Buddha,... on Vulture Peak (Gṛidhrakūṭa) in the western country, India, among an assembly of millions, picked up an *uḍumbara* flower *(yōutánhuá),* and winked (an eye). At that time the face of Venerable Mahākāshyapa broke into a smile. Shākyamuni Buddha said, "I possess the right *dharma*-eye treasury and the fine mind of *nirvāṇa.* I transmit them to Mahākāshyapa."
>
> This is the truth of the *buddhas'* and the patriarchs' face-to-face transmission *(menju)* of the right *dharma*-eye treasury. Authentically transmitted by the seven *buddhas,* it reaches Venerable Mahākāshyapa. Through twenty-eight transmissions from Venerable Mahākāshyapa, it reaches Venerable Bodhidharma. Venerable Bodhidharma personally descends into China and gives face-to-face transmission *(menju)* to Great Master Taiso Shōshū Fukaku, Venerable Eka. Through five transmissions, it reaches Great Master Daikan Enō of Sōkeizan. Through seventeen transmissions, it reaches my late master, the eternal *buddha* Tendō of Daibyakumyōzan in the district of Keigenfu in the great kingdom of Sòng.
>
> On the first day of the fifth lunar month, in the first year of the great Sòng era of Hōgyō (1225), Dōgen first burns incense and does prostrations on the elevated stage in the *myōkōdai* to the late master Tendō, the eternal *buddha;* and the late master, the eternal *buddha,* first looks at Dōgen. Then, indicating the face-to-face transmission *(menju)* and bestowing it upon Dōgen, he says, "The gate of *Dharma* transmitted face to face by the *buddhas* and the patriarchs has been realized."
>
> This is just the picking up of an *(uḍumbara)* flower on Vulture Peak;... it is the transmission of the robe on Ōbai Mountain, and the face-to-face transmission *(menju)* on Tōzan Mountain. This is the face-to-face transmission *(menju)* of the eye treasury of the Buddhist patriarchs. It is present only in our house; others have never experienced it even in a dream.
>
> *Eihei Dōgen, Shōbōgenzō, Menju, T2582 82:214a3–23, SDT3 (57) pp.209–10*

Dōgen goes on to intimate something of the nature of this kind of transmission. Without it, he maintains, a master is not really a master; but nothing can match the first face-to-face transmission of the Buddha to Mahākāshyapa, not even Mahākāshyapa's subsequent transmission of the *Dharma* to the Buddha's cousin and close disciple Ānanda, nor even the Buddha's initiation of his son Rāhula, nor the spiritual blessings of the celestial *bodhisattvas.* Nor was the Buddha in any way diminished by passing on the mantle of buddhahood; rather it was the way in which all *buddhas* behave:

> Without the face-to-face transmission *(menju)* from the Buddha's face, we are not (real) *buddhas.* Shākyamuni Buddha's direct meeting with Venerable Mahākāshyapa is the immediate transmission. Even Ānanda and Rāhula cannot match the direct intimacy of the transmission to Mahākāshyapa. Even the great *bodhisattvas (dai bosatsu)* cannot match the direct intimacy of the transmission to Mahākāshyapa; they cannot sit in the seat of Venerable Mahākāshyapa. The World-Honoured One saw the sharing of his seat and the sharing of his robe with Mahākāshyapa as the epitome of *buddha* behaviour.
>
> *Eihei Dōgen, Shōbōgenzō, Menju, T2582 82:214a26–b4; cf. SDT3 (57) p.210*

Mahākāshyapa obtained the privilege of this direct transmission through complete surrender to the Buddha and the utter annihilation of his own small sense of self. When one of these great beings looks at another, they *really* look. When they look at each other, they see deep into each other's heart and mind, and there is a flow of spiritual energy between them:

> The Venerable Mahākāshyapa, through face transmission, mind transmission, body transmission, and eye transmission, has intimately received the face-to-face transmission *(menju)* of the World-Honoured One; he has served offerings to, venerated, made prostrations to, and served homage to Buddha Shākyamuni. In thus pulverizing his bones and shattering his body, he has been through an unknown thousand myriad changes. His own countenance is beyond face and eyes; he has received the face-to-face transmission *(menju)* of the countenance of the Tathāgata. Shākyamuni Buddha really looks at Venerable Mahākāshyapa. Venerable Mahākāshyapa looks directly at Venerable Ānanda. Venerable Ānanda prostrates himself directly before the *buddha*'s face of Venerable Mahākāshyapa. This is face-to-face transmission *(menju).*
>
> *Eihei Dōgen, Shōbōgenzō, Menju, T2582 82:214b4–13, SDT3 (57) p.210*

By face-to-face transmission, Mahākāshyapa passed on the *Dharma* to Ānanda, and Ānanda to Shāṇavāsa, as the first three Indian patriarchs. Had they failed to do so, says Dōgen, the lineage would have come to an end. "The face alone, together with the face" echoes a familiar phrase from the *Lotus Sūtra,* "the *buddhas* alone, together with the *buddhas*",[1] meaning that this is something unique to the *buddhas:*

> Venerable Ānanda abides in and maintains this face-to-face transmission *(menju)* and, through contact with Shāṇavāsa, he transmits it face to face. Venerable Shāṇavāsa directly serves Venerable Ānanda, during which time "the face alone, together with the face" transmits and receives the face-to-face transmission *(menju).* In this way the true ancestral masters of successive generations have each passed on the face-to-face transmission *(menju)* through the disciple seeing the master and the master seeing the disciple. If even one ancestor, one master, or one disciple failed to give or to receive the face-to-face transmission *(menju),* they would not be the *buddhas* and the patriarchs.
>
> *Eihei Dōgen, Shōbōgenzō, Menju, T2582 82:214b13–21, SDT3 (57) pp.210–11*

Therefore, Dōgen maintains, to look at the face of any of the patriarchs is to be looking directly at the Buddha himself:

> This being so, we have amassed an age of days and nights looking directly at Shākyamuni Buddha, and have amassed a generation of days and nights being illuminated by the presence of the Buddha's face. We do not know how countlessly many times this has continued, back and forth. We should quietly consider it, and be glad. It is the Buddha's eyes and the Buddha's countenance which have done prostrations to the *buddha* face of Shākyamuni Buddha, which have moved the *buddha* eyes of Shākyamuni Buddha into our own eyes, and which have moved our own eyes into the Buddha's eyes. That which has transmitted this state face to face until the present, without missing a single generation, is this face-to-face transmission *(menju).*
>
> *Eihei Dōgen, Shōbōgenzō, Menju, T2582 82:214b24–c7, SDT3 (57) p.211*

Metaphorically, all the patriarchs – Indian, Chinese and Japanese – are expressions of the Buddha's eyes or face. They receive their spiritual power and mandate directly from the Buddha. To venerate any of the patriarchs is therefore to venerate the Buddha himself and the "seven *buddhas*" that came before him:

> The present several tens of generations of right successors are individual instances of the Buddha's face, and they receive the face-to-face transmission *(menju)* from the original Buddha's face. To make a prostration to this traditional face-to-face transmission *(menju)* is just to make a

> prostration to the seven *buddhas* and to Shākyamuni Buddha. It is to make a prostration and to serve offerings to the twenty-eight Buddhist patriarchs from Venerable Mahākāshyapa. The features and eyes of the Buddhist patriarchs are like this. To meet these Buddhist patriarchs is to meet Shākyamuni Buddha and the rest of the seven *buddhas*. It is the very moment in which Buddhist patriarchs intimately bestow the face-to-face transmission *(menju)* of themselves; and it is *buddhas* of the face-to-face transmission *(menju)* giving the face-to-face transmission *(menju)* to *buddhas* of the face-to-face transmission *(menju)*.
>
> *Eihei Dōgen, Shōbōgenzō, Menju, T2582 82:214c7–16, SDT3 (57) p.211*

While in the physical body, through face, eyes and mind, the patriarchs convey spiritual power, enlightenment and the mandate of successorship to their successors:

> Opening their eyes, they give the eye-to-eye transmission and receive the eye-to-eye transmission through the eyes. Showing their faces, they give the face-to-face transmission *(menju)* and receive the face-to-face transmission through the face – the face-to-face transmission *(menju)* is received and given at the place of the face. Utilizing the mind, they give the mind-to-mind transmission *(ishin denshin)* and receive the mind-to-mind transmission *(ishin denshin)* through the mind. Realizing the body, they give the body-to-body transmission of the body.
>
> *Eihei Dōgen, Shōbōgenzō, Menju, T2582 82:214c18–21, SDT3 (57) pp.211–12*

In other parts of the world, Dōgen seems to suggest, there have been other *buddha* lineages of the same nature, but in China and further east, the only true lineage goes back to the Buddha, the Tathāgata, and the seven *buddhas* before him. And it is as if they are all present in each successor; to see one is to see them all simultaneously:

> Other nations in other directions also see this transmission as their original ancestor. But east of China, the giving and receiving of the face-to-face transmission *(menju)* is present only in this house of the Buddha's true tradition. We have clearly received the transmission of the true eye with which to see the Tathāgata. When we do prostrations to the face of Shākyamuni Buddha, the fifty-one patriarchs (from Mahākāshyapa to Dōgen) and the founding seven *buddhas* are neither aligned side by side nor aligned in succession; rather, their face-to-face transmissions *(menju)* are all present in the same moment. One who never in a lifetime meets a master is not a disciple, and one who never meets a disciple is not a master. When master and disciple have

> definitely seen each other, have been seen by each other, have given the face-to-face transmission *(menju),* and have succeeded to the *Dharma,* that is the realization of the truth that resides in the patriarchs' face-to-face transmission *(menju).* Thus, master and disciple have directly taken on the brightness of the Tathāgata's face. In sum, even after thousands of years, or myriad years, or hundreds of *kalpas* (vast ages), or *koṭis* (tens of millions) of *kalpas,* this face-to-face transmission *(menju)* is the appearance of the face of and the realization of the transmission from Shākyamuni Buddha.
>
> *Eihei Dōgen, Shōbōgenzō, Menju, T2582 82:214c22–215a7; cf. SDT3 (57) p.212*

Realization of this is realization of the inner state of all the patriarchs:

> When this state of the Buddhist patriarch has been realized, it is the realization of the images of the World-Honoured One, Mahākāshyapa, the fifty-one patriarchs, and the seven founders; it is the realization of their brightness, the realization of their body, the realization of their mind, the appearance of the tips of their toes, and the appearance of the ends of their noses. Even before a word is comprehended and even before understanding of half a word is transcended, when the master has seen the back of the disciple's head, and the disciple has regarded the master through the crown of the head, that is the authentic face-to-face transmission *(menju).* Revere a face-to-face transmission *(menju)* like this.
>
> *Eihei Dōgen, Shōbōgenzō, Menju, T2582 82:215a7–15, SDT3 (57) p.212*

Consequently, he says, all those who revere the Buddha should likewise honour the means by which his spiritual power and his *Dharma* have been transmitted throughout the ages:

> Therefore, those who revere Shākyamuni Buddha and long for Shākyamuni Buddha should revere and should honour this authentic tradition of the face-to-face transmission *(menju);* we should do venerative prostrations to that which is hard to encounter and hard to meet.
>
> *Eihei Dōgen, Shōbōgenzō, Menju, T2582 82:215a26–b1, SDT3 (57) p.213*

This remarkable accolade to and description of the way in which one patriarch or *buddha* transmits his spiritual power to another is deeply mystical in character. Put in simple terms; Dōgen is saying that all the *buddhas* are one, and in one *buddha,* all other *buddhas* are present. But it requires a particularly developed eye and mind to be able to see this. The significance placed upon this tradition in China and Japan no doubt reflects the importance given to family hierarchies and lineages in those countries, but it does not diminish the exalted nature of the spiritual heritage of true *buddhas.*

The Japanese *Zen* tradition may be familiar in the West, yet it owes its origins to Chinese *Chán* Buddhism, which still exists in China, Taiwan, and Hong Kong. *Dharma* transmission remains a key aspect of these traditions. In practice, however, in most cases it is a much watered-down version of the deeply mystical transmission envisaged by Dōgen. There are also many variations on the same basic theme, with the significance and meaning of *dharma* transmission varying from school to school. In some instances, *dharma* transmission is simply recognition that the student has a basic grasp of the *Dharma,* while acknowledging that he still has far to go on the path to enlightenment. Sometimes, *dharma* transmission indicates that a person is suited to play a significant part in the hierarchy of the monastery or particular school. Often, it is a means to establish the authenticity of the lineages of the abbots or head monks of the various monasteries and schools. In a practice known as *in'in ekishi* ('changing lineage in accordance with one's temple'), monks who move from one monastery or temple to another to assume the position of abbot, switched their lineage to that of the institution they have joined. This may happen more than once if the monk takes a position in another monastery. To be the recipient of *dharma* transmission in present times does not imply infallibility or the attainment of the highest enlightenment.

See also: **inka shōmei**, **ishin denshin**, **patriarch** (7.1), **uḍumbara**.

1. *Lotus Sūtra* 2, *T9* 262:5c.

mondō (J), **wèndá** (C) *Lit.* questions and answers; dialogue, discussion; in *Zen* and *Chán* Buddhism, a dialogue with the master as opposed to listening to a discourse. Often a period devoted to *mondō* is scheduled before or after the master or abbot has delivered a discourse or *Zen* talk. Disciples ask questions concerning the Buddhist Way or some other existential problem and, in accordance with *Zen* and *Chán* principles, the master attempts to answer without recourse to theory, doctrine, or intellectual and conceptual analysis. A private interview between master and disciple *(sanzen, dokusan)* may also take on the character of a *mondō.* Often a master will answer a question with a question, or at least with a complete *non sequitur;* sometimes, the reply is a gesture, a shout, or a slap; sometimes the master might challenge a disciple or the entire assembly with a question. Interactions of this nature became a common feature of *Chán* Buddhism during the Chinese *Táng* dynasty (618–907).

The intention behind such, often cryptic, replies, is to throw the essence of the question back at the questioner and at the same time cut off intellectual speculation – to jolt the disciple out of his or her conceptual mode of thinking in order that they might understand the matter directly, intuitively, and for themselves. Many notable exchanges have been remembered and handed down by tradition, often preserved in Buddhist classical literature, for use as *kōans* (C. *gōng'àn*). In China, Korea and Vietnam, they are often made the focus of reflection, commentary, or debate; in Japan, the *kōan* has become the meditative focus of particular schools, notably *Rinzai Zen.* A well-known example of such an exchange concerns the ninth-century *Chán* Buddhist master Dòngshān Liángjià (J. Tōzan Ryōkai), regarded as founder of the *Cáodòng* (J. *Sōtō*) lineage. On being asked by a monk, "What is Buddha?" the Dòngshān replied, "Three pounds of flax."[1]

Other examples include:

> A monk asked Joshu, "What is the one ultimate word of truth?" Joshu replied: "Yes."
>
> "What is my self?" – " What would you do with a self?"
>
> "What is *Dào?*" – "Usual life is very *Dào.*" "How can we accord with it?" – "If you try to accord with it you will get away from it."
>
> "All things are such as they are from the beginning; what is that which is beyond existence?" – "Your statement is quite plain. Why ask me?"
>
> *Traditional Mondō, in CMMD pp.241–42*

In recent times, exchanges of *mondō* have often become stylized, following a habitual pattern, lacking the spontaneous expression of wisdom that arose from spiritually evolved masters of the past.[2]

A particular kind of *mondō* or *wèndá* is known as an encounter dialogue (J. *kien mondō,* C. *jīyuán wèndá*). *Kien* and *jīyuán* mean chance, opportunity or destiny, and this kind of dialogue is regarded as an auspicious or special encounter in which the two parties meet by the force of their mutual destinies and engage in a dialogue in quest of Truth.

See also: **kōan** (▸3), **sanzen, wendá**.

1. See "Mondō," *Shambhala Dictionary of Buddhism and Zen, SDBZ.*
2. See "Mondô," *Illustrated Encyclopedia of Zen Buddhism, IEZB;* "Questions and Answers," *Seeker's Glossary of Buddhism, SGB.*

nargis, **chashm-i nargis** (P) *Lit.* narcissus *(nargis);* narcissus *(nargis)* eye *(chashm);* in Sufi symbolism, the enchanting and intoxicated eyes of the divine beloved, which irresistibly attract the lover; the glance of the master, either inner or outer; often, *nargis* is used as a short form of *chashm-i nargis,* and means the beautiful eye of the beloved. The narcissus or narcissus eye signify beauty, physical or divine. In Islamic poetry, the narcissus, the narcissus eye, the rose, the moon, and so on, are all commonly used to epitomize beauty.

In Greek mythology, Narcissus is the name of a young man who falls in love with his own reflection in a pool of water, gazing into his own eyes. Pining away, he becomes the flower that bears his name. In Western thought, based upon th Greek myth, the narcissist is one who is entirely absorbed in admiration of himself. In Sufism, the myth is understood in a more esoteric manner. The narcissus eye *(chashm-i nargis)* signifies the irresistible attraction of the divine beloved. Gazing into the eyes of the beloved, the lover sees there the divine Beauty. On contemplating this Beauty in the beloved, he comes to see the same divine Beauty within himself.

Ḥāfiẓ says that the master's look unleashes a deep yearning in the hearts of lovers, causing many to experience the anguish of separation from the Divine:

> When that eye *(nargis)* cast a single amorous glance,
> your beguiling eye unleashed a hundred calamities on the world.
>
> *Ḥāfiẓ, Dīvān, DHA p.24, DIH p.71; cf. DHWC (63:3) p.155*

ʻAṭṭār says that absorption in the divine beauty of the inner beloved focuses the inner eye upon Him alone:

> His notorious eye *(nargis)* has closed
> the eye of the heart to everything else.
> Whatever his eyes do, even if they carry off the soul,
> is admirable.
>
> *ʻAṭṭār, Dīvān 71:4430, DASN p.137; cf. in SSE1 p.34*

One glance from the master fills the devoted soul with love:

> The entire horizon filled with yearning and joy
> when you, O idol, opened your narcissus eye *(chashm-i nargis).*
>
> *ʻAṭṭār, Dīvān 296:4910, DASN p.266; cf. in SSE1 p.35*

Rūmī says that if you have no experience of this spiritual intoxication, then look into the beloved's eyes:

> If you know not the intoxication of the heart,
> and wonder what it is,
> seek understanding from the intoxicated eye *(nargis).*
>
> *Rūmī, Maśnavī VI:1298; cf. MJR6 p.330*

Indeed, he says that if you want to stir up the hearts of drunken lovers, you need only speak to them of the beloved:

If you want to disturb the rest of drunkards,
speak of that intoxicated eye *(nargis).*
Rūmī, Dīvān-i Shams-i Tabrīz 2191:23258, KSD5 p.50

See also: **chashm** (▸3).

naẓar (A/P) *Lit.* sight, vision, eyes; look, glance, gaze, regard; insight, perception, viewpoint; consideration, thought, thinking; looking at, examination, investigation, inspection; inner vision, spiritual contemplation, clairvoyance. *Naẓar* covers a broad spectrum of meanings. When used in the sense of 'consideration', it is almost synonymous with *fikr* (cogitation, reflection, thinking). Hence, such expressions as *ahl al-naẓar* (people of consideration, intellectuals), a term used synonymously with *ahl al-fikr* (people of reflection) and *aṣḥāb al-afkār* (lords of reflection), *ahl al-'uqūl* (people of rational faculties), and *'uqulā'* (rational thinkers). However, in a mystical context, *ahl al-naẓar* also means 'people of mystical vision'.

In the sense of a look or glance, *naẓar* implies a purposefully directed look, with attention and love. One such look from a master has great spiritual benefit, for a master can open the spiritual eyes of a seeker simply through the power of his own attention. According to a Sufi saying, a look of this nature is of more value than arduous devotional practice:

Forty retreats! Oh, forty retreats and forty retreats!
One glance *(naẓar)* from the master is better than forty retreats!
Sufi Saying; cf. in SSE2 p.165

Rūmī says much the same thing in his *Maśnavī:*

In all places of assembly,
always seek among intellects *('uqūl)*
such an intellect *('aql)* as existed in the Prophet.
For the only heritage of the Prophet is that which perceives
the unseen things of past and future.
Among eyes, too, always seek that eye
which this epitome (the *Maśnavī*) has not the power to describe.
That is why the majestic (Prophet) forbade monkery,
and going to live as a hermit in the mountains,
so that this kind of meeting (with saints) should not be lost:
For their look *(naẓar)* is fortune and an elixir of immortality.
Rūmī, Maśnavī VI:2617–21; cf. MJR6 p.403

For the spiritual seeker, the possibility of receiving such a glance *(naẓar)* from the master (the "helper") is what turns despair at ever being able to control the *nafs* (lower mind) into hope:

> What help is there, then, but refuge with the helper? Despair is copper, and the elixir for it is a glance *(naẓar).*
>
> *Rūmī, Maśnavī II:3386; cf. MJR2 p.397*

To bolster their hope, disciples like to relate stories concerning the effects of a glance from their master or other evolved souls:

> One day a man from among the men of God directed his glance of favour at our Shams al-Dīn-i Mārdīnī in such a way that, due to that blessed glance *(naẓar),* Shams al-Dīn became without compare *(bī-naẓīr)* in the world and was made into a friend of God.
>
> *Aḥmad al-Aflākī, Manāqib al-ʿĀrifīn 3:318, MASA1 p.386, FKG (3:317) p.267*

Aflākī tells a story concerning Rūmī's father Bahā' Valad who taught Islamic religious law:

> The religious scholars among the companions related that one day Sulṭān Valad (Rūmī's son) said: "The king of those who have lost their wits, our Faqīh Aḥmad – God have mercy on him – was engaged in studying jurisprudence with Bahā' Valad. He (Faqīh Aḥmad) was a Turk, a simple-hearted man, and he was also his (Bahā' Valad's) disciple. Due to one glance *(naẓar)* from my grandfather, he became incomparable *(bī-naẓīr)* in the world, and such a state came over him that he threw the book from his hand. He became filled with (spiritual) passion and set out on the road to the mountains.
>
> Engulfed in the ocean of bewilderment and divine omnipotence, he wandered about for many years in the mountains practising ascetic austerities. In the end, the secret of ʿUways-i Qaranī – God be pleased with him – was manifested to the famous jurist, and he became completely drawn to God *(majdhūb)* and deprived of reason. A group of people asked Bahā' Valad about the man's states and his madness. Bahā' Valad replied: "From those brimming cups of ours, which Sayyid-i Sirr-Dān (Burhān al-Dīn) quaffed, a single drop reached this man."
>
> Likewise, my father also said one day: "The intoxication of Faqīh Aḥmad is but a single whiff from the ocean of intoxication of Mawlānā Shams al-Dīn Tabrīzī, and no more."
>
> *Aḥmad al-Aflākī, Manāqib al-ʿĀrifīn 1:36, MASA1 pp.39–40, FKG pp.30–31*

Rūmī himself tells a story concerning the far-reaching effect of such a glance:

> A saint went on a retreat to seek a sublime goal. A voice came to him, saying: "Such a sublime goal cannot be attained by means of retreat. Leave your retreat so that a great man's gaze *(naẓar-i buzurg)* may fall upon you, and cause you to reach your goal."
>
> "Where am I to find this great man?" he asked.
>
> "In the congregational mosque," he was told.
>
> "How am I to recognize him among so many people?"
>
> "Go!" said the voice. "He will recognize you and gaze *(naẓar kunad)* upon you. And the sign of his gaze *(naẓar)* shall be this, that a ewer shall fall from your hand and you shall fall unconscious, whence you shall know that he has gazed *(naẓar)* upon you."
>
> And so he filled a ewer with water and, going from row to row, gave drink to the assembly at the mosque. Suddenly he had a strange sensation and, uttering a loud shriek, dropped the ewer. While he was lying unconscious in a corner, the congregation departed. When he came to his senses, he saw that he was alone. He never saw that 'king' who had cast his glance *(naẓar)* upon him, but he did attain his goal.
>
> God has men who never show themselves because of God's excessive jealousy of them, but they do bestow gifts and exalted goals upon those who seek them. Such great kings are rare and precious indeed.
>
> *Rūmī, Fīhi mā Fīhi 10:7–14, KFF p.41, SOU pp.42–43; cf. DRA p.53*

The essence of such stories has become enshrined in Sufi poetry. Kamāl Khujandī speaks of Sufis living in a *khānaqāh:*

> Scarcely had your eye cast a glance *(naẓar)* upon the monks,
> than every monk in the cloister let out a drunken shout.
>
> *Kamāl Khujandī, Dīvān, DKK p.52; cf. in SSE2 p.165*

Conversely, *naẓar* applies to the gaze of the lover at the beloved. Sa'dī says that his "body" – symbolizing his material existence – previously robust like the "full moon", has all but disappeared out of the love for and the sight *(naẓar)* of the beloved:

> If the sun's rays turn a crescent to a full moon,
> why has the full moon of my body become a crescent
> through the sight *(naẓar)* of you?
>
> *Sa'dī, Badāyi' 80:4, KSSS p.365; cf. BOS p.90*

Likewise, he says that even if the lover is in grave danger, but is able to gaze upon the beloved, yet the lover could not wish for anything more:

O Saʿdī! Have no fear:
Even if you are in the jaws of a crocodile,
yet within sight *(naẓar)* of the beloved *(dūst),*
it is the height of one's desire.

Saʿdī, Ṭayyibāt 47:9, KSSS p.253; cf. TOS p.67

Ḥāfiẓ, too, longs for the glance of his beloved:

Intoxicated and ruined though I may be, do me a little kindness:
Cast your glance *(naẓar)* upon this perplexed and ruined heart.

Ḥāfiẓ, Dīvān, DHA p.135, DIH p.238; cf. DHWC (309:5) p.535

Seated in meditation within himself – "on the threshold of hope" – he remains hopeful of a single glance:

On the threshold of hope in you, I have opened my eye,
that you may cast a glance *(naẓar)* upon me;
For you have cast me away from your glance *(naẓar).*

Ḥāfiẓ, Dīvān, DHA p.171, DIH p.296; cf. DHWC (378:3) p.652

See also: **naẓar** (▸3).

nigāh (P) *Lit.* look, aspect, glance; observation, custody, watch, care, caution; in Sufism, the transformative glance of grace from the beloved – inner or outer – that confers an inward attraction towards God and a spiritual awakening, culminating ultimately in the annihilation *(fanā')* of the lover's sense of individual self.

Many Sufi poets, longing for the sight of their own master – inner or outer – have spoken of the power and effect of his glance:

A clever beauty stole my heart with a glance *(nigāh),*
my days turned black because of his dark eye *(chashm-i siyāh).*

Sarmad, Rubāʿīyāt 283, RISP p.48, RIS p.41

With but a glance *(nigāh),* that dark-eyed one *(chashm-i siyāh)*
will pillage heart and religion;
That playful one will ruthlessly slaughter innocent captives.

Sabzavārī, Dīvān, DMHS p.60, in FNI5 p.108; cf. in SSE5 p.110

Bestow one glance *(nigāh)* from your two eyes,
so that, running quickly,
they may bring an easy death to the heart-torn.

Ḥāfiẓ, Dīvān, DIH p.179; cf. DHWC (135:9) p.279

Whether he bestows a glance *(nigāh)* on poor me, or not,
he is the beloved, and I his obedient slave.

Sa'dī, Badāyi' 15:4, KSSS p.348; cf. BOS p.18

nigurā (H/Pu) *Lit.* without *(ni)* a master *(guru);* a person with no *guru* or master. Because liberation is deemed impossible without a suitable *guru,* and because the tradition of devotion to a *guru* was so strong in India, to call someone *"nigurā"* – at least until recent times – was considered an insult. Guru Amardās writes:

You shall never have to regret and repent, you fool,
if you listen to the teachings *(updes)* of the *satguru....*
Without the *satguru,* there is no *guru* at all:
one who is without a *guru (nigurā)* has a bad reputation.

Guru Amardās, Ādi Granth 435, AGK,

One who has no *guru (nigurā)*
dies over and over again, only to be reborn;
One who has no *guru (nigurā)*
continues coming and going in reincarnation.

Guru Amardās, Ādi Granth 117, AGK

In traditional Hindu culture, it is regarded as inauspicious to look at the face of someone who is in mourning. Tukārām draws a parallel with a person who has no master:

Without a master *(nigurā),*
all scriptures are like the whispering of ghosts,
says the sage Vyāsa in his *Purāṇas.*
One without a master *(nigurā)* is like one perpetually in mourning –
do not even glance at his face.
No efforts will ever liberate him from the wheel of births and deaths –
know that his human life was in vain.
So say the holy books, declares Tukā, and so said all the saints in history.

Tukārām, Gāthā 4341, STG3 p.516, TCSD p.137

Nonetheless, Sahajobāī counsels discrimination when seeking a true *guru,* otherwise the soul will continue to wander in the eighty-four hundred thousand *(lakh)* forms of creature in this world:

Sahajo says, there are hordes of *gurus* wandering around:
ignorant men, who know nothing of meditation.

They reach out to many, and cannot save any.
These *gurus* are common: cheats, villains, men who want your money.
Sahajo says, find a true *guru (satguru),*
who can give you the fruits of the abode of liberation.

All are ensnared by the web of attachment,
animals, birds, humans – all fall into the trap.
Says Sahajo, only those who take refuge in the *satguru* are saved:
those without a *satguru* remain forever entangled.
Over and over again, they enter into relationships
among the eighty-four thousand species,
because they have no *satguru,*
who can reach out and set them free.

He who is in the company of the *guru*
day and night, throughout his life,
he always remains united to the Lord.
Sahajo says, without a *guru,* you will never have rest.

Sahajobāī, Bānī, Guru Mahimā 61–65, SBB p.10; cf. SPBS p.51

Contrasting those who have a *guru* with those who do not, Dādū says that a *guru* is necessary in order to be purified of all past *karma* and present imperfections – essential prerequisites on the path to God:

A distinction is made between one with a *guru (sagurā)*
and one without a *guru (nigurā);* thus do all saints *(sādh)* declare.
In the court of the Lord, one with a *guru (sagurā)* is proved true,
whereas one without a *guru (nigurā)* is found false. . . .

One with a *guru (sagurā)* observes truth and discipline,
and the Creator appears to him face to face.
One without a *guru (nigurā)* is greedy and covetous,
and he is engrossed in sensual defilements, says Dādū.

Dādū, Bānī 1, Pārikh ko Ang 31–32, DDB1 pp.218–19, DCMU p.78

Employing a selection of colourful parallels, Kabīr is characteristically forthright concerning the fate of those who have no *guru* to extricate them from the cycle of birth and death:

I see religious people counting their beads
and offering great works of charity,
but this I find is an utter waste.

All their good deeds prove futile
because they worship without a master *(guru)* –
A fact that even the scriptures admit.

I see masterless ones *(nigurā)* repeating their prayers,
performing their rituals hundreds of times a day.
Should a prostitute seek to become a *satī*
(immolating herself on her husband's funeral pyre),
for which husband would she leap into the fire?...

I've seen a wealthy woman without devotion to a *guru*
return to this world as a dog.
She hungrily begs from door to door
but no one gives her even a morsel of bread.

Kabīr, I've seen a king without devotion to a *guru*
come back to earth as a poor donkey
that silently bears loads of potter's clay.
No one feeds it for its heavy labour,
for as a king it lived on others' toil.

Kabīr, Sākhī Sangrah, Nigurā kā Ang 1–2, 7–8, KSS p.15;
cf. KGME pp.197–98

See also: **guru**.

nimba (S/Pa), **nīm** (H), **nimm**, **nimb** (Pu) *Azadirachta indica,* the margosa tree or Indian lilac, native to India, Pakistan, and Bangladesh; anglicized as 'neem'; a large tree, all parts of which are used by human beings: the leaves have antiseptic properties and are also used as a natural insecticide; the fruit and seeds yield a medicinal oil; the bark is used to make a tonic, and the trunk exudes a gum. Its leaves, branches, bark, fruit and even its smell (like that of onions, especially in the rains) are all bitter, but, according to folklore, if it grows near a sandalwood tree, it loses its bitterness, acquires the fragrance of sandalwood, and is even called sandalwood. *Azadirachta indica* is a close relative of and very similar in appearance to the chinaberry, bead tree or cape lilac *(Melia azedarach),* originally from China and sharing many of the same medicinal properties, both of which are popularly known on the subcontinent as neem trees.

Referring metaphorically to the neem tree's property of picking up the fragrance of sandalwood, it is said that impure human beings can become pure by remaining in the company of a saint:

Time spent in a saint's company is never spent in vain;
In the vicinity of the sandalwood,
even the *nīm* tree becomes fragrant.
No longer is it known by the bitter tree's name.

Kabīr, Sākhī Sangrah, Satsang kā Ang 7, KSS p.49; cf. KWGN p.635

Kabīr also says that just as insects seem to love the bitter taste of the neem tree, so are human beings happy with the bitter taste of the senses, treating it as though it were nectar. They do not discriminate between the bitterness of the senses and the sweetness of the divine Name.[1]

The neem tree is similarly represented in the Buddhist *Jātaka,* stories of the Buddhas past births, although in this case it is the mango tree whose fruit picks up the bitter flavour of the neighbouring neem. According to the story:

> A young *brāhmaṇ*... had mastered the three *Vedas,* and used to teach sacred verses to a number of young *brāhmaṇs* and *kshatriyas.* In time, he settled down as a married man. His thoughts now busy with wealth and ornaments, serving men and serving women, lands and substance, cattle and buffaloes, sons and daughters, he became subject to passion, error, and folly. This obscured his wits, so that he forgot how to repeat his *mantras* in due order, and every now and then the words did not come clearly to his mind.
>
> *Jātaka 2:185.5, Anabhirati-Jātaka, PTSJ2 p.99; cf. JSBB2 p.68*

One day, the young man goes to visit the Buddha, and in the course of conversation, he admits to the Buddha that he is no longer able to recall all the verses. The Buddha responds:

> *Bhikkhus,* association *(sannivāsa)* with the wicked is evil and injurious; but what use is it to speak about its perniciousness to human beings of bad company *(pāpa-sannivāsa)?* In days gone by, even the sweet-flavoured, senseless mango tree, whose fruit was a dish fit for the gods, turned sour and bitter through association *(sannivāsa)* with a disagreeable and bitter *nimba* tree.
>
> *Jātaka 2:186.6, Dadhivāhana-Jātaka, PTSJ2 p.101; cf. FJFC p.20, JSBB2 pp.69–70*

The Buddha then relates a long story to illustrate the effect of bad company. Towards the end of this story, a certain King Dadhivāhana chances upon a mango fruit floating down the river, and being delighted with its taste, he has its stone planted in his gardens, and tended with great care ("milk-water was poured around it"). Within three years, the mango tree bears its first fruit. The fruit tasted so good and looked so fine that King Dadhivāhana would send some to the neighbouring kings. Before doing so, however, the king

> used to prick with a thorn that place in the stone where the sprout would spring forth, for fear of their growing the like by planting it. When they ate the fruit, they used to plant the stone, but they could not get it to take root. Upon asking why this should be, they learnt what was going on.
>
> *Jātaka 2:186.6, Dadhivāhana-Jātaka, PTSJ2 p.105; cf. FJFC p.28, JSBB2 p.72*

One of the kings therefore asks one of his gardeners if he would be able to destroy the flavour of the mango tree. The gardener replies in the affirmative, and is forthwith given a large sum of money and is dispatched upon his errand. The gardener goes to King Dadhivāhana's kingdom, announces his presence to the king, and by singing his own praises, he gets himself hired as a gardener in the king's gardens. By forcing fruits and flowers out of season, he manages to make the gardens more beautiful, with the result that the previous head gardener is dismissed and replaced by the new upstart, who is placed in sole charge of the gardens:

> No sooner had this man got the gardens into his own hands than he planted *nimbas* and creepers about the choice mango tree. By and by, the *nimbas* grew. Above and below, root with root, and branch with branch, they became completely entangled with the mango tree. Thus this tree, with its sweet fruit, grew bitter as the bitter-leaved *nimba* by the company *(sannivāsa)* of this disagreeable and sour plant. As soon as the gardener knew that the fruit had gone bitter, he took to his heels.
>
> King Dadhivāhana went walking in his gardens, and took a bite of the mango fruit. The juice in his mouth tasted like a disgusting *nimba;* swallow it he could not, so he coughed and spat it out. Now, at that time, his temporal and spiritual counsellor was Bodhisatta. The king turned to him and asked: "Wise Sir, this tree has been as carefully tended as ever, and yet its fruit has gone bitter. What is the meaning of it?" and asking this question, he repeated the first stanza:
>
> This mango tree was formerly endowed
> with colour, smell and flavour,
> so what has caused its bitter flavour,
> for we tend it as we have always done?
>
> Then, explaining the reason for it, Bodhisatta recited a second stanza:
>
> Your mango tree, O Dadhivāhana, is surrounded by *nimbas:*
> The root of the one is united with the root of the other,
> the branches of the one embrace the branches of the other.

> It is because of its close association *(asāta-sannivāsa)*
> with the bad *(nimbas),* that the mango tree has bitter fruit.
>
> Upon hearing this, the king caused all the *nimbas* and creepers to be cut down and their roots to be pulled up, the sour earth to be completely removed and sweet earth to be put in its place, and the mango tree to be tended with milk water, sugar water, and fragrant water. Thus, by absorbing the sweet juices, its fruit once again became sweet.
>
> *Jātaka 2:186.6, Dadhivāhana-Jātaka, PTSJ2 pp.105–6; cf. FJFC pp.29–31, JSBB2 p.73*

The king then reinstates his former head gardener. After finishing the story, the Buddha adds, "At that time I was the wise counsellor."

See also: **bhṛingī**, **ḍhāk**, **kūnj**.

1. Kabīr, *Granthāvalī, Ramainī, KG* p.176.

ninbō (J) *Lit.* personal *(nin)* method or *dharma (hō);* personal transmission; the practice of basing a *Zen* temple lineage on the lineage of the abbot such that the lineage changes whenever a new abbot is appointed, if his lineage differs from the temple lineage at the time of his appointment.

See also: **garanbō**, **in'in ekishi**.

nubuwwah, **nubūwah** (A), **nubuvvat** (P) *Lit.* prophecy, prophethood; the teaching of the divine Reality from an experiential knowledge or gnosis of the spiritual realms, of the divine Acts, Attributes, Names, and of, in some instances, the divine Essence Itself; the prophetic mission or ministry of a *nabī* (prophet); from the Arabic *naba'a* (to impart knowledge, to give news); also called *risālah* and *payghambarī,* both meaning 'messengership'; commonly reserved for Muḥammad, but also used for the mission of other prophets.

Prophecy can originate from any place in the inner realms, according to the spiritual reach of the individual prophet. Lāhījī explains this from a Sufi and Islamic viewpoint. The inner reality of the highest prophet is the divine creative power, the *'Aql-i Kull* (Universal Intelligence), also called the *Ḥaqīqat-i Muḥammadī* (Reality of Muḥammad):

> The Arabic word for prophecy *(nubuwwah)* is based on a root connoting the giving of news or tidings. The prophet *(nabī)* is one who

expounds upon the divine Essence, Attributes, Names, and Decrees, as they are revealed to him.

He is a realized one, who is primally and essentially the Universal Intelligence *('Aql-i Kull),* delegated by God to inform the universal mind *(nafs-i kull)* directly, and the individual soul *(nufūs-i juzvī)* indirectly. Each of the prophets *(anbiyā'),* from the time of Ādam to that of Muḥammad, represents a different manifestation of the prophecy *(nubuvvat)* of the supreme Spirit *(Rūḥ-i a'ẓam),* which is the Primal Intelligence *('Aql-i Avval).*

The prophecy *(nubuvvat)* of the Universal Intelligence *('Aql-i Avval)* is lasting and essential, while the prophecy *(nubuvvat)* of (lower) manifestations is phenomenal and accidental. The Reality of Muḥammad *(Ḥaqīqat-i Muḥammadī)* represents the Primal Intelligence *('Aql-i Avval)* or supreme Spirit, as indicated in the Prophet's statements: "First, God created the Intelligence *(al-'Aql),*" "First, God created my Light,"[1] and "First, God created my Spirit." It is the Muḥammadan form in which the supreme Spirit has appeared with all its Names and Attributes.

The essential prophecy *(nubuvvat źātī),* which makes known the divine Essence and Attributes, primally and essentially, belongs to the supreme Spirit, which is the Reality of Muḥammad *(Ḥaqīqat-i Muḥammadī).* In the end, the seal of prophecy *(khatm-i nubuvvat)* is manifested in both the (human) form and the spiritual Reality of Muḥammad. So prophecy *(nubuvvat)* has belonged to Muḥammad in his essence, from the very beginning, appearing in his (human) form, as well, at the end. Each of the other prophets represents a manifestation of the various perfections of the Reality of Muḥammad.

Lāhījī, Sharḥ-i Gulshan-i Rāz, SGR p.23; cf. in SSE3 p.62

Some Sufis have categorized different forms of prophecy largely based upon the level of attainment of the various prophets and whether or not they taught the practice of external religious observances.[2]

Nubuwwat al-ẓāhirah (outer prophecy), for example, also called *nubuwwat al-khāṣṣah* (particular prophecy), *nubuwwat al-tashrīḥ* (legislative prophecy), *nubuwwat al-muqayyadah* (delimited prophecy), *nubuwwat al-taklīf* (prophecy of religious law) is prophecy or teaching that includes a system of external religious law, which will last only for a particular period of time. Prophets endowed with this kind of prophethood are those who are sent to promulgate and establish a new religion.

On the other hand, *nubuwwat al-bāṭinah* (inner prophecy), also called *nubuwwat al-'āmmah* (general prophecy), *nubuwwat al-ikhbār* (informative prophecy), *nubuwwat al-muṭlaqah* (absolute prophecy), and *nubuwwat al-wārith* (inherited prophecy), is a prophecy or teaching that does not include external religious observances.

Nubuwwat al-risālīyah (prophecy of the apostolate), also called *nubuwwat al-shamsīyah* (solar prophecy) by Ibn al-ʿArabī, is the prophecy of the prophets and messengers. This is contrasted with *nubuwwat al-ʿāmmah* (general prophecy), also called *nubuwwat al-qamarīyah* (lunar prophecy) by Ibn al-ʿArabī. This is the prophecy of the friends of God and the spiritual heirs of the prophet.

Nubuwwat al-barzakhīyah (prophecy of the intermediate realm) is a prophecy that comes from *ʿālam al-mithāl* (world of patterns). *Nubuwwat al-taʿrīf* (descriptive prophecy) includes a description of the divine Essence, Names, and Attributes. And *nubuwwat al-sāriyah* (all-pervasive prophecy) is not really prophecy at all, but is the manner inherent in creation by which God inspires each creature to perform its allotted role. As the *Qur'ān* says:

> Your Lord inspired the bee, saying, "Make your homes in hills, on trees, and in the hives they build for you. Feed on every kind of fruit, and follow the ways of your Lord laid out for you. Then there comes forth from its belly, a drink of various hues, wherein is healing for mankind. Truly, in this there is a sign for those who would reflect.
>
> *Qur'ān 16:68–69; cf. AYA, KPA, MGK*

See also: **nabī** (7.1), **risālah**.

1. *Ḥadīth, AMBF* 342; *cf.* in *SSE3* p.62.
2. For the summary that follows, see Suʿād al-Ḥakīm, *al-Muʿjam al-Ṣūfī* 591–602, *AMAS* pp.1048–52; Shāh Niʿmat Allāh Valī, *Rasā'il, RNV4* pp.36, 79, in *SSE3* pp.62–65.

pañha-vyākaraṇa (Pa) *Lit.* answer *(vyākaraṇa)* question *(pañha);* four ways of answering questions, according to the Buddha in the Pali texts:[1]

> There are these four ways of answering questions *(pañha-vyākaraṇa).* Which four? There are questions that should be answered categorically. There are questions that should be answered with an analytical (qualified) answer. There are questions that should be answered with a counter-question. There are questions that should be put aside. These are the four ways of answering questions *(pañha-vyākaraṇa).*
>
> *Anguttara Nikāya 4:42, Pañha-vyākaraṇa Sutta, PTSA2 p.46, ANTB*

A categorical answer implies a straightforward response such as "yes," "no," "this," or "that." An analytical or qualified answer implies some redefining or clarification of the question before it can be answered. Some questions are best answered by another question, and some questions by making no reply at all. Mystics such as the Buddha are fully aware of the questioner and all that is passing in his or her mind, which will also determine the kind of answer that is given. The intention is always to expand the understanding of the questioner rather than to tie them up in intellectual knots.

See also: **avyākṛita-vastu**.

1. See also *e.g. Anguttara Nikāya* 3:67, *Kathāvatthu Sutta, PTSA1* p.197.

paramparā (S/Pa), **brgyud pa** (T) *Lit.* beyond *(parama)* the other *(para),* one after the other; lineage, succession, transmission, series; tradition, passed on by tradition; a dynasty; a royal lineage in which the son succeeds the father as king for many generations, or an unbroken spiritual tradition passed on by successive teachers; in Buddhism and *yoga,* a lineage of masters or *gurus,* each appointing a suitable successor from among his disciples in an unbroken line – a conduit for the transmission of spirituality from master to disciple.

Traditionally, it is regarded as important for a yogi to be accepted by a *guru* from an established lineage. Buddhist monasteries and temples likewise have a chain of transmission. There are many such lineages among the yogic, tantric, and Buddhist schools. In the *Bhagavad Gītā,* Kṛishṇa tells Arjuna:

> This *yoga* handed down (from master to disciple)
> in succession *(paramparā),*
> was known to the royal sages *(rājashayaḥ).*
> But owing to long lapse of time, it was lost to the world.
>
> You are my devotee and friend –
> today, therefore, I have explained to you even that ancient *yoga.*
> For, it is a noble secret (only imparted by a teacher to a worthy disciple).
>
> *Bhagavad Gītā 4:2–3; cf. BGT*

The *Kulārṇava Tantra* maintains that liberation from the wheel of birth and death cannot be obtained without initiation from a *guru* who is a part of an ancient lineage and an ancient tradition:

> It is said in the teaching of *Shiva* that there can be no *moksha* (liberation) without *dīkshā* (initiation), and no initiation without a teacher from the lineage *(āchārya-paramparā).* Without a teacher, all philosophy, knowledge of the tradition *(sampradāya),* and *mantras* are fruitless. Only that *guru* is protected by the gods who keeps alive what is handed down by tradition *(pāramparya),* who is well versed in the *mantras* and *āgamas* (scriptures), and guards the way of the traditional

> teachings. While he himself remains detached, the *guru,* after testing his disciple for some time, shall, at the Lord's command, deliver (the Truth) to his disciple, in order to imbue him with authority. Verily, for him who is thus imbued with authority, there is union with the supreme *Shiva;* at the end of his bodily life is eternal liberation – this is declared by the Lord. Therefore, one should make all possible efforts to seek a *guru* of unbroken tradition *(sampradāya-avichchhinna),* born of the supreme *Shiva* himself.
>
> *Kulārṇava Tantra 14:3–8, KTAA pp.308–9; cf. KTAA (10) p.101*

The same *tantra* also speaks of those who purport to teach, and even take on the role of a *guru,* while they themselves have no *guru:*

> Lacking instruction from a *guru* and being thoroughly confused themselves, such people confuse everyone else. Some rogues who are fond of wrong conduct hold forth, but how can such a person be a master *(svāmin)* or his disciples *(sevaka)* not be of the same sort? Many who lack transmission *(paramparā)* and are duped by false knowledge imagine the *kaulika* (ancestral) teaching according to their own mind. If men could attain perfection *(siddhi)* merely by drinking wine, every wine-bibbing rogue would (readily) attain perfection.
>
> *Kulārṇava Tantra 2:114–17, KTAA pp.155–56; cf. in TPEF p.231*

Swami Vivekananda says much the same. The spiritual power of an authentic lineage must be present with any *guru* who is to do his work effectively, because he carries the burden of his disciples' *karma:*

> A *sadguru* is one on whom the spiritual power has descended by *guru-paramparā,* or an unbroken chain of discipleship. To play the role of a spiritual teacher is a very difficult thing. One has to take on oneself the sins of others. There is every chance of a fall in less-advanced men. If merely physical pain ensues, then he should consider himself fortunate.
>
> *Swami Vivekananda, Questions 7, CWSV5 p.322*

Likewise, in Buddhism, the lineage and the *dharma* transmission, especially in Chinese *Chán* and Japanese *Zen,* is of great significance, where lineages are commonly traced back to Bodhidharma, and thence to the Buddha himself. Bodhidharma is credited with bringing Buddhism to China, from where it spread to Japan.

Looking at tradition from a different perspective, in the *Kālāmā Sutta,* the Buddha speaks to a group of people (the Kālāmās) who are confused after listening to the many viewpoints put forward by the various schools of thought of the day. He observes that nothing should be accepted merely because it is a part of tradition or because others say so. What is required is a spirit of free enquiry, blended with an inner honesty regarding what works and what does not, what leads to tranquillity and what leads to suffering:

> Of course you are uncertain, Kālāmās. Of course you are in doubt. When there are reasons for doubt, uncertainty is born. So in this case, Kālāmās, do not go by hearsay *(anussava),* nor by what has been passed down *(paramparā),* nor by legends *(itikirāya),* nor by scriptures, nor by logical reasoning, nor by surmise, nor by analogies, nor by agreement reached by considering various viewpoints, nor by a person's cleverness, nor by the thought, "This holy man *(samaṇa)* is our teacher." When you know for yourselves that "These qualities are unskilful; these qualities are blameworthy; these qualities are criticized by the wise; these qualities, when adopted and carried out, lead to harm and to suffering" – then you should abandon them.
>
> *Anguttara Nikāya 3:65, Kālāmā Sutta, PTSA1 p.189; cf. ANST, ANTB*

See also: **ishin denshin**, **menju shihō**.

parishad (S), **parisā** (Pa) *Lit.* sit *(sad)* around *(pari);* assembly, company, community, group, retinue, following; in Buddhism, the four groups *(chatush-parishad)* comprising the Buddha's following *(buddhaparisā), viz.* monks *(bhikkhu),* nuns *(bhikkhuṇī),* laymen *(upāsaka),* and laywomen *(upāsikā),* whether ordained or not, regardless of spiritual attainment; also used in expressions such as *bhikkhu-parisā* (assembly of monks), *tīrthika-parishad* (assembly of heretics), *Brahmapārisajja* (retinue of the deity *Brahmā*); in a Hindu context, a *parishad* is also an *āshram,* a spiritual hermitage or retreat, as well as an assembly or community.

In the Pali *suttas, parisā*[1] has a broader meaning than *sangha* (community),[2] referring simply to those who assembled around the Buddha. *Sangha* generally refers more specifically either to the community of ordained monks and nuns *(bhikkhu-sangha, bhikkhuṇī-sangha)* or to the community of 'noble ones *(ariya-sangha)*' – those who have at least attained the level of stream-entry *(sotāpanna),* the first stage of the transcendent path leading to enlightenment.

It has been suggested that the term *bhikkhu-parisā* originates from an earlier period, before it became necessary to introduce more rules to provide guidance on behaviour for the monks.[3] It is generally agreed that the very detailed monastic code, with its lists of multiple rules, originated after the Buddha's time. But the real history of the Pali texts is too uncertain to be sure how much organization the Buddha introduced during his own lifetime.

Although the *suttas* use the term *parisā,* in modern times, the term that is widely used in the West for the entire Buddhist community is *sangha. Sangha* does appear in one of the earliest Buddhist texts, the *Dhammapada,* as one of the three 'places' where a Buddhist can seek spiritual refuge: the Buddha, the *Dhamma* (Teaching, Path), and the *sangha.*[4]

See also: **saṃgha**.

1. *E.g. Dīgha Nikāya* 4, *Soṇadaṇḍa Sutta, PTSD1* pp.125–26, *TBLD* p.132.
2. *E.g. Dīgha Nikāya* 2, *Sāmaññaphala Sutta, PTSD1* pp.50–51, *TBLD* pp.92–93.
3. I.B. Horner, *Book of the Discipline, BDV2* pp.xvi–xviii.
4. *Dhammapada* 14:12–14.

parivāra (S) *Lit.* retinue, followers; family; in Jainism, among *Shvetāmbara Mūrtipūjaka* monks, a small group, each with its own *āchārya* (leader), after whom the *parivāra* is named. A *parivāra* contains around 25 to 35 monks and 35 to 50 nuns. They may be divided into smaller groups from time to time, particularly during the four months *(chatur-māsa)* of the rainy season, when monks remain at one place, since walking about would cause harm to many insects and other invertebrates on the ground.[1]

In Buddhism, the *Parivāra* is the name of the summary and recapitulation that comprises the fifth and final part of the *Vinaya Piṭaka,* which contains the code of monastic discipline.

1. See "parivāra," *A to Z of Jainism, AZJW.*

prāsāda (S), **báluósuōduò** (C), **barashada** (J) *Lit.* sitting *(sāda)* forward *(prā);* being seated conspicuously; a high or conspicuous seat or platform; a grand temple or mansion approached by steps; in Buddhism, a monastic hall for assembly and confession.

See also: **fǎtáng**.

pravachana (S), **pravacana** (Pa) *Lit.* foremost *(pra-)* words *(vachana);* excellent words; a sermon or spiritual discourse; in Buddhism, a scripture believed to be either the actual words of the Buddha *(buddhavachana)* or containing a correct presentation of his teachings; in Jainism, a sermon or spiritual discourse given by a monk or (among *Digambaras*) by an advanced layperson. Some *Shvetāmbara* nuns *(sādhvīs)* are also permitted to give discourses. Jain monks are generally expected to lead itinerant and mendicant lives for eight months of the year, remaining in one place during the four months *(chaturmāsa)* of the rainy season. During their travels, sermons are delivered at the request of the laity; during the rainy season, discourses are delivered daily at the place of residence, usually by the most senior monk present, often as a series based upon one particular text.

See also: **buddhavachana**, **vachana**.

raft parable, raft simile A frequently cited example given by the Buddha to illustrate that the *Dharma* – the path and the body of teachings – are not an end in themselves. They are not the goal, but are intended to help in reaching liberation and enlightenment.

The parable appears in the *Alagaddūpama Sutta* ('Parable of the Water Snake *Sutta*'). The essence of the story is of a traveller who wishes to cross from the dangerous bank of an expanse of water (*saṃsāra,* transmigration) to the other bank (*nirvāṇa,* enlightenment), which is peaceful. To do so, he makes a raft or coracle for himself out of grass, twigs, branches, and large leaves, and paddles across using his hands and feet. The Buddha then asks his disciples whether or not it would make sense for the man to carry the raft, once he had safely reached the other bank:

> "*Bhikkhus* (monks), I shall show you how the *Dhamma* is similar to a raft, being for the purpose of crossing over, not for the purpose of grasping. Listen and attend closely to what I shall say."
>
> "Yes, venerable sir," the *bhikkhus* replied.
>
> The Blessed One said this: "*Bhikkhus,* suppose a man in the course of a journey comes to a great expanse of water, whose near shore is perilous and fearful, while the other shore is safe and free from danger; but there is no ferryboat or bridge by which to cross over to the other shore. He therefore thinks: 'Here is this great expanse of water, whose near shore is perilous and fearful, while the other shore is safe and free from danger; but there is no ferryboat or bridge by which to cross over to the other shore. Suppose I collect grass, twigs, branches, and leaves and bind them together into a raft, and supported by the raft and labouring with my hands and feet, I cross safely to the other shore.'
>
> "And so the man collects grass, twigs, branches, and leaves and binds them together into a raft, and supported by the raft and labouring with his hands and feet, he crosses safely to the other shore. Then, when he has crossed over and arrived at the other shore, he thinks: 'This raft has been very helpful to me, for with its support and by labouring with my hands and feet, I have crossed safely to the other shore. Now suppose I were to hoist it onto my head or load it on my

shoulders, and then go wherever I want to go.' Now, *bhikkhus,* what do you think? By doing so, would that man be doing what should be done with that raft?"

"No, venerable sir."

"What then, *bhikkhus,* would be the right thing to do with the raft? In this case, *bhikkhus,* when that man has crossed and has arrived at the other shore, he might think: 'This raft has been very helpful to me, for with its support and by labouring with my hands and feet, I have crossed over in safety to the other shore. Suppose I were to haul it onto the dry land or set it adrift in the water, and then go wherever I want to go.' Now, *bhikkhus,* it is by doing this that that man would be doing what should be done with that raft. So I have shown you how the *Dhamma* is similar to a raft, being for the purpose of crossing over, not for the purpose of grasping.

"*Bhikkhus,* when you know the *Dhamma* to be similar to a raft, you should let go even of the teachings *(dhammas),* to say nothing of false teachings *(adhammas)."*

Majjhima Nikāya 22, Alagaddūpama Sutta, PTSM1 pp.134–35; cf. MDBB pp.228–29, MNNP

This parable follows on from the parable of the snake, and is a part of the same thought process. The Buddha observes that if a man goes in search of a snake, but when he finds one, he grasps it by the tail, then the snake will coil around his arm and bite him. The correct way to take hold of a snake is behind its head, so that it cannot bite the one who holds it. In the same way, those who learn the *Dhamma* for the sake of showing off, or for argument, or to criticize others are like those who grasp a snake by the tail. It will do them no good, and they will get bitten by it. On the other hand, those who grasp the snake in the right way are like those who correctly grasp the real meaning of the *Dhamma* and put it into practice. They are the ones who will truly benefit from the *Dhamma.*[1]

The parable of the raft illustrates the case of those who fail to use the *Dhamma* in the right way, but carry it around on their heads, rather than enjoying the peace and safety that it can bring to them. The point is that the form of the *Dhamma* is only a means to an end; it is not a dogma to be adhered to, but only a helper along the way. This does not mean that the moral precepts or other aspects of the path are to be abandoned once the goal is reached. It implies that once the Reality has become an experience, the essence of the *Dhamma* is then known and lived, rather than believed in and applied. The religious or doctrinal perspective of the *Dhamma* is replaced by direct spiritual experience.

The parable is also an example of 'expedient means *(upāya-kaushalya)*'. It highlights the fact that having a conceptual understanding of the *Dhamma* and of Reality is simply a means that leads to the cessation of suffering. The *Dhamma* is not something to cling to; rather it needs to be let go of when its purpose has been fulfilled. Clinging to doctrine and the outer aspects of the *Dhamma* is like carrying the raft on one's back.

See also: **upāya-kaushalya**.

1. *Majjhima Nikāya* 22, *Alagaddūpama Sutta, PTSM1* pp.133–34, *MDBB* pp.227–28.

re´aḥ (He) *Lit.* fragrance; mystically, divine grace and blessing; more specifically, the spiritual fragrance or blessing emanating from the Tree of Life, which symbolizes the divine creative power; the spiritual fragrance or perfume emanating from spiritually elevated souls; related to *ru´aḥ* (wind, spirit, Breath of God), the second level of the soul as described in the Kabbalah.

Spiritual purity manifests as a fragrance so subtle that it is perceptible only to another spiritually awakened and sensitive soul. Jewish mystics have written of their experience of the fragrance emanating from their spiritual masters. The *Zohar* recounts that when three legendary rabbis died, a scent of perfume was exuded everywhere. Then Rabbi Simeon himself disappeared, and in his place wafted the scent of "perfumes from the spices of the Garden of Eden":

> Rabbi Simeon said something, and his visitors realized that he was no longer present. They were astounded, and none of them could utter a single word because of the deep fear that had fallen upon them. While they were sitting there, perfumes from many spices wafted over them, and they began to regain their courage, and at last they saw Rabbi Simeon talking, but they did not see anyone else except him. After a while Rabbi Simeon said to them: "Did you see anything?"
>
> "No," said Rabbi Pinḥas, "but we were all astounded that we could not see you for a long time in your sickroom. And when we did see you, perfumes from the spices of the Garden of Eden wafted over us, and we heard your voice speaking, but we do not know with whom you were talking."
>
> *Zohar Ḥadash, Bereshit 29b–d, Midrash ha-Ne'elam, in HFJD p.155*

See also: **fragrance** (▸3), **re´aḥ** (▸3).

ribāṭ (A) *Lit.* binding; fort, stronghold; hospice, hostel, caravanserai; a small frontier post housing military volunteers, where relays of horses were also kept, built during the first years of the Muslim conquest of North Africa, later serving to protect trade routes, and acting as centres for isolated Muslim communities; evolving into hostels or caravanserais for travellers, and spiritual retreats; becoming an Arabic name for a Sufi meeting place or place of communal residence, as Sufism spread into North Africa, and from there, across the Sahara to West Africa; hence also, the home of a religious (usually Sufi) teacher *(murābiṭ,* marabout, one who lives in a *ribāṭ)* in North and West Africa;[1] also, a hospice for the poor and elderly.

Ribāṭ comes from the verb *rabaṭa* (to bind). Garrison duty at the frontiers of Islam was regarded as a pious duty. In later Islam, those who performed this duty of vigilance were called *al-murābiṭūn* (those of the *ribāṭ, lit.* bound ones), since they were bound to their duty at the *ribāṭ. Al-Murābiṭūn* later became the name adopted by the Muslim Berbers who founded an empire during the eleventh century CE extending from what are now Western Sahara, Mauritania, Mali, and Morocco to southern Spain and Portugal. The most famous of their forts was known as Ribāṭ al-Faṭh (the camp of victory), which has given its name to the present capital of Morocco – Rabat.

The historian Maqrīzī (1364–1442 CE) says that a *ribāṭ* is "a place wherein dwell the people of the Way". The name, he maintains, came from the tying up or binding up of horses, each one separately, and was later adopted as the name for the religious houses of the Sufis, who shared one dwelling, and were in this sense like the homeless. The inhabitants, he says, had a single purpose, and lived in a manner befitting their calling.[2]

See also: **khānaqāh**.

1. See "Ribat," *Wikipedia,* ret. December 2010.
2. Maqrīzī, *al-Khiṭaṭ* 2, *KMA4* p.302, in *RM* p.172.

risālah (A), **risālat** (P) (pl. *rasā'il) Lit.* messengership, apostleship, apostolate, mission; also, treatise, essay, discourse, letter, as in the titles of many Persian and Arabic books (*e.g.* 'Treatise on…'); from *rasila* (to send – specifically, a missive, message, or letter); the prophetic mission or ministry of a *rasūl,* a divine messenger, a term that shares the same derivation; also called *nubuwwah* (prophecy), *payghambarī* (messengership).

The term is generally applied to the mission of Muḥammad, but can also be applied to that of other messengers:

> Apostolate *(risālah)* signifies God's sending a perfect man *(insān)* to His devotees, whether to preach to them or not; in either case, apostolate *(risālah)* is in the same category as prophecy *(nubuwwah).* Sometimes an apostolate *(risālah)* may be specifically for the preaching of religion, or the descent of Gabriel, or for the revelation of a

book or new law, or to introduce a law that abrogates previous laws brought by previous prophets *(anbiyā')*.

Tahānawī, Kashshāf Iṣṭilāḥāt al-Funūn, KIFT2 p.255; cf. in SSE3 p.58

For Rūmī, prophecy and prophethood usually refers to the perfect saints, whenever they may have come. All sainthood originates with God:

Consort with Him who created human nature
and fostered the natures of the prophets *(khū'hā-yi anbiyā')*.
If you give Him a lamb,
He will give you back a flock:
Truly, the Lord is the fosterer of every good quality.

Rūmī, Maśnavī VI:1420–21, MJR6 p.337

See also: **nubuwwah**, **rasūl** (7.1).

samava-sharaṇa (S) *Lit.* refuge *(sharaṇa)* for all *(samava);* a square or circular enclosure or assembly hall in which a Jain *Tīrthankara* teaches and delivers discourses after attaining *kevala-jñāna* (knowledge of the Absolute, omniscience). According to traditional belief, the hall is built by the gods soon after the *Tīrthankara* has reached enlightenment. He sits on a jewelled throne, located upon a circular, three-tiered dais in the centre of the hall, simultaneously facing all directions. The hall is surrounded by three walls. Monks and deities *(devas)* sit in the innermost enclosure, with animals between the second and third walls. In descriptions reminiscent of the characteristics of a *buddha,* hostility, anger and jealousy, together with diseases and sights of an unpleasant worldly nature are all absent from the halls and the surrounding area. *Samava-sharaṇas* feature prominently in Jain art, and large-scale reproductions may be erected in temple compounds, especially pilgrimage sites.[1]

1. See "samavasaraṇa," *A–Z of Jainism, AZJW.*

saṃgha (S), **sangha** (H/Pa), **sogya** (J), **dge 'dun** (T) *Lit.* group, collection; congregation, community, brotherhood; multitude, assemblage; the Jain and Buddhist term either for a particular community of disciples, followers or monks, or for the followers of a particular Jain or Buddhist school.

In Jainism, the term is used in several ways. The Jain *sangha* is said to have four main divisions: monks *(sādhus),* nuns *(sādhvīs),* laymen *(shrāvakas),* and laywomen *(shrāvikās)*. Together they comprise the complete community *(sakala sangha)*. Sometimes, just the community of monks and nuns is known as the *sangha.* Particular orders of *Digambara* and *Sthānakavāsī*

(Shvetāmbara) monks or nuns are also known as *sanghas*. The *Mūla Sangha,* for instance, is the main extant order of *Digambara* monks, which is further subdivided into four main groups or *gaṇas.*[1]

The Jain *sangha* is understood as the foundation upon which spiritual progress is based:

> A *sangha* is the accumulation of virtues: a *sangha* frees people from the pollution of *karma,* and unites right faith, right knowledge, and right conduct....
>
> The *sangha* grants assurance, evokes confidence, and gives peace like a cool chamber. It is affectionate like the parents and affords shelter to all living beings. So be not afraid of the *sangha.*
>
> Blessed are those who reside lifelong in their preceptor's entourage as they acquire knowledge and specially attain stability in faith and conduct.
>
> What is the use of residing in the preceptor's entourage for him who does not have a sense of devotion, respect, reverence, regard and affection, and feels no awe of his preceptor.
>
> May the lotuslike *sangha* prosper – keeping itself aloof from the karmic dirt just as a lotus keeps itself away from the mud and water. The *sangha* is a lotus whose long stalk is scriptures, the pericarp is represented by the five great vows, the filaments are the other virtues, and the petals are the *munis* (monks). As black bees hover around the lotus, similarly householders frequent the *sanghas.* As the lotus blossoms on account of the sun's rays, similarly the *sangha* grows on account of the precepts of the *Jina* ('conqueror', enlightened one).
>
> *Samansuttam 25, 27–31; cf. SSJV*

The origin of the term in Buddhism stems from the time of the Buddha. According to tradition, the *sangha* came into being when the Buddha taught the *Dharmachakra-Pravartana Sūtra* ('Turning the Wheel of the Law *Sūtra*') to five men who had been his companions while he was practising the intense asceticism that led to his enlightenment. These were his first five disciples, and from this time forward, the *sangha* began to grow, attracting people from all walks of life, from the poor to wealthy merchants and kings.

After the death of the Buddha, with the passage of time, the *sangha* developed a more pronounced organizational hierarchy, resulting inevitably in disagreements that lead to schisms and the formation of the various Buddhist schools. The spread of Buddhism throughout Sri Lanka, India, Tibet, China, Korea, Thailand, Burma, Japan and elsewhere likewise gave rise to different teachings and groupings within the *sangha,* all differing in some respects, yet all founded upon the same basic teachings of the Buddha – the quest for *nirvāṇa* (extinction of desire, tranquillity).

According to the traditional Buddhist history, around a hundred years after the Buddha's death, certain differences of opinion arose in the *sangha,* leading gradually to the development of a number of monastic groups or fraternities *(nikāyas).* Each had developed differing monastic codes and schools of thought *(vādas).* Although all branches of Buddhism trace their origins to these early fraternities, the only one to have survived to present times is the school that has become known as *Theravāda* ('Path of the Elders').

Sangha is used in several senses. Originally, the *sangha* referred to the fourfold community of monks *(bhikkhus),* nuns *(bhikkhuṇīs),* laymen *(upāsakas),* and laywomen *(upāsikās).* More restrictively, *sangha* came to mean the *pātimokkha-sangha* (monastic-code *sangha*), the community of ordained monks and nuns, whatever their attainment, who follow over 200 rules of monastic conduct. The laity, on the other hand, are expected to adhere only to the *pañca-sīla* (five moral precepts). There is also the *ariya-sangha* (noble *sangha*), comprised of those noble persons *(ariya-puggala)* – lay or otherwise – who have at least reached the level of *sotāpanna* (stream-enterer), the 'stream' being the noble Path *(ariya-magga)* that leads to enlightenment. In more recent times, especially in the West, *sangha* or *mahāsangha* (greater *sangha*) is used for the community of all Buddhists. There is also the *bodhisattva-sangha,* a name for the eight foremost *bodhisattvas.*

The *sangha* is one of the three jewels or three precious things *(ratanattaya),* faith in which is a basic requirement for acceptance into the *sangha.* The three jewels are the Buddha himself – the teacher of the Path; the *Dhamma* – his teachings and the Path itself; and the *sangha.* These three are mentioned in one of the earliest Buddhist texts, the *Dhammapada:*

> But he who takes refuge in the Buddha, the *Dhamma,* and the *sangha,*
> he perceives, in his clear wisdom, the four noble truths:
> Suffering, the origin of suffering, the cessation of suffering,
> and the noble eightfold path which leads to the cessation of suffering.
> That indeed is a safe refuge, that is the best refuge:
> by attaining such a refuge, one is delivered from all suffering.
>
> *Dhammapada 14:12–14; cf. DPN, DPR*

Taking refuge in the *sangha* implies that the *sangha* is for mutual support on the spiritual path. It is for this reason, says the Buddha, that a united and harmonious *sangha* is a happy and blessed *sangha:*

> Blessed is the birth of the *buddhas;*
> Blessed is the teaching of the true *Dhamma;*
> Blessed is harmony in the *sangha* (community);
> Blessed is the discipline of those who live in harmony.
>
> *Dhammapada 14:16; cf. DPN, DPR*

The *Dhammapada* also says that a good disciple who is spiritually awake always keeps in mind the spiritual values represented by the *sangha* of which he is a part:

> The disciples of Gotama are always wide awake:
> day and night, their thought remains focused upon the *sangha.*
>
> *Dhammapada 21:9*

Nevertheless, since all human beings have different natures, a greater or lesser degree of disharmony is inevitably prevalent in most human societies, spiritual or otherwise. Disharmony, however, cuts at the root of spirituality, and it is clear that the Buddha advocated harmony for the sake of both happiness and spiritual progress:

> One thing, when arising in the world, arises for the detriment of many, for the unhappiness of many, for the detriment and unhappiness of many beings, both human and divine. Which one thing? Schism in the *sangha.* When the *sangha* is divided, there are arguments with one another, there is abuse of one another, ganging up on one another, abandoning of one another. Then those with little confidence lose all confidence, while some of those who are confident become otherwise:
>
> Doomed for an aeon to deprivation, to hell,
> is he who has divided the *sangha.*
> Delighting in factions, injudicious –
> he is barred from safety from bondage.
> Having disturbed the harmony of the *sangha,*
> he cooks for an aeon in hell....
>
> Blissful is harmony in the *sangha.*
> He who assists in harmony – delighting in harmony, judicious –
> is not barred from safety from bondage.
> Having brought harmony to the *sangha,*
> he rejoices for an aeon in heaven.
>
> *Itivuttaka 18–19, PTSI pp.10–12; cf. KNTB*

A monk who finds himself in a harmonious situation is aware that the situation can change, making meditation difficult. The wise monk therefore seeks enlightenment now, so that should things change for the worse, he will remain unaffected. He thinks to himself:

> At present, the *sangha* – in harmony, on friendly terms, without quarrelling – lives in comfort with a single recitation (*i.e.* monks of a

particular *sangha* come together fortnightly to hear a recitation of the *pātimokkha,* the monastic code). The time will come, however, when the *sangha* will split. When the *sangha* is split, it is not easy to pay attention to the Buddha's teachings. It is not easy to reside in isolated forest or wilderness dwellings. Before this unwelcome, disagreeable, displeasing thing happens, let me first make an effort for the attaining of the as-yet-unattained, the reaching of the as-yet-unreached, the realization of the as-yet-unrealized, so that – endowed with that *Dhamma* – I will live in peace even when the *sangha* is split.

Anguttara Nikāya 5:78, Anāgata-Bhayani Sutta, PTSA3 p.105, ANTB

See also: **sanga, satsanga**.

1. See "saṅgha," *A–Z of Jainism, AZJW.*

sampradāy(a) (S/H) *Lit.* rightly transmitted; that which is correctly passed on; from the verb *saṃpradā* (to offer completely, to transmit); a bestower, a presenter; a tradition; an established and living doctrine, teaching, belief and practice, transmitted in an unbroken line from one teacher and his pupils to another, often within the framework of a more encompassing religious or spiritual tradition; a particular school of thought and spiritual practice; a means of preserving the vitality of a teaching and practice; a way to preserve the treasures of the past; "the uninterrupted succession of pupils and teachers by which scriptural knowledge is conserved and transmitted;"[1] often named after the originator of the *sampradāya,* such as the Vedantist Nimbārka (founder of the *dvaitādvaita* or duality in unity school) and Rāmānuja (founder of *Vishishṭa Advaita* or qualified non-dualism school), or after a *sant* (saint) such as Kabīr; used to identify a particular group, such as the *nātha-sampradāya* or the *siddha-sampradāya* – *nāthas* and *siddhas* being particular kinds of yogic and tantric practitioners; also, a term used for mendicant lineages by Jain *Sthānakavāsīs* (hall-dwellers).

See also: **gachchha**, **pantha** (▸4).

1. Uddyotakara, *Nyāya-Vārttika,* in *PU* p.288.

samudāya (S) *Lit.* emerging *(udāya)* together *(sam);* co-arising; those having the same origin; a Jain term for a present-day, autonomous sub-lineage of *Shvetāmbara Mūrtipūjaka* monks, each with its own *gachchhādhipati* (leader) within a larger group *(gachchha).* Each *samudāya* (which can include several *āchāryas* or teachers) may be further subdivided into smaller groups of monks who travel together. These smaller groups are known as *parivāras,* each with their own *āchārya*. A *samudāya* originates due to the practicalities of location or the attractive power of a charismatic or of a truly spiritual leader.[1]

See also: **gachchha**, **parivāra**.

1. See "samudāya," *A to Z of Jainism, AZJW.*

sang(a) (S/H/Pu), **samāgama**, **sat-samāgama** (S), **sangati** (S/H), **satsangat(i)** (H), **sangat** (H/Pu) *Lit.* coming together *(sanga, samāgama);* joining, meeting, union, association; company, contact; attachment, affection, desire;[1] company of a holy man or saint *(sādhu, sant).* Since the mind is powerfully affected by the company a person keeps, Indian traditions recommend or insist that the company of a *sādhu, sant, guru* or holy man is essential for making spiritual progress. The terms appear in a wide variety of combinations, such as *sādhu-sang, sādhu-samāgama, sādhu-sangati, sādhsang, sādh-sangat, sādh kī sangat, sādhū kai sang, sādh kai sang, sangat sādh kī,* and *sant-sang,* which all mean the company of saints or holy men. There are also the terms *su-sanga* (good company) and *du-sanga* (bad company).

The company of saints is listed as one of the essential aspects of developing true devotion *(bhakti)* for the Divine. The *Adhyātma Rāmāyaṇa* lists nine such aspects or limbs:

1. Association with holy men *(satām sangati).*
2. Remembering and talking about God.
3. Praising the glories of God.
4. Elucidation of scriptures.
5. Devoted service to one's *guru,* and seeing God in him.
6. Steadfast daily worship of God.
7. Repetition of a sacred *mantra.*
8. Worshipful service of devotees.
9. Discussion of spiritual truths.[2]

Of these nine, association with other devotees and with one's *guru* are regarded as the most essential. The *Yoga-Vāsishṭha* is elaborate in extolling the benefits of the company of saints:

> The company of saints *(sādhu-samāgama)* is everywhere of the greatest benefit to men for crossing over the ocean of the world. It is the arbour of the company of the saints *(sādhu-sangata)* that produces the fresh blossom of discrimination; that being cherished by high-souled men, yields to them its fruits of prosperity.... It is the society of saints *(sādhu-samāgama)* that wards off all tribulations (that otherwise

invade the lotus beds of our hearts like frost) and thwarts the icy breath of (spiritual) ignorance.

Know the society of the holy *(sādhu-samāgama)* to be the best improver of the understanding, the destroyer of the tree of ignorance, and the remover of all our mental ailments. The society of the holy *(sādhu-sanga)* produces the light of reason, as charming and fair as a cluster of flowers washed by rainwater. It is the influence of holy company *(sādhu-sanga)* that teaches us the best way to live, never impaired or obstructed by anything, and ever full in itself.

Let no man ever keep himself from association with the holy *(sādhu-sangati),* though he may find himself in utmost distress, and cast in the direst of circumstances. The society of the holy *(sādhu-sangata)* sheds light upon the right path. It destroys the internal darkness of man by the rays of the sun of knowledge.

Whoever has bathed in the cold, clear stream of good company *(sādhu-sangati)* is not in need of the merit derived from acts of charity, pilgrimage, austerity, and sacrifice. Of what use are austerities or pilgrimage to those who enjoy (the company of) holy men *(sādhus),* and whose lives are free from passions and sins, doubts and tangles? Blessed are the peaceful in mind, whom (wise) people regard with as great an ardour as (unwise) people fondly dote upon gems and jewels.

The intelligent mind, with a gracefulness derived from good company *(sat-samāgama),* always shines like the goddess of riches *(Kamalā)* in the company of fairy nymphs *(apsaras).* Therefore, that blessed man is renowned as having attained the crown of a clear understanding who never absents himself from the company of the holy *(sādhu-sangati).*

Hence devout believers, holy men and those revered by people should be served in every way as a means of crossing over the ocean of the world. Those who neglect the company of the saints *(santo),* which is known to be like rainwater that extinguishes the flames of hell, surely serve as dry fuel for hellfire. The medicine of holy association *(sādhu-samāgāma)* serves to allay entirely all the afflictions arising from poverty and death, and the tribulations of worldly affairs.

Yoga-Vāsishṭha 2:16.1–2, 4–17; cf. YVV1 pp.131–33

While the company of holy men elevates the mind, keeping company with the materially minded can lead to worldliness. According to a Vaishnavite devotional work, the *Nārada Bhakti Sūtras:*

Evil company *(du-sanga)* is to be avoided by every means, for it leads to lust, anger, attachment, loss of remembrance, loss of discrimination, and ultimately to utter ruin. Arising first as ripples, by company

> *(sanga),* these things become like an ocean. Who crosses over? Who crosses over *māyā* (illusion)? – He who relinquishes such company *(sanga),* who serves a person of great spirituality *(mahānubhāva),* and is free of all worldliness.
>
> *Nārada, Bhakti Sūtras 43–46; cf. NBST pp.11–12*

The *Haṭha Yoga Pradīpikā* and *Shiva Saṃhitā* both identify worldly company as a negative influence on spiritual progress:

> Overeating, exertion, talkativeness, adhering to rules, being in the company of common people and a vacillating mind are the six things that destroy *yoga.*
>
> Enthusiasm, perseverance, discrimination, unshakable faith, courage, and avoiding the company *(sanga)* of common people, are the six things that lead to success in *yoga.*
>
> *Haṭha Yoga Pradīpikā 1:15–16; cf. HYPM pp.50, 54*

> When in a gathering *(saṃsad),* the wise *yogī* should utter words of the highest wisdom, but he should not talk much. He should eat little, sufficient to maintain his physical frame. And he should renounce human company *(sanga):* let him firmly renounce it, otherwise he cannot attain *mukti* (salvation). Verily, I tell you the truth.
>
> *Shiva Saṃhitā 5:184; cf. SSV p.82*

Many of the mystics and devotees of the *sant* tradition have also spoken of the benefits of the saints' company. The *darshana* (sight, vision) and company of a true holy man, together with initiation into the divine Word, the "one Letter", lead to God and escape from rebirth:

> Whoever has his *darshana* in silence, merges in the boundless Supreme,
> crossing the ocean of birth and death.
> Good deeds and religious observances are of no avail:
> only the company of saints *(sādhu-sang)* can help.
> Initiation *(dīkshā),* duty with detachment *(nishkāma dharma),*
> and devotion *(bhajana)* to the one Letter *(eka Akshara)* help.
> Where God reigns, there is no rising or setting:
> says the helpless Bhīma, the darkness is otherwise impenetrable!
>
> *Bhīma Bhoi, Tahanku Jebana; cf. in SSI8 pp.268–69*

Things take on the characteristics of whatever they associate with, good or bad:

> Just as a Malayagiri sandalwood tree imparts its fragrance to the tree near it, and makes it also sweet-scented, similarly those who frequent

the company of a *sādh,* escape from the afflictions of the world and one day become *sādhs* themselves. Blessed are those who enjoy *sādhsang* (company of *sādhs*) and thus make the best use of the human life.

Swami Shiv Dayal Singh, Sār Bachan Prose 2:233, SBAT p.127

Something becomes sweet when mixed with sugar,
it becomes salty when mixed with salt.
O Dādū, such is human nature, such indeed is the way we are....

In the company *(milai)* of the unholy *(asādh),* a barrier is created,
and the taste of piety and devotion disappears.
In the company *(milai)* of the holy *(sādh),* bliss is generated,
and one overflows with joy.

If obtained, it bears the divine fruit of immortality.
But if the company *(sangati)* of the worldly *(sansārī)* is obtained,
it yields the fruit of poison, says Dādū.

In the assembly *(sabhā)* of a saint *(sant),* noble thoughts arise,
but while sitting in the assembly *(sabhā)* of worldly people *(sākat),*
knowledge parts company with the body....

That which does not arouse piety and devotion,
wherein the Lord is not talked about,
whereby the blemishes of sensuality are not shaken off,
by what measure can that be called *satsang* (true association)?

Dādū, Parchā ko Ang 188, Sādh ko Ang 68–70, Sāch ko Ang 134, DDB1 pp.59, 154–55, 138; cf. DCMU pp.80–81

The company of a saint inspires the heart with bliss. Fortunate are those who are able to enjoy such an opportunity:

The company *(samāj)* of a saint *(sant)*
is always the source of the highest bliss,
where the glory of devotion descends on one's head....
Only the fortunate ones recognize the value
of such holy company *(sādhu sangati),*
where they shed their evil thoughts.
They thus become pure and, through their own mouths,
they begin to utter words of praise for true company *(sat ankā).*

Dariyā Sāhib, Gyān Ratan, Chaupāī 1721, DG2 p.233, Gyān Dīpak 461–62, GDDS p.97; cf. DSSK pp.235–36

To meet a master is a significant landmark on the spiritual journey. Until then, the mind flits from one thing to another, constantly distracted, to such an extent that it is a rare person who truly understands the nature of life and its purpose:

> The mind becomes pure *(shuddha),*
> the mind finds its true direction,
> in the company of a mystic *(santa sangha).*
> To discover your own essence –
> this is why you serve a master.
> In the company of mystics *(santa sangha),*
> faults are destroyed and the ego dies.
> In the company of mystics *(santa sangha),*
> you will see your true self, the secret will be known.
> Discovering your self, you will discover liberation.
> Be with one who is bound to none, says Bahiṇā –
> then you will learn the art of meditation.
>
> *Bahiṇābāī, Gāthā 220, BBAV p.264, in MVOS p.275*

The company of a saint is entirely transformative. It brings joy, inspiration and leads ultimately to liberation:

> The company of the saints *(satsangat)* is the root of joy and blessings:
> spiritual endeavours are its flowers, and its fruit is perfection.
> Even the wicked are reformed by the company of the saints *(satsangati),*
> as base metal is transmuted by the touch of the philosopher's stone....
>
> The company of the saint *(sant-sang)* is the road to salvation,
> while that of the sensualist paves the way to endless transmigration;
> So say the saints, wise men, and the learned,
> as well as the *Vedas,* the *Purāṇas,* and other scriptures.
>
> *Tulsīdās, Rām Charit Mānas 1:2.4–5, 7:33; cf. RCML pp.6–7, 990*

> It is only with the grace of God, O Tulsī,
> that the saint's company *(su-sang),* like the holy Ganges, is obtained.
> Any water flowing into the Ganges becomes the Ganges:
> likewise, whoever comes to the saint becomes a saint.
>
> *Tulsīdās, Dohāvalī 363, DTDG p.122; cf. TGTD p.192*

> The company of a saint *(sādhsang)* brings light and dispels darkness:
> but such company is difficult to obtain....
> *Sādhsang* is a true place of pilgrimage
> where the water of discernment flows;

Bathing in it, one attains all four goals *(chār padarath)* (of Hindu life),
and thus attains salvation.
Whosoever comes to the *satsang* of a saint *(sādh)*
loses the sense of caste, creed and colour,
just as muddy waters that become pure and clear
by joining the Ganges.
Through the company of saints *(sādh-sangat),*
a crow becomes a swan (*hans,* pure soul):
Giving up filthy food, it picks up pearls as its repast.

Sahajobāī, Bānī, Sādh Mahimā 6, 8–10, SBB p.12; cf. in PMS1 p.135

Those who have kept company with a saint find that he is there to help them at the time of death:

O Kabīr, to obtain help at the time of death,
keep the company *(sangat)* of saints *(sādh).*
Shun the company of the wicked, which causes dismay at the end.

Kabīr, Samagra 140, KSS1 p.519; cf. in PMS1 p.117

It is through the company of saints that the soul can come into contact with the divine Name or Word, the creative power of God that draws souls out of the cycle of rebirth and back to their original home. According to Indian belief, a person acquires merit by visiting pilgrimage places. The saints counter this by saying that "pilgrimage" to the "holy feet" of a saint – meaning ascent to his inner spiritual form and consequent contact with the divine power – is what truly destroys the *karma* of previous births:

(The merit of) millions of pilgrimages
are contained in a *sādhu*'s holy feet:
all sins are destroyed by devotion to those feet.
All places of pilgrimage are said to be located near a *sādhu,*
yet the world wanders in delusion.
A person who has not realized the Name remains in delusion,
and moment by moment loses his (spiritual) capital....
O brother, develop love for a saint:
seeing and loving a saint is never in vain.

Dariyā Sāhib, Dariyā Sāgar, Chaupāī 455–57, 916, DG2 pp.45, 92; cf. DSSK p.236

Conversely, remaining away from the influence of saints leads to misfortune and lost opportunity:

You never kept the company *(sādh)* (of saints):
you have frittered away the wealth of a human birth
that was in your hands.

You did not realize the value of the company of saints *(sādhu sang):*
you have frittered away the fortune that lay in your hands.
Now hell will be your home,
for day and night you kept company *(pāsā)* with the vile and false.
Seeing everyone rushing to his doom, Kabīr loudly calls:
"Wake up, wake up, O men! You are being robbed in broad daylight."

Kabīr, Bījak, Ramainī 44, KSB p.17; cf. KWGN p.414

How can you be saved when you don't accept the way out?
The *satguru* has come as your benefactor,
but you do not cherish his company *(sang).*
He is the merciful Lord,
he will teach you the method to free yourself.
He is always busy cutting the heavy chains
of the five elements and three *guṇas.*
Overcome your misgivings, seek his company *(sangat),*
and you'll find yourself in a state of unique bliss.
Believe me, this whole world is a web of deceit,
and you have made friends *(yārī)* with the foolish mind.
Keep trying, every moment, to give up its company *(sang),*
or it will take possession of your soul.
Then you will drift farther away from your home,
and be tossed around in the cycle of birth and death.

Swami Shiv Dayal Singh, Sār Bachan Poetry 15:11.8–15, SBP p.120, SBPS pp.146–49

Of your close companions, not one is your true friend.
Why are you sleeping among these thieves *(ṭhagiyan)?*
Wake up, and find love in the *satsang:*
then the *guru* will dye you in the hueless hue of *Nām.*

Swami Shiv Dayal Singh, Sār Bachan Poetry 15:5.1–2, SBP p.116; cf. in DL p.85

Nonetheless, the mind is driven by the impetus of past habit and even in the company of a saint, it can take a long time to really change its character:

If all this fails to convince your mind,
then you are on your own – do as you like!
You are under the control of *Kāl* (negative power, universal mind),
and that is why your mind fails to respond.
One thing I have learned about you, brother,
is that you are remarkably dishonest with yourself.
Even so, if you continue to keep the master's company *(sang),*
your mind may gradually come around.

Swami Shiv Dayal Singh, Sār Bachan Poetry 18:12.17–20,
SBP pp.140–41, SBPS pp.190–91

The company of a saint *(sādh kai sang, sādhū kai sang, sādhsang),* as Guru Arjun says in the *Ādi Granth,* results in a great many benefits:

This human body has been given to you:
  this is your chance to meet the Lord of the universe.
Nothing else will work:
Join the *sādh-sangat* (company of the saints),
  contemplate on the Name alone.

Guru Arjun, Ādi Granth 12, AGK

Lord's meditation is attained
  in the *sādh kai sang* (company of the saints):
All wealth, O Nānak, is in God's love.

Guru Arjun, Ādi Granth 262, AGK

By meditating on God, the supreme joy,
  in the company of saints *(sādhsang),*
  you shall have salvation, happiness, calmness, and bliss

Guru Arjun, Ādi Granth 295, MMS

In the *sādh kai sang* (company of the saints),
  one's face becomes radiant;
In the *sādhsang,* all impurity is shed;
In the *sādh kai sang,* egotism is eliminated;...
  God is understood to be near at hand;...
  all conflicts are settled;...
  one obtains the jewel of *Nām;*...
  one's efforts are directed toward the one Lord.
What mortal can speak of the glorious praises of the *sādhs* (saints)?
O Nānak, the glory of the *sādhs* merges into God.

In the *sādh kai sang* (company of the saints),...
  one meets the incomprehensible Lord;...
  the five passions are brought to rest;...
  one enjoys the essence of ambrosia;...
  one becomes the dust of all;...
  one's speech is enticing;...
  the mind does not wander;...
  the mind becomes stable;...
  one is rid of *māyā;*
In the *sādhsang,*
  O Nānak, God is totally pleased.

In the *sādhsang,* all one's enemies become friends;...
there is great purity;...
no one is hated;...
no one seems evil;...
supreme bliss is known;...
the fever of ego departs;...
one renounces all selfishness;
He Himself knows the greatness of the *sādhs* (saints):
O Nānak, the *sādhs* are at one with God.

In the *sādh kai sang,* one obtains everlasting peace;...
one grasps the incomprehensible;...
one can endure the unendurable;...
one attains the mansion of the Lord's presence;...
one dwells with the supreme Lord God;...
one obtains the treasure of the Name *(Nām).*
O Nānak, I am a sacrifice to *sādhūs* (saints).

Guru Arjun, Ādi Granth 271, AGK

In the *sādh kai sang,* there is no suffering,
their *darshan (darsan)* brings a sublime, happy peace.
In the *sādh kai sang,* blemishes are removed;...
hell is far away;...
one is happy here and hereafter;...
the separated ones are reunited with the Lord,
and the fruits of one's desires are obtained;...
no one goes empty-handed.
The supreme Lord God dwells in the hearts of the *sādhs* (saints):
O Nānak, listening to the sweet words of the *sādhs* (saints),
one is saved.

Guru Arjun, Ādi Granth 272, AGK

In the *sādh kai sang* (company of the saints),
listen to the Name of the Lord;...
sing the glorious praises of the Lord;...
do not forget Him from your mind;...
you shall surely be saved;...
God seems very sweet;...
He is seen in each and every heart;...
we become obedient to the Lord;...
we obtain the state of salvation;...
all diseases are cured.
O Nānak, one meets with the *sādh* (saints) by highest destiny.

Guru Arjun, Ādi Granth 272, AGK

It is sometimes said in Indian tradition that if one person in a family keeps the company of a saint, then this will result in salvation for several generations of the entire family. But this does not mean that family members can behave as they please and the saint will take care of them. When someone in a family meets a saint and starts to follow a spiritual path and to meditate, this may inspire other family members to do likewise. Through their attachment they are also drawn to the saint. It is only in this sense that the belief can have any true meaning. To attain salvation, all souls have to follow and practise the spiritual path for themselves. No one else can do this for them. It is also said that the company of a true saint eliminates past *karma.* This is because the company of a saint draws the soul inside, to his inner company, which is where *karma* is truly destroyed. Mere external company alone does not destroy *karma:*

In the *sādh kai sang,* all one's family are saved....
one's friends, acquaintances, and relatives are redeemed;...
one's sins are washed away;...
all places (inner realms) are within reach.
O Nānak, in the *sādh kai sang,*
one's life becomes fruitful.

Guru Arjun, Ādi Granth 271–72, AGK

Kabīr's choice of expression is equally direct:

Keep the company of saints *(sant kī sangati),* O Kabīr,
their minds are pure and clean.
They give beyond measure the rare wealth of *Nām.*

Keep the company of saints *(sādh kī sangat),* Kabīr,
for they heal all spiritual sickness and, in the end, make you divine.
The company *(sangat)* of lovers of the world *(asādh),* however,
brings nothing but unending woe.

Keep the company of saints *(sangat sādh kī),* Kabīr,
even if you must live on dry bread.
Run from the company *(sang)* of the worldly *(sākat),*
even if rich banquets are spread before you.

Keep the company of saints *(sangat sādh kī),* Kabīr:
It is like visiting the shop of a perfumer –
even if he gives you no perfume,
you will still enjoy the fragrance....

Keep the company of saints *(sangat sādh kī),* Kabīr:
the time you spend with them is never wasted.

The bitter neem *(nīm)* tree is made fragrant
when it grows beside the fragrant sandalwood.
So the company of a perfect saint makes you a saint as well....

Go to Mathurā, Dwārakā, or Jagannāth Puri as you please:
without the company of a saint *(sādh sangati),*
and without meditation, you will never gain a thing....

Those days were completely wasted
when you lived without the company of a saint *(sant sangati),*
For life without love for a saint, without devotion for the Lord,
is merely life as a beast....

The company of a saint *(sangati sādh)* for even half an hour,
or even a quarter-hour – even moments –
destroys millions of sins, says Kabīr.

Kabīr, Sākhī Sangrah, Satsang kā Ang 2–5, 7, 9, 16, 23, KSS pp.49–50; cf. KGME pp.187–89

See also: **sanga** (▸4).

1. *E.g. Bhagavad Gītā* 2:47, 62; 3:9, 13:21, 18:26; Patañjali, *Yoga Sūtras* 3:52.
2. *Adhyātma Rāmāyaṇa, Āraṇya Kāṇḍa* 10:23–27, *ARSR* p.168.

sangati (H), **sangat** (Pu) *Lit.* company, society (of a person or group), group; meeting place, confluence, centre, congregation, community, brotherhood, gathering.

Sang, sangat and *sangati* all mean company or group, and are often used interchangeably; *sangati* also means visiting, frequenting, meeting, joining. *Sangat* is also used for the community comprising the followers of a particular lineage of *gurus;* equivalent to the Jain and Buddhist *sangha* (Pa).

Disciples of a master, each to a greater or lesser extent, share a fellow feeling and experience. They not only share beliefs in common, but – more importantly – they share the same high aspirations, and are all struggling to overcome their human limitations and rise to higher spiritual levels. They can, therefore, be a considerable source of strength and encouragement to each other.

Only those who have been inwardly touched by a master's grace know the happiness and joy that it brings. Even though they may not speak outwardly of it, such joy and love shine on their faces and in their eyes and communicates itself to others. But only another disciple can really understand the depth of it. This also creates a great bond of genuine affection and understanding between disciples.

There is also a mystical aspect. All disciples are initiates. They are all inwardly connected to the divine Word. They are thus all destined to become one with their master, one with the Word, one with each other, and one with God. Hence, when disciples meet, though they may outwardly be strangers, they inwardly feel very close to one another in a very short space of time. This is a unique kind of closeness, often far closer than they may feel to members of their own family.

Ravidās speaks of the benefits of the company *(sangati)* of a saint:

I have sought refuge in Your company *(sangati),* O Lord,
Sustainer and Protector of the world!
Just as rain water flowing from street to street
merges into the Ganges and becomes pure –
So due to the company *(sangati)* of saints *(mahātmās)*
I have drunk the pure Ganges water of Your Name!

When raindrops fall upon the head of a serpent, they turn to poison:
when the same drops fall into a shell, they give rise to pearls –
It is good company *(sangati)* that makes the difference!

Just as the fragrance of the sandalwood
spreads even to a nearby neem *(nīm)* tree,
so does Your fragrance now abide in me.
My caste is low, my lineage low, and low is my occupation,
but by your grace, says Ravidās the cobbler,
I have been exalted to this position.

Ravidās, Vāṇī, Rāg Āsā 116, SGRV p.116; cf. GRPS p.110

Maharaj Sawan Singh describes something of the effect of a true master on his *sangat:*

Where a *satguru* lives, the entire environment is spiritualized by his body, mind, intellect, and the mode of his life. His very presence greatly influences the people around him. When a *satguru* speaks, or makes a movement of the hands, or confers a gracious look, a special current of attention emanates from him and creates a powerful influence on the minds of the audience. This is subject to the condition that those in the audience are not entirely devoid of loving devotion or, like pieces of flint, are not incapable of understanding or accepting it. Such a current of attention helps the soul to ascend, and the person listening to such spiritual discourses greatly expands his esoteric knowledge.... The audience *(sangat)* that partakes of the fragrance of the spirituality of saints becomes saturated with its sweet perfume.

Maharaj Sawan Singh, Philosophy of the Masters 1, PMS1 p.114

See also: **saṃgha, sang, satsang**.

sangha (H/Pa) See **saṃgha**.

sanzen (J) *Lit. zen* meditation; a meditative consultation between a monk and the head abbot of a *Zen* Buddhist monastery; in the *Rinzai Zen* tradition, a private interview *(dokusan)* between a disciple and a master *(rōshi);* also known as *nyūshitsu,* an abbreviation of *dokusan nyūshitsu.*

The main purpose of *sanzen* is for the master to offer direction and encouragement, to facilitate the disciple's progress in meditation or any aspect of *Zen* practice, and especially to gauge his or her grasp of the meaning of the *kōan* (paradoxical question) that the master has given. The character of the meeting is naturally influenced by the disciple's spiritual condition and his or her capacity to understand and absorb the master's instruction. Much, too, will depend on the spiritual elevation of the master.

Sanzen may take place two or more times a day. During *sesshin* (intensive meditation, traditionally lasting seven days and seven nights), the number of *sanzens* can be several times a day. It may include the practice of *zazen* meditation with the master or contemplation of a *kōan* under the master's personal guidance.

While bland descriptions of such meetings may seem dry, the actual experience is nothing of the sort, as various accounts make clear. In fact, it is evident that *kōan* meditation, far from being an intellectual exercise, requires a deep stillness of mind:

> At first the meditator simply concentrates on the internally vocalized question, ... harmonizing this with watching the breath at the *tanden* (just below the navel). This dampens down wandering thoughts, and may be taken all the way to dhyanic (contemplative) 'serene observation'. The *Rinzai* tradition, however, says that the meditator will lose interest in 'solving' the *kōan* if he enters this state too soon, so he should not let his mind become quite so still, but keep it in a kind of active *samādhi* (concentration) where he slowly recites the words of the question and watches it as a cat watches a mouse, trying to bore deeper and deeper into it, till he reaches the point from which it comes and intuits its meaning.
>
> While practising thus, the meditator consults with the master at least twice a day in *sanzen* interview, to offer an 'answer' to the question. At first, he attempts intellectual answers, based on what he has read or heard, but these are useless and may be rejected with shouts or blows. He then tries to give 'Zennish' answers by bringing articles to the master or doing some absurd action. These are also rejected, thus

driving the student into a state of baffled perplexity, where the habit-structures and constructs of his mind are starting to be undermined. One record of a *Zen* interview with Master Cāoshān Běnjì (840–901), itself used as a *kōan,* goes:

> Someone asked, "With what sort of understanding should one be equipped to satisfactorily cope with the cross-examination of others?"
>
> The master said, "Don't use words and phrases."
>
> "Then what are you going to cross-examine about?"
>
> The master said, "Even the sword and the axe cannot pierce it through!"
>
> He said, "What a fine cross-examination! But aren't there people who don't agree."
>
> The master said, "There are."
>
> "Who?" he asked.
>
> The master said, "Me."[1]

In *sanzen,* the role of the master is crucial: only he can assess the answers of the pupil, and knock away his reliance on anything beyond his own intuition. By progressing through *kōans* over many years, the best pupils then become masters themselves.

The meditator must 'solve' each enigmatic question by himself. Some *kōans* may be solved by relatively simple intuitions. Others require the meditator to struggle on with the question till he reaches the end of his tether. In a profound state of perplexity, he meets the 'doubt-sensation': a pure, contentless, existential 'great doubt'. The mind attains one-pointed concentration on this, with no distinction between doubter and doubt. The meditator is then in a stupefied, strangely ecstatic state, where he feels as if he is walking on air, not knowing if he is standing or walking. Nothing is what it seems to be, 'a mountain is not a mountain and water is not water,' yet all is bright and suddenly complete.

In this condition, the meditator is said to be prone to a number of '*Zen* sicknesses', whereby he will cling to some aspect of his experience, or take the lights or visions he may have as signs of revelation. These features seem akin to those of the 'pseudo-*nibbāna*' on the *Theravāda* path. After the master helps 'cure' him, the meditator can progress. Only when he pushes on and on, throwing himself into the abyss of doubt, will an 'answer' spontaneously arise from the depths of his mind. The deeper he goes into the doubt, the more thorough will be the 'great death' – the death of aspects of ego.

Peter Harvey, Introduction to Buddhism, IBTH pp.273–75

The first-hand accounts of neurologist James Austin provide an even greater insight into the interaction between master and disciple during *sanzen:*

> It is now a few weeks after I began formal sitting in the meditation hall at Ryōkoin. The *rōshi* is starting to conduct his brief private interviews, called *sanzen* in the *Rinzai* tradition. These take place during the second of the three morning meditation periods. They are devoted mostly to problems the trainee is having in practice. Just before entering his chamber, you kneel and pick up a small wooden mallet. Your next task is not easy. It is to announce your presence by striking two authentic notes on a small bronze bell. The *rōshi,* having listened to the bell and observed your subsequent bowings, prostrations, and behaviour, knows only too well exactly where you are in your practice. He conducts the interview with all seriousness, and with gradually increasing formality and firmness, especially during the meditative retreats called *sesshin.*
>
> At my first *sanzen,* he focuses on breathing correctly. "Are you breathing down in your lower abdomen? Are you breathing *out* on 'one'? Are you really *concentrating* on 'one'? Not on the idea of 'one,' but on the *total* reality of it?" I have not consistently done any of these. "Heal thyself, physician," I mutter to myself on the way out.
>
> By the second *sanzen* things are better. Thoughts are much less of a problem, and so it is with misplaced optimism that I now ask for a *kōan* to work on. I have no idea what to expect. He says, "When every phenomenon is reduced to one, then where is that one reduced to?"
>
> My brain reels! My gaze shifts away. What on *earth* did this mean? He waits until my gaze returns, and then looks at me directly, saying, "Not what, not why or how. Not when, but *where* is that one?" I am utterly baffled.
>
> Seeing my bewilderment, he rephrases it slightly: "When all things return to the one, *where* is the one returned to?" This sounds vaguely better, but it still means absolutely nothing. "Because you are a scholar," he continues, "you will try to concentrate on this *kōan* using your mind and your knowledge. It won't work. You must take the *kōan* inside yourself and penetrate it. This is no small thing; it is a major undertaking. You must concentrate on your *kōan* everywhere, but take care not to do so near automobiles. Once when I was a young monk concentrating on my *kōan* – which, by the way, took years – a passing automobile almost struck me down. This story tells you how deep your concentration must be."
>
> At the next *sanzen* he begins by asking gently, "Where is 'one'?" I shake my head, saying "I really can't get anywhere *near* this *kōan.*" He replies, "Your problem is that you've encapsulated your 'one'

inside layers of ideas and ten thousand other conditioned things. You must strike through these layers, break away from any philosophical approach. Finally you will get down to the deeply religious insight. Then it will be no separate matter. It will be something that you will find totally and consciously acceptable."

"But," I reply, "I am still having trouble even defining what 'one' means." He says, "If you find that unity is a better word, use unity." This helps not at all. "Be clear about one thing: the answer to 'where' will not be 'everywhere', and it will not be 'nowhere'. Such answers are things out of the conscious, conditioned mind. When you finally reach your answer, it must be *clear, definite.* Your answer cannot be shaken by *anyone.*"

Another *sanzen.* He begins with a firm question: "If all ideas are melted into one, *where* does that one come from?" No answer from me. I am learning. I am sitting more and talking less. He continues, saying, "The *kōan* is contradictory; you cannot find the answer by logic. Head and body working *together.* That's what you need to penetrate the *kōan.* You will finally find this union of mind and body inside *Zen.*"

In the following months, head and body do not come together. I cannot crack this *kōan.* Reading about *Zen* is not supposed to be helpful. I read, anyway. In one place, I find that this "Where is one?" *kōan* was attributed to Master Zhàozhōu (778–897) back in the early *Táng* dynasty. Reading elsewhere, I come across a vague but potential word answer to the *kōan.* It dates back to the time of Sēngcàn (*d.*606), the third *Zen* patriarch, who lived even earlier. There, in the *Hsin hsin ming (Xìnxīn míng),* I find the statement: "When all things are viewed in their oneness, we return to our original nature." I'm confused. Could this be the answer? If so, how could an answer precede a question? For if Sēngcàn's statement were to be regarded as an answer at all, then it had arisen almost two centuries *before* Zhàozhōu had posed his question. So I keep wondering: Does 'one' mean 'oneness'? Does 'oneness' mean 'unity'? And, by the way, what *is* my original nature?

All my word problems are self-inflicted, and they multiply. At another *sanzen,* still perplexed, I bring up yet another puzzling paradox. "How is it," I ask, "that emptiness – this central Buddhist concept – can exist if supposedly, at the same time, everything in the universe is all linked together? Doesn't the latter imply that there is a very high degree of fullness?" "You are getting diverted," he answers. "You have to *know* emptiness," he replies. "You must stop splashing along the surface with all your words and concepts. You cannot understand emptiness with words or with ideas. You must dive down deep into *zazen.* There, forget about emptiness. Forget about fullness. Get back to working on your *kōan,* on 'one'. Keep on thinking: 'where' does that 'one' come from? This is your problem; keep to it." Trying to help, he then closes by saying, "If you continue your *zazen,* 'one' will finally become itself, and others, and everything else in the universe." I continue sitting, but nothing like this happens.

Next, we begin a short, three-day retreat. It involves sitting several times in the morning and evening of each day. Maybe I can't pierce this *kōan,* but I have been developing an almost palpable perception of being 'in touch' with everything going on. By the third day, perception is becoming clear, immediate. The word 'now' seems to symbolize this immediacy.

Sanzen again. No preliminaries. As soon as I enter, the *rōshi* demands, "Where is 'one'!" "Now!" I blurt out. He raises his eyes, looks at me sharply. I meet his gaze. He nods slightly. "A little better," he says. "But much too logical. You must get inside the *kōan,* immerse yourself in it like it was a tub of warm water."

December arrives all too soon. I have come to see him for my last, long farewell interview before leaving Kyōto. "I'm disappointed," I say, "that I didn't make more progress with the *kōan.*" He reassures me, replying, "I worked over a six-year period on my first *kōan,* with four years taken up during the war." I mention, lamely, that the term, 'original nature' might seem to be a kind of 'word answer' to the *kōan.* He dismisses this casually, saying, "Of course, no word answer is relevant. Stay with the *kōan* itself. Break down through the where of the *kōan,* and then it will open up."

He illustrates. He points down and in, extending both arms into a long V. But at the bottom, he leaves a gap of three inches or so between the tips of his outstretched fingers on both sides. "A deep valley of the mind will open up like this," he explains. "Once you've gone through one of the experiences, a valley is cut in the mind, and it will stay open. Go into that opening."

James Austin, Zen and the Brain, ZBMC pp.107–9

See also: **dokusan nyūshitsu**.

1. Línjì Yìxuán, *Línjì lù,* in *BTIC* p.235.

satsang(a) (S/H/Pu) *Lit.* company *(sanga)* of Truth *(sat);* communion with the Real, contact with the Truth, contact with the Real; true association; specifically, the company of the virtuous or holy, the company of devotees; the company of realized souls or saints *(sants, sādhus);* the company of one who has realized the mystic Truth within himself, and has thus become Truth incarnate; also, contact with the mystic Truth within; contact with the divine creative power or Word; a term used in India by the followers of many spiritual paths.

The value of *satsanga* is depicted in Hindu texts. Says Kṛishṇa in the *Bhāgavata Purāṇa:*

> Neither *yoga,* nor *Sāṃkhya* (analysis of the elements of material nature), nor *dharma* (practice of non-violence and other virtues), nor chanting of the *Vedas,* nor austerities, nor renunciation, nor religious sacrifices, nor service to others, nor charity, nor observance of severe vows, nor worship of deities *(yajñas),* nor repetition of secret *mantras,* nor ablution in sacred waters, nor observance of *niyamas* (rules of mental and bodily discipline) can capture Me (in the heart) and can destroy all external attachments as effectively as association *(satsanga)* with My devotees.
>
> *Bhāgavata Purāṇa 11:12.1–2; cf. BPT5 p.1974, SB16 pp.790–91*

And likewise:

> One who obtains devotion through association *(satsanga)* with My devotees is My true worshipper. Such a person easily goes to my abode, revealed by My pure devotees.
>
> *Bhāgavata Purāṇa 11:11.25; cf. BPT5 pp.1969–70, SB16 p.757*

In these verses, *satsanga* implies association with saints and with the devotees who automatically gather around them.

In common parlance, *satsang* has developed a wide spread of meaning. It refers to a meeting at which someone discourses on spiritual topics. It also refers to the spiritual discourse itself. Even to think or read about spiritual teachings has come to be known as *satsang.*

Satsang is both inner and outer. Inner *satsang* is a meeting of the disciple with the spiritual form of the master on the inner planes. This is the highest form of *satsang.* Outer *satsang* ultimately leads, through meditation, to inner *satsang.* Inner *satsang* is a mystic experience, entailing contact with the divine sound and light of the divine Word *(Shabd)* or Name *(Nām)* of God.

The twentieth-century mystic Maharaj Sawan Singh discusses the meaning of *satsang* in his *Gurmat Siddhānt* ('Philosophy of the Masters'):

> Today, *satsang* usually means a gathering where either music or singing, or the recitation of epics and stories, or discussions of spiritual subjects take place. A discourse by a learned person is also referred to as *satsang.* When four or more persons sit together and sing the praises of the Lord, with or without the aid of an instrument, even this is known as *satsang.*

But in the eyes of the saints, *satsang* connotes a much deeper meaning and has a much higher and purer aim. The gathering of worldly minded people is not termed *satsang*. *Sat* means truth and *sang* means company. One who has the ideal of Truth established in his heart is the image of the Lord. Vedic scriptures affirm that one who has the knowledge of *Brahm* is himself also *Brahm*.[1]

Similarly, one who has inculcated Truth within himself is himself the Truth. There is no difference between the Truth and the true Lord *(sat Purush)*. The *satguru* (true master) is the light of the Truth.

Different persons exert different kinds of influences. The virtuous create an atmosphere of virtue, while the wicked create an atmosphere of evil.

The mind is a wonderful thing. It takes on the colour of the company it keeps. It imbibes the attributes of what it dwells upon. If it keeps the company of worldly people, it also becomes worldly. On the other hand, if it lives among spiritual people it acquires spiritual tendencies. Therefore, if one is keen to gather spiritual knowledge, he must keep the company of those who are spiritually advanced and must keep his mind fixed on them.

Where a *satguru* lives, the entire environment is spiritualized by his body, mind, intellect, and the mode of his life. His very presence greatly influences the people around him. When a *satguru* speaks or makes a movement of the hands or confers a gracious look, a special current of attention emanates from him and creates a powerful influence on the minds of the audience. This is subject to the condition that those in the audience are not entirely devoid of loving devotion or, like pieces of flint, are not incapable of understanding or accepting it. Such a current of attention helps the soul to ascend, and the person listening to such spiritual discourses greatly expands his esoteric knowledge....

The audience that partakes of the fragrance of the spirituality of saints becomes saturated with its sweet perfume. The greatness of *satsang* is unique indeed. All scriptures and holy books sing its praises....

Through *satsang* a person becomes free from the influence of the negative power (universal mind) and the evil designs of his mind. *Yama* – the angel of death – does not come near him, and he is emancipated.

A person who keeps the company of saints *(sādhū sangat)* gains his object and is sustained at the time of his death. The company of evil persons *(sākat dī sohbat)* leads to ruin. Therefore, we must give up bad company *(sākat dī sangat)*....

One who enjoys the *satsang* of spiritually advanced souls goes beyond the domain of matter and mind. Whoever attends *satsang* forgets himself. Just as a melon takes on the colour of its neighbour, so does the *satsang* – a fountain head of spirituality – bestow its benign drops on all who join it, and they become the embodiment of love. Where love abides, there appears a strange and unworldly love-intoxication. Whoever partakes of it burns away his cares and the dross of his mind, and begins to shine in his pristine glory.

Satsang is a unique boon which the master distributes free to both the learned and the ignorant. His overpowering grandeur, his refulgence and magnetic force attract each person according to his merit, with the result that he becomes oblivious of the world and its objects and completely loses track of time and the manner of its passage....

Satsang is so unique that even God is enamoured of it and it is incumbent on one, therefore, to try to find a saint and either attend his *satsang* or keep his company. For this alone can be the means of his salvation. If one obtains the company of a saint and develops faith in him, the fulfilment of his life's mission is ensured. So long as one does not find a perfect master one should prepare oneself by leading a chaste life, studying religious books and keeping the company of those who are spiritually inclined. But if, by the grace of God, one is able to find a saint who has attained God-realization, one should imbibe his teachings and mould one's life accordingly. This is real *satsang*.

Sat (Truth) is another name for God. It abides in the saints and their gatherings. In communities where persons who profess a particular faith live together, there are institutions for imparting their faith. As it is true that education can be had only in schools and colleges, that medicines can be procured only in hospitals, that heat is associated with ovens, and that moisture is inseparable from water, so also God resides where His devotees live.

There rise the waves of love and devotion. There bliss and grace confer peace upon all. The world is a furnace ablaze, where all creatures suffer torture. Their pitiable condition is deserving of mercy. The *satsang* of saints is a priceless blessing, and is the haven of the agonized. Those who depend on it with all their being cross the ocean of the world and realize *Nām*.

If the waters of rivers and rivulets, on joining the Ganges, lose their own identity; if the knife of the butcher turns into gold on touching the philosopher's stone; if a margosa tree growing near a sandalwood tree imbibes its fragrance; if it is true that whatever is kept in a salt mine becomes salt; then there need be no doubt that whoever goes to *satsang* is dyed in its colour. You may be good or bad. There is nothing to worry about. You should gain the company of a saint and listen to his *satsang*. The fresh air of his invigorating spirituality will bestow upon you the same spiritual health and freshness, and in a short time you will become good yourself. Then the qualities of virtue will manifest themselves within you. Listening to the *satsang* with your mind and heart, relishing it, you will easily gain control over your senses, and your soul will become steady in the company of saints and *sādhus*....

The ever-merciful Lord abides within the master. By following his precepts, we are released from the cycle of birth and rebirth. Such is the greatness of *satsang* that, like the philosopher's stone, it transforms the iron-like sinner into a gold-like being of virtue. The lowly is raised on high. One who is worthless becomes precious. Go to *satsang* and lovingly contemplate upon the master and the Lord. Your thoughts, words and deeds will automatically become pure. You will find that through *satsang* the spiritual wealth that can be obtained as a result of following the various kinds of *yoga* will come your way without any difficulty or effort on your part.

Those who attend *satsang,* automatically listen, ponder over, and visualize the form of the *satguru* who is giving the discourse. They do not need to read any outside books, because *satsang* deals with spiritual matters in a practical way. It is not the books alone that are a medium for attaining knowledge. Knowledge can be gained by listening to *satsang*.

Look at a blind man. By listening alone he has become learned. By intently listening, we can imbibe new knowledge. When a particular subject is discussed in *satsang* all the listeners think of the same subject simultaneously, with the result that the entire environment is saturated with their thought currents. The entire audience benefits thereby, and the subject leaves an indelible impression on the minds of those present.

Together with the thought currents, the waves of spirituality that emanate from the master during his discourse help to make the subject matter clear, so that everyone can comprehend it thoroughly. In this way, the dirt of evil thoughts gets washed away, the gloom of ignorance vanishes, and in its place emerges the light of knowledge.

If a person is able to attend the *satsang* of a master with attention, steadfastness and faith, the filth of his mind is easily washed away, and he becomes capable of increasing faith and understanding.

So long as the mirror of one's mind is not cleansed, the words of the master do not have their full effect. As the purity of the mind increases, the words of the *satguru* begin to have a more penetrating effect within. By listening to his words, one becomes absorbed in them, so much so that he even beholds glimpses of the master's radiance within. It appears as if there were two bodies, but only one breath. The vision of the same light enlivening both comes into view. One who attends satsang begins to imbibe the qualities of the master and finally assume his form. When this happens, all is accomplished. Whatever wealth of goodness one has gathered, it is entirely the fruit of the company of the virtuous. *Satsang* is a very powerful means, and through it one rapidly gains emancipation.

Sat also means life. The company of a living master is *satsang*. The scriptures point out that wherever there is a master there is *satsang*. *Satsang* is dependent upon a master, and it can be had only through him.

By remaining in the company of a spiritually awakened soul one is virtually reborn. The animal life in him comes to an end, and he begins to realize his spiritual kinship with God. He becomes *karmaless* (actionless), and the dross of evil wears away. A person who boards the ship of *Nām* easily crosses the ocean of phenomena.

Even as iron floats when it is in association with wood, so also, by keeping the company of saints, one is automatically filled with remembrance of the Lord and develops an intense yearning to realize Him. In *satsang,* the master, through his spiritual currents, bestows the gift of new life on the devotees, with the result that, like moths, they sacrifice themselves on the fountainhead of light and become one with it. For then their life does not remain their own. It becomes that of the master. Thus they attain the state of completely merging in the master....

There is no *satsang* worthy of the name without a master, because the *satguru* (true master) is the bestower of *Shabd,* and without *Shabd* nobody can cross the ocean of life. While eulogizing *satsang,* the scriptures hold that that alone is *satsang* where *Nām* is exalted and discussed. Such a *satsang* can be obtained only from a master....

The lives of saints exercise a powerful influence. They possess a magnetic force. Their mind, body and spirit radiate waves of noble and virtuous thoughts. They have complete control over their minds and senses. In their company *(sangat),* our own mind and senses become stable and no longer wander, with the result that we begin to be dyed in the Lord's grace....

The two kinds of *satsang,* outer and inner, may be explained thus: one (outer *satsang*) is an effort to kindle a fire, while the other (inner *satsang*) is like sitting near a fire and escaping from the cold while also accomplishing many other tasks. One who associates with a saint has his soul awakened by the spiritual currents emanating from him. The second state (inner *satsang*) is therefore supremely superior....

Satsang is a powerful spiritual school or college, where practical lessons are imparted in spirituality and love. *Satsang* is a wonderful workshop where the tangles of the mind are set straight, and one is so chiselled that he can realize himself and God....

Satsang is an exalted place of pilgrimage. It removes millions of sins of numerous past lives, making the mind pure and clear. Just as fire

> burns away the dross of gold and makes it pure, so does the company of saints burn away the sins of past lives and make a person pure.
>
> There is no more complete and useful a machine for transforming evil thoughts into noble ones than *satsang*. In the company of the virtuous, one imbibes virtue and becomes free of all blemishes and sins. Spiritually evolved souls always fill the environment in which they live with currents of purity. Even the worst of sinners cannot escape their influence but turn noble; and in the company of saints, one is dyed in the hue of the Lord.
>
> *Maharaj Sawan Singh, Philosophy of the Masters 1; cf. PMS1 pp.113–36*

Following a spiritual path means going contrary to the worldliness of the majority. Readily affected by the company it keeps, the mind is easily swayed to the worldly side. Masters therefore recommend that disciples meet together regularly to listen to an exposition of the teachings they aspire to follow. Such meetings are also known as *satsang*. Maharaj Sawan Singh writes to disciples in America:

> Initiation is sowing the seed, which needs the water of *satsang* and concentration for sprouting. Love and faith are necessary for its growth. If an initiated soul fails to get this water and is attracted towards the world, the seed will not become a plant; but it is never destroyed. The weight of *karma* becomes heavier and obstructs its growth. But when this weight of *karma* becomes light, some day the seed will begin to sprout. *Karma* is removed by Sound (*Shabd,* Word) practice.
>
> *Maharaj Sawan Singh, Spiritual Gems 165, SG p.269*

> When we are away from the master and the *satsang,* the world imperceptibly impresses itself on us so much that, in spite of our regularly giving time to *simran* and *Nām* (*i.e.* to meditation), we often begin to feel discouraged, dry, and desolate. In such a state, faith and love are our support; and if faith is firm, the master responds. He is always with us – within us – watches as a mother watches her child. So long as we are on this side of the focus (the eye centre or third eye), we do not see him working. But he is doing his duty.
>
> *Maharaj Sawan Singh, Spiritual Gems 117, SG pp.172–73*

Maharaj Charan Singh, disciple of Maharaj Sawan Singh and subsequently appointed master, speaks in a similarly practical manner of the benefits of *satsang*. In addition to other benefits, questions and doubts that naturally arise in the mind are resolved:

> Those souls whom the saints wish to liberate from the ocean of this world and unite with the Lord are first brought by them into their company *(sangat)* and *satsang*. When we attend their *satsang,* various doubts and difficulties disappear. We come to know our origin, our home, and then a longing for union with the Lord is awakened in us. *Satsang* and good company *(sohbat)* are necessary preludes for devotion to the Lord. The mind is easily influenced by the company it keeps. If we keep bad company *(sohbat),* we become wicked; and if we keep the company of saints *(santān dī sangat)* and devotees, we follow their example and, like them, we become devoted to the Lord. If perchance we are kept away from the *satsang* of saints, then we should continue to read their writings so that the mind may remain detached from worldly objects and free from all desire to dominate anyone or to obtain power, position, wealth, *etc.*
>
> *Maharaj Charan Singh, Light on Sant Mat, Discourses 3, LOSM pp.29–30*

> It is the nature of the mind to be open to all sorts of doubts, but if one keeps in *satsang* and reads *sant mat* literature, those doubts or difficulties are automatically cleared and one feels impelled to work on the spiritual path. Huzur Maharaj Ji (Maharaj Sawan Singh) used to compare *satsang* to the fence around the crop – the crop of *bhajan* and *simran* (*i.e.* meditation). By *satsang* is meant a discussion and explanation of *Nām.* In *satsang,* there is no distinction between high and low, nor any distinction of class, colour, or creed; and all meet in a loving, friendly atmosphere. We should, therefore, pray to the Lord to give us the company of holy people so that we will always think of God.
>
> *Maharaj Charan Singh, Light on Sant Mat, Discourses 5, LOSM p.44*

Many other saints have described the benefits of *satsang*. Much, however, depends upon the attitude of attendees:

> *Satsang* is like the *pāras* (philosopher's stone). Just as iron is changed into gold by mere contact with it, those who sincerely follow *satsang* are turned into the gold of immortal life. But a hypocrite with mental reservations, in spite of *satsang,* remains the same iron as before. *Satsang,* however, is *pāras* all the same. . . .
>
> Just as a diamond will pierce a pearl but not a stone, so the discourses of a saint will affect only the deserving. Others derive no benefit. However, if even the undeserving constantly attend *satsang,* they would finally become fit and deserving. But there is a snag here in that it will not be possible for them to stay in the *satsang*. . . .

Satsang comes first. Those who remain in *satsang* receive many benefits. A stone which remains in water keeps cool although the water does not penetrate it; still it is better than the stones outside the water. Likewise, the worldly people come to the *satsang* and are not affected by it, but this does not matter. Anyway, they are better than the out-and-out worldly people. In course of time they will begin to accept the influence....

Mere attendance at *satsang* cannot destroy *karma.* It is only by acting on the teachings of *satsang* that the effects of *karma* can be nullified....

It is very difficult to keep in the *satsang* of the saints. Some attend the *satsang* but are really inattentive; that is, they seem to be sitting and listening to what it said but do not listen or accept it. What good will *satsang* then do to them? They alone truly hear and understand whose minds are affected and also their conduct, more or less....

Vain and haughty people who attend the *satsang* do not enjoy it because they come with the idea of finding fault, and do not grasp the things explained to them.

Swami Shiv Dayal Singh, Sār Bachan Prose 2:15, 29, 35, 69, 164, 205, SBAT pp.55, 59–61, 67, 95, 115

The purpose of outer *satsang* is to lead the mind and soul to inner *satsang:*

Exceedingly exalted is the glory of *satsang,*
  but difficult it is to find an aspirant fit for it....
People sit in *(sat)sang* as a stone in water,
  and are not absorbed in it as sugar in water.
When the external *satsang* is such
  that none appears as dear as the *satguru,*
  only then does one become immersed in internal *satsang;*
The *surat* (soul) then ascends within, and the heavens resound.

Swami Shiv Dayal Singh, Sār Bachan Poetry 38:6.20, 24–26, SBP p.342; cf. in TGTD p.190

Catch the inaccessible current of *Shabd,*
  attach your soul to it, and be always absorbed in this (inner) *satsang.*

Swami Shiv Dayal Singh, Sār Bachan Poetry 20:27.4, SBP p.168, SBPS pp.238–39

Listen to me: keep the company *(satsang)* (of the saints),
  so that both your (inner) vision and hearing are opened,
  so that you see the dazzling flame within,
  so that you hear the wonderful harmony of the heavens.

Swami Shiv Dayal Singh, Sār Bachan Poetry 20:5.19–20, SBP p.157, SBPS pp.226–27

Through *satsang,* the soul comes into contact with the divine Name; and through the Name, the soul returns to its divine source:

> Without *satsang,* the Name of the Lord remains unknown:
> without His Name, attachment to the world does not depart.
> Until attachment goes, there is no release from bondage:
> without release, longing for the Lord does not awaken.
> If longing is absent, devotion will not blossom:
> without devotion, love will not be kindled in the heart.
> Without love, there is no Name, and without the Name, no saint.
> Seek, therefore, O Paltū, the gift of *satsang* from the Lord.
>
> *Paltū, Rekhtā 21, PSB2 p.8; cf. SPLT p.173*

> My contact with *satsang* has dyed me in the hue of my master.
> The delusion of countless ages has been dissolved,
> and I have reached my original home.
>
> *Tulsī Sāhib, Shabdāvalī 1, Kakahrā 10, TSH1 p.25, TSSH p.61*

Certainty, inner purity, and spiritual understanding grows:

> Without *satsang* one does not develop understanding:
> without the *satguru* one does not find the way.
>
> *Tulsī Sāhib, Ghaṭ Rāmāyaṇ 2, GR2 p.129; cf. in TGTD p.195*

> This is the fruit of *satsang* – that no doubt whatsoever is left.
> The mind becomes guileless, pure and steady,
> and one is no more drawn to misery.
>
> *Tulsīdās, Tulsī Satsaī 6:541, TSTD p.51, in TGTD p.191*

Through *satsang,* suffering is ended, inner darkness becomes light, a person becomes pure and universal, and the cycle of rebirth comes to an end:

> When I met the saint *(sādh),* all my sorrows ceased,
> my body became whole;
> When I heard his words,
> the pain of many births and many deaths ended.
> There is moonlight in *satsang,*
> though the rest of the world is in darkness;
> Says Sahajo, it is difficult to find a place
> in the company of the saints *(satsangat).*
> Men and women, place your trust in the boat of *satsang:*
> use the powerful oar of devotion, says Sahajo,
> to take you to the other side.
>
> *Sahajobāī, Bānī, Sādh Mahimā 5–7, SBB p.12; cf. SPBS p.59*

Whoever keeps the company of the holy *(satsang),*
loses all sense of colour, caste, and ancestry.
Sahajobāī, Bānī, Sādh Mahimā 9, SBB p.12; cf. SPBS p.61

The atmosphere surrounding the saints is blissful. In a comparatively short time, *satsang* leads the soul into the divine presence:

Taste the nectar of *satsang,* O friend,
savour the elixir of *satsang.*
At the outset, it tastes sharp and acrid,
but soon, like mango, it is juicy and sweet....
In a few minutes, *satsang* leads to salvation:
thus say the *Vedas* and all holy books.
Mīrābāī, Satsang, Updesh ke Pad 66:1, 4, MSS p.772; cf. MDLS p.127

It is a rare good fortune to obtain the company of a true saint:

In this world, it is hard to obtain
the company of a saint *(satsangati)* even once,
whether for a moment or for half an hour....
Blessed is the time spent in *satsang....*
Only by great good fortune does one happen to obtain *satsang,*
whereby the cycle of birth and death
is brought to an end with little effort.
Tulsīdās, Rām Charit Mānas 7:122.3, 126.4, 32.4;
cf. RCML pp.1091, 1096, 989–90

Satsang is a source of true spiritual bliss and ecstasy:

I am entrapped in the city of thieves (the body and the material world),
while my life is athirst for *satsang.*
In *satsang* lies much benefit, for it swiftly leads you to the True.
But fools do not understand its significance.
During *satsang* is showered a veritable rain of ambrosia.
Kabīr, Shabdāvalī 1, Satguru aur Shabd Mahimā 3:1–3, KSS1 p.2, KGME p.153

If one's mind is always given to *satsang,*
one tastes the immortal nectar of love.
The saint provides this immortal nectar.
Dariyā Sāhib, Bhakti Hetu, Chaupāī 24–25, DG2 p.279, DSSK p.242

Satsang is the source of true bliss,
the basis of love and the ambrosial Sound Current.
It offers the imprint of the hidden realm, beyond the three worlds.

> It burns all evil thoughts,
> and bestows the fortune of the inner vision of the master.
> With the *guru*'s wisdom one beholds his celestial form,
> full of radiant beauty;
> One obtains true love, the philosopher's stone that destroys all karmas.
>
> *Dariyā Sāhib, Gyān Dīpak, Chhand Tomar 27, GDDS p.251; cf. DSSK p.242*

See also: **sang**, **sangat**.

1. *E.g. Bṛihadāraṇyaka Upanishad* 1:4.10, 2:5.19; *Chhāndogya Upanishad* 6:8.7, 7:23.1–25.2; *Māṇḍūkya Upanishad* 1:2.

satsang ghar (H/Pu) *Lit.* a hall or building *(ghar)* in which *satsangs* are held. From a mystic perspective, there is nothing special or sacred about any building, their purpose is entirely practical. In modern, international Buddhism, halls with a similar function are commonly known as *dharma* halls (C. *fătáng,* J. *hattō*), and are used for gatherings of various sorts – meditation, discourses, and so on.

See also: **saṃgha**, **satsang**.

shafāʻah (A), **shafāʻat** (P) *Lit.* intercession, mediation; to intercede on behalf of another person; to ask forgiveness for another person; intercession before a king or on behalf of a debtor; in popular Muslim belief, the intercession of the Prophet on Judgment Day, on behalf of his *Ummah* (community of believers); also, the intercession of the prophets and saints. According to the *Qur'ān:*

> On that Day, no intercession *(shafāʻah)* will avail except from him who has received permission from the Beneficent, and whose word is pleasing to Him.
>
> *Qur'ān 20:109; cf. KPA, MGK*

This is repeated several times.[1] On the other hand, a warning is also repeated[2] against arriving at Judgment Day and expecting an intercession that is unavailable. The idea of intercession is developed in the *ḥadīth* and later popular Muslim belief. It is frequently said in the *ḥadīth* that Muḥammad will intercede for his community on the Day of Judgment.[3] Another *ḥadīth* has the Prophet going to the graveyard in the middle of the night to intercede on behalf of the dead.[4] Other *ḥadīth* also state that if a group of Muslims (either a hundred or three rows) come together and offer prayers for the forgiveness of the sins of another, their petition will surely be granted.[5]

According to a number of *ḥadīth,* on the Day of Judgment, God assembles all the believers, who turn to Adam for intercession. Adam refers them to Noah, who refers them to Abraham, and thence to Moses, and finally to Jesus, who refers them to Muḥammad. In this way, Muḥammad is established as the greatest and final prophet.[6]

Among the Sufis and the general Muslim population, it is believed that holy men can also intercede on behalf of others, even after their death. The tradition of offering prayers and petitions at the tombs of holy men and women remains very much a part of Muslim life. In Syria, at least until the end of the twentieth century, Muslims and Christians shared some of their saints, both praying together at the same shrines.[7]

According to Rūmī, the saints and prophets can make intercession for others. Muḥammad can also intercede for sinners, even saving them from the "heavy torment" of hellfire.[8] Addressing his own master Shams-i Tabrīz, Rūmī writes:

> You who are my soul's comfort in the season of sorrow:...
> to you belongs mercy and intercession *(shafāʿat)*
> for the sin of unbelievers.
>
> *Rūmī, Dīvān-i Shams-i Tabrīz 207:2303, 2308, KSD1 pp.128–29; cf. SDST (VI) pp.22–23*

Rūzbihān says that intercession is possible through one who has been drawn close to God, someone whom al-Ḥallāj identifies as a "divine master":

> When a dweller (*sālik,* wayfarer) in contemplative vision is loved by the Almighty, He draws him near to Himself, and dresses him in the garb of holiness and dignity, making him majestic through His own majesty. Thus is he given rank and standing through God's will....
>
> At this stage, if he appeals for intercession *(shafāʿah),* his intercession *(shafāʿah)* is accepted. Such a dear one of God *(sālik)* is merciful to God's devotees *(ʿibād Allāh)* through the Lord's mercy, and his intercession *(shafāʿah)* is not rejected....
>
> The gnostic (al-Ḥallāj) said, "The station of intercession *(shafāʿah)* is only for divine masters, free of jealousy, and graced with benevolence and compassion for all creation.
>
> *Rūzbihān, Mashrab al-Arwāḥ 9:24, MARB p.177; cf. SSE3 pp.199–200*

1. See also *Qur'ān* 19:87, 53:26.
2. *Qur'ān* 2:48, 123, 254; 36:23; 39:43–44; 43:86; 74:48.
3. *E.g. Ḥadīth Ṣaḥīḥ al-Bukhārī* 1:3.98, 1:7.331, 1:8.429, 8:76.571, 9:93.566, 601, *HSB.*
4. *E.g. Ḥadīth Ṣaḥīḥ Muslim* 42:7149, *HSM.*

5. *E.g. Ḥadīth Ṣaḥīḥ Muslim* 4:2071, *HSM; Musnad Aḥmad ibn Ḥanbal* 4:79, 100.
6. *E.g. Ḥadīth Ṣaḥīḥ al-Bukhārī* 4:55.556, 581, 6:60.3, 6:60.236, 9:93.532, *HSB.*
7. William Dalrymple, *From the Holy Mountain, HMJS* pp.166–71.
8. Rūmī, *Maśnavī* III:1772*ff., MJR4* p.99*ff.*

shajarah (A), **shajarat** (P) *Lit.* tree; genealogical tree; in Sufism, the line of successive *shaykhs* (masters), maintained by each Sufi order, from Muḥammad down to the current master of the order; also called *shajarat-i mashyakhah, mashāyikh,* or *mashā'ikh* (line of *shaykhs*).

See also: **silsilah**.

shihō (J) *Lit.* to inherit *(shi)* the *Dharma (hō);* a ceremony or series of ceremonies in the *Sōtō Zen* school of Japanese Buddhism in which a monk receives a certificate of succession *(shisho),* thus being given formal recognition of having inherited the *Dharma* from his own master and being qualified to take on disciples and teach the *Dharma. Shihō* is also used to mean inheriting the *Dharma* itself *per se.* The ceremony and certificate are only the outward form and external recognition of what has already been given to the disciple by his master.

During the course of the ceremony, the master confirms that the disciple is living the precepts in his daily life. He is then given official recognition that he has received the *Dharma,* and has the authority to transmit it to others. Among other things, he receives a robe and a bowl, together with a certificate of transmission *(shisho)* containing a family tree in the form of a circular graphic image representing the lineage, sometimes tracing the spiritual ancestry back to Bodhidharma, and thence to the Buddha himself. Bodhidharma is credited with having introduced Buddhism to China, whence it spread to Japan.

There are variations in the form and duration of the ceremony among different groups. In the *Zen* lineage of Hakuyū Taizan Maezumi, the complete sequence of ceremonies comprising *shihō* can last between one and three weeks.

See also: **sīshū**.

shōken (J) *Lit.* seeing one another, mutual seeing; the first formal interview *(dokusan)* or ceremony that a prospective disciple has with his or her master *(rōshi)* in a *Zen* monastery, during which the formal request is made for acceptance as a disciple and to join the monastery. Should the master find the disciple sincere, the request will usually be granted. The individual will generally have already passed some time in the monastery as a novice, and a master may not always accept him at the first time of asking. It is traditional to make a small monetary donation at the same time.[1]

See also: **dokusan nyūshitsu**.

1. See "Shôken," *Illustrated Encyclopedia of Zen Buddhism, IEZB.*

shōsan (J), **xiǎocān** (C) *Lit.* small *(xiǎo)* participation *(cān);* small group, small assembly; sermon, talk; an informal talk given by the abbot or master of a *Zen* or *Chán* monastery or temple to a small number of monks or nuns in his own quarters; contrasted with *daishū* (great assembly), which is given in the main hall *(hattō),* and is attended by the entire monastic community.[1]

See also: **daishū**.

1. See "Shôsan," *Illustrated Encyclopedia of Zen Buddhism, IEZB.*

silsilah (A), **silsilat** (P) (pl. *salāsil*) *Lit.* chain; an ancestry, genealogy, or line of succession; from the same root as *salsala* (to link together; a chain, a series); in a Sufi order, the chain or line of transmission (through initiation) of divine grace or blessing *(barakah)* from one master to another master; the chain of masters through which spiritual power, knowledge and teachings have been transmitted within a particular Sufi order, traced back to Muḥammad.

Traditionally, and for the legitimacy of their claim, the *shaykhs* of all Sufi orders must have a *silsilah* that goes back to Muḥammad, usually through the Prophet's successors Abū Bakr and ʿAlī ibn Abī Ṭālib. ʿAlī especially, independently of his place in Shiʿism (where he is regarded as the Prophet's rightful successor), is regarded by Sufis everywhere as the source of mystical knowledge. They are therefore regarded as Muḥammad's spiritual inheritors. The Prophet is believed to have received *barakah* direct from the angel Gabriel; and Muḥammad, in turn, taught mystical Islam to his companions, who passed on the blessing and the teaching to succeeding generations.

The *silsilahs* are believed to have originated in three pacts of allegiance *(bayʿah)* made with Muḥammad, these being the first and second pacts of ʿAqabah, plus, especially, the pact of felicity *(bayʿat al-riḍwān),* a renewal of the oath of allegiance exacted by the Prophet from 1,500 of his companions at al-Ḥudaybīyah,[1] during the early days (Medinan period), when the Prophet had resolved to conquer Mecca but the success of their mission was still in the balance.

The *silsilah* is an attempt to legitimize Sufism in the eyes of orthodox Islam. The fortunes of Sufism within Islam have varied with the passage of time. In the past, a number of prominent Sufis have even been executed as heretics. At the present moment, Sufism is generally regarded as heretical, although, partly because of the prominence and popularity of the Persian Sufi poets, it is tolerated in Iran and Turkey. In most other Muslim countries, however, especially those with Islamic governments, Sufism is deemed heretical, and even books on Sufism are difficult to obtain.

Since *silsilahs (salāsil)* may contain forty or more names, their authenticity is difficult to determine. Even so, they demonstrate the Sufi belief that every master must have had a master from whom they received the blessing of initiation. It is fundamental to Sufism that the Sufi Way *(Ṭarīqat)* cannot be learned from a book. It can only be followed under the guidance of a living *pīr* or *murshid.* The Way to the Divine is regarded as divinely ordained. God can be approached only through these spiritual descendants of the Prophet. Only they are qualified to show the Way to others, and the attempt to reach Him by any other means is considered a great discourtesy towards God and His Prophet.

Speaking of the chain of masters, Rūmī describes them as the spiritual "sons" of Muḥammad:

> A hundred thousand blessings be upon his (Muḥammad's) spirit,
> and upon the advent and the cycle *(dawr)* of his sons!
> Those fortunate caliph-born sons of his
> are born of the substance of his soul and heart.
> Whether they be of Baghdad or Harāt or Rayy,
> they are his spiritual progeny *(nasl).*
> Wherever the rose blossoms on the stem,
> it is still a rose;
> Wherever the wine jar ferments,
> it is still wine.
> If the sun were to rise in the west,
> it would still be the same sun, not something else.
>
> *Rūmī, Maśnavī VI:175–179; cf. MJR6 p.267*

See also: **bay'ah** (7.4).

1. *E.g. Ḥadīth Ṣaḥīḥ al-Bukhārī* 4:52.207; 5:57.48; 5:59.395, 471, 475, 477, 480–83, *HSB.* The number of companions who pledged allegiance varies between 1,300, 1,400, and 1,500.

siṃhanāda (S), **sīhanāda** (Pa), **shīzǐhǒu** (C), **shishiku** (J) *Lit.* lion's *(siṃha, sīha, shīzǐ, shi)* roar *(nāda, hǒu, ku);* metaphorically, a brave speech; a war cry; a speech full of strength, confidence, and authority; in Buddhism, an exposition of the *Dharma* (Way) from a *buddha* or an advanced *bodhisattva.* When it is said that the Buddha "roars his lion's roar *(sīhanāda)* in the assemblies" – often followed by "and sets rolling the wheel of *Brahmā (brahmachakra)*" or the "wheel of *Dharma (dharmachakra)*" – it means that he is teaching the *Dharma* in his characteristically powerful and forthright manner.

The expression makes frequent appearances both in the Pali and later *Mahāyāna* and *Vajrayāna* texts, and the names of a number of *suttas* contain the term. These include, for example, the *Cakkavatti-Sīhanāda* ('Lion's Roar of the Wheel-Turning Emperor'), the *Kassapa-Sīhanāda* ('Lion's Roar of Kassapa'), and the *Udumbarika-Sīhanāda* ('Lion's Roar to the Udumbarkans') *Suttas* of the *Dīgha Nikāya;* the *Cūlasīhanāda* and *Mahāsīhanāda Suttas* ('Shorter and Longer Lion's Roar *Suttas*') of the *Majjhima Nikāya;* the *Sīhanāda Sutta* of the *Anguttara Nikāya;* and *Mahāyāna sūtras* such as the *Shrīmālā-Devī-Siṃhanāda* ('Lion's Roar of Queen Shrīmālā') *Sūtra.*

The discourses of a *buddha* or an advanced *bodhisattva* are likened to a lion's roar because popular belief credits the lion as the fearless king of beasts, able to dominate and overcome all other animals. In the same manner, the spiritual discourses of a *buddha* overcome all doubts, confusions, and erroneous viewpoints. Additionally, because of its fearless and regal reputation, the lion often figures on royal banners and crests. In the same way, a *buddha* or spiritually advanced being is seen as a spiritual king, the natural sovereign of other human beings; also, because a *buddha* has overcome all lower human tendencies and acquired a knowledge of both life and death, he is naturally fearless. Again, it is said that when a lion roars, all lesser creatures are reduced to silence – they stop what they are doing, and listen. Likewise, a *buddha*'s manner of speech is such that everyone automatically listens to what he has to say. At least for a short time, the busy rush of life is stilled and the mind is calmed to some extent, as the message of the *buddha* takes hold.

The advent of a *buddha* in this world is likened to a lion emerging from its lair, and the lion's roar is his setting in motion the wheel of *Dharma (dharmachakra)* or the wheel of *Brahmā (brahmachakra),* which means beginning to teach the *Dharma* and spreading spirituality in the world. In the case of the historical Buddha, according to the traditional story, he gave his first discourse at the Deer Park in Vārāṇasī, where he explained the four noble truths, *viz.:* human life is full of troubles and suffering of one kind or another; the origin of this suffering is self-centred desire; suffering can come to an end in liberation or true freedom, in a state of consciousness known as *nirvāṇa;* and there is a Path that leads to liberation and the cessation of suffering.[1]

There are several variations on the theme. According to one version, it is because he possesses the ten powers unique to a *buddha (dasa tathāgata-*

balāni) that he utters his lion's roar. *Tathāgata* ('Thus come one') is a common epithet of the Buddha and of all *buddhas:*

> Monks, the lion, king of beasts, comes forth from his lair in the evening. Having come forth from his lair, he stretches himself. He then surveys the four directions all around. Having done so, he sounds thrice the lion's roar *(sīhanāda).* And why? (Because he thinks:) "That I may not cause the death of small creatures that are lost!"
>
> 'The lion' – this, monks, is a name for the *tathāgata,* the holy one *(arahanta),* the perfectly enlightened one. When, monks, the *tathāgata* expounds the *Dhamma* in an assembly, that is his lion's roar *(sīhanāda).*
>
> There are, monks, these ten *tathāgata* powers *(dasa tathāgatabalāni)* of a *tathāgata,* endowed with which the *tathāgata* claims the foremost rank, utters his lion's roar *(sīhanāda)* in the assemblies, and sets rolling the wheel of *Brahmā.* What are these ten *tathāgata* powers?
>
> Firstly, the *tathāgata* understands, as it really is, cause as cause and non-cause as non-cause. This is a *tathāgata* power of the *tathāgata,* and because of that power he claims the foremost rank, utters his lion's roar *(sīhanāda)* in the assemblies, and sets rolling the wheel of *Brahmā.*
>
> *Anguttara Nikāya 10:21, Sīhanāda Sutta, PTSA5 pp.32–33; cf. ANNP*

The text then goes on to describe the other ten powers. Another *sutta* adds:

> The Tathāgata has these ten *tathāgata's* powers, possessing which he claims the herd-leader's place, roars his lion's roar *(sīhanāda)* in the assemblies, and sets rolling the wheel of *Brahmā.*
>
> *Majjhima Nikāya 12, Mahāsīhanāda Sutta, PTSM1 p.71, MDBB pp.166–67*

The "herd-leader's place" refers to the lead animal in a herd of cattle, another image conveying power and authority. It is also said that it is because the *tathāgata* possesses the four kinds of fearlessness *(vesārajja)* that "he claims the herd-leader's place, roars his lion's roar in the assemblies, and sets rolling the wheel of *Brahmā,*" something that no "*samaṇa* (holy man), or *brāhmaṇ,* or *deva,* or *māra* (devil), or *Brahmā* or anyone else at all in the universe" is able to do.[2]

The metaphor is further elaborated in the *Sīhopama Sutta* of the *Saṃyutta Nikāya:*

> *Bhikkhus* (monks), in the evening, the lion, the king of beasts, comes out from his lair. Having come out, he stretches himself, surveys the four quarters all around, and roars his lion's roar *(sīhanāda)* three times. Then he sets out in search of game.

> When the lion, the king of beasts, roars, whatever animals hear the sound are for the most part filled with fear, a sense of urgency, and terror. Those who live in holes enter their holes; those who live in the water enter the water; those who live in the woods enter the woods; and the birds fly up into the air. Even those royal bull elephants, bound by strong thongs in the villages, towns, and capital cities, burst and break their bonds asunder; frightened, they urinate and defecate, and flee here and there. So powerful, *bhikkhus,* is the lion, the king of beasts, among the animals, so majestic and mighty.
>
> So too, *bhikkhus,* when the *tathāgata* arises in the world, an *arahanta,* perfectly enlightened, accomplished in true knowledge and conduct, fortunate, knower of the world, unsurpassed leader of persons to be tamed, teacher of *devas* and humans, the enlightened one, the blessed one, he teaches the *Dhamma* (regarding the transience of all things)....
>
> Then, *bhikkhus,* when those *devas* who are long-lived, beautiful, abounding in happiness, dwelling for a long time in lofty palaces, hear the *tathāgata*'s teaching of the *Dhamma,* they are for the most part filled with fear, a sense of urgency, and terror, (saying): "It seems, sir, that we are impermanent, though we thought ourselves permanent;... unstable, though we thought ourselves stable;... non-eternal, though we thought ourselves eternal." So powerful, *bhikkhus,* is the *tathāgata* over this world together with its *devas,* so majestic and mighty.
>
> *Saṃyutta Nikāya 22:78, Sīhopama Sutta, PTSS3 pp.84–85, CDBB pp.913–14*

Similar themes run throughout the later *Mahāyāna sūtras.* In the *Avataṃsaka Sūtra,* the ten vows of a *bodhisattva* are referred to as the "ten kinds of lion's roar":

> A *bodhisattva-mahāsattva* (great-being *bodhisattva*) has ten kinds of lion's roar *(shīzǐhǒu).* He declares, "I will surely attain perfect and complete awakening." This is the great lion's roar *(shīzǐhǒu)* of a mind devoted to enlightenment. "I will save those who are not yet saved, liberate those who are not yet liberated, bring peace to those who have yet to find peace, and enable those who have not attained *nirvāṇa* to attain it." This is the great lion's roar *(shīzǐhǒu)* of great compassion.
>
> *Avataṃsaka Sūtra 38, T10 279:304b23–26*

And so on through the other ten vows. The *Mahāratnakūṭa Sūtra* says that it is because the Buddha has overcome all weaknesses and all lesser powers and has attained perfect enlightenment that he is "able to make the true lion's roar", and to proclaim that he is no longer subject to transmigration:

Only when all impurities *(klesha)* and consequent passions – which are as many as the sands of the Ganges – that should be eliminated, have been eliminated, can one realize the inconceivable *buddhadharma,* which is likewise as vast as the sands of the Ganges. Independent of all things *(sarvadharma),* he realizes unimpeded supernatural power *(shéntōng),* attains wisdom and freedom from all faults, acquires all merits and virtues, and becomes a great *dharma* king, who has attained mastery of all *dharmas*.... He is then in a position to proclaim the real lion's roar *(shīzǐhǒu):* "My rebirths are ended; I have achieved pure living; I have accomplished what had to be accomplished; I am no longer subject to conditioned existence *(i.e. saṃsāra).*" This is why the World-Honoured One can make his continuous and unwavering proclamation in a lion's roar *(shīzǐhǒu)* founded upon the ultimate Truth.

World-Honoured One, there are two kinds of wisdom by which to attain freedom from conditioned existence *(i.e. saṃsāra).* What are these two?

The first is the vanquishing power of the *tathāgatas* by which they have subdued the four demons (the four *māras: kleshamāra* – of the defilements, *mṛityumāra* – of death, *skandhamāra* – of the aggregates, and *devaputramāra* – of the craving for sensual pleasure and comfort) and have transcended all realms. Revered by all sentient beings, they have realized the inconceivable and pure *dharma* body.... They have reached perfection and supremacy; they have nothing further to accomplish and no further stage to realize. Endowed with the ten powers *(dashabala),* they have ascended to the supreme realm of fearlessness, observing all *dharmas* without impediment. Therefore, they can proclaim the true lion's roar *(shīzǐhǒu)* that they are no longer subject to conditioned existence.

The second (wisdom by which one attains freedom from *saṃsāra*) is that of the *arhat* and *pratyeka-buddhas.* They have obtained transport across the boundless river of transmigration and have no further fear of life and death. They have achieved salvation and bliss. Therefore they say, "I am no longer fearful of transmigration and will endure no more suffering."

Mahāratnakūṭa Sūtra 48 (Shrīmālā-Devī-Siṃhanāda), T11 310:676a17–b2

A number of Buddhist *suttas* speak of the interaction between the Buddha and other spiritual teachers of his time, of whom it seems there were many. As is the nature of such anecdotes, since the stories are related in Buddhist texts, the Buddha always comes off best, demonstrating thereby that he is the most spiritually advanced of all. In one instance, the ascetic Pāṭikaputta challenges the Buddha to a miracle and debating contest. But when encouraged by a disciple to go and meet the Buddha, Pāṭikaputta finds himself unable to get up from his seat. Seeing Pāṭikaputta's reluctance to follow through on his challenge, the disciple relates a story of the lion and the jackal who had made a good living off the lion's leftovers, and who thought one day that he too could be a lion:

> Once long ago, the lion, king of beasts, thought: "Suppose I were to make my lair near a certain jungle. Then I could emerge in the evening, yawn, survey the four quarters, roar my lion's roar three times, and then make for the cattle pasture. I could then pick out the very best of the herd for my kill and, having had a good feast of tender meat, return to my lair." And he did accordingly.
>
> Now there was an old jackal who had grown fat on the lion's leavings, and he...was proud and strong. And he thought: "What difference is there between me and the lion, king of beasts? Suppose I were to make my lair near the jungle."...So he chose a lair accordingly and emerging in the evening, he surveyed the four quarters, and then thought: "Now I will roar a lion's roar *(sīhanāda)* three times," and he gave out the howl of his kind, a jackal howl. For what has the wretched howl of a jackal in common with a lion's roar?
>
> In just the same way, Pāṭikaputta, you live off the achievements of the Sugata and feed on the Sugata's leavings, imagining you can set yourself up beside the *tathāgatas, arahantas,* and fully enlightened *buddhas.* But what have wretched Pāṭikaputtas in common with them?
>
> *Dīgha Nikāya 24, Pāṭika Sutta, PTSD3 pp.23–24, TBLD pp.378–79*

The Buddha, who is relating the story, then concludes:

> Then I said: "Pāthikaputta is not capable of meeting me face to face unless he takes back his words, abandons that thought and gives up that view.... Even if the good Licchavis were to think: 'Let us bind him with thongs and try to drag him here with yoked oxen,' he would burst the thongs. He is not capable of meeting me face to face.... If he thinks otherwise, his head will split in pieces."
>
> *Dīgha Nikāya 24, Pāṭika Sutta, PTSD3 pp.26–27, TBLD p.380*

The point is that there are many imitators, imposters and charlatans who make a living by reproducing the spiritual teachings they have heard from the very few who are genuinely spiritually perfect and who truly understand what they are talking about. But their true nature is revealed to themselves and others when they are put to the test. Only a true *buddha* can speak with authority and true understanding – can roar like a lion. Others can only make whatever sound reflects their actual nature.

See also: **dharmachakra**, **siṃhāsana**.

1. *Saṃyutta Nikāya* 56:11, *Dhammacakkappavattana Sutta, PTSS5* pp.420–24.
2. *Majjhima Nikāya* 12, *Mahāsīhanāda Sutta, PTSM1* pp.71–72; *cf. MDBB* p.167.

siṃhāsana (S), **sīhāsana** (Pa), **seng ge'i khri** (T), **shīzǐzuò** (C), **shishiza** (J) *Lit.* lion *(siṃha, seng, shīzǐ, shishi)* seat *(āsana, khri, zuò, za),* lion throne; a throne, a king's throne; metaphorically, a position associated with a lion's strength, regality, dominion, and power; in *haṭha yoga, siṃhāsana* is also the name of a physical posture.

Some Indian deities, such as *Shiva,* regarded as the first yogi, are also often portrayed as seated on a lion throne. Some tantric meditation practices involve imagining the *guru* or some *deva* (deity) seated on an ornate lion throne. In Buddhism, ornate and exotically bejewelled thrones, adorned by lions, whereon the *buddhas* and *bodhisattvas* sit when teaching, are a common image in *Mahāyāna* literature, sculpture, art, and iconography. A lion throne is the seat on which they sit when delivering a discourse on the *Dharma.* In Jainism, the *Jinas* or *Tīrthankaras* are generally portrayed in pictures or sculptures as seated on lion thrones.

The lion is a common symbol in Buddhism. The discourses and teachings of the Buddha are described as a lion's roar *(siṃhanāda)* because of the strength and authority of their delivery, while the *siṃhāsana* symbolizes the Buddha's spiritual kingship and enlightenment, as well as his birth into a royal family as Prince Siddhārtha Gautama. According to the traditional story, his father the king kept the young crown prince away from the sight of suffering. Though heir to the lion throne of this world, when confronted by the sight of suffering, he abandoned his royal inheritance, and embarked on the spiritual quest. Known as Lion of the *Shakyas* and Shākyamuni (Sage of the *Shakyas*), he attained supreme perfect enlightenment *(anuttara-samyak-saṃbodhi),* ascending symbolically to the spiritual throne.

Exotic lion thrones, often conjured up out of nowhere as suitable seats for majestic cross-legged *buddhas* and *bodhisattvas* in the celestial realms, make frequent appearances in *Mahāyāna* and *Vajrayāna* texts such as the *Lotus Sūtra* and the *Avataṃsaka Sūtra.* Lion thrones are also included in some of the names of the countless *buddha*-lands (paradises, heavens), such as 'Lofty Lion Throne of the Gods', 'Lion Throne Illumining Everywhere', 'Jewel Adorned Lion Throne', 'Jewel Lotus Lion Throne', and of celestial *buddhas* such as 'Ascending the Lotus Platform of a Lion Throne'.[1]

Life in the celestial realms, as depicted in the *Avataṃsaka Sūtra* and some other Buddhist texts, is of an extraordinary character. In this *sūtra,* the writer gives full rein to his imagination in the attempt to depict something of his understanding and beliefs concerning these heavenly regions. In a long description concerning the activities of celestial *bodhisattvas,* he paints a picture of lion thrones of great and beautiful magnificence:

> When a *bodhisattva-mahāsattva* (great-being *bodhisattva*) bestows the gift of thrones, he gives a lion throne *(shīzǐzuò)* that is tall and wide, supreme and wondrous. Its legs are fashioned of lapis lazuli, its seat inlaid with gold. It is arrayed with soft fabrics, adorned with jewelled banners, scented with many exquisite perfumes, ornamented with numerous and varied jewels, and covered by a canopy of golden nets. Jewelled bells swing in the breeze, producing exquisite sounds. The throne is adorned with numerous embellishments of unusual design, so magnificent that people look upon it in awe. A crowned king takes his seat upon the throne by himself, and proclaims laws that are followed respectfully in every state.
>
> *Avataṃsaka Sūtra 25, T10 279:141b20–26*

Another passage describes the arrival of the seeker Sudhana at Sunlight Park, where he is to meet a certain *bhikshuṇī* (nun), Siṃha-vijṛimbhita, who is "expounding the *Dharma* for the benefit of countless beings". Sunlight Park is of great beauty, containing many ornate lion seats:

> In the grove, spring water flowed through lotus ponds decorated with seven precious treasures (gold, silver, sapphire, crystal, ruby, emerald, and coral).[2] Black sandalwood clay on the bottom of the ponds was covered with layers of wonderful golden sand. The ponds were filled with the water of eight virtues, covered with green, red, yellow and white lotuses, and surrounded by rows of countless treasure trees.
>
> Arranged under the treasure trees were lion seats *(shīzǐzuò)* decorated with various wonderful treasures. They were spread with heavenly fabrics, perfumed with delightful fragrances, draped with precious silks, surrounded by exquisite enclosures, and covered by canopies comprising layer upon layer of golden netting. Bejewelled bells swung slowly, giving forth beautiful sounds. Beneath one treasure tree, Sudhana saw a lion seat *(shīzǐzuò)* in the centre of a bejewelled lotus; beneath another, a lion seat *(shīzǐzuò)* in the midst of a fragrant diamond lotus; under another, a lion seat *(shīzǐzuò)* in the midst of a diamond lotus embellished with dragons;... (*etc.,* the text depicting several varieties of jewel and diamond lotuses). Each seat was surrounded by tens of thousands of bejewelled lion seats *(shīzǐzuò),* each of which was richly ornamented.
>
> *Avataṃsaka Sūtra 39, T10 279:363b3–16*

There is a passage in the *Lotus Sūtra,* written in a similar vein, in which the Buddha tells his disciples how the *buddha* Victorious through Great Universal Wisdom finally attained enlightenment, seated on a lion throne several miles high, prepared for him by the (Hindu) deity *Indra* and his retinue:

> The *buddha* Victorious through Great Universal Wisdom had a life-span of five hundred and forty myriad millions of *nayutas* (myriads) of *kalpas* (ages). But when this *buddha* first sat in the place of practice, after having smashed *Māra*'s (the devil's) army, and was about to attain *anuttara-samyak-saṃbodhi* (supreme, perfect enlightenment), the *buddhadharma* (*buddha* Way) still did not appear before him. In this way, from one minor *kalpa* up through ten minor *kalpas,* he sat cross-legged, body and mind unmoving; yet still the *buddhadharma* did not appear before him.
>
> At that time, the heavenly beings of *trayastriṃsha* (*Indra* and his thirty-three million) had prepared for that *buddha,* under the *bodhi* tree, a lion throne *(shīzǐzuò),* one *yojana* (several miles) in height, intending that the *buddha* should sit upon it when he attained *anuttara-samyak-saṃbodhi.* As soon as he sat upon that throne, the *Brahmā*-kings rained down a multitude of heavenly flowers, covering the ground for a hundred *yojanas* around. From time to time, a fragrant wind sprang up, blowing away the withered flowers, and raining down new ones. This went on ceaselessly for ten minor *kalpas* as an offering to the *buddha.* These flowers rained down until the very moment of his passage into extinction *(nirvāṇa).* The heavenly beings in the train of the four kings, as an offering to the *buddha,* constantly beat heavenly drums, while the other heavenly beings likewise played skilful heavenly music for ten full minor *kalpas,* until his passage extinction *(nirvāṇa).*
>
> *Lotus Sūtra 7, T9 262:22b20–22c1; cf. LBFD pp.131–32*

The *Mahāyāna* Buddhist philosopher Nāgārjuna (*c.*150–250 CE), faced with many *sūtras* that speak of the lion throne, questions its significance, and also provides an answer:

> **Q.** What is this *siṃhāsana?* Did the Buddha create a lion? Is a real lion present, or did he make a lion out of gold, silver, wood, or stone?…
>
> **A.** The lion in question is not a real lion but, since the Buddha is a lion among men *(purusha-siṃha),* the seat where he sits down, whether it be on a bed *(āsana)* or on the ground *(bhūmi),* is called the lion's seat *(siṃhāsana).* In the same way, even today the seat where the king is enthroned is called a lion's seat *(siṃhāsana),* the chief who commands warriors is called a lion-man *(purusha-siṃha)* and people call the king of the land *purusha-siṃha.* Just

> as a lion among animals is strong, fearless and can conquer all *(abhibhavati),* so the Buddha triumphs over all ninety-six heretical systems and is called *purusha-siṃha.*
>
> *Nāgārjuna, Mahāprajñāpāramitā Shāstra 14:1, TVW1 p.347*

Many, he observes, aspire to sit on such a seat from unworthy motives; yet it is not attained by ambition, but by the certainty that arises from inner knowledge of the Truth and Reality:

> The person of little merit and without wisdom
> is unable to occupy a high seat.
> He is like a wolf in the face of a lion
> that crouches down and does not dare to come out.
>
> The great sage is without fear,
> he can occupy the lion's seat *(siṃhāsana).*
> He is like the lion whose roar
> makes all the beasts tremble.
>
> *Nāgārjuna, Mahāprajñāpāramitā Shāstra 10:17, TVW1 p.289*

The *Zen* master Dōgen recalls the similar observation of his own master concerning the many spiritual teachers who really do not know what they are talking about:

> My late master once said, "Nowadays there are many who ascend the lion seats (C. *shīzǐzuò*) of many districts, and many who act as teachers of human beings and gods; but there are none at all who know the truths of the *buddhadharma.*"
>
> *Eihei Dōgen, Shōbōgenzō, Butsudō, T2582 82:186c25–28; cf. SDT3 (49) p.100, STHT (51) p.637*

See also: **siṃhāsana**.

1. *Avataṃsaka Sūtra* 5, *FOSC* pp.228, 232, 241.
2. *Avataṃsaka Sūtra* 39, *T10* 279:332b14–15.

sīshū (C), **shisho** (J) *Lit.* personal *(shi, sī)* document *(sho, shū);* private certificate; transmission certificate; certificate of succession in *Zen* and *Chán* Buddhism; a document given to a disciple by his master certifying that the holder has received *dharma* transmission and is qualified to teach the *Dharma.*

Traditionally, a *shisho* will contain a circular graphic representation showing the complete lineage of the patriarchs together with the more recent masters, up to the present master and the new *dharma* heir. Sometimes, the lineage may be traced back to Bodhidharma, and thence to the Buddha himself. Bodhidharma is credited with having introduced Buddhism to China, whence it spread to Japan. Often, a *shisho* will also contain a ritual dialogue underlining the essential unity of master and disciple. In ancient times, a *shisho* certified the succession of one truly qualified master by another, and would have been issued only rarely. In modern times, however, *dharma* transmission possesses a spectrum of meaning and significance across the various *Zen* schools and lineages, and understanding of its true nature of has been downgraded. Consequently, a *shisho* can be readily obtained from a master and its issue may only confirm (in the opinion of the master) that a particular monk is qualified to be the abbot of a *Zen* monastery or temple and to take on disciples.

This decline in significance was exacerbated by the introduction to the *Sōtō* school in medieval times (1185–1600) of a practice (known as *garanbō*), in which an abbot would adopt the lineage of a new posting regardless of his relationship with the lineage of his new monastery or temple. Under such circumstances, the recommended practice was either to return the *shisho* to the master who had issued it, or if this was not possible, to burn it. The same practice was also adopted to a lesser extent by the *Rinzai* school.

Later reforms during the Tokugawa period (1600–1867) attempted to reverse the custom, reverting to the purely mystical understanding of *dharma* transmission envisioned by the *Sōtō* founder Eihei Dōgen, regarded as the fifty-first patriarch in a line stretching back to the Buddha himself. Dōgen himself explains the importance of the "seal of certification":

> *Buddhas,* without exception, receive the *Dharma* from *buddhas, buddha* to *buddha;* and patriarchs, without exception, receive the *Dharma* from patriarchs, patriarch to patriarch. This is their direct experience of what has been promised. It is the simple, direct, one-to-one transmission, and for this reason it is the unsurpassed state of *bodhi* (enlightenment). If one is not a *buddha,* one cannot give the seal of certification *(shisho)* to a *buddha,* and no one ever becomes a *buddha* without receiving a *buddha*'s seal of certification *(shisho).* Who but a *buddha* can esteem this state as the most honoured or certify it to be unsurpassed?
>
> *Eihei Dōgen, Shōbōgenzō, Shisho, T2582 82:67c22–28; cf. SDT1 (16) p.245, STHT (15) pp.159–60*

Even so, although emphasizing elsewhere the manner in which the enlightenment experience is passed directly from the mind of one *buddha* to the mind of his successor, the experience is interior and entirely one's own. Whatever part the master may have to play, the experience will always be the disciple's very own experience. It is also an experience in which the "self" is absent:

When we receive the *buddha*'s seal of certification *(shisho),* we realize the state independently, without a master, and we realize the state independently, without our self. For this reason, we speak of *buddhas* really experiencing the succession, and of patriarchs really experiencing the same state. The essential meaning of this truth cannot be clarified by anyone other than *buddhas.* How could it possibly be like what is surmised by those at any of the various stages along the *bodhisattva* path, to say nothing of what doctrinal teachers or mundane commentators on scriptural texts may reckon it to be? Even if we explain it to them, they will not be able to hear it, because it is something that is transmitted between *buddhas,* from *buddha* to *buddha.*

Eihei Dōgen, Shōbōgenzō, T2582 82:67c29–68a8;
cf. SDT1 (16) pp.245–46, STHT (15) p.160

Although a *shisho* is only (traditionally) a document consisting of ink on silk, and from a spiritual perspective may be discounted as 'just another piece of paper', it is clear that Dōgen understood its value to lie in what it represented in terms of the spiritual status of the holder; and in the authentication of the successor by the predecessor, and hence of the entire lineage.

See also: **garanbō**, **in'in ekishi**, **menju shihō**.

sthānak(a) (S/H/Pk) *Lit.* position, situation, rank, dignity; place, city, town; by extension, especially in Jainism, a hall, a dwelling; a Jain *Shvetāmbara* term for a hall of residence and meditation, and also used for a variety of religious activities; also called an *upāshraya* (shelter, refuge).

Sthānaka also means a foundation or something fundamental, and is used in Jainism to refer to the six fundamental truths *(shaṭ-sthānaka):* there is a soul; the soul is eternal; the soul performs *karma;* the soul bears the consequences; there is liberation; and there is a path to liberation. It is also used for twenty *sthānakas* or truths described in the universal or legendary history text known as the *Trishashṭi-Shalākā-Purusha-Charitra.* The twenty *sthānakas* include the worship of *Arhats* (worthy ones, enlightened souls who have departed) and their images; caring for mendicants and *gurus* by gifts of food, medicine, clothes, and so on; service to one's *āchāryas* and religious superiors; freedom from doubt; the earnest attempt to avoid transgressions; the practice of "pure meditation every minute and every second"; learning the scriptures; propagation of the doctrine, and so forth.[1]

See also: **Sthānakavāsī** (7.1), **upāshraya**.

1. Hemachandra, *Trishashṭi-Shalākā-Purusha-Charitra* 1, *TSP1* pp.80–84.

ṣuḥbah (A), **ṣuḥbat** (P) *Lit.* companionship, comradeship, friendship, association, relationship, company, society; in Sufism, the relationship between master and disciple; also, companionship and mutual support among fellow disciples of a master; also, a close inward relationship and contact with the Divine:

> Associate *(muṣāḥabat)* with God. If you cannot, then associate *(muṣāḥib)* with one who associates *(muṣāḥib)* with God.
>
> *Tamastānī, in Mashrab al-Arwāḥ 9:34, MARB p.182, in SSE10 p.84*

Disciples who had close personal contact with a master were sometimes called *aṣḥāb-i ṣuḥbat* (disciples of close association, close disciples), *yārān-i ṣuḥbat* (friends of close association, close friends), or *aṣḥāb-i ṣuḥbat* (companions of close association, close companions).[1]

Ṣuḥbat is sometimes contrasted with *'uzlat* (retreat). Some Sufis have advocated the necessity of companionship with other disciples. They have held that learning to prefer the wishes of others over one's own desires is essential for spiritual progress.[2] Others have maintained the necessity of seeking solitude *('uzlat)* for spiritual progress.[3] Yet others say that it is best to learn to live in the world, in companionship with others, while at the same time maintaining inner peace and solitude.[4]

All these points of view relate to the fact that the mind is soon distracted and affected by the company it keeps. Therefore, mystics have generally advised their disciples to choose their company wisely. As Rūmī enigmatically observes:

> Through the company *(ṣuḥbat)* of the rose,
> the thorn is safe from fire;
> Through the company *(ṣuḥbat)* of the thorn,
> the rose enters the fire.
>
> *Rūmī, Dīvān-i Shams-i Tabrīz, Rubā'īyāt 579, KSD8 p.98; cf. TSR p.92*

And:

> The laughing pomegranate makes the garden laughing:
> Companionship *(ṣuḥbat)* with holy men
> makes you one of the holy men.
>
> *Rūmī, Maśnavī I:721, MJR2 p.41*

Using a different metaphor, Ḥāfiẓ says much the same:

> That by whose ray base metal becomes gold
> is an alchemy found in the company
> of dervishes *(ṣuḥbat-i darvīshān)*.
>
> *Ḥāfiẓ, Dīvān, DHA p.31, DIH p.76; cf. DHWC (36:5) p.98*

Ḥāfiẓ also counsels avoiding the company of those who will lead you astray:

> Our cup-bearing master – may his soul be in bliss! – said:
> "Avoid the company *(ṣuḥbat)*
> of covenant breakers *(paymān shikanān).*
>
> *Ḥāfiẓ, Dīvān, DHA p.214, DIH p.346; cf. DHWC (457:6) p.762*

Bad companions can be avoided, but to find that one who radiates light and bliss, says Ḥāfiẓ, is a blessing from God:

> For God's sake, ask, "Who is the moth
> that enjoys the good fortune of association *(ṣuḥbat)*
> with that bliss-radiating candle?"
>
> *Ḥāfiẓ, Dīvān, DHA p.44, DIH p.104; cf. DHWC (53:7) p.133, in SSE10 p.84*

See also: **jamāʿah**, **pīr** (7.1), **ʿuzlah** (▸3).

1. *E.g.* Aḥmad al-Aflākī, *Manāqib al-ʿĀrifīn* 3:49, 88, 112, *MASA1* pp.133, 173, 202, *FKG* (3:49, 89, 113) pp.94, 121, 140.
2. See *e.g.* in Hujwīrī, *Kashf al-Maḥjūb* XIV:5, *KMM* p.236, *KM* p.189.
3. See *e.g.* in Hujwīrī, *Kashf al-Maḥjūb* XIV:3, *KMM* p.234, *KM* p.188.
4. *E.g.* Hujwīrī, *Kashf al-Maḥjūb* VII:2, *KMM* p.81, *KM* p.72.

tajāhul al-ʿārif (A), **tajāhul-i ʿārif** (P) *Lit.* feigned ignorance *(tajāhul)* of a knower *(ʿārif);* the pretended ignorance of someone who knows; applicable to anyone feigning ignorance; from the verb *jahila* (to be ignorant); often used as a poetic device. The poet Saʿdī for instance, feigns ignorance of the source of the beloved's fragrance:

> Are those aloes under your skirt,
> or roses in your sleeve,
> or is it musk in your collar?
> Show us what it is you have.
>
> *Saʿdī, Ṭayyibāt 359:5, KSSS p.327; cf. TOS p.481*

Likewise, he pretends to confuse the beauty of the beloved with other beautiful things, all of which are symbols for the inner beloved:

> Is it a rose, or an idol, or a moon, or the beloved's face?
> Is it night, or jet, or musk, or his dark tresses?
>
> *Saʿdī, Ṭayyibāt 381:1, KSSS p.333; cf. TOS p.507*

Mystically, *tajāhul al-ʿārif* is the feigned ignorance of a gnostic or mystic, such as the kindness and seeming unawareness of a saint concerning the imperfections of his disciples and others. Rūmī, for instance, tells the tale of two magicians who try to steal Moses' rod while he is peacefully asleep. But the rod becomes a dragon and terrifies them. When they ask Moses' forgiveness, he addresses them as "O nobles" and "O my two friends", and pardons them as if he had no idea of their wrongdoing, and as if he were unaware of any attempted offence against him.[1]

Rūmī also warns that a disciple should not presume too far on the feigned ignorance of his master. The temptation is to believe that the master does not actually know of one's imperfections. Such deceptions include a lack of spiritual practice, together with feigned love and longing:

> You have brought dry manure to one endowed with vision,
> saying, "Buy this instead of a sachet of musk."
> O you of stinking brain and stinking marrow,
> you place camel's dung beneath your nose and say,
> "O, delicious!"
> O squint-eyed crazy fool, you have exclaimed in delight,
> "Oh! Oh!" so that your defective wares may find a ready sale,
> and that you may deceive that spiritual organ of smell,
> which finds pasture in the celestial rose garden.
>
> Though his forbearance has feigned stupidity *(gōl sākht),*
> you must know yourself a little. . . .
> If that glorious one has feigned sleep *(khuftah kard),*
> he is really very much awake:
> Do not run off with his turban!
>
> *Rūmī, Maśnavī IV:2084–88, 2090; cf. MJR4 p.387*

Feigned ignorance is an aspect of a saint's incomprehensible love and humility. Being all-powerful, he still portrays himself as one of the disciples, one of the struggling souls, giving credit for everything that happens to his own master.

Rūmī also equates feigned ignorance with the Socratic method of teaching, posing as someone who knows nothing and asking a series of probing questions to bring out the truth:

> That Kalīm (Moses) became like an ignorant enquirer *(aʿjamī),*
> so that he might acquaint the ignorant with this mystery.
> Let us too feign ourselves to be ignorant *(aʿjamī)* thereof,
> and elicit the answer to it as unknowing strangers.
>
> *Rūmī, Maśnavī IV:3012–13; cf. MJR6 p.438*

1. *Maśnavī* III:1229–44, *MJR4* p.70.

teishō (J) *Lit.* presentation, recitation; sermon, lecture, discourse, talk, address; a talk or commentary, generally from a *Zen* text, given by the abbot of a *Zen* monastery or temple; a *dharma* talk that comprises the first part of a *daishū* (great assembly); often used for the talks given by a *Zen rōshi* (master) during a *sesshin,* a period of intensive meditation, traditionally lasting seven days and nights; a regularly scheduled talk; an inspirational address on the Buddhist *Dharma,* given to monks and other attendees, the presence and atmosphere surrounding the *rōshi* adding significantly to the hearers' experience. The ideal *teishō* follows *Zen* principles and is not so much a logical and analytical lecture, but more a presentation without recourse to theory, doctrine, or intellectual and conceptual analysis.[1]

In a question-and-answer session, *Zen* teacher Shunryu Suzuki (1904–1971) explains the significance of *teishō* as an expression of Reality, helping the listeners towards that experience:

> *Teishō* is to give encouragement. It is not just to talk about something, but to give some suggestions and to help people have a good understanding of our practice. The words must come from the actual experience of – I hesitate to say – the actual experience of enlightenment. These are big words. The actual experience of Reality is *teishō.* The words should not be dead; they should not be something that we study or read in a book. That is the difference between *teishō* and lecture. Strictly speaking, lectures give some knowledge of some thing; *teishō* helps people's actual practice and enlightenment. So pushing people toward real practice is *teishō.* "Here is something you must have as a Buddhist. Look!" That is *teishō.* We must have something real to talk about. If you read this book, even memorize it, that is not *teishō. Teishō* is something that comes from inside, from the bottom of the heart. Because I must use words, I must follow logic and use special, technical philosophical terms. But sometimes, ignoring those terms, we can speak directly about reality. Sometimes it may not be with words. This is *teishō.* To talk about something that is not possible to talk about is *teishō.* Excuse me. I cannot explain it so well. . . .
>
> To give something directly is *teishō.* Usually your attitude in listening to *teishō* is to think about whether it is good or bad. You wonder, "What is he speaking about? If it is good, I will accept it. If it is not good, I will not accept it." That is extra; you don't need to be so careful. If you just listen, you don't even need to try to understand it. If you don't understand, it is okay; if you do understand, it is better, that's

> all. There should be no special intention in listening. Just to listen is how you should receive *teishō*. It is different from studying something.
>
> *Shunryu Suzuki, Zen Talks, BSFD pp.187–88*

See also: **daishū**.

1. See "Teishô," *Illustrated Encyclopedia of Zen Buddhism, IEZB.*

tekke (Turkish) A Sufi meeting place or place of residence. See **khānaqāh**.

uḍumbara (S), **udumbara** (Pa), **yōutánbōluó** (C), **udon** (J) A species of fig tree, *Ficus glomerata* or *Ficus racemosa,* that bears fruit on or close to its trunk, rather than on its branches. Like all fig trees, the flowers are out of sight, enclosed within the fruit, giving rise to the ancient Indian belief that they flower only once in 3,000 years. Its fruit are known as *gular* in North India and as *atti* in the South. In Vedic times, the wood of the *uḍumbara* was believed to possess sacred qualities, and was used for various sacrificial and ritual implements such as ladles, amulets, and so on. In Chinese texts, the *yōutánbōluó* is often abbreviated to *yōutánbō* or *yōután,* sometimes with the addition of *huá* (flower).

Metaphorically, the *uḍumbara* flower denotes something of great rarity. It is frequently used in later *Mahāyāna* Buddhist texts to illustrate how rare it is to come into contact with a *buddha* and to encounter the true *Dharma.* According to the *Lotus Sūtra:*

> The Buddha said to Shāriputra, "A wonderful Law *(Dharma)* such as this is preached by the *buddhas,* the thus come ones *(tathāgatas),* at certain times. But like the blooming of the *uḍumbara (yōutánbō),* such times come very seldom. Shāriputra, you and the others must believe me. The words that the *buddhas* preach are not empty or false."
>
> *Lotus Sūtra 2, T9 262:7a16–17, LSOC p.64*

Similarly, in the *Avataṃsaka Sūtra,* the celestial *bodhisattva* Samantabhadra says:

> Full of great happiness, a *bodhisattva-mahāsattva* (great-being *bodhisattva*) thinks, "The *buddhas* and *tathāgatas* are encountered as rarely as the *uḍumbara* flower *(yōután).* One can hardly meet them even once in countless *kalpas* (ages). But in the future, I will be able to see a *tathāgata* whenever I want to. The *buddhas* and *tathāgatas* are always with me and will never abandon me. They permit me to

> see them and they expound the *Dharma* to me continually. When I hear the *Dharma,* my mind becomes pure and tranquil, free from deviousness, upright, and without falsehood. Always keeping the *buddhas* in my thoughts, I can see them." Entertaining such thoughts, they become very happy.
>
> *Avataṃsaka Sūtra 38, T10 279:284b6–12*

According to a story related by the Buddha in the *Lotus Sūtra,* two spiritually advanced sons of Shubhavyūha want to leave home to become *shramaṇas* and disciples of the *buddha* Meghadundubhi-Svararāja. When the parents of the two sons express their concern, the two sons place their hands together in supplication, saying:

> We beg our mother to permit us
> to leave the household and become *shramaṇas.*
> The *buddhas* are very hard to encounter:
> we will follow this *buddha* and learn from him.
> Rare as is the *uḍumbara* flower *(yōutánbōluó),*
> rarer is it to encounter the *buddha,* . . .
> we beg you to allow us to leave the household.
>
> *Lotus Sūtra 27, T9 262:60a22–25, LSOC p.355*

Their mother then says to them:

> I will permit you to leave household life. Why? Because the *buddha* is difficult to encounter.
>
> *Lotus Sūtra 27, T9 262:60a26, LSOC p.356*

The two sons then thank their father and mother, explaining that they have met the Buddha due to their good deeds in past lives:

> Excellent, father and mother! And we beg you in due time to go to the place where the *buddha* Cloud Thunder Sound Constellation King Flower Wisdom (Meghadundubhi-Svararāja) is, attend him in person and offer alms. Why? Because encountering the *buddha* is as difficult as encountering the *uḍumbara* flower *(yōutánbōluó).* Or as difficult as it is for a one-eyed turtle to encounter a floating log with a hole in it. We have been blessed with great good fortune from past existences, and so have been born in an age where we can encounter the *buddha*'s Law *(buddhadharma).* For this reason, our father and mother should permit us to leave household life. Why? Because the *buddhas* are difficult to encounter, and the proper time is also hard to come upon.
>
> *Lotus Sūtra 27, T9 262:60a27–b3, LSOC p.356*

The *Lotus Sūtra* also adds that the same rarity even applies to a true seeker of the *Dharma:*

> The times when the *buddhas* appear in the world
> are far apart and difficult to encounter.
> And even when they appear in the world,
> it is difficult for them to preach this Law *(Dharma).*
> Throughout incalculable, innumerable *kalpas* (ages),
> it is rare that one may hear this Law *(Dharma);*
> And a person capable of listening to this Law *(Dharma)* –
> such a person is likewise rare.
>
> It is like the *uḍumbara* flower *(yōután),*
> which all the world loves and delights in,
> which heavenly and human beings look on as something rare,
> but which appears only once in many many ages.
> If a person hears this Law *(Dharma),* delights in and praises it,
> even if he utters just one word, then he has made offerings
> to all the *buddhas* of the three existences.
> But a person like this is very rarely found,
> rarer than the *uḍumbara* flower.
>
> *Lotus Sūtra 2, T9 262:10a24–b3, LSOC pp.79–80*

According to Buddhist legend, the Buddha is said to have indicated the appointment of Mahākāshyapa as his successor by giving him an *uḍumbara* flower. In China and Japan, this is understood as a symbol of face-to-face transmission (J. *menju*) of the *Dharma* from a *buddha* to his successor. The *Zen* master Dōgen Zenji (1200–1253), founder of the Japanese *Sōtō Zen* school after training in China with the master Rújìng, describes how the *Dharma* was transmitted from the *buddhas* preceding Shākyamuni Buddha to the Buddha himself, and thence to his disciple Mahākāshyapa. From there, the *Dharma* was passed on until it reached Bodhidharma, who is credited with bringing Buddhism to China, from where, through the Chinese patriarchs, it came to Dōgen Zenji himself.[1]

See also: **menju shihō**.

1. Eihei Dōgen, *Shōbōgenzō, Menju, T2582* 82:214a3–23, *SDT3* (57) pp.209–10.

ummah (A), **ummat** (P) *Lit.* community, people, nation; in Islam, the community of Muslims. A distinction is made between *ummat al-daʿwah* (the called community, the community to whom Muḥammad was sent) and *ummat* *al-ijābah* (the responding community, the community who responded to his call). *Ummat al-mahdīyah* means the rightly guided community, as in the *ḥadīth,* "I was a hidden mercy and I was sent to a rightly guided community *(ummat al-mahdīyah).*"

Rūmī quotes another *ḥadīth,* "The likeness of my community *(ummah)* is the parable of the ship (ark) of Noah: whoever clings to it is saved, and whoever rejects it is drowned."[1] Rūmī expands:

> The Prophet said, "I am like a ship in the storm of time.
> I and my companions are like the ship of Noah:
> whoever catches hold will gain spiritual graces."
>
> *Rūmī, Maśnavī IV:538–39; cf. MJR4 p.302*

And he goes on to speak of the benefits of the spiritual protection of the *shaykh* (master).

1. Rūmī, *Maśnavī* IV:538 (heading); *cf. MJR4* p.302, *AMBF* 334.

upadesh(a) (S/H), **updesh**, **updes** (H/Pu), **man-ngag** (T) *Lit.* instruction, teaching, information, dialogue, discussion, advice, admonition, preaching, sermon, exhortation; spiritual instruction or direction; also, initiation into a spiritual path, which includes advice and instruction on how to meditate and follow that particular path, and which varies in content and intention between different spiritual schools and traditions. Hence, an *upadeshī* or *upadeshaka* is one who gives *upadesha* – an instructor, a teacher, a preacher, one authorized to give initiation. Since the term can mean both teaching as well as initiation, it is sometimes difficult to be certain of the meaning intended by the writer.

In the *Upanishads, upadesha* means teaching or instruction in a general sense. Summarizing its teaching, the author of the *Taittirīya Upanishad* writes:

> This is the command. This is the teaching *(upadesha).* This is the inner meaning of the *Veda.* This is the commandment (given by God and spiritual teachers). Thus should one meditate. Thus indeed should one meditate.
>
> *Taittirīya Upanishad 1:11.6*

Later texts use *upadesha* in a similar manner. Thus, the ninth-century Shankara entitled a concise introductory treatise of a thousand verses, *Upadesha-Sāhasri* ('A Thousand Teachings'); and, in his *Vivekachūḍāmaṇi,* he writes:

> By the way of a dialogue *(upadesha)* between master and disciple has the nature of the *Ātman* (Self, Soul) been ascertained for the easy comprehension of seekers after liberation.
>
> *Shankara, Vivekachūḍāmaṇi 578; cf. VCSM p.214*

In Buddhist texts, *upadesha* generally means discussion or dialogue. *Upadesha* is the ninth of the twelve divisions of *Mahāyāna* Buddhist scriptures in the Pali canon. Such texts contain discussions of teachings or a commentary on a *sūtra,* often presented in a question-and-answer format between the Buddha and his disciples. A text written in the cryptic style of a *sūtra* or root text, however, may also be understood as an *upadesha,* when it contains a highly concentrated instruction from master to disciple. Patrul Rinpoche, in his commentary on the *Three Statements of Garab Dorje,* refers throughout to Dorje's root text as a *man ngag,* Tibetan for *upadesha.* Born around 184 BCE, Dorje was regarded as the first teacher of *Dzogchen* ('Great Perfection'), which proclaims itself as the highest path to enlightenment:

> This *upadesha,* which is like highly refined melted gold, is in truth the essence of the mind. I am reluctant to reveal it to persons who do not practise; but to those individuals who would cherish these teachings as much as their own lives and who, having practised the essential points, might attain buddhahood within a single lifetime, I would not hesitate to reveal them. Hence, it says in the text, "and should be given to the sons of one's heart and sealed".
>
> *Patrul Rinpoche, Special Teaching, GLTS p.63*

The English translator explains:

> The text we have here is pre-eminently an *upadesha (man ngag),* a secret instruction, that is to say, an instruction communicated in private and in confidence from a master to his disciple. An *upadesha* is based more on the personal experience of the master in meditation practice than on philosophical analysis and scholastic tradition. The Sanskrit term *upadesha* is translated in Tibetan as *man ngag,* that is, 'not *(man)* to be spoken aloud *(ngag)* in public'. Thus an *upadesha* is not as such a philosophical treatise or an exegesis, which would be a *shāstra* (T. *bstan bcos*) – a text that constructs *(bcos pa)* a doctrine *(bstan pa)*. . . .
>
> In the Tibetan context, the presence of an oral tradition is very likely, since such oral traditions exist even today. Originally, all *upadeshas* were orally transmitted; only later were they written down. It is merely the bias of most modern scholars to think that something does not exist unless it is written down in some text. In the early days, the masters relied less on written texts than on memory. Often their

> texts were merely mnemonic devices. Only at a later time were these root texts, composed in a highly terse and elliptical language, written down and explicated by commentaries authored by monk-scholars resident in monasteries supported by royal patronage. Thus these monks had the leisure for engaging themselves in this sort of literary activity, which was not the case with the *mahāsiddhas,* who were the actual sources of these *upadeshas.*
>
> Nowadays, in our urban industrial civilization, books are commonplace, but in ancient times, and in general before the advent of printing and a ready supply of paper, they were not. Often a text served…as a mnemonic device, an aid to memory, rather than as an elaborate treatise. Moreover, large books, consisting of many pages, were heavy and therefore were difficult to carry about easily from place to place before modern means of transportation appeared. The lifestyle of the early Buddhist *mahāsiddhas,* like that of contemporary Hindu *sādhus,* was itinerant and peripatetic. It would be impossible in those days for a master, wandering from place to place, to carry a large collection of books with him.…
>
> All of the evidence suggests that…Garab Dorje transmitted these teachings as *upadesha (man ngag),* or secret oral instructions, only to his close disciples, and not publicly. This is not at all unusual in the context of *tantra.* Generally, *upadesha* is very private and intimate instruction given by a master to a disciple, offering advice on practice drawn from his or her own personal experience.
>
> *John Reynolds, Golden Letters, GLTS pp.119, 203, 265–66*

See also: **dīkshā** (7.4), **upadesha** (7.4).

upāshray(a) (S/H) *Lit.* leaning against, resting upon; support, pillow, cushion; shelter, refuge; a dwelling, a lodging house, a guest house; in Jainism, especially in the *Shvetāmbara Mūrtipūjaka* tradition, a dwelling and eating place in the vicinity of a temple for both monks and laypeople, also used for meditation, prayer, ceremonies, the holding of discourses and sermons, and for other religious activities; a place where itinerant monks stay during the four months *(chatur-māsa)* of the rainy season, when walking about would cause harm to many insects and other invertebrates on the ground; a place where laypeople can stay to be free of a householder's responsibilities while temporarily observing mendicant vows, such as fasting, and so on; also called a *sthānaka* (dwelling).

In medieval times, an *upāshraya* was a residence for temple-dwelling *Shvetāmbara Mūrtipūjaka* monks, known as *chaityavāsīs* and later as *yatis,* who did not take the full mendicant vows and led a comfortable lifestyle, a practice that lasted until the latter part of the nineteenth century. In times past, *Mūrtipūjaka upāshrayas* were administered by the local *shrīpūjyas,* some of whom were rich and influential, having elaborate thrones and offices. Nowadays, *upāshrayas* are in the hands of the laity.

In the *Sthānakavāsī* tradition, an *upāshraya* is a hall of both residence and meditation. In keeping with their principles, *Sthānakavāsī* halls are of simple design, large and spacious with few rooms, and separate from the main temple complex, where the monks sit in silent mental worship *(bhāva-pūjā)* of the Jain *Tīrthankaras* (ascended masters).

See also: **chaityavāsin** (7.1), **Sthānakavāsī** (7.1).

upāya-kaushalya (S), **upāya-kosalla** (Pa), **thabs-mkhas** (T), **quán fāngbiàn** (C), **gon hōben** (J) *Lit.* skilfulness *(kaushalya, mkhas, quán, gon)* in means *(upāya, thabs, fāngbiàn, hōben);* cleverness in means; skilful use of expedient means or devices, ingenious methods, ingenuity, clever stratagems; also translated by expressions such as 'skill-in-expedients', 'skill-in-means', 'convenient means'; sometimes abbreviated to *upāya, thabs, fāngbiàn* or *hōben,* and translated as 'skilful means' or 'expedient means'. The Pali *upāya-kosalla* is uncommon and does not convey the same meaning as the Sanskrit *upāya-kaushalya.* It is used to denote the 'skill' required to achieve something, such as teaching the *Dharma* or making spiritual progress.[1]

Upāya-kaushalya is a *Mahāyāna* Buddhist term that refers to the various pragmatic means adopted by *buddhas* and *bodhisattvas* to convey their message to spiritually dull and ignorant human beings, according to the particular circumstances, mentality, personal preferences, *etc.* of their hearers. 'Expedient means' is enumerated as the seventh of the ten *pāramitās* (perfections) – the *upāya-pāramitā* – to be attained by *bodhisattvas* in the course of their spiritual evolution.

Although *Theravāda* (Way of the Elders) doctrines are founded upon the early Pali texts that are regarded as a record of the actual words of the Buddha, *Mahāyāna* Buddhism portrays the earlier *Theravāda* teachings as restricted, as a doctrine given to people of limited spiritual capacity. The notion of 'expedient means' or 'skilful means' is an early *Mahāyāna* innovation, introduced as an explanation or justification of new doctrine. *Mahāyāna* Buddhism maintains that the Buddha tailored his teachings to the people he was addressing, and that the teachings he gave at one time were for that time only, and would be different and not appropriate for the people of other times and cultures. Specific formulations of the teachings are only 'expedient means', dependent on the particular context. It is like a medicine that is given to a particular patient for a particular condition, and is not applicable to all sick patients; or it is like the many different gateways to an ancient city – they all lead to the same place.

The concept of 'expedient means' is founded upon the *Mahāyāna* understanding that all teachings are relative and do not in themselves contain the absolute Truth. Upon attaining liberation, or even while travelling the Way, it becomes clear that the *Dharma* is only a means to reach that goal, devised and expressed according to the needs of the people, their times, and their way of life.

Whatever works as a way of reaching people and getting them to understand the *Dharma* and inducing them to follow it is regarded as 'expedient means', even if it means telling 'white lies' or otherwise contravening normally acceptable human behaviour. It is simply a matter of explaining the *Dharma* in a way that the hearer can understand. Such means may apply to the overall teachings and path laid out at a particular time or to the individual approach that a *buddha* or *bodhisattva* adopts towards a particular individual or to a small group. Different teachers will interact differently with different disciples. They are not bound by any rules, other than those arising from love and compassion. Everything is regarded as legitimate if the spiritual condition of those being taught warrants that approach and is benefited by it.

In some instances, as in the *Upāya-Kaushalya Sūtra, bodhisattvas* are described as committing deeds that contravene Buddhist precepts and the norms of moral conduct. This *sūtra* is devoted to explaining some of the many legendary stories concerning the Buddha both in his past births and in the life in which he became the Buddha. These explanations may be generally classified as far-fetched. It is related, for example, how the Buddha in a previous life as a *brahmachārin* (young celibate) who had "cultivated pure conduct for four billion two hundred million years", agreed to marry a girl who pleaded that she would otherwise die for love of him. In another instance, the Buddha, as an aspiring *bodhisattva,* kills a man to prevent him from killing five hundred others, and from subsequently burning in the lowest hell in payment for his misdeeds. As a result, not only does the man escape hell, but he is reborn in a heavenly region, while the *bodhisattva,* because his act was motivated by pure compassion, also escapes hell and is enabled to progress spiritually.[2] All this is condoned in the name of their deep compassion, and the higher purpose they have in mind.

The Buddhist tradition is replete with stories concerning the interaction between disciples and masters, and the ways used by these masters to bring spiritual insight and realization to their disciples. For example, *Zen kōans* – statements or questions that seem to have no logical meaning – where the intention is to lead the disciple out of his habits of analytical and conceptual thought. *Zen* masters are also well known for their unexpected behaviour – suddenly shouting at their disciples, or slapping them, or giving nonsensical replies to questions. All these are regarded as 'expedient means'.

Some support for the teaching is derived from the early Pali *suttas* where the Buddha indicates that individuals need to be taught in different ways, according to their background and their level of spiritual development. At the outset, seekers may not be ready to accept or may simply not understand the entire truth, and it therefore becomes expedient to teach them a lesser truth, sufficient to get them started on the spiritual path. As well as being known as *upāya-kosalla,* the notion is also embodied in the concept of progressive or gradual instruction *(ānupubbi-kathā),* in which the Buddha explains his teachings by degrees. As he perceives that a person's mind is ready, he gives them progressively more advanced teachings.[3] An instance is related in which the Buddha teaches two young *brahmaṇs* according to their Vedic beliefs. *Brāhmaṇs,* he says, speak about knowledge of and union with *Brahmā,* while neither they, nor their teachers, nor the many successive generations of teachers have ever met *Brahmā* face to face. Then, having gained their confidence, he puts forward his own understanding, which they readily accept.[4]

There is also the well-known parable of the raft. The Buddha gives the example of a traveller who finds himself on the dangerous bank of a river or lake, and wishes to reach the other side, which is safe. To do so, he builds a temporary raft or coracle out of branches and large leaves, and by paddling with his hands and feet, he crosses safely. The Buddha then asks whether it would then be better for the man to hoist the craft onto his shoulders and continue on his way, or to leave it at the water's edge. The point is that once it has been used for crossing the river, the purpose of the raft has been fulfilled, after which the traveller has no further need of it. In the same way, concludes the Buddha, the *Dharma* is only a vehicle, only a means, to cross the ocean of transmigration *(saṃsāra),* and a wise person will let go of it once it has served its purpose.[5] Later *Mahāyāna* interpreters used the story as an example pointing to the Buddha's overall endorsement of the theory of 'expedient means'.

'Expedient means' are a common feature of *Mahāyāna* texts, where they are sometimes discussed at considerable length. Such *sūtras* include the previously mentioned *Upāya-Kaushalya,* together with the *Vimalakīrti-Nirdesha, Vairochana-Abhisaṃbodhi, Avataṃsaka* and *Lotus Sūtras.* The *Lotus Sūtra,* like many others, follows the tradition of being written as if spoken by the Buddha although the text itself, penned by a number of authors, probably dates from between 100 BCE – 200 CE, several centuries after the Buddha's death. The text presents itself as a discourse delivered by the Buddha towards the end of his life, of a higher order than the teachings to be found in the Pali canon, but held in safekeeping for five hundred years by the *nāgas* (serpent deities). Humanity at that time, declares the *Lotus Sūtra,* was unable to understand the higher teaching it reveals.

In the second chapter, the Buddha addresses Shāriputra, one of his foremost disciples, mentioned in the earlier Pali texts:

> Shāriputra, you should know that the *buddhas' Dharma* is like this:
> By resorting to myriads of millions of expedient means *(fāngbiàn),*
> in accordance with what is appropriate to the situation,
> they preach the *Dharma.*
>
> Those who are unfamiliar with the matter cannot understand this.
> But all of you – knowing now that the *buddhas,* the teachers of the ages,
> in accordance with what is peculiarly appropriate,
> have recourse to expedient means *(fāngbiàn)* –
> need have no further doubts or uncertainties.
> Great joy should arise in your hearts,
> since you know that you yourselves will attain buddhahood.
>
> *Lotus Sūtra 2, T9 262:10b15–20; cf. LBFD pp.46–47*

Later, the Buddha adds:

> Did I not tell you earlier that when the *buddhas,* the world-honoured ones, cite various causes and conditions, and use similes, parables and other expressions, employing expedient means to preach the Law *(Dharma),* it is all for the sake of supreme perfect enlightenment *(anuttara-samyak-saṃbodhi)?* Whatever is preached is all for the sake of converting the *bodhisattvas.*
>
> *Lotus Sūtra 3, T9 262:12b10–11, LSOC p.91*

He also explains why it is necessary for him to make use of stratagems and devices:

> The wisdom of the *buddhas* is infinitely profound and immeasurable. The gateway to this wisdom is hard to understand and hard to enter. No *shrāvaka* (hearer) or *pratyeka-buddha* (one who attains enlightenment for himself alone) has ever been able to comprehend it.
>
> Why is this? In his past lives, a *buddha* has personally attended a hundred, a thousand, ten thousand, a million, a countless number of *buddhas,* and has exhaustively practised the *dharmas* of those *buddha*'s ineffable paths. His fame for bold and earnest effort having spread everywhere, he has practised profound *dharmas* that had never previously been practised. What he teaches accords with what is appropriate, yet the end point of its meaning is hard to understand.
>
> Shāriputra, since attaining buddhahood I have, by a variety of means and by resorting to a variety of parables, widely expounded my teachings, and have used countless expedient means *(fāngbiàn)* to guide living beings and cause them to abandon their attachments.
>
> *Lotus Sūtra 2, T9 262:5b25–c3; cf. LBFD p.22*

And again, in greater detail:

Shāriputra, listen carefully,
for the Law *(Dharma)* that the *buddhas* have attained,
through the power of countless expedient means *(fāngbiàn),*
they preach for the benefit of living beings.
The thoughts that are in the minds of living beings,
the different types of paths they follow,
their various desires and natures,
the good and bad deeds they have done in previous existences –
All these the Buddha takes cognizance of,
and then he employs causes, similes and parables,
words that embody the power of expedient means *(fāngbiàn),*
in order to gladden and please them all.

Sometimes he preaches *sūtras,*
verses, stories of the previous lives of disciples,
stories of the previous lives of the Buddha, of unheard-of things.
At other times he preaches regarding origins,
uses similes, parables, passages of poetry, or discourses.
For those of dull capacities, who delight in a lesser teaching *(dharma),*
who greedily cling to birth and death,
who, despite the innumerable *buddhas,*
fail to practise the profound and wonderful way,
but are perplexed and confused by a host of troubles –
For these I preach *nirvāṇa.*
I devise these expedient means *(fāngbiàn)*
and so cause them to enter into the *buddha*-wisdom.

Lotus Sūtra 2, T9 262:7c19–8a2, LSOC pp.67–68

The *Lotus Sūtra* is not shy to promote its own authenticity and its standing among other *sūtras:* "I have preached various *sūtras,* and among those *sūtras* the *Lotus* is foremost!" says the Buddha and, "Among the *sūtras,* it holds the highest place."[6] This confidence is evident in its treatment of other doctrines *(dharmas).* Much of the second chapter is devoted to promoting the idea that there is only one Buddhist vehicle (*Ekayāna,* One Vehicle, One Way). It maintains that the three vehicles *(triyāna)* – the vehicle of the hearer *(shrāvakayāna),* the vehicle of the privately enlightened *buddha (pratyeka-buddhayāna),* and the vehicle of the *bodhisattva (bodhisattvayāna)* – are really only a single *buddhayāna* (vehicle of the Buddha).

Pratyeka-buddha is a term much used in *Mahāyāna* texts for someone who focuses on his own enlightenment, in contrast to the *Mahāyāna* ideal of the *bodhisattva,* who vows to postpone his entry into *nirvāṇa* until all other sentient beings have attained enlightenment. Imputing selfish motives to the *pratyeka-buddha,* often disparagingly, *Mahāyāna* promoted the *bodhisattva* ideal. *Mahāyāna* thus identified two paths within the earlier *Theravāda* school – that of the regular hearers or seekers of enlightenment, and those who had attained that stage. The *Lotus Sūtra* maintains that these two, together with the *bodhisattvayāna,* are really only One Vehicle. The earlier teachings were an 'expedient means' introduced by the Buddha at a particular time for a particular group of people.

Theravāda is thus portrayed as an expedient means for teaching those who were less spiritually evolved, while *Mahāyāna* (Great Vehicle) is promoted as the higher path, and the Buddha goes on to explain why "I must decisively preach *Mahāyāna.*" While promoting the unity of all paths in one *buddhayāna, Mahāyāna* is given the superior position, *Theravāda* being dubbed *Hinayāna* (Lesser Vehicle), a pejorative name probably coined by *Mahāyāna* for earlier Buddhism:

> Up to now I have never told you
> that you were certain to attain the *buddha* Way.
> The reason I never preached in that manner
> was that the time to preach so had not yet come.
> But now is the very time
> when I must decisively preach the Great Vehicle.
> I use these nine devices,
> adapting them to the living beings when I preach,
> my basic aim being to lead them into the Great Vehicle,
> and that is why I preach this *sūtra.*
>
> There are sons of the Buddha whose minds are pure,
> who are gentle and of acute capacities,
> who, under innumerable *buddhas,*
> have practised the profound and wonderful Way.
> For these sons of the Buddha,
> I preach this *sūtra* of the Great Vehicle.
>
> And I predict that these persons
> in a future existence will attain the *buddha* Way.
> Because deep in their minds they think of the Buddha,
> and practise and uphold the pure precepts,
> they are assured they will attain buddhahood,
> and hearing this, their whole bodies are filled with great joy.
> The Buddha knows their minds and their practices,
> and therefore preaches for them the Great Vehicle.

When the voice-hearers *(shrāvakas)* and *bodhisattvas,*
hear this Law *(Dharma)* that I preach,
as soon as they have heard one verse,
they will all without doubt be certain of attaining buddhahood.

In the *buddha*-lands of the ten directions,
there is only the Law *(Dharma)* of the One Vehicle *(Ekayāna).*
There are not two, there are not three,
except when the Buddha preaches so as an expedient means *(fāngbiàn),*
merely employing provisional names and terms
in order to conduct and guide living beings,
and preach to them the *buddha*-wisdom.

Lotus Sūtra 2, T9 262:8a3–20, LSOC pp.68–69

Buddhas come to the world for the sole purpose of helping the spiritually ignorant, and the often arrogant and hostile beings who dwell here. Seeing their condition, a *buddha* has to resort to expedient means in order to help them understand the situation they are in, and to make an effort towards liberation:

The *buddhas* appear in the world
solely for this one reason, which is true –
the other two (vehicles) are not the truth.
Never do they use a lesser vehicle
to save living beings and ferry them across.
The Buddha himself dwells in the Great Vehicle,
and adorned with the power of meditation and wisdom
that go with that Law *(Dharma)* he has attained,
he uses it to save living beings.

I myself testify to the unsurpassed way,
the Great Vehicle, the Law *(Dharma)* in which all things are equal.
If I used a lesser vehicle to convert even one person,
I would be guilty of stinginess and greed,
but such a thing would be impossible.
If a person will believe and take refuge in the Buddha,
the Thus Come One (Tathāgata) will never deceive him,
nor will he ever show greed or jealousy,
for he has rooted out evil from among the phenomena.
Therefore, throughout the ten directions,
the Buddha alone is without fear....

I have converted all living beings,
and caused them all to enter the *buddha* Way.

If, when I encounter living beings,
  I were in all cases to teach them the *buddha* Way,
  those without wisdom would become confused,
  and in their bewilderment would fail to accept my teachings.
I know that such living beings
  have never in the past cultivated good roots,
  but have stubbornly clung to the five desires,
  and their folly and craving have given rise to affliction.
Their desires are the cause
  whereby they fall into the three evil paths,
  revolving wheel-like through the six paths of existence
  and undergoing every sort of suffering and pain.
Having received a tiny form in the womb,
  in existence after existence they constantly grow to maturity.

Persons of meagre virtue and small merit,
  they are troubled and beset by manifold sufferings.
They stray into the dense forest of mistaken views,
  debating as to what exists and what does not,
  and in the end cling to such views....
They are profoundly committed to false and empty doctrines,
  holding firmly to them, unable to set them aside.
Arrogant and puffed up with self-importance,
  fawning and devious, insincere in mind,
  for a thousand, ten thousand, a million *kalpas* (ages),
  they will not hear a *buddha*'s name,
  nor will they hear the correct teaching *(dharma)* –
Such people are difficult to save.

For these reasons, Shāriputra,
  I have for their sake established expedient means *(fāngbiàn),*
  preaching the way that ends all suffering,
  and showing them *nirvāṇa.*

Lotus Sūtra 2, T9 262:8a20–b23, LSOC pp.69–71

This is the method that all *buddhas* have employed in the past and will continue to do so in the future:

The world-honoured ones of the future
  will be of an incalculable number,
  and these thus come ones *(tathāgatas),*
  by resorting to expedient means *(fāngbiàn),*
  will also preach the Law *(Dharma).*

All these thus come ones *(tathāgatas),*
by resorting to innumerable expedient means *(fāngbiàn),*
will save and bring release to living beings,
so that they too may enter into the Buddha's wisdom,
free of outflows (*āsrava,* impurities).
Among those who hear the Law *(Dharma),*
none will fail to attain buddhahood.
This is the original vow of every *buddha:*
"Whatever *buddha* Way I may have trodden,
I wish it to be universally shared among living beings,
so that all alike may attain this Way as well."

Lotus Sūtra 2, T9 262:9a28–b5; cf. LBFD pp.40–41

Though the Buddha may "employ various different doctrines" in order to reach people, according to their way of thinking, he has only one end in view, which he pursues with an undying persistence born of his great compassion:

In order to bring peace and comfort to living beings,
I employ various different doctrines
to disseminate the *buddha* Way.
Through the power of my wisdom,
I know the natures and desires of living beings,
and through expedient means *(fāngbiàn)* I preach these doctrines,
causing all living beings to attain joy and gladness.

Shāriputra, you should understand
that I view things through the *buddha* eye.
I see the living beings in the six paths,
how poor and distressed they are, without merit or wisdom,
how they enter the perilous road of birth and death,
their sufferings continuing with never a break,
how deeply they are attached to the five desires,
like a yak enamoured of its tail,
blinding themselves with greed and infatuation,
their vision so impaired they can see nothing.
They do not seek the Buddha, with his great might,
or the Law *(Dharma)* that can end their suffering,
but enter deeply into erroneous views,
hoping to shed suffering through greater suffering.
For the sake of these living beings,
I summon up a mind of great compassion.

Lotus Sūtra 2, T9 262:9b21–c3, LSOC p.76

Both the *Lotus Sūtra* and the *Avataṃsaka Sūtra* contain fantastical material, in celestial settings outside of human time and history, relating to billions of celestial *buddhas* and *bodhisattvas,* dwelling in an infinity of *buddha*-lands (paradises), addressing vast numbers of beings, mostly heavenly. Many of the specific *buddhas* and *bodhisattvas* encountered have names symbolizing aspects of enlightenment and liberation, such as 'Subtle Light of Flames of Universal Jewels', 'Banner of Oceans of Qualities of Universal Sounds', 'Undefiled Treasury of Light of Oceans of Cloudlike Sounds', 'Realm of Enlightenment of Radiance of Universal Knowledge', and 'Joyfully Uttering Sublime Sounds'.[7] They possess the power to move about and manifest themselves in more or less any way they deem expedient. A passage from the *Avataṃsaka Sūtra* depicts a *buddha's* complete understanding of all beings, and his consequent flexibility in teaching them. Because he sees into the hearts and minds of all, he can readily devise 'expedient means' to teach them:

> All *buddhas* and world-honoured ones possess ten kinds of omniscience. What are they?
>
> All *buddhas* are simultaneously aware of the mind and mental traits of all living beings of the past, present, and future.
>
> All *buddhas* are simultaneously aware of the *karmas* and their consequences accumulated by all living beings of the past, present, and future.
>
> All *buddhas* are simultaneously aware of the needs of all living beings of the past, present and future, turning the three wheels (of diagnosis, prescription, and spiritual power) to reform, teach, and transform them.
>
> All *buddhas* are simultaneously aware of the mental traits of all living beings in the universe. As an expedient means *(fāngbiàn)* of attracting and saving those beings, they manifest themselves everywhere so that those beings can see the *buddha.*
>
> All *buddhas* can, of their own will, descend and take form in order to convert all living beings in the universe, expounding the *Dharma* to them according to their various capacities, inclinations, understanding, and desires.
>
> All *buddhas* are simultaneously aware of the tendencies of the minds of all living beings in the universe, and reveal to them their spiritual power.
>
> All *buddhas,* by their own will, can simultaneously manifest themselves in suitable *buddha*-forms (S. *nirmāṇa-kāya*) to all living beings everywhere; yet they explain that *buddha*-forms are not to be clung to.
>
> All *buddhas* can simultaneously appear to any being, anywhere in the universe, whatever path they may be following.

> All *buddhas* respond instantly to all living beings who think of them, anytime, anywhere.
>
> All *buddhas* are simultaneously aware of and understand the desires of all living beings, and manifest countless physical forms for their benefit.
>
> *Avataṃsaka Sūtra 33, T10 279:250c29–251a16*

The power to manifest simultaneously in multiple places refers to another *Mahāyāna* innovation – the three bodies *(trikāya)* of the Buddha or of any *buddha,* in which it is said that he manifests himself. The *dharmakāya* (Truth or Reality body) is his essence, from which his *sambhoga-kāya* (subtle body, celestial body) is manifested, as well as his *nirmāṇa-kāya* (created body, human body). The simultaneous manifestation of these multiple bodies is also viewed as 'expedient means':

> The *tathāgata*'s spiritual body *(dharmakāya)* is immense –
> it has no limit in all the ten directions.
> His expedient means *(fāngbiàn)* are without end. . . .
>
> The *tathāgata*'s state of being is boundless –
> by expedient means *(fāngbiàn),* he manifests it everywhere.
> Yet it is still and tranquil, without form. . . .
>
> The immense radiance of the *buddha*'s spiritual body *(dharmakāya)*
> manifests in the world through expedient means *(fāngbiàn):*
> He nurtures all sentient beings with a rain of *dharmas* (teachings)
> suited to their natures and to the inclinations of their minds.
>
> *Avataṃsaka Sūtra 1, T10 279:9a13–14, 15c17–18, 22c17–18*

Likewise, the many *dharmas* or forms of teaching that he uses are also viewed as "expedient means":

> A *buddha* creates great clouds of *dharmas* (teachings),
> suited to the nature of beings' minds.
> By various expedient means *(fāngbiàn),*
> he instructs, trains, and enlightens them.
>
> *Avataṃsaka Sūtra 2, T10 279:30c7–8*

Bodhisattvas also make use of "expedient means":

> Uncontrolled body, mind and speech are aspects of *karma:*
> it is impossible to attain anything if one is not free from them.

With the help of expedient means (*fāngbiàn, i.e.* meditation),
they eliminate ignorance and unconsciousness,
thereby cultivating and attaining perfect wisdom.

Avataṃsaka Sūtra 25, T10 279:130c14–15

The *Lotus Sūtra* uses a number of similes and parables in order to explain the nature of 'expedient means' and to justify the changes in doctrine. The *Dharma,* for example, is compared to rain that falls alike upon plants, herbs, grass, shrubs and trees of different sizes that grow in various habitats and utilize the rain in different ways, according to their differing natures. The parable demonstrates that although the rain (the *Dharma*) is the same, the different species receive it differently. "Though all these plants and trees grow in the same earth and are moistened by the same rain, each has its differences and particulars." Just so do sentient beings receive the *Dharma* differently according to their various abilities, interests, and circumstances:[8]

When living beings hear the Law *(Dharma)* of the Thus Come One (Tathāgata), though they may embrace, read, recite, and practise it as preached, they themselves do not understand and are unaware of the blessings they have received. Why so? Because only the Thus Come One (Tathāgata) understands the kind, the embodiment, the substance and the nature of these living beings, what they have in mind, how they think, what things they practise. He knows what *dharma* they have in mind, what *dharma* they think about, what *dharma* they practise, and what *dharma* they attain by resorting to what *dharma.*

Living beings live in a variety of environments, but only the Thus Come One (Tathāgata) sees them clearly and fully understands them without any difficulty. It is like those plants and trees, thickets and forests, and medicinal herbs that do not themselves know whether their own nature is superior, middling, or inferior. But the Thus Come One (Tathāgata) knows that this is a Law *(Dharma)* of one character and one flavour, namely, the character of emancipation, the character of detachment, the character of extinction, the character of ultimate *nirvāṇa,* of everlasting tranquillity and *nirvāṇa,* which in the end leads to emptiness. The Buddha understands all this; but because he can see the desires that occupy the minds of living beings, he guides and protects them, and for this reason does not immediately teach them the all-embracing wisdom.

Lotus Sūtra 5, T9 262:19b25–c6; cf. LSGR p.161, LBFD pp.102–3

One of the themes running throughout the *Lotus Sūtra* is that of the Buddha as the father of all beings. In another parable, the Buddha gives the example of a father whose many sons are playing inside a burning house, but are too engrossed in their play to be aware of the danger. Because he knows and understands the mind of each of his children, he is able to offer each one something that will entice him out of the house. He tells them that rare and enchanting carriages drawn by various animals await them at that very moment outside the gates. Only with this enticement can he persuade his children to leave the burning house. Having done so, because he is wealthy and because he loves his children very much, he gives them carriages even more magnificent than those he had promised. But his main intention had been to get his children out of the house, not to give them wonderful gifts. The Buddha explains that ordinary people are unaware of the suffering in which they are embedded, and the very real danger they are in of remaining in the cycle of birth and death. So he resorts to 'expedient means' – to whatever works – to induce them to take steps to help themselves:

> "Shāriputra, suppose that in a certain town in a certain country there was a very rich man. He was far along in years and his wealth was beyond measure. He had many fields, houses, and menservants. His own house was big and rambling, but it had only one gate. A great many people – a hundred, two hundred, perhaps as many as five hundred – lived in the house. The halls and rooms were old and decaying, the walls crumbling, the pillars rotten at their base, and the beams and rafters crooked and aslant.
>
> "At that time a fire suddenly broke out on all sides, spreading through the rooms of the house. The sons of the rich man, ten, twenty, perhaps thirty, were inside the house. When the rich man saw the huge flames leaping up on every side, he was greatly alarmed and fearful and thought to himself, I can escape to safety through the flaming gate, but my sons are inside the burning house enjoying themselves and playing games, unaware, unknowing, without alarm or fear. The fire is closing in on them, suffering and pain threaten them, yet their minds have no sense of loathing or peril and they do not think of trying to escape!
>
> "Shāriputra, this rich man thought to himself, I have strength in my body and arms. I can wrap them in a robe or place them on a bench and carry them out of the house. And then again he thought, this house has only one gate, and moreover it is narrow and small.
>
> "My sons are very young, they have no understanding, and they love their games, being so engrossed in them that they are likely to be burned in the fire. I must explain to them why I am fearful and alarmed. The house is already in flames and I must get them out quickly and not let them be burned up in the fire!
>
> "Having thought in this way, he followed his plan and called to all his sons, saying, 'You must come out at once!' But though the father

was moved by pity and gave good words of instruction, the sons were absorbed in their games and unwilling to heed him. They had no alarm, no fright, and in the end no mind to leave the house. Moreover, they did not understand what the fire was, what the house was, what danger was. They merely raced about this way and that in play and looked at their father without heeding him.

"At that time the rich man had this thought: the house is already in flames from this huge fire. If I and my sons do not get out at once, we are certain to be burned. I must now invent some expedient means *(fāngbiàn)* that will make it possible for the children to escape harm.

"The father understood his sons and knew what various toys and curious objects each child customarily liked and what would delight them. And so he said to them, 'The kind of playthings you like are rare and hard to find. If you do not take them when you can, you will surely regret it later. For example, things like these goat-carts, deer-carts and ox-carts. They are outside the gate now where you can play with them. So you must come out of this burning house at once. Then whatever ones you want, I will give them all to you!'

"At that time, when the sons heard their father telling them about these rare playthings, because such things were just what they had wanted, each felt emboldened in heart and, pushing and shoving one another, they all came wildly dashing out of the burning house.

"At this time, the rich man, seeing that his sons had gotten out safely and all were seated on the open ground at the crossroads and were no longer in danger, was greatly relieved and his mind danced for joy. At that time each of the sons said to his father, 'The playthings you promised us earlier – the goat-carts and deer-carts and ox-carts – please give them to us now!'"

"Shāriputra, at that time the rich man gave to each of his sons a large carriage of uniform size and quality. The carriages were tall and spacious and adorned with numerous jewels. Railings ran all around them, and bells hung from all four sides. Canopies were stretched over the tops, which were also decorated with an assortment of precious jewels. Ropes of jewels twined around, fringes of flowers hung down, and layers of cushions were spread inside, on which were placed vermillion pillows. Each carriage was drawn by a white ox, pure and clean in hide, handsome in form and of great strength, capable of pulling the carriage smoothly and properly at a pace fast as the wind. In addition, there were many grooms and servants to attend and guard the carriage.

"What was the reason for this? This rich man's wealth was limitless and he had many kinds of storehouses that were all filled and overflowing. And he thought to himself: There is no end to my possessions. It would not be right if I were to give my sons small carriages of inferior make. These little boys are all my sons and I love them without partiality. I have countless numbers of large carriages adorned with seven kinds of gems. I should be fair-minded and give one to each of my sons. I should not show any discrimination. Why? Because even if I distributed these things of mine to every person in the whole country, I would still not exhaust them, much less could I do so by giving them to my sons!

"At that time each of the sons mounted his large carriage, gaining something he had never had before, something he had originally never expected. Shāriputra, what do you think of this? When this rich man impartially handed out to his sons these big carriages adorned with rare jewels, was he guilty of falsehood or not?"

Lotus Sūtra 3, T9 262:12b14–13a3, LSOC pp.91–94

So the Buddha asks the key question. Was the rich man guilty of deception?

Shāriputra said, "No, World-Honoured One. This rich man simply made it possible for his sons to escape the peril of fire and preserve their lives. He did not commit a falsehood. Why do I say this? Because if they were able to preserve their lives, then they had already obtained a plaything of sorts. And how much more so when, through an expedient means *(fāngbiàn),* they were rescued from that burning house! World-Honoured One, even if the rich man had not given them the tiniest carriage, he would still not be guilty of falsehood. Why? Because this rich man had earlier made up his mind that he would employ an expedient means *(fāngbiàn)* to cause his sons to escape. Using a device of this kind was no act of falsehood. How much less so, then, when the rich man knew that his wealth was limitless and he intended to enrich and benefit his sons by giving each of them a large carriage."

The Buddha said to Shāriputra, "Very good, very good. It is just as you have said. And Shāriputra, the Thus Come One (Tathāgata) is like this. That is, he is a father to all the world. His fears, cares and anxieties, ignorance and misunderstanding, have long come to an end, leaving no residue. He has fully succeeded in acquiring measureless insight, powers, and freedom from fear, and gaining great supernatural powers and the power of wisdom. He is endowed with the *pāramitās (bōluómì)* of expedient means *(fāngbiàn)* and of wisdom, his great pity and great compassion, constant and unflagging; at all times he seeks what is good and will bring benefit to all.

"He is born into the threefold world, a burning house, rotten and old, in order to save living beings from the fires of birth, aging, sickness and death, care, suffering, foolishness, misunderstanding, and the three poisons; to teach and convert them and enable them to attain supreme perfect enlightenment *(anuttara-samyak-saṃbodhi).*

"He sees living beings seared and consumed by birth, aging, sickness and death, care and suffering, sees them undergo many kinds of pain because of of the five desires and the desire for wealth and profit. Again, because of their greed and attachment and striving they undergo numerous pains in their present existence, and later they undergo the pain of being reborn in hell or as beasts or hungry spirits. Even if they are reborn in the heavenly realm or the realm of human beings, they undergo the pain of poverty and want, the pain of parting from loved ones, the pain of encountering those they detest – all these many different kinds of pain.

"Yet living beings drowned in the midst of all this, delight and amuse themselves, unaware, unknowing, without alarm or fear. They feel no sense of loathing and make no attempt to escape. In this burning house that is the threefold world, they race about to east and west, and though they encounter great pain, they are not distressed by it.

"Shāriputra, when the Buddha sees this, then he thinks to himself, I am the father of living beings and I should rescue them from their sufferings and give them the joy of the measureless and boundless *buddha*-wisdom so that they may find their enjoyment in that.

"Shāriputra, the Thus Come One (Tathāgata) also has this thought: if I should merely employ supernatural powers and the power of wisdom; if I should set aside expedient means *(fāngbiàn)* and for the sake of living beings should praise the Thus Come One's (Tathāgata) insight, powers and freedom from fear, then living beings would not be able to gain salvation. Why? Because these living beings have not yet escaped from birth, aging, sickness and death, or care and suffering, and are being consumed by flames in the burning house that is the threefold world. How could they be able to understand the Buddha's wisdom?

"Shāriputra, that rich man, though he had strength in his body and arms, did not use it. He merely employed a carefully contrived expedient means *(fāngbiàn)* and thus was able to rescue his sons from the peril of the burning house, and afterward gave each of them a large carriage adorned with rare jewels. And the Thus Come One (Tathāgata) does the same. Though he possesses powers and freedom from fear, he does not use these. He merely employs wisdom and expedient means *(fāngbiàn)* to rescue living beings from the burning house of the threefold world, expounding to them the three vehicles, the vehicle of the voice-hearer *(shrāvaka),* that of the *pratyeka-buddha,* and that of the Buddha.

> "He says to them, 'You must not be content to stay in this burning house of the threefold world! Do not be greedy for its coarse and shoddy forms, sounds, scents, tastes, and sensations! If you become attached to them and learn to love them, you will be burned up! You must come out of this threefold world at once so that you can acquire the three vehicles, the vehicles of the voice-hearer, the *pratyeka-buddha,* and the Buddha. I promise you now that you will get them, and that promise will never prove false. You have only to apply yourselves with diligent effort!'
>
> "The Thus Come One (Tathāgata) employs this expedient means *(fāngbiàn)* to lure living beings into action. And then he says to them, 'You should understand that these doctrines of the three vehicles are all praised by the sages. They are free, without entanglements, leaving nothing further to depend upon or seek. Mount these three vehicles and with sense organs that are without outflows (*āsrava,* impurities), (and with) powers, awareness, the Way, meditations, emancipations, and *samādhis* (concentrations), you will enjoy yourselves, and will gain the delight of immeasurable peace and safety.'"
>
> *Lotus Sūtra 3, T9 262:13a3–b18, LSOC pp.94–96*

The Buddha now likens the lesser carts that he had promised his sons to the vehicles of the *shrāvaka,* the *prateyka-buddha,* and the magnificent carts that he had in fact given them to the *Mahāyāna* Vehicle – the Great Vehicle of the *bodhisattvas.* This is why the author of the parables has chosen carts or vehicles as the toys to entice the children:

> "Shāriputra, if there are living beings who are inwardly wise in nature, and who hear the Law *(Dharma)* from the Buddha, the World-Honoured One, believe and accept it, and put forth diligent effort, desiring to escape quickly from the threefold world and seeking to attain *nirvāṇa,* they shall be called (those who ride) the vehicle of the voice-hearer *(shrāvaka).* They are like those sons who left the burning house in the hope of acquiring goat-carts.
>
> "If there are living beings who hear the Law *(Dharma)* from the Buddha, the World-Honoured One, believe and accept it, and put forth diligent effort, seeking wisdom that comes of itself, taking solitary delight in goodness and tranquillity, and profoundly understanding the causes and conditions of all phenomena, they shall be called (those who ride) the vehicle of the *pratyeka-buddha.* They are like the sons who left the burning house in the hope of acquiring deer-carts.
>
> "If there are living beings who hear the Law *(Dharma)* from the Buddha, the World-Honoured One, believe and accept it, and put forth diligent effort, seeking comprehensive wisdom, *buddha*-wisdom,

wisdom that comes of itself, teacherless wisdom, the insight, powers, and freedom from fear of the Thus Come One (Tathāgata), who pity and comfort countless living beings, bring benefit to heavenly and human beings, and save them all, they shall be called (those who ride) the Great Vehicle. Because the *bodhisattvas* seek this vehicle, they are called *mahāsattvas.* They are like the sons who left the burning house in the hope of acquiring ox-carts.

"Shāriputra, that rich man, seeing that his sons had all gotten out of the burning house safely and were no longer threatened, recalled that his wealth was immeasurable and presented each of his sons with a large carriage. And the Thus Come One (Tathāgata) does likewise. He is the father of all living beings. When he sees that countless thousands of millions of living beings, through the gateway of the Buddha's teaching, can escape the pains of the threefold world, the fearful and perilous road, and gain the delights of *nirvāṇa,* the Thus Come One (Tathāgata) at that time has this thought: I possess the storehouse of the *buddhas'* measureless, boundless wisdom, powers, fearlessness, and other attributes. These living beings are all my sons. I will give the Great Vehicle to all of them equally so that there will not be those who gain extinction by themselves, but that all may do so through the extinction of the Thus Come One (Tathāgata).

"To all the living beings who have escaped from the threefold world he then gives the delightful gifts of the meditations, emancipations, and so forth, of the *buddhas.* All these are uniform in appearance, uniform in type, praised by the sages, capable of producing pure, wonderful, supreme delight.

"Shāriputra, that rich man first used three types of carriages to entice his sons, but later he gave them just the large carriage adorned with jewels, the safest, most comfortable kind of all. Despite this, that rich man was not guilty of falsehood. The Thus Come One (Tathāgata) does the same, and he is without falsehood. First, he preaches the three vehicles to attract and guide living beings, but later he employs just the Great Vehicle to save them. Why? The Thus Come One (Tathāgata) possesses the storehouse of measureless wisdom, powers, freedom from fear, and other attributes. He is capable of giving to all living beings the Law *(Dharma)* of the Great Vehicle. But not all of them are capable of receiving it.

"Shāriputra, for this reason you should understand that the *buddhas* employ the power of expedient means *(fāngbiàn).* And because they do so, they make distinctions in the one *buddha* vehicle *(buddhayāna),* and preach it as three."

Lotus Sūtra 3, T9 262:13b18–c18, LSOC pp.96–98

In another allegory related in the *Lotus Sūtra,* depicting the use of 'expedient means', the young son of a wealthy man runs away from home, living in a far-off foreign land for many years, where he forgets his father and his origin. As he gets older, he finds himself in poverty, wandering from place to place in search of food and clothing. During his wanderings, he returns by chance to his forgotten homeland, where his father, who has never ceased to look for him, happens to see him in the crowd. Apart from the love that the father bears towards his son, he also wishes to give him the wealth he has accumulated, for he has no one else to whom he can entrust it. But fearing to alarm his son by any sudden disclosure, he resorts to 'expedient means'.

First, he sends a messenger to bring the young man to him. But when accosted by a stranger, the son feels frightened and threatened, thinking that he is about to be arrested although he has done nothing wrong. The father therefore asks the messenger to desist:

> Why did he do that? Because the father knew that his son was of humble outlook and ambition, and that his own rich and eminent position would be difficult for the son to accept. He knew very well that this was his son, but as a form of expedient means *(fāngbiàn),* he refrained from saying to anyone, "This is my son."
>
> *Lotus Sūtra 4, T9 262:17a3–5, LSOC p.120*

Next, the wealthy man "decided to employ an expedient means *(fāngbiàn).*" He therefore sends "two men as secret messengers, men who were lean and haggard and had no imposing appearance". The messengers are instructed to offer the son well-paid work, clearing excrement. The young man accepts the job and asks for an advance of wages. After some time, the father then disguises himself as a fellow worker and befriends his son, encouraging him to work hard. Revealing himself as a wealthy man and the young man's employer, he begins to shower favours on his son, and telling him that he likes and trusts him and intends to treat him as his own son. The son agrees to this, still unaware that the wealthy man is actually his own father, and he continues to consider himself of lowly origin and to live in the same humble quarters. And so the story continues. In fact, the son goes on clearing excrement for the next twenty years until at length he at least feels accepted. At this point, the rich man puts his son in charge of the administration of his property, and the son carries out his duties faithfully without ever misappropriating any of the things entrusted to his care, continuing all the while to live in the same humble quarters, "unable to cease thinking of himself as mean and lowly".

By degrees, however, the father notices his son "becoming more self-assured and magnanimous in outlook, that he was determined to accomplish great things, and despised his former low opinion of himself". The father therefore orders his son to arrange a meeting with all his relatives, the king of the country, government ministers and so on, at which he announces that his chief administrator is actually his son, and heir to his fortune. The son is overjoyed at the news, especially since he had never coveted his father's wealth, but had acted only as an agent, and, "Yet now these stores of treasures have come of their own accord!"

The meaning of the allegory is then explained. The rich man is the Tathāgata, the historical Buddha, and the lesser benefits bestowed upon his son represent the lesser vehicles. To add authenticity to the author's point, the story is put in the mouth of Mahākāshyapa, who is regarded in the Pali texts as the Buddha's successor. Mahākāshyapa admits that although he had laboured diligently and had attained *nirvāṇa,* that attainment really amounted to no more than the "day's wages" that the son had been earning by clearing excrement, never aspiring to anything more. But the father, the Tathāgata, was happy to accept the situation and the son's contentment with these lesser doctrines and lesser attainments, knowing that he would ultimately be able to give him the *Dharma* of the Great Vehicle *(Mahāyāna).*[9]

In another parable designed to demonstrate the inferior nature of the *nirvāṇa* of early Buddhism,[10] a man is depicted as leading a group of people along a dreadful and dangerous road, "five hundred *yojanas*[11] (several thousand miles) long – steep and difficult, wild and deserted, with no inhabitants around, a truly fearful place", so that they may reach a place where there are rare treasures. After having covered three hundred *yojanas,* however, the travellers become exhausted and disheartened, and want to turn back. The leader, "a man of many expedients", concerned that his following will abandon the quest for such "rare treasures" when they have already come so far, thinks of an 'expedient means'. He conjures up a phantom city, telling the people, "Don't be afraid! You must not turn back, for now here is a great city where you can stop, rest, and do just as you please. If you enter this city, you will be completely at ease and tranquil. Then later, if you feel you can go on to the place where the treasure is, you can leave the city."

The phantom city represents the *nirvāṇa* of early Buddhism, and when the people are fully rested, he "wipes out the phantom city", and informs them that it was actually a mere fantasy that he had created so that they could rest and would not turn back. But now they must continue in order to attain the true treasure at the journey's real end. The Buddha then explains:

> Monks, so it is with the Tathāgata. Presently, he is acting as your great guide. He knows that the bad road of birth and death and earthly desires is steep, difficult, long and never ending, but that it must be travelled and left behind. If living beings hear only of the one *buddha* vehicle, then they will not want to see the Buddha or approach him, but will immediately think to themselves, "The *buddha* Way is long

and never ending, and one must labour diligently and endure suffering over a long period before success can be attained!"

The Buddha, knowing that the minds of living beings are timid and weak, uses the power of expedient means *(fāngbiàn),* preaching two kinds of *nirvāṇa* to provide a resting place along the way. If living beings choose to remain in these two stages, then the Tathāgata will say to them, "You have not yet understood what you have to do. This stage where you have chosen to remain is close to the *buddha*-wisdom, but you should observe and consider, weigh and measure. This *nirvāṇa* that you have attained is not the real one. It is simply that the Tathāgata, using the power of expedient means *(fāngbiàn),* has taken the one *buddha* vehicle, made distinctions, and preached it as three."

The Buddha is like that guide who, in order to provide a place for the travellers to rest, conjured up a great city, and then, when he saw that the travellers were rested, said to them, "The place where the treasure is, is nearby. This city is not real. It is merely something I conjured up."

Lotus Sūtra 7, T9 262:26a14–24; cf. LBFD p.149, LSGR pp.198–99

All in all, the intention behind these parables is to authenticate *Mahāyāna* doctrine, placing it on a higher pedestal than the Buddha's original teachings, which are depicted as no more than 'expedient means' given to people of limited spiritual capacity. Nonetheless, the *Lotus Sūtra* has been enormously popular and hugely influential in the development of Buddhist thought and doctrine. It became a major text for the Chinese *Tiāntái* school of Buddhism, imported to Japan as the *Tendai* school. Nichiren, a thirteenth-century Japanese Buddhist *Tendai* monk, founded a school based on the teachings of the *Lotus Sūtra,* which he regarded as the ultimate expression of Buddhist doctrine. The *Lotus Sūtra* is also a text commonly quoted by Eihei Dōgen, the thirteenth-century founder of *Sōtō Zen* Buddhism.

While the 'expedient means' discussed in texts such as the *Lotus Sūtra* are largely placed in other-worldly contexts, when it comes to the training of ordinary human *bodhisattvas,* the understanding of 'expedient means' takes on a more personal and practical character. It includes such mundane practices as observing the rules of monastic conduct or the performance of various rituals and worship in order to help engender a spiritual or devotional state of mind, or techniques such as how to remain awake in meditation. In fact anything conducive to spiritual progress can be regarded as an 'expedient means'.

1. *E.g. Dīgha Nikāya* 33, *Saṅgīti Sutta, PTSD3* p.220, *TBLD* p.486; *Anguttara Nikāya* 6:79, *Adhigama Sutta, PTSA3* p.431.

2. *Mahāratnakūṭa Sūtra* 22, *Upāya-Kaushalya Sūtra, T11* 310:596:b25–c16, 310:604b24–605a2; also in *MBDF* p.152.
3. *E.g. Majjhima Nikāya* 56, *Upāli Sutta, PTSM1* pp.379–80; *cf. MDBB* p.485.
4. *Dīgha Nikāya* 13, *Tevijja Sutta, PTSD1* pp.235–52.
5. *Majjhima Nikāya* 22, *Alagaddūpama Sutta, PTSM1* pp.134–35.
6. *Lotus Sūtra* 10, 14, 23, *LSOC* pp.203, 246–47, 327.
7. *Avataṃsaka Sūtra* 1, *FOSC* pp.57, 125.
8. *Lotus Sūtra* 5, *T9* 262:19a19–20b24, *LSOC* pp.134–43.
9. *Lotus Sūtra* 4, *T9* 262:16b8–19a11, *LSOC* pp.117–33.
10. *Lotus Sūtra* 7, *T9* 262:22a19–27b8, *LSOC* pp.174–81.
11. A mythological unit of distance, variously said to be between two and twenty miles.

vachan(a) (S/H), **bachan** (H/Pu) *Lit.* speech, word, sentence; saying, teaching, discourse, instruction, order, command; also used in the plural for words, sayings, teachings, *etc.*, especially the words of some authority; mystically, the creative Word *(Shabd),* the mystic Name, the divine creative power. In religious writings, the actual words or sayings *(bachans)* themselves, as well as their meaning, are often regarded as sacred. The term *pravachana* is used specifically in Jainism for a sermon or spiritual discourse given by a monk or advanced layperson.

The words of a saint can exercise an extraordinary influence on the hearers, especially if they are in tune with spiritual teachings. As Arjuna says to Kṛishṇa in the *Bhagavad Gītā:*

> By your grace, O imperishable One, my delusion has been dispelled,
> my memory (of God) restored!
> Now I stand firm, all doubts resolved,
> ready to execute your command *(vachana).*
>
> *Bhagavad Gītā 18:73; cf. BGT*

Maharaj Sawan Singh explains:

> The words *(bachan)* of the master are not separate from him. The master pervades them. His words *(bachan)* are outpourings of his heart and are permeated with his truth and soul force. Such words *(bachan)* pierce the hearts of spiritually minded persons like arrows and produce a sweet pain, which cannot be described.... The words *(bachan)* of the master bear fruit in accordance with the extent to which you act upon them. To obey the master is to give devotion to him....

> The words *(bachan)* of the master are very sweet and pleasant. You are filled with nectar through them. By acting in accordance with the words of the master one becomes immortal.
>
> *Maharaj Sawan Singh, Philosophy of the Masters 5, PMS5 pp.343–44*

Other saints have said the same:

> The saints' words *(bachan)* are sublime hymns:
> these are invaluable rubies and gems.
> He who hears them and acts thereon, is saved:
> he swims himself, and makes other people swim across.
> Fruitful is his life and profitable his company,
> whose heart is imbued with God's love.
> Hail, hail unto him for whom the celestial Music plays:
> he continually hears it, makes merry (*i.e.* is in bliss),
> and proclaims the Lord's praise.
>
> *Guru Arjun, Ādi Granth 295, MMS*

Following the teachings and advice of a perfect saint will ultimately bring the soul into contact with the divine Name:

> The praise of the Lord's Name is an invaluable treasure,
> which God has deposited with the saint *(sādhū).*
> Whosoever accepts the *guru's* word *(bachan)* as true and abiding,
> taking out this treasure, the *guru* places it before him.
>
> *Guru Rāmdās, Ādi Granth 1326, MMS*

> True are the words *(bachan)* and instruction *(updes)* of the saint:
> true are the persons into whose minds the Lord enters.
> If anyone knows and greatly loves the Truth,
> then he obtains salvation by meditating on the Name.
>
> *Guru Arjun, Ādi Granth 284, MMS*

A master's words soothe the heart and engender love – unlike words of anger and criticism:

> A sharp tongue is like a murderous sword
> or a blaze that reduces the body to ashes.
> But the words *(bachan)* of a saint are cool as water –
> a stream of nectar giving peace and life to all who gather round.
>
> *Kabīr, Sākhī Sangrah, Krodh kā Ang 8, KSS p.132, KGME p.280*

The saints' advice, therefore, is to listen carefully to what they have to say, and then act upon it:

> True are the *guru*'s words *(bachan):*
> enshrine them in your mind.
> Make fruitful your human birth and body.
>
> *Swayyās, Ādi Granth 1401, MMS*

A true disciple will always follow his master's instructions:

> A good disciple always obeys his master,
> and he puts aside all other tasks.
> He holds his master as the one true sovereign,
> and silently bows to him within.
> Says Kabīr: he alone is a good disciple
> who is never disturbed by an order *(bachan)* of his master,
> however strange and unpalatable it may appear.
>
> *Kabīr, Sākhī Sangrah, Gurumukh kā Ang 3–4, KSS p.14; cf. KGME p.221*

The saint's teachings, however, are not meant for everybody:

> People who are steeped in all sorts of worldly desires cannot believe in the words *(bachan)* of the *satguru.*
>
> *Swami Shiv Dayal Singh, Sār Bachan Prose 2:156, SBAT p.93*

Those who have spiritual impressions *(sanskāras)* from past lives will be more interested than others in what the saints have to say:

> If one were to say that a *sanskārī* (one with previous spiritual impressions) does not need the company of saints, that would be wrong. Whether with *sanskārs* or not, both need *sādhsang* (association with or company of *sādhs,* saints). The only difference would be that a *sanskārī* would be affected by the *bachans* (sayings) very soon and would easily accept them, while one without *sanskārs* will not be able to readily accept the *bachan* (of the master) nor to act upon it so well. The seed will, however, be sown in him, and he will practise later on.
>
> *Swami Shiv Dayal Singh, Sār Bachan Prose 2:189, SBAT p.108*

Even with the best of intentions, complete love for and obedience to a master is not so easy to achieve, since the individual mind remains active:

> Every one loves what the *satguru* says and his *līlā* (way of doing things); but it is some rare one who loves the *satguru* himself. The love

which is based upon *bachan* (words) or *līlā* (conduct) only is unreliable. True love is that which is based upon *satguru* himself. But out of those whose love is based upon the *bachan* and *līlā* of the *satguru,* some may develop true love for the *satguru.* This is also a stepping stone to true love.

Swami Shiv Dayal Singh, Sār Bachan Prose 2:225, SBAT pp.124–125

The Buddhist tradition speaks of *buddhavacana* (words of the Buddha), which refers either to words believed to have been spoken by the Buddha or to an accurate expression of his teachings. The *buddhavacana* is also known as *pravacana* (excellent words, spiritual discourse). Buddhism also describes the everyday human language of the Buddha as *vohāravacana* (conventional language). This is the language used by the Buddha when speaking of the things and relationships of this world as if they had a genuine reality. Thus, in Buddhist texts, the Buddha may speak of other people as if they actually possessed a separate identity, while knowing simultaneously that there is a far bigger picture in which the sense of individuality is illusory.

See also: **Bachan** (3.1), **buddhavachana**, **upadesha**, **vāṇī**.

vāṇī (S), **bānī** (H), **bāṇī** (Pu) *Lit.* speech, language, words, sayings, discourse; sound, voice, music, utterance; a text, sacred books, sacred teachings or sayings, especially in poetic or musical form, whether oral or written; any poetic composition from the *Ādi Granth* or other Indian *sants;* the divine creative power, by itself or in such expressions as *ākāsh Bāṇī* (Sound from the sky), *amrit Bāṇī* (immortal Sound), *sachchī Bāṇī* (true Word), and *anāhad Bānī* (unstruck Sound); also, as the Sanskrit *Vāṇī,* a name for *Sarasvatī,* the goddess of speech and learning.

The *bānī* of the saints arises from their own inner knowledge:

Their (saints') teachings *(bānī)* stem from love and inner experience:
but you remain lost in intellectual quibbling.

Swami Shiv Dayal Singh, Sār Bachan Poetry 24:3.6, SBP p.209

The highest saints have all given the same teachings, although the expression of it may differ due to cultural and other circumstances relating to the people to whom the saints are speaking:

Nānak and Kabīr spoke of that (eternal abode),
and Tulsī Sāhib also considered it his true home.

> Their teachings *(bānī)* sing the glory of that dwelling,
> which they reveal as the true region, called *sach khanḍ* or *sat lok*.
>
> *Swami Shiv Dayal Singh, Sār Bachan Poetry 24:1.122–23, SBP p.206*

Just as their teachings arise from inner experience, so too does real understanding only arise from spiritual practice and experience:

> Mere reading and memorizing the *bānī* (teaching) of the saints will avail nothing so long as the teachings are not translated into action. Make the *bachans* (discourses) that you hear, the rule of your life; otherwise, what you hear and understand will be useless.
>
> *Swami Shiv Dayal Singh, Sār Bachan Prose 2:23, SBAT p.57*

See also: **Bānī** (3.1).

walāyah, **wilāyah** (A), **walāyat**, **wilāyat** (P) *Lit.* being master of, controlling; government, jurisdiction, governorship, dominion, lordship, power, authority; a province, a domain; guardianship, protection, tutelage, patronage; sanctity, holiness, sainthood; union with the Divine; commonly translated in Sufi contexts as friendship, divine friendship, godfriendship, or sainthood; the state of being a friend *(walī)* of God; from the same root as *waliya* (to be near to, to be friends with), and *walīy* (A) or *walī* (A/P), both meaning friend. As Sufi terms for sainthood, both imply friendship with or closeness to God, together with His protection.

Walāyah appears in the *Qur'ān* in a parable concerning an unbeliever who has fallen on hard times: "In such cases, the only protection *(walāyah)* comes from God, the Truth."[1]

Some Sufis have distinguished between *walāyat* and *wilāyat* on the etymological grounds that *walāyat* is active and implies the power to give or to dispose, while *wilāyat* is passive and denotes the possession of power.[2] *Walāyat* therefore refers to the spiritual power of a saint, which he actively imparts to his disciples according to his grace and their receptivity. He can also actively bestow his *walāyat* on another individual when he leaves this world, taking that person to the same spiritual level as himself, and making him his spiritual successor. *Walāyat* is also used for the external religious authority of an *imām* or other Muslim cleric.

Wilāyat, on the other hand, refers to a saint's personal relationship of friendship with and protection by the Divine, which is his own personal possession, and goes with him when he leaves this world. As Niẓām al-Dīn Awliyā' once explained:

> The saint possesses both *walāyat* and *wilāyat* at the same time. *Walāyat* is that which masters impart to disciples about God, just as they teach them about the etiquette of the Way. Everything such as this, which takes place between the *shaykh* and other people, is called *walāyat*. But that which takes place between the *shaykh* and God is called *wilāyat*. That is a special kind of love; and when the *shaykh* leaves the world, he takes his *wilāyat* with him. His *walāyat*, on the other hand, he can confer on someone else, whoever he wishes, and if he does not confer it, then it is appropriate for God Almighty to confer that *walāyat* on someone. But the *wilāyat* is the *shaykh*'s constant companion; he carries it with him (wherever he goes).
>
> *Niẓām al-Dīn Awliyā', Morals for the Heart 1:14, FFNA p.22; cf. MHN p.95*

The two terms, however, are not always used in so distinguishable a manner. According to a story related in *Manāqib al-ʿĀrifīn,* while walking to the congregational mosque, Rūmī once happened to meet an executioner, to whom he paid considerable respect. On being asked why he showed the man such cordiality, Rūmī replied that one of the friends of God, whose friendship had remained concealed from others, had been executed as a martyr. This friend had always longed for release from his body, and when he was condemned to death on some pretext, "That friend of God conferred his friendship *(wilāyat)* on the executioner." The executioner had been unaware of this gift, but when Rūmī's disciples told him what their master had related, the executioner repented of his past, begged forgiveness, and "became one of the fortunate disciples".[3]

There is also a Sufi belief that the spiritual authority *(wilāyat)* of a saint covers a geographical area, and that rulers operating within a saint's territory are (unknown to them) subject to the saint's higher authority. It was believed that the mistreatment of a saint by a ruler was likely to bring about his downfall.[4]

The many Sufi discussions of *wilāyat* produced definitions such as *wilāyat khāṣṣah* (elect or special friendship or sainthood), which is that of the spiritually advanced mystic. *Wilāyat ʿāmmah* (general or common friendship), on the other hand, is the friendship or sainthood common to all sincere believers. Abū ʿAbd Allāh al-Sālimī describes such people as

> those who are recognizable by the loveliness of their speech, and fine manners, and submission, and generosity, showing little opposition, and accepting the excuse of everyone who excuses himself before them, and perfect mildness towards all creatures, the good as well as the bad.
>
> *Abū ʿAbd Allāh al-Sālimī, in Nafaḥāt al-Uns, NUJ p.121, in MDI p.199*

Tahānawī explains the difference between the two:

> Friendship *(wilāyat)* is of two categories: general *(ʿāmmah)* and special *(khāṣṣah).* General friendship *(wilāyat ʿāmmah)* is common to all believers, signifying nearness to God through divine grace, all believers being near because of God's grace, for He has brought them out of the darkness of infidelity and illuminated them with the light of faith, as referred to in the verse: "God is the protecting friend *(walīy)* of believers. He leads them from darkness to light."[5]
>
> Special friendship *(wilāyat khāṣṣah)* specifically relates to those on the Path who have attained union with God. It cannot be experienced by those who are at the beginning or intermediate stages of the Path. It signifies the devotee's annihilation in God and subsistence through God. Annihilation in God means that one is no longer conscious of that which is other than God, and subsistence through God means awareness through God and not being aware of that which is other than God.
>
> *Tahānawī, Kashshāf Iṣṭilāḥāt al-Funūn, KIFT4 pp.391–92; cf. in SSE3 pp.66–67*

Other Sufis have differentiated between *wilāyat muṭlaq* (absolute friendship), which is possessed only by God, as indicated by the *Qur'ān:* "He is the protecting Friend *(al-Walīy),* the Praiseworthy,"[6] and *wilāyat muqayyadah* (delimited friendship), which is that of the friends of God. Among the friends of God, there are degrees of *wilāyat,* depending on their spiritual advancement.[7]

God's absolute friendship is also called *wilāyat-i shamsīyah* (friendship of the sun), since God is the divine Source. The friendship of the saints is also called *wilāyat-i qamarīyah* (friendship of the moon), since the saints reflect the light of the divine Sun. The moon was also regarded in Persian and Arabic poetry as being of great beauty, and a symbol of the master and the divine beloved.

A possessor of *wilāyat* is a *walī* (friend of God), and a possessor of *nubuwwah* is a *nabī* (prophet). A *nabī,* such as Abraham, Moses, Jesus, and Muḥammad, is a lawgiver, one who has been given a particular message to deliver. While *Sunnīs* and *Shīʿahs* both agree that Muḥammad was the last *nabī, Shīʿahs* and Sufis maintain that guidance is still available through the initiation and tutelage of a *walī.* Sufis have further debated the relationship between *nubuwwah* (prophethood) and *wilāyat,* and opinions vary. According to Ibn al-ʿArabī, sainthood *(wilāyah)* is an essential inward aspect of prophethood *(nubuwwah).* Every *nabī* is also a *walī,* but not every *walī* is a *nabī.* On the other hand, the Quranic story of Moses (the *nabī*) and Khiḍr (the *walī*)[8] – in which Moses' ignorance of the future is contrasted with Khiḍr's foreknowledge – indicates that sometimes not all the secrets of the divine will are revealed to the *nabī,* although the *walī* may know them.

Since *nubuwwah* (prophethood) is associated with giving a message to humanity, it is temporal, limited to the lifetime of the particular prophet. *Wilāyat,* on the other hand, goes with the prophet when he leaves this world.[9]

Among the special *awliyā'* or friends of God, Sufis differentiated a vast spiritual hierarchy – "officers of the divine court" – headed by the *quṭb* (axis) or *ghawth* (helper), and including three *nuqabā'* (leaders), four *awtād* (supports), seven *abrār* (the righteous), forty *abdāl* (substitutes), and three hundred *akhyār* (the good), and four thousand hidden friends of God.[10]

See also: **nabī** (7.1), **nubuwwah, walī** (7.1).

1. *Qur'ān* 18:44; *cf. AYA, KPA, MGK;* see also *Qur'ān* 8:72.
2. *E.g.* Hujwīrī, *Kashf al-Maḥjūb* XIV, *KMM* p.266, *KM* p.210.
3. Aḥmad al-Aflākī, *Manāqib al-'Ārifīn* 3:316, *MASA1* p.384, *FKG* (3:315) p.265.
4. See Leonard Lewisohn *et al., Legacy of Medieval Persian Sufism, HSL2* p.30.
5. *Qur'ān* 2:257; *cf. AYA, KPA, MGK.*
6. *Qur'ān* 42:28, *MGK; cf. Qur'ān* 42:9.
7. Rukn al-Dīn, *Nuṣūṣ al-Khuṣūṣ, NKTF* p.208, in *SSE3* pp.67–68.
8. *Qur'ān* 18:65–81.
9. Shāh Ni'mat Allāh Valī, *Rasā'il, RNV2* p.19.
10. Hujwīrī, *Kashf al-Maḥjūb* XIV, *KMM,* pp.269–70, *KM* pp.213–14.

wèndá (C) *Lit.* questions *(wèn)* and answers *(dá);* a dialogue; a format often used by Daoist teachers to convey their teachings, either orally or in written scriptures.

Many of the stories found in the *Zhuāngzǐ,* for instance, incorporate *wèndá* exchanges between teacher and student, master and disciple. One example is the lengthy and fictitious exchange between Zhòngní (Confucius) and his favourite disciple Yán Huí. At one point in this interchange, Yán Huí says he has gone as far as he can in his spiritual practice, and cannot go any further:

> Yán Huí said, "Master, what must I do to go forward."
>
> Zhòngní replied, "The way forward is to be found in fasting *(zhāi).* But will you find it easy to practise it?"
>
> "For months together we don't drink alcohol, nor do we eat proscribed foodstuffs," Huí said. "Can this be regarded as fasting?"
>
> "That kind of fasting," answered Zhòngní, "is the kind associated with offering sacrifices *(jìsì);* but it is not the fasting of the mind *(xīn zhāi).*"

"What is 'fasting of the mind'?" asked Huí.

Zhòngní explained, "When you empty *(xū)* your mind *(xīn)* (of all thought), this is fasting of the mind."

Zhuāngzǐ 4; cf. TT1 pp.208–9

A collection of dialogues, poems and discourses of thirteenth-century Daoist master Lǐ Dàochún includes a long *wèndá* exchange with his disciple Qióngchánzǐ:

Q. How do you explain the statement, 'One *yīn* and one *yáng* constitute the *Dào?*'

A. *Yīn* and *yáng* are heaven and earth. Heaven and earth come from the Absolute; the Absolute bifurcates into the two modes; the two modes are the celestial and the terrestrial.

Q. Heaven is *yáng,* earth is *yīn;* why do you also speak of the celestial and terrestrial using the ordinary terms for heaven and earth?

A. The celestial and the terrestrial are heaven and earth; heaven and earth are *yīn* and *yáng; yīn* and *yáng* are one Absolute; the Absolute is basically infinite.

When we speak in terms of the Absolute, we say 'celestial' and 'terrestrial'. When we speak in terms of the changes as represented by the *Yìjīng,* we say heaven and earth. When we speak in terms of the *Dào* we say *yīn* and *yáng.*

Lǐ Dàochún, Zhōnghé jí, BBH p.39

The *wèndá* exchange continues, allowing master Lǐ Dàochún to give his disciple Qióngchánzǐ a full explanation of the meaning of the *Yìjīng* trigrams that represent heaven *(qián)* and earth *(kūn).*

See also: **mondō**.

whakapapa (Mo) *Lit.* ancestry, genealogy, lineage, descent; a table of genealogy.

As enshrined in various legends, the ancient Māori believed that the deity *(atua) Tāne Mahuta* (also called *Tāne nui a Rangi* and by several other epithets) was the progenitor of humanity, and that they were therefore descended from the gods *(atua).* Knowledge of this ancient and extensive lineage was hence regarded as being of great significance, especially since the *mana* (power) of the gods and all the ancestors was understood to be passed down through this line of ancestry.

Handed down, cumulatively, to each firstborn son of the chiefs, the *mana* passed from one generation to the next, accumulating as it moved forward.

Preserved as an oral tradition by means of recitations in which several hundred names were often recited, the ancient Māori, throughout their history, have diligently maintained a record of their descent from the gods, as well as a chronicle of their own family genealogy. The resulting *whakapapas* of the various tribes and family groups are a complex lattice of interconnecting genealogies. Rather than possessing just his own personal *mana,* the Māori was thus empowered by all those who had preceded him in his *whakapapa.* This knowledge of ancestry was preserved and shared with chosen ones in the *whare wānanga* (school of sacred learning).

To the Māori, the world is a manifestation of the *wairua* (spirit) that breathes life and power into the ancestral line, the *whakapapa,* which is itself understood to be imbued with the intuitive knowledge and understanding of *Io* and the gods. As a Māori poem describes it, the *whakapapa* is closely connected to the ever-changing cycle of life, which keeps on revolving, while resting upon an "axle of strength":

Te ao hurihuri (the changing world)
is a world revolving,
a world that moves forward
to a place it comes from,
a wheel that turns on an axle of strength.

James Irwin, Introduction to Maori Religion, IMRI p.7

Every aspect of existence is understood to be closely associated with the spiritual world, a relationship that is encapsulated in the *whakapapa.* This is not, as some might suppose, a superstitious projection of an ignorant people. It is an acknowledgement – within the framework of the Māori culture, mythology, and mindset – that all life has a spiritual foundation – is essentially spiritual, and only makes sense when understood in that context. Johannes Andersen is speaking here of the Māori warrior in particular, but of the traditional Māori understanding in general:

> He (the Māori) was kept fully aware, not only of the existence of the gods *(atua),* but also of their constant proximity, of their participation in every affair of his life. And the reason for the *karakia* (incantations, prayers) being addressed to them (the *atua*), and for their taking the interest they did in the individual person as in the tribe, was that every member of the tribe was, through long lines of ancestors, directly descended from those same gods. That was the Māori's pride of ancestry, and his genealogies were kept meticulously, his often-checked memory being his 'Burke's (Peerage)', and his *tohungas* being his 'College of Arms'. *Noblesse oblige* was no empty phrase to

> him; through *Tāne,* creator and impregnator of man, he was literally descended from the gods.
>
> *Johannes Andersen, Maori Religion, MRJA p.519*

The ramifications of the many genealogies became understandably complex, with gaps and obscurities representing difficult times:

> In the minds of this 'College of Arms' – a heraldry graduating in the *whare kura* (the school of learning) – over a complex lattice of genealogies spread the many-branching vines of ancestry, their roots striking away in the dim past. The details of the trellis must necessarily be dim in the times when the origins struck their roots, but they became clearer and clearer as the vines reached forward into the light of the present and, for a span of twenty generations or so from the present, the prolific vines of descent or lines of descent, with all their many branching and collateral ramifications, are so clearly seen that there is more or less agreement as to the details. Beyond the twenty generations, there occur dim or blurred areas, no doubt indicating unsettled or violent times when the teachings of the *whare kura* might be suspended; but the dim areas are often brightened, and the vines picked up again further back, by checks supplied by the records of other scattered tribes of Polynesians.
>
> *Johannes Andersen, Maori Religion, MRJA pp.519–20*

The *whakapapa* provides more than a framework for the perceived transmission of *mana.* It also furnishes an identity with the past and a pattern for the future:

> It has become a truism to say that Western man since Descartes draws his identity from within himself, "I think, therefore I am," whereas the Māori speaker says "I belong, therefore I am." . . . When making a historical allusion, a Māori speaker will refer to *ngā wā ō mua,* which is usually translated as 'the old times' or 'in days gone by'. Yet this translation is inaccurate, for the word *'mua'* means 'in front', and this gives an essential clue to the Māori understanding of history. The past is not something which lies behind, but something which is spread out in front of the speaker – beginning as it were at his feet. He sees his parents, grandparents and forebears spreading out in front of him and, seeing, participates in what is an ongoing participation by his sharing. There is a strong cyclical rhythm here, but only in terms of the *te ao hurihuri,* for it does not leave the past behind. It gathers it up and moves forward. This is plainly not a static view of history as

> each person is added to the story *(whakapapa)* and moves forward in the growing community of past, present, and that which is to come
>
> *James Irwin, Introduction to Maori Religion, IMRI p.7*

Mitaki Ra, a contemporary New Zealand writer, expands the notion of identity to include that of the spiritual source from which the *whakapapa* originates:

> If we asked ourselves the question, "Who am I?", we would soon discover that the blanket of ignorance is lifted before our very eyes. Then we would see clearly the nature of our journey in the physical world and the meaning and purpose of our *whakapapa.* To open the door to *whakapapa* in this way allows us to recognize that we are not alone in the physical world but are accompanied by the ancestral line who joyously would assist us in the goal of the return to our spiritual home, Ngā Hawaiki, if we had the courage to ask this of them....
>
> *Whakapapa* preserves everything that our ancestral line carries. If we are to discover for ourselves the true meaning and values of being Māori, we must unlock the doors to this vast tome of experience, knowledge, understanding, and wisdom that *whakapapa* holds for us. By unlocking the doors of *whakapapa,* much will be revealed, and the tools given to us that we may learn co-operation one with the other, and find unification of purpose in all that we do.
>
> *Mitaki Ra, Kingitanga, KODW pp.16–17*

> The nature of all things Māori is rooted in *whakapapa,* the codes of the gods, from which the understanding of who we are is found. If we forget our *whakapapa,* we forget our roots and close the door to our return home to our *Tūrangawaewae,* Ngā Hawaiki (ancestral home). The goal of Māori has ever been preservation of the sacred record shared with us.
>
> *Mitaki Ra, Kingitanga, KODW p.9*

whakauki (Mo) *Lit.* towards *(whaka)* distant times *(uki);* the transferring of mediumship from one person to another, usually from a father to his eldest son, or from a *tohunga* (priestly adept) to a worthy recipient.

New Zealand anthropologist and ethnologist Elsdon Best (1856–1931) refers to the transfer of mediumship between those who performed the ceremony of *kumanga kai* – of leaving food for consumption by the Māori *atua* (ancestral deities) – a ritual performed by a medium:

> Should your father be a medium of the *kumanga kai,*... the same office will probably be transferred to you *(whakauki).* This would be done by the aged father laying his hand on you and speaking in a peculiar

> manner; that is to say, no words are distinguishable, it sounds like nonsense *(kōrero pōrewarewa)*. That is all. The *atua* will now pass to you, his son.
>
> *Elsdon Best, Spiritual Concepts of the Maori, SCM2 p.1*

See also: **tohunga** (7.1).

whare wānanga (Mo) *Lit.* school *(whare)* of sacred learning *(wānanga)*. See **initiation (Māori)** (7.4), **tohunga** (7.1).

wilāyah (A) See **walāyah**.

yār-i ghār (P) *Lit.* companion *(yār)* of the cave *(ghār)*, the friend of the cave; an epithet given to Abū Bakr by Muḥammad after the two of them had passed three nights in a cave south of Mecca, on their way to Madīnah, when in danger from the Quraysh, and where they were miraculously saved from harm by a spider who spun a web across the cave entrance, leading their pursuers to think there was no one inside. The incident is mentioned in the *Qur'ān.*[1]

The expression has come into common use for a familiar, close, trusted, sincere, or loyal friend. As Rūmī says, addressing his reader regarding the limitations of his own writing:

> O companion of the cave *(yār-i ghār)*,
> these intermediary words are,
> in the sight of one united with God,
> thorns, thorns, thorns.
> Much tribulation and pain and waiting was needed
> for the pure soul to be delivered from words.
>
> *Rūmī, Maśnavī IV:2984–85; cf. MJR4 pp.436–37*

Rūmī also uses the expression for his own master Shams-i Tabrīz, as the divine beloved within, with whom he lives in intimate spiritual communion, as in a hermit's cave, detached from everything and everybody of this world:

> My heart is the cave and Shams-i Tabrīzī
> is the companion of the cave *(yār-i ghār)*.
>
> *Rūmī, Dīvān-i Shams-i Tabrīz 1663:17435, KSD4 p.24*

He deems himself of little worth if his soul does not journey frequently to witness the spiritual glory of the divine beloved:

I am a cold and worthless stone
  if I do not journey oft to rubiness *(laʿl);*
I am a dark and narrow cave
  if I flee from the companion of the cave *(yār-i ghār).*

Rūmī, Dīvān-i Shams-i Tabrīz 1429:15113, KSD3 p.200

ʿAṭṭār, too, speaks of seeking the divine beloved in the inner "cave" of selflessness and divine unity:

Give up the intellect for love and see
  in one brief moment all eternity;
Break nature's frame, be resolute and brave,
  then rest at peace in unity's black cave *(ghār).*
Rejoice in that close, undisturbed dark air –
  the Prophet will be your companion *(yār)* there.

ʿAṭṭār, Conference of the Birds 639–41, MTAN p.260, CBD p.30

1. *Qur'ān* 9:40.

zāwiyah (A), **zāviyat** (P) (pl. *zawāyā*) *Lit.* angle, corner; an oratory, a small mosque; a quiet corner of a mosque where people would retreat from the distractions of everyday life to focus themselves in the remembrance of God; subsequently, a secluded and remote place used as a spiritual retreat and for learning; even a room set aside in a house for prayer or meditation; in Sufism, a monastery, hostel, or meeting place; in North Africa, often the mausoleum associated with a saint of a particular Sufi order; the North African equivalent of the Sufi *khānaqāh* (in eastern Islam) or the *dargāh* (in Turkey); sometimes, the residence of a Sufi *shaykh,* his family, and close circle; may also function as or contain a school, a library, a hostel for pilgrims, a sanctuary offering asylum, a local vegetable garden during times of famine, and so on; also, an organizational division or group within a Sufi order, each with its own *muqaddam* (leader) appointed by the leading *shaykh* of the order.

See also: **khānaqāh**.